THE
Department of State

A HISTORY OF ITS ORGANIZATION, PROCEDURE, and PERSONNEL

By

GRAHAM H. STUART

Drawings by Gloria E. Anderson

THE MACMILLAN COMPANY

New York : 1949

CARL A. RUDISILL
LIBRARY
LENOIR RHYNE COLLEGE

353.1
Stad

Copyright, 1949, by

THE MACMILLAN COMPANY

All rights reserved—no part of this book may be reproduced in
any form without permission in writing from the publisher, except
by a reviewer who wishes to quote brief passages in connection
with a review written for inclusion in magazine or newspaper.

FIRST PRINTING

Printed in the United States of America

25926
jan '50

To

NORMAN ARMOUR

able representative of his country

at home and abroad

FOREWORD

This volume attempts to present a brief but comprehensive history of the organization, personnel, and procedure of the Department of State from its beginnings to the present time. Policy problems are discussed only where they are vitally connected with, or illustrative of, the methods employed by the Department officials in the performance of their duties. Every effort has been made to evaluate the work of the Department objectively, but at the same time sympathetically.

The author wishes to acknowledge his grateful appreciation to the personnel of the Department of State for their assistance, over a long period of time, in the preparation of this volume. Space precludes individual mention, but the members of the library staff were particularly helpful and the author is deeply grateful to them.

The author is particularly indebted to former Assistant Secretary of State Norman Armour, who read much of the manuscript and was constantly available for information and advice, and to his colleague, Professor Thomas A. Bailey, who read the entire manuscript and was most helpful in his suggestions. Secretary of State Marshall afforded every facility and gave generously of his time. Assistant Secretary Dean Rusk and Robert M. McClintock made several very useful suggestions and the late Charles Evans Hughes read the chapter on his administration and was most helpful in his comments. Former President Herbert Hoover and former Secretary of Interior Ray Lyman Wilbur gave the author the benefit of their criticism for the period in which they were particularly concerned. The author wishes to express his thanks to Miss Gloria Anderson for her very original drawings and end-cover design, to Miss Grace McClimans for her careful checking of references and many helpful suggestions, and to the Social Science Research Council for its grant-in-aid to help carry on the research in Washington, D.C. The author assumes sole responsibility for all statements, both of fact and opinion.

CONTENTS

ILLUSTRATIONS

1

The Beginnings

The Committee of Secret Correspondence

It is a far cry from the elaborate organization of the Department of State today with a staff of about six thousand, to the Department of Foreign Affairs established in 1781 with a secretary and two clerks; nevertheless, there is a very visible thread of continuity. The original Department stemmed from the Committee of Secret Correspondence, consisting of five members, which was created by the Continental Congress in 1775, with the renowned Benjamin Franklin as its chairman and John Jay one of its members. This committee was directed to correspond with various individuals abroad who might be of service to the Colonies. There was no restriction as to the nationality of these potential friends. Some of them were American, but more were foreign. Franklin, with his cosmopolitan background, carried on much of this correspondence— a correspondence as remarkable for its wisdom as for its wit. The committee at times also sent representatives abroad. Silas Deane was the first agent thus dispatched, but as a precautionary measure he went in the guise of a merchant rather than as a public minister of the Colonies. It was Franklin who wrote Deane's instructions.

Since the Committee of Secret Correspondence was a committee of the Congress, the latter regularly decided the matters to be discussed and the policy to be followed, thereby limiting considerably the importance of the committee. In fact, upon many occasions when the policy was of particular importance, the Congress in the Committee of the Whole took complete charge. For example, it was the Congress that prepared in the minutest detail the instructions to Franklin when he was elected commissioner on September 27, 1777, to negotiate a treaty with France. On other occasions special committees were appointed to consider questions of foreign policy, which were clearly within the jurisdiction of the Committee of Secret Correspondence. A special committee of five, containing no member of the Committee of Secret Correspondence, was named in December, 1776, to prepare and report on a plan to obtain assistance from abroad.[1] When it is realized that during the year 1776 Congress employed 169 special, and 14 standing committees,[2] it is not surprising that the conduct of foreign affairs was highly decentralized, and the Committee of Secret Correspondence largely by-passed.

The Committee for Foreign Affairs

Two years after its establishment, on April 17, 1777, the Committee of Secret Correspondence became the Committee for Foreign Affairs; and under this title it functioned just as intermittently and ineffectively for the next five years as had its predecessor. An evaluation of the work of the Committee for Foreign Affairs, by its most active member, James Lovell, gave evidence of its weakness:

There is really no such thing as a Committee for Foreign Affairs existing —no secretary or clerk further than I presume to be one and the other. The books and papers of that extinguished body lay yet on the table of Congress, or rather are locked up in the Secretary's private box.[3]

Under these circumstances the Committee for Foreign Affairs was wholly ineffective. John Jay, writing from Madrid in October, 1780, declared that he would throw stones with all his heart if he thought that they would only hit the committee with injury to the members of it.[4] But it was the Congress rather than the committee which was at fault. The Congress simply refused to give the committee jurisdiction over matters within its power. During the years 1779 and 1780, at least fifteen different special committees were elected to carry out functions which pertained wholly to the field of foreign affairs.[5] The result was a constant tug of war at home between the radical and conservative factions of these committees, with a corresponding diversity of instructions, which made for uncertainty of policy abroad.

On May 15, 1780, a committee was elected to consider and report upon the establishment of a Department of Foreign Affairs. It reported out a plan on December 17, and its report was debated in Congress beginning January 10, 1781.[6] Although both Arthur Lee and Robert Livingston were nominated immediately, it was not until August of the same year that Livingston was elected Secretary.

Robert R. Livingston—Secretary of Foreign Affairs

The new Secretary of Foreign Affairs, Robert R. Livingston, had been trained in the law, and in the Continental Congress he had served as a member of the Foreign Affairs Committee. Fortunately, he was a very good friend of

Franklin's and placed implicit confidence in the Colonies' most able representative abroad. This new agency of government, the Department of Foreign Affairs, was justified by the opinion of the Congress that "the extent and rising power of these United States entitles them to a place among the great potentates of Europe while our political and commercial interests point out the propriety of cultivating with them a friendly correspondence and connection." [7]

To accomplish this end, the Secretary of Foreign Affairs, who was to head the new office, was specifically directed to correspond with the representatives of the United States at foreign courts and with the ministers of foreign powers with a view to obtaining useful information relating to foreign affairs to be laid before Congress when required. The Secretary of Foreign Affairs, who was in reality an agent of Congress, was also instructed to submit such communications as the Congress directed, to our agents abroad. To carry on these functions the more effectively and intelligently, he was granted the liberty to attend sessions of Congress, a privilege that his successor under the Constitution did not possess.[8] However, since he was not authorized to ask questions, our first Secretary of Foreign Affairs confessed that he was puzzled oftentimes as to what were exactly the sentiments of Congress.

Not willing to continue indefinitely in this fog of uncertainty, Livingston, on August 10, 1781, prepared a letter to Congress pointing out certain gaps in the legislation setting up the Department. He was very emphatic in his insistence upon the need for greater powers and additional help. A Congressional committee received his report favorably and reported out the Act of February 22, 1782. The new legislation, slightly modified to permit the appointment of two Undersecretaries of Foreign Affairs, was, on the whole, satisfactory to Livingston. He could now control Departmental matters and settle private complaints against foreign states without consulting Congress. He could attend the sessions of Congress, ask and answer questions, explain his policies, and have access to the records of Congress. He was given a salary of $4,000, considered very munificent in those days; his two undersecretaries received respectively $800 and $700, and a clerk and a translator were employed at $500 each.[9]

An excellent idea of the general work of the newly established Department is given by the report of a Congressional committee which summarized the functions performed from October, 1781, to July 1, 1782. Some thirty-nine letters had been dispatched to our ministers plenipotentiary at Versailles, Madrid, The Hague, and St. Petersburg. Others had gone to consuls and agents in various capitals and ports. A certain amount of correspondence had also been carried on with the governors of the states, particularly the communication of Congressional resolutions. In conclusion the report declared that the business of the Department had been conducted "with much industry, attention and utility." [10]

The principal defect in the situation in which Livingston found himself was the interference of Congress. The duties of the Secretary had never been clearly defined and he was never given a free hand in the conduct of foreign relations. Congress passed resolutions directing the policy which foreign ministers were to pursue, and even dealt directly with foreign representatives in Philadelphia. Special committees were constantly appointed which infringed upon the powers supposedly delegated to the Secretary.

In addition to the interference, which produced a feeling of futility, the duties were arduous in the extreme. It is difficult today to appreciate the drudgery required to carry on the routine duties of the office in those days. All correspondence was in longhand and every dispatch had to be copied several times in anticipation of loss. It was regularly the custom to send a duplicate of the preceding dispatch with the first copy of a dispatch, just in case the preceding dispatch had not arrived. Communications were so slow and irregular that the Secretary never knew how many intermediate dispatches were still on their way or how many had been intercepted by the enemy. A minimum of six weeks was the time required to get a dispatch to Europe, and oftentimes it took as many months. As a consequence, both the Secretary and the United States representatives abroad had to work quite independently. It has been estimated by an American historian that approximately one-third of American diplomatic correspondence of the Revolutionary period failed to reach its destination, and on one occasion when the Continental Congress had twelve paid agents in Europe, eleven months elapsed without a word from any of them.[11] Such a situation at times was very embarrassing to Livingston, and he complained to Franklin that he blushed when he met a member of Congress who inquired as to what was passing in Europe. When General Washington applied to him for advice, Livingston confessed that he had to inform him that he had no information but what he had seen in the papers.

Nevertheless, the achievements of Livingston as Secretary of Foreign Affairs were considerable. Perhaps of greatest importance was the stand which he took from the very beginning in placing the conduct of our foreign relations firmly upon the basis of international law. In a private letter written to the Governor of Virginia on February 18, 1782, he declared: "While we hold an intercourse with civilized nations we must conform to laws which humanity has established and which custom has consecrated among them." [12] He saw the futility of sending representatives to countries which were unwilling to receive them and opposed this procedure as being both unwise and in violation of international law. Franklin felt the same way, and he declared upon one occasion that "a virgin state should preserve its virgin character and not go about suitering for alliances, but wait with decent dignity for the application of others." [13]

Livingston organized the Department of Foreign Affairs so that it functioned smoothly and effectively. He played a leading role in shaping the foreign policy of the country. He insisted constantly that the foreign representatives of the United States, both ministers and consuls, should report regularly and in detail. He favored strongly the appointment of Americans only in foreign diplomatic posts—a policy that was accepted after he left office and has been followed ever since. He believed that diplomatic salaries should not depend upon the fluctuations of exchange, and supported Franklin's stand upon this issue in the Congress. He did his best to speed up Congressional action in foreign affairs, and when he resigned Congress thanked him for his services and showed its appreciation for "the ability, zeal, and fidelity with which he hath discharged the trust reposed in him."

Various reasons were assigned as the cause of Livingston's resignation. Congress was niggardly in its salary appropriations, and Livingston pointed out that his expenses exceeded his annual salary of $4,000 by $3,000, or by 75 per cent. He had been appointed to the post of Chancellor of the State of New York, and he felt that while holding that office he could give more attention to his family and to his property interests. The emergency had passed and he no longer believed that he was essential to the public interest.

Although Livingston had originally signified his desire to resign in November, 1782, it was not until the following June that he was permitted to leave the office; and even then Congress seemed unwilling or unable to name a successor. In fact, the position remained unfilled for more than a year, and during that period foreign relations were handled by Congress directly. In conducting the foreign relations of the Colonies, the Congress would discuss and formulate policy in reference to questions raised by United States agents abroad, and then assign the matter to the proper committee to prepare a suitable reply. This response was passed in the form of a Congressional resolution, and after being signed by its president, it was immediately dispatched to the appropriate diplomatic representative abroad. Unfortunately, many of the dispatches from our representatives abroad went wholly unanswered.

Our diplomatic corps at the time of Livingston's resignation consisted of five ministers plenipotentiary, all of whom, except Jefferson, were engaged in negotiating peace in Paris. Benjamin Franklin was the American minister in Paris. John Adams had been accredited to The Hague, John Jay to Madrid, and Henry Laurens and Thomas Jefferson [14] were elected specifically as commissioners for the negotiation of the peace and accorded the same rank as their colleagues. All received salaries of $11,111 per annum; considering the purchasing power of the dollar at the time, this was a relatively larger sum than was paid to their successors. Francis Dana, our unrecognized envoy at St. Petersburg, was rated as minister and his salary was $4,440.40, the same amount as received by William Carmichael, secretary to the legation at Madrid. C. W. F. Dumas, the Swiss secretary and translator for Minister Adams in The Hague, although he served as chargé d'affaires when Mr. Adams went to Paris, had to be content with the small salary of $920. During this period the ceremonial duties normally performed by a Department of Foreign Affairs were assigned to the Superintendent of Finances, or to the Secretary of War.

The physical plant of the first Department of Foreign Affairs was exceedingly modest. It consisted of a small residence at 13 South Sixth Street in Philadelphia. A large room on the ground floor was occupied by the clerk and interpreter. The Secretary had the front room on the second floor. Under Livingston the office remained in this building from its establishment in 1781 until June, 1783, when Livingston finally quit the position. Inasmuch as Congress again took charge, no quarters were needed until John Jay assumed the duties of the office in December, 1784. After Livingston's resignation the Department's papers were turned over to the departmental secretary, Charles Thomson, and kept under seal until Henry Remsen, Jr., was elected Under Secretary in March, 1784. Lewis R. Morris, the first Under Secretary of the Department, left his office soon after the departure of his chief.

John Jay—Secretary for Foreign Affairs

It had long been realized that the committee system left much to be desired in the conduct of foreign relations, and on May 7, 1784, Congress elected John Jay of New York as Secretary for Foreign Affairs. Jay, at the time, was still in England, where he had gone after his arduous work in Paris in helping to negotiate the treaty of peace. It is doubtful that he was pleased when he landed in New York on July 24, 1784, and learned of his appointment. He had been an original member of the Committee of Secret Correspondence, and as such he had realized that government by Congress was both cumbersome and inefficient. As a precautionary measure, Jay insisted that he be allowed to choose his own clerks—a function which Congress had presumably kept in its own hands.[15] The fact that the Congress was moving the seat of government from Trenton, New Jersey, to New York City made the position somewhat more acceptable. Jay realized that he was exceedingly well equipped to serve in the post which had been offered to him, and he was not disposed to shirk responsibility where the possibility of substantial achievement was afforded.

At this time, although John Jay was only thirty-nine years of age, he had a long career of public service behind him. Trained for the law, he had served in both the first and second Continental Congresses as representative of New York and had been elected president of the second. In 1779 he had been selected as minister to Spain, and although his mission was a failure in that he was

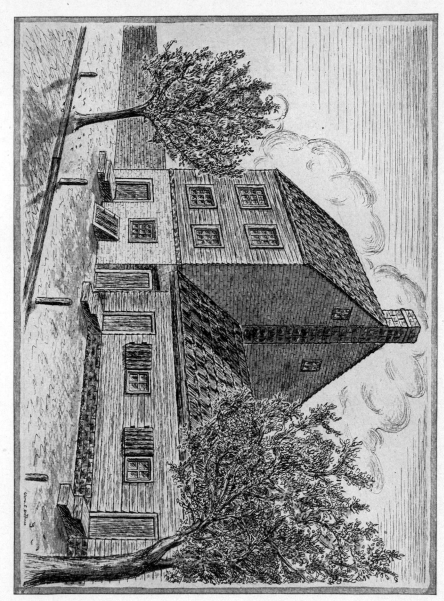

The Department's First Home 1781–1783
13 South Sixth Street, Philadelphia

never officially received, his stalwart efforts to obtain recognition and a loan never weakened in the two years that he remained in Madrid. Jay's subsequent services in Paris in the negotiations for a treaty of peace were clouded by his ever present suspicions of France, which although they were not wholly unwarranted, hardly excused his opening negotiations with Great Britain behind Franklin's back. Even the meticulous John Adams supported Jay upon this occasion in his nonobservance of protocol.

It would have been difficult to have found any person available at the time better qualified for the office of Secretary of Foreign Affairs than John Jay. Having returned to America, in the words of John Adams, "like a bee to his hive, with both legs loaded with merit and honor," he was well equipped to make the position count for something in the conduct of foreign affairs. His first act was to inform the Congress that he had come into the office of Secretary of Foreign Affairs "with ideas of its duties and rights somewhat different from those which seemed to be entertained by the Congress." Sensing his insistence upon the need for channeling all matters pertaining to foreign relations through the Secretary's office, Congress, in a resolution dated February 11, 1785, reaffirmed the preceding resolutions of February 22, 1782, requiring that all communications both to and from the United States on the subject of foreign affairs be made through the Secretary, and that all letters, memorials, or other papers on the subject of foreign affairs for the United States be addressed to him. The Secretary was authorized to appoint an interpreter so that in the future all papers written in a foreign language which might be communicated to Congress from the Department of Foreign Affairs should be accompanied with a translation into English.

That this policy of centralization of the duties of the office in the Secretary was recognized as vitally essential is shown by a letter written by Madison to Monroe on March 21, 1785, in which he declared:

If the office of foreign affairs be a proper one, and properly filled, a reference of all foreign dispatches to it in the first instance is so obvious a course, that any other disposition of them by Congress seems . . . to affront the minister in office and to put on him a label of caution against that respect and confidence of the ministers of foreign powers which are essential to his usefulness.[16]

Hardly had Jay entered upon his duties on December 21, 1784, when it was necessary to move his office to New York. His first location was a room above the Council chamber in the City Hall which the Common Council had obligingly permitted the Congress to use as a temporary meeting place. In April the Congress leased a building at the southeast corner of Broad and Pearl streets, the former location of Fraunces's Tavern, and the Department of Foreign Affairs was assigned two rooms—one for the Secretary and one for an assistant and a clerk. The Department remained in this location until 1788, when a new location on Broadway, near the Battery, was provided. Shortly after Jay took charge, the Department was granted another clerk and an interpreter, and in the last year of his incumbency still another employee, who served in the dual capacity of doorkeeper and messenger. Jay's original salary was $4,000, but it was later reduced to $3,500. The doorkeeper received an annual salary of $150.

Jay appreciated the necessity for carefully collecting and filing the official correspondence of the Department—a task which Livingston was inclined to overlook. He informed John Adams that he had collected his public letters and dispatches because loose and detached papers were easily lost or misplaced, and "it is to papers in this office that future historians must recur for accurate accounts of many interesting affairs respecting the late Revolution." [17] A Congressional report on the Department made in 1788 noted that the clerk had recorded five volumes of Adams's letters, and was working on the sixth. Two volumes of Jay's letters extending from December 20, 1779, to July 25, 1785, had been copied. Other volumes already recorded were the letters of Dana while in Russia, the correspondence of Henry Laurens, minister to the Netherlands, who had been captured and imprisoned in the Tower of London and when released made commissioner of peace; the special mission of John Laurens at Versailles, and the correspondence of Arthur Lee, and of Silas Deane.[18]

The daily transactions of the Department were copied into a journal, the Secretary's letters to our representatives abroad were bound in a Book of Foreign Letters, the correspondence with foreign ministers and others in the United States was recorded in the American Letter Book, and reports to Congress were placed in a Book of Reports. Letters of evidence and commissions of foreign ministers, chargés d'affaires, and consuls were kept in the Book of Foreign Commissions.

Unquestionably the routine work of the Department imposed a considerable amount of sheer drudgery upon the Secretary. He must not only determine what papers should be submitted to Congress but he must annotate and analyze them, and if he felt it necessary, appear in person to present and defend the policies which he thought should be followed. His influence over Congress was very considerable. The French chargé d'affaires described the influence of Secretary Jay to Vergennes, French Minister of Foreign Affairs: "Congress seems to me to be guided only by his directions, and it is as difficult to obtain anything without the cooperation of that minister as to bring about the rejection of a measure proposed by him." [19]

The diagnosis was not entirely correct, because Congress at times refused very definitely to be guided by the Secretary of Foreign Affairs. When the Spanish chargé d'affaires, Don Diego de Gardoqui, was approached by Secretary Jay regarding a commercial treaty, he was very willing to negotiate, but only if the United States agreed to give up navigation of the Mississippi. Jay, who while in Madrid had insisted that Americans believed that "Almighty God had made that river a highway for the people of the upper country to go to the sea by," [20] after much hesitation agreed to accept the Spanish demands to the extent of not exercising the right of navigation for a period of thirty years. When he tried to persuade the Congress to support his compromise, Congress was not impressed by his reasoning and there was strong opposition, particularly on the part of the Southern delegates. Jay then urged the Congress to make a public declaration of United States rights to the Mississippi, and if it were refused to be prepared for war. The Congress thereupon declared that the navigation of the Mississippi was an "essential right of the United States," but referred the treaty to the new Federal government. Jay later admitted that his acceptance of the Spanish thesis was an error of judgment.[21]

Diplomatic Problems

Jay found that our relations with Great Britain were most unsatisfactory. The British had placed onerous restrictions upon American foreign commerce even while they were profiting exceedingly by their trade with the States. The state of commercial relations was so critical that Jay thought it advisable to write to the president of Congress recommending that Mr. Temple be received as consul general of His Britannic Majesty, lest a refusal might be thought to be based upon "pique and irritation, which though nations may feel, they ought not expressly or impliedly to declare." [22] The northern frontier posts which were to be freed from British garrisons by the terms of the treaty remained occupied as before, and no apparent intention to withdraw was indicated. When the Congress protested, British Foreign Minister Carmarthen replied that the Americans were neither paying the British debts nor giving the promised protection to the Loyalists. Congress turned over the matter to Jay, who prepared a long and comprehensive report upon the subject, pointing out the failures on both sides and urging the Congress to make the treaty the law of the land, enforceable by the Courts.[23] Jay conceded to our minister in London, John Adams, that his inquiries led him to believe that the conduct of the states in relation to the treaty was such "that there has not been a single day since it took effect on which it has not been violated in America by one or other of the states." [24] Unfortunately, Jay allowed this objective attitude of his to become known to the British consul in New York, Sir John Temple, who was thus able to strengthen his government's hands in refusing to carry out the British commitment.[25]

Jay was more successful in his dealings with France; in fact, according to an outstanding authority on the subject, John Jay's greatest achievement as Secretary of State was to revise substantially a consular convention with France which Franklin had negotiated in 1784.[26] Franklin had undoubtedly exceeded his instructions; and although in respect to the extraterritorial jurisdiction of consuls Franklin had strengthened the position of American courts in giving them jurisdiction over criminal cases of nationals living in the territory of the other party, he allowed France many privileges which, even though reciprocal, were of little benefit to the United States. Jay, who believed in centralized authority, objected particularly to the provision requiring the French consuls to present their commissions to, and receive their exequaturs from, the various states, instead of dealing with the Congress directly. Jay's case against ratification was so effective that Jefferson negotiated a new convention with Vergennes which eliminated the features which Jay opposed. This treaty was the consular convention of 1788, approved by the Senate in 1789—the first agreement of its kind to be approved for ratification by that body.

It was during the incumbency of Jay that the United States for the first time decided that a foreign representative was *persona non grata* and requested his recall. The situation was the more delicate in that the individual was the Count de Moustier, the first minister sent to the United States by France. Secretary Jay had been very insistent that the United States was not satisfied that France should be represented by a mere chargé d'affaires and urged the exchange of diplomats of ministerial rank. The French Ministry of Foreign Affairs finally agreed, and in 1787 accredited the Count de Moustier to the United States. No *agrément* was needed, since he came with cordial letters of introduction from both Jefferson and Lafayette. He was accompanied by his sister-in-law the Marquise de Bréhan, who came in search of health and a more simple environment to educate her son. The count was ostentatious and discourteous and quickly made himself thoroughly detested. When it became bruited about that an "improper connection" existed between the count and the marchioness, Jay wrote to Jefferson suggesting the count's recall. The French Foreign Minister did not wish a public scandal, and so, interpreting a statement of De Moustier's in one of his letters that he wished a leave of absence, a new chargé d'affaires was appointed and De Moustier returned to France.

Procedure and Protocol

The social side of diplomatic life was recognized as a very important adjunct of successful foreign policy, and from the very beginning those in control of American diplomacy utilized it effectively. John Jay built a house on lower

Broadway and entertained often and lavishly. He had a large circle of friends in the colonial society of the day who were always welcome, and Tuesday nights were set aside for the members of the diplomatic corps. Foreign visitors regularly called upon the Secretary of Foreign Affairs, and his home was one of the chief centers of New York society. Mrs. Jay, the former Sara Livingston, was a very pleasing hostess and her cuisine was so excellent that even such a *bon vivant* as the Count de Moustier could appreciate her dinners. The Spanish chargé d'affaires, Don Diego de Gardoqui, was very fond of dining and dancing with her and felt that his mission was more satisfactorily accomplished through his friendly relationship with his delightful hostess.

Perhaps it may not be amiss to indicate here the etiquette observed in the reception of foreign envoys at this time. In a letter to Don Diego de Gardoqui dated June 21, 1785, Secretary Jay outlined the procedure to be followed:

At such time as may be appointed by Congress for a public reception, the Secretary for Foreign Affairs will conduct you to the Congress chamber, to a seat to be placed for you, and announce you to Congress; the President and members keeping their seats and remaining covered. Your commission and letters of credence are then to be delivered to the Secretary of Congress who will read a translation of them to be prepared by the Secretary for Foreign Affairs from the copies to be left with the President. You will then be at liberty to speak and, if you please, deliver to the Secretary of Congress in writing what you may think proper to Congress, who will take what you may say into consideration, and through the Secretary for Foreign Affairs will communicate whatever answer they may resolve upon.

When you return, you will be reconducted by the Secretary for Foreign Affairs. A visit will be expected by every member of Congress, as well those who may be in town, as others who may afterward arrive during your residence here.[27]

There is no doubt that throughout his term of office Jay felt that the whole governmental organization was quite unsatisfactory. Even before he returned from abroad, he had shown on many occasions his belief in a strong national government which could act directly on the people rather than through the states. His experience as Secretary for Foreign Affairs only strengthened his views. He was one of the founders of the *Federalist* and contributed five of the papers. His greatest contribution, however, was an "Address to the People of New York," which had a profound effect. His summary of the weakness of Congress, particularly in the field of the conduct of foreign relations, was a masterly indictment:

They [the Congress] may make war, but are not empowered to raise men or money to carry it on. They may make peace, but without power to see the terms of it observed. . . . They may form alliances, but without ability to comply with the stipulations on their part. They may enter into treaties of commerce, but without power to enforce them at home or abroad. . . . They may appoint ministers and other officers of trust, but without power to try or punish them for misdemeanors. They may resolve, but cannot execute either with dispatch or with secrecy. In short, they may consult, and deliberate, and recommend, and make requisitions, and they who please, may regard them.[28]

The people of the United States were convinced that the new Constitution hammered out in Philadelphia was a step forward, and it was adopted in 1788 and entered into effect in March, 1789. The last specific action taken by Congress in the field of foreign affairs was a resolution passed on September 16, 1788. It was resolved that "no further progress be made in the negotiations with Spain, by the Secretary of Foreign Affairs; but that the subject to which they relate be referred to the federal government, which is to assemble in March next." [29]

Although many defects of the Department of Foreign Affairs under the Articles of Confederation would be remedied under the Constitution, the very weaknesses that had been disclosed were advantageous in building the new Department upon a foundation tested by experience. Nor should the achievements of the Committee of Secret Correspondence, the Committee of Foreign Affairs, and the Department of Foreign Affairs be discounted. Perhaps never in our history have we had a more brilliant galaxy of diplomatic representatives abroad than in this early period: Benjamin Franklin, who with Jay and Adams negotiated the Treaty of 1783 with Great Britain which, Wharton declared, "of all treaties that have ever been negotiated . . . has been of the greatest benefit to civilization as a whole";[30] John Adams, who persuaded the States General of Holland to sign a treaty of commerce with the colonies even before the peace treaty was concluded, and later became our first American minister plenipotentiary to the court of St. James's; John Jay, who was willing to sacrifice his pride and his personal interests in remaining at the Spanish post where he was not wanted and was treated accordingly; and Thomas Jefferson, who succeeded Franklin in Paris and was to be the first Secretary of State under the new Constitution.

Nor was the young Republic content with representation at the courts of the great powers with which its interests were particularly bound. Holland, Prussia, Tuscany, and even inhospitable Russia of Catherine the Great were approached by commissioners of the Congress in the hope that contacts of advantage might be established.

The committee system of control of foreign relations was gradually supplanted, and the power to deal with foreign nations and even to make treaties was delegated by the Congress to the Secretary of Foreign Affairs. The Department of Foreign Affairs had so clearly proved its value that its reestablishment in modified form was always contemplated in the many and various proposals for executive control of foreign relations in the new government under the Constitution.

2

The Department of State Is Established

The Department of Foreign Affairs ·

The need for a Department of Foreign Affairs under the Constitution was so urgent that until one could be established, the former Department, with John Jay at the head, continued to function. Although various proposals in the Constitutional Convention had specifically mentioned a Department of Foreign Affairs headed by a Secretary, the real beginning of the Department of State under the Constitution stemmed from a motion by James Madison on May 19, 1789, before the Committee of the Whole of the House of Representatives, to the effect "that there shall be established an Executive Department to be denominated the Department of Foreign Affairs at the head of which there shall be an officer, to be called the Secretary to the Department of Foreign Affairs."

After considerable debate in both Houses, the Act setting up the Department of Foreign Affairs was passed and became law with the signature of President George Washington on July 27, 1789. The functions of the office as enumerated in the Act were to the effect that the Secretary should perform such duties as the President might assign to him relative to correspondence, or negotiations with public ministers or consuls from the United States or from foreign states, and it was specifically provided that the Secretary should conduct the business of the Department "in such manner as the President of the United States shall, from time to time order or instruct." He was to have charge of all records, books, and papers in the existing office and he was authorized to appoint a Chief Clerk who should take charge of all the records, books, and papers of the Department in the absence of the Secretary.[1]

The Department of Foreign Affairs lasted in the form originally established by the Congress less than two months. The founding fathers quickly discovered that certain duties had to be performed correlating the Federal government with the states. At first it was proposed that a home department be established to correspond with the states, keep the Great Seal and the accounts and records of the United States, and to provide for the publication of the Acts of Congress; but the Congress was not disposed to be reckless in establishing administrative machinery. Rather was it felt that the Department of Foreign Affairs would not be so overburdened with work but that it could perform these domestic tasks in addition to those pertaining to foreign affairs already prescribed. Consequently, a bill was passed and approved by the President on September 15, 1789, changing the name of the Department and augmenting its functions.

The Department of State

The new designation of the Department of Foreign Affairs was the Department of State, and the principal officer was to be called the Secretary of State. In addition to the duties pertaining to foreign affairs, the Secretary was now directed to receive from the President the bills, orders, and resolutions of Congress, have these printed, deliver a printed copy to each senator and representative and the authenticated copies to the governor of each state. He was made custodian of the Great Seal of the United States and given authority to affix the seal to all civil commissions of officers to be appointed by the President. He was also given custody of all books, records, and papers that pertained to the Department.[2]

A statute approved on September 11, 1789, had already taken care of the financial needs of the new Department. The Secretary's salary was fixed at $3,500, the salary of the Chief Clerk at $800, and other clerks at not over $500 each. In his estimates made on May 7, 1789, before the Department of Foreign Affairs was officially established under the Constitution, Secretary Jay had proposed a budget of $5,950 allocated as follows: Secretary, $3,500; Under Secretary, $800; two clerks at $450 each; a French interpreter, $250; allowances for other interpreters, $150; office rent, $200; doorkeeper and messenger, $150. The Department of Foreign Affairs was the first executive department to be established under the Constitution, and Jay was given the opportunity to carry on as Secretary if he so desired. However, since he was given also the privilege of choosing any other high position of trust in the new government, he picked that of Chief Justice of the Supreme Court, a position more fitted to his judicial temperament.

Thomas Jefferson—First Secretary of State

In picking his cabinet, Washington not only looked for ability and absolute integrity, but he wanted men who had already distinguished themselves in their work. He chose men "already of marked eminence before the country; not only as the more likely to be serviceable, but because the public will more readily trust them." [3] For the top executive position in the new cabinet, Washington was doubly desirous that these criteria should be met. Thomas Jefferson seemed to Washington to be ideally equipped to fulfill these requirements as the first Secretary in the new Department of State. Although only forty-six years of age, Jefferson had already achieved a great name in political affairs, both at home and abroad. It was he who had been called to draft the Declaration of Independence, and he had also prepared the resolution ratifying the peace treaty with Great Britain. He succeeded Franklin as minister to France, where he found himself immediately at home in the cosmopolitan society of Paris. Although he was a bit diffident as to being able to succeed adequately his great predecessor, Jefferson's own broad outlook and keen interest in matters of science and philosophy quickly gave him an enviable position among the cultured circles of the French capital. Except for the constant strain due to the weak financial situation of Congress, Jefferson was faced with no serious problems in Paris; in fact, he was so contented with the position that he was not at all eager to give it up.

Washington was quite aware of this predilection, and taking advantage of the fact that Jefferson had returned to the United States on leave to take care of certain private matters, he wrote him a personal letter urging him to accept the position of Secretary of State. Jefferson informed the President frankly that he would have preferred to return to Paris, but that if it was believed that he could be more useful in the administration, he would sacrifice his own inclinations without hesitation. Washington's reply was a masterly appeal in which he emphasized the importance of the office and Jefferson's special aptitude to fill it acceptably:

I consider the office of Secretary for the Department of State as very important on many accounts and I know of no person who in my judgment could better exercise the duties of it than yourself. . . . But in order that you may be better prepared to make your ultimate decision on good grounds I think it necessary to add one fact which is this, so far as I have been able to obtain information from all quarters your late appointment has given very extensive and very great satisfaction to the Public.[4]

Organization and Personnel

Although Jefferson was commissioned on September 26, 1789, he did not enter upon his duties until March 22, 1790. In the meantime Jay, as requested by President Washington, performed the essential tasks of the office. The routine matters and care of the papers pertaining to foreign affairs were under the direction of Henry Remsen, Jr., who had been named Under Secretary of Foreign Affairs on March 2, 1784. The custody of the Great Seal and such public papers as were not connected with foreign affairs, finance, or war, were assigned by the President to Roger Alden, who had served as Deputy Secretary of Congress. Since these two officers were of equal rank and performed equally important duties, and since the law provided for but one Chief Clerk, Jefferson was in a quandary as to which one he could do without. Neither was willing to take a secondary appointment, and "they were each so well acquainted with their respective departments and the papers in them, that it was extremely desirable to keep them both." [5] Jefferson solved the problem by appointing them both Chief Clerks, and the Act of June 4, 1790, authorized their employment at a salary of $800 each per year. The dual arrangement, however, did not last long; Alden found the remuneration inadequate and he resigned on July 25, 1790. Thereupon the Home Office and the Foreign Office were merged and Remsen became the only Chief Clerk.

One of Jefferson's appointments to the small staff of the new Department proved to be most unfortunate. A French translator was necessary, and at the suggestion of certain friends, including James Madison, Jefferson gave the appointment to Philip Freneau, a well known poet and journalist. Freneau, to supplement his inadequate government salary of $250 per year and to express his very definite political ideas, became the editor of the National Gazette, a newspaper which was to become the leading antiadministration organ. Although serving as a translating clerk in the Department of State, Freneau, as editor of the National Gazette, never hesitated to attack President Washington and his policies. He castigated the monarchical ways of the President and even found fault with the regal splendor of Mrs. Washington's social affairs. Inasmuch as Secretary of the Treasury Hamilton, Jefferson's chief opponent in the cabinet, was the principal object of Freneau's malevolence, Jefferson made no effort to discharge his clerk. On one occasion at a cabinet meeting, Washington declared that the rascal Freneau had sent him three copies of his papers every day in order to insult the President, and intimated that Jefferson should get rid of him. Jefferson, however, refused to withdraw his appointment.[6] In fact, it is not certain but that Jefferson gave Freneau certain items from the foreign dispatches which were quite useful to his press activities.[7]

Jefferson had long been antipathetic to Alexander Hamilton and he distrusted Hamilton's conservative tendencies and monarchistic theories. Undoubtedly the fundamental cause of disagreement between the two men was their completely different attitude toward the government under the Constitution. Hamilton favored a strong, centralized government, and was willing to use almost any means to obtain it. Jefferson believed in the people, in democratic control and states' rights, and would not compromise his principles.

During the first two years of their services as members of the cabinet, Jefferson and Hamilton got along fairly well, partly as a result of Washington's efforts and also because each was equally desirous to see the new government succeed. The first serious breach came as the result of Freneau's caustic criticism of Hamilton in the *National Gazette*. Hamilton, writing in the *Gazette of the United States* under various pseudonyms, attacked Jefferson severely, centering his accusations on the allegation that Jefferson had hired Freneau to attack those who opposed him in the government. Although Freneau made an affidavit that Jefferson had neither written a line in his paper nor had attempted in any way to influence it, Hamilton continued his attacks. Relations with France brought matters to a head.

Jefferson hated England and was fond of France; Hamilton much preferred the staid and loyal British to the excitable and revolutionary French. With both men in the cabinet and each consulted by Washington on all important questions of policy, an outbreak was bound to occur. Washington clearly recognized that by the Constitution the President was responsible for the conduct of foreign affairs, but he wanted the support of his advisors and usually asked for written opinions from the members of his cabinet. Jefferson and Hamilton were almost invariably upon opposite sides. Jefferson realized that this situation was most unsatisfactory, and in a letter to Washington dated May 23, 1792, suggested that he wished to retire at the end of Washington's first term. It was only the serious situation in France, brought about by the establishment of the Republic and the execution of Louis XVI, joined with Washington's earnest request that he remain, that prevented his resignation.

Jefferson on Recognition and Neutrality

The question as to whether the United States should recognize the new republican government of France inspired Jefferson to prepare one of his greatest state papers—a classic presentation of the case for the recognition of a new government, regardless of its form or the method of its establishment. Writing to Gouverneur Morris, the United States minister to France, Jefferson declared:

We surely cannot deny to any nation that right whereon our own government is founded—that everyone may govern itself according to whatever form it pleases and change these forms at its own will; and that it may transact its business with foreign nations through whatever organ it thinks proper, whether king, convention, assembly, committee, president, or anything it may choose. The will of the nation is the only thing essential to be regarded.[8]

In April, 1793, the United States learned that France had gone to war with England and Spain. Since the United States was still bound by the Treaty of Alliance of 1778 with France, the question of our policy was a vital one, and Washington called a cabinet meeting to get the opinions of his advisors. He found that although all seemed to favor a policy of neutrality, there was complete disagreement as to procedure. A declaration of neutrality was vigorously opposed by Jefferson, and in its place a proclamation setting out the duties of Americans toward the belligerents which would not mention neutrality was finally agreed upon. It was also unanimously agreed that the new French minister be received. The proclamation itself was the work of Randolph, although it was undoubtedly based upon an earlier draft prepared by Jay. It would seem to have been the duty of Jefferson to have prepared it, but Washington, knowing that Jefferson was not too enthusiastic about the policy, gave him no opportunity. In fact, although Jefferson supported the policy officially, he personally characterized the proclamation as an act of pusillanimity [9] and felt that Washington had exceeded his constitutional powers in issuing it.

Inasmuch as Washington wished to have a specific answer as to whether the French representative, Edmond Genêt, should be received with or without qualifications, and whether the United States was still bound by her treaties with France, he requested Jefferson and Hamilton to present him their opinions in writing. Hamilton favored a complete neutrality, the denunciation or suspension of our treaties with France, and the reception of the French envoy, with substantial qualifications. Jefferson disagreed with him on all points, taking the sound position that treaties were made with states and a change in government changed neither their obligation nor their force. He recommended an unqualified reception to Citizen Genêt, thereby recognizing the validity of the treaties. Washington recognized the cogency of Jefferson's arguments; he received the French envoy without qualification.

Unfortunately, the French representative, in spite of Jefferson's predilection in his favor, so comported himself that the Secretary of State could not support his actions. Genêt not only violated every semblance of neutrality, but was insolent in his attitude toward the President. When Genêt in requesting an exequatur for a French consul addressed his letter to the Congress rather than to the President, Jefferson, who believed firmly that the transaction of foreign relations was vested solely in the President, made a pronouncement that has held to the present day. He wrote:

The President is the only channel of communication between this country and foreign nations, and it is from him alone that foreign nations or their agents are to learn what is or has been the will of the nation; and whatever he communicates as such, they have a right, and are bound to consider as the expression of the nation and no foreign agent can be allowed to question it, to interpose between him and any other branch of Government under the pretext of either's transgressing their functions.[10]

Jefferson's Resignation

Jefferson sensed that Washington was tending more to the Hamiltonian point of view in foreign affairs, and in July, 1793, he insisted upon retiring from the cabinet. Again Washington opposed his going, but compromised upon a delay until the end of the year. It was during this last six months that Jefferson completed his last and one of his most important state papers, a voluminous report on "Commercial Privileges and Restrictions," [11] which was meant to serve as the basis for Congressional retaliatory action against British goods as a means of compelling the British to agree to a more advantageous commercial agreement with the United States. Hamilton not only ignored completely the jurisdictional rights of the Department of State, but a decent sense of propriety as well, by keeping himself and the British minister informed upon the principal proposals of the report.

On December 31, 1793, Jefferson sent in his letter of resignation. In his reply President Washington, after once more expressing his regret at Jefferson's resignation, declared:

I cannot suffer you to leave your station, without assuring you, that the opinion which I had formed of your integrity and talents, and which dictated your original nomination, has been confirmed by the fullest experience; and that both have been eminently displayed in the discharge of your duties.[12]

In evaluating Jefferson's work as the first Secretary of State, it must be conceded that he does not perhaps rate a position as one of the greatest who has held the office. Washington to a considerable extent was his own Secretary of State, and Jefferson cooperated willingly upon this basis. Hamilton was constantly attacking Jefferson both openly and covertly; and upon the occasion when Jefferson completely confounded the British minister, Hammond, by his brilliant defense of the American position with regard to the failure of the states to restore Loyalist property and to pay their debts, Hamilton nullified the effect by telling Hammond that Jefferson's note did not fairly represent the attitude of the administration. Hamilton's constant opposition made Jefferson's position very difficult and detracted from his effectiveness.

Nevertheless, as administrative head of the Department of State he did a superb job. His relations with our representatives abroad were highly felicitous, and he was usually inclined to oppose the sending of special agents when a regularly accredited representative was doing his work effectively. If Washington had listened to Jefferson's advice, John Jay would not have been sent on his special mission to Great Britain which was destined to have such momentous consequences.[13] Appreciating the difficulties caused by the low salaries allowed by the government to American representatives abroad, Jefferson tried to have the law of July 1, 1790, which governed the cost of the foreign service, so interpreted as to permit certain expenses to be allowed as an additional charge. In a memorandum submitted to the President on July 17, 1790, Jefferson informed Washington that he had had a conference the day before with the Vice President, who was familiar with the residences at London and The Hague, and with the Chief Justice, who was acquainted with that at Madrid; and all three concurred in the opinion that the salaries fixed by the Act—$9,000 for ministers and $4,500 for chargés d'affaires—were much below those of the same grade at the courts of Europe and less than the public good required. It was therefore unanimously agreed that the cost of couriers, gazettes, translations, printing necessary papers, and aid to poor Americans should be allowed as an extra charge.[14]

The Department of State Under Jefferson

It was well that Jefferson was a natural administrator, because the Department of State was the catchall of duties which were not definitely assigned elsewhere. In fact, Jefferson himself described the Department of State as embracing the whole domestic administration (war and finance excepted).[15] President Washington deposited official letters, even those concerning other departments, in the State Department; and all applications for office were turned over to it. When civil appointments were made by the President, he used the Secretary of State as the agency for the transmission of the commissions of appointment. Originally, Jefferson expected the postal service to be under his jurisdiction, and with Postmaster General Pickering worked out a scheme to accelerate the mail service; but Washington preferred the post office to be under the Treasury Department. On the other hand, the mint, which seemingly was closer to the Treasury Department, was definitely assigned to the Department of State. Perhaps Washington remembered that it was Jefferson who had proposed the Spanish dollar as the unit for the United States and had supported the decimal system as a rational and easy means of computation. Jefferson had also thought it wise to coin silver half dollars, a "bit," or tenth of a dollar, and cents of copper, valued at a hundredth of a dollar. He established a mint in Philadelphia and the first coins were struck in October, 1792.

Another function which the first Secretary of State had to perform was to issue letters of patent. The Chief Clerk of the Department was in charge of preparing the papers, and final action was taken by a board which usually consisted of the Secretary of State and the Attorney General. The story is told that when a certain Isaacs requested a patent for a process of converting sea water into fresh water, he was invited by Jefferson to perform his operation before certain members of the Philosophical Society. No patent was issued because the process utilized was merely one of distillation.

The Department of State was also responsible to some extent for the carrying out of the copyright laws. Inasmuch as the law prescribed that within six months after publication of the title of a book, chart, or map, a copy be deposited in the Department of State for preservation, the Department became the depository of all books written in the United States. Subsequently, engraved prints and musical compositions were included, and the collection soon became a very large one. The State Department fulfilled this function until 1859, when the Department of Interior was given jurisdiction. In 1870 the Library of Congress took charge and is still in control.

Another function performed for a time by the Department of State was the printing of the census from the returns which were deposited in the Department. The first census, taken in 1790, was a simple affair largely limited to an enumeration of the population divided into free white persons, male or female, and slaves. The results were published in a fifty-two-page pamphlet, and the entire cost of the census was $44,337.18.

The Department of State was not a heavy drain upon the finances of the country, in spite of its manifold activities. In June, 1790, Jefferson sent to the Congress an estimate, amounting to $7,961, of the probable expenses of the Department for one year. Of this amount $7,300 was for the salaries of the Secretary, five clerks, the French interpreter, and two messengers. The remaining $691 covered office rent, firewood, stationery, newspapers, and gazettes.[16] The Act of December 3, 1791, fixed the budget of the Department for the ensuing year at $6,300; but this was not to include the amounts paid to messengers and laborers, nor did it include rental or other maintenance expenses. When Jefferson, at the end of 1793, turned over the office to his successor, Edmund Randolph, the cost of the Department had increased to $9,661.67. The cost of foreign intercourse was considerably higher, inasmuch as ministers were paid $9,000, and chargés d'affaires $4,500. By 1791 the United States had a regularly organized diplomatic service, with Thomas Pinckney as minister in London, Gouverneur Morris as minister to France, William Carmichael as chargé d'affaires in Madrid, William Short as minister resident to The Hague, and David Humphreys as the first United States minister resident to Portugal. Although in 1790 Jefferson had appointed some sixteen consular officers, they were self-supporting, since their remuneration was obtained from their fees. Jefferson, in a report made in November, 1792, estimated that the $40,000 appropriated for the Foreign Fund was ample for existing needs of our service abroad.[17]

Jefferson made a notable contribution to diplomatic and consular practice by his carefully prepared instructions to our diplomatic and consular representatives abroad. From diplomats he declared that he expected regular communications once or twice a month, as well as newspapers and gazettes and other public documents which might prove informative to the Department.[18] Since Congress had not yet acted as regards the duties of consuls, Jefferson, in a lengthy circular dated August 26, 1790, gave most elaborate instructions as to consular deportment and duties. In addition to information pertaining to all American ships entering the ports of their districts, the consuls and vice consuls were to provide

information of all military preparations and other indications of war which may take place in your ports; and when war shall appear imminent, you notify thereof the merchants and vessels within your district, that they may be duly on their guard; and in general, that you communicate to me such political and commercial intelligence as you may think interesting to the United States.[19]

It was Jefferson's skill as an administrator that led a contemporary, William Wirt, afterward Attorney General in the administration of President Monroe, to state:

As an evidence of universal admiration of the matchless skill and talent with which he [Jefferson] discharged the duties of this office [the Department of State], when at a subsequent period he was put in nomination by his friends for the office of President, his adversaries publicly objected "that Nature had made him only for a Secretary of State." [20]

Edmund Randolph—Secretary of State

The man whom Washington picked to succeed Jefferson was Attorney General Edmund Randolph, a handsome Virginian of excellent family, trained in the law, fluent in French, and a man who had early attained a high political reputation as Attorney General and Governor of Virginia, and head of the Virginian delegation to the Convention of 1787. Chosen as the first Attorney General of the United States by Washington, Randolph had delivered many opinions on international law and was thoroughly conversant with the international situation. As a jurist, he was disposed to consider cases on their merits rather than upon the basis of political expediency; hence he was not too popular with either Federalists or Republicans. In accepting the position, Randolph emphasized this objective attitude. In a letter to President Washington dated January 2, 1794, Randolph assured the President that

let the consequence be what it may, in this perilous office no consideration of party shall ever influence me; that nothing shall ever relax my attention or warp my probity, and that it shall be my unremitted study to become an accurate master of this new and important business.[21]

Although Randolph only served from January 2, 1794, until August 19, 1795, when he resigned under unfortunate circumstances, his direction of the State Department in a most troublesome period was not without honor. Relations of the United States with both Great Britain and France were very unsatisfactory—the two countries were at war and each wished to use the United States as a cat's-paw to injure the other. Our declaration of neutrality had antagonized the French without creating any improvement in our relations with Great Britain. Citizen Genêt, representing revolutionary France, had publicly criticized Washington and had openly flouted American neutrality, while Gouverneur Morris, the aristocrat, had never been *persona grata* to revolutionary France, nor had he shown any desire to become so. Joseph Fauchet, who succeeded Genêt and was instructed to arrest him and send him back to France, proved to be more injurious to Randolph than Genêt had been to Jefferson.

In Randolph's few official encounters with Genêt—his recall had been requested by Jefferson—the new Secretary of State did not find the French minister sympathetic. Randolph reproved Genêt for his failure to address Randolph by his official title, and he considered Genêt's strictures regarding the President as even less excusable. Nevertheless, Randolph favored Genêt's recall rather than his dismissal. [22] The new French minister Fauchet arrived the same month and on February 21 had his first official conference with Randolph. The ceremony of presentation of letters of credence as arranged by Randolph was simple in the extreme. Secretary Randolph had sent a copy of the letters to the President, who examined them and agreed to see the minister the following day at noon. Accompanied by Randolph in the Secretary's carriage, Fauchet was ushered into the President's room and introduced by Randolph. The minister presented his sealed credentials to the President, who opened them and gave them to the Secretary of State to read. The President thereupon declared that he received the French envoy as minister plenipotentiary of the French Republic, and expressed his friendly regards. After Fauchet had thanked the President, all three sat down and chatted informally for a few minutes. The Secretary and minister then left the President and entered another room to meet Mrs. Washington. After this brief ceremony Mr. Fauchet was recognized as the official French envoy to the United States.[23]

In reply to Randolph's queries as to Fauchet's relations with the American minister in Paris, Randolph learned that Fauchet had left France without seeing Morris—in fact, Fauchet seemed very vague about the American representative. It was not wholly unexpected when Fauchet soon afterward made a request for the recall of Morris. It is a tribute to Randolph's innate kindliness that he was able to inform Morris that his recall had been asked by the French government in such terms as to soften the blow considerably, as well as to retain Morris's respect and affection. In fact, Morris had congratulated Randolph upon his appointment as Secretary of State and had indicated that it might "produce a more active correspondence with the public servants abroad." [24] Monroe, who succeeded Morris, offended in the other direction. He was such an ardent supporter of revolutionary France that his address at his reception by the French government was so much more enthusiastic than his instructions warranted that Randolph informed him that it was his duty "to cultivate the French Republic with zeal but without any unnecessary éclat." [25]

The Jay Mission

Washington was quite inclined to make his own decisions on international affairs, although he regularly consulted not only the Secretary of State, but also other cabinet members. Hamilton usually had the most influence with the President and Randolph did not like this any more than did his predecessor, Jefferson. An excellent example of this situation was given by the appointment of John Jay as minister extraordinary to Great Britain. Apparently the Federalists had the intention of proposing Hamilton as an envoy extraordinary to go to England to complain of British injuries and to obtain redress. It is not surprising that Randolph supported the idea of a special mission, because he felt that the British seemed to pay no attention to the representations made by Mr. Pinckney; furthermore, it would please the merchants, who would appreciate that their interests were being supported; and the mission would prove our peaceful intentions, particularly as it came directly from the United States.[26] There was so much opposition to Hamilton as special envoy that Hamilton asked Washington to withdraw his name from consideration. However, Hamilton, without consulting Randolph, suggested John Jay. Randolph, although a friend of Jay's, opposed the nomination so long as Jay held the office of Chief Justice. Nevertheless, Hamilton's wishes prevailed and Jay was chosen for the mission.

Although it was the duty of the Secretary of State to prepare the instructions for the Jay mission, again Hamilton interposed with certain points for consideration by the President. One of these was to authorize Jay to negotiate a commercial treaty. Randolph opposed this power on the ground that it abridged the power of the Senate, since the Senate would be expected to approve ratification of the treaty. In this instance Randolph took a very untenable position. As finally prepared, the instructions included the power to sign a commercial treaty, leaving it to Jay's discretion as to whether he should make the proposal. It was particularly required of Jay that he should make no commitment which would in any way interfere with the United States' obligations to France. Randolph, who had to consider the attitude of France, was most insistent upon this point.

The Jay mission was a dubious effort to reconcile divergent national viewpoints in a period of crisis when resentment was so great that only a miracle of diplomacy could prevent war. Even Jay himself feared for the result. The procedure was most unorthodox. Hamilton's personal letter to Jay was regarded as of greater importance than Randolph's instructions. Jay was given a very free hand and corresponded more often with Washington and Hamilton than with the Secretary of State. It must be conceded that the preliminary draft of September 30 [27] took a strong stand for American rights, but when Lord Grenville learned from his minister in Washington (who had been informed by Hamilton) that the United States had no intention of joining the armed neutrality which Randolph had insisted upon as a potential threat, Jay had to retreat. The final draft was signed on November 19, before Jay had received Randolph's criticisms of Grenville's proposals. It gained practically nothing and conceded much. Its principal achievement was to preserve peace and to reintroduce arbitration, since certain questions, such as the northeastern boundary and pre-Revolutionary debts, were to be submitted to mixed arbitral commissions. But its weakness was due more to Hamilton's inexcusable interference than to Jay's alleged pro-British attitude, or to Randolph's instructions.

The Jay Treaty, sent by special courier, was given to Randolph on March 6, after the Senate had adjourned. A brief perusal indicated that it would be a very unpopular document and that it would be difficult to obtain Senate approval. Washington and Randolph agreed that it should be kept secret, even from members of the cabinet, until the Senate could consider it in secret session. Before Washington authorized publication of the treaty, Senator Stevens gave it to the press, and a veritable storm of abuse descended upon Jay and Washington. The opposition was strengthened by the issuance by the British of a new order in council authorizing the seizure of all vessels laden with provisions if bound to any port in France.[28] Washington, following the urgent injunction of Randolph, agreed not to sign the treaty until the British provision order was rescinded.

Randolph's Forced Resignation

An unexpected, and for Randolph a tragic, incident caused a complete reversal of policy. A confidential letter written by Fauchet to his government had been captured by a British man-of-war.[29] It was a very rambling, discursive report on conditions in the United States and intimated that Randolph had made overtures of a questionable nature to Fauchet. The British sent the document to Mr. Hammond, the British minister, and he gave it to Hamilton's successor, Secretary of Treasury Wolcott. The latter showed the incriminating document to his colleagues, and they urgently summoned Washington back to Philadelphia. Instead of discussing the matter with Randolph, Washington called a cabinet meeting and in spite of Randolph's opposition declared that he would ratify the Jay Treaty. Subsequently, Washington consulted with the other members of the cabinet—Wolcott, Pickering, and Bradford—in regard to the compromising dispatch and asked their opinion as to how best to proceed. Washington himself finally decided to present the dispatch to Randolph in a cabinet meeting without any advance notice, so that his colleagues could watch his reactions.

The test took place on August 19, five days after the decision to ratify the treaty. Secretary of War Pickering and Secretary of Treasury Wolcott were already present when Randolph arrived. This surprised Randolph, since he had requested an earlier meeting and his request had been refused. After a very formal greeting the President rose, and extracting from his pocket a large letter, handed the dispatch to Randolph and asked whether he could explain it. Randolph read the document but apparently found no particular reason for worry, and since references were made to other dispatches, suggested that he obtain them before attempting an explanation. However, when he was asked to step into another room while the others considered the case, Randolph became very resentful at the procedure and at the acceptance of his guilt, implied without even a hearing. He decided to resign immediately and did so the same day.

Inasmuch as there was a vague implication in the dispatch that money was involved, Randolph got in touch with Fauchet before he left for France and obtained an affidavit stating categorically that Mr. Randolph had never received directly or indirectly any money, nor had any overture been made in this respect.[30] Not the slightest proof of dishonest or improper action on Randolph's part was ever found subsequently in any document, yet Randolph resigned under a cloud of suspicion that still clings to his memory. Perhaps the most serious accusation was a statement made by Randolph's successor, Timothy Pickering, in relating the reaction of President Washington directly after he had read Randolph's *Vindication*. Pickering declares that Washington, after violently castigating Randolph, denounced him in these words:

He, the Secretary of State, to whose trust the foreign relations of the country are confided, has been conducting an intrigue with the ambassador of a foreign government to promote the designs of that government which were to overthrow the administration of which he Randolph was a trusted member, receiving from that ambassador money to aid in accomplishing this object; soliciting from him more to accomplish the same purpose.[31]

Randolph's dealings with Fauchet were perhaps injudicious, but compared with Hamilton's relations with Hammond, they were far less worthy of condemnation.[32] Randolph's case is unique in American diplomacy, and considering the fact that Fauchet denied any wrongdoing and explained the implications in his dispatch, it would appear to the unbiased observer that Edmund Randolph was more sinned against than sinning.

Washington was more than ever his own Secretary of State while Randolph was in office, and more inclined to follow the advice of Hamilton than that of his Secretary of State. In fact, Randolph had very little influence upon the development of policy; his function was to advise and then to prepare statements in accordance with instructions. On one occasion Randolph was not able to receive certain refugees from France, although they came with letters of introduction from Pinckney and Jay, because Washington opposed it. Randolph confessed that he would have liked to have received them, but he sacrificed his personal feelings for political considerations. [33] Randolph was a middle-of-the-roader in a time of fanatical party loyalties, and his objectivity made him unpopular with both factions.

3

Timothy Pickering and John Marshall

Secretary of War Pickering Becomes Secretary of State

Washington discovered that it was no easy matter to find a suitable successor to Randolph. He offered the post first to William Patterson, a senator from New Jersey, but the latter was not interested; he next approached Thomas Johnson, a judge of the Supreme Court, with equal lack of success. Charles Pinckney, who had played a prominent role in the Convention of 1787, was the next to refuse. The fourth to be asked in vain was Patrick Henry of Virginia, who at first had not been too friendly to the new government, which he thought "squinted towards monarchy." The fifth invited to accept was Rufus King, who was later to serve as minister to Great Britain, but he, too, refused. In desperation Washington turned to Timothy Pickering, Secretary of War, and asked him to take over the State Department in addition to the War Department. Pickering was averse to accepting the position but he could not refuse the request of his Commander in Chief. In a letter to a Mr. Higginson dated September 22, 1795, Pickering declared: ". . . you will believe the President not so unwise as to have tendered and me not so imprudent as to have accepted an office to which I am so little competent. The business of the office could not be suspended and from necessity I have by the President's direction undertaken the temporary conduct of it." [1] He compromised, however, by suggesting that he would serve in either War or State as the public good might require but he would not give up War until a satisfactory incumbent could be found. As a result, Pickering served as Secretary of State ad interim from August 20, 1795, to December 10, 1795; and he did not give up the War Department until James McHenry was appointed February 6, 1796.

Although Pickering was a graduate of Harvard and admitted to the bar, he was more interested in military than political affairs; he was commissioned in the Continental Army, where he served successively as colonel, adjutant general, and quartermaster general. His army background gave him a rather gruff and harsh manner—in fact, he was much more inclined to be dictatorial than diplomatic.

The Department of State was constantly in difficulties in its efforts to preserve our neutrality, and Pickering felt very keenly that the United States needed a navy to compel respect for our rights. However, since the United States lacked adequate means to enforce her will, Pickering realized the advantage of prudence and discretion, and one of his instructions to the American legation in London emphasizes strongly the necessity for the *suaviter in modo* approach:

When in the correspondence from this office, the feelings and resentments of the people of the United States are expressed in warm and indignant terms, it is by no means intended that the language of such letters should be used in addressing a foreign court. The prudence and discretion of the minister or agent is relied on to express those feelings and resentments . . . for while this passion repels whatever wears the semblance of reproach, it often yields to mild language, and firm but respectful representations; and always, where peace and friendship are the objects of pursuit, words as well as actions must be conciliatory.[2]

On the other hand, Pickering supported vigorously the rights of neutrals. In his intercourse with Mr. Adet, the French minister, he insisted upon the right of neutrals to trade in articles which were contraband of war, either by selling at home or abroad. He also insisted that the belligerent's sole means of redress was to seize such contraband on the high seas or in his own country— "the country of exportation was not compelled by international law to prohibit such exportation." [3] Pickering also declared that the sale of prizes brought into the ports of the United States by the armed vessels of the French Republic was not justified either by the law of nations or by the treaty of amity and commerce with France.

One of Pickering's harshest notes was sent to the British chargé d'affaires, Mr. Bond, in reference to the unwarranted action of Captain Rodham Home in searching a vessel of the United States in the territorial waters of the United States in order to seize Mr. Fauchet, the French minister, on his return to France. Pickering denounced the British captain for this flagrant violation of international law and also for his insulting language to the Governor of Rhode Island and for his threats of reprisals in case he should not be able to purchase provisions. Pickering demanded that Captain Home be withdrawn from American waters henceforth, and he revoked the exequatur of the British vice consul who had served as intermediary for Captain Home's unfriendly communications.[4]

Subsequent to the ratification of the Jay Treaty with Great Britain, relations with France steadily deteriorated. Adet continued to fulminate against the United States' policy of maintaining its neutrality and condemning French privateers which violated it, and he saw to it that his complaints were published in the press, so as to appeal indirectly to the American people. Pickering was gracious and sympathetic in his replies, but he refused to concede on principles. At the same time, feeling that Monroe, "a partisan of the Revolutionists," then minister to Paris, was not emphasizing sufficiently the determination of the United States to avoid being drawn into the European cross currents, Pickering requested his recall and sent General Charles C. Pinckney in his place. Pickering's instructions to Pinckney were a masterly survey of the entire situation and a very effective defense of the American position. They have been regarded by some authorities as Pickering's "most famous state paper." [5] The French government, however, had become increasingly hostile: the Directors, having already recalled their minister, Adet, refused to receive the new envoy from the United States.[6] They went even further, and by a threat of arrest forced Pinckney to leave the country.

In the meantime John Adams had been elected President, and he was faced with the possibility that the rupture of diplomatic relations between the United States and France might soon be followed by war. He was strongly averse to any such catastrophe taking place; yet he retained both Pickering and Wolcott in his cabinet, although he must have known that both were resigned to, if not eager for, war. However, President Adams did not follow Washington's precedent of conferring with his cabinet members on all matters of policy —perhaps he sensed their opposition. Adams, determined to make a final effort to prevent war with France, felt that if he could send a special mission headed by an outstanding friend of France, such as Jefferson, he might be successful. Jefferson, however, was now Vice President and under the circumstances could not leave the country. Madison was the next choice, but he refused to go. Jefferson strongly favored the sending of a mission, and as Hamilton also thought well of the idea, Pickering and Wolcott had to ride with the tide.

The three envoys finally chosen were: first, Pinckney, to compensate for his unseemly previous treatment; second, John Marshall, an outstanding Federalist who had previously refused the Secretaryship of War; and third, Francis Dana, who had had previous diplomatic experience in Russia and was now Chief Justice of Massachusetts. When Dana refused to accept, Adams turned to his friend Elbridge Gerry, who was more of a Republican than a Federalist. It was evident to all that Adams had not consulted his Secretary of State before making the last appointment—in fact, the entire cabinet had already shown strong opposition to the appointment of a Federalist.

Inasmuch as instructions to all diplomatic missions are issued by the Department of State under the signature of the Acting Secretary, Pickering's name was appended to the instructions given to the members of this special mission to France. Since Pickering was opposed to sending the mission and the instructions were not couched in his ordinary style, Professor Henry J. Ford gives it as his opinion that the instructions were probably drafted by Marshall.[7] The mission was a complete failure—the Directory made it clear that the commissioners would not be received until a redress of grievances had been made. Talleyrand, who was then foreign minister, tried to get rid of Pinckney and Marshall and to carry on negotiations with Gerry alone. The latter, unwisely and against the objections of his colleagues, agreed to remain as a private citizen. In the meantime the American mission's dispatches had reached Philadelphia, and Pickering could feel that his attitude had been correct from the beginning. He instructed the three envoys to demand their passports and to return. When he learned of Gerry's action, he censured him severely and ordered him home immediately. Pickering showed himself to be most intemperate in declaring publicly that Gerry was a man of duplicity and treachery, pusillanimous, and worthy of impeachment. He even proposed to deprive him of his pay for the period after his colleagues had left.[8]

Pickering felt himself becoming more and more incompatible with President Adams, and he made very little effort to conceal it. In fact, his harsh undiplomatic methods and caustic language got him into one difficulty after another. Nor did he hesitate to give his statements or correspondence to the press upon occasion. He characterized the French government as "devils out of pandemonium." As regards the Spanish minister, the Chevalier d'Yrujo, with whom he had been corresponding in a sarcastic vein, Pickering, in a letter to Secretary of War McHenry, called the envoy a Spanish puppy for whom he had perfect contempt.[9]

When Monroe upon his return from his unappreciated mission to France asked for a room in the Department of State and the assistance of a clerk to prepare his vindication, Pickering refused to grant it. Neither would Pickering state in writing, at Monroe's request, the grounds for his recall. Pickering's anger toward a Quaker, Dr. George Logan, who had visited Paris in an unofficial capacity in order to avert war, was more easily justified. The State Department refused to receive him, and Pickering urged Congress to pass a law punishing with fine and imprisonment any person who engaged in unauthorized negotiation with a foreign government. The law of January 30, 1799, which carried these provisions, is generally known as the Logan Act, and is still in force.

Pickering Dismissed

Pickering's dismissal from the cabinet came as a result of his efforts to bring about war with France; but Adams had long since lost all confidence in his holdover cabinet members, and particularly in his Secretary of State. He knew that they were counseling with Hamilton behind his back, and matters came to a climax when Adams decided that he was justified in sending a second mission to France as a result of Talleyrand's more friendly attitude. Pickering did all in his power to prevent such a move, and when he saw this was impossible, to postpone it. However, informed by Secretary of Navy Stoddert that Pickering would prepare letters of instruction with too much acrimony, Adams called a cabinet meeting on October 15, 1799. Without giving any indication of his plans, he had the instructions considered, and the next day he notified Pickering that the envoys should depart immediately. Pickering resented this summary procedure, but his hands were tied. Henceforth, Adams had only the most formal relations with Pickering, and on May 10, 1800, Adams wrote the Secretary of State suggesting that he resign. When Pickering declined to resign, Adams wrote him a curt note on May 12, as follows: "Divers causes and considerations essential to the administration of the government, in my judgement, requiring a change in the Department of State, you are hereby discharged from any further service as Secretary of State." [10]

Although other secretaries of state have been relieved of their duties by various means, Pickering still enjoys the dubious distinction of being the only Secretary of State who was dismissed from office. Some years later, in a letter to William Cunningham, Adams declared that Pickering's removal "was one of the most deliberate, virtuous, and disinterested acts of my life." Adams also felt that it was only because he had ousted Pickering that he was able to negotiate a peace with France and an amicable agreement with England.

The Department of State Under Pickering

Secretary of State Pickering neither enhanced his own reputation nor did he improve the position of the Department of State during his incumbency; nevertheless, he carried on the duties of the Department effectively and fearlessly. He himself was the first to concede that he had too quick a temper to be a good diplomat. Pickering was much more at home as Secretary of War than as Secretary of State, and he could work with Washington more satisfactorily than with Adams. The Department never had more than eight or nine clerks and other employees while Pickering was Secretary, and he did a vast amount of clerical work himself. Jacob Wagner, who was already a senior clerk and familiar with the duties of the position, was appointed Chief Clerk on February 8, 1798. Wagner was a Federalist, but he did his job very creditably and held it until 1807, despite the change in the political front of the administration. The Department was still in charge of patents, still the depository for copyrighted books, and the authority for the taking of the census. The Act of

March 2, 1799, required the Secretary of State to furnish the Congress with an annual statement containing an abstract of all returns received by him from the collectors of customs at the various ports, also all reports from American agents abroad concerning the impressment of American seamen.[11] During the brief undeclared war with France, it was required of the Department that it issue letters of marque and reprisal to private armed vessels commissioned as privateers. The Department issued exequaturs for foreign consuls in the United States, and passports to Americans who wished to travel abroad. The first passport which is to be found in the files of the Department was issued on July 8, 1796, and was signed by Timothy Pickering.[12]

The huge task of copying documents and the correspondence with American ministers abroad was farmed out to all officials of the Department when their other specific tasks permitted; nevertheless, a vast amount of the correspondence was carried on in the handwriting of the chief of the office. It should be noted that in addition to the correspondence with American ministers and agents abroad and with representatives of foreign governments in this country, the Secretary of State had supervision over territorial offices and he was frequently called upon to advise with judges, attorneys, and marshals of the district courts of the United States. When Pickering's successor took charge, the Department had nine clerks and other employees, making a total cost of $11,500 for maintenance, of which the Secretary now received $5,000.

Throughout Pickering's administration of the Department, it was housed at the corner of Fifth and Chestnut streets in Philadelphia except for the period from August to November, 1798, when, because of an epidemic of yellow fever in Philadelphia, the Department was temporarily moved to the State House in Trenton, New Jersey.

John Marshall—Secretary of State

Adams's cabinet house cleaning included both the Secretary of War and the Secretary of State, and the troublesome European situation required that both posts be filled immediately. John Marshall was offered the Secretaryship of War the day it became vacant, but he refused it without hesitation. Exactly a week later Adams tendered him the State Department headship. Marshall again was by no means eager to accept; in fact, he debated with himself for almost two weeks as to whether he should take the position. His excellent work on the recent mission to France had convinced Adams of his superlative ability, and this background and Marshall's desire to bring his labors to a successful conclusion may have been the factors which finally gained his acceptance. The Senate approved his nomination on May 13, 1800, but Marshall did not enter upon his duties until June 6 of the same year. In the meantime the essential duties of the office were performed by the Attorney General, Charles Lee.

The holdover cabinet member from the previous administration, Secretary of Treasury Oliver Wolcott, felt that Marshall would find himself out of his proper element in his new position, while the newspaper *Aurora* declared that Marshall was "more distinguished as a rhetorician and as a sophist than as a lawyer and a statesman." [13] Both were completely mistaken.

The position at this time had manifest disadvantages. The capital had been moved from Philadelphia to Washington before the new location was ready. The archives of the Department had been brought to Washington and were at first stored in the Treasury Building, although this edifice was not yet completed. The hot, humid climate of Washington in the summertime was not appealing, the salary of $5,000 was not overly tempting, and the routine work, which, since President Adams was at his summer home most of the time, included the task of taking care of office seekers, was thankless and exhausting. Nevertheless, the diplomatic problems were serious and an able man was urgently needed to try to keep the United States out of war.

Relations with France were still unsatisfactory, and a second mission had been dispatched, after Talleyrand had promised that it would be promptly and properly received, to conclude a new treaty. However, when a long delay ensued, Adams was seemingly ready to ask Congress to declare war; and only the logical, patient arguments of Marshall restrained him. When finally the envoys obtained an arrangement which recognized the right of American neutrality, Marshall, although not satisfied with it, advised that it be ratified as a means of avoiding war.

It was with our relations with Great Britain that Marshall was most concerned. He had the difficult task of attempting to change the British policy by a forceful exposition of the fundamental principles of international law. Marshall set himself to this task, and his lengthy instructions to our minister, Rufus King, under date of September 20, 1800, in which in a clear, cogent, and forceful manner he summarized our position, is one of the great papers in the history of our foreign relations.[14] Even though not immediately accepted, the principles enunciated were later sustained and ultimately accepted as sound principles of neutral rights.

President Adams leaned very heavily upon his Secretary of State, although, according to Bayard, the Secretary of State knew as little of the intentions of the President as any other person connected with the government.[15] Nevertheless, Senator Beveridge in his classic study of Marshall says that Marshall was "the practical head of the Government," and it seems to be a reasonable assumption that it was Marshall who wrote Adams's farewell address to Congress, which was delivered on December 3, 1800.[16]

In spite of his excellent record, Marshall was not to remain long as Secretary of State. The position of Chief Justice of the United States became vacant in December, 1800, with the retirement of Chief Justice Ellsworth, and when John Jay refused to accept a reappointment, Adams decided upon Marshall. This was a position that Marshall could not refuse; he accepted immediately and carried on the duties of both positions until the Jefferson administration took charge in March, 1801. His contributions to the development of international law in his great decisions, such as *The Exchange* v. *McFadden, The Nereide, Thirty Hogsheads of Sugar* v. *Royal,* and in *The Antelope,* proved that if given the opportunity he would have been a great Secretary of State. Fortunately, his abilities were not lost to the United States by his transfer.

The Department at the End of the Century

In the eleven years since it had been established under the Constitution, the Department of State had not grown rapidly, nor had its personnel changed to any considerable extent. Foreign policy was controlled by the President, but he had to sense the feeling of Congress before he took any important action. The relationship between the President and his Secretary of State depended considerably upon the personality and interests of the two men. Washington was on the whole his own Secretary of State, whereas John Adams leaned more heavily upon his advisors. Even with its domestic duties, the work of the Department was not particularly heavy. When Marshall resigned the total personnel was only ten and the total salary quota was $11,500. The office of Chief Clerk had become quite important, because in the absence of the Secretary he assumed all of his routine duties. The other assistants, clerks, employees of no designated status, and the messenger took care of recording and copying the correspondence, collating the laws, recording land patents, making out exequaturs for consuls, issuing passports, superintending and issuing patents and granting copyrights and performing any other functions assigned to the Department.

The diplomatic service of the United States had not expanded more than the Department. In 1800 the following diplomatic representatives were abroad with the designation of envoy extraordinary and minister plenipotentiary: Rufus King of New York in Great Britain, and Charles Cotesworth Pinckney of South Carolina in France; William Smith of South Carolina was minister plenipotentiary to Portugal, and David Humphreys of Connecticut held a similar rank in Spain; William van Murray of Maryland was our minister resident to the Netherlands.

Although by no means elaborate, the United States had adequate machinery both at home and abroad to carry on effectively a foreign policy aimed primarily at the maintenance of peace and neutrality; and considering the fact that the Government had no army and a most inadequate navy whereby to enforce its will, the results of its diplomacy were such that the new Republic could feel encouraged to carry on as it had begun.

4

James Madison, Robert Smith, and James Monroe

James Madison—Secretary of State

With the advent of Thomas Jefferson as the successful candidate of the Republican party, the Federalists were discredited, and a complete change in both cabinet and policy could be expected. It was known in advance who would be Secretary of State if Jefferson should win the presidency, because at Mr. Jefferson's "pressing desire" James Madison had agreed before the election to accept the position of Secretary of State in Jefferson's cabinet. Not only had the two men been good friends for many years, seeking each other's counsel and advice, but Madison by his background, experience, and ability was peculiarly well equipped for the position.

Madison's interest in foreign affairs was long standing and continuous; in fact, it was he who as leader of the House introduced a resolution to establish the Department of Foreign Affairs as the first of the Federal executive departments, and while serving in the Continental Congress Madison had always shown a keen interest in this Department. In 1782 he had moved to enlarge the Secretary's power in order to retain Livingston's services as Secretary, and it was Madison who in 1785, in a letter to Monroe, strongly insisted that all foreign dispatches should be referred first of all to the Department of Foreign Affairs, instead of to a committee of Congress.[1]

Madison, who in the beginning had been regarded by Hamilton as a supporter, soon turned Republican and became a bitter partisan opponent of the Secretary of the Treasury and his Federalist friends. It was undoubtedly Jefferson's influence that dominated Madison. Washington, who strove constantly to remain nonpartisan, consulted Madison on many occasions, even though he was not a member of the cabinet. In fact, when Jefferson retired from the State Department, Washington declared that Madison was his first choice to replace him; but he knew that Madison was unwilling to serve in an executive office.[2]

President Adams also had a high regard for Madison's ability and would have appointed him on the mission to France if he had not known of the strong opposition which such a move would have raised among his Federalist supporters. Thus, having been wholly free from any official relationship to the foreign field, Madison could enter upon his duties as Secretary of State with a completely open mind and with no commitments of an international nature to handicap him. He was on excellent terms with the diplomatic corps in Washington, and Sir Augustus Foster, the British minister, thought that Madison was better informed than Jefferson. It was generally conceded that as a speaker and writer Madison ranked among the best of his time. He liked society, and with his amiable and popular wife he was well equipped to entertain the diplomatic corps and the government set.

Although Madison was commissioned Secretary of State on March 5, 1801, he did not enter upon his duties until May 2. His father had died in February and since his private affairs necessitated his attendance at his home, the Attorney General, Levi Lincoln, acted as ad interim Secretary of State until Madison could take over.

The Department remained practically unchanged during the eight years of Madison's incumbency. A letter accusing Chief Clerk Jacob Wagner of ridiculing Republicanism was received by President Jefferson in 1801 and turned over to Secretary Madison, but he took no action upon it and Wagner remained until he voluntarily retired from the position in 1807. As Wagner's successor Secretary Madison appointed Mr. John Graham, whom he knew very well personally and who had served from 1801 to 1804 as secretary of legation and chargé d'affaires at the American legation in Madrid. The new appointment made by Madison was that of Dr. William Thornton, a highly educated scientist, who in 1802 was placed in charge of the Patent Office as superintendent and who held this position until he died in 1828.

In a report made by Secretary Madison on January 1, 1807, he listed the personnel of the Department of State for the year 1806, giving a brief statement of the duties of each official and the compensation granted. Mr. Wagner, the Chief Clerk, whose salary was $2,000, distributed the business among the others and superintended its execution. Next to him was listed Mr. Brent, at a salary of $1,000, who was responsible for the business of impressed seamen and for the collating of laws preparatory to their publication. Mr. Pleasanton, who received $906, made out and recorded patents for military bounty lands, issued exequaturs for consuls, civil and military commissions for the District of Columbia, recorded the correspondence with our ministers in foreign countries, and transmitted the laws to the printers for promulgation. Mr. Thom, whose salary was $881, recorded Virginian military land patents, paid out awards, and kept the contingent accounts of the Department. Mr. Smith, whose compensation was $800, aided Mr. Brent with seamen's cases, recorded correspondence (except with ministers abroad), and collated laws. Mr. Forrest, at the same salary, made out and recorded patents for land under the direction of the registers and issued passports for citizens going abroad. A Mr. Gardiner received $25 for occasional services in recording land patents. Dr. Thornton received $1,400 for his services in issuing patents and securing copyrights. Miscellaneous copying was distributed as the other work permitted. The salary of the Secretary at this time was still $5,000, and the total sum for personnel amounted to $12,812.

The Louisiana Purchase

Perhaps the most important diplomatic problem which the President and State Department had to grapple with during Madison's incumbency was the question of Louisiana. In the very month that Madison took over the office of Secretary, a dispatch from Rufus King, American minister in London, dated March 29, 1801, noted the fact that the French Directory was considering with Spain the exchange of Tuscany for Louisiana; King was of the opinion that a treaty had already been entered into. Owing to the domestic political situation, the United States had no minister in Paris at this time. James A. Bayard, who had been named by President Adams to replace Pinckney, had no opportunity to serve, due to Jefferson's election a month after his appointment. Jefferson, even before his inauguration, had offered the Paris legation to Robert R. Livingston. Livingston had indicated that he would be unable to proceed immediately to his post, but with the control of the Mississippi at stake Madison urged him to take charge as quickly as possible. Having previously served with distinction as Secretary of Foreign Affairs under the Articles of Confederation and subsequently as Chancellor of the State of New York, Livingston was well equipped to uphold the diplomatic interests of the United States, even with the redoubtable Talleyrand.

Livingston arrived in France early in November, 1801, and immediately made inquiries of Talleyrand regarding the transfer of Louisiana. Talleyrand denied that anything more than conversations had taken place. Yet at this very time Rufus King, our minister in London, was sending to Secretary Madison a copy of the treaty, concluded eight months previously, which established the retrocession of Louisiana from Spain to France. At about the time that Madison learned of Talleyrand's duplicity, the American consul general in Santo Domingo informed the State Department of the arbitrary and illegal confiscation of American goods by General Leclerc. When General Leclerc followed this action by imprisoning American ship captains and expelling the American consul general, Jefferson and Madison decided to act.

Jefferson wrote on April 18, 1802, a dispatch to Livingston declaring: "The day that France takes possession of New Orleans fixes the sentence which is to restrain her forever within her low water mark. . . . From that moment we must marry ourselves to the British fleet and nation." [3] This dispatch was entrusted to a Frenchman, Du Pont de Nemours, who was returning to France. A covering letter from President Jefferson to Du Pont de Nemours urged him "to impress on the Government of France the inevitable consequences of their taking possession of Louisiana." [4]

Three news items which reached Washington in November, 1802, strengthened the administration's intention to act: the death of General Leclerc, the decimation of his army in Santo Domingo by yellow fever, and the action of the Spanish intendant at New Orleans in abrogating the right of Americans to deposit their merchandise as authorized by the Treaty of 1795. The western states were aroused and the Federalists in Congress introduced a resolution in February, 1803, authorizing the President to take military action to seize New Orleans.

Jefferson was unwilling to let matters drift further toward war, and on January 11, 1803, he requested the Senate to approve the nomination of James Monroe as minister extraordinary to both France and Spain to aid ministers Livingston and Pinckney in "enlarging and more effectually securing our rights and interests in the river Mississippi and in the territories eastward thereof." [5]

The instructions to Monroe, as well as those to Livingston, were dated March 2, 1803, and were drawn up by Secretary Madison and included a draft treaty for the cession of East and West Florida and the island of New Orleans to the United States. Before these instructions reached Paris or Monroe had presented his letter of credence, Talleyrand proposed to Livingston the sale of Louisiana. Livingston was startled; but while appreciating the opportunity, his instructions were for the purchase of territory east rather than west of the Mississippi, and he could only offer to sound out his government. Two days later, the very day that Monroe arrived in Paris, the French minister of finance, Barbé-Marbois, made a definite offer to Livingston to sell the whole of Louisiana for sixty million francs provided the United States would also appropriate twenty million francs to pay for all claims of American citizens against France.

Since Monroe was in Paris as minister extraordinary and plenipotentiary, he seemingly outranked Livingston and would therefore be the accredited leader in the negotiations.[6] Nevertheless, since both Napoleon and Talleyrand preferred to deal with Livingston, and as Monroe had not yet been officially received, Monroe could only act through the accredited minister. Fortunately, although jealous of Monroe, Livingston cooperated loyally, and the two envoys, without any instructions authorizing it, finally accepted Napoleon's offer. Unquestionably, Monroe's presence was unnecessary, because Napoleon had already decided to get rid of the territory; but by sending him, Jefferson strengthened his position at home with the West and was able to give support to Livingston if he needed it.

No achievement in the foreign policy of the United States has been more productive of profitable development than the purchase of Louisiana, "the biggest real-estate transaction in history." Yet it must be conceded that Secretary of State Madison at first did not seem to appreciate the magnitude of the bargain, although after delaying two weeks he wrote Livingston and Monroe that the purchase of Louisiana "would be regarded on the whole as highly advantageous." [7] Jefferson fortunately had greater vision, and in spite of his strict constructionist tendencies regarding the Constitution—he at first thought an amendment would be necessary to acquire the territory—he quickly decided that legal title could be achieved by a treaty. In a note to Secretary Madison he wrote: "The less that is said about any constitutional difficulty [respecting Louisiana] the better; and it will be desirable for Congress to do what is necessary, *in silence*." [8] The Senate was of the same opinion and approved the treaties for the Louisiana Purchase on October 20, 1803, three days after the special session had met.

Commercial Restrictions and Impressment

Although in most of the important problems of foreign policy arising during his administration Jefferson was his own Secretary of State, in the question of commercial restrictions in time of war the attitude of Jefferson was identical with that of Madison, and it was the Secretary of State who took the initiative in the attempt to protect American trade against British and French restrictions. Great Britain had found it profitable to favor the so-called Rule of 1756, which forbade neutrals from trade in time of war which was closed to them in times of peace. Such trade was very profitable to American shipowners, and Madison was sympathetic to their operations and made every possible diplomatic effort to protect their interests. In 1806 he wrote and published anonymously a lengthy and scholarly monograph under the title, "Examination of the British Doctrine Which Subjects to Capture a Neutral Trade, Not Open in Time of Peace." [9] But although it was good theory, it was, in the caustic words of John Randolph, like a shilling pamphlet hurled against eight hundred ships of war.

The practice of the British in impressing American seamen on the ground of indefeasible allegiance was protested even more bitterly by the Secretary of State, particularly when the enforcement occurred upon American vessels upon the high seas, where the British captains could seize any able-bodied seaman on the alleged grounds of being a British deserter. Secretary Madison sent a veritable barrage of instructions to the successive American ministers in London, demanding a cessation of the impressment of seamen,[10] but neither Rufus King nor James Monroe was even partially successful. Finally, William Pinckney was sent as minister extraordinary to see if Monroe and he together could get results. The British remained obdurate. A climax was reached when the British fired upon the American frigate *Chesapeake*, killing and wounding a score, and then boarded her and took off four alleged deserters, three of whom were American citizens. This flagrant violation of international law brought forth one of Madison's most violent denunciations of British conduct. He demanded a formal disavowal, return of the seamen, cessation henceforth of impressment, and declared that all other negotiations were suspended in the meantime.[11]

Jefferson now took over the control of foreign relations, ordered all British warships out of American waters, and summoned a special session of the Congress. He knew that Madison had long favored an embargo: Jefferson decided to try it. He persuaded the Congress to pass an embargo act which virtually stopped the export trade of the United States, but it proved to be a boomerang which hurt the United States as much if not more than the British at whom it was aimed. It was a complete failure in effecting a change in British policy.

Ultrademocratic Protocol

Although Madison was not successful in carrying through any major foreign policy during his incumbency as Secretary of State, unless he be given some credit for the purchase of Louisiana, he retained the wholehearted support of Jefferson to the end. He unquestionably deserved this support, because Jefferson's tendency to dictate and control, whenever he felt so inclined, made Madison's position at times a most unsatisfactory one. If in questions of policy this was perhaps justified, in the matter of protocol it was not. In his insistence upon an ultrademocratic procedure in social matters, Jefferson often placed his Secretary of State, as well as himself, in a most unenviable position.

Washington had perhaps established a more ceremonious social procedure than was appropriate to an undeveloped and theoretically very democratic governmental system, but it coincided with Washington's conception of the dignity of the presidential office. John Adams, although less inclined to elaborate levees, made no radical changes. Jefferson, although fond of the social graces and conversant with the most exacting requirements of worldly society, was an ardent believer in simplicity and had an abhorrence of snobbery of any sort. He therefore decided to abolish all social distinctions and follow the rule of *pêle-mêle* at White House gatherings. Such a procedure was particularly obnoxious to the diplomatic set; nevertheless, the Department of State could hardly do otherwise than follow the presidential lead.

On the occasion of a White House dinner, the British minister, Anthony Merry, became so incensed that he created a diplomatic incident. At the moment when the dinner was announced, President Jefferson happened to be talking with the wife of the Secretary of State; without further ado he conducted her into the dining room. Inasmuch as Secretary Madison had customarily, through courtesy rather than protocol, given precedence to foreign ministers, the British representative resented the action. A few nights later, at a dinner given by Secretary Madison, the Secretary of State, following the precedent set by Jefferson, escorted the wife of the Secretary of the Treasury to the dinner; and on this occasion, since Mrs. Merry found herself without an escort, her husband joined her and they sat where they could find places. Merry protested to his government and Madison had to explain the situation to Monroe so that he might inform the British government that no slight was intended. Madison was considerably relieved when Monroe informed him that Mrs. Monroe had been preceded in London by the wife of an under-secretary.[12]

Upon a subsequent occasion Jefferson, to placate the British minister, made inquiry through the Swedish chargé whether, if invited to a family dinner with the President, he would accept. Merry agreed, but upon receiving an invitation in the President's handwriting he wrote Secretary Madison to find out whether he was invited officially or unofficially. If officially, he must be assured that he would be received with those "usages of distinction" due to His Majesty's ministers. Secretary Madison curtly replied that the President's invitation, "being in the style used by him in like cases, had no reference to the points of form which will deprive him of the pleasure of Mr. Merry's company at dinner." [13]

A frank appraisal could not place Madison high among American Secretaries of State. Nevertheless, his record did not prevent him from succeeding Jefferson as the fourth President of the United States. To serve with as brilliant and changeful a man as Jefferson for eight years and to retain his wholehearted support to the very end was a feat in itself. The Secretary of State was still practically the entire State Department as far as policy was concerned, and yet the Secretary himself was dominated wholly by the President whenever the latter cared to interpose his wishes.

Robert Smith—Secretary of State

The failure of the embargo and its great damage to American commercial interests darkened Jefferson's last days as President. His former popularity had largely disappeared, and the Senate had harshly refused his last official request: to send William Short as minister to Russia. In advancing from the head of the State Department to the Presidency of the nation, Madison realized fully the difficulties ahead. Neither Great Britain nor France was disposed to relinquish its belligerent rights, even when they were concededly disastrous to neutral interests. Never did a President have greater need for an able Secretary of State to advise and support him. Madison wanted the Secretary of the Treasury, Albert Gallatin, to head the Department of State, a statesman whose ability and qualifications easily transcended all others suggested. He learned to his consternation that a cabal of senators, led by Senators William B. Niles and Samuel Smith, was determined to prevent Gallatin's appointment. In order to circumvent them, Madison offered to name Secretary of the Navy Robert Smith, brother of Senator Samuel Smith, as Secretary of the Treasury provided Senator Smith would support Gallatin for the State Department position. Gallatin, knowing Smith's lack of ability, refused categorically, on the ground that he would have to carry on the work of both positions; let Madison rather appoint Smith Secretary of State. Although appreciating Smith's deficiencies, Madison wished to avoid a party struggle at the outset of his administration, and he named Robert Smith as Secretary of State. Inasmuch as Madison had held the office so long and expected to retain the conduct of foreign relations in his own hands, the appointment was excusable. Gallatin, however, resented the sacrifice of ability for political expediency and scarcely concealed his contempt for his cabinet colleague.

Robert Smith was a native of Pennsylvania, a college graduate trained in the law, and a specialist in admiralty. The fact that he served continuously as Secretary of the Navy during Jefferson's two terms and was in charge of the Navy Department when the successful war between the United States and Tripoli was fought indicates that he had a certain proved competence.[14] The fact that Madison had little confidence in Smith's ability and had appointed him under pressure was not conducive to a satisfactory administration of the Department, regardless of the Secretary's ability.

Shortly after Smith assumed the office of Secretary of State—he was commissioned March 6, 1809 [15]—the British minister in Washington, David M. Erskine, who sincerely wished to cultivate more friendly relations, informed Secretary Smith that the British government was willing to disavow the action of the captain of the *Leopard*, return the men taken from the *Chesapeake* (except the deserter, who had been hanged), and make suitable recompense for the sufferers. In reply Smith accepted the offer, but declared that President Madison, while not insisting upon further punishment of Admiral Berkeley, who was responsible for the captain of the *Leopard's* action, felt that if an example were made of him "it would best comport with what is due from His

Britannic Majesty to his own honor." [16] Smith later declared that Madison had supplied the last sentence against his wishes. It was an unfortunate statement, and the British foreign minister, Canning, not only repudiated the agreement, but censured the unhappy Erskine who had accepted it. The well meaning Erskine was recalled and a much less friendly envoy replaced him.

The new British minister, Francis James Jackson, quickly showed his disdain for diplomatic language by insinuating that the United States had made the agreements with Erskine when it was known that he had exceeded his instructions. Madison, who had never had much faith in the ability of his Secretary of State, decided to reply under Smith's name. His answer, dated October 19, 1809, which Adams characterizes as "perhaps the best and keenest paper that Madison ever wrote," [17] showed surprise that the British government had given no reasons for not fulfilling its pledges, nor could he understand why Erskine's efforts to work out a reasonable compromise should be regarded as inadmissible.

Madison felt that he must have a new Secretary of State, for, complained the President, the papers drafted by Smith were "so crude and inadequate, that I was in the more important cases generally obliged to write them anew myself, under the disadvantage, sometimes of retaining, thro' delicacy, some mixture of his draft." [18] The State Department itself, in the words of the outstanding historian of the period, "stood helpless in the face of intolerable insults from all the European belligerents. Neither the diplomatic nor the consular system was better than a makeshift, and precisely where the Government felt most need of ministers—at Copenhagen, Stockholm, Berlin and St. Petersburg—it had no diplomatic and but few consular agents, even these often of foreign allegiance." [19] Madison, however, was slow to act; and it was not until March, 1811, when Gallatin submitted his resignation rather than endure the disaffection in the cabinet caused by factional differences which he declared could only be settled by the resignation of the Secretary of the Treasury or the Secretary of State, that Madison moved. He refused Gallatin's resignation and suggested that Gallatin approach James Monroe as to whether he might be interested in taking the Secretaryship of State.

As soon as Madison was assured that Monroe looked upon the offer favorably, he summoned Smith to inform him that his services as head of the Department of State did not measure up to its requirements. Madison was almost brutally frank. After accusing Smith of sabotaging the policies of the government, he informed him that "the business of the Department had not been conducted in the systematic and punctual manner that was necessary, particularly in the foreign correspondence, and that I had become daily more dissatisfied with it." Since, as Madison informed him, Smith evidently did not possess the talents adapted to his station, it was better that he serve in some other capacity. Madison thereupon offered him the post of minister to Russia.[20] Smith seemed at first willing to accept the sop, but after several days' consideration he decided that he had been shamefully abused and he rejected the offer as a contemptible proposal. He placed his case before the public in an "Address to the People of the United States," and tried in every way possible to weaken Madison's position; but as a private citizen his political influence was small, and today he is one of the Secretaries of State whose name is practically forgotten.

James Monroe—Secretary of State

Robert Smith retired from the Department of State on April 1, 1811; James Monroe was commissioned Secretary of State the following day and entered upon his duties on April 6. It was an ideal appointment, both from an international and national viewpoint. Monroe had served as American minister at Paris on two different occasions, he had been minister to Spain, and he served still later as minister at London. Although his diplomatic missions were not conspicuously successful—Henry Adams declared that he was singularly unfortunate in diplomacy—it is questionable whether anyone else would have obtained more satisfactory results under the circumstances. Madison, who as Secretary of State had failed to support Monroe's British policy, had temporarily estranged the two men, and Monroe's hopeless bid for the Presidency against Madison had not improved their political relations. However, Madison, having been overwhelmingly successful in gaining the Presidency, could afford to be generous; and he could use advantageously Monroe's political influence in Virginia. In the short correspondence between the two men, Monroe made it clear that if he took the position he would wish to be Secretary in fact as well as in name, and be given a free hand to try to reconcile the serious difficulties which existed with the British.

Secretary Monroe Fails to Prevent War

It is difficult to evaluate the definite responsibilities for the break with Great Britain. In his letter to Monroe discussing the foreign policies of the administration, President Madison had insisted that all concerned desired a "cordial accommodation with Great Britain," and declared that no commitments precluded such an arrangement. Secretary Monroe was wholly inclined in the direction of England, and he made it plain on numerous occasions. But the British seemed determined to precipitate a crisis. Their successor to Jackson, Augustus Foster, although seemingly desirous of following a more conciliatory policy, unfortunately made his diplomatic debut by protesting vigorously against the evident intention of the United States to seize West Florida. Since Monroe had always insisted that West Florida was included in the purchase of Louisiana, such an approach was hardly the correct one to propitiate the Secretary of State. Foster next declared that unless the Nonintercourse Act of the United States were repealed, the British government would retaliate further. Inasmuch as Monroe had expected that it would be the British who would make concessions by repealing their illegal orders in council, he could hardly brook this transfer of the onus of guilt to the shoulders of Uncle Sam. Monroe's letter of July 2, 1811, to the British minister's demands seemed to close the door to further argument. Britain must concede or accept the consequences.[21]

Thus Monroe, who came into the cabinet determined to reverse Madison's policy of seemingly greater antagonism to Great Britain than to France, was quickly brought round to support the anti-British policy with even greater determination. At times he was almost ready to recommend that the United States sever relations at the same time with both Great Britain and France, inasmuch as both were violating flagrantly and with impunity the lawful rights of American merchants that both Madison and Monroe had promised to protect.

The Congress met in November, 1811, a month before its regular session, and Madison sent in a message extremely critical of Britain's policies. The so-called War Hawks were eager to cease arguing and proceed to arms, and Monroe went along with them. It is alleged by a contemporary editor that Monroe went so far as to declare: "We must fight. We are forever disgraced if we do not." [22] In a meeting which Monroe held with the House Committee on Foreign Relations on March 31, 1812, he told them that the President thought war should be declared before Congress adjourned.[23] When the new British foreign minister, Lord Castlereagh, showed no change in policy, both Madison and Monroe were convinced that Great Britain had no intention of making the concessions demanded. A war message was prepared and given to the Congress on June 1, 1812. The House promptly passed a war resolution, but the Senate took two weeks to debate the matter, and seriously considered including France. The majority, however, supported the President, and war against Great Britain was declared on June 18, 1812.

Secretary of State Monroe was not too happy at the result, even though he had become satisfied that there was no other way out. In an apologetic letter to his friend Colonel John Taylor, Monroe declared that he had been afraid to write because he knew that better things had been expected of him than he had been able to perform.[24] Even after war was declared, Monroe authorized the able and experienced American chargé d'affaires in London, Jonathan Russell, to declare that the United States would suspend hostilities if the British would repeal their orders in council and cease their practice of impressment.

In fact, two days before the United States had declared war, Lord Castlereagh promised that the orders in council would be repealed; and on June 23 the order of repeal was issued. But no cable or radio was available to carry the news to Washington. It has been argued that the Senate would never have approved the war resolution if Castlereagh's concession had been received;[25] and it should be noted that diplomatic relations were never completely severed, since Russell remained as American chargé in London throughout the period of the war.

Great Britain was not eager either to enter the war or to continue it after it had begun, but Madison and Monroe would not consider an armistice until the British ended impressments. Monroe, who already had his eyes fixed upon the Presidency, and his chief, Madison, who was determined to have a second term, were undoubtedly somewhat moved by domestic political reasons. They knew that the West wanted Canada and was unwilling to make peace without a try for it. The Chief Clerk of the State Department, John Graham, who had been appointed by Madison when he was Secretary of State, had made a trip through Ohio, Kentucky, and Western Virginia to sound out public sentiment for the Department. He wrote to Monroe that the early disasters of the war had only aroused the people to greater exertions.

Nevertheless, the war was hardly more popular in America than in Britain, and both the Department of State and the President appreciated this fact. No outstanding victories stimulated either side. On the contrary, the British perpetrated an irreparable act of vandalism when they captured and partially destroyed the new capital of the United States. The White House, the Capitol, and the various Department buildings were burned by the specific orders of the British General Ross.[26] Secretary Monroe, who had seen military service during the Revolution, and upon the resignation of Secretary of War Eustis had acted as Secretary of War from December 3, 1812, until January 13, 1813, had gone forward to scout the enemy when their approach toward Washington had been announced. Upon sighting the enemy on August 14, 1814, he sent an orderly to the Department of State instructing Mr. Graham, the Chief Clerk, to remove the records to a place of safety. Mr. Graham, aided by two other State Department officials, had bags of coarse linen made in which they packed the books and records of the Department. They were then placed in carts and taken by the Commission Clerk of the Department, Mr. Pleasanton, to an unoccupied grist mill on the Virginia side of the Potomac, a few miles above Georgetown. The papers carted off included the Declaration of Independence, the secret journals of Congress, the correspondence of George Washington, and all the laws, treaties, and correspondence of the Department of

State from the adoption of the Constitution to that time. Later the records were moved to an empty house in Leesburg, Virginia, for greater safety.[27] It was fortunate that these irreplaceable records were removed, because in a report made by Secretary Monroe on November 14, 1814, on the loss of books and papers resulting from the incursion of the enemy, he declared that the volumes of laws and many of the books of the Department library shared the fate of the building in which they were deposited.[28]

The United States can claim little glory in the conduct of the War of 1812. It is not surprising that when the czar of Russia proposed mediation both Madison and Monroe welcomed the suggestion. Without awaiting the British reaction, Madison appointed Gallatin and Bayard as envoys extraordinary to join John Quincy Adams, the United States minister to Russia. The British, however, were unwilling to bring Russia into the matter and proposed a direct settlement with the United States. Monroe, who after the fiasco in the defense of Washington had taken over the War Department and held both the Secretaryships of War and State, was in an excellent position to carry on the war and work for peace simultaneously.[29] The peace commissioners, who now included Henry Clay and Jonathan Russell as well as the three previously appointed, were to support the continuance of war until honorable terms of peace were obtained.

The American commission for peace, which after long and arduous negotiations worked out the terms of the Treaty of Ghent, was so expert and highly regarded that Monroe gave its members a large degree of discretion in interpreting his instructions. Inasmuch as the United States was willing to accept the territorial status quo, and there was small desire in Britain to continue a war for colonial aggrandizement, the two countries finally found it possible to reach an agreement. The fact that the British were represented at Ghent by envoys of little talent compared with the American delegation permitted American diplomacy to win where its arms had failed.

The Department Under Monroe

Although the Department of State under the Secretaryship of James Monroe had been largely subject to President Madison in the development of foreign policy, there was no derogation of the Secretary's powers, since both President and Secretary usually possessed the same point of view. The Secretaryship of State served again as an excellent ladder to political preferment, since just as Madison had done before him, Monroe left the Department to become President.

Monroe made no radical changes in the Department, either in organization or personnel. John Graham of Virginia served as Chief Clerk throughout

Monroe's period of service. In regard to procedure Monroe made a few contributions. He made it clear—and the precedent has been followed—that the Department of State can receive no communication from subjects of another country on international matters except through the official representative of the country concerned.[30] He was perhaps the first Secretary of State who suggested that the United States use the *alternat* in the signing and exchange of treaties.[31] He strongly supported adequate salaries and allowances for American representatives abroad. In a letter to the chairman of the Ways and Means Committee of the Congress, Secretary Monroe wrote:

A minister can be useful only by filling his place with credit in the diplomatic corps and in the corresponding circle of society in the country in which he resides which is the best in every country. By taking the proper ground, if he possesses the necessary qualifications and is furnished with adequate means he will become acquainted with all that passes and from the highest and most authentic sources. . . . Deprive him of the necessary means to sustain this ground, separate him from the circle to which he belongs and he is reduced to a cipher.[32]

As other Secretaries before and after him, he had to explain that freedom of speech in the United States means that criticism is permitted of foreign as well as domestic officials. When at a public dinner in Baltimore the local postmaster gave a toast which allegedly reflected upon the character of the French government, the French minister in Washington requested of Monroe that he be dismissed and an apology be rendered. Monroe informed him that the Government of the United States exercised no control in such matters. Angered at Monroe's refusal to act, the French minister suspended the French consul in Baltimore and the French government informed Mr. Gallatin, the American minister in Paris, that henceforth no French consul would reside in Baltimore and that the Government of France might be indisposed to take the steps toward paying for Napoleon's spoliations.[33]

In all, James Monroe served as Secretary of State for about five and a half years. The Department of State was faced with many serious international problems during this period, but all were handled in a creditable and on the whole in a satisfactory manner. Monroe's administration of the Department was conservative and effective. He retired from the State Department on March 3, 1817, and the next day he was sworn in as President of the United States.

5

The Department's Greatest Secretary—
John Quincy Adams

Basis of Adams's Appointment

Strangely enough, President Monroe, although he had served as Secretary of State and realized the importance of the position, picked the most important member of his cabinet upon a political and geographical basis, rather than upon outstanding qualifications for the office.[1] Nevertheless, if Monroe had weighed the qualifications of every potential candidate then available, he could have found no one who was better equipped by background, training, experience, and ability to take over the administration of the Department of State than John Quincy Adams. When only eleven years of age, he had accompanied his father, John Adams, to Paris on a mission for the Continental Congress, and inasmuch as no provision had been made for secretarial help, he assisted his father in that capacity. At the age of fourteen young Adams served as private secretary to Francis Dana, the American minister at St. Petersburg. Two years later he was one of the secretaries of the American plenipotentiaries sent in 1783 to negotiate a peace treaty with Great Britain. In 1794, at the age of twenty-seven, John Quincy Adams was named by President Washington as minister to the Netherlands. He served in that capacity for three years, and he was then transferred to Berlin.

After returning home and serving in the Senate, he was again asked to represent his country abroad. This time he was to be the first accredited American minister to Russia. Adams might well have accepted this post with some trepidation, because it will be remembered that Francis Dana had spent two years at St. Petersburg without ever being received at court. However, Adams served for almost six years in Russia, where he outgeneraled the great French ambassador Coulaincourt, and won great diplomatic laurels. Madison appreciated his services and nominated him to head the peace commissioners at Ghent to make peace with Great Britain in 1814. In January, 1815, Adams

JOHN QUINCY ADAMS

was named minister to Great Britain, and he was representing his country at this post when he was informed of his appointment as Secretary of State by President Monroe.

In spite of his long experience, John Quincy Adams was by no means the ideal diplomat. According to the historian John Fiske, "his manners were stiff and disagreeable; he told the truth bluntly, whether it hurt or not, and he never took pains to conciliate anyone." Dexter Perkins characterizes him as "acrid, suspicious, and overbearing." Adams said of himself, "I am a man of reserved, cold, austere, and forbidding manners; my political adversaries say, a gloomy misanthropist, and my personal enemies, an unsocial savage. With a knowledge of the actual defect in my character I have not the pliability to reform it." [2] Nevertheless, Adams was scholarly, keenly intelligent, and legally trained. His education and long sojourns abroad had made him fluent in both French and German. No living American had a better knowledge of the complex European political problems. He was courageous and stubborn and could be depended upon to maintain his country's interests as he saw them. Well might Monroe declare that respect for Adams's "talents and patriotic services" had induced him to commit the Department of State to his care.

The offer of the Secretaryship of State did not come as a surprise to Adams. In a letter to John Adams dated January 3, 1817, the American Minister to Great Britain noted the fact that in November last he had heard that rumors were circulating in Washington that the next President planned to offer him the State Department position.[3] Monroe's letter asking Adams to serve was dated March 6, two days after Monroe's inauguration, and Adams received the proposal on April 16, 1817. He accepted immediately, although he confessed to his mother that he doubted his competency for the place, and this doubt weighed more heavily upon his mind than upon the occasion of any former appointment.[4] Although Adams's commission was dated March 5, he did not arrive in the United States until August 6, and entered upon his duties September 2, 1817. John Graham, the Chief Clerk, served as ad interim Secretary from March 4 to March 9, and the new Attorney General, Richard Rush, carried on in the same capacity until Adams was ready to assume the office.

The Department's First Reorganization

The first problem facing Adams was the appointment of a new Chief Clerk. John Graham, who had served for ten years most creditably in this capacity, had retired on June 18, 1817,[5] and Daniel Brent, who had been in the Department for over a decade, had been given the position temporarily. Inasmuch as both President Monroe and Acting Secretary of State Rush strongly recommended his appointment upon a permanent basis, Adams willingly accepted their suggestions and appointed him Chief Clerk. Two other clerkships were open, and Adams, in spite of requests by relatives and friends, was determined to make the appointments on the basis of merit alone. In fact, he declared that he would appoint none of his own relatives to any office under his control.[6] Adams followed this policy rigidly and was able to say a year and a half later (March 18, 1819) that there had not been a single appointment of any consequence, even in his own Department, made at his recommendation.[7] In fact, Adams felt at times that much went on in regard to appointments under the Department of State of which he had not been informed.[8]

The position next to that of the Chief Clerk was offered to a Mr. Bailey solely because his recommendations were best, in spite of the fact that Bailey was unknown to Adams and that one of his friends demanded the position for his son. The demands for appointments abroad were far more numerous and bothersome. Although President Monroe made all diplomatic and consular appointments, the Secretary of State was constantly importuned by the "beggars for office" or, as he called them, "door-bursters of public confidence."

Adams found, as he had expected, that the duties of the office of Secretary of State were onerous in the extreme. On his first day in the office he was informed that the business of the Department was much in arrears. Writing to his mother about six weeks after assuming direction of the Department, he commented upon the business which could not be committed to the clerks. "Business crowds upon me from day to day requiring instantaneous attention, and in such variety that unless everything is disposed of just as it occurs, it escapes from the memory and runs into the account of arrears." [9] In a letter to a friend dated June 22, 1818, Adams wrote: "It was considered by Mr. Madison that the public duties of the Department of State were more than sufficient for one man. . . . For myself I can only assure you that I have found the duties of the Department to be more than I can perform. Some of them therefore are not performed." [10]

Apparently no adequate filing system was maintained and no record was kept of letters received in the Department. Thus, important documents were misplaced and unavailable when needed. Adams gave instructions immediately that a record of letters as they arrived be kept in a book, but he soon discovered that this was not enough. On one occasion he had eleven dispatches from Richard Rush in London to answer at once, and almost as many from Stockholm, Paris, and Madrid. The idea occurred to him of keeping an index of diplomatic correspondence in which each dispatch from a minister abroad would be entered as received, and a minute of its contents and enclosures added preparatory to its being answered. A similar register should be maintained for consular correspondence.[11]

Two days after Adams had decided that he must have a more systematic procedure for correspondence, he had occasion to read over the correspondence of Jonathan Russell while negotiating a treaty of commerce with Sweden; and he discovered the principal letter concerning claims on the Swedish Government was missing, as well as the English translation of the treaty. Adams declared: "So it is with almost every correspondence in the Department. All is disorder and confusion." [12] When he found it necessary to leave at the end of August, 1818, for a short visit to see his father and mother, he confessed that he had to leave a great number of letters unanswered, some of them important. Even Sundays were not free from the cares of the Department. Adams complained that he was "compelled reluctantly to devote this day [Sunday, November 1, 1818] to the duties of my office to prepare the draft of a dispatch with instructions to A. Gallatin and R. Rush conformably to the decisions of the late Cabinet meetings." Even after he became more experienced in the duties of the office, Adams found that the preparation of instructions for a minister going out on a foreign mission was "one of the most arduous and difficult duties of a Secretary of State." [13]

In order to aid in the dispatch of business, the organization of the Department was somewhat clarified in 1818. By an executive order the duties and salaries of a number of the clerks were specifically stated. It was decreed that "all the directives of the Secretary of State" were to be carried into effect through the Chief Clerk. He was to assist in the correspondence of the office under the orders of the Secretary and he was responsible "for the care and superintendence of every part of the Department." Daniel Brent held this position and his salary was fixed at $2,000 a year.[14] Directly under the Chief Clerk came Mr. Bailey, who was charged with consular correspondence and kept a record of domestic and foreign correspondence other than diplomatic. His salary was $1,500 a year. Next in order were three clerks: Richard Forrest, John B. Colvin, and Josias W. King, each receiving $1,250 annually. The first, Forrest, copied letters, made out personal passports and ciphers, filled out certificates for the Secretary's signature, had charge of abstracts of registered seamen, and made out and recorded exequaturs for foreign consuls. Colvin prepared the Acts of Congress for publication, made out and recorded pardons and emissions of fines, and had the care and arrangement of papers relating to the pecuniary claims of individuals on foreign governments. It should be noted, however, that the Secretary himself was often involved in the question of claims. Adams lamented the fact that individual claims formed "the most troublesome and most embarrassing portion of the business of my office. To examine them thoroughly often demands an examination of documents as voluminous and complicated as any affairs of the highest national concern." [15] King made out and recorded commissions [16] and letters of credence, copied letters, forwarded newspapers and public documents to our own and foreign ministers, and had charge of the books and papers of the old Congress. A sixth clerk, John H. Purviance, drew two salaries, one of $1,250 for copying and recording correspondence, and $350 for serving as translator of the office. Since his health was feeble, and in spite of the fact that he was the only good interpreter of Spanish in the Department, Adams sent him as a special messenger to Madrid with a duplicate copy of the treaty with Spain as a relaxation from the labors of the Department and for the healing properties of a sea voyage.

Two clerks, Moses Young and Andrew McCormick, were approximately keepers of the files and archives as well as copyists. The first was responsible for the arrangement of the papers of the office, copied and recorded reports to the President and to the Congress, while the second also assisted in collating the Acts of Congress and served as treasurer of the office. These clerks received an annual stipend of $1,250. The Patent Office was still under the direction of Dr. William Thornton, who seemed to be in trouble constantly with both Secretaries and inventors. In a letter to Secretary Adams dated December 13, 1817, Thornton hoped "if there be a purgatory, that the Superintendent of the Patent Office will be exempt from many sufferings in consequence of the dire situation he has experienced on earth." Adams on one occasion, after a visit to the Patent Office, wondered whether it was not among his duties as Secretary of State to devise means of rendering the Patent Office more conducive to the public service and of more extensive usefulness. However, he decided that the hurry of the hour left him so little time that at the close of his career he would have merely gone helter-skelter through the current business of the office and left no trace behind of his having ever been in it. The total personnel, including messengers and assistants, after Adams had filled all the vacancies authorized by law, still numbered only about a dozen persons.

Adams was determined to put in order the accounts of the Department for contingent expenses, which had been kept in a "very loose and slovenly manner." He directed Bailey to obtain an account book and, beginning with the year 1817, to open an account for every appropriation placed under the direction of the Department of State.[17] Adams also noted a failure on the part of the Department in recording the laws and resolutions of Congress as provided by law. He immediately ordered Brent to see to it that this duty was carried into effect.[18]

Secretary Adams quickly learned that the entire cabinet, as well as the chairman of the Committee of Foreign Relations of the Senate, was consulted by President Monroe in every important question concerning foreign relations. Monroe was oftentimes much more willing to compromise to secure a quick result than was his Secretary of State; nevertheless, Adams at the same time noted a "slowness, want of decision and a spirit of procrastination in the President." [19] On occasions Adams found himself at odds with the President and the other members of the cabinet, as when he defended singlehandedly the conduct of General Jackson in Florida. In drafting dispatches, Adams regularly put in expressions which he knew Monroe would criticize and expunge, thereby absorbing "that portion of the objecting spirit which must exercise upon something and which if alloy be not provided for it to cast off is apt to fall upon the pure metal itself." [20]

While Adams was head of the State Department, there arose a question of protocol which he settled upon a common-sense basis. The question was whether heads of departments and their wives should make the first call upon senators and their wives, or the reverse. Adams pointed out that he considered the government as an agency established for the transaction of business and that any ceremonial which interfered with this essential function would be contrary to the fundamentals of democratic government. It should be left to the individuals to maintain these friendly relationships as dictated by their sense of propriety.

The Department Takes the Census

The Congress had by an Act of March 14, 1820, placed the full responsibility for the taking of the census upon the Secretary of State. In comparing the current law with the three preceding Acts, Adams found that the first census, that of 1790, was a mere counting of the population by the several United States marshals and their assistants, with the results forwarded to the President. He forwarded the figures to the Congress, which directed them to be printed under the direction of the Secretary of State. In the census of 1800 the Secretary of State was authorized to furnish the necessary instructions to the marshals, who were instructed to transmit the returns directly to the Secretary of State. The census of 1810, which was much more elaborate, since it attempted to obtain statistics of manufactures as well as a more complete enumeration of persons, was placed under the jurisdiction of both Treasury and State, the former responsible for the account of manufactures and the latter for the enumeration of persons. Inasmuch as by the 1820 law the Secretary of State was made wholly responsible, Adams spent considerable time in preparing the instructions for the marshals. He was unable to find any record of the census taking in the Departmental files, but fortunately the work had been largely done under the direction of one of the clerks, Colvin, who was still in the Department. Furthermore, the instructions from both State and Treasury had been printed in the *National Intelligencer* of 1810.

Adams consulted the abstract of the 1810 census prepared by Tench Coxe of Philadelphia in 1813, also Seybert's statistical tables and forms, the latter of which Adams adopted. This census was to ascertain the sex, color, age, and condition of life of the inhabitants, the number of foreigners not naturalized, and the number of persons engaged in agriculture, commerce, and manufactures. In order that the Department might in the future have the advantage of his procedure, Adams directed that a special record be kept of all the correspondence covering the execution of the law, and a memorandum book in which should be noted all incidents of importance in the making of the enumeration.[21]

Although even less connected with the appropriate duties of a foreign office than the census, Congress had requested in 1817 that the Secretary of State make a complete report on weights and measures. For four years Adams spent a good part of his time, not essential for other duties, on this assignment, reading exhaustively and investigating procedures and usages abroad. His report for standardization of weights and measures in the United States was a remarkable piece of research which was long rated as the standard work on the subject.

Procedural Improvements

In many ways Adams sought to improve the filing system of the Department. He found the register of governmental employees, published once every two years, wholly unsatisfactory due to the many changes. To keep it up to date, he had the latest copy interleaved with blank leaves, upon which every change resulting from death, resignation, or removal, and every new appointment should be entered as soon as known. He also ordered copies of a volume containing a digest of the commercial regulations of foreign nations to be sent to every minister and consul of the United States abroad, with instructions to collect and transmit to the Department any further information relating to the subject. Mr. Bailey was instructed to keep a corrected up-to-date master copy of this digest.

He also thought it advisable to prepare in two parts the instructions to all ministers and agents going abroad, the one a general or standing letter of instructions which would be the same for all, the second a personal letter limited to the special problems of the particular post. In the first were included such matters as the method of writing dispatches, the keeping of accounts, deportment to the sovereign to whom they were accredited and to the members of the diplomatic corps; their relations with the consuls of the United States, duties with regard to the granting of passports, the use of the *alternat* in the signing of treaties, and the rules regarding the acceptance of gifts.[22]

During the summer of 1820 Adams took in hand the library of the Department. He found that the various removals, the fires, the British invasion of 1814, and the want of system in administration had made the library almost worthless. Inasmuch as the Department had moved to its new building at the corner of 15th Street and Pennsylvania Avenue in January, 1820, Adams took two rooms for the library. Shelves were prepared and Adams charged the most recently employed clerk, Thomas L. Thurston, with the care of the library. No book was henceforth to be taken out without a record being made and the person informed that he was responsible for its return. He then wrote a circular letter to all Federal district attorneys, requesting a complete set of the statutes of the states where they were stationed, and to the governors of the states, requesting a copy of the laws from session to session.

Early in 1821 the Congress embarked upon a retrenchment program, and Senator Dana of Connecticut came to see Secretary Adams to complain that the cost of the Department was twice as much in 1820 as it had been in 1800. He wanted to know what justification there was for this situation. Adams pointed out that his salary of $6,000 lacked from $4,000 to $5,000 of being enough to take care of his individual and domestic expenses. However, if the Congress wished to increase the contribution which he was paying for serving the public he would acquiesce in it. He did object to cutting the salaries of the clerks, who only received a subsistence wage and one which was inadequate compensation for the qualifications which they must possess. Adams then pointed out that although the foreign correspondence had remained approximately the same, the interior correspondence which in 1800 was with sixteen states was now with twenty-four. At that time two or three octavo and one folio volume constituted all the documents printed at a session, whereas in 1820 from fifteen to twenty volumes were published every year. Furthermore, with 230 members of Congress now as against 130 then, there were five calls from Congress for information and documents from the Department where formerly there was one. The Department, in fact, needed very badly one or two more clerks to carry on its essential business. Senator Dana seemed to be satisfied with the Secretary's defense.[23]

The copying of correspondence at a time when typewriters and carbon paper were unknown was a very arduous duty for the Department. When it was the question of a treaty in a foreign language which required absolute exactness and several handwritten copies, the drafting and copying gave "anxious occupation." A very careful comparison then had to be made with the printed copies. In the case of the treaty with Spain regarding Florida, Adams himself executed three originals. His account of the ratification of this treaty is an interesting example of the protocol of the period. The Spanish minister, General Vivés, came to the Department of State with a secretary of legation. Adams took the treaty with the king of Spain's ratification and General Vivés took the treaty with the President's ratification. The Spanish secretary read the Spanish original and the other Spanish copies were compared with it. Adams read the

English original, which was compared in the same way. The ratifications were then examined and found correct, and triplicate certificates of the exchange were signed and sealed with the *alternat* procedure of signing maintained. General Vivés took away the treaty ratified by the President and Secretary Adams retained the treaty ratified by the king of Spain. Adams took his copy to the President, who immediately proclaimed it.[24]

Although John Quincy Adams was not a sociable person, his relations with the members of the Department of State were friendly and pleasant. On occasions he made clever use of his clerks. The British minister, Stratford Canning, declared that Adams had a trick of leaving the door open into the room occupied by his secretaries whenever some point of difference between the two governments arose, and by giving utterance to some expression that the British diplomat could not pass over, Adams would give the officials of the Department a high opinion of his national spirit.[25]

No one in the Department worked as hard as the Secretary himself, but all were expected to do the work assigned efficiently and promptly. When one of the clerks, John B. Colvin, failed to report to the office regularly and neglected his duties, Adams refused to tolerate it. Although Adams knew that Colvin would become a bitter enemy, he dismissed him summarily. Colvin retaliated by writing a series of articles in the *Washington City Gazette* in which he attempted to ridicule Adams's pretensions to the Presidency.

Adams had no illusions as to his lack of the graces of a courtier and he refused to seek popularity, even to achieve the Presidency. Writing to his wife, Louisa Catherine, he once confessed that he had "no powers of fascination; none of the honey which the profligate proverb says is the true fly catcher;" he also appreciated the fact that it would not be good policy on his part to affect it.[26] When a friend in a confidential letter to Mrs. Adams complained that Adams showed a disposition to discourage any efforts of his friends to make him President, he agreed and quoted Macbeth: "If chance will have me king, why, chance may crown me, without my stir." Nevertheless, he was politically ambitious, but he wished recognition to be accorded him solely upon his ability and his achievements. That he attained the Presidency in spite of his rigid refusal to deviate a step from his principles to obtain it is a tribute to the quality and character of the members of Congress who nominated him.

The Purchase of Florida

John Quincy Adams's contribution to the formulation of foreign policy during his two terms of office was outstandingly notable. He was an inveterate nationalist who put his country first at all times. Appeasement was anathema to him and he believed in a frank declaration of principles, regardless of the outcome. One of his greatest state papers was his determined defense of General Jackson's invasion of Florida when the President and the entire cabinet were of the opinion that Jackson had violated his instructions. Concededly it was *ex parte* pleading, and in places the foundations of historical fact were unstable; nevertheless, as a whole, the argument was sound and brilliantly and cogently presented.

Monroe had vainly tried to purchase the Floridas in 1803, when Louisiana was obtained, and President Madison had obtained West Florida largely by fiat aided by local uprisings and conquest. Adams proposed to obtain the rest of Florida by treaty. Monroe was sympathetic to the idea, particularly as rumors had reached him that Spain had authorized her minister to the United States, Luis de Onís, to dispose of them for the best terms obtainable. Adams, after arduous and prolonged negotiations, obtained the signature of the Spanish minister to a treaty which gave the United States a clear title to East Florida in return for assuming claims of its citizens against Spain amounting to $5,000,-000 and surrendering its tenuous title to Texas. Adams regarded the signing of this treaty as the most important event of his life and "an event of magnitude in the history of the Union." [27] Although the Senate approved the treaty quickly and unanimously, the Spanish government, in its *mañana*-like manner, delayed ratification for two full years. Adams's determination, patience, and pertinacity were such that Spain finally acceded to his insistence.

Adams and the Monroe Doctrine

Adams's preeminent claim to fame will, however, rest upon his policies regarding the recognition of the colonies of Spain in the New World and his participation in the formulation of the doctrine enunciated by President Monroe. President Monroe was early inclined to recognize the independence of the Latin American colonies, whereas Adams, when the question was first raised, took a strong stand against it. His statement to President Monroe of August 24, 1816, is a logical, accurate formulation of the international law on the subject:

I am satisfied that the cause of the South Americans, so far as it consists in the assertion of independence against Spain *is just*. But the justice of a cause, however it may enlist individual feelings in its favor, is not sufficient to justify third parties in siding with it. The fact and the right combined can alone authorize a neutral to acknowledge a new and disputed sovereignty." [28]

When by the end of 1818 it seemed as though the Republic of La Plata had definitely established its independence and given proof of its stability, Adams was willing to go along with Monroe and accord recognition. In fact,

Adams's draft to the American minister in London, Richard Rush, was so definite on the subject that President Monroe suggested that it be changed to read that recognition was contemplated unless any material change of events should occur.[29] Bolívar and San Martín were inflicting a series of defeats upon the Spanish arms. The fact that the Florida Treaty had been ratified in 1821 removed an important reason for further delay on the part of Adams. On March 8, 1822, President Monroe sent a message to the Congress declaring the time for recognition had come and asking for the necessary funds to make it effective. On March 28, 1822, the House voted approval 167 to 1.

It will always be a disputed issue as to just how much Adams was responsible for the Doctrine which was promulgated in 1823 by President Monroe. Rumors of intervention on the part of the powers of the Holy Alliance to restore the colonies in the New World to Spain had reached Washington early in 1818. Adams, a cold realist, was skeptical of such a move because it seemed like a most unreasonable policy and did not accord with the purposes of Alexander's Holy League. Consequently, at a cabinet meeting held on May 13, 1818, when the question came up, Adams opposed making a proposal to Great Britain for concerted efforts to promote South American independence. It would be a violation of neutrality; and Great Britain, even if acquiescing in South American independence, would avoid any appearance of supporting it and would not only decline our overture, but would use it to injure us with the other European powers.[30] Nevertheless, Adams wished to make it clear that the United States was opposed to European intervention; and in his instructions to Albert Gallatin, the American minister to France, Adams proposed that he approach the French foreign minister informally and let him understand that "we can neither accede to nor approve of any interference to restore any part of the Spanish supremacy in any of the South American provinces." [31]

It was not until the spring of 1823 that the Holy Alliance, by intervening in Spain, changed Great Britain from a friendly cooperator into an active opponent and aroused the latent fears of the United States. In a discussion with President Monroe on June 20, 1823, Adams noted the changed attitude of the British toward their former allies and wondered whether this was not "a suitable occasion for the United States and Great Britain to compare their ideas and purposes together with a view to the accommodation of great interests upon which they had hitherto differed." [32]

George Canning, the new foreign minister of Great Britain, had never been as sympathetic to the Holy Alliance as Lord Castlereagh, his predecessor. He perceived that Great Britain and the United States thought alike in regard to opposing the return of the colonies of the New World to the Spanish yoke and suggested joint action against it to Richard Rush, the American minister.

Rush immediately communicated the proposals of Canning to the State Department and they were received early in October. Secretary Adams had left Washington to visit his father, and in his absence President Monroe carried on the most important duties of the Secretary of State. The British proposal seemed so important that President Monroe decided to consult the two living ex-Presidents, both of whom had served as Secretaries of State. In his letter to Jefferson dated October 17, 1823, Monroe said that it was his own impression "that we ought to meet the proposal of the British Government and to make it known that we would view an interference on the part of the European powers, and especially an attack on the Colonies by them, as an attack on ourselves." [33] Jefferson, although against entangling ourselves in the embroilments of Europe, favored cooperation with Great Britain on this occasion, because if it brought war—which he doubted—it would be our war.[34] Madison was even more emphatic in urging acceptance of the British proposal for joint action.[35]

When the matter was first discussed at a cabinet meeting in Washington on November 7, 1823, Adams felt that Britain was more eager to forestall the acquisition by the United States of a part of the Spanish-American possessions than to gain a public pledge from the United States against interference by the Holy Alliance. Using a recent communication from Czar Alexander announcing his refusal to receive any minister from the South American governments as a "convenient opportunity for us to take our stand against the Holy Alliance and at the same time decline the overture of Great Britain," Adams spoke the phrase which has been rightly quoted so often as evidence of his epigrammatic way of presenting a vitally important suggestion: "It would be more candid, as well as more dignified, to avow our principles explicitly to Russia and France than to come in as a cock boat in the wake of the British man-of-war." [36]

It should be noted that Adams had already taken a strong stand against Russian expansion in the New World. The emperor of Russia in September, 1821, had issued a ukase claiming the northwest coast of North America as far as the fifty-first degree. This would have included a part of the Oregon Territory to which the United States had a substantial claim. On the occasion of a visit by the Russian minister, Baron Tuyll, on July 17, 1823, Adams informed him that the United States would "contest the right of Russia to any territorial establishment on this continent and that we should assume distinctly the principle that the American continents are no longer subjects for any new European colonial establishments." [37]

These statements of Adams prove conclusively that he played perhaps the most vital role in the formulation of the Monroe Doctrine. Nevertheless, it was President Monroe who was responsible for announcing the policy; it was he who decided to present it as a part of his presidential message rather than, as Adams suggested, through diplomatic notes to the foreign offices. That he was himself completely convinced of the wisdom of a unilateral declaration was shown by a letter written to Jefferson early in December, 1823, when he declared that it was more creditable to our government to move alone rather than with England; otherwise, both the Latin American states and the allied powers might think that we acted at Britain's instigation and under her influence.[38]

Adams's Contribution to International Law

Adams's contributions to the development of international law, although not as important as those in the formulation of policy, were by no means inconsiderable. He believed that "the more of pure moral principle is carried into policy and conduct of a government, the wiser and more profound will that policy be." [39] Consequently, he believed that the President should see to it that the laws of nations should be faithfully executed without waiting for an Act of Congress. On one occasion he had a very spirited argument with Attorney General Wirt concerning extradition. Adams felt that since international law required that fugitives charged with heinous crimes should be delivered up, it was the duty of the President to see that the law of nations be faithfully executed. Wirt found such a doctrine too bold for him.[40]

Secretary Adams's greatest contribution to existing international practice in maritime war was in regard to neutral rights. He felt very strongly that the seizure of enemy property in the vessel of a friend was a "relic of the barbarous warfare of barbarous ages." He characterized it as a "system of licensed robbery bearing all the most atrocious characters of piracy." He persuaded Monroe to allow him to draft the project of a convention to regulate neutral and private belligerent rights in time of war. He proposed to abolish privateering, to restrict contraband, that free ships make free goods and persons, and that neutral property should be free even though found in the vessel of an enemy.[41] The draft was discussed in the cabinet and sent to all the leading European states through the American ministers. Adams conceded that it might be the dream of a visionary, but he preferred to consider it "the great and practicable conception of a benefactor of mankind." Rarely did he manifest such enthusiasm over any project as he did on this proposal. He felt that he could "die for it with joy . . . with a consciousness of not having lived in vain for the world of mankind." [42] It was not until 1856, when the Declaration of Paris was accepted by the principal powers of Europe, that his dream was realized; and at that time the United States was unwilling to accept it.

Comparing John Quincy Adams with his predecessors in the high office of Secretary of State, he must be ranked at the top or very close to it. His background, experience, and ability, coupled with his straightforward honesty and sincerity, gave him a natural priority in the cabinet. Although he declared that except for his personal controversy with Jonathan Russell he always submitted his own judgment to that of the President, his determination verging upon obstinacy usually carried sufficient weight to overcome any misgivings in Monroe's mind. In the case of General Jackson's acts in Florida, he won over both President and cabinet.

Few men could have maintained his working schedule, which meant rising between six and seven and working until midnight, with time out only for meals and a swim or a walk. He prided himself upon never refusing to receive a visitor, even though he conceded that they wore him out. He met as many as 264 visitors personally in a single month. This perpetual drain upon his strength undoubtedly made him at times a bit irascible, both in his speech and in his writings. Adams confessed to Monroe that his communications to Great Britain might seem unnecessarily harsh, but considering the British language, the tone was justified. Mr. Crawford, Secretary of the Treasury, felt that "the tendency to estrange us from all foreign powers, which the style of the notes of the State Department has uniformly had, has been so often demonstrated, yet so often permitted, that I have almost given up the idea of maintaining friendly relations with those powers." [43] Adams was a strong nationalist, he believed in his country's greatness and he would brook no disparagement of it. The Department of State, under his direction, was respected even if grudgingly, both at home and abroad.

6

Henry Clay, Martin Van Buren, and Edward Livingston

<hr>

Henry Clay—Secretary of State

The failure of John Quincy Adams to receive a majority of the electoral college votes, and his election to the Presidency by the House of Representatives when General Jackson had received a plurality of the popular votes, was not a propitious beginning for a successful administration. The choice of John C. Calhoun as Vice President did not improve the situation for Adams. But the appointment of Henry Clay as Secretary of State proved to be the most serious mistake of all. Not that Clay did not merit the appointment. He had served as a member of the American peace commission with Adams at Ghent in 1814, where he fought successfully both the British and his colleagues against giving the British the right of navigation of the Mississippi. He had been elected senator before he was old enough to take office, and he had served as a most eloquent Speaker in the House of Representatives. He had always been keenly interested in foreign affairs, and particularly in closer relations with Latin America. One of his great speeches in Congress was a brilliant exposition of the justification of recognizing the independence of the Latin American states.

Years later, Adams thus justified the appointment of Clay:

As to my motives for tendering to him the Department of State when I did, let that man who questions them come forward. Let him look around among statesmen and legislators of this nation and of that day. Let him then select and name the man whom, by his preeminent talents, by his splendid services, by his ardent patriotism, by his all-embracing public spirit . . . by his long experience in the affairs of the Union, foreign and domestic, a President of the United States, intent only upon the welfare and honor of his country, ought to have preferred to Henry Clay.[1]

Unfortunately, the presidential election had been bitterly contested and Clay had thrown his support to Adams in the House, thus insuring his election.

When Adams appointed Clay Secretary of State, an office which was the ideal springboard to the Presidency, Jackson's followers suspected a secret deal and made the accusation of "bargain and corruption." John Randolph of Roanoke, a bitter opponent of Clay on the floor of the Senate, characterized the appointment as the "coalition of Blifil and Black George . . . the Puritan with the blackleg." This allusion to Clay's propensities for drinking and gambling brought a challenge from Clay which resulted in a duel with pistols. Even this drastic effort on Clay's part failed to destroy the venomous campaign of his political enemies, and although there was no proved justification for the accusation that any sort of bargain had been made between Adams and Clay, the adherents of Jackson used it as a cudgel to belabor Clay throughout his four years of office.

Clay himself was not happy in the position of Secretary of State. He was essentially a great parliamentary leader and not interested in administration. He was fond of speaking and was noted as one of the outstanding orators of his time. He was brilliant in debate and apt at repartee, but he confessed that he had "an unaffected repugnance to any executive employment." His poor health and the death of his two daughters all conspired to make his incumbency an unsatisfactory one as compared with his achievements in the Congress.

Departmental Reorganization Proposed by Clay

Mr. Clay had hardly been inducted into office before he made an urgent request for additional help. On January 14, 1826, he sent a communication to Louis McLane, chairman of the Committee of Ways and Means of the House of Representatives, pointing out the great increase of work required of the officers of the Department as a result of recognizing and sending missions to seven new American powers to the south. Besides, since these states conducted all their correspondence in the Spanish and Portuguese languages, much more translating was required. The time was propitious for obtaining an increase in personnel, inasmuch as a select committee of the House had requested each of the four existing executive departments to submit a statement "whether any and if any, what part of the public service under their control suffered, or was liable to suffer for want of suitable means and provisions for the proper performance of such service." Secretary Clay was thus given an excellent opportunity to suggest changes in the organization of the Department and to request the additional personnel needed.

In his letter dated February 16, 1826, to Daniel Webster, chairman of the Special Committee of the House, Clay first gave a brief summary of the work of the office and the organization existing to perform its functions. He divided the work of the Department into fifteen categories, pointing out that only eight of the fifteen pertained to the conduct of foreign affairs and were therefore suitable for assignment to the Department of State. The other seven were of a purely domestic nature and might much more suitably be assigned to a home department.

The subjects which Clay thought should be continued under the jurisdiction of the Department of State were the following:

First, Correspondence with fourteen American Ministers of both grades in foreign countries; with four consuls to the Barbary Powers, charged also with diplomatic duties; with two agents of claims at Paris and London; and with one hundred and ten consuls abroad, and including numerous translations; and likewise an extensive correspondence concerning claims of citizens of the United States.

Second, Correspondence, occasional treating and frequent official interviews on business with Foreign Ministers, accredited to this Government whose number varies from ten to fourteen; and also correspondence with Foreign Consuls admitted in our port, whose governments have no diplomatic representatives.

Third, The issuing and distributing to applicants personal passports, and the preparation and distribution of sea letters and Mediterranean passports.

Fourth, A compilation from official returns of lists of passengers arriving in the United States and of registered seamen and of commercial information.

Fifth, The custody of the Great Seal and the recording of all the commissions to American Ministers and Consuls, and of foreign consuls residing in the United States, and the making out and the recording of their exequaturs.

Sixth, Examination and liquidation of accounts for foreign and other services under the Department . . . and the application and disbursement of the fund for the relief and protection of distressed American seamen.

Seventh, Custody and care of the books and papers belonging to various Commissions, which are now dissolved, under different treaties . . . and the occasional exhibition and making extracts from some of those papers, on the application of individuals.

Eighth, Reports to Congress and complying with calls for information, and other orders of the Senate and House of Representatives.

The other seven classes of duties assigned to the State Department were clearly of a wholly domestic character and would logically belong to a domestic or home department. These seven classes, according to Clay, may be briefly summarized as follows: correspondence with governors of states and territories and with Federal officials; the preservation of the rolls of Congress; the recording, printing, and distribution of the laws and public documents; the Patent Office; the reception and preservation of books published in the United States and giving of necessary certificates to procure the copyrights; the making out and recording of commissions and the compiling of the biennial register of officers; the authentication by certificate of records, papers, and documents and the issuance and recording of pardons, remission fines, and penalties; care of the original manuscript journal, books, documents, and papers of historical value, and the superintendence of the taking of the census.[2]

Although no immediate action was taken to relieve the Department of State of these seven groups of incongruous activities, all but the first were ultimately assigned to other agencies of the government. The suggestion that a home office be established did not appeal to Congress, which was already looking askance at the increasing tendency of the Federal government to usurp undelegated powers. However, the number of regular clerks by 1827 had been increased to thirteen, and extra clerks were added from time to time as need arose, either by single acts or by joint resolutions of Congress. For example, we note that by the Act of March 2, 1827, some $3,400 was authorized to be expended as compensation for four additional clerks in the State Department. The annual appropriation for the Department during the years 1825 and 1826 had been fixed as $24,050, which was $10 less than had been appropriated for the Department in 1819. Secretary Clay's salary was $6,000, the same as that of his predecessor, while Daniel Brent remained as Chief Clerk with no increase in his salary of $2,000.

The period from 1825 to 1829, when Clay served as Secretary of State, gave little opportunity for a brilliant diplomatic performance. The Congress of Panama, called by Bolívar to discuss the common problems of the Western World, offered what appeared to be glorious possibilities; but due to opposition on the part of the representatives of the slaveholding states, there was so long a delay in securing approval for the appointed delegates and the financing of the mission that the Congress of Panama had adjourned before the delegates from the United States arrived. Secretary Clay had shown his power of persuasion by convincing President John Quincy Adams of the great opportunity afforded to participate. In his instructions to the American delegates, Clay penned perhaps his greatest state paper. Unfortunately, the Congress of Panama was ahead of its time and its failure was a blow to Bolívar, who conceived it, and to Clay, who did his part to make it succeed.

Perhaps the most concrete achievement of the Department of State under Clay's administration was the negotiation of a considerable number of treaties. Clay himself declared that while he was Secretary of State, "more treaties between the United States and foreign nations had been actually signed than had been during the thirty-six years of the existence of the present Constitution." [3] There were a dozen in all, including treaties with Mexico, Central America, Brazil, Great Britain, Sweden and Norway, Denmark and the Hanseatic republics. Most of them were commercial agreements, with most-favored-nation treatment accorded. However, if President John Quincy Adams, whose diplomatic ability was renowned, was unable to make a record of achievement during this period, Clay's failure to do more cannot be laid to inability. As one of his biographers says, "Diplomacy was in the doldrums." Henry Clay could negotiate ably and write effectively, and no Secretary of State was more popular with the diplomatic corps. But no opportunity was afforded to play a great role on the international stage, and Clay returned to his parliamentary career with a feeling of relief. He had found President Adams most friendly and cooperative and was able to write to a friend, "I have found in him since I have been associated with him in the executive government as little to censure and condemn as I could have expected in any man." [4]

Martin Van Buren—Secretary of State

President John Quincy Adams, like his father before him, proved to be a one-term President. General Andrew Jackson was the picturesque hero of the people and he rode into the Presidency on a swelling wave of mass popularity. The man who according to Daniel Webster did more than any other ten men to prevent Adams's reelection was Martin Van Buren, and in return President Jackson offered him the first post in his cabinet. Van Buren, an "immovable, obstinate, and imperturbably good-natured" Dutchman, according to his own definition, had had no diplomatic experience, but he was an excellent lawyer and a shrewd politician. He had served as state legislator, Attorney General, senator, and had just been elected Governor of New York. It would appear that he expected to be Secretary of State under Jackson even before he campaigned for the governorship—a procedure which aroused considerable criticism.

Van Buren was not able to enter upon his duties immediately after he was commissioned, due to his desire to complete certain reforms as governor, before coming on to Washington. Instead of permitting the Chief Clerk to serve as Secretary ad interim, in accordance with previous practice, Van Buren recommended that President Jackson name James A. Hamilton of New York, a close friend and supporter, to carry on for about a month, from March 6 until April 5, 1829, when Van Buren could take charge.

The appointment of Martin Van Buren as Secretary of State was purely political, and President Jackson made no pretense that it was otherwise. "I called him to the Department of State," he declared, "influenced by the general wish and expectation of the Republican party throughout the Union." [5] However, in his letter to Van Buren, Jackson declared that he wished men in whom he could repose trust under all exigencies, and then he abruptly concluded with a typically Jacksonian statement: "Trusting in your intelligence and sound judgment my desire is that you shall take charge of the Department of State." [6]

Political Appointments

It has been alleged that Van Buren was the originator of the extension of the spoils system of New York to the national government,[7] and that one of the clerks in the Department of State became insane at the thought of being removed from his position.[8] A careful check of the clerical personnel would seem to indicate that Francis Q. Smith of Virginia was referred to: Mr. Smith had been appointed in 1822; on May 1, 1829, his salary was reduced from $1,600 to $800, and on June 30, 1829, he resigned. Of the others who resigned, Thurston had served 11 years, Bronner 6 years, Slade 5 years, and Fendall 2 years.

Van Buren declared that when he arrived in Washington the hotel was surrounded by a crowd of applicants for office who followed him into, and filled his room. He promised to examine their papers but declared that he was indisposed to see persons who desired appointments by seeking them in person in Washington.[9] In the case of Daniel Brent, the Chief Clerk and a "thorough old Federalist," Van Buren kept him in office in spite of the remonstrances of many of the supporters of the administration, on the ground that his "gentlemanly manners and the truthfulness and integrity of his character were especially invaluable in the role of duties he had long and well discharged." [10] Other clerks of long experience, such as Josiah Wilkins, John Martin Baker, Andrew T. McCormick, were also retained. In fact, a comparison of the clerical personnel in the Department for the years 1829 to 1831 would indicate that a majority of those who held office in 1829 were still in office in 1830 and 1831.[11]

Van Buren's first difference with President Jackson occurred because of Jackson's hasty and ill advised methods of making important appointments. Even before Van Buren's arrival in Washington, Jackson had appointed one L. W. Tazewell as minister to England and Edward Livingston as minister to France. By insisting upon an early departure in each case, Van Buren obtained the appointee's resignation, and henceforth the President accepted Van Buren's suggestions regarding further diplomatic appointments. That Van Buren's own judgment was not too reliable in making appointments was shown when he persuaded President Jackson to appoint John Randolph of Roanoke as minister to Russia. The latter's conduct in spending a good part of his term in London was so disturbing to the administration that Jackson had to make a graceful excuse for it in his annual message to the Congress.

Problems Social and Diplomatic

Another immediate problem which faced Secretary Van Buren was the hesitant attitude of the diplomatic corps to accept the new administration as socially sound and politically dependable. At the suggestion of Van Buren, the entire diplomatic set was invited to meet with the President and Secretary of State at the Executive Mansion, with a view to their presentation. The President delivered a very informal address emphasizing his friendly feeling to all nations, and it was followed by an excellent dinner and entertainment. The result, according to Van Buren, was that "the anxieties of these gentlemen were completely relieved and their prejudices materially softened by the most approved diplomatic machinery." [12]

When Van Buren assumed office, he found that although the administration had been organized for over a month, no one pertaining to it had called upon the defeated President. With the approval of the President, Van Buren thereupon called upon Mr. Adams and was cordially received. As the Secretary was leaving, Adams said he would give him a useful hint; namely, that no secrets could be kept in the State Department, for the representatives of foreign powers were always sure to find out what was going on concerning their governments.[13] Profiting by this suggestion, in the first diplomatic negotiations which Van Buren engaged upon to establish commercial relations with Turkey and obtain the admission of American vessels to the Black Sea, he kept all the papers in his private rooms while the matter was in progress.

Van Buren, being a widower, could act independently in the petticoat war waged by the wives of the other members of the cabinet against "Peggy O'Neill," the wife of Secretary of War Eaton. He quite regularly took Mrs. Eaton in to dinner when the occasion permitted and ingratiated himself still more strongly in the President's favor by so doing. As might be expected in such a campaign, the women won and neither Jackson nor Van Buren could force Washington society to accept the lady with a past upon whom the Secretary of War had bestowed his name.

Remarkably enough, President Jackson and Secretary Van Buren were able to settle the thorny and long-contested dispute with Great Britain over trade with the West Indies, in regard to which President John Quincy Adams and Secretary Clay had tried in vain to obtain an agreement. As a real effort toward compromise, Van Buren instructed our minister in London, Louis McLane, to agree to the provisions of the British Act of 1825; and Jackson simultaneously requested that he be permitted to open the ports of the United States to British vessels and their cargoes coming from British possessions upon the same terms that American vessels and their cargoes received coming from the same ports. The issue was settled upon this basis, and by the fall of 1830 British colonies were once again opened to American shipping. However, Van Buren, by frankly conceding that the United States was wrong in her previous position and by unpatriotically criticizing to a foreign government the position taken by the previous administration, antagonized a considerable number of senators, who retaliated later by refusing to approve his appointment as minister to Great Britain.[14]

Van Buren Resigns

Van Buren was by far the ablest member of Jackson's cabinet, and the two were much together in a social as well as a political way. The Department of State and problems of foreign relations interested Van Buren much less than domestic affairs, and after two years he decided to resign. He knew that Jackson wanted him to be the next President. Jackson had even suggested that Van Buren run for the Vice Presidency when Jackson tried for his second term, and that after a year or two he would resign because of ill health and Van Buren take charge. Jackson was at first adamant against his resignation, and when he finally became reconciled to it, insisted that Van Buren remain in public life by serving as minister to Great Britain.

Before the resignation could be made public, it was necessary to pick a successor. After canvassing the situation thoroughly, Jackson and Van Buren decided to offer the position to Edward Livingston—the same Livingston whom Jackson had named two years previously as minister to France, but whose appointment Van Buren had opposed, primarily because it had been made before he had entered upon his duties and without any consultation with him. On this occasion it was Van Buren who insisted and President Jackson who reluctantly "yielded . . . to my earnest solicitations."

A letter dated April 9, 1831, was immediately dispatched to Livingston, who had recently been elected senator from Louisiana. The letter, signed by Secretary Van Buren, informed him: "We wish to see you here at the earliest practicable moment on an affair of deep interest. The President will be obliged if you will start the day after you receive this, under circumstance which will work to avoid speculation by preventing its being known that your destination is Washington." [15] Apparently Livingston had no idea of what was wanted of him, and when the offer was made he asked for time to consider it. Writing to his wife, he expressed serious doubts of his ability to fill the office with credit, as he knew nothing of the details and would be worried by political intrigue. Another letter, written a month after he had been commissioned, indicates that he appreciated the honor conferred upon him:

Here I am in the second place in the United States,—some say the first; in the place filled by Jefferson and Madison and Monroe and by him who filled it before any of them,—my brother; in the place gained by Clay at so great a sacrifice; in the very easy-chair of Adams; in the office which every politician looks to as the last step but one in the ladder of his ambition; in the very cell where the great magician, they say brewed his spells.[16]

Van Buren had often been called the "Little Magician," and no soothsayer able to read the future could have pursued a more inspired policy looking toward the presidential goal than did Van Buren in his resignation from the Department of State and acceptance of the post as minister to Great Britain. Both his nomination and that of Livingston were recess appointments, and when Congress convened in December, it confirmed all appointments except those of Livingston and Van Buren. The delay in confirming Livingston by the Senate Committee on Foreign Relations was due to a motion of Henry Clay's to have a statement from the Treasury as to whether Livingston had cleared the debt which he owed the government. This referred to an old debt assumed by Livingston through the defalcation of a subordinate official whose accounts had not been audited carefully by Livingston. Livingston had agreed to make full payment and had already paid over $90,000 on an original defalcation of less than $50,000. Clay should have been familiar with the facts, and although he withdrew his motion and Livingston was confirmed, the latter never forgave Clay for the unnecessary humiliation. The Senate refused, however, to confirm Van Buren's nomination, although he had already established himself in London and was carrying on successfully important diplomatic negotiations with Great Britain which he had initiated as Secretary of State. The narrow petty partisanship evinced by the Senate in this action so aroused Jackson's anger that he made Van Buren his vice-presidential running mate; and with the successful outcome of the election, Van Buren not only became presiding officer over the Senate which had refused his confirmation, but built up a popular support that later carried him into the Presidency.

Edward Livingston—Secretary of State

Although he possessed no diplomatic training or background, few Secretaries of State have been endowed with greater natural talent or have shown greater ability in diversified fields than Edward Livingston. Graduated from Princeton at the age of seventeen, he began the study of law and was admitted to the New York bar when he was twenty-one. At thirty he was elected to Congress, where he served three terms as representative of New York. He next served as district attorney and mayor of New York City. It was in the office of the district attorney that financial irregularities occurred, which, since they were due to carelessness, he assumed fully and paid off completely. However, it necessitated a drastic change in his mode of life. He moved to New Orleans, where he soon became an outstanding member of the legal profession. As a member of the Louisiana Assembly, he revised the civil and criminal codes of the state and established a remarkable new penal system that received world-wide acclaim. Sir Henry Maine regarded him as the "finest legal genius of modern times."

Perhaps it was unfortunate that no outstanding diplomatic problems were presented to him in his two years of service as Secretary of State. However, even if there had been, it is doubtful whether he would have been given a free hand, since Jackson liked to keep both foreign and domestic policies closely within his own hands and he still advised with Van Buren in all matters which he considered of importance. In fact, Jackson suggested Van Buren's return to the Department and the sending of Livingston abroad even before Livingston had completed his first year of service.

Livingston was not sympathetic to the Jacksonian spoils system, either in the Department of State or in the diplomatic or consular service. Very few changes occurred in the State Department personnel during his incumbency, and he avoided as far as possible making purely political appointments abroad. When requested by a senatorial friend to give a consular post to a person of doubtful qualifications, Livingston pointed out that

really his appearance is not fitted for public life. Imagine him in a consular uniform marching with his sword dragging on the pavement to a national entertainment. He is a good poet and novelist you say but this last title to celebrity has convinced him most unfortunately that every man who can write a good novel must be a diplomatist. The consulate given to Cooper, the secretaryship to Irving are colors in Westminster Hall to him, they will not let him sleep. I did everything I could to make him understand that his literary talent would be obscured by mercantile associations into which he would be led by a consulship but I fear without success.[17]

Livingston took a particular interest in the foreign service and felt very strongly that our representation abroad was insufficient and that the representatives were ill paid and unappreciated. In a communication to President Jackson, dated January 31, 1833, the Secretary of State pointed out that no diplomatic relations existed between the United States and Austria, Prussia, Bavaria, Saxony, and the other members of the Germanic Confederation, the Hanse towns, Switzerland, Sardinia, the Papal Dominion, Naples, the rest of Italy and Greece; that the cost of our foreign relations annually was about $200,000, while the foreign commerce it superintended abroad was always more than \$171,000,000. Concerning salaries, he felt that if the representative were forced to live in a manner that would not allow him to associate on an equal footing with others of the same grade, "he is deprived of many of the advantages which social intercourse affords to perform essential duties and to gain important information which can only be obtained by mixing in the first circles." He then noted that the government provided its representative with none of the necessaries for the transaction of business; he had to do all the drudgery of the office with his own hands and he was forced to live in some obscure place where his countrymen blushed to find him. As a partial remedy, he suggested that additional representation and a reasonable allowance be granted, so that books could be kept regularly and the representative be relieved of the expense of copying all documents and correspondence in the Department of State necessary for completing the archives of the several legations abroad.[18]

The position of Secretary of State had not banished from Livingston's mind his desire to serve as minister of the United States in Paris. His second wife, a French Creole from Jamaica, and of excellent family, was more French than American; in fact, she spoke only French when Livingston married her. His close and cherished friend, the Marquis de Lafayette, constantly urged him to come to Paris. In the spring of 1833 he was chosen foreign associate of the Institute of France as recognition for his outstanding work on the code of criminal law. Jackson was not blind to Livingston's interests, and since the French post had been vacant since the return of William Rives in 1831, the move was a natural one. On May 29, 1833, Livingston resigned as Secretary of State, and the same day he was named minister to France. In accepting his resignation, President Jackson, after expressing appreciation for his services, declared that as he would still have the benefit of his experience and talents in the branch of the public service with which he had been particularly charged during the past two years, "the regret which I would otherwise feel of your retirement from that station is greatly diminished." [19]

7

Louis McLane and John Forsyth

Louis McLane—Secretary of State

As to how important a role was played in the transfer of Livingston to Paris by Louis McLane, Livingston's successor as Secretary of State, is somewhat difficult to say. Martin Van Buren declares that McLane visited him in New York in the fall of 1832, and proposed, with the consent of the President, to discuss "sundry grave matters," including the transfer of Livingston to France, and the elevation of McLane to be Secretary of State. Van Buren then goes on to remark that these two movements "had ceased to be open questions and wanted only the expedient moment for their execution." [1] McLane desired the position, but only as a step toward the bench of the Supreme Court, or even, if Fortune were propitious, to the Presidency.

At the time of his nomination as Secretary of State, McLane was Secretary of the Treasury, an office which interested him only slightly. McLane was an able lawyer, had served creditably in both houses of Congress, and as minister to Great Britain had effectively carried out Van Buren's instructions in obtaining a treaty opening up trade with the West Indies. He was therefore as well qualified for the position as Secretary of State as his immediate predecessors. The only important diplomatic issue that faced him in his year's administration was the failure of France to make her payments of the spoliation claims in accordance with treaty provisions, and here Livingston in Paris and President Jackson in Washington played the leading roles.

McLane, however, took a very important part in the administrative improvement of the Department of State by his reorganization plan of 1833. In his first annual message to the Congress, dated December 8, 1829, President Andrew Jackson declared:

The great and constant increase of the business in the Department of State forced itself at an early period upon the attention of the executive . . .

the remedy proposed was the establishment of a home department—a measure which does not appear to have met the views of Congress. . . . I am not, therefore, disposed to revive this recommendation, but am not the less impressed with the importance of so organizing that Department so that its Secretary may devote more of his time to our foreign relations.[2]

Nothing had been done to reorganize the Department by either Van Buren or Livingston, but Secretary McLane, by his order of June 30, 1833, made the first over-all reorganization of the Department since its establishment in 1789. Under the new regulations the Chief Clerk's functions were administrative and supervisory. He served in reality as an Acting Under Secretary of State. Under his general direction seven bureaus were to be set up: diplomatic; consular; home; archives, laws and commissions; pardons, remissions, copyrights, and library; disbursing and superintending; translating and miscellaneous. With the exception of matters pertaining to accounts, all communications between the Secretary and the Department were to be made through the Chief Clerk, unless otherwise directed by the Secretary. Daniel Brent, who had served as Chief Clerk since 1817, was commissioned as consul of the United States in Paris in August, 1833, and in his place Secretary McLane appointed Asbury Dickins of North Carolina.

Secretary McLane felt very strongly that the position of Chief Clerk was of such great responsibility that the salary of $2,000 allocated to the office was wholly inadequate. In a letter to the Committee of Ways and Means of the House, dated February 3, 1834, he pointed out that "the Chief Clerk is in fact, though not in name, an assistant or undersecretary; and in the absence of the head of the Department always charged with the care and preservation of the archives and most generally with all the official duties." He also indicated that the duties of the State Department are strictly confidential "and of a very delicate nature requiring not only great fidelity, but talent and education of a high order, general information, and an accurate knowledge of public officers both foreign and domestic, not necessarily required in other inferior officers of the Executive Government." He urged that the salary be increased to an amount between $2,500 and $3,000. Congress did not see fit to accept the recommendation.[3]

The Reorganized Department of State

The first and most important bureau was the Diplomatic Bureau. Three clerks were assigned to it: the first, W. S. Derrick, had charge of our missions in England, France, Russia, and the Netherlands; the second, A. O. Dayton, was responsible for the other missions in Europe, and to these the Regulations of 1836 added countries in Asia and Africa and consular affairs with Tripoli, Tunis, and Morocco. William Hunter had charge of the missions in North and South America. Notes and instructions were to be prepared and indexed, dispatches received, filed, and registered, letters of credence made ready and treaties prepared for ratification and exchange. The business of the bureau was to be carefully indexed, and a survey of the state of each mission abroad was to be made immediately and thereafter kept up to date. A weekly correspondence with each of the missions abroad was to be maintained, giving general information concerning conditions at home and abroad. A full and accurate record was to be kept of the arrival of ministers, chargés d'affaires, and consuls general. An interesting regulation required that all foreign newspapers, after having been perused by the Secretary and Chief Clerk, be committed to the Diplomatic Bureau, where they were to be examined by the gentlemen to whose division they appertained; and such articles in a foreign language as were deemed proper for the Secretary to be acquainted with were to be marked and sent to the Translator for translation. The Diplomatic Bureau was to be responsible for the filing and preservation of foreign newspapers, and no such newspaper could be loaned to a person not connected with the Department without the permission of the Secretary.

The Consular Bureau had approximately the same responsibility for consular correspondence as the Diplomatic Bureau had for diplomatic correspondence. In addition it was charged with the issuing and recording of exequaturs, a function which was transferred to the Home Bureau by the regulations of the following year. The Consular Bureau was responsible for keeping indexes and registers and a synopsis of the state of relations with each consulate. Although at the time the regulations were issued there were 152 officers designated as consuls, consular agents, or commercial agents, as against 19 diplomatic representatives, only two officers were assigned to consular activities: Francis Markoe, Jr., and Benjamin C. Vail. However, by 1836 a third clerk was added, T. W. Dickins, and the allocation of work was placed upon a geographical basis similar to that of the Diplomatic Bureau.

The Home Bureau, as its name implies, was charged with filing and registering all domestic correspondence with the Department. It authenticated certificates under the seal of the Department. It kept and preserved registers of seamen to whom protection was given and kept a record of the arrival of passengers from foreign ports. The two clerks assigned to this bureau were Andrew T. McCormick and Lewis Randolph.

The Bureau of Archives, Laws, and Commissions was charged with the Department's archives. It was responsible for making out and recording commissions and furnishing copies of them; it also prepared statements of vacancies occurring by the expiration of terms for which commissions were granted, and received and filed all applications for office. It took care of the rolls of the laws and saw to it that they were published and distributed. The bureau also distributed the messages of the President and the reports of heads of departments. Thomas P. Jones, formerly superintendent of the Patent Office, was in charge of this bureau, and he was assisted by George Hill.

The Bureau of Pardons and Remissions and Copyrights and of the Care of the Library was given such heterogeneous duties that it was an administrative monstrosity and was reorganized on a more logical basis the following year. Its first duty was the preparation of pardons for signature and to care for correspondence connected with them. It received and deposited all copyrights in accordance with law. It collected the statutes of the different states and kept an accurate record of them. It had charge of the library and its catalogues and it was responsible for the arrangement and preservation of books, documents, and maps. Arthur Shaaff was placed in charge of this bureau. In 1834 the bureau was abolished; the duties relating to pardons, remissions, and copyrights were transferred to the Home Bureau and those relating to the library to the Translator and Librarian.

The Disbursing and Superintending Bureau made purchases for the Department and made disbursements from various appropriations under the control of the President and the Secretary of State. It kept a record of the correspondence on accounts and money transactions and arranged for the payment of the drafts of our ministers and agents abroad. It kept the Great Seal of the United States and the seal of the Department. Edward Stubbs, who was assigned to this position at a salary of $1,400, received an extra $250 annually as superintendent of the North East Executive Building.

The Translating and Miscellaneous Bureau was required to translate all letters, papers, and documents which in any way related to the business of the Department. Translations were to be made immediately after the material was received and then filed with the original in the proper bureau. The miscellaneous functions included the making out of special and personal passports and taking care of the correspondence concerning them; also entering upon the mail books all communications received by the Department and filing miscellaneous letters. Robert Greenhow, who was the Translator, received $1,600 a year, a sum equal to that of the head of the Diplomatic Bureau.

A few general regulations covered extra clerks and their utilization. No change was made in the Patent Office organization, which, although still under the jurisdiction of the State Department, was administered separately. The hours of duty for officers of the Department were prescribed to be from 10:00 A.M. to 3:00 P.M., and no clerk was permitted to be absent during these hours without special permission. Requests for leaves of absence for more than twenty-four hours were to be submitted to the Secretary in writing. All business was to be regarded as strictly confidential and was to be disposed of on the day of reference unless impracticable for good cause. All papers and documents were to be regarded as confidential.

Although this reorganization seemed at first to be quite drastic, in reality the duties were not materially changed nor procedures modified to any great extent. Nevertheless, the fact that duties were more specifically prescribed, jurisdictions mapped out, and responsibilities assigned made for operational efficiency. Such changes as proved unsatisfactory were modified by the subsequent regulations of 1834 and 1836, as will be noted below.

One other improvement in diplomatic procedure by Secretary McLane was the request issued to the representatives of foreign nations that they reside in the capital and furnish a list of all persons attached to their missions to the Department of State.

The resignation of Louis McLane as Secretary of State on June 30, 1834, after serving just a year and a month, was sudden and unexpected. He had openly opposed President Jackson in regard to rechartering the Bank of the United States, an attitude which had brought rumors of his resignation in September, 1833, and in February, 1834. A letter from Washington Irving to Martin Van Buren, dated March 11, 1834, indicated that Irving was much concerned over McLane's position but hoped that he would not retire.[4] The real cause of the resignation, according to Van Buren, came as a result of McLane's insistence upon drastic action to compel France to pay the draft drawn upon the French government under the Treaty of 1831. Undoubtedly the dismissal of McLane's friend, William J. Duane, as Secretary of the Treasury, was a bitter blow to McLane, but when it seemed evident that Jackson would name Roger Taney to the Supreme Court—the goal of McLane's ambitions—McLane decided that he had had enough.

John Forsyth—Secretary of State

President Jackson, without any delay, accepted McLane's resignation and named John Forsyth of Georgia as his successor. In many ways Forsyth was an excellent appointment. He was a staunch supporter of the President, had his fullest confidence, and was on most cordial terms with Van Buren, whom Jackson consulted so constantly in matters of foreign policy. While in Congress he had shown a keen interest in foreign affairs and had served for a period during the administration of President Monroe as chairman of the Committee on Foreign Affairs. In 1819 he was appointed by President Monroe as minister to Spain, where he remained until 1823, when he was again elected to Congress. Subsequently he became governor of Georgia, and at the time of his appointment as Secretary of State he was serving as senator for Georgia.

Although the Department of State had been reorganized completely by Secretary McLane in the direction of operational efficiency, Secretary Forsyth, who, having served as governor of Georgia, was familiar with administrative problems, found the need for certain changes which might improve the effectiveness of the administration. By a departmental order, effective on October 31, 1834, he materially increased the size and scope of duties of the Home Bureau. In addition to the duties already assigned to it, such as filing and registering domestic correspondence, registering seamen, recording the arrival of passengers from foreign ports, and the making and authenticating of documents, there was added the following: making out and recording of passports, exequaturs, and commissions; taking care of pardons and remissions, and the seals of the United States and of the State Department; filing and preserving the returns of copyrights; keeping a daily register of all letters other than diplomatic and the action taken thereon; the forwarding of dispatches to ministers and consuls and keeping a register of them; and recording reports to the President and to the two houses of Congress. The Bureau of Pardons, Remissions, and Copyrights was immediately abolished. The Bureau of Archives, Laws, and Commissions was also eliminated, and in its place there was substituted the Keeper of the Archives, whose function was to keep the archives, to take care of the rolls of the laws, and to distribute public documents, including the messages of the President and the reports of the heads of departments. The Disbursing and Superintending Bureau became the Disbursing Agent, who also served as superintendent of the building. The care of the library was given to Mr. Greenhow, the Translator. Although there were now only four bureaus instead of seven, the Home Bureau being the largest, with four clerks, there were still seven divisions and fourteen clerks, counting the Chief Clerk. The personnel in 1835, under Secretary Forsyth, remained practically the same as it had been in 1833, under Secretary McLane.

Just as Secretary McLane before him, Secretary Forsyth was much concerned over the low salary scale prevailing in the State Department. He wrote once in 1835 and twice in 1836 to the chairman of the Ways and Means Committee of the House, urging an increase of salary for the Chief Clerk. He also wished to equalize the salaries of the three clerks in the Diplomatic Bureau at $1,600, since they shared the work equally. Their current salaries were $1,600, $1,500, and $1,400. In the same way he requested that each clerk in the Consular Bureau receive $1,400. However, except for making all salaries in the Consular Bureau $1,400, no change in the salary schedule occurred during Forsyth's incumbency.

Subsequent regulations [5] under Secretary Forsyth, which became effective on November 30, 1836, made very few changes. The Translator was relieved of the library, which was put under the Home Bureau; more elaborate directions were given concerning the functions of the bureaus, and more attention was paid to the security regulations of the Department. The organization of the Department now met all requirements so satisfactorily that except for a few slight changes the arrangement held until 1870, when Secretary Fish made another thorough reorganization.

The following tabulation summarizes the clerical personnel of the Department as of 1836, noting the dates of appointments, the salaries and ages of the officials:

1. Asbury Dickins, appointed Chief Clerk on August 8, 1833, salary $2,000, age 55.
2. William S. Derrick, appointed on March 3, 1827, salary then $800, now $1,600, age 33.
3. Aaron Ogden Dayton, appointed July 1, 1833, salary $1,500, age above 21.
4. William Hunter, Jr., appointed May 4, 1829, salary then $800, now $1,400, age 30.
5. Francis Markoe, Jr., appointed May 12, 1832, salary $1,400, age 35.
6. Benjamin C. Vail, appointed Feb. 12, 1833, salary $1,400, age 36.
7. Thomas W. Dickins, appointed October 1, 1833, salary then $800, now $1,000, age 26.
8. Andrew T. McCormick, appointed January 1, 1818, salary then $1,250, now $1,400, age 60.
9. George Hill, appointed December 2, 1831, salary then $1,000, now $1,400, age 35.
10. Robert S. Chew, appointed July 10, 1834, salary $800, now $900, age 23.
11. Jacob Broom, appointed March 19, 1835, salary $800, age 27.
12. Thomas P. Jones, appointed April 12, 1828, salary $1,500, now $1,400, age 63.
13. Robert Greenhow, appointed September 1, 1831, salary $1,000, now $1,600, age 35.
14. Edward Stubbs, appointed May 3, 1829, salary $1,150, now including extras for superintendent of North East Executive Building, $1,700, age 50.

In addition to these clerks, the Patent Office had Henry L. Ellsworth as superintendent, beginning May 12, 1835, at a salary of $1,500. He was assisted by three clerks, two of whom received $1,000 a year, the other, $800.[6]

The above tabulation shows only one so-called "old-timer," Mr. McCormick, with a period of service of eighteen years; the next oldest in time of service are Mr. Derrick with nine years and Mr. Jones with eight. Two others, Stubbs and Hunter, had served seven years, and the others five years or less. The total salary disbursement, including the Secretary's salary of $6,000 and $4,300 for the Patent Office, amounted to $29,500.

President Jackson Settles with France

It had taken the Department of State some twenty years to obtain an agreement with France regarding the illegal losses, amounting to about $12,000-000, suffered by our commerce during the Napoleonic Wars. Secretaries Van Buren, Livingston, and McLane had tried in vain to obtain the payments promised by the treaty. This was one of the first problems facing Secretary Forsyth when he took office on July 1, 1834. The French Chamber of Deputies had refused in April, 1834, to appropriate the money to make the first payment. Livingston, who was representing the United States in Paris, felt that only a strong stand on the part of the United States would get results. Such a situation was tailored to a President like Andrew Jackson. He ordered the navy for sea duty and promised a strong message on the subject to the Congress. He instructed Secretary Forsyth to inform the French minister, who was much concerned over the situation, that President Jackson was deeply mortified by the refusal of France to pay her obligations and that he intended to place the situation before the representatives of the people. In his message to Congress on December 1, 1834, the President did not mince words:

It is my conviction that the United States ought to insist on a prompt execution of the treaty and in case it be refused or longer delayed, take redress into its own hands. After a delay on the part of France of a quarter of a century in acknowledging these claims by treaty it is not to be tolerated that another quarter of a century is to be waited in negotiating about the payment.[7]

He then suggested the seizure of sufficient French property, public or private, to pay the debt.

The French government was incensed at Jackson's language, and Minister Sérurier, in a note to Secretary Forsyth, declared that it would be "superfluous to say" that the message of President Jackson was received in Paris with a "sentiment of painful surprise." He then declared that the complaints of the President on account of the *pretended* nonfulfillment of the engagements entered into by the French government were strange, not only from the total inaccuracy of the allegations, but because the situation had been explained fully to Mr. Livingston in Paris and to the cabinet in Washington by M. Sérurier himself. Secretary Forsyth objected violently to the word "pretended" as an attack upon the integrity of the President. He declared:

In all discussions between Government and Government, whatever may be the differences of opinion on the facts or principles brought into view, the invariable rule of courtesy and justice demands that the sincerity of the opposing party in the views which it entertains should never be called in question.

Facts may be denied, deductions examined, disapproved, and condemned without just cause of offense; but no impeachment of the integrity of the Government in its reliance on the correctness of its own views can be permitted without a total forgetfulness of self-respect.[8]

Both countries instructed their ministers to depart and both legations were left in the hands of chargés d'affaires. In the meantime the French Chamber appropriated the necessary funds but made payment subject to an apology by President Jackson. When the French chargé, M. Pageot, wished to read the bill passed by the Chamber to Forsyth, Jackson refused to permit Forsyth to hear it, on the ground that foreign nations were not justified "to arrogate to themselves the right to take offense at the mode, manner, or phraseology of the President's message or any official communication between the different coordinate or other branches of our government." [9] In his next message to Congress, although Jackson declared that the "honor of my country shall never be strained by an apology from me for the statement of a truth or the performance of duty," he did concede that his message of the preceding year was not intended "to menace or insult the Government of France." [10] However, by this time the American chargé had requested his passports and the French chargé followed suit. Great Britain now offered to mediate, and the matter was quickly settled when it was decided that *prétendu* in French meant "alleged" and not "pretended," and so no offense could be taken where none was meant. During the whole affair President Jackson was his own Secretary of State and Secretary Forsyth did exactly as he was told. Few episodes in our early diplomatic history show more conclusively that in the conduct of foreign relations the President is absolutely supreme in any instance where he wishes to assume direction.

Van Buren Becomes President

President Jackson had named Martin Van Buren his first Secretary of State, had brought about his choice as Vice President, and finally maneuvered him into the Presidency. As a consequence, Van Buren as President tended to maintain in office the Jackson appointees and to carry out the Jacksonian policies. Since he had suggested Forsyth as Secretary of State to Jackson, it was natural that he should invite Forsyth to continue in office. In fact, no changes whatsoever were made in the cabinet except the appointment of Joel R. Poinsett as Secretary of War to fill the position vacated by Lewis Cass when he accepted the appointment of minister to France.

As Secretary of State under President Van Buren, Forsyth made very few changes in the Department of State personnel. Asbury Dickins had resigned his position as Chief Clerk on December 12, 1836, to accept the position as

Secretary of the Senate of the United States. In his place, Forsyth promoted Aaron Ogden Dayton to serve as Acting Chief Clerk, but he resigned on June 25, 1838, to accept a position as fourth auditor of the Treasury Department. Aaron Vail of New York was thereupon appointed and he remained as Chief Clerk until July 7, 1840, when he resigned to serve as chargé d'affaires in Madrid. The two other changes in the clerical force of the Department which occurred during 1837 were the resignations of Jacob Broom and Thomas P. Jones and the appointment of Horatio Jones, James S. Ringgold, and Alexander H. Derrick to fill the positions vacated.

A survey instituted by the House Committee on expenditures in the State Department, presented on May 26, 1838, gave some interesting sidelights on the cost of administration of the Department for the years 1829 to 1838. The greatest annual sum expended for incidental and contingent expenses of the Department, including the publishing and distribution of the laws, was $31,542.39 during the year 1832, and the smallest amount was $20,213.92, spent in 1831. The total amount spent for these purposes during these years was $225,942.66. The annual expenditures for our missions abroad, which covered the salaries and expenses of four ministers and fifteen chargés d'affaires, amounted to $147,159. The minister to Great Britain received the largest salary, $9,000, and his outfit and return allowances averaged $7,509. The chargés each received a salary of $4,500 and their outfits varied from $1,000 to $2,000. The amounts expended for the relief and protection of American seamen in foreign countries, which had averaged $47,722 per annum for the years 1815 to 1824 inclusive, averaged $26,422 per annum for the years 1829 to 1837 inclusive.[11]

Few diplomatic problems of importance faced the Department of State during the period of Van Buren's administration. The destruction of the *Caroline*, an American-owned steamship chartered by Canadian rebels and their sympathizers to run men and guns into Canada, caused a considerable flurry. President Van Buren issued a proclamation urging observance of our neutrality laws, and Secretary Forsyth protested against "an extraordinary outrage committed . . . on the persons and property of citizens of the United States within the jurisdiction of the State of New York . . . at the moment when . . . the President was anxiously endeavoring to allay the excitement and earnestly seeking to prevent any unfortunate occurrence on the frontier of Canada." [12]

Extraneous Activities

Before concluding this account of the work of the Department of State during the administrations of Jackson and Van Buren, note should be taken of two tasks imposed upon the Department which were strictly domestic in character and wholly alien to the normal duties of a department primarily concerned with foreign affairs. The first of these was a report from the Secretary of State in compliance with a Senate resolution directing him to ascertain and report to the Senate the number of suits on the trial docket of each of the circuit courts of the United States and of the district courts when exercising circuit-court powers, and second, to report the number of miles traveled by each judge of the Supreme Court in attending the circuit allotted to him. This required that letters requesting the information and its subsequent compilation be sent to the forty-one district attorneys of the United States, and that letters be sent also to the Supreme Court judges, requesting the mileage traveled. It is of interest to note that Roger B. Taney, whose district included Washington, listed 458 miles; whereas John McKinley, who made his trips to Little Rock, Mobile, and New Orleans, estimated that he had to travel 10,000 miles annually.[13]

A much more arduous task, which by an Act of Congress the Secretary of State was directed to perform, was the taking of the sixth census of the United States. In a report to President Van Buren, dated December 23, 1839, Secretary Forsyth pointed out a number of discrepancies in the census law, the problems faced by the district marshals in making the enumeration and by the Department of State in examining and correcting the returns and condensing and printing them. He made a number of suggestions for improving the procedure.[14] Fortunately for the Department this was the last census taken under its direction, because by the law of May 23, 1850, the seventh decennial census was placed under the jurisdiction of the Department of the Interior. The establishment of the Department of the Interior in 1849 also relieved the Department of State of the Patent Office. For a considerable period of time this agency had been administered separately, although until the time of its removal, all patents had to be signed by the Secretary of State as well as by the Commissioner of Patents.[15]

The Jacksonian era had brought new blood into the Department of State, and the first thorough reorganization of the administration of the Department. President Jackson completely dominated the diplomatic picture, although Secretary of State Van Buren undoubtedly was permitted to play a more important role than Secretaries Livingston, McLane, or Forsyth. No difficult diplomatic problems of great importance faced the Department during this period. Secretary of State Forsyth and President Van Buren remained sympathetic to the Jacksonian principles, giving the State Department a coherence and stability which made for successful routine diplomacy. Secretary Forsyth remained in office until March 3, 1841, when he turned over his duties to the

Chief Clerk, Jacob L. Martin, who served as Secretary ad interim until Daniel Webster took charge on March 5, 1841.

Although John Forsyth will never rank as one of the great Secretaries of State, he was more than mediocre. He drafted easily and reasoned cogently. He worked with President Van Buren with never a semblance of a clash, and no evidence is available that he ever saw otherwise than eye to eye with the President. His forensic ability was of little value while he was Secretary of State, but as an administrator and advisor he served creditably, if not brilliantly.

8

Daniel Webster and Abel P. Upshur

Daniel Webster—Secretary of State

The administration of Martin Van Buren had not achieved notable success, either abroad or at home, and it succumbed to the Whigs, who had chosen General William Henry Harrison as their candidate for the Presidency and John Tyler of Virginia as his running mate. Henry Clay and Daniel Webster were the real leaders in the anti-Democratic crusade, and undoubtedly Webster's ingenious and effective campaigning was a potent factor in the overwhelming victory. In a letter to his friend Mr. Jaudon, dated June 23, 1840, Webster intimated that in the event of General Harrison's election he would leave the Senate and would have something to do with the government.[1] He was not disappointed, because early in December he received a letter from General Harrison offering him the choice of becoming either Secretary of State or Secretary of the Treasury. Webster preferred to head the State Department, because he did not feel qualified to administer the technical subjects required by the Treasury. Nominated as Secretary of State on March 5, 1841, Webster was confirmed immediately by the Senate. Inasmuch as Forsyth had retired on March 3, Jacob L. Martin of North Carolina, who had been appointed Chief Clerk on July 16, 1840, served as Secretary ad interim on March 4 and 5.

Although Daniel Webster had never held a diplomatic appointment, he was well equipped for his new position. Well trained in the law, a remarkable speaker, a man of fine physique and personality, he had served in both Houses of Congress and had been a candidate for the Presidency. Although renowned as perhaps the greatest constitutional lawyer of the day, Webster was also keenly interested in international affairs. To better acquaint himself at first hand with the European situation, in 1839, after the adjournment of Congress, he made a trip to England with his wife and family as a private citizen. He was received hospitably by most of the leading statesmen of the day, such as Lord Melbourne, Disraeli, Palmerston, the Duke of Wellington, Sir Stratford

Canning, and Sir Robert Peel. He was presented to Queen Victoria and found her pleasant and intelligent. Although relations between the United States and Britain were troubled by several serious diplomatic controversies, Webster gained both admiration and respect by his gracious manners and tactful attitude. He was equally well received in Paris, and Louis Philippe complimented him highly upon his excellent speeches. His first-hand encounters with statesmen abroad and the opportunity afforded to appreciate the foreign point of view proved to be an excellent background for his subsequent work in the field of diplomacy.

The Department Under Webster

One of Webster's first administrative acts smacked strongly of nepotism, when he appointed his son Fletcher to the important post of Chief Clerk. This was the one position in the Department where previous experience was of particular value. As a partial excuse it might be noted that the incumbent, J. L. Martin, had held the position less than eight months and was equally inexperienced when appointed. An unfortunate development of this appointment was a tendency for Webster to take vacations from time to time, leaving his son Fletcher as Acting Secretary of State, with full powers to conduct important negotiations. But while making this very partisan appointment, Webster at the same time issued a civil-service circular forbidding employees to display partisanship in Federal or state elections or to make any contribution to campaign funds.[2]

The sudden death of President Harrison exactly one month after he had been inaugurated, thereby making Tyler President, threatened to relegate Webster to private life immediately. As senators, Tyler and Webster had never agreed, and it was very problematical whether Tyler would carry on with a Harrison cabinet. However, Tyler invited all the heads of the executive departments to remain and he expressed his complete confidence in Webster in a personal conference with him. The Whigs, particularly those of the Clay faction, were not satisfied with Tyler, and in September, five out of the six cabinet members resigned—Webster being the sole exception. It was only a strong sense of duty and his desire to work out a solution of the difficult problem of Anglo-American relations which kept him in office.

The report of Secretary Webster of April 2, 1842, gave a complete picture of the organization and work of the Department at that time. With reference to the Chief Clerk, after listing his duties as assigned in 1836, Webster noted that he was specifically given a number of others, such as: to draft letters on official business for the consideration of the Secretary; to write letters on matters of minor importance and to revise those written in the various bureaus; to execute duties not assigned to a specific bureau; to receive and execute orders of the Secretary and superintend the daily business of the Department and on the absence of the Secretary to assume his duties. As indicated above, Daniel Fletcher Webster, the Secretary's son, held this very important post.

The Diplomatic Bureau now employed four clerks to take care of all diplomatic correspondence. W. S. Derrick had charge of all matters pertaining to our relations with Great Britain, France, Russia, and the Netherlands. Francis Markoe, Jr., was responsible for matters pertaining to the other countries of Europe and to Asia, Africa, and the Sandwich Islands. William Hunter, Jr., had jurisdiction over affairs concerning Texas, Mexico, and Central and South American countries. A fourth clerk, unnamed, receiving a salary of $900, prepared letters of ceremony and treaties, did copying, kept the secret journal of the Department, and took care of matters pertaining to exequaturs, full powers, and letters of credence.

Three clerks, Messrs. Vail, Ringgold, and Chew, did similar work with the Consular Bureau. Inasmuch as Congress, by an Act of August 16, 1812, required the Secretary of State to report all changes and modifications in foreign commercial systems annually, Webster recommended that one clerk be appointed to arrange and condense such information from the reports made by the American consuls abroad. When no action was taken by Congress, Secretary Webster on his own authority directed one of the extra clerks to perform this duty.[3]

The Home Bureau consisted of seven clerks: the Disbursing Agent, Mr. Stubbs, who served also as superintendent of the North East Executive Building and as disbursing officer for those taking the census until its completion; Mr. Greenhow, Translator and Librarian, who also recorded, when they were not in English, commissions of consuls and vice consuls upon which exequaturs were issued; Mr. Dickins, keeper of the archives, who also was charged with the publication and distribution of the laws of the United States; and finally Messrs. McCormick, Jones, and Derrick, Jr., who took care of all such domestic matters as copyrights, pardons and remissions, domestic letters and reports to the President and Congress, authentications, and matters requiring the use of the seals. They also had to register returns of passengers and seamen and record special and general passports and keep a register of all letters other than diplomatic. Finally, Mr. Hill served simply as a copying clerk.

Considerable additional help was employed at this time for special tasks of a temporary nature: three clerks were employed on a report for the House of Representatives on restrictions on commercial intercourse of the United States which when completed proved to be a document of almost six hundred pages, and seven clerks were needed for the census. Adding the messengers, laborers, watchmen, and agents in forwarding dispatches in New York, Boston, and Liverpool, we find a total of some thirty persons employed, not counting the Patent Office.

Secretary Webster thought it "wholly impracticable without positive detriment to the public service to effect any retrenchment of expense by diminishing the number of persons employed in the Department." He pointed out that as a consequence of the increased number of states and territories, the domestic duties of the Department were constantly increasing. Also, improved means of transportation had increased the correspondence with ministers and consuls.[4] The appeal of the Secretary of State was effective and no cuts in the staff were made—in fact, two additional clerks were added by Secretary Webster, but Congress failed to authorize any increases in the salary scale.

In his letter to the chairman of the Ways and Means Committee, dated December 24, 1842, Webster again emphasized the absolute necessity for more permanent clerks or else the right to employ temporary help when required. He noted the fact that although the business of the Department had been steadily increasing, there had been no addition to the number of its regular clerks since the year 1831, yet "there were then twenty-five states and two territories—now twenty-six states and three territories; then thirteen foreign missions—now twenty-one; then almost one hundred and thirty consulates—now more than one hundred and sixty." To emphasize the seriousness of the legislative fiscal strait jacket imposed upon the Department, Webster pointed out that the "Department, upon which there is devolved a vast amount of business requiring labor, which occupies thirty-two rooms, having sixteen fires, is prohibited the employment of messenger, laborer, or other person with the exception of the messenger and assistant messenger authorized by law." [5] In his report for the year 1842, made on January 20, 1843, Webster indicated that in addition to fifteen regular clerks and a substitute and the regular messenger and assistant messenger, the State Department had employed nineteen extra persons in various capacities and for periods ranging from four days to nine months.[6]

Diplomatic Problems

The first diplomatic problem which faced Webster was the case of Alexander McLeod, an outgrowth of the *Caroline* affair, which was bequeathed to the new administration in an unsettled, unsatisfactory state. One of the participants of the foray against the *Caroline*, a Canadian named Alexander McLeod, was alleged to have boasted, while visiting in New York, that he personally had fired the shot which had killed an American citizen. He was immediately arrested and tried for murder. The British government demanded his release on the ground that since McLeod was engaged in an act of a public character he could not be made responsible, particularly since the British government had already informed the United States government that it had accepted responsibility for the destruction of the *Caroline*. Webster realized the legality of the British position and attempted to have McLeod liberated. However, when the New York court having jurisdiction refused to release McLeod, public opinion in Great Britain became inflamed, and British Foreign Secretary Palmerston notified our minister in London that if McLeod were executed it might well be regarded by Great Britain as a legitimate *casus belli*. Webster was much worried and informed the British minister, Fox, that the Federal government had afforded the prisoner authentic evidence that his own government had assumed responsibility for the attack on the *Caroline* and that in the opinion of the United States government this avowal protected the prisoner from personal liability.[7] Although the New York court insisted upon trying McLeod in spite of Webster's efforts to obtain a writ of habeas corpus, the jury acquitted the prisoner and a serious situation was averted. To prevent such threats to peace in the future, Webster drafted a bill giving Federal justices the power to issue writs of habeas corpus and to discharge from custody or to remove from state to Federal court jurisdiction any person accused of an unlawful act proved to have been committed under the instructions of a foreign country. The act was passed by Congress on August 29, 1842, and became the law of the land.

Webster wished to settle all outstanding disputes between the United States and Great Britain by friendly negotiation and reasonable compromise. A change in ministry in Great Britain, which supplanted the crotchety Palmerston as foreign minister by the cooperative Aberdeen, was an important factor in Webster's success. He was also aided by the fact that his good friend Edward Everett had been appointed minister to Great Britain at his instigation, and the British had sent as a special envoy to the United States, Lord Ashburton, a statesman of rare charm as well as of outstanding ability.

Ashburton's instructions gave him a general authorization to settle all differences between the two nations. Webster, knowing that Ashburton was wealthy and socially inclined and quite familiar with and partial to the American way of life,[8] determined to make Ashburton's visit a pleasant one. Having been informed that Ashburton would bring a large retinue and would want a rather large house, the Secretary of State rented the Clark House on Lafayette Square, close to Webster's own residence, for the British mission. He also arranged a series of dinners and entertainments which did much to compensate for the long and arduous negotiations which lasted into the heat and humidity of a typically Washington summer. The result more than compensated for the careful preparations and the months of tedious parleying.

The two diplomats felt that the more informal the discussions were, the better was the chance of a settlement. To quote Mr. Legaré, in their conferences "the mere etiquette, the unnecessary mystery and mummeries of negotiations were dispensed with." [9] It must be confessed however that Webster did not lay all of his cards on the table. Webster had been informed by the historian Jared Sparks that he had noted a map in the French archives upon which the boundary of the United States was marked in a heavy red line. He sketched this map from memory for Webster and it substantiated the British claims. Inasmuch as this boundary purported to be the one accepted by Franklin in 1782, such a map would have been exceedingly useful to the British. Webster also had another map, the so-called Mitchell map, which supported the British case. He kept these maps secret from the British but sent Sparks to use them with the Maine authorities as a means of obtaining a more reasonable attitude on their part. The ruse was successful and both Maine and Massachusetts accepted the compromise line agreed upon by Webster and Ashburton. Later research, however, indicated that there was a copy of the Mitchell map in Madrid, with Franklin's red-line boundary almost identical with the American claims.[10]

Success crowned the efforts of the two able negotiators, and Webster was just as successful in having the Treaty of Washington approved by the Senate as he was in getting its acceptance by Maine and Massachusetts. Although some opposition arose based upon the informal procedure employed by the negotiators, and although there were some objectors who wanted "whole hog or none," the Senate approved the treaty by the overwhelming majority of 39 to 9.

Expressions of Policy

Although the Treaty of Washington proved to be the permanent monument to Webster as a great Secretary of State, he made, in addition, numerous declarations of policy and enunciations of the principles of international law in the development of American foreign policy which merit being noted. With regard to the Sandwich Islands, he took a strong antiimperialist stand. He declared that "no power ought either to take possession of the islands as a conquest or for the purpose of colonization, and that no power ought to seek for any undue control over the existing government, or any exclusive privileges in preferences with it in matters of commerce." [11] In other words, he advocated a Monroe Doctrine and an Open Door Policy simultaneously for these islands of the Pacific. In one of his letters of instruction to the American minister to Great Britain, Secretary Webster declared with regard to intervention:

The great communities of the world are regarded as wholly independent, each entitled to maintain its own system of law and government, while all in their mutual intercourse are understood to submit to the established rules and principles governing such intercourse. And the perfecting of this system of communication among nations requires the strictest application of the doctrine of non-intervention of any with the domestic concerns of others.[12]

It was Webster's antiexpansionist attitude that was the principal cause of his retirement. President Tyler was an ardent apostle of "manifest destiny" and was eager to add Texas, together with certain portions of Mexico, to the territory of the United States. Webster was strongly opposed to any such policy and Tyler well knew his attitude. At the same time, Webster was under continuous criticism for supporting Tyler when the Whigs were now in violent opposition to him. Webster decided very reluctantly that he would have to resign, and to cushion the resignation he tried to persuade Everett to accept the position of commissioner to China so that he might be named as minister to Great Britain. However, Everett liked the post in London and was not willing to leave the solid comforts of the Court of St. James's for the romantic but distant court of the Celestial Emperor in Peking. On May 8, 1843, Webster sent in his formal resignation as Secretary of State and it was accepted by President Tyler on the same day. After thanking Webster for his zeal and ability in discharging his duties, the President declared: "I do not mean to flatter you in saying that, in conducting the most delicate and important negotiations you have manifested powers of intellect of the highest order." [13]

The remarkable success of Daniel Webster as Secretary of State stemmed both from his ability and from the fact that President Tyler was so unpopular with his party and in such hot water politically during his term of office that he was neither desirous nor in a position to pay much attention to problems of foreign policy. It must not be overlooked, however, that upon occasions President Tyler aided his Secretary of State materially by his sustained support and helpful suggestions. During the Webster-Ashburton negotiations when the British envoy, completely discouraged, was almost ready to depart, President Tyler called him in and gave him renewed confidence in achieving a satisfactory agreement. Webster gave President Tyler full credit for his effective support in a letter dated August 24, 1842:

I shall never speak of this negotiation, my dear sir . . . without doing you justice. Your steady support and confidence, your anxious and intelligent attentions to what was in progress, and your exceedingly obliging and pleasant intercourse both with the British Minister and the commissioners of the States have given every possible facility to my agency in this important transaction.[14]

Webster's dominating personality was an important asset in achieving his ends. This, joined with his fine mind, tenacity of purpose, and judicial objectivity, made him an ideal head of the Department of State. Henry Cabot Lodge, who was not prone to extravagant statement, thus characterized Webster and his work: "It may be fairly said that no one with the exception of John Quincy Adams has ever shown higher qualities, or attained greater success in the administration of the State Department than Mr. Webster did while in Mr. Tyler's cabinet." [15]

Ad Interim Secretaries Legaré and Derrick

After the resignation of Webster on May 8, 1843, the Department of State remained in a state of flux for almost a year. The first incumbent to act as ad interim Secretary was Hugh S. Legaré of South Carolina, a brilliant lawyer who was serving as Attorney General in the reorganized cabinet of President Tyler and who agreed to assume the additional duties of Secretary of State until Tyler could make a permanent appointment. Legaré, who had studied French in Paris, Roman law in Edinburgh, and had served for four years as chargé d'affaires in Belgium, was eminently well qualified for the position. A little over a month after his appointment, however, he became fatally ill and died on June 20, 1843.

The Secretaryship was thereupon temporarily assumed by William S. Derrick, who had been appointed Chief Clerk at the resignation of Fletcher Webster. Derrick, who had already served in the Department of State for about sixteen years, had the unique experience of serving for two days as Chief Clerk ad interim and Secretary of State ad interim simultaneously. He subsequently reverted to his former position as clerk in the Department.[16]

Abel P. Upshur—Secretary of State

The next appointee was Abel P. Upshur of Virginia, who, since he was already serving as Secretary of the Navy, was at first named as Secretary ad interim. Exactly one month later, on July 24, 1843, he was commissioned as Secretary of State, and since the Senate was in recess, he was recommissioned on January 2, 1844. Upshur had no particular qualifications fitting him for the head of the State Department—in fact, believing as he did that the only natural law was the law of force—his appointment might be regarded as ill advised. The reason for the transfer from the Navy to the State Department is not clear, other than that an emergency existed and he was available and known to be sympathetic to President Tyler's desire for the annexation of Texas.

Texas had already signified her desire for annexation to the United States during the administrations of Jackson and Van Buren, but without success. It was alleged that Tyler thought that his chances for reelection to the Presidency would be substantially enhanced if he were able to strengthen the United States by gathering in the vast territory embraced by the sovereign state of Texas. The fact that the British chargés d'affaires in both Mexico City and Galveston, Texas, were promising to urge Mexican recognition of her independence provided Texas would free her slaves and adopt a policy of free trade stimulated the Tyler administration to take some sort of protective action. Secretary Upshur moved promptly both through American representatives in Mexico and Texas and through the Texan representative in Washington. In a confidential letter to Mr. Murphy, the chargé of the United States in Galveston, he declared that Texas must not be permitted to throw herself into the arms of England, for "she may rest assured that the very moment that she shall commend herself to British protection, she will be the lamb in the embrace of the wolf." [17] Texas, however, now became somewhat coy and refused all embraces, including that of the United States, until her future security was assured. Before the union was finally consummated, Upshur had been killed and John C. Calhoun had been appointed Secretary of State.

In the course of this policy looking toward the annexation of Texas, Secretary Upshur engaged in a diplomatic duel with the Mexican minister in Washington in which the buttons were taken off the foils and during which Upshur can hardly be excused for the following riposte:

The undersigned reminds General Almonte that this Government is under no necessity to learn from that of Mexico what is due to its own honor or to the rights of other nations. It is therefore quite unnecessary that General Almonte in his future communications to this department should admonish this Government whether to respect its duties or to take care of its regulations.[18]

Under no circumstances could such a statement be said to conform to the accepted diplomatic formula, *fortiter in re, suaviter in modo*.

In his short term of office Upshur utilized the existing personnel of the Department of State: W. S. Derrick, who had been in the Department since 1827, served as Chief Clerk, and no important changes occurred in either organization or personnel. Shortly before Upshur's separation from the Department by his untimely death, the House Committee on Foreign Affairs, "with a view to the diminution of the public expenditures," made several radical and ill advised recommendations regarding our foreign missions which would have seriously injured the foreign service. At the time (January 17, 1844) that Secretary Upshur reported to the committee, at its request, the United States had nine ministers extraordinary and plenipotentiary—including the China mission and one minister resident in Turkey—and twelve chargés d'affaires. The maximum salary for ministers was $9,000 plus $9,000 for an outfit, plus $2,500 maximum for contingent expenses annually and $2,250 allowed for the return to the United States. The total cost of our representation abroad amounted yearly to about $180,000. To reduce this amount the committee made, among others, the following novel suggestions and observations:

The missions to China, to Austria and to Turkey the Committee considers useless: all the good they do may be done better otherwise. . . . The thirteen subordinate missions as chargés d'affaires, viz., eight in Europe and five in America, may all be abolished—with the triple advantages of strengthening our foreign relations, reducing their cost, and diminishing that executive patronage which is in this respect the most arbitrary and detrimental.

The committee then presented its plan: the ministers plenipotentiary to England, France, and Russia to remain as at present; one and the same minister plenipotentiary to Spain and Portugal, the Executive to direct when he shall officiate in Spain and when in Portugal; one minister plenipotentiary to all the states of the German Empire; one minister plenipotentiary to all Italy and to Turkey; one and the same minister resident to Holland and Belgium; one minister resident for Sweden and Denmark; one minister plenipotentiary to Mexico and Texas; one minister resident for Brazil, Montevideo, and Buenos Aires; one minister resident for Venezuela, New Granada, and Ecuador; and one minister resident for Bolivia, Peru, and Chile.

The committee felt that by raising the rank of our representatives "not only will our negotiation be more effective but our negotiators more respectable." The committee noted that duplicate and moving missions were becoming common in Europe and that stationary and permanent foreign missions were contrivances of not very long standing. The committee apprehended "that American foreign ministers are prone to sink into social neglect of public duty; and that frequent changes of their residence and revival of their functions will tend to improve their services." The committee then conceded that of the $40,000 saved from the annual expenditure for salaries it might take $20,000 to defray the charges of transportation from place to place as directed by the Executive. The report was read and laid on the table.

Upshur's death occurred on February 28, 1844, just eight months and four days after he became Secretary of State. He, with other notables, including President Tyler, Secretary of Navy Gilmer, and Senator Benton of Missouri, were guests of Captain Stockton aboard the battleship *Princeton* on the Potomac River. A large new cannon—the Peacemaker, which carried a 225-pound projectile—was fired many times to impress the guests. On what was to have been the last charge, the gun burst and several of the spectators, including Secretary of State Upshur and Secretary of the Navy Gilmer, were killed and others seriously injured.

Secretary ad Interim John Nelson

Not wishing to be stampeded in the appointment of a new Secretary of State, President Tyler requested his Attorney General, John Nelson of Maryland, to serve as Secretary of State ad interim. Nelson acted in this capacity for exactly one month, from February 29 to March 31, 1844. During his short incumbency, as the result of a Senate resolution, he made a very valuable report on the consular service. This report gave a complete list of the names, fees, and nationality, when known, of all American consuls serving on February 22, 1844, and a statement showing the number of destitute American seamen relieved by American consuls during the years 1842 and 1843. In the latter case Liverpool outdistanced London, the second in number, by over 100 per cent—Liverpool 1202 as against London's 540. The report regarding consular fees for 1842 placed Havana in the lead with $9,231.26; Liverpool was second with $8,400.02; Rio de Janeiro was third with $4,776.00; Le Havre was fourth with $3,626.00; Paris was fifth with $2,286.14; and London a close sixth with $2,233.13.[19]

9

John C. Calhoun and James Buchanan

Secretary of State—John C. Calhoun

The naming of John C. Calhoun as Secretary of State by President Tyler was unique in that Calhoun did not want the position, nor did Tyler wish to give it to him. The *deus ex machina* in this instance was a Virginia congressman, Henry A. Wise, who had just been nominated and confirmed as minister to Brazil. Wise, a close friend and trusted adviser of the President, was very eager that Calhoun be appointed Secretary of State, and he had persuaded Calhoun's former law partner, Senator McDuffie of South Carolina, to write to Calhoun urging him to accept the Secretaryship when it should be offered. McDuffie did so, thinking that the offer had come from the President through Mr. Wise. Wise then went to Tyler to persuade him to nominate Calhoun for the post of Secretary of State. Tyler at first refused, but when Wise confessed that he had already asked Senator McDuffie to urge Calhoun to accept the offer, which would arrive shortly, Tyler angrily succumbed and made the nomination.[1] Tyler, once committed to the appointment, couched his offer of the post to Calhoun in such cordial and urgent terms that Calhoun, wholly ignorant of the real basis of the appointment, decided to accept, although a bit hesitantly.[2] In his letter of acceptance dated March 16, 1844, he declared that he returned to public life with reluctance, and nothing short of the magnitude of the crisis occasioned by the pending negotiations (concerning Texas) could induce him to leave his retirement.[3]

The office of Secretary of State could scarcely be regarded as a step upward politically for a person with the background of John C. Calhoun. Except for the Presidency, he had held almost every political position which his country could offer him. Seven years in the lower house of Congress, eight years as Secretary of War under President Monroe, Vice President for seven years, senator for ten years, and a perennial candidate for the Presidency, Calhoun had run the gamut of political preferment. As might have been expected, Calhoun's nomination was immediately and unanimously approved by the Senate on March 6, 1844. He was in temporary retirement in his home at Fort Hill, South Carolina, and not in the best of health, so he traveled leisurely north to the Capital, where he was commissioned Secretary of State on April 1, 1844.

Calhoun's Departmental Recommendations

One of the first acts of the new Secretary of State was to appoint his friend Richard K. Crallé, editor of the Lynchburg *Virginian*, as Chief Clerk in place of the long-experienced W. S. Derrick. The latter, after having been Secretary and Chief Clerk ad interim, now reverted to the status of senior clerk in the Diplomatic Bureau. Crallé subsequently edited the *Works of John C. Calhoun*, published in 1851 in six volumes. On the whole, Calhoun was against the dispensing of patronage. When Robert Greenhow, the Translator and Librarian of the Department and a friend of Calhoun's family, requested a post of chargé, Calhoun, while expressing appreciation of his worth and capabilities, held out no hopes for an appointment. Calhoun did, however, later take care of his son-in-law Thomas G. Clemson, the husband of his daughter Anna, by offering him the post of chargé d'affaires to Belgium.[4]

In his report on the Department dated January 13, 1845, Secretary Calhoun indicated that the Department was badly understaffed with permanent officials and as a result had been compelled to employ during the year 1844 thirty-one persons on a temporary basis. This did not include the Patent Office, for which a separate report was made.[5] In the following month Calhoun amplified his report in a statement to the chairman of the Ways and Means Committee. He noted that for the years 1818 to 1845, a period of twenty-seven years, there had been added only four regular clerks to the Department, and only one of these during the last eighteen years. During this period the number of missions and consulates had nearly trebled, and the duties of the Department had probably been quadrupled. He then noted the requirement imposed by the Act of August 16, 1842, to make a report annually on the changes in foreign commercial systems. In order to fulfill this requirement, an irregular commercial and statistical bureau, composed exclusively of extra clerks, had grown up in the Department. Since these clerks had to be familiar with foreign languages, foreign moneys, and foreign weights and measures, as well as possessed of much other general information, he felt it desirable that a permanent bureau be connected with the Consular Bureau and that its officers be suitably compensated for their labors. He therefore suggested that an Act be passed authorizing the establishment of a Statistical and Miscellaneous Bureau, with a clerk at an annual salary of $1,450 in charge. He also requested an additional $2,000 for extra clerical hire and copying.

CARL A. RUDISILL
LIBRARY
LENOIR RHYNE COLLEGE

The first diplomatic task facing Calhoun in the Department was the completion of the negotiations for the annexation of Texas, which had been interrupted by the untimely death of Secretary Upshur. Calhoun had long been an advocate both of recognition of the independence of Texas and of her admission to the Union. The Treaty of Annexation was signed on April 12, 1844, just eleven days after Calhoun assumed the Secretaryship.

The overwhelming defeat of the Treaty of Annexation in the Senate was the cause of great discouragement to Calhoun, and it looked temporarily as if Tyler, who did not view kindly this pessimistic attitude of Calhoun's, would ask for his resignation. The question was also disastrous for the two leading candidates for the Presidency. Van Buren lost the nomination of the Democrats to James K. Polk, and Clay, who was the nominee of the Whigs, was defeated because he tried to straddle the issue. Polk's platform had as its most important plank the reannexation of Texas and the reoccupation of Oregon, and his narrow victory seemed to indicate public support of both issues. This gave President Tyler his opportunity, and he urged in his annual message of December 3, 1844, that Congress accept the people's mandate and annex Texas by a joint resolution. Congress responded favorably and Tyler signed the joint resolution annexing Texas on March 1, 1845, just three days before he retired from office.

Calhoun's diplomatic dealings with Great Britain have been much criticized due to his violent censure of British policy regarding the abolition of slavery, particularly when it spread to the shores of Texas. However Calhoun was a Southerner, an ardent believer in slavery, and he felt that abolition in Texas would be the first step toward abolition in the United States. Believing, as he did, that such a result would mean exclusive British control of the cotton trade, he could perhaps hardly be blamed for his undiplomatic correspondence with the British minister in Washington and his pronounced belief that Britain united in herself "the ambitions of Rome and the avarice of Carthage."

The election of President Polk raised the question of whether Calhoun would be invited to remain in the cabinet and if so, whether he would accept. Calhoun was quite passive in his attitude but indicated that he would refuse to stay even if invited unless the organization was satisfactory. However, President Polk informed him that he desired to form an entirely new cabinet. At the same time Polk expressed his respect for, and confidence in, Calhoun and offered him the post of minister to England. Calhoun refused the proffered post and informed Polk that he was not dissatisfied with the opportunity to return to the repose of private life earlier than he had anticipated but not than he desired.[6] He thereupon sent in his resignation to take effect as soon as his successor was ready to take over.

The Department of State, except for the appointment of Mr. Crallé as

Chief Clerk, remained practically unchanged during Calhoun's year of administration. Although President Tyler appointed him against his better judgment, the two men worked together without friction and with a feeling of mutual appreciation. They were equally eager to secure the admission of Texas and it was their effective cooperation which brought success to their efforts. Domestic politics were so important throughout the year that Calhoun served as Secretary of State that it is not strange that he was not in a position to make a record that his personality and past advancements warranted.

James Buchanan—Secretary of State

The appointment of a successor to Calhoun was made by President Polk fully two weeks before Calhoun was informed that he would not be invited to remain. The invitation to accept the position of Secretary of State as made to James Buchanan by President Polk on February 18, 1855, was couched in most peculiar language. After announcing the fact that in making up his cabinet he desired to select gentlemen who would agree with him and cooperate cordially, the President specified that "should any member of my cabinet become a candidate for the Presidency or Vice Presidency of the United States it will be expected upon the happening of such an event that he will retire from the cabinet." Polk then declared that he disapproved of the practice of cabinet members absenting themselves for long periods of time from the seat of government and leaving the management of their department to chief clerks. Having thus made clear his position, Polk invited Buchanan to become Secretary of State providing he concurred in the President's views.[7] Buchanan approved heartily of the views of the President but declared that while he would not raise a finger to become President, he refused to proclaim to the world that in no contingency would he be a candidate. If such a situation should arise, Buchanan agreed to retire from the cabinet.[8] Buchanan became Secretary of State under these conditions.

The new Secretary of State was better qualified for the position by background and experience than any of his immediate predecessors. He had served creditably in 1832 and 1833 as minister to Russia, where, to his own surprise and to the consternation of the British, he was successful in negotiating a commercial treaty. He had always been particularly interested in foreign affairs while representing Pennsylvania in the Senate, and for a number of years he was chairman of the Committee on Foreign Relations of the Senate. One of his ablest and longest—it took two days to deliver—speeches in the Senate was on the treaty with France.

Calhoun graciously agreed to remain in office until Buchanan could take charge, hence no Secretary ad interim was needed. Since Mr. Crallé, the Chief

Clerk, was a personal friend of Calhoun's and had been appointed as such, he resigned on March 10, 1845, simultaneously with his chief. As upon previous occasions, William S. Derrick was thereupon made Chief Clerk ad interim. Again his appointment proved to be of short duration, because, on August 28 of the same year, Secretary Buchanan appointed Nicholas P. Trist of Virginia to the position of Chief Clerk. Although a political appointee, Trist was a fairly able man, with previous experience both as a clerk in the Department and for eight years as consul to Havana. He had been investigated in this latter post by both Congress and the Department on charges of failing to support adequately the rights of American citizens. Although the charges were not sustained, he was recalled as a result of partisan party politics in 1841. He remained as Chief Clerk until April 14, 1847, when he was appointed to accompany General Scott's army as "commissioner plenipotentiary" to Mexico to negotiate peace. Trist quarreled with Scott and was recalled by Polk. Nevertheless, without powers and exceeding his instructions, he signed the Treaty of Guadalupe Hidalgo with Mexico. Polk thereupon dismissed the diplomat and accepted his treaty.

As did many of his predecessors, Secretary Buchanan found the staff of clerks in the Department wholly inadequate to the demands made upon their time. However, he was not inclined to endure the situation without making a vigorous protest against it, coupled with countersuggestions to remedy it. In a report to the House Judiciary Committee, which had requested certain information regarding the organization of the Department, Buchanan made some comparisons which he hoped would stir up some action on the Hill.

He pointed out that our diplomatic correspondence with all the nations of the world was carried on by three clerks assisted by two copying clerks while the consular section was even worse off, with only two clerks. He then noted the fact that of all the persons belonging to the Department, he was the only one with authority to sign a single paper or to decide on any question, however trivial it might be. "The consequences of this accumulation of business upon the head of the department must be manifest to everyone. He must either neglect the national interests or the subordinate but pressing business involving the rights of individuals. . . ." He realized that the Secretary of State should be familiar with all international relations bearing upon his country's interests —he should have time to read and reflect. Yet in spite of his industry he had no time even for the perusal of the leading foreign journals. Only the most urgent dispatches were written to our ministers abroad, and the vast amount of information collected by our consuls was useless because no one was available to digest, arrange, and publish it. After outlining the work of the Chief Clerk, the tasks performed by the first clerk in the diplomatic branch, the duties of two clerks in the consular branch, and the six covering miscellaneous activities,

Secretary Buchanan showed that whereas the personnel of our missions abroad in twenty-eight years had increased 236 per cent and that of our consulates 153 per cent, the personnel in the Department had increased only 36 per cent. The British Foreign Office, he indicated, with no functions of a domestic nature, had a force more than two and one-half times larger.

His suggestions for remedying the situation followed:

Let the Chief Clerk be converted into an assistant secretary authorized by law under the general supervision of the Secretary to transact all the business of the department except that of a purely diplomatic character. The salary of this officer the Secretary would propose to fix at $3,000. Relieve the Secretary from the judicial and other business connected with the Patent Office . . . by transferring it to the Attorney General to whom it could appropriately belong. Let provision be made for the employment of three additional clerks in the diplomatic branch. These men ought to be men of intellect and information competent to prepare despatches . . . and to examine claims and to receive a salary not less than $2,000. . . .

In the consular branch two additional clerks at least are required, one at a salary of $2,000 and the other at $1,400.[9]

Secretary Buchanan was hardly more successful than his predecessors in obtaining relief from the Congress. It was not until 1853 that the position of First Assistant Secretary of State was established and the salary of the Chief Clerk increased to $2,200. The one recommendation adopted was the authorization by the Act of August 12, 1848, for the appointment of a clerk at $2,000 to examine the claims of American citizens presented to the Department. This position was requested urgently by Secretary Buchanan as a vital requirement for the cause of justice. William Hunter, Jr., of Rhode Island was appointed Acting Claims Clerk on October 1, 1848, and Claims Clerk on March 16, 1849. His successor was Abel French of New York. Although the position of Claims Clerk was abolished by the Act of March 3, 1855, it was reestablished later under the title of Examiner of Claims and was the precursor of the Office of the Legal Adviser.

Diplomatic Problems

The first diplomatic problem faced and solved by the new Secretary of State, the status and boundaries of Oregon, was a carry-over from the Webster-Ashburton negotiations. In his first inaugural address, President Polk claimed that the United States had a clear title to the Oregon Territory; nevertheless, privately he was willing to compromise and authorized Buchanan to accept the forty-ninth parallel as the dividing line.

Buchanan made a very good case for the claim of the United States to the entire Oregon Territory, but declared that the President was willing to compromise only because of the concessions already agreed upon by his predecessors.[10] Instead of referring Buchanan's offer to the British Foreign Office, the British minister Pakenham rejected it on his own responsibility. Polk now took charge of the matter, withdrew the offer, and reverted to the claim to the entire territory. In his next inaugural address he requested that the existing joint occupation be terminated, and Congress took him at his word. However, neither country could afford a war, and when the United States gave notice of the termination of joint occupation, the British offered to compromise on the forty-ninth parallel. The United States, already at war with Mexico, accepted promptly. The credit for this outstanding diplomatic victory must be given to President Polk rather than to Secretary Buchanan, because Polk in this case took both the initiative and the responsibility.

It is somewhat more difficult to apportion the responsibility, as far as the United States is concerned, for the war with Mexico. President Polk undoubtedly again played the leading role, since he not only directed foreign policy but also gave orders to the armies in the field. The annexation of Texas to the United States, the *casus belli* as far as Mexico was concerned, had been achieved before Polk and Buchanan took office. The Mexican minister, General Almonte, had already protested against the resolution of annexation and had broken off diplomatic relations. Buchanan, whose task it was to reply to the Mexican minister's protest, although declaring that the admission of Texas had been irrevocably decided, expressed his sincere regret that Mexico should have taken offense and assured the Mexican envoy that President Polk would make the most strenuous efforts toward the amicable adjustment of every cause of complaint between the two governments. To prove that these were not empty words, toward the end of March, 1845, President Polk named W. S. Parrott as confidential agent to Mexico and empowered him to use every honorable effort to restore friendly relations. Polk followed this by sending as minister plenipotentiary John Slidell of Louisiana, with instructions to release Mexico from certain financial obligations if she would accept the Rio Grande as the boundary line. When Mexico refused to receive Slidell, General Taylor was ordered into the disputed territory and the Mexicans attacked.

Unquestionably both Polk and Buchanan were willing to have a showdown with Mexico. They felt that Mexican opposition to the annexation of Texas was unreasonable; and they were also interested in obtaining the California Territory, because prompt action was needed here to prevent either Great Britain or France from taking it and because "the possession of the bay and harbor of San Francisco is all-important to the United States." In fact, Slidell was authorized to pay $25,000,000, in addition to assuming the claims of American citizens, if Mexico would agree to a boundary running west from the extremity of New Mexico to the Pacific Ocean.[11] Nevertheless, Slidell's instructions indicated very clearly that peace with Mexico was desired and that only if diplomatic methods failed was a recourse to force justifiable.

During the course of the war, the Department of State made several serious efforts to negotiate peace, but they all proved abortive. Thereupon, in order that peace might be achieved immediately after victory, Polk proposed to send an envoy with the army to negotiate immediately after hostilities ceased. He at first thought of Secretary Buchanan in this connection but quickly realized that Buchanan could not be spared. His next choice was the Chief Clerk, Nicholas P. Trist, whom he named as commissioner with full powers to conclude a definite treaty of peace. The results proved the wisdom of this procedure. Although both Polk and Buchanan were much disturbed over Trist's controversy with General Scott in regard to status, and Trist was severely reprimanded and recalled, nevertheless, when Trist found that he was able to obtain an agreement upon the conditions demanded by Buchanan, he violated his instructions and signed the peace that ended the war with Mexico.

Few Secretaries of State have been plagued with more headstrong envoys representing the United States abroad than was Buchanan. As a result, he spent considerable time in censuring his representatives for unbecoming conduct or flagrant violation of instructions and then even greater effort to repair the damage which they caused American diplomacy. The United States almost broke off diplomatic relations with Brazil as a result of the intemperate conduct of Henry A. Wise, the American minister in Rio. Although the United States refused to recall Wise at the earnest request of Brazil, a previous request of his to return to the United States was granted with enthusiasm by Secretary Buchanan. William Brent, Jr., the United States representative to Buenos Aires, offered mediation in the name of the United States between the governments of Buenos Aires and Paraguay without authority and in opposition to the established policy of the United States. Elijah Hise, sent by Secretary Buchanan to Central America to conclude treaties with Guatemala and El Salvador, signed treaties instead with Nicaragua and Honduras, although specifically instructed not to do so.

On the other hand, there were some outstanding figures in American diplomatic annals in the foreign service of the United States during Buchanan's incumbency of the Department. Henry Wheaton in Berlin and his successor Andrew Jackson Donelson were exceedingly able diplomats. George Bancroft, our minister to Great Britain, and Richard Rush in Paris would have added prestige to any foreign mission. Having served as a foreign minister himself, Buchanan appreciated the need of an adequate foreign service, both diplomatic and consular. A report which he made on the consular system of the

United States was critical in the extreme. A few of his comments and suggested improvements are well worth noting.

He urged strongly that a single law should provide: (1) for the number, appointment, and compensation of all consuls, consuls general, and vice consuls, and (2), it should clearly define all the duties of these officers and specify the fees to be received for their performance. Due to political pressure and the system of payment by fees, Buchanan felt that many more consulates existed than were necessary. At the time there were 168 consulates and 10 commercial agencies—he thought that 74 consuls and 55 vice consuls would be more than adequate, provided that these officers might appoint consular agents. He recommended the authorization of the appointment of consuls general in the more important ports of Europe and the Near East. He indicated that by not having this title our consul at Alexandria could not hold personal intercourse with the viceroy of Egypt. He urged reduction and regulation of the payment of consuls by fees and encouragement of salaries. A consular code defining the powers and duties of consuls he held to be vitally necessary. They were, at the time, left to the discretion of the consuls. Effective enforcement of the extraterritoriality privileges in the Far and Near East was required, as were greater restrictions upon expenditures for the relief of destitute American seamen in foreign countries. Finally, he felt that the whole consular system should be utilized for more adequate information of all sorts which might be useful both to the Congress and to the people.[12] Although not acted upon immediately, most of his suggestions were subsequently incorporated into legislative enactments.

James Buchanan served four full years as Secretary of State in spite of a rather uncongenial relationship between himself and President Polk. The latter was headstrong and stubborn. He was inclined to take charge of the conduct of foreign relations upon any subject where his interest was involved and disregard the advice of his Secretary of State. Upon one occasion President Polk wrote in his diary: "Mr. Buchanan will find that I cannot be forced to act against my convictions and that if he chooses to retire, I will find no difficulty in administering the Government without his aid." [13] Nevertheless, Buchanan undoubtedly gave many a directing turn to the tiller of the ship of state, and on many occasions he was in complete control. He took perhaps the most vigorous position up to his time as regards an unqualified right of expatriation and equal protection to citizens, whether naturalized or native.[14] His direction of the Department of State was of such a character that it served as one of the steps leading ultimately to the Presidency.

10

John M. Clayton, Daniel Webster, and Edward Everett

John M. Clayton—Secretary of State

Just as his predecessor, Calhoun, had carried on the duties of Secretary of State until Buchanan was commissioned, so Buchanan remained in his position until his successor, John M. Clayton, took over. The new President, General Zachary Taylor, was a Whig who wanted a Whig administration, and as a consequence, in making appointments, merit gave way to political considerations. Although Clayton had played an important part in securing the election of Taylor, the President offered the position of Secretary of State first to John J. Crittenden who had just been elected Governor of Kentucky. Crittenden refused the offer and suggested Clayton's name. President Taylor thereupon offered the post to Clayton, who accepted immediately. A particularly successful trial lawyer with some political experience, Clayton was named entirely upon the basis of partisan politics. His principal assets for the position were an engaging personality and a keen intellect. He was not conversant with foreign affairs and had never shown any predilection for them. Inasmuch as in this field the President also knew little and cared less, it could hardly be expected that foreign affairs would be a dominant factor in the administration. Clayton was not apprehensive, however, as to his ability to handle the situation, for in one of his letters to Crittenden he declared: "I will give you leave to hang me like an acorn, if I do not bring out the glorious old man's administration in its foreign policy without cause for complaint even from his enemies." [1]

Although the spoilsmen were besieging the Department of State as they were other government agencies, Clayton resisted their attack. His first very creditable appointment was to name William S. Derrick as Chief Clerk on April 5, 1849. On four different occasions Derrick had been appointed Acting Chief Clerk or Chief Clerk ad interim and once, Secretary of State ad interim, so that his nomination as Chief Clerk was a well deserved reward for long and meritorious service. He died in office on May 15, 1852. William Hunter, Jr., was made Claims Clerk and other old employees, such as Francis Markoe, Jr., Alexander H. Derrick, Robert S. Chew, George Hill, William C. Qantzinger, and Robert Greenhow, remained in the Department. It should be noted that the number of clerks employed was materially increased by Secretary Clayton's new appointments; and at the end of the year 1849, twenty-four clerks, one messenger and two assistant messengers, two extra clerks, seven packers, and a laborer were listed as employed by the Department of State.[2]

Shirt-Sleeve Diplomacy

Persons unfamiliar with diplomatic usage are often inclined to scoff at its seemingly archaic expressions and the importance given to protocol. Nevertheless, experience has shown on many occasions that these procedures have a very definite proved value and that a reckless disregard for them can lead to serious consequences. President Taylor—"Old Rough and Ready," as he was appropriately named—and Secretary Clayton, more familiar with the courtroom than with the chancellery, were not long in learning that "shirt-sleeve" diplomacy was not only unproductive but even dangerous. The incidents causing the trouble were insignificant in the extreme, but the methods used almost brought two great countries to a severance of diplomatic relations.

A certain Frenchman had made a considerable profit through a sale of tobacco illegally auctioned off to him by mistake by the United States Army. The mistake discovered, he was reimbursed by military court action the original cost plus interest, but deprived of his profits. Dissatisfied, he appealed to the French minister in Washington, William T. Poussin, who championed his cause somewhat overzealously. In his support of the army action, Clayton impugned Poussin's veracity. Poussin replied in such a manner that Clayton showed the letter to President Taylor, and the latter insisted that the French minister withdraw the communication or leave. The obnoxious part was eliminated but both parties were resentful.

A little later, the commander of the United States naval vessel *Iris*, having rescued a French vessel from a reef in the Gulf of Mexico, held it temporarily to secure salvage. When the French consul protested and the American consul at Vera Cruz felt that salvage was not justified, the vessel was released. Poussin again protested in rather undiplomatic language and demanded that Commander Carpender of the *Iris* be reprimanded. Secretary Clayton did not take the affair very seriously and merely forwarded certain papers from the Navy Department which he thought would explain the commander's action. Poussin once more wrote a caustic letter declaring that he was induced to believe that the United States government subscribed to "the strange doctrine professed by Commander Carpender." Instead of requesting the recall of Minister Poussin, President Taylor instructed Clayton to lay the whole matter before the French government. In turn, the French government felt that the United States had been decidedly undiplomatic in the tenor of its correspondence and that while Poussin had been somewhat at fault, he had already been censured for his too spirited expressions and he would in future be more courteous if reciprocity could be expected. Taylor thereupon told Clayton to dismiss Poussin and to inform the French foreign minister, De Tocqueville, that he had not been asked to decide as an arbiter upon the way in which the American government conducted its correspondence.

Such a communication sent directly to the French foreign minister was like a thunderbolt out of a clear sky, and De Tocqueville decided to present the entire case before the Council of Ministers. In a letter dated October 11, 1849, De Tocqueville requested an explanation from the United States, since otherwise the French government did not know whether to consider the situation as a misunderstanding to be repelled or an intention to wound the French government and to derogate from the just respects due it. Instead of receiving the olive branch thus offered, Taylor regarded the communication as an ultimatum; and in spite of Secretary Clayton's pleas that a reply be sent so worded as to permit France to withdraw from a situation now becoming critical, the President decided to force a showdown. The reply which Clayton dispatched curtly declared: "The President finds nothing in the conduct of this Government which requires the expression of his intentions, views or wishes beyond that contained in my note to your excellency of September last." [3]

Thereupon Secretary Clayton notified Rives, the newly arrived American minister, that if he were not received within a week after receiving the instruction he should quit Paris and go either to Berlin or St. Petersburg. Since the breaking of diplomatic relations is often the preliminary to war, the situation had clearly got out of hand. Fortunately for all concerned, a shakeup occurred in the French government and Louis Napoleon decided to receive Mr. Rives and forget the whole matter. Both Taylor and Clayton were glad to settle on this basis, and in his message to Congress of December 24, 1849, President Taylor expressed his sincere satisfaction over the renewal of diplomatic relations with France, "the sister republic to which we have so long been, and still remain, bound by the strongest ties of amity."

It is hardly credible that the Congress would have declared war over such a trivial incident, but Secretary Clayton now appreciated the fact that diplomatic amenities were worthy of observance and that he could not hope to conduct the foreign policy of the United States without serious interference on the part of the Executive upon any subject which caught his attention.

The Clayton-Bulwer Treaty

The one accomplishment of his administration which Secretary Clayton regarded as an achievement of the highest order was the treaty signed with Sir Henry Bulwer looking toward the construction and neutralization of a canal joining the Atlantic and Pacific by way of Nicaragua or Panama. Clayton had long been interested in an interoceanic canal and shortly after becoming Secretary of State had dispatched an emissary, E. George Squier, to negotiate a treaty for the right of transit across Nicaragua. At the same time, he was attempting to make an arrangement through the American minister in London whereby the United States and Great Britain would each agree to forego exclusive claims to the Central American region and work out some plan for internationalization of the projected interoceanic canal. Great Britain, appreciating the almost fanatical support of the Monroe Doctrine by American public opinion, was not averse to a joint guarantee for the protection of a transit route open to all nations upon terms of equality. Clayton was so eager to obtain an agreement that he decided to work out the arrangement in Washington with the new British minister, Sir Henry Bulwer. To avoid complications, the two men worked secretly and informally, each equally determined to gain the advantage over the other. The result was that the treaty provisions were deliberately ambiguous in those clauses where national interests were opposed.

President Taylor, who was keenly interested in the negotiations, almost provoked a breakdown by demanding a complete renunciation of the British claims of a protectorate of the Mosquito Territory. Bulwer could not possibly accept any such categorical requirement, and Clayton finally persuaded the President to recede from a direct demand when the same results could be obtained indirectly. The treaty as finally drawn merely prohibited further occupation according to the British interpretation, whereas the United States expected, or at least hoped for, the renunciation of existing British claims. Perhaps no treaty ever concluded, except the Treaty of Versailles, has received more criticism than has been heaped upon the Clayton-Bulwer Treaty. Clayton's predecessor, Buchanan, declared that Bulwer had earned a British peerage for his successful negotiations. A later Secretary of State, James G. Blaine, characterized it as "misunderstandingly entered into, imperfectly comprehended, contradictorily interpreted and mutually vexatious." The eminent diplomatist, historian, and Secretary of State, John W. Foster, declared that it has generally been regarded as the most serious diplomatic mistake in our history. Even today historians differ as to whether it was a justifiable compromise. However, looking backward, it must be conceded that, although criticized as a violation of the Monroe Doctrine, the treaty ultimately forced a renunciation of British claims and placed the United States in a position to play a leading role in the construction and control of any interoceanic canal.

The Clayton-Bulwer Treaty was approved by the Senate on July 5, 1850, and four days later President Taylor died after a short illness. Secretary Clayton, who had already contemplated retiring to private life on at least two previous occasions, did not delay to send in his resignation. His health was becoming steadily worse, the heavy burden of carrying on the duties as Secretary with the limited clerical force authorized by Congress, and the need to take care of his private interests all combined to strengthen his resolution. In a letter to his good friend Crittenden, he declared:

I feel like a man with a mountain taken from his shoulders. . . . I have worked and toiled as man never toiled before, amidst embarrassments and difficulties unequalled . . . the situation I have filled during the period of President Taylor's administration was more difficult, more thorny and more liable to misrepresentation and calumny, than any other in the world.[4]

Secretary Clayton retired from the Secretaryship on July 22, 1850, after sixteen and a half months' service. Although not a great Secretary of State— in fact, few Secretaries have been more harshly criticized—he instituted and carried out the policies that he believed essential fearlessly and effectively. He made a valiant effort to strengthen the Department by increasing both salaries and personnel. His work and achievements merit greater attention than they have hitherto received.

Webster Again Heads the State Department

Daniel Webster, who had already served as Secretary of State under two Presidents, William Henry Harrison and John Tyler, was now invited by President Millard Fillmore, who as Vice President succeeded to the Presidency upon the death of Taylor, to serve a second time. This was the first time in American history that such a signal honor had been accorded; and to the present, it has only been repeated once, in the case of James G. Blaine. Webster was now sixty-eight years of age, but his faculties were as keen as ever.

Bequeathed the problem of carrying out the ambiguous and evasive terms of the Clayton-Bulwer Treaty, Webster followed a conciliatory policy with both Bulwer and his successor Crampton. Believing, as he did, in a firm policy of neutrality and that filibustering expeditions aimed at destroying Spanish power in the island of Cuba were not only contrary to national and international law but to the best interests of the United States, he did all in his power to prevent the third and fatal venture of Narciso López. When López and many of his American followers were executed by the Spanish government in

Cuba, sympathizers in New Orleans mobbed the Spanish consulate, destroyed considerable property, and ripped the Spanish flag to pieces. Webster handled the situation with excellent judgment and avoided a serious diplomatic incident. He characterized the action as unjustifiable and disgraceful and expressed the deep regret of the Federal government that it had occurred. He noted at the same time that the outrage was perpetrated by a mob and that no officer agent of either Federal or state government took any part in it or in any way countenanced it. He also adroitly pointed out that the news of the hasty and wholesale execution of many people well known in New Orleans produced an outbreak that the authorities were unable to control. As a demonstration of respect, a salute would be given to the flag of the ship of the Spanish consul and a recommendation would go to Congress for proper indemnification for the losses sustained.[5]

This procedure was in marked contrast to the bombastic and rabble-rousing language used by Webster in a letter to the Austrian chargé d'affaires, the Chevalier Hülsemann, where the position of the United States was quite unjustifiable but where, as Webster himself confessed, he wished to write a paper which touched the national pride.[6] The Taylor administration had instructed A. Dudley Mann to proceed to Hungary and to report on the revolutionary activities going on there and to promise the recognition of the United States if he thought the situation warranted it. In some way the instructions were obtained by the Austrian government and the Chevalier Hülsemann protested privately to Secretary Clayton at this unwarranted intervention in Hungary's domestic affairs. When President Taylor, on March 28, 1850, communicated the instructions and correspondence pertaining to the affair to the Senate, and it was made public, Hülsemann protested vigorously to Secretary Webster, who had just succeeded Clayton. One sentence of Hülsemann's note was particularly irritating to Webster:

The Imperial Cabinet had deemed it proper to preserve a conciliatory deportment making ample allowance for the ignorance of the Cabinet of Washington on the subject of Hungarian affairs and its disposition to give credence to the mendacious rumors which are propagated by the American press.

Webster decided to make a brutally harsh response.

After insisting that in communicating the correspondence to the Senate of the United States, President Taylor was engaged in a strictly domestic transaction and that therefore the Hungarian remonstrance was interfering in the domestic concerns of a foreign state, Webster engaged in a boastful comparison between the United States and Hungary wholly inexcusable in a note to the representative of a friendly government. One sentence will illustrate: "The power of this republic at the present time is spread over a region one of the richest and most fertile of the globe, and of an extent in comparison with which the possessions of the House of Hapsburg are but as a patch on the earth's surface." His conclusion had all the jingoism of a Fourth of July oration delivered in a political campaign rally:

Nothing will deter either the Government or the people of the United States from . . . forming and expressing their own opinions freely and at all times upon the great political events which may transpire among the civilized nations of the earth. Their own institutions stand upon the broadest principles of civil liberty; and believing those principles . . . to be eminently favored to the prosperity of States—to be in fact the only principles of government which meet the demands of the present enlightened age—the President has perceived with great satisfaction that in the constitution recently introduced into the Austrian Empire many of these great principles are recognized and applied.[7]

The fact that the note was received with acclaim in the United States does not excuse its vainglorious pomposity; it detracts from Webster's status as a great Secretary of State, even though it gave a temporary fillip to his popularity.

Departmental Improvements

A few months before death brought an end to his services as Secretary of State, Webster prepared a report on the classification and compensation of clerks in the Department that was a milestone in the long struggle to provide sufficient personnel and to grant adequate compensation to the underpaid officers of the Department of State. He declared that "few things are more prejudicial to the public service than the removal from office of experienced and faithful clerks of proved ability and industry. . . . While the Department has been under my care no removal has been made without proof of notorious incapacity or inattention to duty." He pointed out that "no one in coming new into any one of the various branches of this Department can learn in a short time the actual state of things in the bureau to which he may be assigned." He argued that a great present want was an Assistant Secretary who should be a person of accomplishments and knowledge of diplomatic usages, with a salary of $3,000—equal to that allowed the Assistant Secretary of the Treasury. He wanted an increase in the salary of the Translator and Librarian and the appointment of an assistant translator. He thought that all clerks in the Department of State should possess higher qualifications than copyists: they should understand modern languages, be persons of literary attainments, and possess a good knowledge of geography, laws, and history. He emphasized the need of very competent clerks on claims. It should be noted that Webster's report on the numbers and salaries of clerks for the year 1851 indicated that the Department had only nineteen clerks, of whom only four received salaries of $1,600 or over. Of these, only two received $2,000—the Chief Clerk and the Clerk of Claims.[8]

The Congress was finally moved to act, but it was not until March 3, 1853, that the position of Assistant Secretary of State was established at a salary of $3,000; the salary of the Secretary of State was raised to $8,000. The salaries of the Chief Clerk, William Hunter, and the Claims Clerk, Abel French, remained at $2,000; but the salaries of the principal clerk of the Diplomatic Bureau, Francis Markoe, and the principal clerk of the Consular Bureau, Robert S. Chew, were also raised to $2,000. The Translator, Louis F. Tasistro, continued to receive $1,600. The total personnel of the Department for the year 1853, including the Secretary, Assistant Secretary, Translator, Disbursing Officer, and clerks, numbered twenty.

On May 15, 1852, W. S. Derrick, who had entered the Department of State on March 3, 1827, died in office after having served for about twenty-five years. He had begun at a salary of $800 and had finally reached the position of Chief Clerk at $2,000. Incidentally, during the period 1841 to 1852, he had served as Acting Secretary of State at twelve different times with no increase of salary. When his widow some years later petitioned for the difference in salary between that of Chief Clerk and Secretary for the 263 days on which he served as Secretary, amounting to $2,882.20, her petition was rejected upon the ground that

the Government for the salary fixed by law expects and requires the best services of its officers of all grades; and if the exigencies of the public service frequently required the performance of novel and additional duties, as is the case in a country as growing and extensive as ours, they must be performed as promptly and as ably as the talents, and time, and physical ability of the officers will allow.[9]

During the fall of 1852, the duties of the Secretary of State were carried on for the most part by the Chief Clerk, William Hunter, because of the increasing weakness of Secretary Webster, who finally passed away on October 24, 1852, at the age of seventy years. Webster's second incumbency did not give him the same opportunities as did his first, but nevertheless, even relatively minor matters were handled so as to establish important precedents for the future. For example, in the Lobos Islands controversy with Peru, Secretary Webster, by his definite stand, practically settled the question that the sovereignty of the islands outside of the three-mile limit cannot be based upon contiguity but must rest upon other rights. He also maintained effectively that at nonofficial dinners the established rule of protocol might be waived without being made the subject of diplomatic representations.[10] The entire

United States mourned the loss of one of its truly great statesmen in the death of Daniel Webster.

Edward Everett—Secretary of State

President Fillmore did not delay in "gracing his administration" by offering the position of Secretary of State to his good friend Edward Everett of Massachusetts. As there were only four months of Fillmore's administration left, the offer was one requiring service rather than bestowing honor. Everett accepted immediately, but as he could not assume the duties till November 6, 1852, Charles M. Conrad, the Secretary of War, served in an ad interim capacity. The appointment of Everett was an excellent one. He had been a good friend of Webster's and was sympathetic to his point of view; he knew Europe well from firsthand observation and had served brilliantly as minister to Great Britain. His service as chairman of the Committee on Foreign Affairs of the House gave him an additional advantage which could not help but be useful.

Everett's one outstanding contribution as Secretary of State was to pen a note to Great Britain and France refusing to join in a tripartite pact to renounce all intention to obtain possession of the island of Cuba. His letter was not only a masterful presentation of good reasons against such an action on our part, but in its marshaling of historical factors and the picturesque phraseology employed, it is a unique contribution to our diplomatic annals. His conclusion that "it would be as easy to throw a dam from Cape Florida to Cuba in the hope of stopping the flow of the Gulf Stream as to attempt by a compact like this to fix the future of Cuba now and for hereafter" was so irrefutable that no serious effort was made to discuss the matter further.[11] The historian James Ford Rhodes, ordinarily not given to eulogies, declared: "Never had the success of a Secretary of State been more complete." [12]

Perhaps because Everett was in office but four months, he experienced the pressure of work and the inadequacy of trained personnel even more than those accustomed to the situation. Some time after leaving his office he wrote in his journal: "I am even now terrified at the thought of the amount of work done by me and of the necessary haste with which important documents were turned off." [13] It is not surprising, therefore, that he, too, put in his plea for an Assistant Secretary of State, even though he knew that his party would not have the advantage of making the appointment: "I am decidedly of the opinion that the time is near at hand when the Department can hardly get on without such an officer. . . . It may seem to be gratuitous magnanimity on our part to increase the patronage of our successors; but this is a small thing as to amount of patronage; and is incontrovertibly desirable for the dispatch of public business." [14]

11

William L. Marcy, Lewis Cass, and Jeremiah Black

William L. Marcy—Secretary of State

Everett retired as Secretary of State on March 3, 1853, and William Hunter, Jr., the Chief Clerk, acted as ad interim secretary until William L. Marcy was commissioned on March 7. The newly elected President, Franklin Pierce, did not make his cabinet appointments hastily. In fact, after much deliberation, he first offered the post of Secretary of State to John A. Dix, former senator from New York, and later withdrew the offer when he found strong Southern opposition to the appointment. His second choice was Senator Robert M. T. Hunter of Virginia, but Hunter was unwilling to resign from the Senate to accept a cabinet position. Marcy was very eager to have a cabinet post, and his friends had been working hard in his behalf. He had been notified to be in Washington not later than February 10 by Pierce's secretary and was unquestionably asked to serve shortly afterward as Secretary of State in the new cabinet.

Few Secretaries of State have held the office whose training and experience were less directed to the position of foreign minister than Marcy's. He had represented New York State in the Senate for two years, he had served as Governor of New York for three terms, and he had been Secretary of War for four years in President Polk's cabinet. His only experience pertaining to the conduct of foreign relations was a two-year term as member of the Mexican Claims Commission. His friend Buchanan, who knew the State Department at firsthand, criticized the appointment very frankly in a personal letter to a friend: "I know no public man of experience and character who is more ignorant than he is of all which relates to our foreign affairs. He has never made them any portion of his study. But he has a cool head and a strong intellect and I place great reliance on his capacity. He may and I trust will succeed." [1] Even Marcy himself conceded his lack of background: "I had not given until recently much attention to our foreign affairs and really was not qualified for the position assigned me. I have been obliged to make up this deficiency—with really no leisure to do it and without much assistance from any quarter." [2]

Diplomatic Appointments and Problems

Although Marcy was the author of that very expensive political slogan, "To the victor belong the spoils," he did not follow the precept as far as the clerks in the State Department were concerned. The first important position to be filled was that of the newly established Assistant Secretaryship. Inasmuch as both Marcy and Pierce were wholly unfamiliar with foreign affairs, it was decided to appoint Ambrose Dudley Mann, a career diplomat of the period, as Assistant Secretary. Mann had had over ten years of diplomatic and consular experience in Germany, Hungary, and Switzerland and was therefore already familiar with the European policies of the Department and could be expected to master quite quickly its technical procedures. With the able and responsible William Hunter, Jr., as Chief Clerk, and the equally well experienced Francis Markoe as head of the Diplomatic Bureau and Robert S. Chew of the Consular Bureau, the Department was in a position to navigate the Ship of State, even with a neophyte helmsman. Another official with diplomatic experience and well trained in the field of international law was the Attorney General, Caleb Cushing. Cushing proved to be a pillar of strength to Secretary Marcy in assisting in the diplomatic forensic contests in which the Secretary was soon engaged.

The administration was very slow in making its diplomatic appointments to the ten posts which received ministers plenipotentiary, and the only outstandingly suitable appointment was that of James Buchanan as minister to Great Britain. In the place of the very successful William C. Rives, minister to France, Pierce chose his old friend conservative Judge John Y. Mason, and for the Spanish post, the erratic fire-eating Frenchman, Pierre Soulé. Two other appointments, one diplomatic and the other consular, were of little importance at the time, but their incumbents ultimately became world-renowned: the enigmatic but incredibly crude Daniel E. Sickles, Secretary of Legation in London, and the erudite literary light, Nathaniel Hawthorne, as consul in Liverpool.

One of the first diplomatic problems which Secretary Marcy faced was that of diplomatic costumes, a technical question of protocol in which he should never have become involved. While going through the instructions issued to our representatives abroad, he noted that various regulations had been drawn prescribing suitable uniforms for our diplomats when attending court functions. The circular issued in 1817 provided for quite an elaborate costume, whereas the circular issued in 1829, at the suggestion of President

Jackson, recommended a costume more in keeping with democratic institutions. Secretary Marcy now decided to go the whole way toward democratic simplicity, and a circular issued on June 1, 1853, stated that the Department would encourage as far as practicable, without impairing his usefulness to his country, the appearance at court of the representative of the United States in the simple dress of an American citizen. All previous instructions were thereby withdrawn and every envoy was allowed to regulate the matter according to his own sense of propriety.[3]

Buchanan in London wore a plain dress suit but buckled on a sword; Mr. Mason in Paris wore an embroidered coat, a cocked hat, and carried a sword; Mr. Soulé in Madrid was a symphony in black; Mr. Vroom in Berlin followed the rules prescribed by the Prussian *chef de protocol*. Mr. Fay, the American minister at Berne, wrote the Secretary that the "absurd and expensive" uniform necessary to be worn at a royal court was never required in the ancient republic of Switzerland. Mr. Belmont at The Hague, who wore only ordinary evening clothes, was the only diplomat honored at the royal ball by the Queen, who danced a quadrille as his partner. On the other hand, "Townsend Harris in his mission to Japan in 1857 completely disregarded the suggestion and arranged himself and his cohorts in finery almost Oriental in its lavishness." [4] Senator Sumner, who had strongly urged the sending of the instructions, succeeded in having all the diplomatic uniforms prohibited by law in 1867.

A more serious problem concerning the foreign service faced Secretary Marcy when, at the instance of the House Committee on Foreign Affairs, the Congress on March 1, 1855, passed a law prescribing grades, posts, and salaries in both diplomatic and consular services, limiting all such appointments to citizens of the United States. It did away with outfits and infits, did not mention chargés d'affaires, and provided that the President raise all ministers resident to the rank of ministers plenipotentiary. The Act had many excellent features, particularly the provision placing consuls upon a salary basis and requiring all fees to be turned over to the government, but it was not satisfactory to either the President or Secretary of State Marcy. Marcy particularly objected to the provision requiring the President to raise all ministers resident to ministers plenipotentiary and to give each minister a secretary of legation. He felt that not more than five out of the twenty ministers plenipotentiary could have much use for a secretary of legation.[5] Marcy also thought that the act was unconstitutional in that it encroached upon the discretionary rights of the President and appealed to the Attorney General for an opinion. Cushing supported the views of the Secretary and declared that Congress could not compel the President to raise the rank of all ministers resident nor could it restrict his powers of appointment.[6] Congress accepted the criticism and passed a new

Act on August 18, 1856, which remedied the defects of the previous law and was so well drawn that it remained practically unchanged for the next fifty years.

The law of August 18, 1856, made a considerable change in the status of the personnel in the Department of State. In the first place a new position, denominated "Superintendent for Statistics," was officially created. In actual fact the Department had already set up a statistical office in 1854 to carry on the work which had been assigned to the Department by the Act of August 16, 1842, which required an annual report on changes and modifications of foreign commercial systems. Secretary Webster had assigned an extra clerk to this task, and Calhoun had urged the setting up of a statistical bureau while he was Secretary. The other notable change was a new grading of clerks into four classes which, although it improved the status of some clerks, meant a reduction in salary of such experienced clerks as Francis Markoe and Robert S. Chew, whose salaries of $2,000 were cut to $1,800. On the other hand the Department had now eight clerks of Class 4 at $1,800, ten clerks of Class 3 at $1,600, three clerks of Class 2 at $1,400, and four clerks of Class 1 at $1,200. The Chief Clerk was now raised to $2,200 and the disbursing officer remained at $2,000. If we add to this list the Superintendent for Statistics and the Assistant Secretary and Secretary, we now have thirty regular officials in the Department of State. The messenger, extra clerks, packers, and laborers add twenty-seven more, making a total personnel of fifty-seven in the Department for the year 1856.[7]

Diplomatic Mistakes and Achievements

Marcy's inexperience with diplomacy was shown by his naïve instructions to Soulé, the American minister to Spain, in regard to Cuba. Granted that both Pierce and Marcy were eager to obtain Cuba and were justified in attempting to buy it, they cannot be excused for specifically authorizing Soulé to try to "detach the island from the Spanish dominion" if Spain refused to sell. The result was the so-called Ostend Manifesto, a unique curiosity of American diplomacy. The three American diplomats Buchanan, Mason, and Soulé, having conferred together at Ostend, Belgium, as to what policy should be followed regarding Cuba, proposed that if Spain refused to accept a sum of $120,000,000, "then by every law human and Divine we shall be justified in wresting it from Spain." [8] When this recommendation for the United States to engage in international brigandage reached Marcy, he realized that his suggestion to detach the island had been too liberally interpreted, and his reply was so cool to the proposal that Soulé resigned in disgust. Two questions still remain unsettled: How did Soulé inveigle the wary and experienced Buchanan to sign the document and why did Pierce and Marcy permit its publication?

Marcy's most striking achievement as Secretary of State was his success in maintaining the neutrality laws of the United States against an attempted violation by the British minister, John F. T. Crampton. In his effective handling of this matter Marcy was assisted continuously and ably by Attorney General Cushing. The British fortunes in the Crimean War were so low that an Act of Parliament permitted the enlistment of soldiers abroad. The British Foreign Office gave instructions to this effect to its representatives but at the same time warned them against violating domestic laws. Crampton flagrantly violated the laws of the United States by recruiting, and continued to do so even after instructed by his government to cease. Marcy at first gave the British an opportunity to recall their minister, but when the Foreign Office attempted to defend him he was summarily dismissed.

The Department of State under the direction of Secretary Marcy had not only increased materially in personnel but it had taken on certain additional functions. We have already noted the office of Superintendent of Statistics. Another innovation resulting from the Act of March 1, 1855, was the first issue of a book entitled *General Instructions to the Consuls and Commercial Agents of the United States, Prepared Under the Direction of the Department of State*. The utility of this publication was so great that the regulations were revised from time to time and finally were issued in a loose-leaf form so that the volume could be kept up to date.

Recent developments may be noted at this time. Subsequent to the Acts of 1924 and 1931 combining the diplomatic and consular services into the Foreign Service of the United States, the diplomatic instructions and consular regulations were combined and revised. This work was begun in 1938 under the direction of career foreign-service officers assigned temporarily to the Department of State, and the first issue of the *Foreign Service Regulations of the United States* appeared in 1941. The Act of 1946 again made many changes, so that the current *Regulations* consists of two large volumes of loose-leaf pages —some printed, some typed, and some mimeographed. The volume is marked "Confidential" and is only available to officials of the Department of State and regularly accredited foreign-service officers.

With the close of the Pierce administration, Marcy was seventy years of age. Considering his lack of background and experience in the field of international affairs, he had served very creditably as Secretary of State and could be proud of his record. He retired on March 6, 1857, and planned an extended trip to Europe with his wife. However, the onerous duties of the Department had sapped his strength, and he died three months after giving up his duties.

Lewis Cass—Secretary of State

When James Buchanan became President on March 4, 1857, it made very little difference as to who would be named Secretary of State. Buchanan had certain very definite ideas as to the future destiny of the United States and he intended to conduct the foreign policy of his country in accordance with his views. His previous training and experience at least partly warranted this attitude. Having followed foreign affairs closely in the Senate, with an excellent record as minister to Russia and Great Britain, and having served a full four years as Secretary of State, it was but natural that he should consider himself better equipped than any man whom he could appoint. The sole factors considered in appointing Lewis Cass as Secretary of State were political expediency and an amenable disposition. Geography had to be considered and Cass came from Michigan. Cass had a very kindly disposition, and having reached the age of seventy-five, it was hardly likely that he would be either aggressive or ambitious. Buchanan was not concerned over the fact that Cass had long been a violently vocal Anglophobe. Neither did he care that while minister to France, Cass had shown little indication of diplomatic aptitude and had bitterly attacked Secretary of State Webster in a matter wholly outside of his proper jurisdiction. Since Buchanan would be his own Secretary of State, he wanted a man who would enhance the prestige of the cabinet but who, at the same time, would take orders gracefully.

Lewis Cass, although not personally compatible with Buchanan, met all political requirements. He had risen to the rank of brigadier general in the regular army, he had been appointed governor of the Northwest Territory, he had served ably as Secretary of War under President Jackson, and although not a diplomat, he had had diplomatic experience. He was regarded as a very able senator and in 1848 he had been nominated by the Democrats for the Presidency. Although at the time the fact that he had written, while he was minister to France, a famous pamphlet against the right of search in times of peace was not thought to be important—in fact John Quincy Adams denounced it as "a compound of Yankee cunning, of Italian perfidy, and of French *légèreté*, cemented by shameless profligacy, unparalleled in American diplomacy" [9]—he proved its importance later while Secretary of State. In fact the position which he took, and as Secretary effectively maintained, became ultimately the recognized and accepted rule on the subject in international law.

Departmental Personnel

When Secretary Cass took charge of the Department of State, he found General John A. Thomas of New York serving as Assistant Secretary, a man who, according to Buchanan, had discharged his duties with much ability as American agent on the British-American Claims Commission. Thomas had been appointed a few months after the retirement of A. Dudley Mann. In the interim between Mann's resignation and the appointment of Thomas, May 8 to October 31, 1855, William Hunter, Jr., served as Assistant Secretary of State and Robert S. Chew as Chief Clerk. When Secretary Marcy made these appointments, the following unique written statement was prepared and signed by Secretary Marcy and Messrs. Hunter and Chew:

It is to be understood that the appointment of William Hunter as Assistant Secretary of State and Robert S. Chew as Chief Clerk in this Department are of a temporary character only and that upon the appointment of another Assistant Secretary they may resume those positions in the Department from which they have respectively been promoted.

President Buchanan appointed as Assistant Secretary of State a very able officer in the person of John Appleton, an official who already possessed considerable diplomatic experience. Appleton had served as a clerk in the Department of State for a very short period when Buchanan was Secretary of State and had then been appointed chargé d'affaires to Bolivia. He found his diplomatic assignment unimportant and dull and resigned in 1849. He served one term in Congress and then went to London to serve as Secretary of Legation while Buchanan was minister. He was well qualified to serve as Assistant Secretary and unquestionably he was responsible for a considerable amount of the Department's diplomatic correspondence.

The personnel of the Department remained practically unchanged during the administration of Buchanan and Cass. The tried and true William Hunter continued as Chief Clerk, Francis Markoe—or as he was sometimes dubbed Don Magnifico Markoe—remained as head of the Diplomatic Bureau, and Robert S. Chew as head of the Consular Bureau. The number of clerks increased slightly as the needs required. As of September 30, 1857, we find eight clerks of the fourth class, nine of the third class, three of the second class, and three of the first class, all of which, including the Secretary, Assistant Secretary, Chief Clerk, Disbursing Clerk, and Superintendent of Statistics, but not counting messengers and watchmen, made a total of twenty-eight officials.[10] Two years later the list was unchanged in numbers and almost unchanged in personnel. It should be noted that the position of Disbursing Clerk had been abolished by the Act of March 3, 1855, but it was reestablished in 1857, and under the title of Disbursing Agent or Bureau, or Division of Accounts, it has existed to the present time.

Diplomatic Problems

Buchanan was determined to maintain friendly relations with Great Britain at all costs. His recent service as minister at the Court of St. James's was to prove a great asset in carrying out this policy, since he was thoroughly conversant with the situation abroad and had many close friends among the members of the British Foreign Office. A few days before he was inaugurated, Buchanan in a personal letter to Lord Clarendon assured his friend that no uneasiness need be felt because of the Anglophobia of General Cass, who was to be named Secretary of State—since "if it ever existed, it no longer exists."[11] Buchanan felt that the Clayton-Bulwer Treaty ought to be abrogated and said so frankly, although privately, to Lord Clarendon. But he knew that the British would not consent to such a renunciation and so he tried to work out problems arising under it in accordance with the interpretation which we supported. In the case of the San Juan Islands, Buchanan, who had negotiated the Treaty of 1846, was adamant against British claims to their possession. Here he would make no compromise, and the decision of the German arbitrator many years later proved that he was right in his stand.

Secretary Cass had an opportunity while Secretary of State to maintain the principles of the freedom of American vessels which he had so vigorously championed while he was minister to France. When a British warship off the coast of Africa seized an American vessel suspected of carrying on the slave trade, Cass protested strongly to the British government. Buchanan supported Cass in his stand; and when reports continued to arrive indicating that British cruisers were boarding American merchantmen, not only off the African coast but in the Caribbean, on the allegation that they were slave traders, the President ordered every American ship of war in the vicinity of the Gulf of Mexico to protect all American vessels from search or detention. When the British attempted to make a distinction between the right of visitation and the right of search, Cass objected. He insisted that the distinction between

an entry for the purpose of examining into the national character of a vessel and the entry for the purpose of examining into the objects of her voyage could not be maintained upon any recognized principle of the law of nations. . . . The United States deny the right of the cruisers of any other power whatever, for any purpose whatever, to enter their vessels by force in time of peace.[12]

The British now decided to recede from their position and Cass was informed by Lord Napier, the British minister to the United States, that "Her Majesty's Government recognize as sound those principles of international law which have been laid down by General Cass in his note of the 10th of April." [13] In his annual message of December 6, 1858, President Buchanan declared that the "long-pending controversy between the governments relative to the question of visitation and search has been amicably adjusted." [14] This brilliant diplomatic victory, in which Cass played the stellar role, raises the position of Secretary Cass above the many mediocre incumbents of this office.

One of the most famous state papers emanating from the Department of State during this period was the circular dispatch of June 27, 1859, sent by Secretary Cass to our various representatives in Europe, outlining the position of the United States on the subject of blockades, contraband, and the rights of neutral commercial vessels on the high seas in times of war.[15] It was a brilliant disquisition on behalf of neutral rights against belligerent action and has been often quoted by the authorities in international law. Unfortunately the Civil War came only two years later, and the United States, as a belligerent, violated most brazenly many of the principles of blockade and contraband that Secretary Cass had so recently insisted should be regarded as essential bases of the international law of maritime warfare.

In concluding an account of the services of Lewis Cass as Secretary of State, one matter of foreign-service administration deserves attention. The Department of State was in receipt of many bitter complaints from its consular officers in many parts of the world who were unable to live even in the most niggardly fashion upon the salaries established by the Act of August 18, 1856. Secretary Cass, on January 25, 1858, wrote to the chairman of the House Committee on Foreign Affairs an urgent request that Congress authorize the President to allow consular officers clothed with the judicial function in countries granting extraterritoriality the expenditure for the rent of jails, and to appoint marshals who should be entitled to compensation for their services. He also requested that the President be authorized to appoint consular clerks where required, their compensation to be paid from consular fees. From the letters which Secretary Cass sent as exhibits with his request, we find that the consul at Liverpool had received a cut of over 50 per cent in income at the same time that his expenses had increased 20 per cent. The consul at Calcutta, with a salary fixed at $5,000, estimated his annual expense at the post as $9,600 plus $2,000 for passage to India and back. The American consul at Pernambuco, Brazil, presented his case in most picturesque and fervid language. With a salary of $2,000 a year, he declared that with bread at 15 cents a pound, turnips and carrots at 56 cents per pound, turkeys from $4 to $6 each, fruits too high for general use, and hack hire from $5 to $10 per hour, the salary paid did not afford "the actual means of a scanty and miserable existence." Of his predecessors he declared that one had resigned his commission when he had received "such mournful account of this place as to disgust him in advance of his arrival; four others have left their bones to fade in these fearfully hot sands, without a slab of stone or a stick of wood to point the stranger to their graves." [16]

Secretary Cass did not serve out the whole of President Buchanan's term of office. He resigned not on a question of foreign policy, but because Buchanan failed to take a strong enough stand against secession. Buchanan accepted the resignation immediately, pointing out that neither the Secretaries of War nor Navy supported Cass in his stand for the immediate use of force. It might have been expected that the Assistant Secretary of State, William Henry Trescot,[17] would have assumed office; but as a native of South Carolina, Trescot was ardently in support of the Southern position, and he resigned four days after Secretary Cass. Chief Clerk William Hunter, Jr., served as Secretary of State ad interim for the two days of December 15 and 16, 1860, when he was succeeded by Attorney General Jeremiah Black.

President Buchanan had never had a high regard for General Cass as his Secretary of State. After his resignation, Buchanan had this to say of him: "So timid was he and so little confidence had he in himself that it was difficult for him to arrive at any decision of the least consequence. He brought many questions to me which he ought to have decided for himself. When obliged to decide for himself he called Mr. Cobb and Judge Black to his assistance." [18] Judge Black, as a fellow member of the cabinet and later as the successor to Cass, felt that Buchanan was not always fair to Cass—he thought harshly of his faults and was unkind to his virtues. He himself felt that Cass was the "most honest, upright, patriotic gentleman that I have ever known."

Jeremiah Black—Secretary of State

When Jeremiah Sullivan Black assumed the duties of Secretary of State on December 17, 1860, Abraham Lincoln had already been elected President and war clouds were piling up on the horizon. Buchanan chose him because he trusted him implicitly, and Black had already proved himself intellectually superior to any other member of the cabinet. Although he possessed no experience in the field of international relations, he was an able lawyer, and Cass regularly sought his advice on questions involving both national and international law. His opinion in the case of Christian Ernst—a naturalized American citizen who while visiting his home in Germany had been forced to enlist in the Hanoverian Army—strongly upheld the rights of expatriation and naturalization and formed the basis of a circular dispatch on the subject to our representatives abroad as expressing the views of the United States. In this instance the Hanoverian government dismissed Ernst from military service but declared that similar conflicts in the future could only be avoided by the United States' renouncing its view. The United States maintained its policy, although during the Civil War, with conscription in force, it was found inexpedient to enforce the claim of protection in the case of forced military service when the naturalized citizen voluntarily returned to his country of birth.[19]

When Assistant Secretary of State Trescot resigned, Secretary Black attempted to secure in his place the services of Thomas F. Bayard of Delaware, who was later to serve as Secretary of State under President Cleveland. When Bayard refused, Black decided that he could get along, for the short time during which he would serve, with the assistance of capable and experienced Chief Clerk William Hunter. He carried on the routine duties of the Department but his real interest was in the fateful domestic situation. In fact, he clashed with President Buchanan in regard to the answer to be made to the envoys from South Carolina regarding the seizure of Fort Moultrie, and offered his resignation as Secretary of State less than two weeks after he was commissioned. President Buchanan, rather than accept it, revised his response to the Southern envoys in accordance with Secretary Black's suggestions. Black's last official act was to instruct our representatives abroad to make every effort to prevent recognition being accorded to the envoys of the newly established Confederate government. He surrendered his office on March 5, 1861, to President Lincoln's choice for Secretary of State—Senator William H. Seward of New York. However throughout the administration of President Buchanan, whether the able Marcy or the hesitant Cass or the legalistic Black held the Secretaryship of State, it was the President who directed and controlled foreign policy.

WILLIAM H. SEWARD

12

William H. Seward

William H. Seward—Secretary of State

With the outbreak of the Civil War the Department of State was faced with an entirely new set of problems. Whereas until then slavery had been a powerful underlying factor in the diplomacy of the period, now the primary interest in foreign relations was to prevent the recognition of the Confederacy by the great states of Europe—particularly Great Britain. If ever an outstanding Secretary of State and an equally able diplomatic corps were needed, now was the time.

President Lincoln in his choice of a Secretary of State felt himself somewhat circumscribed by national political requirements and by the fact that the crisis at home far outweighed any visible dangers abroad. Almost immediately after his election, Lincoln began to consider possible candidates for the cabinet and he seems to have picked William H. Seward as his first choice for Secretary of State. From the standpoint of ability and political prestige, few men of the day could equal Seward. An able lawyer, onetime Governor of New York, outstanding senator, and Lincoln's rival as candidate for President in the nominating convention, Seward would be a pillar of strength in any administration. Although Seward possessed no diplomatic experience, he had served on the Senate Committee on Foreign Relations and in the year 1859 he had traveled widely in Europe and the Near East. There was some question as to whether he would accept a cabinet position. He had written in a letter in 1849: "The post of a Minister, and even of a Premier, has no temptations for me." [1] On the other hand, his position in the Senate was such that he might well question whether he could be of greater influence in the cabinet.

President Lincoln proffered the post of Secretary of State to Seward on December 8, 1860, and accompanied the official offer with a confidential letter in which he declared that he had thought of Seward for this office from the time of his own nomination and believed that Seward's "position in the public eye, your integrity, ability, learning and great experience all combine to render it an appointment preeminently fit to be made." [2] Before accepting, Seward consulted his wife and Thurlow Weed, and on December 28 he wrote a very brief note to the President that "after due reflection and much distrust," if he were nominated to the position of Secretary of State and the nomination should be confirmed, it would be his duty to accept the appointment.[3] A short note to his wife on the same day indicated clearly that he felt it his duty to accept, and another letter a few weeks later indicated that he regarded his role as the most vital one in the cabinet: "It seems to me that if I am absent only three days, this Administration, the Congress, and the District would fall into consternation and despair. I am the only *hopeful, calm* and *conciliatory* person here." [4] Just before the inauguration, Seward tried to resign from the proposed cabinet when he learned that Salmon P. Chase was to be a member, but at Lincoln's urgent solicitations he decided to remain and not "leave the country to chance."

Seward's Appointments at Home and Abroad

William H. Seward was commissioned Secretary of State on March 5, 1861; he entered upon his duties the following day and remained in this position for the next eight years under Presidents Lincoln and Johnson. His son, Frederick W. Seward, who had been acting as associate editor of Thurlow Weed's *Albany Evening Journal* for the previous ten years, was named Assistant Secretary of State and was commissioned with him. An accusation of nepotism disturbed Seward not in the least. One of his son's principal duties at first was to take care of office seekers and Secretary Seward frankly acknowledged that he had placed him "where he must meet the whole array of friends seeking office—a hundred taking tickets when only one can draw a prize." With neither the Secretary nor the Assistant Secretary familiar with the Department's routine, Chief Clerk William Hunter was even more indispensable than usual. Frederick Seward notes in his biography of his father that Secretary Seward issued his first summons for Mr. Hunter, who "was and for years had been the personification of the Department work. He was its memory, its guiding hand. . . . His life had been devoted to its service; and in return it had come to regard him as an indispensable component part of its existence. . . ." [5] Writing many years later, after having served as Assistant Secretary under Johnson and Hayes, Frederick Seward was even more enthusiastic regarding Hunter:

Every secretary trusted him and depended upon him. He was a walking encyclopedia of the decisions and precedents and questions arising out of our foreign relations . . . conversing fluently in French or Spanish he was an excellent medium for intercourse with the foreign representatives,—most of whom liked to have a private unofficial interview with Mr. Hunter when they were not sure whether their carefully studied English would correspond with the customary American idioms.[6]

Since the Republican administration was in for the first time, a clean sweep of officeholders was expected and Washington was crowded with applicants for positions on the government payroll. Seward, however, made only one inquiry of his clerical force—were they loyal to the Union or did they favor the Secessionists. Every one of the latter was dismissed and orders given that access to archives and papers should be denied to them. All others, regardless of party, were kept, and their future, they were informed, would be determined by their fidelity to their official duties. A careful check of the personnel of the Department after this loyalty purge indicates that quite a number of changes occurred. The names of clerks of long experience, such as Francis Markoe and Edward Stubbs, no longer appeared; on the other hand, we find George E. Baker, Seward's old friend and biographer, as Disbursing Clerk, and his former townsman, J. C. Derby, was made Librarian. The new Superintendent of Statistics, John A. Jones of Illinois, was also a political appointee. Of the eight clerks of the fourth or highest class in the Department as of September 30, 1861, four, including Robert S. Chew, had been carried over and two had been promoted from Class 3. The total number of clerks now numbered twenty-four as against twenty-six in 1859.

No changes were made in the organization of the Department except for the fact that a temporary bureau was created to take care of political prisoners and rebel correspondence under the direction of E. D. Webster. Seward asked for no change or increase of the regular force but did request an appropriation for temporary clerks when they were required. This was authorized and the temporary personnel varied from five to twenty-five. Frederick Seward felt that the Department of State functioned very effectively during the war and reconstruction period—"no duty of the Department was ever neglected; no paper ever lost; no State secret ever betrayed."[7]

We have already noted that the Department of State's building had been located since 1820 at the corner of Fifteenth Street and Pennsylvania Avenue —the only one of the four Federal buildings which had remained completely unchanged. Assistant Secretary Seward gives an excellent description of it as it looked when he entered the Department in 1861:

The Department of State, at this period, was in the old two-story brick building which used to stand on ground now occupied by the northern end of the Treasury Department. It was substantial and convenient, without being either stately or imposing. Its exterior was painted a plain drab color, and exhibited little attempt at ornamentation, except a portico of six white columns on the northern side. Under this portico was the main entrance, which however was little used. . . . Within, its finish was equally simple. It had but thirty or forty rooms, not large though well arranged for their purpose; and these, during the preceding half century, had been found ample for the needs of this branch of government; though the accumulation of books and archives was now beginning to cramp the space of some of the clerks. The two rooms in the northeast corner of the second floor were usually occupied by the Secretary —one for study, the other for receiving visitors. Messengers were just outside his door; and across the hall, within convenient reach, were the rooms of the Assistant Secretary and Chief Clerk.[8]

The problem of choosing diplomatic representatives to protect the interests of the United States abroad was particularly important at this time of crisis, yet sectional and political interests had to be considered. By far the most important post at this time was that of minister to Great Britain. Lincoln had already mentioned William L. Dayton of New Jersey for that position when Seward countered by suggesting Charles Francis Adams, the "reserved but emphatic" son of John Quincy Adams, for whom Seward had great admiration and respect. Lincoln, after some argument, accepted the suggestion, a decision fraught with momentous and most fortunate consequences. Former Senator William L. Dayton was thereupon nominated for France. Although unversed in diplomacy and unable to speak French—he wore a court uniform rather than fuss over buttons—Dayton became very popular with the French government, and Seward thought highly of his work. The great German liberal, Carl Schurz, was sent to Madrid in spite of Seward's opposition. His political addresses had so moved the President that he declared that, considering their short acquaintance, no one stood nearer to his heart. At the urgent solicitation of Senator Sumner, the erudite and urbane historian, John Lothrop Motley, was named minister to Austria. Perhaps the most logical appointment, and a most excellent one, was that of George P. Marsh to Italy. Marsh was a brilliant scholar, spoke most of the European languages fluently, and had already served as minister to Turkey, Greece, and the Scandinavian states. He was to remain twenty-one years at his post in Italy—a record achievement for a politically appointed diplomat. The experienced and successful Townsend Harris remained at his post in Japan. Anson Burlingame was at first sent to Austria but soon after was transferred to China where his services were unique in relations between the states of the Occident and Orient. One of the questionable appointments was that of the fiery crusading abolitionist from Kentucky, Cassius Clay, who wanted to be Secretary of War. President Lincoln, although his good friend, had other ideas for his cabinet and persuaded Clay to take the post of minister to Russia.

Seward unquestionably expected to take complete charge of the foreign relations of the United States and as Lincoln's "prime minister" to dictate foreign policy and to administer the Department of State as he saw fit. Frederick W. Seward, Assistant Secretary of State, tells that on the first Sunday after his arrival in Washington President Lincoln informed Secretary Seward that he depended upon him to take care of matters of foreign affairs and that gradually Lincoln signed the papers from the Secretary, which the Undersecretary brought to him, without even reading them.[9] Many authorities cite as proof of Seward's intention to try to run the government a memorandum entitled "Some Thoughts for the President's Consideration," which Seward handed to Lincoln on April 1, 1861.[10] The opening sentence, "We are at the end of a month's Administration and yet without a policy either domestic or foreign," might be regarded as critical of the President's procedure, yet in the next sentence Seward conceded that this was "unavoidable." In regard to foreign nations he would demand satisfactory explanation from Spain and France (regarding their intervention in Mexico), and if they refused to give satisfactory explanations he would convene Congress and declare war upon them. The concluding sentences are the most remarkable:

But whatever policy we adopt, there must be an energetic prosecution of it. For this purpose it must be somebody's business to pursue and direct it incessantly. Either the President must do it himself . . . or devolve it on some member of his cabinet. . . . It is not my especial province; but I neither seek to evade nor to assume responsibility.

Frederick Seward, who copied the memorandum for his father, explains it as merely the basis for subsequent interviews between the President and Secretary of State and useful hints for cabinet discussions. Nevertheless, the suggestion of declaring war upon Spain and France at the very moment when war was threatened between North and South seems hardly worthy of discussion. President Lincoln acknowledged the memorandum in a kindly fashion, stating definitely, however, that if these things had to be done he would do them.

Seward and Great Britain

One of the first tasks facing the new Secretary of State was the preparation of instructions to our diplomats proceeding to their posts abroad. The burden of these instructions was to the effect that no form of recognition be accorded the seceding states by any foreign nation. Those to Charles Francis Adams, who was going to Great Britain, were the most elaborate because his task involved "the responsibility of preventing the commission of an act by the government of that country which would be fraught with disaster and perhaps ruin to our own." In describing the condition of affairs existing when the new administration came into office, Seward declared: "Disaffection lurked, if it did not openly avow itself, in every department and every bureau, in every regiment and in every legation and consulate from London to Calcutta." [11] Unfortunately for the success of Adams in his mission, Seward was suspected as a warmonger by Downing Street: it was remembered that he had told the Duke of Newcastle while he was visiting America that if he (Seward) ever became Secretary of State it would be his duty to insult England and he would most surely do so. In some of his earlier instructions to Adams, it appeared as though Seward were carrying out his earlier promises. In fact one instruction, if delivered as Adams received it, might have brought about war between the two powers "before the carriage of the American minister had rattled out of Downing Street."

The metamorphosis of these instructions indicates how important is the foreign representative of a government who is in a position to evaluate the foreign reaction. Before Adams had reached his post in London, the British government had received unofficially certain representatives of the Confederate States and had issued a proclamation of neutrality which gave the Confederacy the status of a belligerent power. When Secretary Seward received news of this action which appeared both hasty and unfriendly, he wrote a dispatch to Adams which was so lacking in diplomatic courtesy that if delivered verbatim to the British Foreign Office, as Seward meant it to be, no further correspondence might have been possible. However Lincoln made numerous changes and insisted that the instructions were for the guidance of Adams only and should not be shown to anyone. Thus Adams was permitted to present the context of the instructions in his own words, which he did most effectively.[12]

Although not too familiar with diplomatic protocol, on one occasion Secretary of State Seward made excellent use of it to prevent a joint effort on the part of the British and French ministers to make an offer of mediation for peace. Having been informed by a messenger that the British and French ministers wished jointly to see him, he asked that they be shown into the room of the Assistant Secretary. Seward then went in, and seeing them seated together, he smilingly shook his head and said: "No, no, no! This will never do. I cannot see you in that way." They insisted that they were obeying instructions, but Seward invited the French minister to dine with him that evening and suggested that Lord Lyons come in and discuss what he had to say. The interviews were held separately, and after a mere glance at the papers, Seward refused to hear them read or to receive them officially.[13]

The *Trent* Affair was perhaps the problem which taxed the diplomatic ingenuity of the Department of State more than any other problem during the Civil War. Two commissioners of the Confederate States, James M. Mason of Virginia and John Slidell of Louisiana, and their secretaries who were traveling on the *Trent,* a British mail steamer bound from Havana to St. Thomas, were seized on the high seas by Captain Charles Wilkes of the United States warship *San Jacinto.* These well known men—both had been senators of the United States—were being sent to Britain by the Confederacy to replace the previous envoys, who had not been too successful. Although Captain Wilkes had acted without instructions, he was commended by the Secretary of the Navy, his act was declared to be legal by former Secretary of State Everett, and the press of the country wildly applauded. Secretary Seward made no public statement, but in a confidential letter to Adams he indicated that there might be serious repercussions and that, fortunately for the government, Captain Wilkes had acted without instructions. [14] Before the official British protest arrived, news had come of the hostility aroused in England, and it was evident that what the United States thought of as merely a clever coup against the Confederacy, the British saw as a deliberate insult to the empire. Seward took an entire day to draft a reply and cleverly based his disavowal of Captain Wilkes's action on a maintenance of the long established doctrine of visit and search. To save face as much as possible, Seward argued that Captain Wilkes under international law might have seized the *Trent* for carrying contraband and brought her into an American prize court, but he conceded that the seizure as it occurred was illegal and that the United States therefore would surrender the commissioners to the British authorities.[15] Seward's argument that persons were contraband was a bit flimsy, but his adroit acceptance of the British claims as finally supporting our long established policy gained popular favor. Instead of calumny being heaped upon him as he feared, Seward was praised for his "infernal cunning."

The other critical situation arising between the United States and Great Britain as a result of the construction of warships in Britain for the Confederacy was handled almost entirely in London. Seward had implicit confidence in Charles Francis Adams, and rightly so. It was well that he had, because the British were ever suspicious of Seward—they felt he might favor a war abroad as a possible means of bringing the United States together against a foreign foe. Adams had the advantage of having the provisions of the British Foreign Enlistment Act wholly on his side. However the law could be flouted, technically at least, by building ships in Britain but equipping them on the high seas. Adams kept the Foreign Office completely informed of what was going on and documented his representations thoroughly. After the *Alabama* had been turned over to the Confederacy, the next order was for two ironclad rams, which, if obtained, might have broken the blockade and won the war. Seward's instructions now were explicit—in fact almost threatening. However Adams informed Seward courteously that "as minister and on the spot, he thought he understood the men and situation best and accordingly he would assume the responsibility of acting on his own judgment and as circumstances might seem to require." [16] Nevertheless, Adams thought he had lost, and in his final memorable note to Lord Russell, dated September 5, 1863, he declared: "It would be superfluous in me to point out to your Lordship that this is war." [17] But Russell had already issued an order to hold the rams, and Adams had won.

Unusual Diplomatic Procedure

Perhaps it should be noted in passing that the Secretary of State engaged in two ventures in the conduct of the diplomacy of the war period which were highly questionable both as to procedure and possible results. The first was the sending of several unofficial envoys on confidential and secret missions abroad to try to influence public opinion as regards the war. They were to have no diplomatic status, were not to deal with foreign governments, and they were to receive no compensation except for expenses. Fortunately, the three who accepted the missions were extremely able and dependable persons: Archbishop Hughes of the Roman Catholic Church, Bishop McIlvaine of the Protestant Episcopal Church, and Seward's good friend and counselor, Thurlow Weed. Their reports, which were private and confidential and have never become a part of the official archives, were of considerable value to the Department.[18] The second venture was inexcusable in procedure if not in purpose. Two irresponsible American bankers were dispatched to London with United States bonds to the value of $10,000,000 and authorized to purchase the ironclads being built for the Confederacy by outbidding them on price. Adams fortunately was not apprised of their errand or it would have been a serious blow to his effort to prove illegal a similar action on the part of the Confederacy.

The case of William M. Evarts, sent to London by Secretary Seward to assist the legation on legal matters, was more regular but still not too well appreciated by Minister Adams. In fact Adams felt very strongly that "the almost constant interference of government agents of all kinds has had the effect, however intended, of weakening the position of the minister." [19] His son, who served as his secretary, wrote caustically that because "of other diplomats, roving, poaching and volunteer, Mr. Adams had grave and just cause of complaint; they were officious, they meddled and they were to the last degree indiscreet." [20]

While the Civil War was in progress, a serious violation of the Monroe Doctrine occurred which Seward did not overlook, but he found the time inauspicious for effective action. When Napoleon III established Maximilian upon the throne of Mexico, the House of Representatives on April 4, 1864, passed a resolution refusing to recognize "any government erected upon the ruins of any Republican government in America." The Department of State had been instructing the American representative in Paris to keep Napoleon III apprised of American sentiment and to counsel against permanent intervention, but it was to be done discreetly and diplomatically. When the French minister in Washington asked for an explanation of the House resolution, Seward replied that while the resolution interpreted the sentiment of the American people, the administration had in no way changed its policy of hands off.

Changes in Personnel and Location

It was just a month after Lincoln was inaugurated for his second term that Seward, while out for his customary drive, was thrown from his carriage and seriously injured. Nine days later, while hovering between life and death in the hospital, he was set upon by an assassin and his face and throat were slashed and hacked with a bowie knife. Assistant Secretary of State Frederick Seward was even more seriously injured in attempting to protect his father. It was the same night that President Lincoln was murdered and was unquestionably a part of the same plot. Chief Clerk William Hunter took charge of the Department and carried on until both the Secretary and Assistant Secretary had recovered. Vice President Johnson, after taking the oath of office, declared his intention of carrying on the Lincoln policies; and Seward, although the Radical Republicans soon broke with the President, decided to remain in charge of the Department of State. He returned to his work while still swathed in bandages and was carried to his office by his assistants. One of his first dictated letters was to Minister Bigelow in Paris, informing him that President Lincoln's two secretaries, John Hay and John G. Nicolay, had been appointed secretary of legation and consul for Paris.

Unquestionably the most important change in the personnel of the State Department was that brought about by the Act of July 25, 1866, when a Second Assistant Secretary of State was authorized at a salary of $3,500—the same as the First Assistant Secretary currently received—and Chief Clerk William Hunter was named to this post. No promotion was more popular or well deserved. Robert S. Chew, who had also grown up with the service—he had been appointed on July 10, 1834, at the age of twenty-one—was promoted to the position of Chief Clerk. Another temporary addition to the administrative organization of the Department had come about as a result of the Act of July 4, 1864, which authorized the President to appoint a Commissioner of Immigration under the direction of the Secretary of State. He was to receive a salary of $2,500 a year and to be assisted by three clerks. One of these was stationed in New York as Superintendent of Immigration. The arrangement was temporary and by the Act of March 30, 1868, it was abolished.

It was during Seward's administration that the Department of State changed its location. The Department of the Treasury had grown to such an extent that it needed the site occupied by the State Department, and the old two-story brick building had to be torn down. Since no public building was immediately available, an orphan asylum on 14th Street which was in process of construction was rented and equipped for the Department. The fiscal officer, Mr. Baker, took charge of the moving, and each bureau officer and clerk was instructed to move all papers and documents for which he was responsible. A single night was sufficient to transfer all the records and the voluminous correspondence of the Department. The story is told that shortly after the old building was torn down, one of the officers presented to Secretary Seward a cane of plain dark wood with the statement: "That stick, Mr. Secretary, has been in the hands of every President of the United States, of every Secretary of State and every cabinet officer. It has been handled by every foreign minister accredited to the government or commissioned by it. It has been touched by nearly every senator and by the majority of all the representatives in Congress, to say nothing of thousands of civil, military, and naval officers and private citizens." When Seward showed his incredulity, the clerk explained that it had been carved out of the handrail of the old stairway leading to the Secretary's office.[21]

Imperialistic Impulses

It was during the Johnson administration that Seward had the opportunity, long desired, to try to expand the territorial limits of the United States. Even before becoming Secretary of State he had cast envious eyes upon the Russian possessions in the Northwest, and during the Civil War he felt that the lack of naval bases in the North Pacific was a severe handicap. He was also familiar with the fact that in 1859 Assistant Secretary of State Appleton had raised the question of the purchase of Alaska for $5,000,000 but the Civil War put an end to all negotiations. During the Civil War Russia showed a friendly attitude toward the Union and indicated a willingness to discuss the cession of Alaska. When the Russian minister came to Seward's residence one night, saying that a treaty for the purchase of Alaska was authorized and that he would come to the Department in the morning, Seward said: "Why wait

The State Department in the Washington Orphan Asylum 1866–1875 Fourteenth Street near S Street, Washington, D.C.

until tomorrow? Let us make the treaty tonight." Baron Stoeckl at first demurred, but at Seward's insistence he and his aide appeared at the Department about midnight, and by five in the morning the treaty was signed and sealed. In this instance, although the press called it "Seward's Folly" and "Johnson's Polar Bear Garden," the Senate wisely approved its ratification.

Seward was not so successful in getting the support of Congress for the annexation of the Hawaiian Islands, although the United States did take possession of the Midway Island, even farther to the west. Nor was he more successful in carrying out his imperialistic designs in the Caribbean. President Johnson gave him a free hand and supported him in arranging for the purchase of St. Thomas and St. John from Denmark, and the Danes agreed to take $7,500,000 for the islands. The Congress thought any price too high at this time, but in 1917 the United States was glad to get them for $25,000,000. His efforts to obtain Santo Domingo, or at least the Bay of Samaná, were no more successful. The House of Representatives looked askance at further expenditures for territorial expansion, and Seward had to be content with Alaska.

Seward's eight years of service as Secretary of State ended with the inauguration of President Ulysses S. Grant. On the day before the change of administration, Seward was very pleased to receive a letter of appreciation from the officers of the Department for the courtesy which he had shown toward his subordinates. Of the forty officers who signed the letter, eleven had been clerks in the Department when he had entered upon his duties eight years before. These officials had no doubt as to the outstanding achievements of their chief in his administration of the Department of State in the difficult period in which he served. The impartial historian, viewing Secretary Seward's contributions as a whole, must unhesitatingly place him among the great Secretaries of State. His ardent devotion to duty, his limitless energy, the unfailing optimism and faith in the United States which colored all his instructions, his courage and his vision outweigh overwhelmingly the few serious errors in judgment which might be assessed against him. In the words of one of his successors, "He betrayed no trust, he deserted no duty, he quailed before no danger, he recoiled from no labor."

13

Hamilton Fish and William M. Evarts

Hamilton Fish—Secretary of State

With the advent of General Ulysses S. Grant as President, cabinet members were chosen in complete disregard of special capacity, public opinion, or even party interests. The President apparently consulted only his own ideas on the subject. For Secretary of State he chose Congressman Elihu B. Washburne, who had supported him constantly and effectively throughout the Civil War and had campaigned for his Presidency far more vigorously than he had himself. It had generally been expected that Washburne would receive a cabinet appointment—the office of Secretary of the Treasury seemed to be most suitable, considering Washburne's interests—but to pick him as Secretary of State at a time when the foreign interests of the United States were increasingly important aroused widespread and vocal criticism. When Grant was approached on the subject, he confessed that the appointment had been made as a token of gratitude and that after a very short occupancy Washburne would be sent as minister to France and James F. Wilson of Iowa would take his place as Secretary of State. However, when Washburne resigned five days after he had been appointed, Wilson refused the position. It was alleged that he was disgruntled because Washburne had already made certain appointments which were not justified, considering his temporary status.

President Grant now gave some consideration to the appointment of John Lothrop Motley, the historian, as Secretary of State. Motley was a good friend of Charles Sumner's, chairman of the Foreign Relations Committee of the Senate, and he had served as secretary of legation at St. Petersburg and later for six years as minister to Austria. But according to one story, after an interview, Grant, noting that Motley's hair was parted in the middle and that he wore a monocle, said that he might as well get the Earl of Clarendon to run the State Department.

It is not quite clear why Grant then decided to offer the position to Hamilton Fish of New York. He only knew him casually and Fish had had no training or experience in foreign affairs.[1] Furthermore, Fish had retired from the political arena and was not interested in reentering it. He had served as Governor of New York and as representative and senator in the Congress of the United States; he was quite wealthy and was about sixty years of age. He had made his contribution to society; he now wished to look on rather than participate. When Grant wrote Fish a very informal note suggesting that he might like to accept the State Department portfolio, Fish, much surprised at the offer, decided after some thought that he would be unwise to accept. He thereupon sent Grant a courteous note of refusal. Meanwhile, the very next day, March 11, 1869, Grant sent Fish's name, with several others, to the Senate for confirmation. When Fish's note reached him too late for its withdrawal, he urged Fish to reconsider. Fish, who had given his wife's health as one of his reasons for refusing, found that his wife now felt that he should accept. So, hesitantly and with the full expectation of withdrawing after the adjournment of Congress, Hamilton Fish took over the Department of State. Although he was commissioned on March 11, 1869, Fish did not enter upon his duties until March 17, and in the meantime Secretary Washburne carried on the work of the Department.

It must be conceded that Fish was not qualified particularly for the position which he had agreed to fill. Other than the fact that he spoke French fluently and had spent two years traveling in Europe, his background and experience were wholly domestic. He clearly realized his limitations and entered upon his duties, for which he had "little taste and less fitness," with a full appreciation of the need for caution and careful consideration. A first requirement was to choose a First Assistant Secretary to take the place of Frederick W. Seward. J. C. Bancroft Davis, nephew of the historian George Bancroft, who had served in London for three years as secretary of the legation, applied for the position. Bancroft Davis, as he was known, was trained in the law and had acted as American correspondent for the London *Times* from 1854 to 1861. The choice proved to be an excellent one and Davis was invaluable to the United States in the *Alabama* claims arbitration, which was to be one of the outstanding diplomatic achievements of the Grant administration. While Davis was serving as agent in the Geneva arbitration, the position of Assistant Secretary was held for somewhat less than a year by Charles Hale of Massachusetts, a journalist who, although he had served for six years quite satisfactorily in Egypt as consul general, was wholly unfamiliar with the Department of State and did not get along very well with Secretary Fish. Davis was reappointed Assistant Secretary on January 25, 1873, and remained in office until June 30, 1874, when he was named minister to Berlin to succeed his more famous historian uncle.

The able and experienced William Hunter remained as Second Assistant Secretary and Robert S. Chew continued as Chief Clerk. The organization of the Department in actuality had not changed substantially since the reorganization of Secretary Forsyth, even though the Act of March 3, 1855, had abolished all bureaus officially. In practice it was found necessary to carry on the work through such agencies, although in the *United States Official Register* between the years 1855 and 1870 we find no bureaus listed. One of the first innovations inaugurated by Secretary Fish was the publication of the *Register of the Department of State*, which contained a listing of all officials and employees of the Department, both at home and abroad. It also listed the foreign legations and consulates in the United States and gave certain regulations of the Department which might be useful to the officers.[2] There had been previous listings of the officers of the Department of State and the diplomatic and consular officials abroad,[3] but Secretary Fish decided to make this an annual publication with more extensive and detailed information.

Secretary Fish was a stickler for accuracy and regularity, and one of his first orders imposed a stricter regime in the Department for all of its employees. Issued on October 20, 1869, under the title "Regulations of the Department of State," the order notified officers and employees that the regular hours of the Department were from 9:30 A.M. to 4:00 P.M., but longer if the business required it, and at least one clerk had to remain in each bureau until the mail for the day was signed by the Secretary. An accurate daily account must be kept of absences; clerks were not allowed to receive visitors or visit each other during office hours; no information of any sort regarding the business of the Department should be given out; smoking was taboo in the halls and parts of the building open to the public. The violation of any of these rules was to be regarded as sufficient cause for removal.[4]

Secretary Fish Reorganizes the Department

Of far greater importance was the reorganization of the Department which Secretary Fish effected in 1870. The Congress had become economy-minded and had reduced the number of clerks from forty-eight to thirty-one for the fiscal year beginning July 1, 1869. Secretary Fish in a note to Speaker James G. Blaine noted that this was more than one-third of the personnel and that with such a large reduction the business of the Department was seriously embarrassed.[5] On January 17, 1870, in a letter to N. P. Banks, chairman of the House Committee on Foreign Affairs, Secretary Fish urgently requested the appointment of a solicitor of claims for the Department of State and three additional clerks for indexing records and papers received by the Department. He pointed out that there was no comprehensive alphabetical index of the

Department's papers and that as a result the Department had to depend upon the memories of the more experienced employees for information regarding the contents of the archives. Much time was thus taken by the clerks in searching for papers wanted by the Secretary or Assistant Secretaries, which meant an equal amount of time spent in waiting for the papers.[6]

Some time afterward, Secretary Fish had a graphic illustration of the need to rely upon the memory of Assistant Secretary Hunter. The Dutch minister made a claim under a treaty of 1782 which apparently had not been abrogated. However, when Fish mentioned the matter to Hunter the latter was sure that it had been denounced. He thought that it was Secretary Adams who had denounced it but found that it was Secretary Monroe.[7]

Fish obtained his solicitor under the designation of Examiner of Claims by a Congressional resolution of May 27, 1870, but less than a month later, by the Act of June 22, 1870, the officer was placed under the Department of Justice and in the reorganization scheme he was listed under the heading of Law Bureau. The incumbent was E. Peshine Smith and his salary was $3,000 a year. No appropriation was made for the extra clerks, so that Fish worked out his reorganization on a basis of thirty-one officers.

The new organization plan distributed the business of the Department under nine bureaus, two agencies, a translator, and a telegraph operator— making a total of twenty-nine. Two clerks were unassigned and were under the direction of the Chief Clerk to be allocated for the general work of the Department. The Chief Clerk was also authorized to transfer a clerk from one bureau to another when the pressure of work demanded it. Inasmuch as the organization of the Department of State as established by Secretary Fish remained, with some changes, the basic arrangement for the next thirty-nine years, a brief summary of the arrangement is warranted.[8]

CHIEF CLERK'S BUREAU This bureau was given custody of the archives and rolls, the receipt and distribution of correspondence, and the indexing of the records. Under R. S. Chew, who still served as Chief Clerk at $2,200 a year, there were a senior index clerk, two index clerks, a Keeper of the Rolls, and an Assistant Keeper of the Rolls.

FIRST DIPLOMATIC BUREAU This bureau had jurisdiction over the diplomatic correspondence with eleven European countries: Austria, Belgium, Denmark, France, Great Britain, the Netherlands, North Germany, Portugal, Spain, Sweden and Norway, and Switzerland, also with China and Japan in the Far East. The Chief was Henry D. J. Pratt, who had entered the Department on November 1, 1851. The bureau was also under the superintendence of Assistant Secretary of State J. C. Bancroft Davis. Two clerks were assigned to this bureau.

SECOND DIPLOMATIC BUREAU This bureau had charge of correspondence with seventeen Latin American states: Argentina, Bolivia, Brazil, Chile, Colombia, Costa Rica, Ecuador, Guatemala, Haiti, Honduras, Mexico, Nicaragua, Paraguay, Peru, El Salvador, Venezuela, and Uruguay; also with Greece, Italy, Russia, Turkey, Egypt, the Barbary States, Liberia, and the Hawaiian Islands. Robert S. Chilton, who entered the Department on January 1, 1852, was Chief of the Second Diplomatic Bureau and it was under the superintendence of the Second Assistant Secretary of State, William Hunter. This bureau also had two clerks assigned to it.

FIRST CONSULAR BUREAU This bureau was charged with the correspondence with the consulates in those countries which were under the direction of the First Diplomatic Bureau. The Chief of the First Consular Bureau was Jasper Smith, who had entered the Department on April 1, 1861, and he was assisted by three clerks. Assistant Secretary Davis had general direction over this bureau.

SECOND CONSULAR BUREAU This bureau had jurisdiction over the same countries as the Second Diplomatic Bureau; its Chief was A. H. Clements, a relative newcomer who had entered the Department on December 1, 1866; two clerks assisted the Chief, and the Second Assistant Secretary, Mr. Hunter, had superintendence over it.

LAW BUREAU This agency was charged with the examination of all legal questions submitted by the Secretary or Assistant Secretaries, and its incumbent, Mr. E. Peshine Smith, known as the Examiner of Claims, was in reality under the jurisdiction of the Department of Justice.

BUREAU OF ACCOUNTS The Disbursement Clerk, George E. Baker, who entered the Department in 1861, was responsible for the custody and disbursement of the Department's appropriations and for the care of the building and property of the Department. Mr. Baker had no regular assistants but he had a certain responsibility for the watchmen and laborers.

THE STATISTICAL BUREAU Charles Payson, the Librarian, and his aid, a temporary clerk, both appointees of the Grant administration in June, 1870, took care of the books and pamphlets and prepared the reports on commercial relations.

TRANSLATIONS The Translator, Henry L. Thomas, was also a newcomer, having entered the Department on September 1, 1869. He made such translations as were requested by the Secretary, Assistant Secretaries, or Chief Clerk.

PARDONS AND COMMISSIONS This agency was responsible for the preparation of commissions and pardons and also applications for office and correspondence pertaining to these matters. The Chief was George Bartel, who had come into the Department on December 1, 1852. He had one assistant.

DOMESTIC RECORDS Edward Haywood, appointed November 1, 1861, the single clerk in this agency, was charged with taking care of correspondence with territorial officers and miscellaneous correspondence not connected with the diplomatic or consular service. The Assistant Secretary had general direction over this unit; there was no assistant.

PASSPORT BUREAU In charge of this bureau was Thomas C. Cox, the passport clerk, whose service in the Department began on January 1, 1856. His duties were to issue and record passports and to collect the internal revenue tax imposed upon them.

TELEGRAPH Thomas Morrison, the operator, sent and received such messages as were ordered by the Secretary and Assistant Secretaries. He was appointed on March 7, 1867.

A few slight changes were made during the next few years: for example, in 1873 the Bureau of Archives and Indexes was established with a chief and three clerks, thus relieving the Chief Clerk of all administrative work other than that of general supervision of the clerks and employees in the Department. R. S. Chew, who had been in the Department for thirty-eight years and was Chief Clerk for six years, retired just before the change was made. His salary had been raised to $2,500 just before his retirement. The new Chief Clerk, Sevellon A. Brown, had entered the Department on December 9, 1864, and was Mr. Chew's assistant at the time of his promotion. Perhaps it should be noted that in 1873 the Secretary's salary was raised from $8,000 to $10,000 and the salaries of the two Assistant Secretaries from $3,500 to $6,000. This increase was very short-lived because the Act of January 20, 1874, reduced the salaries to the previous level.[9] The chiefs of bureaus who formerly received $1,800 as fourth-class clerks now were paid $2,400. The Act of March 3, 1873,[10] which provided for these raises in salaries, also for the first time recognized six bureaus as legally established: Accounts, Indexes, and Archives, and the First and Second Diplomatic, and Consular Bureaus. The other bureaus—Statistical, Domestic Records, and Passport—were abolished. Duties regarding territories were transferred to the newly established Department of Interior. The principal changes occurring in the Department during Grant's second term were the appointment of John L. Cadwalader, an able New York lawyer in whom Fish had absolute confidence, as Assistant Secretary of State on June 17, 1874, when Bancroft Davis was named minister to Berlin; the establishment of the office of Third Assistant Secretary of State by the Act of June 20, 1874, with John A. Campbell so commissioned on February 24, 1875; and the appointment of a clerk of the top class (4) as private secretary to the Secretary of State.

In addition to reorganizing the Department in its administrative units, Secretary Fish issued a series of new rules and regulations to improve and speed up the procedure for making reports, preparing abstracts for the Secretary and Assistant Secretaries, opening the mail pouches, distributing correspondence and acknowledging dispatches and letters. A new system of recording the correspondence of the Department in a central set of index volumes for diplomatic, consular, and miscellaneous communications, incoming and outgoing, replaced the former procedure of indexing each volume of correspondence in the front of each book. Fish also had the vast number of miscellaneous papers classified and bound, and he saw to it that all dispatches were copied promptly. Discipline was strict but fairly administered, and Fish was highly respected by his subordinates for the excellent way in which he directed the Department. Bancroft Davis, who served under him, declared that Fish "had no superior as an executive officer. His great ability made itself felt in every room and at every desk." [11] Finally, by making promotions as far as possible upon a merit basis, Fish raised the morale of the Department and made it an effective instrument for formulating and carrying out the foreign policies of the nation.

Diplomatic Appointments

As was customary at the time—and the practice still exists to a lesser extent—the great majority of ministers representing the United States abroad were changed by the Grant administrations. In spite of Grant's opposition to the spoils system and the efforts of Fish to support merit over political expediency, only five out of thirty-five diplomatic representatives were retained and of these only three were ministers plenipotentiary: the scholarly and brilliant George P. Marsh in Rome, the famous historian George Bancroft in Berlin, and General Alvin P. Hovey in Lima, Peru, whom Grant himself had commended for his services in the Vicksburg campaign. The only appointment which rather unexpectedly proved to be outstandingly good was that of Elihu B. Washburne to Paris. On the other hand, some of the appointments were incredibly bad. J. Russell Jones, who was appointed minister resident to Belgium, had as his qualifications the fact that he was the uncle of Grant's secretary and, according to Senator Oliver P. Morton, was "about the most elegant gentleman that ever presided over a livery stable." Grant's brother-in-law, M. J. Cramer, was named minister to Denmark. The notorious Daniel E. Sickles was sent to Madrid, where he played the role of the "Yankee King." The consul general sent to Alexandria, G. H. Butler, the nephew of Congressman Butler, was accused of drunkenness, brawling, engaging in a shooting affray, and purchasing some dancing girls.[12]

The appointment of the historian John Lothrop Motley as minister to Great Britain came largely as a result of his close relations with Senator Sumner, who as chairman of the Foreign Relations Committee of the Senate wanted him in London to carry out certain ideas in connection with forthcoming negotiations with Great Britain over reparations for the damage caused by the *Alabama* and other Confederate cruisers built in Great Britain. Former Minister Charles Francis Adams remarked that apparently Motley expected to represent two persons abroad, Mr. Sumner and the United States government. On his first interview with Lord Clarendon, Motley violated his instructions by taking a much stronger position than Fish had indicated. Grant wanted to recall him forthwith, but Fish felt that it would antagonize Sumner and make it more difficult to carry out the administration's policy. Grant let Fish have his way and Motley got off with a mild reprimand. However, Fish decided to carry on the negotiations with Great Britain in Washington rather than in London—a greater blow to Motley's pride than the note of censure.[13]

Just a year later, President Grant, smarting under the failure of the Senate to approve his treaty for the annexation of Santo Domingo and Sumner's strong opposition to it, demanded that Fish recall Motley immediately. Fish protested in vain and even contemplated resignation from the cabinet. Fish, on his own initiative, wrote Motley a friendly letter requesting his resignation, instead of recalling him as the President asked. Motley then complicated the situation by refusing to resign on the ground that he would thereby be conceding that his conduct was blameworthy. There was only one solution left—to recall Motley—which the Department did in November, an indignity, according to Motley, to which no public minister of the United States had ever before been subjected.[14]

Strangely enough, President Grant had the greatest difficulty in finding a suitable candidate to replace Motley. He nominated Senator Frederick Freylinghuysen, then learned that he would not accept. Fish had opposed this appointment from the beginning. Many other names were considered, including James G. Blaine and Andrew D. White. Finally it was decided to appoint Senator Oliver P. Martin, and his commission was issued under date of September 23, 1869. However, domestic political reasons finally caused him to withdraw his acceptance. The situation became so ridiculous that one of the newspapers suggested that the government advertise for a minister, stating his qualifications and particularly requiring that he must not part his hair in the middle or write books.[15] Grant finally picked an old friend from Ohio, General Robert C. Schenck, who was equally at home in war, diplomacy, and draw poker.

It will be remembered that in 1866, while Seward was Secretary of State, the Department had been moved temporarily into the newly constructed

Washington Orphan Asylum. An Act of March 3, 1871, authorized the construction of a building to house the Departments of State, War, and Navy. The result was a huge hideous building of solid granite which was to house the Department, at least in part, until 1947. The south wing was the first to be completed and in July, 1875, the Department of State moved in. Unfortunately, since the Department did not need the entire wing, some of its space was given to the Navy and War Departments, which continued to hold them long after the Department needed the space very badly. The entire building was not completed until January 31, 1888, and at the time, with its ten acres of floor space and almost a mile and three-quarters of corridors, it was regarded as one of the finest office buildings in the world.

Diplomatic Problems

The first diplomatic problem which faced Fish was the annexation of Santo Domingo, which President Grant had set his heart upon. The Navy looked with covetous eyes upon the magnificent Bay of Samaná, and Grant could appreciate its interest.[16] Fish was cold to the idea but was clever enough to realize that if Grant spent his efforts in this direction, Fish would have a much freer hand in dealing with the more important claims against Great Britain.

Both Great Britain and the United States wanted to make a settlement in regard to the *Alabama* claims, but the Department of State was handicapped by the fact that Senator Sumner, who was chairman of the Foreign Relations Committee, wanted to use the controversy as a fulcrum to pry Canada loose from the British Empire. In a speech delivered before the Senate on April 13, 1869, blasting the Johnson-Clarendon Treaty for the settlement of claims on both sides, Sumner built up the fantastic amount of damages, direct and indirect, which he felt Great Britain owed to us, to over $2,000,000,000. The repercussions of the speech on both sides of the ocean made the road to a diplomatic settlement temporarily impassable.

Secretary Fish was less aggressive in his views than was President Grant and felt that if Great Britain would express regret for the escape and depredations of the Confederate cruisers—"hell hounds," according to Sumner—and would agree to principles of international law which would prevent such occurrences in the future, the two governments would then be in a position where the problem of claims would not be incapable of a satisfactory solution. To get action, he persuaded Grant to take a rather pessimistic stand in his annual message of December 5, 1870. The British were impressed and in the following spring a joint high commission in Washington worked out a comprehensive

Old State Building 1875–1948
Seventeenth Street and Pennsylvania Avenue

treaty which settled all outstanding disputes between Great Britain and the United States.

Secretary Fish headed the American group and showed both tact and wisdom by refusing the chairmanship in order to keep the negotiations as informal as possible. Fish and de Grey did much work in private and could usually find a basis of compromise—even upon the principles of maritime neutrality, which Fish insisted were the foundation of the American claims. The treaty was signed at the Department of State with most of the clerks present to witness the signatures. Fish brought his task to a brilliant conclusion by insisting that the American arbitrator to fix the amount of claims should be Charles Francis Adams, and although Grant opposed for some time, Fish finally gained his point.

Secretary Fish felt that he had worked so unceasingly and withal so successfully in bringing about the Treaty of Washington that, considering his age and strength, he was justified in resigning from the Department, but the protests of President Grant and his colleagues were so vehement that he agreed to remain.

Diplomatic Personnel Difficulties

Few Secretaries of State have had as much trouble with diplomatic misfits, both at home and abroad, as Secretary Fish. The Russian minister to Washington, Count Constantin Catacazy, caused a series of unpleasant incidents for the Secretary. One of the many fraudulent claims of the day was the Perkins claim against Russia for the purchase of arms. Fish did not support the claim but he objected to Catacazy's procedure in attacking the claim by personally signed articles in the public press. Subsequently it was alleged that Catacazy prepared two forged letters, one censuring his own stand and the other his reply attacking Grant and Fish, in a most violent fashion. When Catacazy interfered in the work of the Anglo-American High Commission and wrote a series of anonymous articles attacking the President, Fish informed the United States minister to Russia that Catacazy had become *persona non grata*.

We have already noted the controversy over instructions between Fish and Motley which led to the latter's recall. His successor General Robert C. Schenck proved to be an even more unfortunate appointment. Schenck was unwise enough to lend his name for a consideration to a fake mining promotion scheme which caused huge losses to British investors. Inasmuch as Schenck had made an excellent showing as a diplomat and had withdrawn from the venture as soon as the question of his position was raised, he was not immediately recalled. However, when several years later a house investigation committee reported the sordid details, Schenck resigned in disgrace.[17] When we add to these the irascible Sickles in Madrid, the irresponsible Jones in Belgium, the garrulous Jay in Vienna, the obstreperous Charles Washburn in Paraguay, and the violent paranoiac Rumsey Wing in Ecuador, it is easy to understand that Fish finally revolted against President Grant's appointments to positions for which the Department of State was responsible. When finally Grant proposed to appoint as minister to Moscow General M. C. Meigs on the ground that he was ill equipped for his duties as quartermaster general, Fish protested vigorously. He knew that Meigs had done a superlative job as quartermaster general during the Civil War and that his transfer was purely to give a better position to a crony of Grant's and his secretary, General Babcock. His letter to Grant did not mince words:

Pardon me, my dear General, should I seem a little sensitive in respect to having one who is held to be unfit to discharge the duties of a Bureau in the War Department held as competent to discharge the most important diplomatic duties under the Department of State.[18]

When subsequently Grant proposed to transfer Jones, "who never sent the State Department anything but press clippings," from Belgium to Russia, and Read, "a selfish climber," from Greece to Belgium, and Bowman, a farmer friend of Secretary of War Belknap's, as minister to Ecuador, Fish decided to send in his resignation. President Grant was considerably disturbed and after a frank discussion agreed that henceforth outside influence would not be permitted to interfere with matters under the jurisdiction of the Department of State. Fish thereupon withdrew his resignation.[19]

Thereafter Fish was able to raise the standard of diplomatic appointments to a much higher level. He persuaded Grant to appoint the outstanding authority on international law, Richard Henry Dana, Jr., as minister to Great Britain; and when through jealous intrigues the Senate refused confirmation, Fish supported Attorney General Pierrepont for the position. In Russia, with the appointment of the well known playwright and poet George H. Boker as minister and the retention of the able and experienced Eugene Schuyler as secretary of legation, the United States had a remarkably able combination. Boker had made an excellent record as minister to Turkey where he had served for the four years preceding his appointment to St. Petersburg. When Benjamin A. Avery, the United States minister to China, died in 1875, Fish recommended George F. Seward to Grant. The President demurred on the ground that he didn't like the family, but he finally came around to Fish's point of view and early in 1876 appointed Seward minister to China. It proved to be an admirable appointment. Another outstandingly able diplomat, John W. Foster, had been named as minister to Mexico. At Madrid, Caleb Cushing remained as minister and his secretary of legation was Alvey A. Adee. With E. B. Washburne remaining in

France and Bancroft Davis in Germany, Fish could rightly feel that the United States was represented abroad by a group of diplomats ably qualified both to protect its interests and to enhance its prestige.

As Grant's second term drew to a close, Fish was approaching his seventieth year and was more than willing to hand over the portfolio of Secretary of State. His work had been so satisfactory to the President that when Bayard Taylor later declared to Grant that the three greatest statesmen of the age were Cavour, Gorchakov, and Bismarck, Grant insisted upon adding Fish as fourth. Grant further showed his appreciation of Fish by writing a letter urging the nomination of Fish as an excellent nominee for President for the Republican party in case of a deadlock at the Republican Convention.[20] Although assuming the office as a temporary duty, Fish held it during Grant's two terms, and throughout this most difficult period of reconstruction he carried out a consistent and successful foreign policy. Grant always gave the most careful consideration to his opinion and often deferred to him against his own judgment. In the matter of internal organization of the Department, Fish ranks near, if not at, the top. His reorganizational policies were sound and based upon the needs of the Department, and they proved remarkably effective. At the request of President Rutherford B. Hayes, Fish stayed on for a few days after the inauguration to give such advice and assistance as he could to the new administration. He retired on March 12, 1877, with the Department running smoothly and efficiently.

William M. Evarts—Secretary of State

Although Rutherford B. Hayes was not informed of his election as President of the United States until March 2, 1877, he had already prepared a tentative list of cabinet members some months before, and he had noted in his diary under the date of January 17, 1877: "My thoughts rest on Evarts for the first place." [21] There were many excellent reasons for the choice. William M. Evarts was not only one of the most brilliant legal minds of the day, but his work at Geneva in the *Alabama* claims arbitration had given him an outstanding international reputation. But even before this, Evarts had achieved considerable renown for his diplomatic services during the Civil War as a special agent for the Department of State in London and Paris. As to his standing as an international lawyer, John Bassett Moore, writing of the brief presented by Evarts in behalf of the condemned cargo of the British vessel *Springbok*, declared:

It has never been my good fortune to read a better argument in a prize case and I do not ever expect to see a better one. . . . No one but a great lawyer with a profound appreciation of the principles of international law could have made such an argument.[22]

The fact that Evarts presented Hayes's case successfully before the electoral commission may have been the deciding factor, as was alleged by some of Tilden's friends.

In spite of Evarts's high standing, his nomination was opposed strongly by certain outstanding senators, particularly Cameron, Conkling, and Blaine, on narrow political grounds. But when the vote was counted on March 10, 1877, only two votes were cast against Evarts. He himself was not sure that he should have accepted and he wrote his friend Edward Pierrepont, American minister to Great Britain: "I would gladly have seen someone else take the place but there seemed to be no one obvious for it and it might have been critical for me to decline it." [23]

Departmental Personnel

William M. Evarts entered upon his work on March 12, 1877. Although he was not hounded by office seekers to the same extent as Fish, he found it very difficult to follow, in his appointments to office, the civil service regulations that Secretary of Interior Carl Schurz had formulated and which he himself had approved. The demand for positions in the foreign service was particularly insistent: it was estimated that for one vacancy in the consular service there were more than seven thousand applications. It is said that he proposed to carve on the outside of his office door: "Come ye disconsulate," and on the inside: "Abandon hope all ye who enter here." He finally issued a statement to the effect that all desirable consulates would be filled by promotion on a strictly merit basis, and some fifty-four promotions were made within the year.[24] Evarts was particularly interested in the expansion of foreign trade and he attempted to increase American commerce abroad by sending consuls with business experience. In order that businessmen at home and abroad might utilize the commercial reports of the consuls more advantageously and that the consuls might prepare more useful reports, Evarts instituted an elaborate inquiry to the consular corps in Latin America and Europe as to wages, cost of living, and general trade conditions. One result was the publication in 1879 of a volume entitled *Labor in Europe*. A second and even more important result was the beginning of the publication of special consular reports every month in addition to the annual volume of *Foreign Relations*. On the other hand, although Evarts tried to raise the salaries of the diplomatic service and favored a career service with promotions based upon merit, he was not successful, and our representatives abroad were on the whole less able than those who served under Fish.

Evarts, unlike Fish, was not interested in the routine of the Department. In fact he was often criticized for his tardiness in answering important dispatches and notes and for his delays in issuing instructions. Evarts once remarked to Andrew D. White: "There are just two rules at the State Department: one, that no business is ever done out of business hours; and the other is that no business is done *in* business hours." [25] And on another occasion, when President Hayes called his attention to his dilatory methods, Evarts countered, "You don't sufficiently realize the great truth that almost any question will settle itself if you only leave it alone long enough." Fortunately, Fish left the Department very well organized and Evarts made practically no changes in the personnel. The Assistant Secretary, John L. Cadwalader, was a personal friend of Fish's and had no desire to remain as Assistant Secretary under Evarts, his junior in the practice of law. In his place Evarts named the able and experienced Frederick W. Seward, who had served under his father so creditably for eight years in a similar capacity. Unfortunately, in 1879, Seward's health was such that he was forced to resign. However, his successor, John Hay, proved equally able; and on the many occasions when Secretary Evarts was absent, both Seward and Hay filled the position of Acting Secretary most satisfactorily. In the place of John A. Campbell, the Third Assistant Secretary, Evarts chose Charles Payson of New York, Chief of the Diplomatic Bureau, who had been in the Department some seven years. The able veteran William Hunter remained as Second Assistant Secretary, and familiar as he was with every phase of departmental work, the administration of the Department ran very smoothly. One notable addition to the personnel of the Department during the Evarts regime was Alvey A. Adee, who came into the Department in 1877 after seven years' experience as secretary and chargé d'affaires ad interim at the United States legation at Madrid. Adee entered as a clerk of the fourth (top) class but the following year he was appointed Chief of the Diplomatic Bureau. Sevellon A. Brown, who entered the Department in 1864, remained as Chief Clerk. Arthur B. Wood, with ten years' experience in the Department, was retained as Chief of the Consular Bureau, and John H. Haswell, who had been with the Department twelve years, remained as Chief of the Bureau of Indexes and Archives.

In one respect, at least, Evarts established a high reputation for the Department of State—it was "magnificently hospitable." The Evarts liked to entertain and the Secretary was at his best at the dinner table. He was an excellent raconteur and exceedingly apt at repartee. When asked at a diplomatic dinner if drinking so many different wines didn't make him feel seedy the next day, he replied that it was the indifferent wines that produced that result. He rented a fine house at 1507 K Street, where he did most of his entertaining, and when it was not large enough he rented more adequate quarters. Although a believer in diplomatic protocol, he did not follow it slavishly and on one occasion wore a frock coat instead of a dress suit at a White House New Year reception. Evarts liked diplomacy and was adept at it, but he seemed to prefer the form to the content.

Few matters of considerable importance faced Evarts in conducting the foreign policy of the United States. Perhaps his outstanding achievement was his adroit handling of the Chinese immigration problem in such a way as to retain the friendship of the Chinese while at the same time revising the Burlingame Treaty of 1868, which permitted almost unrestricted immigration of Chinese coolies. Both President Hayes and Secretary Evarts felt very strongly that the attempt of Congress to abrogate the treaty by nullifying parts of it was unfair and unnecessary, and it was Evarts who wrote the veto message delivered by Hayes. His next step was to get rid of Minister George F. Seward, who had consistently opposed his policies on China. He then sent a special mission to China headed by President James B. Angell of the University of Michigan. The mission was successful and the new arrangement permitted the United States to "regulate, limit, or suspend the immigration of Chinese laborers."

One of Evarts's last proposals as Secretary of State concerned administration. In a note to President Hayes dated February 18, 1881, Evarts suggested:

If instead of the present rigid definition by law of the number and grade of compensation of the clerks allowed to be employed by the Department of State, there was left to the Secretary of State some discretion in the matter of salaries, the change would be of very decided advantage to the efficiency of its internal service. A certain amount of clerical work of a character involving merely ordinary capacity of manual aptitude might be compensated at a rate even lower than that now paid as fixed by law, and the money thus saved could be used in securing the services of persons of intellectual capacity and education to assist in the more important work, such as the preparation of correspondence and reports which require a degree of ability and attainments for which the ordinary pay of clerkships offers no adequate remuneration.[26]

Although it has been said that in Evarts the lawyer dominated the statesman, in the case of Chinese immigration it was the statesman that prevailed. He had tackled a thorny problem and had solved it quickly and effectively and in such a way that both nations appreciated that justice was the basis of the settlement. It epitomized Evarts's career as Secretary of State—diplomacy based upon equity and mutual consideration.

JAMES G. BLAINE

14

James G. Blaine and Frederick T. Frelinghuysen

James G. Blaine—Secretary of State

When on March 7, 1881, William M. Evarts turned over his portfolio as Secretary of State to James G. Blaine, the Department of State was a well organized efficient administrative unit. Most of the personnel were men of considerable experience in the Department who had secured promotion on the basis of merit. The three Assistant Secretaries of State, John Hay, William Hunter, and Charles Payson, were officers of exceptional ability who had been well trained in their work. The Chief Clerk, Sevellon Brown, had been in the Department for seventeen years and his supervision of the personnel and business of the Department was highly satisfactory. Alvey A. Adee as Chief of the Diplomatic Bureau had a fine background of experience abroad and was a man of superlative ability. Arthur B. Wood, the Chief of the Consular Bureau, and John H. Haswell, Chief of the Bureau of Indexes and Archives, had both arrived at their positions through merit after many years of service. In addition to the Chief of the Bureau of Statistics and the Translator, we find an experienced corps of clerks: twelve in the highest, or fourth, class at $1,800 a year; three in the third class at $1,600; two in the second class at $1,400; and nine in the first class at $1,200, among whom was one woman, Mary Markoe. Of the ten clerks of the $900 and $1,000 classes, three were women.[1] The personnel officers and clerks of the Department now numbered fifty.[2]

Inasmuch as the appointment of Blaine by President Garfield was based entirely upon personal and political reasons and Blaine himself was steeped in politics, some changes in the upper brackets of the Department could be expected. John Hay could hardly wait to be delivered from the "heats of Washington"; and although President Garfield urged him both directly and indirectly to serve as his private secretary with practically the status of a member of the cabinet, Hay courteously but firmly refused. He did remain

155

at his post [3] until May 4, 1881, when he was succeeded by Robert R. Hitt, who had spent the preceding seven years as secretary at the American legation in Paris. Assistant Secretary Hitt was to remain less than a year in the Department; elected to Congress the following year, he became chairman of the Committee of Foreign Affairs of the House and proved himself most useful to subsequent Secretaries of State. Upon Hitt's retirement, J. C. B. Davis, who had had service previously in the Department and with several claims commissions, was named. A less satisfactory appointment was that of Walker Blaine, the son of the Secretary, to the post of Third Assistant Secretary in place of the experienced Charles Payson. Mrs. Blaine, however, writes in one of her letters: "You cannot think how much praise has been showered on Walker for his urbanity and efficiency these last days. Mr. Lamar [United States Senator from Mississippi] says no such young man has been in Washington." [4] However, with William Hunter remaining as Second Assistant Secretary, the Department could carry on its duties with a minimum of lost motion or friction.

From the standpoint of either diplomatic or legal training or experience, Blaine was a complete novice, but his political background could hardly be surpassed. In the political arena for over a quarter of a century, he had been congressman, senator, and a candidate for the Presidency. "He was a gladiator in debate and a spell binder on the hustings," but such capabilities were hardly those necessary to aid the President in the formulation and direction of foreign policy. But Garfield could not overlook the fact that it was the two hundred and fifty Blaine delegates that swung to him at the Chicago convention that had made his nomination possible. Blaine's letter of acceptance of a place in the cabinet is effusive and at the same time self-laudatory almost to the point of incoherence:

Your generous invitation to enter your Cabinet as Secretary of State has been under consideration for more than three weeks. The thought had never once occurred to my mind until you presented it with such cogent arguments in its favor. . . . Your administration must be made brilliantly successful. . . . To that most desirable consummation I feel that next to yourself I can contribute more influence than any other man. . . . It is this fact which has led me to the momentous conclusion embodied in this letter—for however much I might admire you as a statesman, I would not enter your Cabinet if I did not believe in you as a man and love you as a friend. [5]

Many reasons were given at the time for Blaine's acceptance of the position. One of his contemporary biographers, T. C. Crawford, thought that Blaine expected to direct the national administration from his new position.

Another biographer, Edward Stanwood, thought Blaine wished to make the United States supreme politically and commercially in the Western Hemisphere. Garfield suggested that after Blaine's long service in Congress it would be a rest for him. Mrs. Blaine wrote her son Walker as regards the Secretaryship, "Socially, you know, it is about the best position." [6] Congressman Perry Belmont, Blaine's political opponent, relates that when Blaine was offered the appointment he thought the purpose was to "shelve him" and that his political friends urged him to remain in the Senate where he had a better chance for the Presidency.[7] Unquestionably the motives were mixed, but evaluating in retrospect it would appear as though Blaine wanted the position of Secretary of State primarily to introduce a new and dynamic foreign policy in the Western World. He was determined "to bring about peace and prevent future wars in North and South America; to cultivate such friendly commercial relations with all American countries as would lead to a large increase in the export trade of the United States." [8]

Blaine's Latin American Policy

Unfortunately the untimely death of President Garfield by the bullet of an assassin prevented Blaine from accomplishing his plan for hemispheric solidarity. However, considering that his incumbency was just a little over nine months, Blaine's accomplishments were very substantial from the standpoint of the initiation of positive policies. His greatest achievement, although seemingly a failure at the time, was his effort to bring representatives of the nations of the Americas together in a conference to work out a program of mutual cooperation looking toward the maintenance of peace in the Western Hemisphere. Henry Clay had urged a league of freedom for the Americas in 1820 and Bolívar had called a conference for similar purposes to meet in Panama in 1826, but Blaine deserves credit as the sire of the international conferences of the American states which have become such an important factor for the maintenance of peace and security in the Western Hemisphere. Unfortunately his initial attempt was made only three weeks before his resignation; and although President Arthur had originally endorsed the invitations, he reconsidered the matter and finally instructed Secretary of State Frelinghuysen to withdraw the invitations. Blaine was incensed at this inexcusable change of policy and wrote a public letter of protest. Mrs. Blaine, writing to her son on February 2, 1882, bitterly assails the new Secretary:

Undoubtedly the State Department intended the life of your Father which they expected to take with all due regard for the *convenances*. . . . They revoked his instructions though they were Arthur's as well; they kept back his papers, they sent to Congress garbled despatches of Trescot's; they permitted private letters of Christiancy to be sent to Congress.

Mrs. Blaine was certain that her husband would be vindicated and her prophecy was correct, for in less than a decade Blaine had the honor of convening the first international conference of the American states.

Blaine's keen interest in the problem of Latin America was based upon reasons of security as well as prosperity. For this reason he felt very strongly that any isthmian canal should be under the protection of the United States. When Colombia intimated that European powers might be invited to guarantee the Panama Canal which De Lesseps proposed to build, Blaine dispatched one of his strongest instructions to our minister to England, protesting any such action. Since he omitted to mention the Clayton-Bulwer Treaty, the British foreign minister, after a delay of five months, informed Blaine very succinctly that all guarantees of the canal had been settled by the Clayton-Bulwer Treaty of 1850, which was still in force.

Under these circumstances, Blaine decided to get rid of the Clayton-Bulwer Treaty. He gave many good reasons proving the treaty obsolete according to the international law principle of *rebus sic stantibus* and that therefore the United States was no longer bound by it. Lord Granville quickly exposed the weakness of Secretary Blaine's arguments by pointing out that the British possessions in North America had also shown considerable development and the statesmen parties to the treaty had certainly envisaged certain changes of condition. Although Blaine was unsuccessful, he presented the attitude of the United States on the subject in a moderate, dignified, and courteous manner. His approach was anything but jingoistic, and its correctness was proved by the Hay-Pauncefote Treaty of 1901, which followed along exactly the same lines proposed by Blaine twenty years earlier.

With the advent of Vice President Arthur as President upon the death of Garfield on September 19, 1881, it was not expected that Garfield's cabinet would be retained. Arthur was a member of the so-called Stalwart faction of the Republican party, which favored a third term for General Grant. Blaine had been a constant and bitter opponent of this faction and he could hope for no mercy from them. As Blaine's successor, President Arthur named Frederick T. Frelinghuysen of New Jersey. He was commissioned on December 12, 1881, and entered upon his duties a week later. For the first time in twenty-three years Blaine held no political position nor did he have a profession or a business, yet according to Mrs. Blaine he was never happier and had no intention of "going down under the preconcerted attack on the part of the State Department and its friends." [9]

Blaine's influence on the Department of State as an organization was small—it could hardly be otherwise in the brief period that he served—but his influence on American foreign policy was remarkable. He was in perfect accord with President Garfield and he had a free hand to carry out his ideas of Pan American unity and cooperation. He frightened the conservatives with his vigorous and impetuous procedure—his Pan Americanism was "magnificent but it was inconvenient"—he was at times undiplomatic in his correspondence with the British; he was almost jingoistic in his opposition to Chinese immigration. Nevertheless, Blaine mapped out a positive foreign policy, and although he was ahead of his times, the precedent was set and his successors profited thereby.

Frederick T. Frelinghuysen—Secretary of State

President Arthur was not personally antipathetic to Blaine, but political reasons required his resignation. Frederick T. Frelinghuysen, the new Secretary of State, was wholly unfamiliar with the field of foreign affairs. His closest approach to diplomatic experience came when President Grant named him as minister to Great Britain, but he refused the appointment because he wished his children to be reared in an American atmosphere. Frelinghuysen was a conservative lawyer and had represented New Jersey in the Senate of the United States for nine years. He inspired confidence and could be depended upon to consider any diplomatic problem objectively and then to act deliberately. Since Chester A. Arthur had been chosen as are most Vice Presidents, without any expectation of his assuming the Presidency, Frelinghuysen as Secretary of State inspired more confidence than did Arthur as President.

Frelinghuysen was fortunate in finding the State Department well manned with an experienced personnel which he was wise enough to retain intact whenever it was possible. In place of the able but inexperienced Robert R. Hitt, there was named as Assistant Secretary of State J. C. Bancroft Davis, who had acted twice previously as Assistant Secretary. He had served with great distinction as agent of the United States in the *Alabama* claims arbitration and subsequently he succeeded his uncle, George Bancroft, as minister to Germany. When he retired as Assistant Secretary on July 7, 1882, John Davis was appointed. Davis had first entered the Department as clerk in 1870 and had later served as private secretary to Secretary of State Hamilton Fish. At the time of his appointment as First Assistant Secretary he was acting as assistant counsel before the French and American Claims Commission, and more to the point, was married to Sally Frelinghuysen, the daughter of the Secretary. William Hunter was entering his fifty-third year of service in the Department and his twelfth as an Assistant Secretary of State. But the most important appointment of all was that of Alvey A. Adee [10] as Third Assistant Secretary after four years as head of the Diplomatic Bureau. He was to continue as an Assistant Secretary for the next forty-two years and to make a record of achievement that has never been equaled in the annals of the Department.

Alvey A. Adee was a natural genius who was fortunate enough to find the perfect environment for the utilization of his talents. Although he never went to school or college, he was a linguist and a great Shakespearean scholar. He was fond of mathematics and started to become an engineer. Almost by chance he became private secretary to the colorful but notorious General Sickles when he went to Spain as American minister. On four different occasions Adee served as chargé d'affaires in Madrid and it was he who, noting the difficulties involved in extraditing notorious criminals—he had been successful in the case of Boss Tweed—suggested the model extradition convention of 1877. When Adee returned from Spain, Secretary Evarts, appreciating his value to the Department, offered him a temporary position to draft state papers. Within a year he had been named head of the Diplomatic Bureau and four years later, on July 18, 1882, Secretary Frelinghuysen promoted him to be Third Assistant Secretary of State to take the position vacated by Walker Blaine.

Sevellon A. Brown, the Chief Clerk in 1882, added the title of Superintendent of the State Department Building to his name and $250 additional to his salary—making it now $2,750. The rest of the organization remained approximately the same except that the Librarian, Theodore F. Dwight, was now made Chief of the Bureau of Rolls and Library at a salary of $3,100, equal to that of the other bureau chiefs instead of his clerk's salary of $1,800.

The State Department library grew out of a Congressional resolution of September 23, 1789, and Jefferson determined the character of the collection. It included the statutes of the states and territories of the United States; laws of foreign states; general and special works in history, biography, geography, political science, political economy, language, statistics; government documents germane to its field, reference works, and periodicals. According to a system adopted upon the library's reorganization in 1875, books not of particular use to the Department but which came to it as gifts were transferred to the Library of Congress or to other departments. As of the year 1882, the library contained about 18,000 works.

The bureaus now numbered seven: Diplomatic, Consular, Indexes and Archives, Accounts, Rolls and Library, Statistics, and Law. Translations, pardons and commissions, and passports were not yet raised to bureau status, although the Translator received the same salary as the bureau chiefs. The total personnel of the Department as of August 15, 1882, was 61 officers and clerks and 35 other employees, such as a packer, a lithographer, engineers, firemen, "a conductor for elevator," messengers, watchmen, and laborers.[11]

Diplomatic Appointments

The President, rather than the Secretary of State, usually makes important diplomatic appointments in practice as well as in theory. Although Chester A. Arthur was regarded as a New York spoilsman, his was an instance when the office dignified the man. He gave Frelinghuysen a free hand in keeping the spoils system out of the State Department and he was equally averse to its utilization in making appointments of Americans to represent the United States abroad. The death of President Garfield at the hands of a disappointed office seeker had strengthened the demand for civil-service reform, and the Pendleton Act, "the Magna Charta of Civil Service Reform," passed in 1883 with the strong support of the President. However, diplomatic posts abroad have always been regarded as the choice prizes for the victorious party's political bigwigs and the question of training, experience, or even merit has too seldom been given consideration in the making of such appointments.

President Arthur, although not able to resist the spoilsmen completely, made a record of appointments in the foreign service which was highly creditable. The Court of Saint James's is the top position in the American diplomatic service and the most urgently sought. Arthur resisted all efforts to have the minister to Great Britain, James Russell Lowell, removed and thereby endeared himself to men of letters on both sides of the Atlantic. He retained General "Lew" Wallace, the author of *The Fair God* and *Ben Hur*, as minister to Turkey. He also kept in office career diplomatic officers, such as Eugene Schuyler in Rumania, and W. L. Scruggs in Colombia. The eminent financier and Wall Street banker, Levi P. Morton, who had been appointed minister to France by President Garfield, was also retained. Where positions were open, the appointments made were not outstanding. The millionaire William Waldorf Astor was named minister to Rome to fill the post made vacant through the death of that unique character, George P. Marsh, who had represented the United States so ably at that same post for more than twenty years; A. A. Sargent was sent to Berlin and became *persona non grata* because of his overzealous efforts to protect the American pig. It could hardly be claimed that Alphonso Taft, although he had served successfully both as Secretary of War and Attorney General, was well equipped for the ministership to Austria-Hungary. The appointment of Secretary of the Navy William H. Hunt as minister to Russia was regarded by Hunt as a dismissal from office because of his refusal to support congressional abuse of Navy funds. He was offered his choice of Austria or Russia and took the latter solely because it paid $17,000 as against $12,000.[12] The appointment of John Russell Young, the journalist, to China at the request of former President Grant, turned out to be a very happy choice. Young, who was a friend of Li Hung-chang's, was very successful in his new post, particularly in the settlement of American claims.

Dubious Diplomacy

Frelinghuysen's policy as Secretary of State consisted for the most part in reversing the policies of Secretary Blaine. His instructions to the able diplomat William H. Trescot regarding the War of the Pacific were almost incoherent in their apparent contradictions. Apparently the United States was willing to use its good offices but wished to assume no responsibilities, and although we thought Chilean demands exorbitant we were very uncertain as to what we could do about it. The result was that the United States lost the good will and respect of both sides and failed utterly in preventing the seizure of Peruvian territory. The revocation of the invitation to the Latin American states to meet in a conference in Washington was another change in policy hardly conducive to enhancing the prestige of the United States.

Perhaps Frelinghuysen's greatest accomplishment was his courageous acceptance of the invitation to participate in the Berlin Conference of the Congo of 1884. The American representatives, assisted by Explorer Henry M. Stanley, helped materially in securing the acceptance of such principles as the abolition of the slave trade and the neutralization of the area in time of war and freedom of trade and intercourse. Although Frelinghuysen was criticized for having violated the Monroe Doctrine and the United States never ratified the Act, the participation of the United States was a step forward in its slow assumption of international responsibilities. Professor Samuel Flagg Bemis aptly suggests that Frelinghuysen's proposal that the Congo Basin be neutralized and "held in trust for the benefit of all peoples" was "the germ of the idea of international mandate for backward areas." [13]

Under the direction of Frelinghuysen the Department of State followed a policy of meeting problems as they arose and avoiding as much as possible those which might make trouble. It was a negative policy of drifting with the current with the navigation limited to steering clear of diplomatic shoals. According to some, Frelinghuysen had metamorphosed the glorious American eagle into an innocent and timid dove, while others said he looked upon it "as a mere hen—past middle age." [14] Fortunately, no serious problems faced the Department and routine matters were well attended. The social activities of the Department were carried on in a tasteful and dignified manner suitable to the traditions of the office. Frelinghuysen possessed the charm and bearing of a courtly diplomat of the courts of Europe. He was kindly to the staff and they held him in high respect. He was not a great Secretary of State, but rather "a Christian gentleman . . . who labored devotedly to serve what he believed to be the highest interests of America and of all mankind." [15]

15

Thomas F. Bayard, James G. Blaine, and
John W. Foster

Thomas F. Bayard—Secretary of State

When the Democratic party, after twenty-five years in the wilderness, elected Grover Cleveland as President in 1884, the partisan office seekers had visions of a feast after a famine. They completely overlooked Cleveland's famous slogan, "Public office is a public trust"—but they soon learned that he really meant it. He generally allowed neither friendship nor partisan politics to sway him toward making a bad appointment or to prevent him from making a good one. He wished to make his cabinet appointments early so that he might have the reaction of the public before their names were sent to the Senate for confirmation. In looking over the field of eminent Democrats whose advice would strengthen the administration, Thomas F. Bayard ranked among the foremost. He had served Delaware for sixteen years in the Senate of the United States, and on two occasions his name was seriously considered as a nominee of the Democratic party for the Presidency. Even before the new year began, Bayard's name was being discussed as a likely member of the new cabinet, either as Secretary of the Treasury or as Secretary of State. His friends favored the former but were insistent upon his acceptance regardless of the post. Bayard was not eager to leave the Senate and made no effort whatsoever to be considered for a cabinet position. Bayard's friends, Carl Schurz and Horace White, urged Cleveland to make Bayard his Secretary of the Treasury, but Cleveland had already decided upon Daniel Manning for the Treasury portfolio, and he preferred Bayard to take the first position in the cabinet.[1]

Changes in Departmental Personnel

Thomas F. Bayard found the Department of State well organized and functioning effectively. Since Cleveland quickly went on record as not only determined to enforce civil service but also to retain efficient employees regardless of party affiliation, Bayard was not under pressure to dismiss many State Department officers. The only change of the principal officers was the appointment of James D. Porter as Assistant Secretary of State in the place of John Davis, who had retired two weeks before the inauguration. This appointment is hard to justify with men like Hunter and Adee immediately available and superbly qualified for the position. However, the position of First Assistant Secretary, which paid a salary of $4,500 and carried great prestige, was still regarded as a political position. Porter had made a good record as Governor of Tennessee and later was to become renowned as an educator, but his two years as Assistant Secretary of State added nothing to his standing or to that of the Department. Upon Porter's retirement in 1887, George L. Rives of New York was commissioned as Assistant Secretary. Rives came of a diplomatic family—his grandfather had been minister to France and his mother was the granddaughter of the famous Thomas Barclay, British consul general in New York. Rives was that rare combination, a topflight corporation lawyer and an eminent scholar. He did much to improve the business methods of the Department and helped revise the consular regulations.

It was during Bayard's administration that the Department of State suffered an almost irreparable loss in the death of Second Assistant Secretary of State William Hunter after fifty-seven years in the Department. Entering as a clerk in 1829, he worked his way up by the merit route to become Chief of the Diplomatic Bureau, Claims Clerk, Chief Clerk, and on two different occasions ad interim Assistant Secretary of State. It was reported that when the office of Assistant Secretary of State was established in 1853, Hunter was offered the position but refused. However, when the office of Second Assistant Secretary was established in 1866, President Johnson named him as its first incumbent and he held it until his death. He was invaluable in answering questions of precedent and protocol and his encyclopedic memory was tapped constantly by successive Secretaries and their subordinates.

Bayard wisely promoted Alvey A. Adee to Hunter's position as Second Assistant Secretary, little realizing that Adee would make an even more remarkable record than his able predecessor. Bayard made another outstanding appointment when he named John Bassett Moore as Third Assistant Secretary of State. Although Moore was only twenty-six years of age and had been in the Department only a year, he quickly made himself the leading authority in the Department on all questions of international law. Another outstanding appointment of the greatest value to the Department was that of Francis Wharton as Solicitor or Examiner of Claims. Although the Law Bureau under the Department of Justice, with the Solicitor at its head, was not authorized by law until the Act of March 3, 1891, the term Solicitor appears in the *Register of the Department* of 1885 and a report of the Solicitor was made on April

30, 1887.[2] Wharton was a great authority on both criminal law and international law at the time of his appointment. Congress, appreciating the facility of Wharton in scholarly research and writing, authorized him to compile *A Digest of the International Law of the United States*. He completed this assignment in 1886 and the three-volume work, when published, enhanced his reputation both at home and abroad. He was next given the task of editing *The Revolutionary Correspondence of the United States*, which was published in six volumes in 1889. With Francis Wharton and John Bassett Moore in the Department at the same time, the United States could count upon notable legal support in any international law question which might arise.

One of the few flagrant violations of the promises of the Cleveland administration to maintain in office all employees who had given good service occurred in the case of Chief Clerk Sevellon A. Brown. Brown had first entered the Department in 1864 and was appointed Chief Clerk in 1873. After twenty-five years of satisfactory service in the Department, fifteen as Chief Clerk, of which the last three were under Bayard and Cleveland, he was asked to resign. Bayard said that it was Cleveland who requested the resignation.[3] Brown was out of service for about two years and was reappointed by Secretary Blaine.

Diplomatic Appointments

Whereas the personnel of the Department remained almost unchanged in the switch from a Republican to a Democratic administration, the situation was far different in the diplomatic and consular services. Thirty good Democrats, properly endorsed, applied for the position of minister to Belgium, and according to Bayard there were more than one hundred applications for the post of consul general in Paris.[4] These positions were regarded as political assets and served as a very acceptable currency to repay campaign debts. In the thirty-five diplomatic missions maintained by the United States abroad at this time, there was a clean sweep with a single exception—Minister Henry C. Hall, who was accredited to the Central American states. Well trained career diplomats such as John W. Foster, minister to Spain, and W. L. Scruggs, minister to Colombia; outstanding representatives with years of experience, such as Thomas O. Osborn in Argentina and John A. Bingham in Japan, all succumbed to the spoilsmen. Even the famous James Russell Lowell in London was not spared.

On the other hand many of the appointments were excellent from the standpoint of ability if not experience. The very important London post was bestowed upon Edward J. Phelps, a well trained lawyer, Kent professor of law at Yale, and onetime president of the American Bar Association. Realizing the need of an able legal mind to consider some of the questions involving the United States and Great Britain, Bayard persuaded Cleveland to make this appointment. Paris received Robert McLane, perhaps the best, or at least the most easily justified, of the Cleveland diplomatic appointments. McLane, son of the former United States minister to Great Britain, had gone to school in France as a boy, was a close friend of Lafayette's, was intimately familiar with French history and customs, and spoke the language fluently. He had served on two previous occasions in the diplomatic service, first as commissioner to China and later as minister to Mexico. The new minister to Germany, George H. Pendleton, although a "lame duck"—he had lost his Senate seat as a result of his ardent and successful advocacy of civil-service reforms—was a man of great ability. He had studied at Heidelberg and was familiar with Germany and its language. The appointment of Charles Denby to China proved to be most satisfactory—so much so that he continued to serve for thirteen consecutive years.

The most unfortunate political appointment—one that became a *cause célèbre* in all books on diplomatic practice—was the nomination of Anthony M. Keiley as minister to Italy. After Keiley was confirmed by the Senate and was on his way to his post, it was discovered that some fourteen years previously he had made a speech denouncing King Victor Emmanuel of Italy for the invasion of the Papal States. When this information reached the Italian government, the Italian minister immediately informed Secretary Bayard that Keiley was *persona non grata*. Keiley resigned and was thereupon named as minister to Austria-Hungary. Here again he was not wanted because of political reasons, but the principal excuse given was that as Keiley was married to a Jewess, his social position at the court of Vienna would be a most unsatisfactory one. The State Department could not accept this as a valid reason for refusing to receive an American representative and Bayard protested vigorously, declaring that the President felt that to object to our envoy on the sole ground that his wife was alleged to entertain a certain religious faith was a "doctrine so destructive of religious liberty and freedom of conscience, so devoid of catholicity and so opposed to the spirit of the age that it could not be accepted by the great family of civilized nations nor by the people of the United States." The Austrian government thereupon reverted to Keiley's want of political tact and refused to receive him. President Cleveland explained his position in his annual message and declared that no new nomination had been made.[5] The post remained in the hands of a chargé d'affaires for the next two years.

In the place of Lew Wallace at Constantinople, President Cleveland named a deserving Democrat, Samuel S. Cox, whose wife, in violation of regulations, insisted upon accepting the Grand Cordon of the Order of the Shejakat [6] at the hands of the sultan. Cox felt that if it should be returned it would upset his plans for establishing closer relations with Turkey. Secretary Bayard informed him that "husband and wife are one in law" and consequently neither could accept a gift from foreign officials without the consent of Congress. When President Cleveland refused the sultan's gift of two beautiful photograph albums for his fiancée Miss Folsom, the sultan withdrew the Grand Cordon from Mrs. Cox and this solved Bayard's problem.[7] The appointee to Colombia, Charles D. Jacob, who replaced the able and experienced W. L. Scruggs, was completely incompetent and lasted but six months. It was later discovered that he had abstracted some official correspondence from the archives of the legation and the Department was hard put to recover it.[8]

Relations with Britain and Germany

One of the first diplomatic problems facing the Department of State was the northeast fisheries question, which for more than half a century had been a disturbing factor in Anglo-American relations. The problem was complicated by the fact that while it was wholly Canadian, yet the British had to deal with it; also, in the United States both houses of Congress had begun separate inquiries and domestic politics were concerned with it. Bayard was fortunate in having men like Adee, Moore, and Wharton as his counselors in Washington and a very able lawyer in Minister Edward J. Phelps, representing the United States in London. President Cleveland was amenable to reason and a joint commission to study the whole matter seemed a reasonable solution. But the Senate was dominated by a Republican majority which was unwilling to allow a Democratic administration to strengthen itself by a successful adjustment and voted down the President's recommendations for a joint commission. It was finally decided that a mixed commission whose American members would be appointed by the President without consulting the Senate might be the solution, and Great Britain accepted the suggestion. The commission was appointed, met in Washington in the Department of State, and after thirty strenuous meetings signed a treaty. President Cleveland sent the fisheries treaty to the Senate on February 20, 1888, recommending its approval. Bayard had little hope, since the Senate Foreign Relations Committee had usually been uncooperative and obstructive. His fears were confirmed. A majority report condemned the treaty, and the Republican majority in the Senate voted against it on strict party lines. The careful work of the Department of State to settle this dispute, extending over many months, was nullified by a vote not on the merits of the treaty, but upon its value as a domestic political issue.[9]

Although both Cleveland and Bayard were anti-imperialists, both were insistent that American interests in all parts of the world be respected. Bayard was not a swashbuckler and always preferred to attempt friendly cooperation if possible and to avoid threats of retaliation. Compared with Bismarck's iron-fisted policy, Bayard exemplified the policy of the velvet glove. The two policies were to come into conflict in Samoa. The United States, by a treaty made in 1878, obtained most-favored-nation treatment in the islands and the right to establish a naval base at Pago Pago. When in 1884 Germany threatened to set up a regime equivalent to a German protectorate, Bayard protested and proposed a conference of the British and German ministers in Washington to work out an arrangement for the maintenance of Samoan autonomy with adequate protection. Bismarck now authorized the German authorities to establish a semiprotectorate by ousting the king and setting up a regime subservient to the Germans. American public opinion was aroused, the press attacked the State Department for not acting, and Congress requested all information on the subject. Apparently the State Department's characterization of German aggression as leading "to a want of harmonious action," was not emphatic enough to suit the country. Unfortunately the Germans and British refused to permit the publication of the Washington Conference protocols, which would have indicated the strong position taken by the Department.

When a revolution occurred in the islands against the German puppet king and Germany entered into a declared war against the revolutionists, Bayard suggested to the Secretary of the Navy that "a government vessel be sent to Samoa to protect American interests." The situation had become critical and Secretary of the Navy Whitney wanted to know what was the policy of the State Department. Senator Morgan of the Senate Committee on Foreign Relations sarcastically inquired whether the "Senate should indicate their view on the Samoan situation as a guide to the Executive or rather as a means of presenting a firm and solid front on these matters?" Bayard caustically replied: "My experiences of the last five years have made me hopeless of receiving even ordinary comity or courtesy much less firm and steady support from the Senate as that body is at present constituted and controlled." [10] The Department itself was divided as to policy and Assistant Secretary George L. Rives felt strongly that the United States should adopt sterner measures. When Congress appropriated $500,000 to protect American interests and $100,000 to develop a naval station at Pago Pago, the German government decided to take a more conciliatory attitude.

Bayard's policy of peace at almost any price had proved temporarily successful, but it might be questioned whether the stronger stand taken by the President and the Congress did not help considerably. Certainly Bayard was in a difficult position when partisan politics impinged constantly upon delicate questions of foreign policy and the Department of State had to defend itself at home as well as abroad. Bayard's feelings upon the subject appear in a letter to his friend Wade Hampton:

I weary so over the tone of our press and not the press alone but of men high in public councils who propose to deal with the vast issues of war and peace between great states in the spirit of prize fighters or scuffling boot blacks. It has been a pitiable sight to witness the conduct of the Senate Committee on Foreign Relations . . . for the past four years. When the record is reviewed, as one day it will be, I believe you will find that I have no cause to be ashamed of the spirit and manner in which I have sought to arrange the relations of the United States with other nations.[11]

The Sackville-West Affair

One of the most unfortunate diplomatic episodes in this period in which the Department of State was involved was the dismissal of Lord Sackville-West, the British minister, because of certain statements regarding American domestic politics. A Republican adherent in California conceived the idea of entrapping the British minister by writing him under an assumed name as a recently naturalized Englishman as to how to vote in the forthcoming election to serve British interests. The letter intimated cleverly that President Cleveland had in his recent message asked for retaliatory legislation against Canada for purely political reasons and that once reelected he would return to a more conciliatory policy. If the British minister could reassure the writer upon this point, he would cast his vote for Cleveland. The writer assured the British minister that the letter was confidential and the reply would be kept secret. The letter should have aroused suspicion but Sackville-West was taken in. He advised the writer that Cleveland's message undoubtedly had been colored by the political situation and that if reelected he would probably manifest a spirit of conciliation in dealing with the British. The writer thereupon gave the correspondence to the Republican Executive Committee of California, which had it published in the *Los Angeles Times*.

A furor was raised in the Republican press against the British minister for interfering in American domestic politics. Bayard at first was inclined to disregard the affair officially upon the ground that the whole matter was private and confidential. However, the demands for Sackville-West's dismissal were so widespread and the political repercussions so dangerous to the Democrats that the Department had to act. Unfortunately Sackville-West gave several interviews to the press defending his action and resenting American political trickery. He also seemed to impugn the good faith of the President. Bayard cabled the American minister in London, asking that he present the matter to the British foreign minister, suggesting that Sackville-West be recalled immediately. Lord Salisbury, however, thought that he should first receive Lord Sackville-West's explanation, because recall meant the end of his diplomatic career. Bayard consulted his two experts in international law, Francis Wharton and John Bassett Moore, and both agreed that Sackville-West must go. President Cleveland and the cabinet approved, and on October 30, 1888, Secretary Bayard notified the British minister that it would be detrimental to the good relations of both governments for him to hold any longer his official position in the United States.

Lord Salisbury resented the dismissal and questioned the statement of the United States government that the "acceptance or retention of a minister was a question solely to be determined, either with or without the assignment of reasons, by the government to which he was accredited." Bayard requested both Francis Wharton and John Bassett Moore to prepare memoranda which might refute the contention of the British government. With their assistance Bayard prepared an instruction to Minister Phelps which discussed the whole question in an objective and statesmanlike manner and pointed out that international lawyers, including Calvo, agreed that if the diplomatic agent commits a gross offense he may be dismissed without waiting for recall by his own government, nor need the reasons be given.[12] Granted that the whole affair was one of unfortunate political expediency, the position of the Department of State was sufficiently strong to give legal backing to a very questionable diplomatic procedure. Nevertheless, Anglo-American relations were embittered; Cleveland lost the election and the New York Tribune, the leading newspaper of the Republican party, could gleefully have Cleveland tell John Bull the real truth in doggerel:

> Believe me that I made him go for nothing that he wrote,
> But just because, as well you know, I feared the Irish vote.[13]

The election of 1888 was very close—Cleveland received a plurality of the popular vote—but the Republican nominee, Benjamin Harrison, won a majority of the electoral votes and the Republicans were once more in power. Bayard welcomed the return to private life. Both his wife and daughter had died while he was serving as Secretary of State, and he had been vilified by the press and either ignored or abused by the Congress. The quiet practice of law in Wilmington seemed like a haven of refuge. Thomas F. Bayard retired on March 6, 1889, and President Harrison named James G. Blaine as Secretary of State for the second time.

James G. Blaine—Secretary of State

There was no doubt that Blaine was eager to return as head of the Department of State. His wife, writing in 1883, declared that the one thing which Blaine desired was to be once more Secretary of State.[14] Defeated in the 1884 election, he was unwilling to stand again in 1888 but urged his friends to support Harrison, and after the latter's nomination he campaigned brilliantly for him. When Harrison was elected it was expected that he would immediately invite Blaine to serve again as Secretary of State. However, General Harrison was determined to be President in fact as well as in name and he was not too eager to have a popular idol for the top place in the cabinet. It was not until January 17, 1889, that Harrison made the offer briefly and formally and accompanied by a "private" letter expressing his views upon their relationship and upon the foreign policy that he favored. Harrison also was desirous that the civil service should be maintained upon a high plane. He promised that each member of his official family should have his *full* confidence and wrote that he expected his in return.[15]

In his reply, dated January 21, 1889, Blaine declared that he was in the heartiest accord with the principles and policies desired by the President. He then outlined his understanding of their relationship.

The State Department was designed in its original constitution to be at all times in close communication with the President. The Secretary is his certifying officer even for many things that more nearly concern other departments. The foreign affairs are in their inception and management exclusively executive and nothing decisive can be done in that important field except with the President's personal knowledge and official approval.[16]

However, the very fact that Harrison had laid down his ideas in advance in a field where Blaine was a past master indicated that Blaine would not have the free hand in initiating foreign policy that he had had with Garfield.

Personnel Changes

James G. Blaine entered upon his duties as Secretary of State for the second time on March 7, 1889. The Senate paid him the compliment of confirmation without reference to a committee. The first problem was to pick an Assistant Secretary of State to take the place of Mr. Rives. Since Robert R. Hitt, whom Blaine had chosen before, was unavailable because of his position in Congress, Blaine turned to his son Walker Blaine, who had served very successfully as Third Assistant Secretary under his father previously and who had his father's complete confidence. President Harrison, however, whether unwilling to be accused of nepotism or whether he feared a Blaine faction might be built up, refused to name Walker Blaine Assistant Secretary. He was agreeable however to making him Solicitor to take over the duties of the outstanding international lawyer and publicist, Francis Wharton, whose death in February, 1889, deprived the Department of State of a jurist and scholar whom Secretary Bayard characterized as "among the most renowned publicists of our times." Secretary Blaine was keenly disappointed but accepted the compromise. The fact that he had suggested Eugene Schuyler as Assistant Secretary when Walker's name was unacceptable and that he too was rejected indicated that Blaine would not find his relationship with the President quite as satisfactory as he had hoped. Harrison's refusal to follow Blaine's recommendations for positions caused Mrs. Blaine to write: "The idea apparently is that having given Blaine the head of the table, no distinctively personal friend shall also have a seat." [17]

Secretary Blaine, though he did not have his son Walker as Assistant Secretary, was fortunate in having the able and experienced Alvey Adee and John Bassett Moore as Second and Third Assistant Secretaries. At the suggestion of Senator Henry Cabot Lodge, the post of Assistant Secretary was given to William F. Wharton, a Massachusetts constituent who was completely lacking in diplomatic experience and any other special qualifications for the post. It will be remembered that Bayard had asked Chief Clerk Sevellon A. Brown to resign in January, 1888, after fifteen years of excellent service. Secretary Blaine brought him back as Chief Clerk, where he remained throughout Blaine's second term. H. Sidney Everett, who had served as secretary of legation in Berlin for seven years and had been Chief of the Diplomatic Bureau since 1885, remained in office. Francis O. St. Clair, who had entered the Department as clerk in 1865, continued to serve as head of the Consular Bureau, a position which he had held since 1881. John H. Haswell, Chief of the Bureau of Indexes and Archives, had also been in the Department since 1865 and had held his present position since 1873. Francis J. Kiekhofer remained Chief of the Bureau of Accounts, a position which he had held since 1884, with ten years' previous experience in the Department. Michael Scanlan was reappointed Chief of the Bureau of Statistics, a post to which he had been named in 1880 but which he had lost in 1885 when he had to make way for a political appointee. The Chief of Bureau of Rolls and Library was a newcomer, Frederick A. Bancroft, appointed in 1888. The Translator, Henry L. Thomas, had been in the Department since 1869 and Translator since 1875. The clerical force now numbered forty-eight, of whom eleven were women. Including three dispatch agents, messenger, laborers, and a few other workers, the total personnel of the Department as of July 1, 1889, numbered eighty-one.[18]

Secretary Blaine was not consulted in most of the appointments in the diplomatic service, although some of his best friends, such as Whitelaw Reid and W. W. Phelps, received the highest appointments. The mission to Great Britain, which is usually regarded as the top appointment, was expected to go to Whitelaw Reid, editor of the New York Tribune, the Republican party's principal supporter. But since the Tribune had been advocating Irish Home

Rule and had been opposing the prime minister, Lord Salisbury, President Harrison felt that it would be preferable for Reid to accept the position of minister to France. He requested John Hay, as a personal favor, to go to New York to explain the situation to Reid and urge him to accept. Hay accomplished his mission successfully and Reid went as minister to France.[19] The Irish-Americans, it was reported, had not been satisfied with either Lowell or Phelps as ministers to Great Britain and wanted a man thoroughly in sympathy with American institutions and not amenable to British flattery. The first choice of President Harrison was Chauncey Depew, but he refused to accept. Harrison then turned to Robert Todd Lincoln, who although disinclined to take public office accepted and was later characterized by Theodore Roosevelt as the only American minister to London who did not become pro-British.

The appointment as minister to Germany of William Walter Phelps, a lifelong friend and supporter of Blaine, proved to be a most satisfactory one. Phelps had been minister to Austria-Hungary and had served on the Foreign Relations Committee of the House of Representatives for several terms; he spoke German quite fluently and was very wealthy. His wit and friendly manner made him a most popular representative in Berlin. Very few veteran diplomats were appointed by the Harrison administration and these to secondary posts—as, for example, W. L. Scruggs to Venezuela and Eugene Schuyler to Egypt. Charles Denby, appointed to China in 1885, was permitted to remain. On the whole, the politicians had their way and diplomatic appointments were no better than in previous administrations in spite of Harrison's real desire not to submit to the spoilsmen.

First Inter-American Conference

Blaine was most fortunate in that one of the first important duties facing him was to carry on the arrangements for the first international conference of the American states to be held in Washington in October, 1889. It will be remembered that Blaine had conceived the idea and issued the invitations for such a conference in his first term as Secretary of State but that President Arthur, upon the advice of Secretary Frelinghuysen, had withdrawn the invitations, to Blaine's bitter disappointment. It was an act of poetic justice that Secretary of State Blaine was the representative of the United States government who officially received the delegates and was elected chairman of the First International American Conference. Although he was keenly disappointed that the conference was unwilling to accept arbitration as a principle of American international law, he could be justly gratified that a permanent organization was set up at this conference, now officially known as the Pan-American Union, which has acted as a successful liaison agency for the twenty-one republics ever since.

The conference had as one of its objects the betterment of commercial relations. Hardly had it convened before the House of Representatives passed the McKinley tariff bill—the highest tariff in American history. Although Blaine believed in protection, he also felt that reciprocity between the American republics was vitally necessary if commercial relations were to be improved. Blaine had no hesitancy in violating the doctrine of separation of powers. He appeared personally before the Ways and Means Committee of the House and the Finance Committee of the Senate to urge a reciprocity provision. He wrote open letters to congressmen and made speeches which were printed and distributed. His efforts were successful at least to the extent that a reciprocity amendment was added to the McKinley Act, although it was a much more restrictive provision than Blaine wanted.[20]

Diplomatic Problems

The Department of State had inherited a problem in relation to the protection of the seals in the Bering Sea which taxed its powers of diplomatic negotiation to the utmost. The desire of the United States to prevent the wanton destruction of the seal herds of the Pribilof Islands was justifiable but the methods used were difficult to defend. Canadian sealers who engaged in killing seals outside the three-mile limit were seized, imprisoned, and their ships condemned. When the British government protested vigorously, Blaine was hard put to justify a practice which the United States had always refused to permit. He successively argued that the destruction of the herds by pelagic fishing was *contra bonos mores*, that the United States had a property interest in the seals, that since Russia had declared the Bering Sea a *mare clausum*, the United States had a prescriptive right to control the sea fisheries. According to John W. Foster, who later defended the interests of the United States in the controversy, "It is doubtful if any other living American could have made a more brilliant defense of his Government." [21] However, Lord Salisbury was not convinced nor was the court of arbitration which later ruled against the United States upon every point at issue. Nevertheless, Blaine's spirited defense induced the court to recommend certain minimum regulations for the protection of the seals which prevented the complete destruction of the herds which otherwise would have been inevitable.[22]

The most serious problem faced by Secretary Blaine in his second term as head of the Department of State was in the field of Latin American relations. The revolutionary party in Chile resented bitterly the action of American Minister Patrick Egan in giving asylum to a number of government officials whose lives were jeopardized when the revolutionists were successful. The animosity resulted in an attack by civilians and police upon a contingent of American sailors and petty officers who had been given shore leave in Valparaiso by Captain Schley of the U.S.S. *Baltimore*. Two of the Americans were killed, several badly wounded, and some thirty odd were beaten and maltreated while being taken to prison. An investigation showed that the sailors were unarmed and that the attack was due to hostility to the United States and not because of any acts of the sailors. The public authorities not only afforded no protection but aided in the assault. The Chilean government, instead of expressing regret, seemed inclined to regard the matter as a drunken waterfront brawl caused by Captain Schley's imprudently allowing such a large number of sailors to have shore leave.

Secretary Blaine was ill at the time when the incident occurred and Acting Secretary of State William F. Wharton handled the matter. His note to the Chilean government was somewhat peremptory and the reply of the Chilean foreign minister was anything but cordial. When the official inquiry in Chile dragged along, President Harrison, in his message of December 9, 1891, protested both the delay and the offensive tone of the Chilean reply and promised to bring the matter before Congress unless adequate action should be taken by the Chilean government. The Chilean foreign minister thereupon committed a serious diplomatic *faux pas* by making a violent denunciation of the American position to the Chilean senate and sending a copy of his attack to the Chilean minister in Washington to be published in the press. The language was violent and abusive and violated the most elementary canons of diplomatic procedure.[23]

The American public demanded action and President Harrison was inclined to recall Minister Egan, but Blaine had returned to take charge and since a new president of Chile would shortly be inaugurated he counseled delay. The new minister of foreign affairs was somewhat conciliatory but his expression of regret seemed equivocal. When this was followed by a request for the recall of Minister Egan, President Harrison insisted that Blaine send an ultimatum stating that unless the offensive parts of the dispatch of December 11 were immediately withdrawn and a suitable apology offered, diplomatic relations with the government of Chile would be terminated. Some criticism has been made of this ultimatum being sent at a time when Chile was attempting to excuse her previous conduct. Certainly President Harrison was not justified in sending what was virtually a war message to Congress four days after the ultimatum and before there was an opportunity to get a reply from Chile. The very next day the Chilean answer accepted the demands of the United States and the crisis was over.

Less than six months later, on June 4, 1892, Blaine suddenly resigned as

Secretary of State, giving no reasons for his action but merely asking to be relieved from his duties. His health throughout his second period as Secretary had been failing and he had to leave Washington for weeks at a time. He had never been happy in his relations with President Harrison. The President could not help resenting Blaine's preeminent position in the party and never invited him as a guest upon presidential trips. Blaine always regretted not having his son as Assistant Secretary, and although Walker became Solicitor, that position did not permit the same close relationship. The death of Walker on January 15, 1890, severed another tie binding Blaine to the Department. Blaine never gave the reason for his sudden resignation and it is doubtful whether the reason will ever be known.

Blaine as Secretary of State was not a particularly able administrator nor were his achievements in the field of policy notable. If Blaine is given a high place among the Department's Secretaries, it is because he had originality of conception and energy in execution. He brought the United States into closer cooperation with the republics of the Western Hemisphere, he saw the advantages of reciprocity in commercial relations, he fought hard for the conservation of natural resources, and he believed ardently in the settlement of disputes by pacific means. What he conceived and initiated others have carried to fruition and profited thereby. President Harrison, who accepted his resignation without a word of commendation, directed all executive departments in Washington to be closed the day of his funeral and in his address on his death declared: "In the varied pursuits of legislation, diplomacy and literature his genius has added new luster to American citizenship." [24]

John W. Foster—Secretary of State

The resignation of Secretary Blaine came so unexpectedly that for almost a month Assistant Secretary Wharton carried on as Acting Secretary until President Harrison might appoint some one to replace Blaine. Inasmuch as President Harrison's term of office would expire in less than a year and reelection was by no means certain, the position would hardly be sought by anyone interested in political advantage. President Harrison wisely chose an expert in international law and diplomatic practice, John W. Foster, who was actively serving the Department at the time of his appointment by preparing the case for the United States in the Bering Sea controversy. Foster's first diplomatic experience had been when he was appointed minister to Mexico by General Grant in 1873. After seven years in Mexico City he was named by President Hayes as minister to Russia. He served there almost two years, but the financial burden entailed in serving the government abroad and the desire to educate his children at home brought about his resignation. He was again persuaded to serve abroad when President Arthur appointed him in 1883 as minister to Spain to negotiate a commercial reciprocity treaty for Cuba and Puerto Rico. Upon Cleveland's inauguration, Foster tendered his resignation but was persuaded by Secretary Bayard to return and work for a modification of the previous treaty, which had not been approved by the Senate.

Foster's appointment by Secretary Blaine to conduct the reciprocity negotiations under the McKinley tariff bill had enhanced his reputation considerably. Before he completed this assignment, Secretary Blaine became very ill and President Harrison requested Mr. Foster to take over the task of preparing the case of the United States in the Bering Sea arbitration. The immediate problem was whether Foster could serve simultaneously as Secretary of State and as agent for the United States in the Bering Sea case. Although there was an accumulation of work in the Department due to Blaine's illness, Foster undertook to accomplish both jobs. In his short term of less than seven months, Foster reported to the President that all matters relating to foreign affairs pending in the Senate had been dispatched—a condition that had not existed for many years.[25]

The Department organization remained practically unchanged throughout the period of Blaine and Foster with the exception of the appointment of Frank C. Partridge as Solicitor to take the position made vacant by the death of Walker Blaine. Partridge was a successful businessman of Vermont who was trained in the law and had a predilection for public service. He was commissioned Examiner of Claims on June 10, 1890, although the title used in the Department by both Francis Wharton and Walker Blaine was Solicitor. By the Act of March 3, 1891, the title was changed officially to Solicitor. He held the position throughout the rest of Blaine's administration of the Department and through most of Foster's. He was later named minister to Venezuela and consul general to Tangier, Morocco. The position of Third Assistant Secretary, from which John Bassett Moore had resigned in September, 1891, to accept a professorship in international law at Columbia University, remained vacant until William M. Grinell of New York was appointed in February, 1892. He held the position a little over a year.

Foster, with the duties of the Department plus preparing the case for the Bering Sea arbitration, found it necessary to work nights as well as days and to depend considerably upon the assistance of the junior counsels, Robert Lansing and William Williams. An incident occurred in the Department in the preparation of the case which was very embarrassing to Secretary Foster. The State Department Library possessed a large collection of archives of the Russian government of Alaska which had never been translated and it was thought that documentary evidence might be found in them supporting the claim that Russia had exercised exclusive jurisdiction for the protection of the seals in the Bering Sea. Since no American translator was available, a native

Russian scholar was employed. He translated a number of documents and they all confirmed the American position that Russia had exercised exclusive jurisdiction for the protection of the seals in the Bering Sea. After photographic copies in facsimile of the documents were made and the English translations attached and delivered to the British government, a junior clerk in the State Department who had been studying Russian informed Secretary Foster that he did not think the documents were accurately translated. An investigation was made and it was discovered that the Russian translator had deliberately mistranslated the documents to make them support the United States position. Foster immediately notified the British government of the incorrect translations and promised to furnish corrected copies just as quickly as the translation could be checked and revised.[26]

Inasmuch as Foster had prepared the American case, it was thought vital that he should defend the position of the United States before the arbitration tribunal. To do this he was forced to resign from the Department headship about a week before President Harrison's term expired, so as to be present in Paris in time for the opening sessions. For the remaining period, February 24, 1893, to March 7, 1893, Assistant Secretary of State William F. Wharton served as Secretary ad interim.

John W. Foster was Secretary of State for too short a period to compare him with the great Secretaries of State who preceded him. In ability, experience, and in keeping the Department functioning smoothly, efficiently, and at a far greater speed than normal, Foster was among the best. However, it is as a diplomat and a writer on diplomatic history, practice, and procedure that his fame rests. His service as Secretary of State was merely an interlude in his greater service in formulating and interpreting foreign policies of the United States in other capacities.

16

Walter Q. Gresham, Richard Olney, John Sherman, and William R. Day

Walter Q. Gresnam—Secretary of State

With the advent of the second Cleveland administration, the officers with long periods of service, whether at home in the State Department or abroad in the foreign service, were not unduly alarmed regarding their positions. Grover Cleveland had shown himself so opposed to the spoils system in his first administration that even though deserving Democrats might feel that it was their turn to receive the choice political plums, they knew from former experience that Cleveland would never sacrifice a good career officer for a political opportunist. However, even the most ardent supporter of civil-service procedure might well have been surprised when President Cleveland offered the highest political appointment to Walter Q. Gresham, a man who until the last campaign had been a lifelong Republican; particularly to one who had served as Postmaster General and later as Secretary of the Treasury in President Arthur's cabinet and had even been a serious contender for the presidential nomination at the hands of the Republican party. Many thought Cleveland would turn again to Bayard as his Secretary of State—in fact Allan Nevins states that he did offer the post to Bayard, but the latter preferred the position of ambassador to Great Britain.[1] Charles C. Tansill, the biographer of Bayard, disputes this statement and feels that if Cleveland had invited Bayard to serve in the cabinet he would have willingly accepted; and John Bassett Moore concurs in this opinion. In fact, Tansill goes so far as to allege that Cleveland raised the post of minister to London to that of ambassador and then offered it to Bayard so as to gild the pill of disappointment to Bayard because of his failure to receive a cabinet appointment.[2]

Cleveland's letter, dated January 25, 1893, inviting Gresham to become Secretary of State was a very friendly one, and in concluding, the President appealed to his sense of duty: "In really a great emergency, the country needs your services in the place I ask you to fill. In an effort to subserve the interests

of my countrymen I need you. Can you not come to us?" [3] Gresham at first refused the offer, but the pressure of his friends urging him to accept was so
great that when Cleveland wrote him again, urging reconsideration, Gresham
reluctantly agreed to serve.

Walter Q. Gresham was commissioned as Secretary of State on March
6, 1893. He was an able lawyer and had plenty of political courage, as shown
by his suppression of the Louisiana lottery as soon as he became Postmaster
General. His decision to support Cleveland as against Benjamin Harrison also
proved his strong tendency toward political independence. However, he possessed no experience or background in the diplomatic or international-relations
field.

Personnel Changes

A few changes were made in the Department's personnel shortly after the
new administration came into power. Josiah Quincy, a successful lawyer and
scion of the illustrious Quincy family of Massachusetts, was chosen as Assistant
Secretary of State. He had acted as publicity manager for the Democratic
National Committee and was rewarded for his services by the position in the
Department. He held the position less than a year. His successor, Edwin F.
Uhl, an outstanding lawyer and businessman of Michigan, proved to be an ex-
cellent appointment. Alvey Adee continued as Second Assistant Secretary and
he was ably assisted by the newly appointed Third Assistant Secretary, Edward
H. Strobel. President Cleveland during his first term had appointed Strobel
secretary of legation at Madrid, where he remained for approximately five years,
serving on several occasions as chargé d'affaires. He resigned his position as
Assistant Secretary in 1894 to go as minister to Ecuador and then to Chile.
Later he became Bemis professor of international law at Harvard. The new
Chief Clerk, William Woodville Rockhill, was another excellent appointment.
Rockhill had acted as second secretary of legation in Peking and as chargé
d'affaires at Seoul. He was destined to play an important role in the Department's future activities. When Third Assistant Secretary Strobel left the Department for Guayaquil, Rockhill was commissioned Third Assistant Secretary in his place. Edward I. Renick, Chief of the Bureau of Statistics, was
thereupon promoted to the position of Chief Clerk.

An interesting change in the method of appointment of bureau chiefs occurred under Gresham, who was a stickler for strict legality. For eighteen years,
in spite of an opinion of the law officer of the Department to the contrary,
bureau chiefs were appointed directly by the Secretary of State instead of by
the President. Gresham went back to the ruling of the law officer, and the
President, rather than the Secretary of State, nominated Pendleton King, for-

merly secretary of legation at Constantinople, as Chief of the Bureau of Indexes and Archives on June 1, 1894. The procedure was again reversed in 1896
when Secretary of State Olney referred the matter to the Attorney General,
who gave as his opinion that the bureau chiefs were clerks and entitled only
to departmental commissions.[4] Among the clerical force we note a number
of names later to become famous: Kenesaw M. Landis, Frederick Van Dyne,
Gaillard Hunt, and almost at the bottom of the clerical force, Wilbur J. Carr.
Excluding messengers and laborers, the entire personnel of the Department as
of July 1, 1893, numbered sixty-nine.

The outstanding appointment in the diplomatic service made by Cleveland was that of his former Secretary of State Thomas F. Bayard as ambassador
to Great Britain. An unfortunate incident occurred shortly after the reception
of the new American ambassador that was not too creditable to the Cleveland
administration. The first secretary of the London embassy was Henry White,
a remarkably able career diplomat who had served with distinction under Lowell, Phelps, and Lincoln. Unfortunately, he had incurred the enmity of Daniel
S. Lamont, the new Secretary of War, and the latter urged Cleveland to demand White's resignation. It is to Secretary of State Gresham's credit that he
made a valiant effort to change Cleveland's mind on the subject, but the
President was determined to have White's resignation.[5]

The only other diplomatic post with a distinguished minister was at St.
Petersburg, where Andrew D. White had been appointed by Benjamin Harrison. When White sent in his resignation to Cleveland, the President refused
to accept it and urged White to continue at the post. White agreed and continued in the service for almost a year longer. The other diplomatic appointments were either mediocre or bad. Various aspirants to the Paris embassy
were discussed in the press—ex-minister Robert M. McLane, the renowned international lawyer Frederic R. Coudert—but the choice fell upon ex-Senator
James B. Eustis of Louisiana, a good Democrat in need of a job. Here too, both
First and Second Secretaries, Henry Vignaud and Augustus Jay, exceedingly
able men, were dismissed summarily. The ambassador's son, Newton, was
made Second Secretary, but the need of Vignaud was so great that Eustis persuaded President Cleveland to reinstate him. One diplomatic appointment,
that of James J. Van Alen, was opposed so vigorously by the Civil Service Reform League because of his contribution of $50,000 to the Democratic cam-
paign fund, that he resigned in spite of Cleveland's request that he remain.

Secretary of State Gresham refused to have anything to do with making
appointments for the Department, and the burden fell upon Assistant Secretary
Quincy, who believed in civil-service reform. He apparently tried his best to
require that the applicant possess at least reasonable qualifications, but the
Congressmen were so insistent that within five months of the change of ad-

ministration, 117 consular officials out of a total of 317 had been dismissed, and mostly for political reasons.[6] Nevertheless, in the roster of the State Department personnel we find only three new appointees other than the two assistant secretaries already mentioned: Walter D. Dabney as Solicitor; Edward I. Renick as Chief of the Bureau of Statistics; Kenesaw M. Landis as clerk to the Secretary of State.[7]

Annexation of Hawaii

Few problems of vital importance in the foreign policy of the United States came up during Gresham's short term of office. The question of the annexation of Hawaii, however, made considerable trouble for the Department of State. The previous administration was definitely in favor of an expansionist policy, and Secretary Blaine had given his representative, John L. Stevens, considerable discretion in his instructions. But Stevens went even further. He aided in directing the overthrow of the government of Hawaii, he recognized the provisional government prematurely, and practically established an American protectorate over the islands. Gresham believed in morality—public as well as private, international as well as national. According to his wife's statement, he felt that international morality required the restoration of Queen Liliuokalani, and he was able to persuade President Cleveland that since the agent of the United States had helped to depose her, the United States had a duty to restore her.[8] To convince Cleveland was not difficult inasmuch as he was strongly anti-imperialist by disposition. Gresham also suggested that Cleveland send a special commissioner to Hawaii to get all the facts.

The conditions in the islands proved to be such that a return of the queen's rule was impossible without the use of force upon the part of the United States. Both the queen and the provisional government were stubborn and the sentiment for annexation was strong in the United States, regardless of how it should come about. Cleveland and Gresham had attempted to stem a tide of expansion that was irresistible. Even though Cleveland finally placed the responsibility of determining what should be done in the hands of Congress—an unjustifiable diversion of Executive responsibility in the conduct of foreign relations—both Gresham and Cleveland must be credited with making their acts conform to their expressed ideals of justice and fair play.

The even more difficult problem facing the Department, the Venezuela boundary dispute with Great Britain, was not to be settled by Gresham. He was taken ill with pneumonia early in May, 1895, and before the end of the month he was dead. President Cleveland and the members of the cabinet had come to be very fond of their frank and honest colleague and his death was a serious loss to them personally as well as governmentally. No one would argue that

Gresham was a great Secretary of State. He considered himself more of a judge than a diplomat. Even if he had lived, his high and rugged sense of moral value joined to his tendency to idealism might have prevented his achieving success in a field where flexibility and compromise are as essential as uprightness and ability.

Richard Olney—Secretary of State

The unexpected demise of Gresham left the Department under the direction of Assistant Secretary Uhl for about ten days. During Gresham's illness, Attorney General Richard Olney had been given charge of the Venezuela dispute and he had been called in previously in the Hawaiian affair. Cleveland was well satisfied with his recommendations in the Hawaiian matter and it caused no surprise when the President invited him to accept the position of Secretary of State. Richard Olney was no better prepared by training or experience than his predecessor to take over the chief cabinet post. A corporation lawyer, he had not willingly accepted the offer of the Attorney Generalship when it was proffered. However, he had no hesitancy in accepting the post as head of the State Department. In manner he was even less diplomatic than his predecessor. Nevertheless, according to his biographer, Henry James, "in many respects he had presented an agreeable contrast to Gresham's saunterings in hotel corridors, shirtsleeve appearance in the State Department and generally uncouth personal idiosyncrasies." [9]

The only important changes in Departmental organization and personnel in Olney's administration were the following: William W. Rockhill took Edwin F. Uhl's place as Assistant Secretary of State on February 11, 1896, and William W. Baldwin moved into Rockhill's former place as Third Assistant Secretary; Walter E. Faison, who had been a clerk in the Department for ten years, became Solicitor in the place of Walter D. Dabney; a new agency under the term Appointment Clerk was established to consider applications for office and to prepare commissions, exequaturs, and warrants of extradition. The Appointment Clerk was also given custody of the Great Seal. Also there was established the Departmental Board of Promotion with the Chief Clerk as chairman. The clerical force in the Department had now increased to sixty-six in number. If we include the Secretary, three Assistant Secretaries, Solicitor, and the fifteen messengers and laborers, the Department personnel as of January, 1897, was eighty-six.

The Venezuela Dispute

For well over half a century Great Britain and Venezuela had been disputing the boundary of British Guiana, and at least four American Secretaries of State—Frelinghuysen, Bayard, Blaine, and Gresham—had indicated the interest of the United States in the dispute. Good offices, mediation, and arbitration had all been urged upon Great Britain by the United States to no purpose, and Cleveland, in his annual message of December 3, 1894, promised to do all in his power to persuade Great Britain to arbitrate the dispute. Congress on February 22, 1895, passed a joint resolution supporting the President's proposal of arbitration. Gresham was working upon a note to send to Ambassador Bayard but his illness and death put the matter into the hands of Olney. As an able lawyer who considered the Monroe Doctrine as the "accepted public law of this country," Olney felt that the British refusal to arbitrate, unless a substantial part of the disputed territory be conceded to her in advance, was a flagrant violation of the principles of the Monroe Doctrine. Under these circumstances, since previous efforts to persuade Britain had completely failed, Olney concluded that more forceful measures were essential. He prepared the draft of his famous note of instructions of July 20, 1895, to Ambassador Bayard with considerable trepidation. It was his first important diplomatic effort and he had no idea as to how President Cleveland would react to it. But he was so sure that his policy was the only one feasible that he was willing to hand in his resignation if President Cleveland disagreed with him. He was in a state of nervous suspense until he received a personal note from Cleveland commending him highly for his draft. The President felt that it was

the best thing of the kind I have ever read and it leads to a conclusion that one cannot escape if he tries—that is if there is anything of the Monroe Doctrine at all. You show there is a great deal of that and place it, I think, on better and more defensible ground than any of your predecessors—or mine.[10]

At Cleveland's suggestion Olney read his draft to various members of the cabinet, but no changes of any consequence were made. No evidence is available to indicate that Olney either discussed the draft with his assistants in the Department or even showed it to them. The note, which is one of the most famous ever drafted by an American Secretary of State, was a comprehensive, legalistic presentation of the entire case, closing with what was regarded as a virtual ultimatum to the British government. Its most quoted and most criticized statements are the following:

The Monroe Doctrine rests . . . upon facts and principles that are both intelligible and incontrovertible . . . whether moral or material interests be considered it cannot but be universally conceded that those of Europe are irreconcilably diverse from those of America and that any European control of the latter is necessarily both incongruous and injurious . . . the states of America, South as well as North, by geographical proximity, by natural sympathy, by similarity of governmental constitutions are friends and allies commercially and politically of the United States. . . . Today the United States is practically sovereign on this continent, and its fiat is law upon the subjects to which it confines its interposition. . . . Why? . . . It is because in addition to all other grounds, its infinite resources combined with its isolated position render it master of the situation and practically invulnerable as against any or all powers.[11]

The dispatch concluded with a statement that the President hoped that the British would submit the entire question to arbitration, but if not, he wished to know it so that he might lay the whole matter before the Congress in his next annual message. Ambassador Bayard, who had long been an ardent advocate of Anglo-Saxon unity and who felt that the new Salisbury government would give additional impetus to a rapprochement with the United States, was considerably dismayed by the extreme truculence of the phraseology and by the absurdity of some of the generalizations.[12] When Bayard relayed the contents of his instruction to Lord Salisbury, the latter refuted both effectively and caustically Olney's "incontrovertible facts and principles." He found no violation of the Monroe Doctrine and refused arbitration.[13]

When the wholly unsatisfactory reply was brought to Olney on December 7, President Cleveland was away, but he had left instructions that Olney prepare a draft message to Congress. Olney prepared a message without consulting anyone in the State Department, one which was worded harshly because "in the English eyes the United States was then so completely a negligible quantity that it was believed only words the equivalent of blows would be really effective." [14] Upon his return Cleveland rewrote the message, but the bellicose and aggressive tone and the "bumptious" phrases which Olney contributed to it were not substantially modified. The message as sent to Congress on December 17, 1895, was brief but devastating. It requested that Congress provide expenses for a commission to investigate and report upon the boundary. After this report was made and accepted, the message said, it was the duty of the United States to resist by every means in its power the appropriation by Great Britain of territory which we have determined belongs to Venezuela. This meant war unless Great Britain should agree to arbitrate. Congress overwhelmingly approved the naming of a commission and vociferously supported the President in his two-fisted support of the Monroe Doctrine. However, having followed Olney's counsel thus far, Cleveland now selected a boundary commission of outstanding Americans without consulting his Secretary of State. The fact that John Bassett Moore, Carl Schurz, and others were vigorously opposed to the President's position tended to influence Cleveland in spite of the overwhelming popular approval. Meanwhile Great Britain became much more aroused by the Kaiser's telegram to President Kruger than by Cleveland's message to Congress. Great Britain, after the necessary diplomatic jockeying, agreed to arbitration, and the decision was largely in her favor.

The role of the Department of State in bringing about the final settlement was most noteworthy. Olney worked closely with the Washington representative of the *London Times* so that British public opinion might be correctly informed, and he dealt with the British ambassador, Lord Pauncefote, in many off-the-record personal conferences with excellent results. The Secretary of State felt that Ambassador Bayard had not represented adequately to the British government the United States point of view;[15] and when he learned that former secretary of the American legation in London, Henry White, was going abroad, he asked him to "see the important members of the government, to interpret the American position to them and report back his impressions." White speedily saw all the principal British statesmen informally, and his reports were so satisfactory to the Department that Olney wrote White that hitherto the United States had been handicapped by having in England a diplomatic agent "who through sentiment, self-conceit, physical infirmity or otherwise has been practically disabled from rendering the service rightfully expected of him."[16] Secretary Olney's "twenty-inch-gun" dispatch, as Cleveland later called it, settled a long-standing dispute satisfactorily and enhanced materially the diplomatic prestige of the United States.

A Strong-Willed Secretary of State

Olney was not too happy in his relations with Congress and at times he criticized violently its interference with the administration's control of foreign policy. Both Cleveland and Olney, while sympathizing with the Cubans in their efforts to secure independence from Spain, were averse to intervention and opposed vehemently the Cameron resolution favoring the recognition of the independence of Cuba. Olney gave an interview to the press pointing out that such a resolution was merely "an expression of opinion by the eminent gentlemen who vote for it." The President alone could accord recognition and such a resolution would merely inflame passions, jeopardize American lives and property abroad, and make the task of carrying on foreign relations the more difficult.[17]

Olney's administration of the Department was unique in the highest degree. He was a very efficient worker who never hesitated to make decisions. He believed that the Department should close at four o'clock and he saw to it that it did. On one occasion when the British ambassador appeared at four o'clock, as Olney was going to the elevator, he announced to him: "Mr. Ambassador, it's now four o'clock and the Department is closed; so I must ask you to call again tomorrow."[18] Although Olney was not an international lawyer, he usually made his own decisions as to what should go into the Department's important dispatches. In most cases he then turned them over to Adee or Rockhill to put into "the lingo." Upon some occasions, for example, the Venezuelan note, he consulted no one in the Department.

Olney was keenly interested in the improvement of the consular service, and Cleveland, in his message to Congress in 1893, had urged reorganization of the service to improve its efficiency. To speed up the procedure, Olney recommended that a start be made by executive action, and an executive order was issued requiring that all vacancies in a consulate or commercial agency, when the salary ranged from $1,000 to $2,500, should be filled upon a merit system. This order, signed September 20, 1895, was the first step taken by any administration to take the foreign service out of politics. [19] Olney also favored the purchase of official residences for our ambassadors and ministers abroad, and President Cleveland recommended such action in his annual messages of 1895 and 1896. In a communication, dated February 15, 1897, to Vice President Stevenson recommending the acquisition of suitable official residences, Olney enclosed a memorandum showing the inferior position of the United States compared with the principal European countries. At the time the total number of residences owned by the United States for diplomatic or consular purposes was five: at Tokyo, Bangkok, Seoul, Tangier, and Tahiti. In China the United States legation was the only one occupying rented premises. [20]

Secretary Olney made an innovation which if adopted would have been a boon to historians, international lawyers, and political scientists, but one which, unfortunately, has never been carried out since Olney tried it in 1896. This was to be an annual report summarizing the important developments, diplomatic and administrative, which took place under the State Department's jurisdiction during the year. The *Report* for 1896 was a thirty-one-page summary of the diplomatic relations of the United States. It also discussed extradition, official residences for ambassadors and ministers, consular service, and the Department of State. The paragraph devoted to the administration of the Department noted the rearrangement of the earlier archives, a reorganization of the passport service, and a considerable extension of the operations of the Bureau of Statistics. Olney closed with the suggestion that the Department of State would soon need a more commodious building designed with especial regard to the needs of the service. [21]

Although Olney was not a great Secretary of State, he was a most admirable one. He had the courage of his convictions and he stated them clearly and forcefully. He was respected both by his peers and his assistants. He was reticent and unquestionably did not use as completely as he should have the outstanding abilities of such expert assistants as Adee and Rockhill. He was harsh at times and not inclined to overlook what seemed to him inefficiency—his attitude toward Ambassador Bayard is an example. Once he made a decision he never reconsidered: he put his energy into making it work. Such a characteristic may be an asset in a general but it is a liability in a Secretary of State. He was fortunate in serving under a great President and he measured up to Cleveland's highest requirements. His characterization of Cleveland as one who "never failed to maintain the honor of the government or the dignity of his own high office" might be reversed as an apt description of Olney as Secretary of State.

John Sherman—Secretary of State

Political reasons are necessarily paramount in the selection of the Secretary of State, but there is perhaps no instance in American history where a political debt was satisfied with such utter disregard for the public interest as in the case of the nomination of John Sherman by President William McKinley. The fact that Sherman had been chairman of the Foreign Relations Committee of the Senate did not excuse the appointment nor did it have the slightest bearing upon the matter. Mark Hanna of Ohio unquestionably had been the principal factor in making McKinley President, and Mark Hanna wanted very much to be senator. Inasmuch as Ohio had two senators and no election was due for two years, the only solution was for one of the senators to resign and Hanna be appointed in his place. For the good of the party and for Mark Hanna's aggrandizement, Senator Sherman was requested by McKinley to resign from the Senate and serve as Secretary of State.[22] The fact that Sherman was already seventy-four years of age and his memory failing rapidly did not deter the President. William Roscoe Thayer, an eminent and authoritative historian of the period, does not mince words regarding the appointment: "To force the venerable Sherman, whose powers were already failing, into the most important office after that of the President himself, showed a disregard of common decency not less than of the safety of the nation." [23] Henry Adams, who was keenly interested in foreign affairs, was "shocked beyond all restraints of expression;" and although personally friendly to both McKinley and Sherman, he felt that "John Sherman, otherwise admirably fitted for the place . . . was notoriously feeble and quite senile so that the intrigue seemed the betrayal of an old friend as well as of the State Department." [24]

President McKinley made the offer to Sherman on January 4, 1897, and Sherman accepted hesitatingly. In a letter to a personal friend Sherman indicated his uncertainty but felt that he would embarrass the President if he refused to accept. "Personally," he declared, "I have but little choice in my position, whether in the Senate or the Cabinet, but will do whatever is best for the Republican Party if it can be ascertained." [25] With Rockhill and Adee as assistants, the change to a Republican regime was cushioned temporarily. However, a new Assistant Secretary of Republican persuasion and of exceptional ability was needed, considering the status of the aging Secretary. President McKinley turned to his old friend Judge William R. Day, who had already refused a position in the cabinet as Attorney General but was persuaded to become First Assistant Secretary of State out of personal loyalty to the President. Incidentally, it meant a sacrifice of an income of $15,000 a year for a salary of $4,500. Mr. Rockhill remained on until Day's appointment and was shortly afterward named as minister plenipotentiary and consul general to Greece, Rumania, and Serbia. The appointment of Thomas W. Cridler as Third Assistant Secretary to take the place which W. W. Baldwin had held less than a year was essentially one of intrinsic merit. Cridler had been in the Department for a total of twenty-two years and had been Chief of the Diplomatic Bureau since 1889. On the other hand the appointment of William H. Michael as Chief Clerk was a purely political appointment and dispossessed Edward I. Renick, who had become Chief Clerk by promotion. The only change in organization that occurred during Sherman's short tenure of office was in the Bureau of Statistics, which became the Bureau of Foreign Commerce.[26]

Diplomatic Appointments

The change-over to a Republican administration meant another overhauling of the foreign service and new ambassadors and ministers to all parts of the world. In many respects the new Republican diplomatic corps was far superior to its Democratic predecessor. For the London post McKinley chose John Hay, an appointment that could not have been bettered. Hay had ability, charm, wealth, and considerable diplomatic experience. He had served as secretary of legation in Paris, Vienna, and Madrid and he had lived in London and had many friends high in governmental circles. Since he had also served as Assistant Secretary of State for almost two years, he could appreciate the problems of a foreign office. Hay was also fortunate in having the very competent and experienced Henry White return to his position as first secretary of the embassy. In persuading Andrew D. White to serve as ambassador to Germany, McKinley obtained one of America's ablest diplomats in a post that was particularly important. The appointment of General Horace Porter to France proved to be very satisfactory, and James B. Angell as minister to Turkey was an asset to any diplomatic post.

From the beginning of his incumbency, Sherman indicated that he was unable to perform the functions of the Department adequately. As a result the President came to depend more and more upon the services of the Assistant Secretary of State, William R. Day. One of the first problems facing the Department was the annexation of Hawaii. The Attorney General for the islands had come to Washington before the McKinley inauguration to obtain a treaty of annexation, and on June 16 Secretary Sherman signed the treaty. However, it was Assistant Secretary Day who conducted all the negotiations. When a few days before the signature the Japanese minister came to ask about the provisions of the Hawaiian treaty, Secretary Sherman denied that a treaty was being considered. He had apparently completely forgotten the negotiations. When the treaty was signed and notice of it given to the press, the Japanese were highly incensed and protested strongly to the Department.[27]

In regard to the conditions in Cuba, Sherman was caught in a maelstrom from which he could not withdraw. He was opposed to intervention and even more so to war, but events were kindling the conflict. The publication of the Dupuy de Lôme letter criticizing the President, the destruction of the *Maine* in Havana harbor, and the "Butcher" Weyler policy in Cuba all inflamed public opinion in the United States. In this critical situation, since Sherman was in no condition to discuss the foreign policy of the United States at cabinet meetings, President McKinley invited Assistant Secretary Day to attend. Sherman resented this keenly and on April 25, 1898, he resigned and two days later he left the office. Assistant Secretary Day immediately took charge, and although according to Hay neither Day nor President McKinley was satisfied with the new arrangement, it seemed the best solution for the time.

William R. Day—Secretary of State

William Rufus Day, who was to act as Secretary of State for the next five months, was a very close personal friend of President McKinley's. As young lawyers, both had practiced in Canton, Ohio, and when McKinley appointed Day Assistant Secretary, the latter was serving as judge of the United States District Court for northern Ohio. His sole experience in the field of foreign relations was his year's service in the Department under Sherman. However, he had been responsible for so much of the actual work of the Secretary during that period that the new position hardly changed either his work or responsibilities. His first move was to persuade Professor John Bassett Moore to get leave from Harvard in order to act as Assistant Secretary of State. When it is remembered that until the law of July 7, 1898, raised the salaries of Second and Third Assistant Secretaries of State to $4,000, the salary for these top governmental officials was only $3,500 a year, persuasion was often necessary to get highly qualified persons to accept. It should be noted that the Act of April 17, 1900, raised the salaries of the Second and Third Assistant Secretaries to $4,500, placing all Assistant Secretaries upon the same salary level. The salary of the Secretary of State still remained fixed at $8,000. With Adee and Cridler as the other two Assistant Secretaries, Day had three able and experienced assistants to advise him. Another important appointment made just before Day became Secretary officially was the promotion of Sidney Smith to be Chief of the Diplomatic Bureau. Smith had entered the Department in 1881 and had earned the promotion by meritorious services. The even longer experienced Robert S. Chilton, Jr., remained as Chief of the Consular Bureau.

William R. Day entered upon his duties as Secretary of State on April 28, 1898, just two days after war with Spain had been declared. With an authority like John Bassett Moore in the Department, questions pertaining to neutrality, belligerent rights, and other questions of international law were handled by the Assistant Secretary. The Department of State was faced with no outstanding diplomatic problems during this period. It is difficult to determine just how far the Secretary of State influenced the President in the making of the peace. The draft protocol submitted by the Department of State proposed the relinquishment of all of the Philippine Islands to Spain except for a suitable area for a naval base. The President was undecided, but the majority of the cabinet seemed to favor the retention of the islands and the President came around to that view. He jokingly remarked that "Judge Day only wants a hitching post," and when after the cabinet meeting the Secretary of State complained that his motion for a naval base was not presented, the President replied, "No, Judge, I was afraid it would be carried." [28]

It was Secretary Day who, with the assistance of the Departmental experts, drafted the final protocol of the peace terms. When they were accepted, President McKinley appointed Judge Day as chairman of the American commission for the negotiation of the peace and Assistant Secretary Moore as secretary and counsel to the American commission. Considering the part taken by these officials in the preliminaries, their appointment to the commission was highly commendable, but it was necessary to replace them immediately in the Department. McKinley again showed his ability to choose able advisers by naming John Hay Secretary of State, and David Jayne Hill Assistant Secretary. The President had originally proposed to make Adee First Assistant Secretary, but Adee urged the President to await John Hay's arrival before appointing the First Assistant Secretary. The President complied with his wishes and the offer was not repeated.[29]

JOHN HAY

17

John Hay

John Hay—Secretary of State

When John Hay received the telegram from President McKinley inviting him to become Secretary of State, he was much perturbed. He was very happy as ambassador to Britain and the work interested him; he fitted in well with the British officials; he found the atmosphere most congenial; and, above all, he did not want to be Secretary of State. He prepared two replies, one declining on the basis of health, the other accepting on the grounds of duty. He debated the matter at great length with his friends, and they were anything but enthusiastic. Nevertheless, the consensus of opinion was that he must accept. In the apt phraseology of Henry Adams, who looked upon public office as poison: "No serious statesman could accept a favor and refuse a service." Hay sent the cable accepting the appointment, but his letters of the period show his gloomy views of the change. To Senator Henry Cabot Lodge he wrote that he hoped that after he was installed in Mr. Mullett's masterpiece (the State Department Building) he could count upon the same kindness and indulgence for his shortcomings. To his brother-in-law Samuel Mather he wrote:

I have never been so suppressed by a sense of inadequacy before. . . . I did not want the place and was greatly grieved and shocked when it came—but of course I could not refuse to do the best I could. . . . I look forward to the next year with gloomy forebodings.[1]

But his wife received his most pessimistic outburst:

I almost dread to have you come and plunge into this life of dreary drudgery. It is going to be vile—the whole business. The men are bad enough—their wives are worse. All the fun of my life ended on the platform at Euston. I do not mean by that that England was so uproariously gay but this place is so intolerable.[2]

193

The Department Under Hay

John Hay entered upon his duties as Secretary of State on September 30, 1898. At the time, according to Tyler Dennett, the Department was an "antiquated, feeble organization, enslaved by precedents and routine inherited from another century, remote from the public gaze and indifferent to it. The typewriter was viewed as a necessary evil and the telephone was an instrument of last resort." [3] This was a rather harsh picture of the top executive department of the government and it is not entirely fair. The precedents of the Department of State were oftentime based upon the slow-developing principles of international law and diplomatic practice, and in dealing with the members of an international society, established forms and procedures are necessary. Furthermore, it was not until the Spanish-American War that the United States came of age as a world power. Until this time the President and the Secretary of State, with the assistance of a few experts and the necessary clerical personnel, could deal with the problems of foreign policy which faced the nation. It is true that Congress never seemed to allocate sufficient funds to staff the Department adequately, and Hay, like his predecessors, immediately complained of overwork. On his third day in the Department he went to work at ten-thirty but couldn't catch up, and thereafter decided to start at nine-thirty. Two days later, with his hours from nine-thirty to five, he declared that he was disgustingly busy and expected conditions to be worse when Congress met.

The new First Assistant Secretary of State, Dr. David Jayne Hill, formerly president of the University of Rochester, was wholly unfamiliar with the State Department's organization and procedure and Hay depended almost entirely for advice upon Second Secretary Adee. Dr. Hill was keenly interested in international affairs—he had studied public law abroad, particularly in Germany—but his real contribution came later as a diplomat, publicist, and historian. It was quite natural that Hay should have great confidence in Adee. They had served together in Madrid in the legation under the flamboyant General Sickles and had been literary collaborators as well as diplomatic colleagues. Adee had been in the Department twenty-one years and was expertly conversant with every phase of the Department's work. Being a bachelor, he had few outside interests and spent long hours at his desk and often slept in the Department. His ability to draft clear concise instructions made him invaluable to the many secretaries under whom he served. Hay told Adee on many occasions that he couldn't go astray if he tried. According to the historian William Roscoe Thayer

Presidents ignorant of diplomacy and international law felt reasonably safe in appointing as their chief secretaries gentlemen as ignorant as themselves because they knew Adee was there to guard against blunders. He was the master of both the language and practices of diplomacy. . . . His capacity for work, like his cheerfulness, never ran out. Although it took sometimes six and a half hours to "shovel through" the morning mail, and fifty-five minutes to sign the official correspondence, he could still close a letter to his absent chief with the salutation, "Fatiguedly but always chipperly yours." [4]

Hay constantly worried lest Adee break down through overwork, because "One Adee is all we have in the pantry." Adee reviewed all outgoing correspondence before the signature, thus acting as an office of coordination and review, in addition to his many other duties. Hay often referred to him as the "Cinderella" of the Department and at times became incensed that Dr. Hill did not share the work more fully.

The Third Assistant secretary was Thomas W. Cridler, who had been in the Department since 1875 and had served for eight years as Chief of the Diplomatic Bureau before becoming Third Assistant Secretary in 1897. Cridler retired in 1901, and at the request of Senator Lodge, Herbert H. D. Peirce was named as Third Assistant Secretary. Peirce had been serving as secretary of the American embassy at St. Petersburg preceding his appointment. Hay had very little to do with appointments, although, like other executive officers, he was under constant pressure from office seekers. In fact he once humorously remarked that he couldn't even appoint his own private secretary and as for the consular service, Judge Day had "cleaned off the shelf." In a letter written on July 2, 1902, Hay declared that he had made no appointments in the foreign service since entering the State Department and that all other positions are so rigidly covered by the civil service that "the foreign service is like the topmost rock which you sometimes see in old pictures of the Deluge. The pressure for a place on it is almost indescribable." [5]

Even his friend Whitelaw Reid embarrassed Hay in his desire for the ambassadorship to London. Hay refused to interfere with the President's choice and that much sought-after post went to Joseph H. Choate. When Hay did discreetly suggest that Henry White be made ambassador to Italy, his suggestion was not followed.

Hay was not interested in the routine and procedure of the Department and very few changes took place in his seven years of service as Secretary of State. The office of Assistant Solicitor was created on April 21, 1900, and Frederick Van Dyne, who had already served in the Department for twelve years, was named to this post. Another translator was added in 1900 and the Secretary was given a confidential clerk to assist his private secretary. In 1901 a law clerk was authorized to edit the laws of Congress. In the following year Wilbur J. Carr, who had entered the Department as a clerk in 1892, was made Chief of the Consular Bureau. In 1902 a Passport Bureau was established and Gaillard Hunt, who entered the Department in 1887, was named as its head.

Early in 1903 Dr. David Jayne Hill was named as minister to The Hague, and Francis B. Loomis became First Assistant Secretary of State. Loomis, a well known journalist and editor, had served both as commercial agent and consul at Saint-Etienne and later as minister to Venezuela. At the time of his appointment he had been acting for two years as minister to Portugal. The appointment was not entirely satisfactory, for Secretary Hay had first offered the position to Arthur Sherburne Hardy, who was about to go to Spain as American minister, but he preferred the diplomatic post.[6] The President named Loomis; and Secretary Hay, when asked by Herbert W. Bowen, Loomis's successor as minister to Venezuela, how Loomis happened to be appointed, confessed that he knew nothing about it.[7] Subsequently, serious accusations were made against Loomis; and although they were not substantiated, Loomis retired on October 10, 1905, a few months after Root became Secretary of State.[8]

One appointment engineered by Hay, which was outside of the Department but which had an important influence on the Far Eastern policy of the Department, was that of W. W. Rockhill. A close friend to both Hay and Henry Adams, Rockhill had served in the Far East before returning to Washington to enter the Department. While he was acting as Third Assistant Secretary of State, McKinley appointed him minister to Greece, Rumania, and Serbia, but he was not content in the Near East and resigned in 1899. Hay would have liked to have him as First Assistant Secretary, but when that was not feasible Hay successfully urged his appointment as Director General of the Bureau of American Republics. With Rockhill in Washington, Hay was able to use his expert knowledge of the Far East most advantageously; and the opportunity arose shortly after Hay became Secretary.

Hay's Far Eastern Policy

The situation in China when Hay became Secretary of State was most precarious. The great powers had already carved out toothsome concessions and spheres of interest, and *l'appétit vient en mangeant*. The United States was primarily interested in the protection of American missionaries and the right to trade freely with China. The British, whose commercial interests in the Far East were extensive, looked toward the United States for cooperation. Turning to Rockhill for advice, Hay found that he had been convinced by an old British China hand, A. E. Hippisley, that the time was propitious for the United States to take the lead in demanding equal commercial opportunity for all in China. With Hippisley's notes as a basis, Rockhill prepared a memorandum which was used almost verbatim for the notes to the powers which gave Hay his enduring fame as the author of the open-door policy. Although Hay did not originate the idea, he placed the government of the United States squarely behind it and cleverly assumed that the great powers were agreeable, although their replies were evasive and, in the case of Russia, even antagonistic. But having announced to the world that the powers had given a final and definitive assent to his proposal, Hay had placed them in a position where to deny it would have been most embarrassing.

Hay was equally successful in his policy during the Boxer Rebellion. He insisted that the United States was not at war with China but was merely sending a relief expedition against the Boxers to protect American lives and property and to relieve the besieged American legation in Peking. He then made his momentous statement that the United States policy was to seek a solution which might bring permanent safety and peace to China, "preserve Chinese territorial and administrative entity . . . and safeguard for the world the principle of equal and impartial trade with all parts of the Chinese Empire." [9] That he was realistic is indicated by the fact that when he received no direct answer of support for his principle of territorial integrity of China, he authorized the American minister to take up with the Chinese government the possibility of an American naval base at Samsah Bay. The United States would thus be in a better position to bargain in the future. Japan, however, had preempted this area and she did not hesitate to mention Hay's proposal to maintain the territorial integrity of China. Hay was taken seriously ill before the powers finally came to terms with China. Since an international army was contemplated, Hay could depend upon his friend, Elihu Root, Secretary of War, to protect American interests militarily, and Adee would handle the diplomatic side satisfactorily. In fact, on August 9, 1900, Hay complimented Adee for his management of the Chinese problem and declared that Adee and Root would handle it better than he could.[10]

Hay had also to struggle with the domestic political thinking on our commitments in the Far East. The Presidential election was approaching and McKinley felt that it was necessary for the United States to withdraw her troops from China. Hay realized that the United States and Great Britain had similar interests in China and should cooperate, but in a presidential year such a policy would be suicidal. Writing to John W. Foster on June 23, 1900, Hay expressed his discouragement: "How can I make bricks without straw? That we should be compelled to refuse the assistance of the greatest power in the world *in carrying out our own policy* because all Irishmen are Democrats and some Germans are fools, is enough to drive a man mad."

Hay's Canal Policy

Although Hay was sometimes suspected of being too partial to the British, in reality his policy was to utilize the power of Britain as an adjunct of security to the United States. Inasmuch as the Congress indicated the possibility of passing a bill authorizing the construction of a canal by way of Nicaragua regardless of any or all treaty commitments, Hay sounded out the attitude of Lord Salisbury through the American chargé, Henry White, regarding revision of the Clayton-Bulwer Treaty. The British foreign office finally agreed to authorize the British ambassador in Washington to sign a treaty permitting the United States to build and control an isthmian canal but not to fortify it. In its original form the new draft treaty did not satisfy the Senate, and Secretary Hay, completely discouraged, sent in his resignation. President McKinley assured Hay that his administration of the State Department had his warm approval and he refused to accept his resignation. Hay resented the Senate's action almost as a personal affront and wrote: "When I sent in the Canal Convention, I felt sure that no one out of a madhouse could fail to see that the advantages were all on our side. But I underrated the power of ignorance and spite acting upon cowardice." [11]

Theodore Roosevelt, as Governor of New York, had not been satisfied with the original Hay-Pauncefote Treaty, but when he became President he was most eager to build a trans-isthmian canal. At Hay's instance Alvey Adee had already prepared the draft of a new treaty which was discussed by Ambassador Choate and Henry White with the British foreign secretary in Downing Street and put into final shape by Secretary Hay and Ambassador Pauncefote in Washington.[12] The second Hay-Pauncefote Treaty met the Senate objections and was approved by the Senate with a large margin.

The role of the Department of State in the subsequent efforts to obtain the rights to dig a canal by way of either Nicaragua or Panama was primarily one of furnishing technical and legal rather than political advice. By the passage of the Spooner amendment to the Hepburn bill, Congress placed the decision of choosing the route in the hands of the President. Secretary Hay was not particularly eager to build a canal, but if it were done he favored dealing with Nicaragua. When the Panama Canal Company offered to sell its rights for what seemed like a good bargain, Roosevelt swung to the Panama route and instructed Hay to make a treaty with Colombia for a canal by way of Panama. Hay gave what he thought were generous terms, and when the Colombian government refused to accept the Hay-Herran Treaty, Hay was willing to reopen negotiations with Nicaragua. In a letter to President Roosevelt, dated August 16, 1903, Secretary Hay suggested that the President might take "the simple and easy Nicaraguan solution or the far more difficult and multifurcate scheme of building the Panama Canal malgré Bogotá." [13] A month later, on September 13, 1903, Hay guessed that the Panamanians might stage a revolution if the politicians in Bogotá refused the offer of the United States, but again Hay was noncommittal. He merely noted the three possible procedures which the President might follow: (1) await the result of the revolution; (2) help rescue the Isthmus from anarchy; or (3) treat with Nicaragua. He did, however, feel that if a serious insurrectionary movement took place in Panama, the United States must keep the transit clear.[14]

The attitude of the State Department as to the possibility of the United States annexing Panama in case a revolution of secession were successful was shown by a communication, dated August 18, 1903, of Adee to Hay, who was vacationing in New Hampshire: "Such a scheme could of course have no countenance from us—our policy before the world should stand like Mrs. Caesar, without suspicion. Neither could we undertake to recognize and protect Panama as an independent state like a second Texas." [15] However, when the revolution did occur, President Roosevelt ordered American forces to keep the transit open, a course which prevented the Colombian troops from putting down the revolution. Four days after the revolution occurred, the United States recognized Panama as an independent republic. Within two weeks Hay had negotiated a treaty which gave the United States the right to build the canal upon even better terms than those accorded by the Hay-Herran Treaty. Both Roosevelt and Hay were criticized severely for the "rape of Panama," but the President justified his speedy recognition of Panama as an "act justified by the interests of collective civilization," [16] and Hay upon many occasions insisted that the procedure was justified. His only qualms concerned Panama, for he conceded that the treaty was not advantageous to Panama. President Roosevelt boasted later that he "took the canal," and under the circumstances the Department of State could hardly do less than agree.

The respective roles of Roosevelt and Hay in the whole affair of the Panama Canal epitomize their relationship. Roosevelt had great admiration for Hay and respect for his judgment. While Governor of New York Roosevelt had characterized Hay as the greatest Secretary of State that he had seen in his time. Nevertheless, even in the letter which made this statement, Roosevelt criticized Hay for his treaty with Pauncefote and wanted rather a bill to build *and fortify* our own canal. After Hay's death Roosevelt was quite critical of Hay as Secretary of State—"In the Department of State his usefulness to me was almost exclusively the usefulness of a fine figurehead." [17] Yet Roosevelt insisted that Hay remain in office when he began his second term, although Hay's health was such that to carry on meant an almost unbearable burden of suffering. And on the day after Hay's death Roosevelt declared that the American people had never had a greater Secretary of State than John Hay and that his loss was a national calamity.[18] Certainly any fair evaluation of Hay's work would warrant placing him among the half dozen ablest Secretaries of State.

John Hay was never really happy as Secretary of State. He hated the political pressure for positions and he had a violent dislike, amounting almost to contempt, for the Senate. In a letter to Henry White he declared:

It is impossible to exaggerate the petty worries and cares which, added to the really important matters, make the office of Secretary of State almost intolerable. The unrestricted freedom of access which members of Congress and especially Senators insist upon; the venomous greed with which they demand and quarrel over, every scrap of patronage that falls in. . . .[19]

In a letter to his close friend Nicolay, he confessed that "the thing that has aged me and broken me up has been the attitude of the minority of the Senate which brings to naught all the work a State Department can do. . . ." [20] The requirement that treaties receive a two-thirds vote of the Senate before ratification was possible was a cause of perpetual criticism on the part of Hay. "A treaty entering the Senate," he wrote, "is like a bull going into the arena. No one can say just how or when the final blow will fall—but one thing is certain —it will never leave the arena alive." [21] Yet it must be conceded that although the Senate refused to pass the first canal treaty and amended the Roosevelt-Hay arbitration treaties so that Roosevelt withdrew them, the Senate passed fifteen treaties sponsored by Hay—a most enviable record.

Hay did not believe that the Secretary of State should enter into domestic politics actively, since it would have a bad influence upon the diplomatic corps and would injure his influence in the Senate, which had to pass on his treaties and policies. Nevertheless, when President Roosevelt was running for his second term in 1904, he insisted that Hay make a political speech and gave as his reason that if he did not, the election might be lost and Hay would not be Secretary of State for another four years.[22]

Hay had suggested that he resign in July, 1903, and that Secretary of War Root take over the State Department, but Roosevelt refused his request. After Roosevelt's reelection he again insisted that Hay remain for the next four years. But Hay's health became so bad that after the inauguration he turned over the Department to Secretaries Loomis and Adee and went abroad. The trip availed little. Hardly had he taken up his duties upon his return when he was stricken and died on July 1, 1905. One of his last acts was to offer the position of First Secretary to one of the ablest career diplomats, Lloyd Griscom, who had been serving since 1902 as minister to Japan. First Secretary Francis B. Loomis immediately became Secretary of State ad interim until July 19, 1905, when Elihu Root became the new Secretary of State. In reality President Roosevelt was his own Secretary of State during this period. Perhaps his closest advisor was Jules Jusserand, the French ambassador, whom he called John Hay. On one occasion when a senator with whom the President was discussing certain confidential matters seemed surprised at the presence of Jusserand, the President casually remarked, "Never mind, he has taken the oath of Secretary of State." [23]

As has already been indicated, Secretary Hay made very few changes in the Department of State. He took the Department as it was and did the best job possible with the existing personnel. He was very fortunate in having Alvey Adee always available. The Department increased very slowly while he was Secretary. There were 82 on the payroll of the Department when he entered in 1898 and 119 when Root took office. The cost of the Department had increased from approximately $135,000 in 1898 to $191,000 in 1905. The one outstanding innovation which may be credited to Hay was the beginning of the press conferences in the Department. He made it a custom to receive a few of the correspondents accredited to the Department regularly and to explain policies by giving the background. Much of what he said was confidential and only once was his confidence misplaced and then it occurred because a correspondent, coming late, had not been informed of the secrecy injunction. Hay's sense of humor and quick repartee were shown by the way that he handled this situation. When the offending correspondent was accused by Hay at his next conference, he assured the Secretary that he would not have violated his confidence for anything in the world. Hay, knowing that he represented one of the *Journals,* promptly quipped, "Perhaps not for the *World,* but you would for the *Journal.*" [24]

18

Elihu Root and Robert Bacon

Elihu Root—Secretary of State

Upon the death of John Hay, President Roosevelt considered only two persons to replace him, William Howard Taft and Elihu Root. Taft was at the time Secretary of War and Root had preceded him in that position. Roosevelt did not hesitate long because, as he wrote to Senator Lodge on July 11, 1905:

As soon as I began seriously to think it over I saw there was really no room for doubt whatever, because it was not a choice as far as the Cabinet was concerned between Root and Taft, but a choice of having both instead of one.[1]

On the same day President Roosevelt wrote to ex-Senator Beveridge, giving more specific reasons for choosing Root:

I wished Root as Secretary of State partly because I am extremely fond of him and prize his companionship as well as his advice but primarily because I think that in all the country he is the best man for the position and that no minister of foreign affairs in any other country at this moment in any way compares with him.[2]

Roosevelt's opinion of Root was accepted almost universally. Few men had been inducted into the Department of State as Secretary with the eminent reputation for statesmanship that Elihu Root possessed when he was approached by President Roosevelt. He had been an outstanding attorney and counselor at law when in 1899 he was asked by President McKinley to serve as Secretary of War. In his five years' service under McKinley and Theodore Roosevelt he achieved not only a national but an international reputation. His handling of the relations with Cuba, Puerto Rico, and the Philippines was successful in the highest degree. While Secretary of War, he worked constantly and closely with Secretary of State Hay, often taking the latter's place, in fact

Photo Pach Bros., N.Y.

ELIHU ROOT

if not in name, when the Secretary of State was ill. He had been outstandingly successful as the chief representative of the United States in the Alaska Boundary Dispute. Secretary of War Taft accurately expressed the sentiment of the country when he declared: "Happy the country, happy the President, who having lost a Hay, can turn to a Root."

Root, although he had been so successful as Secretary of War, was not overly eager to return to Washington and the responsibilities of a high government official. His hesitation was less due to the huge loss of income from his law practice in accepting the paltry $8,000 offered by the Department of State than the feeling that his ability was overrated and too much would be expected of him. His sense of public duty gave him no option, however, and he accepted Roosevelt's offer promptly and with no reservations. He was sworn in on July 19, 1905, but he did little active work in the Department until September.

Changes in Personnel

When Root took over the Department the first problem was a new First Assistant Secretary. Lloyd Griscom, one of our few career diplomats at the time, had been slated to succeed Loomis if Hay had lived, but Roosevelt and Root now decided to appoint Robert Bacon, a classmate of Roosevelt's at Harvard and at the time a partner in the banking house of J. P. Morgan. It was an appointment based wholly upon personal relationship, because Bacon had had no diplomatic experience and he himself questioned whether he would be able to write a satisfactory dispatch. However, with the ever dependable Adee still at hand, the technical details would always be taken care of adequately and correctly. It was not long before Bacon and Root became very close friends and Bacon carried out instructions so successfully that when Root finally resigned to accept the position of senator for New York he recommended and Roosevelt accepted Bacon as Secretary of State. Bacon possessed an unusually charming personality and with a background of family, wealth, travel, and culture he was particularly well suited to the social side of diplomatic life. Loomis had remained in the Department throughout the summer of 1905 while Root took a much needed vacation, and then spent another month in the fall assisting Bacon in his new duties.

The position of Chief Clerk became vacant, shortly after Root became Secretary of State, with the resignation of William H. Michael, who had held the position almost eight years. In his place Charles Denby was appointed. An expert on Far Eastern affairs, Denby had served for twelve years as secretary and chargé d'affaires in the United States legation in Peking and later as advisor to Viceroy Yuan Shi-kai. Apparently Denby's services in the Far East were of more value to the government than as Chief Clerk in Washington, because in less than two years he returned to China to be consul general in Shanghai. The able and experienced Wilbur Carr was thereupon promoted from his position as Chief of the Consular Bureau to that of Chief Clerk. The change meant not only an increase in responsibility but also an increase in salary from $2,100 to $3,000. A more serious resignation, which occurred shortly after that of Chief Clerk Michael's, was that of Solicitor William L. Penfield. Here a most excellent successor was found in James Brown Scott, who was, when appointed, a professor in the law school of Columbia University. Several years later Root, in a letter to President Nicholas Murray Butler of Columbia University, wrote that he considered it one of the most fortunate events of his administration that he was able to secure Scott for Solicitor. "He came to the State Department without any influence or backing of any kind. I had never known him and nobody spoke for him. He was selected solely for what he had already done, and from what I could learn of him from inquiries I made." [3]

The appointment of Huntington Wilson as Third Assistant Secretary of State upon the retirement of H. H. D. Peirce in June, 1906, who had been named minister to Norway, was not entirely a happy one. Wilson had served in the American legation at Tokyo in various capacities and was very highly regarded by Minister Lloyd Griscom. After seven years' service in Japan, a post which Wilson never liked, Griscom wrote Secretary Hay, urging his secretary's promotion to another post.[4] When nothing came of it, Wilson's young wife, a good friend of Secretary of War Taft, persuaded him to introduce her to Secretary Root so that she could urge Wilson's promotion. According to Archie Butt: "When Root saw the Juno-like form of Mrs. Wilson and watched her sweep across the room like a long limbed Atalanta his eyes began to warm." [5] When the post of the Third Assistant Secretary became vacant, Root appointed Wilson, but the two were never sympathetic. Root regarded Wilson as overly formal and wholly lacking in a sense of humor, quite egotistical and too easy to take offense. On one occasion Wilson tendered his resignation when President Roosevelt refused to deliver an address prepared by Wilson because it was "fatuous and absurd." [6] Root apparently had no confidence in Wilson's judgment, because when he was about to embark on his tour of Latin America, he wrote to President Roosevelt that it was "a great satisfaction to leave Bacon in charge with Adee and Scott to back him up." [7]

On the other hand, Wilson was "naturally horrified at the methods . . . in the Department of State." He found its "antiquated organization pitifully inadequate for the conduct of foreign relations in sorry contrast to the other great powers." [8] Wilson recognized Root's brilliance as a lawyer and his remarkable mind but felt that he was a poor administrator because he found it difficult to delegate authority. He regarded Bacon as a mere shadow of Root without an idea of his own and unable to make decisions. Wilson highly appreciated Alvey Adee, "the perennial and lovable Second Assistant Secretary" who, according to Wilson, was a "veritable encyclopedia of precedent and of all the past business of the Department" and whose wisdom and experience made him "a valuable restraining and conservative influence." [9] In spite of their incompatibility, Secretary Root and Third Secretary Wilson worked together most effectively, and it was Wilson who persuaded Root to begin the reorganization of the Department of State upon a regional basis.

Foreign-Service Reorganization

The first effort of Secretary Root toward the improvement of the machinery of foreign intercourse was a reorganization of the diplomatic and consular services. The latter was particularly vulnerable to the political spoilsmen and was used either to reward political services or to get rid of political rivals. The result was a defective, inefficient organization wholly unfitted for the tasks it was expected to perform. President Cleveland in 1895 had attempted to improve the consular service by an executive order requiring examinations and promotions by merit in the lower ranks, but its administration had been very perfunctory after President Cleveland went out of office.

On November 10, 1905, President Roosevelt issued the executive order which placed both diplomatic and consular positions, except for the posts of ambassador or minister, upon a civil-service basis. Examinations were required for entrance into the foreign service and promotions were to be made upon a basis of merit.[10]

Root thereupon drafted a bill to put the reforms upon a permanent statutory basis; but the law of April 5, 1906, as passed, merely classified consuls and provided for annual inspection of consulates and the payment of consuls by salaries instead of by fees. Root, however, again had recourse to the executive-order method, and President Roosevelt, by an order dated June 27, 1906, extended the civil service merit system to the whole consular service. The examining board recommended by Root consisted of the Third Secretary of State, Huntington Wilson; the Chief of the Consular Bureau, Wilbur Carr; and a representative of the Civil Service Commission. Secretary Wilson felt that his most important contribution to the regulations governing the examinations was his insistence that the examinations be oral as well as written and that the oral examination should count for half of the grade.[11]

The examinations were very strictly graded; and when in 1907 only thirteen out of thirty-eight candidates passed, Assistant Secretary Bacon authorized the board of examiners to permit a reexamination—a policy which has continued up to date. Root never interfered with the examiners but once did suggest to Mr. Carr that they ought to keep in mind that the examinations were not being held for exclusion from the foreign service.[12] Root handled promotions and always read the dossier of each officer whose name was listed as deserving of promotion. He also advocated allowances for rent and other expenses of foreign-service officers and the purchase of buildings for our diplomatic and consular establishments abroad, but the Congress showed a complete lack of interest in his suggestions. One suggestion for the improvement of the foreign service, supposed to have been made by Adee, which did not appeal to Root was a uniform for American diplomats. After noting the suggestions for "silk stockings and satin knee breeches, a silk coat with red satin sash and lace frills," Root suggested one additional improvement: "a spray of mistletoe embroidered on the coat tails." [13]

Departmental Reorganization

Although Secretary Root was not a particularly able administrator, he did make a few important improvements in the internal condition of the Department. He found the arrangement and classification of official documents crude and archaic. Remembering that the War Department had a system whereby all documentary information was made easily and quickly available, Root had an employee, David A. Salmon of the War Department, transferred to the State Department and three State Department employees detailed to the War Department to become familiar with the new procedure. The new system as installed by Mr. Salmon was so highly satisfactory that the Department retained him in charge of the files, and some years later he became Chief of the Bureau of Indexes and Archives. Root also attempted to get higher salaries for the Departmental personnel and additional clerks and assistants to carry the constantly increasing burdens. It was Secretary Root who suggested the plan, subsequently adopted, of making officers of the Department eligible for transfer to positions in the foreign service.

Secretary Root did not hesitate to make changes promptly when the action was warranted. On April 23, 1907, Gaillard Hunt, Chief of the Passport Bureau, prepared a memorandum for the Secretary recommending that the Passport Bureau be rechristened the Bureau of Citizenship. Hunt pointed out that all communications to the Department pertaining to citizenship and protection abroad came to the Passport Bureau, which was authorized to act upon them, and that such action would come more appropriately from a Bureau of Citizenship. Inasmuch as the bureaus were all created by orders of the Secretary of State, Root issued such an order on May 31, 1907, designating the Passport Bureau thereafter as the Bureau of Citizenship.[14]

The most important innovation in a half century in the organization of the Department of State—the establishment of the geographical divisions—

although it was begun during Root's Secretaryship, received very little encouragement from him. Huntington Wilson, then Third Secretary of State, had worked out an elaborate reorganization plan which proposed the establishment of four geographical divisions—Latin American, Far Eastern, Near Eastern, and Western European affairs—each to be administered by an expert brought in from the diplomatic or consular service in those fields who would thus be well acquainted with existing conditions and problems. The plan also concentrated responsibility in the office of the First Assistant Secretary, who became a sort of Under Secretary of State.[15] Root took no action upon the plan for six months and then somewhat grudgingly suggested that Wilson take over Far Eastern affairs as an experiment. Wilson agreed, provided he could have as his assistants William Phillips, second secretary of the American legation at Peking, and Percival Heintzleman, a career officer with five years' experience in the consular service in China. The two officers were ordered home and the Division of Far Eastern Affairs was created in March, 1908. Root finally conceded that it was a step in the right direction, but the full-fledged development of the reorganization as Wilson had proposed did not take place until Philander C. Knox became Secretary of State in March, 1909.

It will be remembered that Secretary Hay had been quite unhappy in his relations with the Foreign Relations Committee of the Senate. In the case of Secretary Root there was no such problem. As Secretary of War he had been accustomed to appear before congressional committees, and when Chairman Cullom suggested that he appear the suggestion was received with enthusiasm. "In fact," remarked Senator Cullom, "he [Root] became so constant and punctual in his attendance at the meetings of the Committee that we grew almost to regard him as a regular member." [16] According to Dr. James Brown Scott, at that time Solicitor of the Department, "Root assured by his personal appearance before the Committee, its approval of all of the conventions of the Second Hague Peace Conference and of his own treaties of arbitration." [17]

Relations with Latin America

Elihu Root served as Secretary of State for three and one-half years, from July 7, 1905, to January 27, 1909. One of his first tasks as he saw it was to improve relations with our Latin American neighbors. He was somewhat handicapped by the fact that it was he who had written the Platt Amendment legalizing the right of American intervention in Cuba, and he had also made a strong defense of Roosevelt's action in regard to the Panama Canal. Nevertheless, Root felt that a good-will trip to Latin America in connection with the Third International American Conference to be held in Rio de Janeiro in July, 1906, would help dissipate suspicion of the Colossus of the North. He saw to all arrangements personally, and his unaffected friendliness and his simplicity and charm of manner did much to counteract the latent fears of our neighbors to the south. His one formal prepared address at the conference was a convincing exposition of the vital need for mutual and sympathetic understanding among the American nations. One paragraph was a clarion call for continental solidarity:

No nation can live unto itself alone and continue to live. . . . There is not one of our countries that cannot benefit the others, there is not one that will not gain by the prosperity, the peace, the happiness of all. . . . We wish for no victories but those of peace; for no territory except our own, for no sovereignty except the sovereignty over ourselves.

Senator Henry Cabot Lodge felt that Root had done more to advance our good relations with South America than had been done in all the years since Henry Clay began it.[18] The beautiful Pan American Union Building in Washington was built and donated to the twenty-one American republics by Andrew Carnegie at the suggestion of Elihu Root. Also, it was Root who urgently insisted that the American republics be invited to participate in the Second Hague Conference.

Throughout Root's administration of the Department of State, relations with the Latin American republics were conducted upon a basis of mutual equality and respect. At Root's instigation the Department of State persuaded Mexico to join in offering good offices to the warring Central American states Guatemala and El Salvador, and a peace convention was signed upon the United States warship *Marblehead*. The peace was short-lived, owing to the intransigeance of President Zelaya of Nicaragua, but Root had Adee keep open the tender of good offices and at length the Central American states agreed to send representatives to Washington to establish a lasting peace. Secretary Root welcomed the delegates, and the result was not only a general treaty of peace and amity, but a convention establishing a Central American Court of Justice based upon a plan for a World Court proposed by Root at the Hague Conference.[19] Roosevelt conceded that the policy of the administration toward Latin America while Root was Secretary of State was wholly directed by the Department of State—all that Roosevelt did was to back up the Secretary of State.[20]

Root's Achievements

Perhaps never in its history was the foreign policy of the United States conducted on a higher plane than when Root was the directing agent. His instructions to the American delegates at the Second Hague Conference were models of fairness and national initiative. Roosevelt and Root worked together to prevent war between France and Germany over Morocco and obtained the consent of the Senate to the Treaty of Algeciras. Root concluded some twenty-five arbitration treaties, the one with Great Britain leading to the settlement of the century-old Newfoundland fisheries dispute. Root helped in bringing about the remission of the unused half of the Boxer indemnity to China, and his agreement with Viscount Takahashi of Japan strengthened the open-door policy and the maintenance of the territorial status quo in the Far East. He worked closely with Roosevelt in trying to protect Japanese in California against local discriminatory legislation, and the gentleman's agreement with Japan to control Japanese immigration was his peaceful solution of a very threatening situation.

The work of Secretary Root was so outstanding that President-elect Taft urged him to remain in the post under the new administration. If Root had consulted only his own inclinations he would have remained, but he felt that Mrs. Root could not continue to endure the Washington climate and the arduous social duties entailed by being the wife of the highest cabinet officer. Inasmuch as the New York State Legislature had elected him to represent New York in the Senate, he felt that such a position would keep him in public life and at the same time require much less time in Washington. At Taft's request that he suggest a successor, he recommended Senator Philander C. Knox of Pennsylvania, and it was Root who approached Knox to obtain his consent to the acceptance of the position. Inasmuch as Root wished a rest before entering upon his senatorial duties, he proposed that President Roosevelt appoint Robert Bacon as Secretary of State to fill out the period from January 27, 1909, until the new President should be inaugurated on March 4. In his letter accepting Root's resignation as Secretary of State, President Roosevelt was even more laudatory than in his praise of Hay. Speaking what he declared to be "the literal truth," President Roosevelt said: "In my judgment you will be regarded as the greatest and ablest man who has ever filled the position of Secretary of State." [21]

Robert Bacon—Secretary of State

Robert Bacon, whom Secretary Root had recommended as his immediate successor for the few weeks remaining of the Roosevelt administration, had served most congenially as Root's right-hand man. In his thirty-seven days as Secretary of State, Bacon had merely to carry on the Root policies. The new Secretary of State, Senator Knox, was very desirous that Mr. Bacon remain as Under Secretary. Mr. Bacon agreed and a bill to create the office of Under Secretary was introduced. When it failed of passage and the embassy in Paris became vacant as a result of the resignation of Henry White, Bacon was appointed as ambassador to France. The only change in the Department of State personnel in the short period of Bacon's incumbency was the appointment of John C. O'Laughlin, an able newspaper man, as Assistant Secretary of State to fill the vacancy created by Mr. Bacon's promotion. A change, just preceding Mr. Root's resignation, which should be noted was the appointment of William Phillips, a career foreign-service officer, as Third Assistant Secretary of State to replace Huntington Wilson, who had been named minister to the Argentine Republic. Phillips had been brought into the Department from his post at Peking to serve first as assistant to the Third Assistant Secretary of State and later as Chief of the Division of Far Eastern Affairs.

19

Philander C. Knox

Philander C. Knox—Secretary of State

Like many a Secretary of State preceding him, Philander C. Knox had held no diplomatic or other position which would have given him experience in the conduct of foreign relations. In fact Lord Bryce, the British ambassador, a very keen and objective commentator on American political affairs, observed that Knox "gave the impression of having cared little, known little, or thought little of foreign politics until he became a minister, and as being, partly from a lack of diplomatic or historical preparation, partly from a certain impatience of temperament, inclined to be autocratic and rapid in his decisions." [1] Root, who had recommended Knox to Taft and thought very highly of him, became somewhat critical of Knox's temperamental tendencies, particularly in his policy toward Latin America.

Knox was a peppery sort of fellow. He got mad very easily. He did mix into things too much. . . . He was absolutely antipathetic to all Spanish-American modes of thought and feeling and action, and pretty much everything he did with them was like mixing a Seidlitz powder. [2]

However, although inexperienced in the conduct of foreign relations and undiplomatic in temperament, Philander C. Knox had many attributes in his favor. In his twenty-four years in the practice of law, he had proved himself to possess outstanding administrative as well as forensic abilities; in his three years as Attorney General he had not only been successful in such complicated domestic issues as the prosecution of the Northern Securities Company, but he had also been able to clear the title of De Lesseps' Panama Canal Company. Finally, in his five years as senator from Pennsylvania, he had to give consideration to many problems of foreign policy and he would thus be able to appreciate the senatorial point of view.

One difficulty which seems to have been overlooked completely in the appointment of Knox was the fact that as senator he had voted for the legislative act, approved on February 26, 1907, increasing the salary of the Secretary of State from $8,000 to $12,000. Inasmuch as the Constitution (Article I, Section 6) specifically prohibits any senator from being appointed to any civil office during the time for which he was elected if the emoluments of that office shall have been increased during such term, the question was not a simple one. That the problem had not occurred to either Root or Knox, both outstanding constitutional lawyers, is rather surprising. The problem was solved by the repeal of Section 4 of the Act which raised the Secretary's salary, thus putting it back to the $8,000 level. The reduced salary scale held until the Act of March 4, 1911, reestablished the figure at $12,000, inasmuch as the six-year term as senator to which Knox had been elected had now expired.

Philander C. Knox entered upon his duties as Secretary of State on March 6, 1909. However, he had known of his prospective appointment months earlier and had immediately given consideration to the personnel in the Department. Among his visitors at this time was Huntington Wilson, former Third Secretary of State, who was making preparations to go to Buenos Aires as minister to Argentina. Knox became keenly interested in Wilson's plans for the reorganization of the Department and just two days before Wilson was to sail for his new post offered him the position of Assistant Secretary of State.[3] Wilson was delighted at the promotion and at the opportunity afforded of getting his plans for the reorganization of the Department adopted under his direction.

Knox and Wilson Reorganize the Department

A very considerable increase of work had been entailed upon the Department by its more extensive relations with Latin America, as well as by an increase of more than 75 per cent in foreign trade and over 100 per cent in immigration. The personnel in the Department, although considerably augmented, was still inadequate and wholly unprepared to take on any additional duties. The following figures for the years 1898 and 1908 indicate the relative ratio of increases: consular fees in 1898 were $532,990.25 and in 1908 they were $1,613,834.65; salaries for Departmental officers in 1898 amounted to $118,038.50 and in 1908 they amounted to $228,386.85; the number on the Department's payroll in 1898 was 82 and in 1908 it was 167; American foreign trade in 1898 amounted to $1,847,531,984 and in 1908 it had reached the sum of $3,055,115,138.[4]

The situation in the Department became critical when the new Tariff Act of August 5, 1909, imposed upon the Department of State the duty of checking the laws and practices of foreign governments with reference to American trade to enable the President to grant minimum rates where the law permitted. Secretary Knox had pointed out the impossibility of the existing personnel and machinery in the Department of State to discharge these additional duties and at the same time safeguard national interests. He declared that an additional $100,000 would be required to reorganize the Department to meet the new situation. Congress, impressed by his arguments, granted the entire amount and Secretary Knox and Assistant Secretary Wilson proceeded to put into effect the most complete reorganization of the Department since the reorganization by Secretary Fish in 1870.

The first new office established under the reorganization plan was Counselor of the Department. This officer was expected to investigate and report on such important questions as required legal and technical skill and uninterrupted consideration. For example, he had the responsibility of negotiating trade agreements under the Act of 1909, of giving consideration to questions raised by the International Maritime Conference and the international congress dealing with the fur seals. The duties imposed required an able and experienced lawyer, and a salary of $7,500 was allocated to the position. Secretary Knox appointed as the first Counselor, Henry M. Hoyt of Pennsylvania, formerly Solicitor General of the United States, who had worked closely with Mr. Knox when he was Attorney General. Hoyt entered upon his new position on August 27, 1909, and held it until his death on November 20, 1910. The next appointee to this position was a prominent New York lawyer, Chandler P. Anderson, who had already served as special counselor to Elihu Root while he was Secretary of State. It has sometimes been erroneously stated that the position of Counselor was equivalent to that of Under Secretary of State, which was created in 1919. As a matter of fact, the First Assistant Secretary of State was in reality the equivalent of an Under Secretary. In his report to Congress on the reorganization, Secretary Knox thus defined the position of Assistant Secretary: "The office of Assistant Secretary, which corresponds to that of Under Secretary or Vice Minister for Foreign Affairs in other foreign offices, shares under the direction of the Secretary in the general direction of the Department." [5] Unfortunately the salary assigned to the Assistant Secretary under the reorganization was only $5,000, so that subsequent First Assistant Secretaries regularly assumed the title of Counselor in order to receive the $7,500 salary which went with that office.[6]

Another new position created in the reorganization was that of Resident Diplomatic Officer, whose duty it would be to assist the Secretary in the formulation and execution of policies from the standpoint of a career officer who had been in actual touch with the problems in the field. Inasmuch as the current problems requiring such assistance were largely Latin American, due to the rapid growth of political relations between the United States and the countries of that area, a Latin American expert was indicated. The officer chosen was

Thomas C. Dawson, who had served as minister to Chile and to Colombia. His previous experience included the position of consul general in Santo Domingo and secretary of legation in Rio de Janeiro. His two-volume work entitled *The South American Republics*, published in 1903, was one of the first scholarly studies made by a North American in the field of Latin American history and government. Since career officers received considerably larger salaries than their equivalent officials in the Department, the salary fixed for this position was $7,500 annually. In 1910 Mr. Dawson was sent to represent the United States in Panama and then transferred to carry out an important mission in Nicaragua.[7] Secretary Knox thereupon appointed H. Percival Dodge as his successor as Resident Diplomatic Officer and Chief of the Latin American Division. Mr. Dodge was a career officer who had served as third secretary in Berlin, as minister to Honduras and El Salvador, and who, when appointed, was American minister to Morocco.

The functions assigned to the Second Assistant Secretary under the reorganization did not differ materially from what they had been formerly. Inasmuch as Alvey A. Adee continued to serve as Second Assistant Secretary, it was taken for granted that he would continue to exercise a directing influence over all matters which concerned the Department.

The work of the Third Assistant Secretary was now made specifically administrative. Whereas previously he had been charged with the immediate supervision of all matters pertaining to the consular service, he was now made responsible for the administrative direction of the diplomatic service. He was also given the direction of matters relating to international conferences and questions of ceremonial. He was charged with the approval or disapproval of expenditures of public moneys in the Department and the foreign service. In addition to these administrative duties the Third Assistant Secretary was given supervision over one of the new geographical divisions created by the reorganization of the Division of Western European Affairs. William Phillips, who was the first Chief of the Division of Far Eastern Affairs, had been appointed Third Secretary of State in January, 1909, but in September of the same year he was named secretary of embassy in London. In his place Chandler Hale, son of Senator Hale of Maine, was named Third Secretary. Hale had served as secretary of the United States embassy in Rome and Vienna and also as secretary of the American delegation at the Second Hague Conference. Although not a man of outstanding attainments, he was familiar with diplomatic procedure and the administration of the foreign service. He was assisted by Charles Lee Cooke, a clerk in the Department who later became the Department's leading authority on all matters of precedence and protocol.

Another new post established at this time was the Director of the Consular Service. We have seen that the Third Assistant Secretary had been divested of all matters pertaining to the consular service and that Wilbur Carr, who had been acting as Chief Clerk for the past two years, was given direction over consular matters. Carr had already served in the Department some seventeen years and had been Chief of the Consular Bureau for a number of years. His directive emphasized the promotion and extension of our foreign commerce through the consular service. The salary for this position was fixed at $4,500.

The work of the Solicitor's office had increased considerably, which warranted the addition of a Third Assistant Solicitor and several law clerks. It was estimated that from 165 to 170 communications were referred to this officer every week. They covered every phase of international law and diplomacy: diplomatic claims, cases of extradition, citizenship, naturalization, expatriation, and passport problems, questions of extraterritoriality, neutrality, asylum, and many questions of municipal law. Questions of claims passing through the Solicitor's office for the preceding two-year period amounted to about $125,000,-000. James Brown Scott, who had been appointed Solicitor in 1906 at an annual salary of $4,500, had his salary increased to $5,000. His two able assistants, J. Reuben Clark, Jr., and William C. Dennis, who were also appointed in 1900, were retained at their existing salaries of $3,000, and a new Assistant Solicitor, Charles F. Wilson, was appointed at the same salary.

The most important innovation in the reorganization of the Department was the establishment of three new politico-geographical divisions—Western European, Near Eastern, and Latin American—in addition to the Far Eastern Division, which was already functioning satisfactorily. Under the reorganization of Secretary Knox, Ransford S. Miller, Jr., who had served as interpreter for the United States legation in Japan for a decade and then as Japanese secretary and interpreter to the embassy, was appointed as Chief of the Division of Far Eastern Affairs at a salary of $4,500 a year. As his first assistant, Edward T. Williams, an outstanding authority in Chinese affairs, was named. Williams, who received the same salary as the Chief, had served as interpreter, consul general, and secretary of the American legation in China and was fully conversant with political and commercial affairs in the Far East. The jurisdiction of the Division of Far Eastern Affairs included Japan, China, and leased territories, Siberia, Hongkong, French Indo-China, Siam, the Straits Settlements, Borneo, East Indies, India, and in general the Far East. In its first year the division sent and received some 9,500 communications covering such questions as commercial undertakings, the open door and equality of commercial opportunity, the problem of the territorial integrity of China, immigration, railway and public works concessions, American missions, schools and hospitals, the reform of the opium traffic, and questions of extraterritoriality.

The new Division of Latin American Affairs was established by a departmental order dated November 19, 1909, under the direction of Thomas C.

Dawson, the Resident Diplomatic Officer, who also held the title of Chief of the Division of Latin American Affairs. He was given as his Assistant Chief, W. T. S. Doyle, an able lawyer who had assisted W. I. Buchanan, the American commissioner charged with settlement of the Venezuela claims and who had served as Secretary Root's private secretary on his tour of South America. Doyle had managed the Central American Peace Conference which had been held in Washington in 1907, and according to Huntington Wilson, he was "the best man the Department of State has ever had in Latin American Affairs." As Assistant Chief, however, his salary was only $3,000 a year. The Division of Latin American Affairs was charged with the duty of carrying on diplomatic, consular, and miscellaneous correspondence relating to Mexico, Central America, South America, and the West Indies. From the beginning the personnel of this division was overworked, even though the work of a routine nature was transferred to the Diplomatic Bureau. It was estimated that Mr. Doyle averaged twenty-seven hours per week of overtime work. As examples of its work, the division aided materially in the settlement of disputes between Panama and Costa Rica, Peru and Ecuador, and revolutionary disturbances in Nicaragua and Honduras. The division took charge of all matters concerning the Fourth Pan American Conference at Buenos Aires, held in August, 1910.

A departmental order, dated December 13, 1909, set up the Division of Western European Affairs under the supervision of the Third Assistant Secretary of State, Chandler Hale. No Assistant Chief was named in 1909 and three clerks constituted the personnel. In 1910 one of the clerks, Charles Lee Cooke, was named Assistant Chief. Mr. Cooke had been in the Department since 1901 and just before his appointment in the Western European Division had served as clerk in the American embassy in London. Since this division was charged with the entertainment of foreign guests of the government, the presentation of newly accredited foreign representatives to the President, and other questions of precedence and etiquette, Mr. Cooke became the State Department's expert in ceremonial and protocol. The jurisdiction of this division included Great Britain and her colonies, Portugal, Spain, France, Belgium, Switzerland, Luxembourg, Norway, Sweden, Denmark, Morocco, the Congo, and Liberia. It was estimated that this division prepared about 4,500 communications annually.

The same departmental order which set up the Division of Western European Affairs also established the Division of Near Eastern Affairs, which was charged with questions arising in connection with Turkey, Greece, Italy, the Balkan states, Germany, Austria-Hungary, Russia, Abyssinia, Persia, Egypt, and the colonies belonging to the countries in this area. Evan Young, a career officer familiar with problems in the Near East, was named Chief of the Division of Near Eastern Affairs at a salary of $3,000. Young was a graduate of the

University of Wisconsin law school and had served as consul at Harput for three years and as consul at Salonika for about a year and a half. This division had as its primary duties the protection of American economic, educational, and religious interests in this region. It was estimated that the division handled about 13,000 pieces of correspondence annually.

An innovation in the reorganization plan was the creation of a new agency called the Division of Information. Its duties as prescribed by the Departmental order required the publication of a pamphlet, called the "Information Series," which should give to every American embassy and legation the pertinent information regarding the negotiations that the United States was carrying on in all parts of the world. The division was also required to read and digest current publications at home and abroad, write a summary of current news of diplomatic or economic importance, and distribute it to Secretaries and heads of divisions and bureaus. Finally, the annual *Foreign Relations* volumes were prepared under the supervision of this division. The editing required considerable care and discretion to prevent the inclusion of material of a confidential nature or material which might be protested by friendly states. As Chief of this division, a well known newspaper man, Philip H. Patchin, was named. Mr. Patchin had served as reporter for the *New York Sun* for a number of years in Washington and in various countries of Latin America. The Chief was assigned an Assistant Chief and four clerks and his salary was fixed at $3,000 annually.

In addition to the new agencies established, some changes and additions were made to the older bureaus. It was recognized that the Bureau of Trade Relations, which had been in existence since 1903, would have to be overhauled and enlarged. As a result of the additional duties imposed upon the Department by the Tariff Act of August 5, 1909, there were needed not only additional clerks but technical advisers. Under the reorganization two commercial advisers were added at salaries of $4,500 each and a total clerical force of thirteen was allocated. As is often the case in reorganization plans, the Chief of the bureau was wholly overlooked and his salary was maintained at its previous level of $2,100. This was the more inexcusable in that the Chief, John B. Osborne, was a man of wide experience and considerable ability. He had served previously in the foreign service, had practiced law, and had been Chief of the bureau since May 17, 1905. The two new expert advisers were Charles M. Pepper and Mack H. Davis, both of whom had served as foreign trade commissioners in the Department of Commerce and Labor. The bureau's work covered two types: (1) matters pertaining to the trade reports and correspondence of American diplomatic and consular officers, and (2) the compilation of commercial information for the use of the Department and the drafting of official correspondence relating to tariff and other commercial questions. A report of the work of the bureau for the year 1910 showed incoming correspondence of 35,000 pieces and outgoing 50,301. Over 9,000 consular and diplomatic reports were edited in the bureau and 13,667 consular trade letters.[8] In supporting the work of this bureau before the sub-committee of the Committee on Appropriations, Secretary Knox declared that the United States had obtained over $200,000,000 of new business for the United States as a result of the direct efforts of this agency.[9]

The Diplomatic Bureau, which remained under the direction of Sydney Y. Smith, remained practically unchanged under the reorganization. However, when Wilbur Carr was made Director of the Consular Service and was relieved of his duties as Chief Clerk, William McNeir, another clerk with a service record dating back to 1881, succeeded him. Herbert C. Hengstler remained in charge of the Consular Bureau. The Bureau of Citizenship was slightly enlarged and placed under the direction of Richard Flournoy, Jr., upon the retirement of Gaillard Hunt in 1908, after twenty-one years of service in the Department. A comparison of the work done in this agency for the years 1901 and 1910 indicated an increase of the number of passports issued from 14,554 to 24,064 and an increase in the number of pieces of mail leaving the bureau from 21,268 to 42,131. As a result of the new procedure of registering in American consulates under the direction of this bureau all Americans living abroad, the certificates of registration for the year 1910 amounted to 6,319.[10]

The Bureau of Indexes and Archives, which received, recorded, distributed, and filed all of the correspondence pertaining to the general business of the Department, continued to grow as the work of the Department increased. A number of improvements, such as changing from a chronological file to a case system and a decimal classification of subjects of correspondence, simplified the work and increased the efficiency of the bureau. The number of clerks in this bureau had increased from 15 in 1900 to 29 in 1910. In 1910 the bureau was handling about 10,000 papers and 1,000 telegrams monthly. John R. Buck, the Chief of this Bureau since 1906, remained in charge.

The Bureau of Rolls and Library which had received no addition to the staff in ten years, still remained unchanged in spite of its increased and very important work. With a collection of about 75,000 volumes and the originals of laws, treaties, proclamations, and executive orders, original manuscript records and papers, the bureau was an indispensable adjunct to the formulation of policy. It was estimated that over 5,000 communications, some requiring extensive research, were answered in the course of a year. When William McNeir was promoted from his post as Chief of this bureau to that of Chief Clerk, he was succeeded by his assistant John A. Towner, who had been a clerk in the Department since 1907.

The Bureau of Appointments, which had charge of all applications for appointments to positions under the Department of State, found its work increased materially by the new and restrictive regulations for the appointment of foreign-service officers after examination issued by President Taft's order of November 26, 1909. Miles M. Shand, who entered the Department as a clerk in 1882, was named Chief of the Bureau of Appointments in November, 1908.

The one agency which still needed overhauling was the Bureau of Accounts, but owing to the necessity of following archaic procedures specifically required by law, no change was immediately possible. Secretary Knox, in a statement to the chairmen of the Senate and House Committees on Foreign Relations and Foreign Affairs on January 7, 1911, pointed out:

A simple, expeditious, and inexpensive system is needed, but such system cannot be adopted so long as the law remains unchanged. If Congress should act favorably upon the recommendations submitted, it is proposed to abolish all unnecessary formalities and reduce the accounting system to such form as will require a minimum of clerical work.[11]

The total personnel of the Department at the end of the year 1909, when the Department had been almost completely reorganized by Secretary Knox, consisted of 35 ranking officers, 135 clerks, 28 messengers, 2 telephone operators, 1 porter, 8 laborers and 1 messenger boy, making a total of 210 persons. The most unsatisfactory feature of the reorganization was the gross inequality of salaries paid in the Department. For example, Huntington Wilson, who in reality was second in command, received a salary of $5,000, and Alvey Adee, Second Assistant Secretary and perhaps the most important man in the Department, received $4,500. On the other hand the new appointees to the positions of Counselor and Resident Diplomatic Officer were granted salaries of $7,500 each. The Chief and Assistant Chief of the Division of Far Eastern Affairs received salaries of $4,500 each, while the Chief of Near Eastern Affairs received $3,000. The Chief of the Bureau of Trade Relations received $2,100, while each of his two assistants received $4,500 as technical advisers. The highly trained lawyer who served as Chief of the Bureau of Citizenship obtained $2,100 annually, while the journalistically trained Chief of the Bureau of Information received $3,000. Such a hodgepodge of inequalities in salaries, all of which were made public, could not but have a serious effect upon the morale of the able and experienced officers so unfairly discriminated against. The salaries of the clerks ranged from $900 to $1,800, that of messengers from $720 to $840, while laborers received either $600 a year or $1.50 per day.[12]

On the whole, however, the reorganization made for a considerable improvement in the efficiency of the Department. The changes were not radical but were made by men familiar with the needs of the Department, and they were based upon a background of experience. A business expert of wide experience in reorganizing corporations, Major Hine, who had been appointed by President Taft to examine the governmental machinery, after making a brief survey of the reorganized administration of the Department of State, stated that "the working of the State Department indicates the most modern type of organization and an intelligent development of the most progressive methods. . . . So far from the State Department needing much expert assistance, it is in a position to set an example as to fundamentals of organization and methods for many large business corporations." [13]

Diplomatic Appointments

Inasmuch as both President Taft and Secretary of State Knox had come into office highly recommended by their Republican predecessors, few changes occurred in important diplomatic appointments abroad. In London Whitelaw Reid continued to represent American interests at No. 10 Downing Street, as he had under the Roosevelt-Hay regime. In Paris, however, where the able and experienced career diplomat, Henry White, was doing a most excellent job, a change was made in spite of every effort on the part of ex-President Roosevelt, Senator Lodge, and other notable Republicans to prevent it. President Taft, when in Paris some years earlier, had not received tickets for an important Parliamentary debate and he blamed the secretary of the embassy for not obtaining them. Henry White happened to have been the unfortunate secretary. Roosevelt never forgave Taft for White's removal and he later declared: "The most useful man in the entire diplomatic service during my Presidency, and for many years before, was Henry White . . . he was removed by Mr. Taft, for reasons unconnected with the good of the service." [14] President Taft, at the request of Senator Lodge, first offered the embassy post in Paris to President Eliot of Harvard. When Eliot refused it,[15] Assistant Secretary of State Bacon was named, and he was very pleased at the promotion. Other posts where no changes occurred were Berlin, where David Jayne Hill had proved himself a very able diplomat, and Copenhagen, where Maurice Francis Eagan, a witty professor of English from Catholic University, was asked to retain his post. It should be noted that many of the changes which were made simply meant the transfer of experienced diplomats from one post to another. For example, William W. Rockhill was transferred from China to Russia, Henry Lane Wilson from Belgium to Mexico, E. V. Morgan from Cuba to Paraguay and Uruguay, and John G. A. Leishman from Turkey to Italy. The new ambassador to Turkey was Oscar S. Straus, who had already served on two different occasions as the United States representative in Constantinople. In a few instances career officers were promoted from their positions of diplomatic secretaries to ministers plenipotentiary, as, for example, Robert S. R. Hitt, who had been secretary of embassy in Berlin, became minister to Panama, and Henry P. Fletcher advanced from his post as chargé d'affaires in Peking to minister plenipotentiary in Chile. On the whole, President Taft and Secretary Knox made a real effort to carry out the merit system in their appointments in both the diplomatic and consular services.

Professor Philip C. Jessup makes an interesting comparison of the manner in which Secretary Root and Secretary Knox handled promotions in the consular service. Root would carefully scrutinize the dossier of each man recommended to make sure that the promotion was justified. Knox, on the other hand, inquired whether the dossiers had been carefully examined and thereupon initialed the memorandum letting the officer in charge know that he was being held responsible for the action taken.[16]

Dollar Diplomacy

Unquestionably, Secretary Knox was responsible for at least one major development in the foreign policy of the Taft administration; namely, "dollar diplomacy." President Taft conceded that it was his Secretary of State who decided foreign policy in his administration and claimed only the merit of selecting him for the task.[17] At times the President became a bit nettled at the overbearing assurance of his Secretary of State, but Taft was easygoing and would merely remark, "There is no lack of confidence in Knox." [18] Both Taft and Knox were sympathetic to American economic expansion, and a former United States consul in Manchuria, Willard D. Straight, who had returned to Washington, was able to persuade the Department of State that the Orient offered the greatest possibilities. Secretary Knox was not hard to convince and he issued a Departmental memorandum declaring:

The nations that finance the great Chinese railways and other enterprises will be foremost in the affairs of China, and the participation of American capital in these investments will give the voice of the United States more authority in political controversies in that country which will go far toward guaranteeing the preservation of the administrative entity of China.[19]

President Taft went so far as to cable the prince regent of China that he had a personal interest in seeing to it that American capital be used in the development of China.[20] The Chinese government agreed, and Straight went to Peking as the representative of the American banking group. Once engaged, the State Department quixotically proposed the neutralization of all the Manchurian railways. Even Great Britain was a bit cold to this proposal, and Russia and Japan flatly refused. The first effort of Secretary Knox in his policy of dollar diplomacy was a complete failure, and it was at least partly due to lack of careful planning on the part of the Department to overcome Russian and Japanese objections. Without an adequate *quid pro quo* or sufficient and available force, success would have been a miracle in this region where selfish nationalism and economic imperialism were in determined opposition to the open door.[21]

Knox's next effort to utilize American dollars to support the commercial expansion of the United States in the Caribbean area was somewhat more successful. Here the policy had two bulwarks of support already fashioned—the Monroe Doctrine as interpreted by Theodore Roosevelt while President, and the Panama Canal, which would soon be open to world trade. Knox approved of the Roosevelt theory that the small republics of the Caribbean must be compelled to fulfill their financial obligations in order to prevent foreign intervention, but he would go a step further and substitute American capital for European and thus eliminate any reason for European intervention.

The State Department urged American bankers to assume the British-owned debt of Honduras. Knox persuaded American interests to invest in the National Bank of Haiti. In the case of stubborn Nicaragua under the domination of the hated Zelaya, the United States used both its power of recognition and a battleship in the harbor to force Zelaya out and an American loan to repay the British.[22] Knox felt sincerely that his policy of substituting dollars for bullets was advantageous to both sides, and in a public address made in New York on December 11, 1911, he declared frankly: "If the American dollar can aid suffering humanity and lift the burden of financial difficulty from states with which we live on terms of intimate intercourse and earnest friendship, and replace insecurity and devastation by stability and peaceful self-development, all I can say is that it would be hard to find better employment." [23]

Knox and the Senate

Although Knox had been a senator and on the whole had little friction with the Senate, his good friend Senator Lodge stymied the Department on one occasion. A Japanese concern was carrying on negotiations leading to the acquisition of some land in Lower California near Magdalena Bay. Senator Lodge introduced a resolution disapproving of the transfer of strategic areas in the Western Hemisphere to non-American companies, and although both Knox and Taft objected to the resolution, it was passed by a vote of 51 to 4. The State Department, nevertheless, did not hesitate to invoke the so-called Lodge corollary to the Monroe Doctrine subsequently when the occasion warranted.

The most serious difference of opinion between the administration and the Senate, however, occurred in reference to arbitration. President Taft authorized Secretary Knox to sign treaties with Great Britain and France which provided arbitration for all legal disputes. Henry Cabot Lodge, chairman of the Foreign Relations Committee, opposed the treaties, while Senator Elihu Root supported them. Secretary Knox apparently made the mistake of not conferring with key senators during the course of the negotiations. Although Senator Root attempted to amend the treaties to safeguard every legitimate American interest, the Senate finally passed the treaties in such a form that they were practically valueless and Taft refused to approve their ratification. He declared later that he hoped that "the Senators might change their minds, or that the people might change the Senate, instead of which they changed me." [24]

Secretary Knox retired on March 5, 1913. Assistant Secretary of State Huntington Wilson remained in office temporarily at the request of Secretary Bryan; but when President Wilson completely revised the Knox policy in regard to the consortium in China, Wilson resigned as of March 19, 1913. Alvey Adee, as Second Assistant Secretary, had become so invaluable that his retention was taken as a matter of course. Chandler Hale remained for something over a month to help prepare his successor for the duties of the office and retired on April 21, 1913.

If an evaluation were to be made of the services of Philander C. Knox as Secretary of State from the sole standpoint of policy, he would not rate among the dozen most important Secretaries of State. If, however, we include his influence on the organization and work of the Department, he would surely rate among the top half dozen. This is the more remarkable in that he detested the routine of the Department and spent as much time as possible away from it. President Taft frequently remarked that laziness was Knox's besetting sin. Taft conceded that Knox made a good Secretary of State, but he declared also that if Knox "were not so lazy he would make a great Secretary of State." [25] Huntington Wilson, who worked closest to Knox during the entire four years of his Secretaryship, had the highest admiration for him and regarded Knox as a great administrator as well as a great lawyer and statesman. His ability to analyze a difficult problem and strip off the nonessentials was remarkable. But as a corporation lawyer Knox was accustomed to emphasize the factors in favor of his case and minimize all others, and as a consequence his policies often lacked objectivity. Once he was convinced of the advantage to the United States and to her Latin American neighbors of commercial expansion in the Caribbean, he became almost ruthless in trying to achieve his ends. He overlooked a fundamental precept of successful diplomacy: *fortiter in re, suaviter in modo.*

20

William Jennings Bryan

William Jennings Bryan—Secretary of State

Perhaps no President has ever appointed his Secretary of State with greater hesitation, nay, even trepidation, than did Woodrow Wilson in appointing William Jennings Bryan. As professor of political science, Wilson was an authority on presidential government and he knew the place of the cabinet in this system, but he also knew the importance of party obligations. Bryan had been the Democratic standard bearer for sixteen years, its candidate for the Presidency three times, and it was Bryan who had turned the tide in Wilson's direction at the convention. Furthermore, Wilson had come to respect and admire the "peerless leader," but he could not help feeling dubious about Bryan's judgment. Wilson intended to be his own Secretary of State and Bryan was not the type of man who would compromise upon any question where he felt that his principles were involved. Bryan made not the slightest effort to obtain a cabinet post. In fact, when his followers were demanding that his great services to the party be given recognition, Bryan wrote an editorial for *The Commoner*, dated January 10, 1913, stating:

> Cabinet positions ought not to be regarded as currency with which to pay debts. . . . We venture to hope that Governor Wilson will be governed by higher motives than gratitude in the selection of his official household. He need not consider any service that Mr. Bryan has rendered him.[1]

The President debated the matter at length with himself and asked the opinion of Colonel House several times before he finally made up his mind.[2] He realized that the opposition to Bryan was strong—in fact, his own campaign manager, William F. McCombs, had telephoned, urging Wilson to state that he would not appoint Bryan as Secretary of State while the Democratic Convention in Baltimore was voting on the candidates for nomination.[3] According to Mrs. Bryan, Wilson's reply was to tell McCombs to go to hell.[4] House

224

felt that Bryan was the logical aspirant and Wilson finally agreed. The appointment was made on December 21, 1912, at a private meeting at Governor Wilson's home after a discussion lasting several hours. Apparently Bryan's only objection was that he might be expected to serve intoxicating beverages, which was contrary to his principles. When Wilson declared that Bryan could serve what he pleased, he accepted the position without further hesitation.[5]

William Jennings Bryan was wholly unsuited by background, experience, and temperament for the top cabinet position. He had been a political leader for many years but had only been in the government as a member of Congress for two terms. His interests were almost wholly in domestic matters. It is true that his advocacy of free trade required a certain amount of consideration of foreign commercial policies and markets, but his nearest approach to international problems came with his strong opposition to imperialism at the close of the Spanish-American War and his advocacy of Philippine independence. His greatest interest in world politics was the maintenance of peace, and he made sure that President Wilson approved his plan for negotiating treaties for the advancement of peace with all the countries of the world who might be interested.

Political Appointments

Inasmuch as the Democratic party had not been in power for sixteen years, the demand for political positions was overwhelming, and both the President and Secretary of State were importuned by thousands of greedy office seekers who deserved well at the hands of the party. In this situation Bryan was more sympathetic to the party wheel horses than his chief, and he felt that as far as possible deserving Democrats should be given consideration. In the State Department all of the clerical force fortunately was under civil-service regulations and it was only in the upper echelons that changes were possible. Here, however, Bryan at first seemed to recognize the need of a trained, experienced personnel and he made no new appointments during the first few weeks of his incumbency. In fact he invited Huntington Wilson to remain as Assistant Secretary of State, and Wilson agreed; but President Wilson's repudiation of the six-power consortium in China after the Assistant Secretary had made a strong plea for its continued support, caused Wilson's resignation on March 19, 1913. Assistant Secretary Wilson resented particularly the failure to consult any member of the Department of State before public announcement of the new policy and showed it in his letter to the President:

I had no reason to suppose that the officials on duty in the Department of State would learn first from the newspapers of a declaration of policy which I

think shows on its face the inadequacy of the consideration given to the facts
and theories involved and the failure clearly to apprehend the motives leading
to and the purposes of the policy superseded.[6]

Assistant Secretary Wilson gives a vivid picture of Bryan's first days in the
Department:

From the first moment his waiting room was overflowing with political
friends from all over the country seeking favors for themselves or their con-
stituents. He was left hardly a moment for Department business, and I even
had to sign most of the mail for him. . . . He had never been interested in
diplomacy; and this made it not only difficult but actually impossible, quickly
to impart to him a conception of foreign relations.[7]

Secretary Bryan's opposition to the spoilsmen for positions in the Department was short-lived. Fortunately for the Department, Second Assistant Secretary Alvey Adee was retained, although he was now seventy-one years of age
and had been in the Department for some thirty-six years. His memory was
excellent and his vitality unimpaired, and if necessary he could still "carry
the whole machinery of foreign policy under his hat." The new Assistant Secretary of State named to replace Huntington Wilson was John E. Osborne.
The only reason for his appointment was the fact that he was a prominent
Democratic politician who at the time of his appointment was a member of
the Democratic National Committee. The Third Assistant Secretary of State,
Dudley Field Malone, a clever New York lawyer, was no more experienced in
the field of foreign relations than was the Assistant Secretary. The only new appointment that indicated the slightest desire to maintain an effective foreign
office was that of John Bassett Moore, who was named Counselor for the Department. Inasmuch as he had already served as Third Assistant Secretary and
First Assistant Secretary, he was authorized by the President to serve as Acting
Secretary of State in the absence of the Secretary. In other words, Moore held
a position equivalent to that of the First Assistant Secretary previously—a position which was later to become that of Under Secretary. The new Solicitor,
Joseph W. Folk, who superseded the able and experienced J. Reuben Clark, Jr.,
was also a political appointee. Wilbur J. Carr remained as Director of the
Consular Service; but the long-experienced Chief Clerk, William McNeir, who
had served the Department ably since 1881 and as Chief Clerk since 1909, was
demoted to the position of Chief of the Bureau of Accounts and Disbursing
Clerk at a salary of $2,300, to make room for Bryan's confidential clerk, Ben
G. Davis, who would thus receive $3,000 annually.
    Even the geographical divisions were not safe from the politicians. The
new Chief of the Division of Latin American Affairs was Boaz W. Long, the

proprietor of a commission company, with no diplomatic or consular experience. As the head of the Division of Near Eastern Affairs, Albert H. Putney, Dean of the Illinois College of Law, was named. A newspaper man, John H. James, became Chief of the Division of Information. It might be noted that these positions had salaries running from $3,000 to $4,500, while the Chiefs of bureaus such as the Diplomatic, Consular, Appointments, Citizenship, Archives, Rolls and Library who were retained received salaries from $2,100 to $2,250. The two new Foreign Trade Advisers, who received $4,500 each, salaries equivalent to Second Assistant Secretary Adee's, were Robert F. Rose, founder and editor of The Shorthand Writer, who had served as Bryan's private secretary in his 1900 and 1908 campaigns, and William B. Fleming, who had been a presidential elector of Kentucky, an associate justice of the United States Court of the Territory of New Mexico, and a law officer of the Treasury Department.

The avid office seekers found even greener pastures in the diplomatic service. Here there were no civil-service regulations to guard the able foreign-service officer who had only his ability and a good record to protect him. Bryan believed in "giving the faithful a chance" and of rewarding as many deserving Democrats as possible. In this respect the President and the Secretary of State did not see eye to eye. In the most important diplomatic posts President Wilson took control personally and able men were sought out. At the Court of St. James's, where Whitelaw Reid had graced the position, President Wilson very much desired ex-President Eliot of Harvard to serve, but with Bryan as Secretary of State the position had no attractions for Eliot. Former Secretary of State Richard Olney was next approached, but personal affairs prevented his acceptance. Finally, at the suggestion of Colonel House, Wilson offered the post to Walter Hines Page, editor of The World's Work and a partner in the publishing firm of Doubleday Page & Company.[8] Page was delighted and was commissioned on April 21, 1913. Wilson wanted his friend Dean Henry B. Fine of Princeton to be ambassador to Germany and, realizing the financial problem, got Cleveland H. Dodge to supplement the salary by an additional $15,000 or $20,000. When even this inducement did not succeed, James W. Gerard, a wealthy New York lawyer who had contributed $13,500 to the Democratic campaign fund, was named. In Paris, Myron T. Herrick had made an enviable record, but the ambassadorship to France was also regarded as a choice political plum. William F. McCombs, Wilson's campaign manager, wanted a cabinet position, but Wilson offered him instead the ambassadorship to France. McCombs could not make up his mind as to whether or not he should accept and finally decided that he could not afford the post. McCombs never forgave Wilson for trying to send him "to St. Helena." More than a year elapsed before Congressman William Graves Sharp was appointed upon the urgent solicitation of Senator Pomerene of Ohio. Although nominated on June 19, 1914, Ambassador Sharp did not reach Paris until after the outbreak of the war, owing to the serious illness of his wife. Ambassador Herrick was requested to remain in charge temporarily and did not leave his post until late in November.

President Wilson was much concerned over the Chinese situation and several weeks before his inauguration he wrote to Mr. Bryan suggesting that John R. Mott would be an ideal person for the position of minister. When Mott refused, Wilson declared that he was profoundly disappointed. He then named Professor Paul S. Reinsch, head of the Department of Political Science at the University of Wisconsin. Other creditable appointments, even though the men were inexperienced in diplomacy, were Thomas Nelson Page, the author, as ambassador to Italy; Dr. Henry Van Dyke, professor of English literature at Princeton, as minister to the Netherlands; and Brand Whitlock, mayor of Toledo, Ohio, as minister to Belgium. In a few rare cases career diplomats were retained, as, for example, Edwin V. Morgan, ambassador to Brazil; Henry P. Fletcher, ambassador to Chile; and in at least one case, that of Arthur Bailly-Blanchard, we find the secretary of the embassy in Tokyo promoted to be minister plenipotentiary to Haiti.

It must be confessed, however, that these were exceptions, and out of some forty-odd diplomatic chiefs of missions twenty-nine were changed within the first six months of the Wilson administration. Of these the majority might be classed as career officers who had either entered the service after passing examinations or entered before examinations were held and were promoted because of excellent service. A few of the most flagrant examples are cited: William Rockhill was ambassador to Turkey when the Wilson administration came into power. He had been in the Department of State, had been minister to Greece, Rumania, and Serbia, minister to China, ambassador to Russia, and in 1911 was appointed ambassador to Turkey. He had served the United States in the State Department or abroad for nineteen years and was probably the most experienced and able diplomat in the foreign service. He was replaced by a New York financier, Henry Morgenthau, who had been chairman of the Democratic Finance Committee and had contributed some $30,000 to nominate and elect Woodrow Wilson. John B. Jackson, minister to Bulgaria, Rumania, and Serbia, with more than twenty years' diplomatic service, was succeeded by Charles J. Vopicka, a Chicago politician. Arthur M. Beaupré had been appointed, after examination, secretary of legation at Guatemala in 1897; by 1903 he had become minister plenipotentiary, and he served in this capacity at various posts until he was named minister to Cuba in 1911. To succeed him, Secretary Bryan named William E. Gonzales, a newspaper man and editor in South Carolina utterly devoid of diplomatic experience. H. Percival

Dodge, a Boston lawyer, had entered the diplomatic service as secretary of embassy in Berlin in 1899. He served in several other posts, became minister to Honduras and El Salvador in 1907, Chief of the Division of Latin American Affairs in the Department of State in 1910, and minister to Panama in 1911. In his place a practicing lawyer, William Jennings Price, from Danville, Kentucky, was appointed.

Perhaps the most notorious case of all occurred in the Dominican Republic. William W. Russell, who had been serving there as consul general since 1910 and minister since 1911, was a graduate of the United States Naval Academy. He had as a lieutenant made several surveys in Latin American countries and had entered the foreign service as secretary of legation in Caracas in 1895. He had subsequently served as minister in Colombia and Venezuela. To this post was appointed James M. Sullivan, a New York "police court lawyer" who, according to a leading member of the New York bar, "was not a member of any of the associations of reputable lawyers in New York." A later investigation showed that he was intimate with New York gambling interests and had been supported for this position by persons having large financial interests in Santo Domingo with the intention of profiting through the incumbency of a minister under obligation. Senator Phelan, who was named by Secretary Bryan to investigate charges made against Sullivan while he was minister to the Dominican Republic, reported that Sullivan had violated his instructions, participated in local politics, obtained pecuniary favors for friends, had not paid his debts, and, in fact, had completely lost the confidence of the Dominican people. Senator Phelan declared that he should be asked to resign and that if he refused, the minister should be recalled.[9]

Secretary Bryan's policy regarding diplomatic appointments was deluged with criticism when a letter which he had written to Walter W. Vick, Receiver General of Customs at Santo Domingo, was published. In it he wrote,

Now that you have arrived and acquainted yourself with the situation, can you let me know what positions you have at your disposal with which to reward deserving Democrats? Whenever you desire a suggestion from me in regard to a man for a place down there, call on me. You know . . . how difficult it is to find suitable rewards for the deserving. . . . You will find Sullivan a strong, courageous, reliable fellow.[10]

One other criticism of Bryan was the result of his continuing to give lectures for pay while he held the position as Secretary of State. It was alleged that before he had completed his first year as Secretary he had been away from Washington seventy-two days, had traveled 31,800 miles, had made forty-three speeches, of which eighteen were commercial.[11] Even the liberal *Nation* declared editorially that it was outraged by the spectacle of the Secretary of State appearing nightly in company with acrobats and vaudeville performers of every kind. We do protest emphatically at a Secretary of State cutting short conferences with foreign ambassadors to rush off to little towns in West Virginia or Maryland to earn his $250.[12]

Bryan's Peace Treaties

In spite of Bryan's much criticized policy of appointing inexperienced politicians to carry out America's foreign policies abroad, he was an idealist in the formulation of policy. As early as 1905 Bryan had supported a plan for world peace by having states agree to submit unsettled disputes to investigation by a commission of inquiry which could find the facts and report them publicly. Bryan had discussed his plan with Wilson when he was offered the cabinet post and had obtained the President's approval to proceed with it. Bryan wisely proposed his tentative plan to the Foreign Relations Committee of the Senate before proceeding further. He received such excellent cooperation here that the very next day, April 24, 1913, the plan, under the heading "President Wilson's Peace Proposal," was presented to the representatives of the foreign governments in Washington.

Although the Bryan treaties did not stall the juggernaut of war, the procedure was a real contribution to the machinery of peace and Bryan considered these treaties his outstanding achievement while Secretary of State. A portrait of him holding a Treaty for the Advancement of Peace was hung in the Diplomatic Room of the old State Department Building on Pennsylvania Avenue.

Unskilled Diplomacy

Secretary Bryan was permitted to take the initiative in few other problems of American foreign policy which immediately faced the United States. The Taft administration had refrained from recognizing Huerta as president of Mexico, although our ambassador, Henry Lane Wilson, urged it and the State Department supported his position. Secretary of Agriculture Houston noted that in the cabinet meeting on March 11, President Wilson read a statement regarding policy toward Latin America which "clearly indicated that the President was going to be his own Secretary of State. I do not know to what extent the President had consulted Bryan, but Bryan had not presented the matter, and the President did the reading." [13] According to Josephus Daniels, Bryan was the only member of the cabinet who had been consulted.[14] Wilson's statement to the press issued after the cabinet meeting was a clear-cut repudiation of the Knox policy of dollar diplomacy. He declared that the United States had nothing to seek in Central and South America except the lasting interests of the peoples of the two continents and that we favored only such trade development as should profit both and interfere with the rights of neither. As regards the recognition of Huerta, the President was opposed to it since the Huerta regime was based upon force and not upon the consent of the governed. Wilson's subsequent policy of "watchful waiting" and the dispatch of his own friend, William Bayard Hale, and later a Californian of Mexican descent, Reginald del Valle, and finally John Lind, a friend of Bryan's, as his personal representatives to Mexico resulted in a complete fiasco. If the President had consulted the experts [15] in the Department, he might have learned earlier that to refuse recognition of a government because of its employment of unconstitutional means to gain control was a form of intervention that Latin America did not appreciate.

Relations with Japan had become critical because of pending legislation in the California legislature restricting the ownership of real property by aliens to those eligible to citizenship. Wilson appealed to Governor Johnson through Bryan, and when that failed he sent Bryan in person to present the government's point of view. Although the legislation was passed, there is no doubt but that the efforts of the Federal government to prevent it had a conciliating effect upon the Japanese government. In preparing the notes to Japan, Bryan depended almost entirely upon John Bassett Moore, Counselor of the State Department, as drafting officer. On the whole, however, both Wilson and Bryan distrusted the State Department as being too slow-moving and conservative.

One result of this suspicion was the utilization of executive agents, instead of diplomatic representatives, to carry out the administration's foreign policies. Colonel Edward M. House, a close friend of the President's, ultimately came to play a more important role in the formulation of American foreign policy than the Department of State. For example, Colonel House was extremely interested in the idea of a League of American States in which the republics of the Western Hemisphere would agree to guarantee each others' territorial integrity. President Wilson liked the idea but wanted it presented to the Latin American diplomats by House rather than by Bryan. House noted: "The President was evidently somewhat nervous about Mr. Bryan's attitude. It was easy to see that he did not want him to interfere in any way with my procedure and yet he was afraid he might be sensitive about it." [16] House thereupon informed Bryan of his Pan American policy but found him only slightly interested. All subsequent negotiations with the Latin American diplomats were carried on by Colonel House. When the European situation became increasingly critical, the President authorized his "silent partner" to go to Europe and report back from there. Ray Stannard Baker points out:

The employment of such "special" or "secret" ambassadors as House, Hale, Lind and others, while it had certain advantages . . . tended to paralyze the normal relationships and understandings between the American State Department and the foreign offices of the other governments.[17]

In spite of Bryan's idealism, he was opposed to the repeal of the Panama Canal Tolls Act, which, by exempting vessels engaged in coastwise trade, was by common consent in violation of the Hay-Pauncefote Treaty. Here, however, Wilson, convinced that the exemption was bad economically as well as in contravention of our international obligations, was determined to act. He had Colonel House discuss the matter with various senators and in a message to Congress, presented personally, he declared: "I shall not know how to deal with other matters of even greater delicacy and nearer consequence if you do not grant it to me in ungrudging measure." [18] Secretary Bryan finally swung over to the President's side and did much to influence the liberal wing of the Democratic party. The question was hotly contested in both Houses, and when the repeal finally passed it was a great personal victory for the President and unquestionably enhanced the prestige of the United States among the nations of the world for its recognition of the sanctity of treaty obligations.

The outbreak of war in Europe was a tragic catastrophe to the United States as well as to Europe. Just a month before it broke, twenty of the Bryan peace treaties had been sent to the Senate for approval of their ratification. Numerous legal problems of neutrality were raised immediately upon which the Department of State was obliged to make decisions. The able counselor John Bassett Moore had not been too happy during the Mexican crisis and early in March, 1914, he resigned from the State Department. He gave no reasons other than previous commitments, and President Wilson, in commending Moore for his work, indicated that the eminent jurist had only agreed to remain a year when he accepted the position. Some years later, in an address before the New York Bar Association, however, Judge Moore made it clear that Bryan's Declaration of Policy of March 11, 1913, "was inspired by a feeling of repugnance to the newly established government of Huerta in Mexico," and he felt that "this declaration constituted a radical and subversive departure from our previous policy and practice and also from the established practice and policy of other governments." [19] The Republican *New York Tribune* was exceedingly caustic in regard to Counselor Moore's resignation and the State Department's status. It fulminated: "The whole service, from its uncertain chief pattering platitudes and coddling cheap politicians to his incompetent horde of retainers now infesting foreign capitals, is the despair of men trained in diplomacy like John Bassett Moore." [20] To make matters worse, Joseph W. Folk, the Solicitor of the Department, whose official relations with Secretary Bryan had never been very satisfactory, had also resigned.

Lansing and Phillips Appointed

President Wilson appreciated the seriousness of the situation and was determined to find a Counselor who had both the ability and legal training to meet the high requirements of the position. On March 27, 1914, Robert Lansing was named Counselor of the Department of State. It was an ideal appointment. Lansing was an international lawyer who had served as counsel for the Chinese and Mexican legations in Washington and had represented the United States in numerous international arbitrations, including the fur-seal arbitration and the North Atlantic coast fisheries arbitration at The Hague. He was familiar with the Department of State and was highly regarded both in the United States and abroad for his contributions to the development of international law. His wife was the daughter of former Secretary of State John W. Foster and he himself had served as special counsel for the Department of State on various diplomatic questions.

Another important appointment had been made in the Department of State just two weeks before that of Lansing. Third Assistant Secretary of State Dudley Field Malone, after serving less than a year, had resigned to become Collector of Customs at the Port of New York, and in his place a very able career foreign-service officer, William Phillips, was named. Phillips had already acted as Third Assistant Secretary in 1909 after several years' experience in the diplomatic service and as Chief of the Division of Far Eastern Affairs. With Lansing, Adee, and Phillips in the Department, President Wilson and Secretary Bryan had available experts familiar with every phase of diplomatic practice and procedure.

The State Department and World War I

The European War now claimed the State Department's entire attention. It had broken unexpectedly in so far as no specific warnings had come from any of America's diplomats in Europe to the Department of State. The one exception seems to have been a report dated July 13, 1914, from Vice Consul Frank E. Mallett in Budapest, who declared that the impression prevailed in Hungary that war between Austria-Hungary and Serbia was unavoidable and would come when the crops were harvested. However, consuls do not send high-priority political reports and Mr. Mallett's was no exception to the rule. It was not until Ambassador Herrick's dispatch of July 28, urging President Wilson to mediate, was read that Secretary Bryan appreciated the seriousness of the situation.[21] The President, informed of Herrick's proposal, had Bryan telegraph to Ambassador Page in London, asking whether an offer of the good offices of the United States would be acceptable. Although Page answered in the negative, an offer of good offices was made on August 4 by the President after a cabinet meeting. Ambassador Herrick in his memoirs declared that he did not receive an answer to his telegram and never knew whether Wilson had received it. In fact, he later asked the President and was informed that he had not. The State Department investigated this incident and found that Bryan's telegram to Page had been sent directly from the White House. The Department explained that "Mr. Herrick was not informed of what was going on since it was not possible for the Department of State, especially in such crowded times, to acknowledge telegrams or to keep Ambassadors informed about the development of policies still under consideration." [22] An interesting sidelight on the influences hampering the Department is shown by a letter from Colonel House to the President dated August 1, 1914: "Please let me suggest that you do not let Mr. Bryan make any overtures to any of the Powers involved. They look upon him as purely visionary and it would lessen the weight of your influence if you desire to use it yourself later." [23]

During the early period of the war Secretary Bryan was often absent making addresses and Lansing served as Acting Secretary. As a trained international lawyer hired to defend the interests of his client, the United States, Lansing favored putting pressure upon Great Britain to compel her to respect American rights on the high seas. Here, however, he was handicapped by the strongly pro-British attitude of Ambassador Page and to a lesser extent by the conciliatory approach of Colonel House. On one occasion when the State Department had prepared a particularly strong protest on British violations of the Declaration of London, House obtained Wilson's permission to arrange a private interview with the British ambassador, Sir Cecil Spring-Rice, at the home of Third Assistant Secretary William Phillips; and House and Spring-Rice rewrote the dispatch to avoid giving offense.[24] Page became almost antagonistic to the State Department and he besought House to deliver him from the Department's "library lawyers." On one occasion when he was instructed to make no shipping agreements with neutral powers, he wrote House: "What damfool in the State Department supposed that I was making agreements with any Govt. . . ." [25] Wilson appreciated the fact that Page was pro-British and criticized him for it, but he was unwilling to threaten his recall.

As a last resort to put a speedy end to the war, President Wilson decided to send Colonel House as his personal emissary to the belligerent capitals on an unofficial peace mission. When House informed Secretary Bryan of the plan, Bryan was much disappointed, as he had expected to go on such a mission himself. House explained that the mission was entirely unofficial, and Bryan then agreed that House was best equipped to undertake it. Although the letter of credentials which House carried made it clear that he was to act in an unofficial capacity, in his last meeting with Wilson before his departure the

President asked him to tell Sir Edward Grey that "while you are abroad I expect to act directly through you and avoid all intermediaries." [26]

Bryan Steps Out

A difference of attitude gradually grew up between President Wilson and Secretary of State Bryan. The latter felt that Great Britain in her seizures of American ships, in establishing paper blockades, in utilizing illegally the American flag should be held just as accountable as Germany was for her use of the submarine. As Ambassador Spring-Rice put it, Bryan regarded the torpedo and the prize court with equal abhorrence. In a letter to President Wilson dated April 23, 1915, Bryan showed clearly the cleavage. Bryan felt strongly that American citizens should not be permitted to travel on belligerent ships, even though international law countenanced it. He also pointed out that the sale of arms and ammunition worked entirely for the benefit of one side and gave Germany an excuse for charging that the United States favored the Allies. The final break came with the sinking of the *Lusitania*. There were 159 Americans on board and 124 perished. Ambassador Page immediately urged that the United States join the Allies, and House cabled from London that he felt that the United States could no longer remain a neutral spectator. Wilson, determined not to be swayed by the hysteria of the moment, went into seclusion and prepared a note of protest without consulting anyone, not even the experts in the Department of State. When it was completed, he called a meeting of the cabinet on May 11 and read them the much belabored draft. Bryan alone objected to its harshness, and Wilson agreed at first to counterbalance it with a supplementary statement affording Germany the procedure of the cooling-off treaties and with a warning to Americans against travel on belligerent ships carrying contraband of war. Bryan thereupon reluctantly signed the note. Lansing, however, felt that such a notice to citizens was unwise at the time and the President accepted Mr. Lansing's point of view. Wilson also changed his mind regarding a supplementary statement.

Secretary Bryan's position was now rendered even more untenable by the unfortunate repercussions of a meeting with the Austrian ambassador, Dr. Dumba. The latter had a conference with Bryan in regard to the strained relations with Germany and came away feeling that Bryan regarded Wilson's protest on the *Lusitania* as largely for home consumption. Dumba hastily relayed his tip to the German government and the next day he informed Third Assistant Secretary Phillips that the country was not behind the President in his *Lusitania* note. Phillips got in touch with Bryan, who immediately called Dumba in to clear up the matter. Unfortunately, the statement had by now become public property abroad, inasmuch as American Ambassador Gerard in Berlin had already been told by an American woman that the *Lusitania* note was only a sop to American public opinion.[27] Although Secretary Bryan had been quoted incorrectly and evidence was available to prove it,[28] the matter caused the administration and particularly Bryan a great deal of criticism in the press.

Germany's reply to the Wilson protest was wholly unsatisfactory, and again Wilson drafted a reply, working alone, and again submitted it to a meeting of the cabinet. In the discussion Bryan became critical of his fellow members because they supported the President in refusing to consider a protest to Great Britain at this time. According to Secretary Houston, the President sharply rebuked Bryan for his unfair remarks.[29] Secretary Bryan could not accept the note as Wilson wanted it. He wrote several letters to the President in the next few days, but the President was unwilling to change his position. Bryan then decided to resign, and neither the President nor Secretary McAdoo was able to persuade him to remain. In his letter of resignation, dated June 9, 1915, Secretary Bryan gave as his reason his inability to sign the note which the President intended to send to Germany. However, in his statement to the press two days later Bryan was more specific. He wanted to delay any final action by utilizing his procedure of investigation by an international commission, and in the second place he believed that Americans should be warned against traveling on belligerent vessels or with cargoes of ammunition and that American passenger ships should be prohibited from carrying ammunition. Mrs. Bryan had frankly explained to Secretary McAdoo that her husband had long been unhappy in his position because of the President's habit of preparing important diplomatic papers himself. "He had come to feel . . . that he was playing the part of a figurehead." [30] Wilson unquestionably regretted Bryan's resignation, particularly at this time. In his letter accepting the resignation, Wilson stated that he deplored it because "our objects are the same and we ought to pursue them together." Some time later, Wilson made a statement which perhaps more accurately expressed his feelings regarding Bryan: "He is absolutely sincere, that is what makes him dangerous." [31]

The resignation of Bryan produced a great sensation in the press, but the country clearly supported Wilson in his stand. "Marse Henry" Watterson, who in his Louisville *Courier-Journal* had accused the German ambassador— "Satan's Ambassador at Washington"—of murder in the sinking of the *Lusitania*, now fulminated against Bryan's resignation even more violently: "Men have been shot and beheaded, even hanged, drawn and quartered for treason less serious!" [32] Ambassador Page wrote House that he had inspired the leader in the *Times* which said that Bryan's departure would make no difference. "There are others who ought to join him—for their country's good—in the Bad Lands of dead men who don't know they are dead. They talked themselves into greatness and not knowing when to stop, also talked themselves out of it." [33] Joseph H. Choate, former ambassador to London, was almost as harsh in his opinion as Ambassador Page. Writing to his daughter, he inquired: "What do you think about Bryan? He has certainly done the State some service at last, by taking himself out of the State Department where he has been much worse than useless." [34]

A fairer evaluation of Bryan's services as Secretary of State has gradually been accepted as historians have been able to view the whole period more objectively. As a sincere advocate of peace, Secretary Bryan could not conscientiously follow a policy which seemed certain to draw the United States into war. He knew that his resignation would be disastrous to him politically, but he placed ethics above politics. Secretary of the Interior Franklin K. Lane sensed the situation when in saying good-by to Bryan he declared: "You are the most real Christian that I know."

21

Robert Lansing and Bainbridge Colby

Robert Lansing—Secretary of State

William Jennings Bryan resigned his position as Secretary of State on June 9, 1915, and on the same day Robert Lansing, Counselor of the State Department, became Secretary ad interim. President Wilson was at first uncertain as to whom he might appoint as Bryan's successor. He thought that Colonel House would be a good man, but his health would not permit him to accept. Page had become too pro-British to be satisfactory. After giving the matter considerable thought, however, Wilson decided that Lansing would be a satisfactory appointment. He discussed the matter with Mrs. Bolling, whom he had already asked to marry him, and when she exclaimed that Lansing was only a clerk in the State Department, Wilson replied: "He is a counselor of the Department and has had a good schooling under old Mr. John W. Foster, his father-in-law, for whom I have great respect. I think he would steer Lansing, and the combination would be of great help to me." [1]

The situation was too critical for delay, and on June 23, 1915, President Wilson called Lansing to the White House and informed him that he would be appointed Secretary of State if he would accept the appointment. When Lansing protested that he had too little political influence to warrant such an appointment, Wilson replied: "By experience and training you are especially equipped to conduct the foreign affairs of the United States. This under present conditions is far more important than political influence." [2] Secretary of the Treasury William Gibbs McAdoo, the President's son-in-law, tersely summarized the reasons for the appointment: He was the best material at hand, he could put diplomatic notes in proper form and advise on international law, and the President had determined for the future to be practically his own Secretary of State. [3]

New Departmental Personnel

With Lansing elevated to the Secretaryship, it was necessary to fill his former position of Counselor. Many names were considered to meet the qualifications which Colonel House considered as essential—firmness, tact, and legal ability. The choice finally fell upon Frank L. Polk, corporation counsel of the City of New York. In recommending Polk to Secretary Lansing, House wrote:

I think you will find him most helpful as a sort of Assistant Secretary of State. He has a good deal of political instinct and can speak the language of the members of Congress. At the same time he is such a cultured gentleman that he will be of great value to you in dealing with the Diplomatic Corps.[4]

After his first interview with Polk, Secretary Lansing declared that Polk was exactly his conception of what a Counselor ought to be, and their future intercourse confirmed the first impression.

Very few changes occurred in the organization of the Department when Robert Lansing became Secretary. Inasmuch as Secretary Lansing was rated as one of the outstanding international lawyers in the United States and Frank Lyon Polk was almost equally renowned in corporation law, the Department of State was never better equipped to handle any legal problem which might come its way. However, as Ambassador Bernstorff succinctly declared: "Since Wilson decides *everything*, any interview with Lansing is a mere matter of form." And since Wilson still employed Colonel House as his principal adviser, we find Ambassador Page and Sir Edward Grey and Ambassador Gerard and Herr Zimmerman writing directly to the President's alter ego regarding important questions of policy. Such a situation could not help but minimize the role of the State Department in the formulation of policy.

Secretary Lansing depended to a great extent upon Lester H. Woolsey for the preparation of papers where fine technical questions regarding the rights of belligerents and neutrals needed consideration. As recognition of Woolsey's valuable services, he was named confidential Law Adviser to the Secretary, which increased his salary from $3,000 to $4,500 annually and his responsibilities correspondingly. As regards Woolsey's appointment as Solicitor for the Department of State, when Cone Johnson retired in 1917, President Wilson explained to Senator Overman:

Mr. Woolsey is and has for some time been one of the Secretary's right hand, indispensable men. . . . I am so much interested to have the State Department operated at a maximum of efficiency that I would not dare to put in a new man from the outside.[5]

The Latin American Division was so overburdened with work pertaining to Mexico as a result of the Mexican Revolution and the problems resulting from it that a Departmental order was issued, dated July 28, 1915, establishing a Division of Mexican Affairs. Leon J. Canova, Assistant Chief of the Division of Latin American Affairs, was made Chief of the new division, while J. Butler Wright, a career officer, became Acting Chief of the Latin American Division. The Assistant Chief of the new division was Richard C. Tanis, who was destined to remain in this division until it was amalgamated with the Division of American Republics in 1937. Mr. Tanis retired, after some thirty-seven years of service, in 1946.

Wilson and Lansing Differ on Neutral Rights

With the information now available, it is evident that from the very beginning Wilson and Lansing did not see eye to eye in the relationship of the United States to the warring powers. Wilson was determined to keep the United States out of the war and at the same time to use every possible means to bring about an early peace. Lansing, on the other hand, felt that German absolutism threatened democracy throughout the world. He prepared a memorandum for his own guidance entitled, "Consideration and Outline of Policies," dated July 11, 1915, in which he definitely declared: "A triumph for German imperialism must not be. . . . Germany must not be permitted to win this war . . . even though to prevent it this country is forced to take an active part." [6] However, Lansing could not at the beginning take this stand openly, nor did he try to do so. Secretary of the Navy Josephus Daniels makes this evident:

In all cabinet meetings he was so deferential to the President's policies that none of his colleagues regarded him as holding other views. . . . When he answered questions he upheld the vigorous demands on Britain in the written note. . . . His colleagues at first thought he was giving expression to his sincere convictions.[7]

In fact, Lansing's note dated October 21, 1915, protested so vigorously against British infringements of American rights on the high seas that Ambassador Page characterized it as "an uncourteous monster of 35 heads and 3 appendices" [8] prepared by "the lawyers of German importers and Chicago porkpackers," [9] with "not a courteous word, nor a friendly phrase, nor a kindly turn in it." [10]

Although the British unquestionably violated previously established international law of neutral rights, Lansing never forgot that the German submarine campaign also violated international law and caused the loss of both

American lives and property. It was the duty of the State Department to prepare the protests and to conduct the voluminous correspondence which followed. At times, as in the case of the sinking of the *Arabic*, Lansing wrote President Wilson, discussing the prospect of war with Germany, which he considered probable. In a memorandum dated August 25, 1915, outlining his own course of action, he decided to "put the matter up to the German ambassador so firmly and emphatically that he will be convinced that unless his government repudiates the brutal act of its submarine commander in attacking the *Arabic* and promises not to repeat the offense it will probably mean war." [11] In this instance Lansing acted without seeking the President's authorization and told Ambassador Bernstorff that unless Germany ceased attacking vessels carrying passengers, the United States would certainly declare war on Germany.

When six months later a torpedo sank the French channel steamer *Sussex* without warning and with a large loss of life, Lansing wrote Wilson, urging the immediate severance of diplomatic relations with Germany and drafting a note accordingly. Wilson, however, thought the language too severe and redrafted it, permitting Germany an opportunity to discuss the question. Lansing attempted to strengthen Wilson's draft, and both Counselor Frank L. Polk and Solicitor Woolsey supported him. Lansing noted that Wilson consistently changed drafts submitted to him, usually to make them more conciliatory or euphonious, thus stamping them with his style; therefore, in submitting modifications, Lansing tried as far as possible to preserve Wilson's language, while changing the sense to conform with his own ideas. In this way it was easier to persuade the President to modify the thoughts expressed.

Preparations for War

One unique development occurred at this time which was brought about by the strained relations with Europe and the imminent presidential elections. As a student of government, Wilson recognized that if he were defeated it meant that the people had repudiated his policies and he would be unable to conduct the foreign policy of the United States effectively during the period between the election and the inauguration of his successor. As a possible solution to this problem, on the day before the election President Wilson wrote a confidential letter to Secretary Lansing, proposing that in case of the election of Charles Evans Hughes, Secretary Lansing should resign immediately and the President would then name Mr. Hughes as Secretary of State. As soon as he should assume office, President Wilson and Vice President Marshall would resign. In this way Mr. Hughes, as Secretary of State, would succeed to the Presidency and be in a position to face any serious crisis with the majority of the people behind him.[12] President Wilson's reelection eliminated the need to try out this novel procedure.

With his endorsement at home to stimulate him, the President decided to make a final effort to bring about peace. Against Secretary Lansing's advice, President Wilson, on December 18, 1916, sent a request that the warring powers make a specific declaration of their peace aims, because, as stated in general terms by the statesmen of the belligerents, their objects were virtually the same.[13] When this statement was much criticized in the press, Lansing tried to explain away any connection between the German peace overture and the Wilson note by intimating that the sending of the note indicated the possibility of the United States being forced into the war. This explanation was most displeasing to the President and he insisted that Lansing issue a second statement to correct any such false impression.[14]

On January 28, 1917, Secretary Lansing wrote a memorandum to summarize his own thoughts. In it he declared: "We can no more avoid entering this war against Germany than we can avoid the progress of time. . . . War cannot come too soon to suit me since I know it must come at last." [15] Three days later, on January 31, Ambassador Bernstorff arranged to see Secretary Lansing in his office and informed him that beginning February 1, 1917, all ships entering a zone around Great Britain, France, and Italy would be sunk. The realist had outguessed the idealist. The renewal of unrestricted submarine warfare would surely involve the United States. Lansing immediately conferred with Polk and Woolsey and all agreed that the only course was to break off diplomatic relations. In the conference in the White House which followed, President Wilson still hesitated to act. It was not until he had discussed the matter at length with Colonel House and again with Secretary Lansing and finally with the entire cabinet that he decided to hand Bernstorff his passports.[16]

At this point let us note the approximate procedure followed by the Department of State in its efforts to maintain our neutral rights. In various technical questions of international law, such as the right of a neutral to trade in munitions of war, it would appear as though Lester H. Woolsey, Law Adviser to the Secretary, and later Solicitor, usually prepared the original drafts and Secretary Lansing would then confer and advise with him on the final form to be submitted to the President. In matters where the British were concerned, when the President felt that Lansing would not be sufficiently vigorous, the communication was the composite work of President Wilson, Counselor Polk, Solicitor Johnson and Assistant Secretary William Phillips. In regard to the violation of the rules governing the conduct of diplomatic agents, as, for example, when Dr. Dumba, the Austrian ambassador, made use of an American war correspondent who was pro-German to smuggle official communications to his government through the Allied blockade, Secretary Lansing took full jurisdiction. In this instance the Secretary of State interviewed the crestfallen ambassador and prepared the request for his recall so promptly that Dumba did not have time to get permission from his government to resign.

As a result of threats to the security of the United States through the activities of foreign agents and their minions, the Secret Intelligence Bureau was organized in April, 1916, under the direction of an able and experienced foreign-service officer, Leland Harrison, and it rendered very valuable services during the period of the war. The Division of Information was also considerably enlarged and by a Departmental order dated May 7, 1917, it was renamed Division of Foreign Intelligence. In addition to its previous duties of sending information to foreign-service officers abroad and editing the *Foreign Relations* volumes, it now prepared news items for the press, controlled departmental publicity, and saw to it that information was available to congressmen, universities, and the public generally, so that they might better understand the policies of the American government. The two men heading the Division of Foreign Intelligence were Philip H. Patchin, a newspaper man with many years' experience in foreign countries, who had been head of the Division of Information for two years from 1909 to 1911, and who was head of the Associated Press in London when he was asked to return to the Department; the other was a trained diplomat of considerable experience, Hugh Gibson, a foreign-service officer in Class 1. One other important change in personnel occurred when John E. Osborne retired as Assistant Secretary of State on December 14, 1916, and Third Assistant Secretary William Phillips was named to succeed him. The new Assistant Secretary had first served for two years as private secretary to Ambassador Choate in London and had then entered the foreign service, where he remained until he had become Chief of the Division of Far Eastern Affairs in the State Department in 1908. He had already served on two different occasions as Third Secretary, so that his promotion was based upon merit and experience. The new Third Secretary was Breckinridge Long, a lawyer from St. Louis, who, although a newcomer wholly without experience, was destined to hold a number of positions both in the State Department and abroad.

Although the United States did not declare war until April 6, 1917, the war conditions in Europe and the neutrality problems of the United States had increased the work of the State Department to such an extent that, even with the addition of a considerable staff of officers and clerks, overtime work became the custom rather than the exception. In fact, Chief Clerk Ben G. Davis declared that the work of the Department increased 400 per cent during the first six weeks of the European War, and according to Director of the Consular Service, Wilbur J. Carr, in the space of a week to ten days the personnel in the Department was increased by at least 150. The space in the State, War, and Navy Building was wholly unable to take care of the expanding Department, and by the first of January, 1918, quarters were being used in the National Savings and Trust Building, in the Southern Building, in the building at 1653 Pennsylvania Avenue, and at 1423 New York Avenue.

War Problems of the Department

At the outbreak of the war in 1914, the State Department received some 60,000 inquiries regarding Americans in Europe which had to be answered and arrangements made for their protection or repatriation. To meet this situation, the Congress passed a joint resolution appropriating $2,750,000 for the relief, protection, and transportation of American citizens in the war zones. These funds had to be administered by the State Department through American ambassadors and ministers abroad. An additional $1,000,000 was appropriated for representation of foreign governments. Practically all of the foreign belligerents put their interests in the hands of the United States, and all communications between the belligerents passed through the Department of State. Our foreign representatives had to visit hundreds of prison camps and make reports through the Department. Before the war most travelers went abroad without passports, but under war conditions no traveler would consider a trip without one and the work of the Bureau of Citizenship more than quadrupled. The officers in the Solicitor's office worked day and night and still needed additional help. In fact every agency in the Department experienced an abnormal expansion, and since experienced men were wholly unavailable the Department almost denuded the diplomatic and consular posts of their experienced officers. The personnel increase in the Department was from 208 in 1914 to 440 in 1918.[17] One graphic illustration of the increased work of the Department is shown by the fact that whereas in 1914 the Department of State telegraphed 28,031 words, in 1918 that number had risen to 217,597.

The problem of preventing leaks of confidential information was most important for the Department. For example, it was alleged that certain persons learned of President Wilson's note of December 18, 1916, to the warring powers and profited thereby in speculations. To prevent any such possibility, the Department reorganized certain bureaus and divisions so that documents of a top-secret character were only handled by a few of the most responsible officials. A system of passes was inaugurated and no person, even an official, could enter the State Department buildings without possessing one. It was further directed that no information should be given to the press by State Department officials except by the Secretary of State at his daily conferences or by the Division of Information. After the United States became a belligerent, all information except that controlled by the Department of State was put in the hands of a Committee on Public Information, consisting of the Secretaries of State, War, and Navy, and a civilian newspaper man, George Creel. The arrangement was not a happy one, for Lansing resented Creel's position and methods of propaganda and Creel disdained the conservative Secretary and his protocol.[18]

Almost immediately after the United States entered the war, a series of Allied diplomatic missions visited the United States. All arrangements for military, naval, and financial requirements were made through the Department of State. Almost of equal importance was the entertainment of these missions, which put a very considerable social strain upon the higher officials of the State Department. Secretary Lansing noted that between December 1, 1915, and March 10, 1916—a period of one hundred days—he attended fifty-eight dinners with his wife and gave eight. Upon the arrival of these missions it was not only necessary for the Secretary of State to entertain at dinner for them, but to be responsible for all of their social, political, and economic requirements.

Ill Advised Peace Feelers

From the time that the United States entered the war, constant efforts looking toward victory or peace through diplomatic means were made by both neutrals and belligerents. The State Department was concerned largely with keeping informed about these proceedings, but on two occasions it was induced to undertake ill advised and futile action. The first was the sending of Henry Morgenthau and Professor Felix Frankfurter in June, 1917, on a special mission to Egypt. The ostensible purpose was to investigate the status of the Jews in Palestine, but there was also the desire to find out if there were any possibility of detaching Turkey from the Central Powers.[19] Apparently the real purpose of the mission leaked out, because Acting Secretary of State Polk cabled on July 14, 1917, instructing the two emissaries under no circumstances to discuss any subject relating to the international situation in Turkey.[20] When Minister Morris cabled from Stockholm, Sweden, on August 30, 1917, that it was rumored that the Morgenthau mission was attempting to obtain the political independence of Palestine for the Jews and that a feeling of uneasiness was being created in Ottoman government circles, it was decided to recall the mission.

The other mission was the dispatch by the State Department of a special agent, Frank E. Anderson, in the guise of a representative of the American Woolen Company. His instructions declared that he was to make a confidential investigation for the Department and for the American legation in Holland with regard to trading with the enemy. His correspondence with the Department, however, indicated that he was to obtain information regarding political conditions, particularly concerning constitutional reforms in Central Europe. He was specifically enjoined not to enter enemy territory without first obtaining the permission of the Department. In spite of his orders he visited Vienna and Budapest and had meetings with Count Apponyi and other Central European statesmen. Secretary Lansing notified Chargé Hugh Wilson in Switzerland that Anderson had exceeded his authority and that Wilson should disavow him if advisable.[21]

The House Inquiry

Due to the overwhelming pressure of wartime activities, the State Department was not staffed to make plans for the peace treaty which would come at the end of hostilities. Instead of adding the necessary personnel to the State Department, the President, acting through House, set up an organization of experts in New York, headed by Dr. Mezes, the son-in-law of Colonel House, which was known as the "Inquiry." Dr. Isaiah Bowman, director of the American Geographical Society, offered its offices and library as well as his own services. The organization included noted experts in their fields, such as Charles H. Haskins, J. T. Shotwell, Charles Seymour, and Stanley Hornbeck. The secretary of the Inquiry was Walter Lippmann, and affiliated with it were James Brown Scott and David Hunter Miller.[22] Apparently the Secretary of State saw nothing unusual in being relieved of this vitally important work, inasmuch as President Wilson informed Colonel House that Lansing was not only content that he should undertake the preparation of data for the peace conference but had volunteered that House was the very one to do it.[23] Secretary Lansing later declared that he had approved the plans for the organization and work of the Inquiry and that he had found the monographs and reports prepared to be of the highest order.[24] Nevertheless, the State Department would have been well justified in resenting the establishment of this *ad hoc* machinery outside of its jurisdiction. Professor Shotwell, one of the key members of the Inquiry, conceded that

throughout the War, the State Department had been so definitely subordinated to the President that apparently it exercised little influence upon the structure of a conference, most of the preparation for which had been made by outsiders whose conclusions were often not even communicated to the Department in the course of their work.[25]

In a somewhat similar fashion President Wilson worked out his plans for a league of nations without discussing the program with the Secretary of State or his advisers. Secretary Lansing notes the fact that previous to the departure of the American commission for Paris on December 4, 1918, the President had not consulted him, had not shown him a copy of his plan, nor had he even told him that one had been prepared.[26] The President at first gave little thought to a definite program for an association of nations because he felt that all of his efforts should be centered upon winning the war. It was therefore Colonel House and the Inquiry who were made responsible for preparing an American program for the peace conference. In fact, President Wilson made his famous speech of January 8, 1918, giving his program of the Fourteen Points almost entirely from the recommendations of the Inquiry followed by a series of conferences with Colonel House. Secretary Lansing was only called in after the address was in final form and permitted to make a few slight verbal alterations.

State Disregarded in Peacemaking

When in the autumn of 1918 it was evident that the Central Powers were nearing collapse and that a peace settlement would soon be in order, Colonel House informed Secretary Lansing that they would both be named plenipotentiaries to the peace conference and intimated that the President would probably head the American delegation. Lansing felt that this would be a grave mistake and informed the President of his views.[27] President Wilson had apparently made up his mind to go and Lansing realized that his advice was unwelcome. If the President had remained in Washington, it would have made Secretary of State Lansing ex officio head of the American delegation, and President Wilson intended to be his own Secretary of State abroad as well as at home.

President Wilson consulted Lansing in regard to the other two members of the peace commission but as usual made the final decision himself. It was considered advisable to name an outstanding Republican, and Root, Taft, and Hughes had been suggested. House and Tumulty both favored Root, and Lansing was agreeable, but Wilson regarded Root as too conservative. When Lansing finally suggested the former diplomat Henry White, Wilson agreed. The fifth commissioner was General Tasker H. Bliss, who had been serving as an American representative in the Supreme War Council in Paris.[28] Although Secretary Lansing was commissioned by the President to organize the American delegation of experts to advise with the five commissioners, it went without saying that the members of the House Inquiry would have a high priority. In fact, although Joseph Grew, a foreign-service officer currently attached to the Office of the Assistant Secretary of State, was named secretary general of the American commission, the commission as finally organized gave the Inquiry members a far more important position than the personnel drawn from the Department of State. In fact, except for Secretary of State Lansing, who theoretically was second in rank on the commission (although actually subordinate to House, Bliss, and White), the only officers of the State Department holding positions of importance at the peace conference were Secretary General Grew and seven members of the secretariat: Leland Harrison, P. H. Patchin, William McNeir, Sydney Y. Smith, Charles B. Walsh, J. K. Huddle, and R. B. Macatee.

Secretary of State Lansing and the personnel of the State Department in Paris played a very small part in the making of the Treaty of Versailles. In the early days as a member of the Committee of Ten, Lansing endeavored to participate constructively in the conference and even went so far as to instruct Dr. James Brown Scott and David Hunter Miller, the legal advisers to the American commission, to prepare a skeleton treaty which might be submitted to the commission as a tentative draft for their consideration. Unfortunately, Lansing had not consulted the President in advance; and when Wilson was informed, he was resentful and told Lansing bluntly "that he did not propose to have lawyers drafting the Treaty." [29] As Lansing was the only lawyer on the Committee of Ten, he was cut to the quick and from then on hesitant to take the initiative.

Wilson's principal interest was the League of Nations and he devoted his every effort to see to it that the Covenant should be made an integral part of the treaty. The drafts of the Covenant which he placed before the conference as chairman of the commission to draft the Covenant were largely the work of Colonel House, David Hunter Miller, and the President himself. Secretary Lansing had prepared and sent to the President on December 23, 1918, several drafts and suggestions for discussion, but he never received either a reply or an acknowledgment.[30] According to Ray Stannard Baker, Secretary Lansing's letter and enclosures remained in President Wilson's files almost as fresh as when the Secretary signed them.[31] A memorandum of January 7, 1919, suffered a similar fate. It was evident that Wilson and Lansing differed so fundamentally on the kind of Covenant and its importance that the President no longer had any confidence in his Secretary of State. Lansing also opposed the exorbitant reparations bill, the Shantung settlement, the treaty of alliance with Great Britain to protect France, and would have resigned if he had not feared that such action would have delayed the peace settlement.

Once the Treaty of Versailles was signed, both Wilson and Lansing returned to the United States. Lansing took over his work in the Department and in addition made many speeches in favor of ratification of the treaty. His relations with the President, however, became even less satisfactory than before. The situation came to a head when William C. Bullitt, one of the experts at the conference, declared before the Senate Foreign Relations Committee on September 12, 1919, that Lansing had told him in Paris that he thought the treaty bad, the League of Nations useless, and that if the Senate really understood the treaty it would surely defeat it.[32] This was not a fair statement of Lansing's remarks, and the latter telegraphed his version. The President, however, felt that Lansing had been disloyal, and Tumulty felt that only the illness of the President prevented a demand for Lansing's resignation.

Lansing Resigns

Inasmuch as Wilson was too ill to perform his duties as President during the fall and winter of 1919-1920, Secretary Lansing suggested to Secretary Tumulty that his disability be certified and the Vice President be called in to act in his stead. Tumulty coldly rejected any such procedure and was supported by the President's physician, Dr. Grayson.[33] Secretary Lansing thereupon, without authorization by the President but after consulting Secretaries Baker and Lane, called meetings of the cabinet a score of times to carry on essential governmental business. This went on for approximately four months with no objections raised by the President. Then, unexpectedly, on February 7, 1920, Lansing received a letter from the President asking whether he had called the heads of departments into conference, an act which by the Constitution was solely a presidential function. Lansing immediately replied that he had done so to discuss matters which could not be postponed, that he had not thought that he was acting unconstitutionally, but if the President felt it desirable he would gladly resign. In his answer, dated February 11, President Wilson, after condemning Lansing's "assumption of Presidential authority," went on to declare that he had felt a constantly increasing disinclination on Lansing's part to follow presidential directions and that therefore it would relieve him of embarrassment if Lansing would resign and thus permit the President to appoint someone whose mind would go along more willingly with his. Secretary Lansing immediately tendered his resignation "with a sense of profound relief" and declared his only reason for not doing so earlier was that he did not wish to embarrass the President either in the peace negotiations or later in his efforts to secure the ratification of the treaty. His resignation was immediately accepted.[34]

The real reason for Wilson's peremptory demand for Lansing's resignation at this time is not clear. Tumulty opposed it as being inexpedient, considering the state of public opinion, but Wilson replied: "Tumulty, it is never the wrong time to spike disloyalty. When Lansing sought to oust me I was on my back. I am on my feet now and I will not have disloyalty about me." [35] Josephus Daniels rejects entirely the President's ostensible reason, because if that were the basis all of the cabinet members who approved were equally guilty. He de-

clares that the immediate reason was Lansing's ultimatum to Mexico to free
Consular Agent Jenkins, who had been captured and was held by bandits. In
issuing the ultimatum, which might have caused war with Mexico, the Secretary of State had consulted neither the President nor any member of the cabinet. President Wilson could stand no more and simply used the abuse of authority as an excuse.

A fair evaluation of Lansing as Secretary of State is difficult, first, because
of the characteristics of President Wilson, which were such that even Colonel
House finally broke with him, and, secondly, because of the war and its aftermath, which placed responsibilities upon the Department which it was not
permitted to assume. Unquestionably, Lansing was an able international lawyer well equipped to perform the normal duties of the Department. But even in
this field his record was not entirely satisfactory. His attitude toward the secret
treaties was naïve in the highest degree. The Department of State should have
known their terms and have been prepared to demand their modification or
abrogation if they were found contrary to American interests. Instead, even
after they had been published in the press, Lansing confessed ignorance and
seeming indifference concerning them. Secretary Lansing in his apologia de-
claims that the "people are sick of whispering diplomats. . . . What the world
asks are honest declarations openly proclaimed." [36] Nevertheless, Ray Stannard
Baker declares that at the peace conference Secretary Lansing was one of the
most difficult of men to approach, and that concerning his own commission
he was the least communicative of any of the commissioners. Conceding that
these were weaknesses, nevertheless Secretary Lansing at times saw further
than his chief. If accepted, some of his suggestions as to the peace treaty might
have made the road to ratification much easier. Perhaps no one had a better opportunity to know and evaluate the work of Secretary Lansing than Colonel
House. In 1928, when he could look back objectively upon the stormy period of
the war and its aftermath, Colonel House wrote:

The country has never quite appreciated Lansing. No other Secretary of
State had so difficult a task. The years of neutrality before we entered the war
presented many delicate and intricate situations and a false step might have
proved disastrous. He made none.[37]

In the words of an eminent American historian who has recently restudied
this entire period:

Lansing was an able rather than an outstanding man . . . he gave serious thought to the problems at hand, spoke cogently when the occasion demanded and grew steadily in the esteem of his colleagues. . . . Lansing was
a stern realist with his feet on the ground.[38]

Departmental Changes

Before taking up the work of Lansing's successors, we should note some of the changes in the Department hitherto not mentioned and the very considerable expansion which occurred during the period of the war and the peace negotiations. During 1916 three additional Assistant Solicitors were added, of whom one, Richard W. Flournoy, Jr., served as acting head of the much expanded Bureau of Citizenship. The Division of Western European Affairs was separated from the Office of Third Assistant Secretary of State and Frederick A. Sterling, an experienced foreign-service officer, was made acting head. As an antidote to Bryan's unfortunate political appointments, another foreign-service officer, Jordan H. Stabler, was appointed Acting Chief of the Division of Latin American Affairs. The office of the Foreign Trade Adviser, with a staff of eighteen, was placed under the direction of Marion Letcher, a foreign-service officer; and a new agency called the Office of the Adviser on Commercial Treaties was created with William B. Fleming at its head. David A. Salmon, who had been transferred to the State Department in 1906, was made Chief of the Bureau of Indexes and Archives, which, with a staff of fifty-one, had become the largest agency in the Department. In 1917 some forty-four additional temporary clerks were added to this bureau and in 1918 the temporary list had reached 143 in order to take care of the vast increase in the Department's correspondence. In 1917 some twenty-nine temporary employees were added to the Bureau of Citizenship, giving that agency a total personnel of sixty, which made it the second largest bureau in the Department. In 1918, by a Departmental order, its name was changed to Division of Passport Control. By the end of 1918 its permanent personnel numbered twenty-two, whereas its additional employees numbered 124. To afford greater facilities, additional Passport Bureaus were established in New York and San Francisco, with eight employees in the first and four in the second.

Because of the horde of emigrants waiting to enter the United States, the government had made it a requirement that all prospective immigrants obtain an American visa on their passports. To take care of this additional work, a Visa Office was set up by a Departmental order dated August 13, 1918, in the Division of Passport Control. A year later, on November 21, 1919, it was made a separate office and given complete jurisdiction over all matters pertaining to visa control.

One result of the war which somewhat altered the complexion of the Department was the largely increased number of women who were employed. At the top of this group was Margaret M. Hanna, who, after having served as a clerk in the Department for twenty-three years, was made Chief of the Correspondence Bureau, which had been set up in the office of the Second Assistant Secretary, to review all outgoing correspondence. Her Assistant Chief was Ruth B. Shipley, who was subsequently to serve as Chief of the Passport Division for almost a quarter of a century. Other women placed in responsible positions were Anna A. O'Neill, serving as a law clerk; Natalia Summers, employed in the Division of Near Eastern Affairs; and Nina G. Romeyn, in the Division of Latin American Affairs. About a dozen women had reached the rank of third-class clerks at $1,600 a year, the second highest clerical classification. About half of the second-class clerks at $1,400 and fully three-fourths of the first class at $1,200 were women.

Personnel Problems

The armistice brought no reduction in the work of the Department of State—in fact, its duties both expanded and increased when it was required to take over the work of some of the temporary war agencies. For example, the War Trade Board, by a Departmental order dated July 1, 1919, was made a section of the Department of State. In fact, the Chief of the Consular Bureau was immediately given jurisdiction over its foreign agents and its reports. In a table submitted by Mr. Carr to a subcommittee of the House Committee on Appropriations the personnel of the Department on December 1, 1919, numbered 788, of which 353 were statutory officials and 435 were additional.[39]

In a letter dated January 20, 1919, Counselor Polk wrote to the chairman of the Senate Appropriations Committee, calling his attention to the fact that twelve heads of offices reported an increase in their work of from 10 to 300 per cent over the amount of January 1, 1918, and that thirteen officers stated that an increase of from one to twenty-four persons was necessary to keep the current work up to date. Four officers reported their work in arrears from three to eighteen months, and six were only able to keep their work up to date by overtime and night service. The Department was faced with the problem of studying thousands of claims amounting to many millions of dollars, of considering questions of international finance, tariff policies, customs difficulties, trade promotion, the welfare and whereabouts of American citizens in enemy territory, the establishment of diplomatic and consular relations with the former enemy countries and with the nations newly established.[40]

Another serious problem was that of trained personnel. Many foreign-service officers who had been brought in from the field would be compelled by law to return to their posts. Many other officers who had left their well paid positions in professions and in business because of patriotic desire to support the government found it necessary to leave their inadequately paid positions in Washington to earn a living wage. It could hardly be expected that law clerks who had private practices would continue in the Department at salaries of

$2,000 to $2,500 a year or that chiefs of bureaus would resist outside offers when their salaries ranged from $2,100 to $2,450. In fact, one official at $4,500 refused an offer of $10,000 but succumbed to $15,000, while one able consul who left the service was soon making $45,000 a year in private business. The Congress refused regularly to appropriate sufficient funds to make it possible for the Department to get trained and capable personnel. Wilbur J. Carr, the able director of the consular service, who after nine years in this position and after twenty-six years in the Department was receiving a salary of $4,500 annually, declared to the House Appropriations Committee on November 22, 1918, that "the trouble with our Department is that the personnel is terribly weak and utterly incapable of doing the things the Department must do." Counselor Polk, in the hearings before a Senate committee, declared:

If you compare our State Department with the foreign offices abroad, the equipment is utterly different. Over there they have men of experience, trained men with adequate help. When I came down here from the corporation counsel's office in New York, the first thing that struck me was that here were these big questions involving many millions of dollars to the American people being handled by boys. . . . It was not the fault of the Department. That is all the equipment they had.[41]

After the resignation of Secretary Lansing there was widespread criticism of the Department because of its failure to serve more adequately during the war and at the peace conference. Many recognized the fact that the cause was partly Secretary Bryan's policy of filling key posts in the Department with inexperienced and incapable political henchmen and also by the refusal of the Congress to appropriate sufficient sums to staff the Department adequately. An additional reason was Wilson's tendency to create and use outside agencies to carry out tasks which lay properly within the purview of the Department. The War Trade Board sent men abroad, organized offices, and carried on activities which might better have been assigned to an enlarged consular corps. The Committee on Public Information also set up foreign agencies which were wholly outside of the foreign service and gave out information at times at complete variance with State Department policies. With the war ended, it was now the task of the State Department to tie up the loose ends and carry on a vastly expanded program of world contacts.

One of Lansing's last acts was to write a letter, dated January 21, 1920, to Congressman John Jacob Rogers of Massachusetts, urging a thorough reorganization of both the Department and the foreign service:

The machinery of government now provided for dealing with our foreign relations is in need of complete repair and reorganization. As adequate as it may have been when the old order prevailed and the affairs of the world were free from the present perplexities it has ceased to be responsive to present needs. . . . American agents in the foreign field must broaden the scope and intensify the nature of their work in order that the Department of State may have at its disposal knowledge of the actual facts of every development or turn of events.[42]

The Department, as we shall see, did little to meet the new requirements, and the reorganization of the foreign service awaited a new administration.

Bainbridge Colby—Secretary of State

When Secretary Lansing resigned on February 13, 1920, Frank Lyon Polk became Acting Secretary of State. Polk had entered the Department as Counselor on August 30, 1915, and by the Act of Congress of March 1, 1919, his title had been changed to that of Under Secretary of State. The Department had long urged this change of nomenclature, but due to the fact that some congressmen felt that such a change would seem to ape the British, the Congress had delayed action. There was much speculation as to whether Under Secretary Polk would be rewarded for his excellent services during his incumbency by being named Secretary or whether President Wilson would again name someone "who would go along more willingly with him." The President's illness and the increasingly important role played by Mrs. Wilson aroused the keenest interest in the appointment. In addition to the name of Frank Polk, suggested by Secretary Houston, the two names prominently mentioned were those of Secretary of War Newton D. Baker and the Jewish financier Bernard Baruch, but to the astonishment of all the mantle fell upon Bainbridge Colby. It was not a popular choice either in Congress or in the press. The New York Times declared that if there was any political reason for choosing Mr. Colby it was not a wise one and that it would be better if President Wilson, in making appointments, could satisfy rather than surprise the public.[43] The Senate reacted very unfavorably to the appointment. The fact that Colby had been a Republican, Progressive, and Democrat in turn was a considerable liability with the old-line Democrats. As one phrased it: "He was a decided Democrat but he only decided lately." As a consequence, although nominated on February 25, the Foreign Relations Committee of the Senate did not report his name favorably until March 20, and then only after a hearing before the committee. His nomination was confirmed by the Senate on March 23 and he entered upon his duties the same day.

Bainbridge Colby was a very able lawyer, a fine speaker, a good administrator, and an excellent drafting officer,[44] but wholly inexperienced in diplomacy or the conduct of foreign relations. However, it was thought that Wilson intended to continue to act as his own Secretary of State in spite of his disabilities and in spite of Colby's reputation for independence.

Three important changes in top personnel occurred during Colby's incumbency. The able Under Secretary, Frank L. Polk, resigned on June 15, 1920, and Norman H. Davis, a New York banker, succeeded him. Mr. Davis had represented the Treasury Department in London and Paris in 1918 and had subsequently served as financial adviser to President Wilson. He was a man of ingratiating personality who had a natural flair for diplomacy, and although not a career diplomat, his background and experience tended to make him one. The First Assistant Secretary of State, William Phillips, a career officer, had been named minister to the Netherlands and left the Department on March 25, 1920. For almost a year this important post remained vacant; in fact, it was not filled until the new administration took charge. Alvey A. Adee continued to act as Second Assistant Secretary of State and celebrated his fiftieth anniversary in the service of the United States government in 1920. Secretary Colby took advantage of the occasion to commend him highly for the impress which his learning and remarkable abilities had made upon the Department of State. In the place of Third Assistant Secretary Breckinridge Long, a New York banker and lawyer was appointed, Van Santvoord Merle-Smith. Inasmuch as the work of the Third Assistant Secretary had become largely administrative and required a firsthand knowledge of the workings of the Department and the foreign service, this was a questionable appointment. Lester H. Woolsey retired as Solicitor of the State Department on March 31, 1920. His successor was Fred K. Nielsen, who had entered the Department of State as a clerk in 1904 and had been made a law clerk in 1913 and Acting Solicitor in 1914. Nielsen had been one of the legal advisers to the American Commission to Negotiate Peace at Paris in 1919 and was well qualified for the promotion.

A new agency had been created on February 6, 1920—just before Secretary Colby took office—to collect and coordinate political information and supply it to the executive officers of the Department. An experienced newspaper man, Prentiss B. Gilbert, was put in charge of this Division of Political Information. A Departmental order the following year, on May 24, 1921, changed its name to that of Division of Political and Economic Information and increased its jurisdiction.

Departmental Problems

Secretary Colby entered the cabinet of President Wilson under most inauspicious circumstances. The President was in such physical condition that Dr. Grayson, his physician, and Mrs. Wilson felt it necessary to keep him to a considerable extent incommunicado. He had broken with Colonel House

22

Charles Evans Hughes

Charles Evans Hughes—Secretary of State

President Warren G. Harding was neither experienced nor interested in foreign affairs. He had engaged in mellifluous double talk in regard to the League of Nations, but once elected he took a stand against the adherence of the United States. As a former senator he was unquestionably influenced by his colleagues, Senators Lodge, Knox, and Brandegee, in the appointment of a Secretary of State who would be acceptable to these bitter opponents of the League. At the same time, thirty-one outstanding Republicans had supported Harding on the ground that he would bring the United States into the League of Nations but with the Covenant so amended as to protect adequately the interests of the United States. Elihu Root was the Republican who drafted this document and was known to be one of the most ardent Republican supporters of the League of Nations. Charles Evans Hughes and Herbert Hoover were also signatories of this appeal but they were not so closely affiliated with the pro-League advocates as was Root. Former President Taft, also a signatory, favored the appointment of Root as Secretary of State and urged his name upon Harding. However, Senators Lodge, Knox, and Brandegee were strongly opposed to Root. President Harding did not wish to antagonize these former colleagues and yet he could not afford to estrange the many Republican supporters of the League. In spite of these vital political requirements, President Harding was so much indebted to Colonel George Harvey for both his nomination and election that he considered offering the post of Secretary of State to this fanatically bitter opponent of the League. Harvey, however, was too intelligent to consider accepting and informed the President that he must choose his premier member of the cabinet from a Republican of long standing.[1] Harding then wisely turned to Charles Evans Hughes as one who had the respect, if not the support, of all factions. Both Root and Hughes had visited Harding in Marion, Ohio, in December, 1920, and it was at that time that President-elect

258

Copyright Harris & Ewing

CHARLES EVANS HUGHES

Harding offered Hughes the State Department portfolio. Hughes asked for a few days to consider and then wrote Harding that he would accept. The arrangement was later confirmed by President-elect Harding in writing, and on February 19, 1921, at a conference in St. Augustine, Mr. Hughes was introduced to the newspapermen as the Secretary of State in the new cabinet. Mr. Harding at this time gave a clue to his future relationship with his Secretary of State when he declared: "From this time on, gentlemen, you will get your news as to the foreign relations of the United States from the State Department." [2]

Charles Evans Hughes, who took office as Secretary of State on March 4, 1921, was just as little versed in diplomacy and foreign relations as the President. Nevertheless, Hughes's appointment was hailed everywhere as most admirable. His reputation as a very able lawyer, a courageous prosecutor, an excellent governor, a scholarly Associate Justice of the Supreme Court, and the near-successful Presidential candidate of the Republican party in 1916 gave assurance that the Department of State would be in most capable hands. His phenomenal ability to digest facts and make a prompt decision based upon sound judgment would be an invaluable asset in the formulation of foreign policy. The eminent Republican senators on the Foreign Relations Committee of the Senate, Messrs. Lodge, Borah, Brandegee, Knox, and Moses, were to find that Hughes intended to be his own Secretary of State.

Hughes's Excellent Appointments

Secretary Hughes quickly showed that he intended to surround himself in the Department with able, experienced, and well qualified assistants. As Under Secretary of State he chose Henry P. Fletcher, who had behind him a long and distinguished career in the diplomatic service of the United States. For First Assistant Secretary a career foreign-service officer was named, Fred M. Dearing, who had been in the American foreign service for some seventeen years. *Semper paratus* Alvey Adee, whom Hughes characterized as "the constant and most trusted adviser of Secretaries of State," continued as Second Assistant Secretary. Robert Woods Bliss, another career officer, with some eighteen years' experience, was appointed Third Assistant Secretary of State. Wilbur J. Carr was retained as Director of the Consular Service, Fred K. Nielsen remained as Solicitor, and Ben G. Davis as Chief Clerk. The career officers acting as chiefs of the geographical divisions—John Van A. MacMurray, Far Eastern Affairs; Warren D. Robbins, Near Eastern Affairs; and Sumner Welles, Latin American Affairs—stayed on at their posts. Matthew E. Hanna, a career foreign-service officer, replaced Charles M. Johnston, a political appointee, as Chief of the Division of Mexican Affairs. De Witt C. Poole, who had served in the consular service for eleven years and had originally been appointed Chief of the Russian

Division and had been supplanted by Arthur Bullard, was now reappointed Chief of the Division of Russian Affairs. In the place of Robert Woods Bliss, who had been named Third Assistant Secretary of State, the new head of the Division of Western European Affairs was William R. Castle, Jr., who had been serving for two years in the Department as a special assistant. The new head of the Office of the Foreign Trade Adviser was Arthur C. Millspaugh, who had already served for several years in the Department and had subsequently entered the consular service.

Herbert Hengstler, who had been in the Department since 1898, remained as Chief of the Consular Bureau. Sydney Y. Smith, one of the oldest men in the Department—he had entered as clerk on July 1, 1881—had been relieved of his position as Chief of the Diplomatic Bureau, which he had held for fourteen years, on July 1, 1919, but had been retained as a drafting officer. He was to remain in the Department in this capacity for another twenty years, making a total period of service of fifty-eight years, a unique record. Worthington E. Stewart, with fifteen years' service in the Department, succeeded Smith as Chief of the Diplomatic Bureau. No change was made in the Division of Passport Control, and a consular officer, J. Preston Doughten, was made Chief of the Visa Office.

Three new divisions, all pertaining to informational activities, were established a month after Secretary Hughes took office. One, called the Division of Publications, created on May 13, 1921, was a reorganization of the Bureau of Rolls and Library, with certain duties added. The Division of Publications had custody of the laws, treaties, and proclamations of the President, supervised the publications of the Department, and had charge of the library. It was authorized to prepare the volumes of *Foreign Relations of the United States* and the *History of the World War*. Gaillard Hunt, who was named Chief of the Division of Publications, had served in the Department for six years as Chief of the Bureau of Citizenship and had then gone to the Library of Congress as Chief of the Division of Manuscripts. He returned to the Department during the First World War and was appointed as special assistant to prepare a history of the war from the standpoint of the Department of State. He remained in the Department as a drafting officer until he was named Chief of the Division of Publications. As reorganized in 1921, the division had as personnel an Assistant Chief, an Editor, and an Assistant Editor of the laws, and fifteen clerks.

The Division of Political and Economic Information, which was established on May 24, 1921, was the Division of Political Information created in 1920, with the addition of extra duties covering the collection of social, economic, and geographical information. It had charge of the map collection of the Department and in 1924 it was assigned the management of the Department library. Prentiss B. Gilbert remained as Chief of the Division.

The Division of Current Information, which was established simultaneously with the Division of Political and Economic Information, had a long history. In the early days, according to Josiah King, a clerk forwarded "newspapers and public documents to our foreign ministers." [3] From 1833 to 1909 the Diplomatic Bureau carried on this function and included the perusal and translation of foreign newspapers. In 1909 it became the Division of Information and took over the editing of the *Foreign Relations* series. Its name was again changed in 1917 to the Division of Foreign Intelligence, and as a war measure it controlled Departmental censorship and publicity and prepared daily press summaries and the pamphlet "Information Series." This division was abolished in May, 1921, and the Division of Current Information created. It was at this time that duties relating to the publication of the *Foreign Relations* volumes were transferred to the Division of Publications. The Division of Current Information continued to function, with some changes during the Second World War, until it was abolished by Secretary Stettinius in his drastic reorganization of February 22, 1944. One of the clerks in the division was Michael McDermott, who was made Chief of the division in 1927 and remained at its head until the division was abolished.

Perhaps the most noticeable feature of Hughes's administration of the State Department was the large number of career diplomatic and consular officers brought in from the field. We have noted that the new Under Secretary of State and the two new Assistant Secretaries were career men. All but one of the chiefs of the geographical divisions were from the foreign service, as were the heads of the Foreign Trade Adviser's Office and the Visa Office. As of December, 1921, there were thirty-six officers in the Department holding important positions who had served previously in either a diplomatic or consular capacity abroad.[4] The excellent record made by Secretary Hughes in formulating and executing a successful foreign policy proved the wisdom of the procedure.

Although Secretary Hughes relied to a very large extent upon his advisers, he never spared himself and did a prodigious amount of spadework when it was necessary. He signed a vast number of letters and instructions daily, but never without reading them carefully enough to know exactly what he had signed. He worked long hours and made every hour count. He required that a brief memorandum be prepared regarding every visitor, which he read before commencing the interview. He believed fully in making available to the press all information pertaining to foreign policy which would not jeopardize the security of the state. He saw to it that two press conferences were held every working day, at which either the Secretary or Under Secretary was present.

Secretary Hughes appreciated the need for close relations with the Congress and regretted that it was not permitted that a Department head go before the Congress to explain in person the policies of his Department.

The Secretary of State appears before committees from time to time and gives the information which is asked. But there is lacking the direct personal relation to the discussions of the Senate when foreign officers are under consideration. The Secretary of State, acting for the President, may negotiate an important treaty but he has no opportunity to explain or defend it upon the floor of the Senate when its provisions are under debate. . . . The advantage of oral explication and of meeting each exigency as it arises in the course of discussion and thus of aiding in the formation of public opinion in the manner best adapted to that purpose is not open to him.[5]

Diplomatic Appointments

Secretary Hughes declared that he had made no changes in the Department of State for political reasons and he was opposed to appointments in the diplomatic or consular service on a purely political basis. The Republicans had been out of office for eight years, however, and President Harding had certain political obligations which only important diplomatic posts could fulfill. The ambassadorship to Great Britain is perhaps the most sought after appointment next to a cabinet post. President Harding offered it to the man who had done so much to make him President, Colonel George B. M. Harvey. It would have been difficult to find a more undiplomatic diplomat than the vituperative Harvey, "a journalistic rough neck" in the words of the Louisville *Courier-Journal*, although its former editor, "Marse Henry" Watterson, supported him for the position. An outstanding journalist historian of the period thus characterized the appointment: "Bumptious, unstable, sensational and loose of tongue the ex-editor . . . was the wrong man in the wrong place at the wrong time." [6] Ambassador Harvey's first public address in London at the Society of Pilgrims' dinner seemed to bear out the criticism. He informed his listeners that the United States had sent its soldiers across the sea solely to save the United States of America "and most reluctantly and laggardly at that. We were not too proud to fight, whatever that may mean. We were afraid not to fight." He concluded by stating categorically that the United States had not the slightest intention of entering the League of Nations.[7] Harvey's biographer declares the address was approved by Harding and others before Harvey left for his post, but Secretary Hughes's name was not mentioned as among "the others."

The post of ambassador to France was Myron T. Herrick's if he wished. Herrick's former outstanding services at this post, his close friendship with Harding, the need to rehabilitate our relations with France after refusing to sign the Versailles Treaty made Herrick the ideal choice. President Harding very much wanted Herrick in his cabinet, but Herrick would never serve in a cabinet of which Harry Daugherty was a member, and Harding would not pass over this intimate political crony and henchman. Herrick's health was not satisfactory and he at first refused any diplomatic appointment, but when both Hughes and Root supported Harding in urging him to accept, Herrick agreed.

Another political obligation which the President had to meet was to take care of Richard Washburn Child, editor of *Collier's Weekly*. He and George Harvey were the President's principal advisers during his speaking campaign, "deftly employing language to conceal thought." Child was offered the choice of three diplomatic posts and chose Italy. Contrary to the experiences of some ambassadors, Child was always able to work well with the Department of State. Writing after he had left the service, Child declared: "The Department of State appeared to me during all my experience in Italy and at international conferences as a very lively catcher willing and able to handle everything thrown from the field." [8]

The post at Berlin was not an urgent matter since no embassy would be opened immediately, and Ellis L. Dresel, the American commissioner, long familiar with the diplomatic problems in Berlin, was serving satisfactorily. Dresel changed his status as American commissioner to chargé d'affaires in November, 1921, and remained in charge of the post until Congressman Alanson B. Houghton was appointed to Berlin as ambassador extraordinary and plenipotentiary on February 10, 1922. Some difficulty was found in filling the post in Tokyo. It was first offered to former Ambassador to Germany David Jayne Hill, but he refused, as did Progressive Senator Albert J. Beveridge, the next to be proposed. It was finally accepted by a Detroit lawyer, Charles Beecher Warren, who had had some international juridical experience and had served in the Judge Advocate General's office during the war. President Jacob Gould Schurman of Cornell University, who had been minister to Greece in 1912, was named minister to China. In similar fashion Cyrus E. Woods, ambassador to Spain, had served previously as minister to Portugal in 1912. Although these were all political appointments, the representatives named were in every instance men of considerable ability who could be expected to represent the United States creditably abroad.

In many instances Secretary Hughes was able to reward able career diplomats by appointments giving recognition to their excellent services, as, for example, Joseph C. Grew, named minister to Switzerland; Hugh Gibson, minister to Poland; Peter Augustus Jay, minister to Rumania; and Charles S. Wilson, promoted from chargé d'affaires to minister to Bulgaria. The able career ambassador to Brazil, Edwin V. Morgan, was retained, as was Ira Nelson Morris, who had been serving creditably as minister to Sweden since 1914. In some cases former diplomats who had left the service after making excellent records were brought back. Outstanding examples were John W. Riddle, ambassador to Argentina; William Miller Collier, ambassador to Chile; and

Laurits S. Swenson, minister to Norway. Although a few appointments were inexcusably bad, considering Hughes's insistence upon the need for trained men in the foreign service,[9] as, for example, Joseph M. Dunning, diplomatic agent to Tangier, Morocco; Joseph Saul Kornfeld, minister to Persia; and William J. O'Toole, minister to Paraguay, the Harding-Hughes regime made a far better record in diplomatic appointments than the Wilson-Bryan administration which preceded it.

Postwar Problems

Among the first problems facing the Harding administration was the need for a treaty of peace to end the war. Since the Senate had repudiated the Treaty of Versailles, the Congress declared the war with Germany to be at an end by a joint resolution. Secretary Hughes appreciated the fact that such a procedure was not sufficient to protect American interests which obtained as a result of her participation in the war as an associated power. His first idea was a revised Treaty of Versailles amended to meet the Senate demands, but he was informed that the Senate would not approve such an arrangement. For a lawyer of Hughes's ability such a problem was simple. He proposed an entirely new treaty to be entered into by the United States and Germany which should embody the text of the joint resolution and such provisions of the Versailles Treaty as were deemed essential to safeguard the interests of the United States. Such a document, preserving the fruits of victory without accepting its responsibilities, was quite satisfactory to the Senate.

Secretary Hughes gave evidence of his legal training in his handling of the allocation of the mandates in the Pacific. As an associated power, Secretary Colby had insisted that the United States should share in all the rights and privileges as regards the mandates as provided for in the treaties of peace. When Hughes learned that mandates in the Pacific had been approved without consulting the United States, he made a strong protest based upon the legal rights of the United States as an associated power, regardless of the fact that we had not ratified the Versailles Treaty. His case was so well reasoned that Japan, Belgium, and France made treaties with the United States recognizing its rights.

The Washington Disarmament Conference

Certainly the most spectacular, if not the most important, achievement of the Harding administration in the field of foreign affairs was the Conference for the Limitation of Armament held in Washington, D. C., from November, 1921, to February, 1922. Senator Borah felt that too much money was being spent on naval armament, and even an isolationist senator appreciated the fact that the United States could not disarm alone. Shortly after President Harding's election, Senator Borah introduced a resolution requesting the President to invite Great Britain and Japan to send representatives to a conference which might work out a plan for mutual reduction of their programs for naval building. President Harding resented Senator Borah's interference with the presidential prerogative and tried at first to sidestep the proposal. However, when the resolution, which had been made an amendment to the Naval Appropriations bill, was being debated in Congress, public opinion in its favor was so overwhelming that the President became an ardent champion of the idea. In the meantime Ambassador Harvey had learned that the British were planning to call a conference on Far Eastern affairs, with reduction of armament as a part of the agenda. He called Secretary Hughes, pointing out the advantage of President Harding's taking the initiative, since the idea had originated in the United States. Hughes acted promptly on Harvey's suggestion and notified the press that the United States had issued invitations for a conference on limitation of armament and matters relating to the Far East, to the governments of Great Britain, France, Italy, and Japan, to be held shortly in Washington.[10]

Secretary Hughes handled both the preliminaries and the conference itself in a masterly manner. The British, eager to get rid of the Anglo-Japanese Alliance, wanted very much to have a preliminary conference on Far Eastern affairs, either in England or in the United States, and used every diplomatic maneuver to get their way. Secretary Hughes was determined that only one conference should be held and that that one should be in Washington and that its agenda should include both limitation of armament and Far Eastern questions. Hughes won his point. He was also successful in obtaining four official representatives for each state instead of the two suggested by the British. Hughes was determined to obtain the cooperation of the Senate, and to achieve this he felt that he needed both Chairman Henry Cabot Lodge of the Senate Committee on Foreign Relations and Oscar Underwood, the ranking member of the minority on the committee, as official delegates. For the fourth representative he wanted Elihu Root, the Republican party's elder statesman. He readily obtained President Harding's approval of his proposed delegation.

President Harding made Secretary Hughes responsible for making concrete proposals for actual reduction of armament. Hughes and his assistants in the Department of State well appreciated that the Navy would not be sympathetic to any radical reduction. Consultations between State Department and Navy Department experts could reach no common basis of security requirements. Secretary Hughes decided that the sole possibility of success was to maintain existing ratios between the great naval powers. At an early meeting of the American delegates, Elihu Root made a similar suggestion and the proposal was approved by both senators and President Harding. The experts of the Departments of State and Navy were given the problem of determining how much of each navy should be scrapped and how far building should cease. The Navy Department agreed to parity with Great Britain but wanted a two-to-one ratio as regards Japan. Secretary Hughes knew this would never be accepted by Japan and persuaded President Harding to accept the approximate naval strength of 100 per cent each for the United States and Great Britain and 60 per cent for Japan.

Having obtained his way with the President and the Navy Department, Secretary Hughes was equally determined to see to it that the problem of disarmament should take precedence over political questions at the conference and that concrete results should be obtained as quickly as possible. His procedure was both original and unique in international conferences. Having been selected as chairman of the conference, according to traditional diplomatic practice, he arranged to have only two addresses at the opening session—the brief, formal welcoming speech by President Harding and his own supporting address as chairman of the conference. Harding's speech was according to formula, but Hughes's was a veritable bombshell. After a conventional introduction, Hughes proceeded immediately to concrete proposals for a ten-year naval holiday and the scrapping of such ships as were built or building to give Great Britain and the United States each approximately 500,000 tons of capital ships and Japan 300,000 tons, with the same rates to be applied to other types of ships. According to Colonel Repington, the British naval expert: "Secretary Hughes sank in 35 minutes more ships than all the admirals of the world have sunk in a cycle of centuries." Before the delegates could recover from their astonishment and protest, the meeting was adjourned until the following Monday. Hughes counted upon public opinion rallying behind his proposals, and he was not disappointed.

By his audacious initiative Hughes was able to put his limitation of armament program through almost intact as far as capital ships were concerned, but owing to French opposition the conference could not agree to include other types of ships. The French delegates resented Hughes's direct-action procedure and became so uncooperative that upon one occasion Hughes had to cable to Premier Briand to secure the acceptance of the French quota of 175,000, which was a larger tonnage than France actually possessed. To obtain Japanese acceptance, the American-British ultimate tonnage was changed to 525,000 and that of Japan to 315,000, thus permitting Japan to retain its most publicized battleship, the *Mitsui*. The Japanese were also unwilling to give up their alliance with Great Britain without a compensatory agreement and the substitute finally accepted was a four-power treaty between the United States, Great Britain, France, and Japan, pledging each to respect the others' insular possessions and dominions in the Pacific. When a reporter asked President Harding as to whether the term "insular possessions" included the homeland of Japan, he replied that it did not. Inasmuch as Secretary Hughes had stated that the homeland of Japan was included, according to the interpretation accepted by the conference, President Harding was compelled to confess that he had been mistaken. Subsequently, the Japanese delegation, under the compulsion of Tokyo, were able to obtain a supplementary agreement which specifically excluded the Japanese homeland from the terms of the treaty.[11]

Hughes's greatest success, however, was the Nine-Power Treaty, which specifically required the signatory powers to respect the territorial integrity and the political independence of China and the maintenance of the open-door policy. Root and Balfour aided materially in putting pressure upon the recalcitrant Japanese delegates, but it was Hughes's persuasiveness and driving force which achieved results. It was at Hughes's suggestion that the hitherto secret protocol to the Lansing-Ichii Agreement of 1917 was incorporated almost verbatim in the Nine-Power Treaty.[12] Hughes also did much to bring about an agreement outside of the regular conference to secure the return of Shantung to China. On one occasion he took the Chinese minister to see President Harding to secure his help in persuading the Chinese minister to take advantage of this opportunity to regain Shantung by making certain economic concessions to Japan.[13]

Throughout the conference Secretary Hughes utilized the personnel of the Department of State for consultation and advice, particularly career men and technical and regional experts. Among the State Department officials who were named as advisers were Under Secretary of State Henry P. Fletcher, Fred K. Nielsen, John Van A. MacMurray, De Witt C. Poole, Warren D. Robbins, and Stanley K. Hornbeck, an expert on Far Eastern Affairs but serving at the time in the Office of the Economic Adviser. Two career officers from the embassies at Paris and London also acted as advisers: Leland Harrison, formerly counselor in the Paris embassy and shortly to become Assistant Secretary of State, and J. Butler Wright, counselor of the American embassy in London. Tracy Lay, a consular officer who had served in both London and Paris and was at the time detailed to the Department of State, was also designated for duty in connection with the conference.

Hughes's Latin American Policy

Although it is often overlooked, Secretary Hughes and the Department of State made a most creditable record in the relations of the United States with the republics of Latin America.[14] The day after he entered office, Secretary Hughes was faced with a threat of war between Costa Rica and Panama over a boundary dispute developing from an arbitral award handed down in 1914 by Chief Justice White of the United States Supreme Court. He immediately sent identic notes to both republics, asking them to suspend hostilities, and on March 15, 1921, he urged Panama to accept the arbitral award. When the President of Panama refused, Hughes informed the Panamanian government that the United States would take physical means to establish the line if necessary. Hughes's position supporting the just claims of Costa Rica against Panama —a sort of protegé of the United States—indicated that the new Secretary of State was forceful as well as juridical.[15] Secretary Hughes showed equal firmness and fairness in dealing with Mexico. He refused to recognize President Obregón until assurances should be given that the confiscatory provisions of the Constitution of 1917 would not jeopardize the legally acquired property rights of American citizens. Hughes was able to make an equitable arrangement bringing about the withdrawal of the marines from the Dominican Republic, and he helped establish better relations with Haiti.

Secretary Hughes had several excellent opportunities to outline the policy of the United States and he took advantage of them. On September 8, 1922, as the representative of President Harding at the centennial celebration of Brazilian independence, Secretary Hughes disclaimed any imperialistic intent on the part of the United States in most categorical terms: "We covet no territory; we seek no conquest; the liberty we cherish for ourselves we desire for others; and we assert no rights for ourselves that we do not accord to others." [16] At the Central American Conference of Washington in 1922 and 1923, to formulate a treaty for the maintenance of peace by peaceful procedures, Secretary Hughes as chairman of the conference declared: "The United States has no ambition to gratify at your expense, no policy which runs counter to your national aspirations and no purpose save to promote the interests of peace." [17]

Secretary Hughes's most important declaration of policy, however, occurred in an address made on August 30, 1923, upon the occasion of the celebration of the centenary of the Monroe Doctrine. After stating that the Doctrine was a policy of self-defense and nonaggression, he conceded that the United States "reserved to itself its definition, interpretation and application." He insisted that the Doctrine did not infringe upon the independence and sovereignty of other American states, but at the same time he noted that as regards the Caribbean area, if we did not have the Doctrine we should have to create one. In conclusion he pointed out that the Monroe Doctrine did not stand in the way of Pan American cooperation; rather it afforded the necessary foundation for that cooperation in the independence and security of American states.[18]

Nonrecognition of Russia

The Department of State made no change in the Wilson policy toward Soviet Russia. Almost immediately after Hughes became Secretary of State, the Soviet government proposed the negotiation of a trade agreement with the United States. Secretary Hughes, without discussing whether such an arrangement might constitute recognition of the Soviet government, declared on March 25, 1921, that the Soviet government did not yet present the guarantees of respect for life and property, the sanctity of contract and the right of free labor which would permit the United States to discuss a trade agreement.[19]

Certain leftist interests in the United States were vocally very critical of the United States policy in refusing recognition of the Soviet government. In order to explain the attitude of the State Department and to reduce criticism as much as possible, Secretary Hughes, on March 21, 1923, received a delegation of the Women's Committee for Recognition of Russia. He noted what had already been done by the United States for the stricken people of Russia from the humanitarian standpoint, but pointed out that the real problem was based upon the fundamental principle that states must recognize the sanctity of international engagements. Unless the Soviet government would return or give adequate compensation for the property of American citizens confiscated after the Revolution of 1917 and recognize the validity of the debts owing to the United States government, there could be no sound basis for international intercourse. It was not enough that the Soviet government had proved its stability, it was also necessary that it cease subversive actions aimed at the stability of the United States and its institutions. The United States was most eager to promote peace in the world, but it must be a peace founded upon good faith.[20] Both President Harding and President Coolidge supported the State Department's position, as did the vast majority of the American people.

The State Department and the League

One widespread criticism of the State Department as it functioned under the direction of Secretary Hughes was its stubborn refusal at first to have any dealings with the League of Nations. Granting that President Harding favored the isolationist position, on the other hand Secretary Hughes was one of the thirty-one eminent Republicans who had urged that the electorate support Harding as a means of getting the United States into the League. For six months the Department of State failed to answer any communication of the League of Nations. When public protests became very vociferous, the League received, in a single batch, fifteen acknowledgments of various communications written in the most noncommittal phraseology that the Department could devise: "The Secretary of State has taken note of this information for any purpose of relevancy to the United States as a state not a member of the League of Nations." In a letter to the author, Justice Hughes made the following explanation:

During the last month or so of the Wilson Administration communications from the League had been allowed to accumulate and went unanswered. That policy continued after I took office. I did not know of this. It was due to the policy of the subordinates in the State Department who had charge of the correspondence files. It was some time later that I learned that these communications, which were largely routine, had accumulated and been unanswered. I at once gave directions that they should be acknowledged and they were. All later communications were acknowledged in due course.

Unquestionably, Secretary Hughes personally favored organized international cooperation, both legally and politically, but as a realist he recognized the fact that the Foreign Relations Committee of the Senate, under the chairmanship of Henry Cabot Lodge and with Borah, Brandegee, Johnson, and Moses as members, would be a difficult obstacle to hurdle. Neither could he overlook the fact that the Senate had attached a reservation to the peace treaty with Germany to the effect that the United States should not be represented or participate in any body, agency, or commission without the consent of Congress. As an evidence of his desire to cooperate where he considered it feasible, he replied sympathetically to the League's communications on white slavery and traffic in arms; and he sent Lewis W. Haskell, a career foreign-service officer, as an unofficial observer to the International Conference on Customs and Transportation, and another career officer, Edwin N. Neville, to attend meetings of the Advisory Committee on the Traffic in Opium and to represent the United States at the International Narcotics Conference which followed.

Finally, Secretary Hughes went so far as to take the initiative in proposing the adherence of the United States to the Permanent Court of International Justice. On February 17, 1923, he sent a communication to President Harding recommending that the United States, which had always favored the peaceful settlement of international disputes, should adhere to the protocol establishing the Permanent Court of International Justice. In order to meet the objections which the Senate might raise, he excluded acceptance of the optional clause for compulsory jurisdiction and laid down four conditions protecting every possible interest of the United States.[21] The Senate Committee on Foreign Relations, with Republicans in control, stalled by adopting a resolution, introduced by Senator Borah, asking certain specific questions and requiring further information. Secretary Hughes put the committee on the spot by answering their inquiry fully and promptly.[22] The committee, however, decided that there was not time to consider the question adequately before the end of the session. Secretary Hughes thereupon placed the matter before the public by an impartial and scholarly exposition of the question in an address delivered before the American Society of International Law at its annual meeting in Washington on April 27, 1923.

Hughes Appeals to the People

Secretary Hughes used his ability as a forceful and convincing public speaker on various occasions to secure public support on controversial issues or to present an explanation of the Department's policies. Perhaps the most far-reaching and effective of these efforts was the address entitled "Some Aspects of Our Foreign Policy," which he delivered at New Haven, Connecticut, on December 29, 1922, before members of the American Historical Association. He had long been worried over the reparations problem and had suggested a nonpolitical solution to France both through the French ambassador in Washington and the American ambassador in Paris, but with no apparent results. He now decided to publicize his suggestion. He interpolated a proposal in his address that outstanding financial experts of the interested countries be appointed to a commission which should recommend a reparations settlement upon a basis of fairness and feasibility and declared that he had no doubt but that distinguished Americans would be willing to serve upon such a commission.[23] President Harding approved the move; and although the suggestion was not immediately accepted, it was the genesis of the Dawes Plan, which came into operation a year later.

Secretary Hughes not only deserves credit for substituting economics for politics in trying to solve the problem of reparations, but in putting pressure upon France and Germany to sign the Dawes Plan once it had been negotiated. He had gone to London in the summer of 1924 as the president and representative of the American Bar Association. Learning that France and Germany were hesitant about signing, Secretary Hughes went to Paris and Berlin, where he made it clear that unless they signed they could count on no further cooperation from the United States. His plea was successful.[24]

An Improved Foreign Service

One of Secretary Hughes's most valuable yet least publicized contributions to the Department was his earnest effort to improve the foreign service of the United States. Congressman John Jacob Rogers of Massachusetts had introduced three bills during 1919 for the reorganization of the diplomatic and consular service, but no action was taken upon them. In April, 1921, he reintroduced a similar bill and after long consultation with the Department of State he agreed to accept certain modifications and suggestions. Both President Harding and Secretary Hughes supported such a reorganization, and on August 22, 1922, Secretary Hughes submitted a draft of a bill for the reorganization and improvement of the foreign service whose main purpose was "to lay the foundation of a broader service of trained men." The bill introduced by Congressman Rogers on September 1, 1922, was based largely upon his previous bills and the recommendations made by Mr. Hughes. In a letter to Mr. Rogers, dated October 13, 1922, Secretary Hughes approved the revised bill and promised his hearty cooperation in securing its early enactment.[25]

At the hearings on the bill held in December, 1922, Secretary Hughes appeared in person and in a lengthy statement supported the bill and explained its provisions in general. The Director of the Consular Service in the Department of State, Wilbur J. Carr, followed his chief and analyzed the bill in the most elaborate detail. Although the bill passed the House, the Senate adjourned before reaching this bill on its calendar. It was reintroduced in the next session of the Congress and again Secretary Hughes went before the committee to support it. Success crowned the joint efforts of Congressman Rogers and the Department of State, and the Rogers bill became law on May 24, 1924. At last the Department of State had a Foreign Service whose members, from vice consul to counselor of embassy, were appointed and promoted strictly on a merit basis, where both consular and diplomatic officers were paid on the same basis and were interchangeable, and one in which any Foreign Service officer could be assigned for duty for three-year periods in the Department of State whenever the occasion warranted it.

Departmental Changes

Such changes in personnel as occurred during Secretary Hughes's incumbency were almost entirely routine changes through promotion, transfer, or retirement. Career officer Henry P. Fletcher was transferred in 1922 from his position as Under Secretary to become ambassador to Belgium. Another career officer, William Phillips, who had already served twice as Third Assistant Secretary of State and once as Assistant Secretary of State, was brought back from the Netherlands, where he was serving as minister, to act as Under Secretary of State. He remained as Under Secretary until 1924, when he was named ambassador to Belgium and another career officer, Joseph C. Grew, currently serving as minister to Switzerland, was recalled to become Under Secretary in his place. In similar fashion, in 1922 Assistant Secretary of State Dearing, a career officer, was commissioned minister to Portugal and Leland Harrison, another career man, took his place. Warren D. Robbins left his post as Chief of the Division of Near Eastern Affairs to serve as counselor of embassy in Berlin and his place was taken by Allen W. Dulles, a career officer who had been assigned to the American High Commission at Constantinople. In 1923 Robert Woods Bliss, Third Assistant Secretary of State, was appointed minister to Sweden and his successor was another career officer, J. Butler Wright.

A Departmental order, dated October 10, 1922, changed the name of the Division of Russian Affairs to Division of Eastern European Affairs in order to include relations with Estonia, Finland, Latvia, Lithuania, and Poland. At the same time De Witt C. Poole, its Chief, was assigned as consul general to Cape Town, and to his position Secretary Hughes named career officer Evan Young, who had been serving in the Baltic Provinces in Russia. Upon the resignation of Sumner Welles in 1922 as Chief of the Division of Latin American Affairs, Francis White, who had been serving in the United States embassy in Buenos Aires, was made Acting Chief, and in 1923, Chief. These transfers all indicated a desire upon the part of Secretary Hughes to carry out the provisions of the Rogers bill by exchanging officers in the Department for officers in the field to the mutual advantage of both.

It was in the year 1924 that the Department of State lost one of its oldest and most valuable officers. In accordance with the provisions of the Rogers Act, which eliminated numerical designations for the Assistant Secretaries, Alvey A. Adee was commissioned Assistant Secretary of State on July 1, 1924. Three days later he passed away at the age of eighty-two. He had been in the Foreign Service or in the Department of State for some fifty-four years. He had served as Third Assistant Secretary of State for four years and as Second Assistant Secretary for thirty-eight years. On one occasion, in September, 1898, when the position of First Assistant Secretary was temporarily vacant, Adee acted as Secretary of State ad interim between the incumbencies of Secretaries Day and Hay. Adee was very useful to Hay during the period of the Boxer Rebellion. Hay, who was not too familiar with the situation in the Orient, was persuaded by Adee to bring back the outstanding authority on the Far East, W. W. Rockhill, to serve as his adviser. It was during this period that Secretary Hay was at a loss to find a satisfactory expression to describe the inchoate Chinese government. He called upon Adee, who suggested the adequate but innocuous phrase, "administrative entity." Adee had worked with twenty-two secretaries of state, and the story was told that when he was informed by Gaillard Hunt, then an official of the Library of Congress, that Congress had authorized the transfer from the Department of State to the Library of Congress of all ancient, historical, and no longer useful material, Adee replied: "If that is so, you will have to take me along too."

Adee was a veritable encyclopedia of information, a master of protocol, and a remarkable linguist, but his greatest forte was finesse in diplomatic phraseology. On one occasion when several drafts of a note failed to satisfy Secretary Hughes, he called upon Adee. When Adee delivered his draft to the Secretary, the latter read it carefully, then, with a smile to Adee, he said: "I shall now give myself the pleasure of a second reading."[26] Unfortunately, Adee ordered all of his papers to be burned at his death, so that posterity will never be able to appreciate just how great a role he played behind the scenes in directing the foreign policy of the United States. Secretary Hughes expressed the universal sentiment of the Department when he declared: "The Government has never had a more faithful and competent servant."

The Rogers Act of May 24, 1924, permitted recognition of the outstanding services of another long-time officer, Wilbur J. Carr, Director of the Consular Service. Section 22 of the Act authorized the establishment of an additional Assistant Secretary of State and at the same time abolished the position of Director of the Consular Service. Mr. Carr, on July 1, 1924, was appointed Assistant Secretary of State, given complete charge of consular activities, and made budget officer for the Department. A substantial but still insufficient increase in salaries was also authorized by the Congress.[27] Whereas previously the First Assistant Secretary received $5,000 annually and the others $4,500, the new salary scale was $7,500 for each of them. No change was made in the salaries of $7,500 for the Under Secretary and $12,000 for the Secretary.

One very unfortunate development in the salary scale arose from the fact that when career officers were brought back into the Department they retained their salaries as Foreign Service officers, which often were considerably higher than those of State Department officials under civil-service regulations who were doing exactly the same type of work. For example, Evan E. Young, Chief of the Division of Eastern European Affairs, a career officer, received $9,000 annually, while William R. Castle, Jr., an experienced official of the State Department, Chief of the Division of Western European Affairs, received only $5,200. Hugh R. Wilson, a career officer, Chief of the Division of Current Information, was paid $9,000, whereas Prentiss B. Gilbert, one of the ablest of the men in the Department, as Chief of the Division of Political and Economic Information received $4,400, and the brilliant Tyler Dennett, Chief of the Division of Publications and Editor of the Department, was paid $3,800. The fact that the Under Secretary of State and the four Assistant Secretaries of State received $7,500 a year while some of their subordinates as Chiefs of Division were paid $9,000, was hardly conducive to an improvement of the morale in the Department. Other well merited but inadequate raises in salary were those which gave the Solicitor, Charles Cheney Hyde, $6,000 instead of $5,000, and the Chief Clerk, E. J. Ayers, $3,800 instead of the $3,000 paid to his predecessor, Ben G. Davis, who had retired after eleven years' service in the office.

The Rogers Act abolished the Diplomatic Bureau and the Consular Bureau, which had been functioning continuously since 1870, and in their place the Division of Foreign Service Administration was established. Herbert C. Hengstler, who had been at the head of the Consular Bureau since 1907, was appointed Chief of the new division. He remained in this position until 1937, when, in recognition of his long and excellent services to the Department, he was appointed Foreign Service officer of Class 1 and assigned as consul general at Toronto, Canada.

One new office established in 1924, which was necessitated by the vast increase in the Department's correspondence, was the Office of Coordination and Review. A somewhat similar agency, called the Correspondence Bureau, had been set up to review outgoing mail in October, 1918, but it had been abolished in 1920. As long as Second Assistant Secretary of State Adee was alive, he saw to it that no conflicts in policy occurred between different divisions and he was equally particular in correcting errors of grammar, orthography, or form. Upon his death it was quickly realized that some agency must be made responsible for checking the outgoing correspondence and to advise with the various bureaus on questions of style and diplomatic precedent. As chief of the new office, Secretary Hughes appointed Margaret M. Hanna, who had served under Assistant Secretary Adee for some twenty-eight years and who was adept in every phase of the work. Miss Hanna chose as her assistant Ruth B. Shipley, who had served in the Department since 1914 and was another of Secretary Adee's able assistants.

A Starved Department

Unquestionably, during Secretary Hughes's administration the Department of State functioned most efficiently, nevertheless a serious situation was developing as a result of a lack of an adequate staff to do the work required. The Bureau of the Budget and the Congress were economically minded and the State Department suffered even more than the other agencies of government in not being able to obtain adequate appropriations. In the hearings before the subcommittee of the House Committee on Appropriations in charge of the State Department's Appropriation Bill for 1925, Assistant Secretary of State Carr gave a clear presentation of the situation. Whereas in 1921 the Department's personnel numbered 714 and the incoming and outgoing pieces of mail amounted to 743,422, in 1922 the personnel dropped to 602, whereas the mail increased to 901,769; and in 1923 the personnel was reduced still further to 590 and the mail increased still further to 948,700.[28] The provision made for personnel was insufficient to enable the work of the Department to be performed adequately. In fact, "45 or more highly paid officers of the foreign service are assigned to the Department to enable it to carry on its work." [29]

In the figures submitted by Mr. Carr, the total appropriations for the Department of State proper for 1923 were $1,185,033; for 1924, $1,258,940; and the budget estimate for 1925 was $1,313,515. The personnel for 1924 and 1925 remained at 590. Including the cost of foreign intercourse and the payment of certain international obligations, such as payments to Colombia and Panama and certain international bureaus and concessions, the total appropriations for the Department of State for 1923 were $16,977,013.47; for 1924, $15,455,691.98; for 1925 the budget estimate was $14,988,446.29. However, excluding the fixed charges due to treaty obligations of the government, which were placed in the State Department's budget arbitrarily, and giving credit for the cash income from passport, consular, and other fees, the actual outlay from the Treasury for the State Department and Foreign Service was as follows: 1923, $1,926,721.91; 1924, $1,539,230.41; 1925, $1,205,805.41. In conclusion Assistant Secretary Carr declared: "The State Department is being run, in my judgment, on an entirely too modest basis for the importance of the work which it has to do." [30]

The Coolidge Administration

Upon the death of President Harding on August 2, 1923, Vice President Calvin Coolidge was inducted into the Presidency, but as President, Coolidge made no immediate changes in either cabinet or policy. The Big Three of the Harding cabinet, Hughes, Hoover, and Mellon, carried on, and it was popularly thought that they would remain in the cabinet after Coolidge was elected President in his own right in November, 1924. Secretary Hughes continued to run the Department with almost as free a hand as under President Harding. The only visible influence of the President was in the appointment of several new ambassadors.

When George Harvey unexpectedly resigned as ambassador to Great Britain in August, 1923, President Coolidge wanted to appoint Elihu Root but learned that he would not accept. He next approached Governor Lowden of Illinois, but he too refused.[31] He finally, to the surprise of many, offered the position to Frank B. Kellogg, who had recently been defeated as candidate for reelection to the Senate from Minnesota. Senator Kellogg declared that while he was a visitor in the White House early in October, 1923, President Coolidge had told him of Harvey's intention to resign and asked his suggestions as to a successor. Mr. Kellogg named Elihu Root, Governor Lowden, James M. Beck, and President Lowell of Harvard among others. The very next week Kellogg was summoned back to Washington and was informed by President Coolidge that he and Secretary Hughes, after canvassing several names, including some of those suggested by Kellogg, had concluded that Kellogg was the man for the position. Kellogg asked for a week's time to consider the offer and at the end of that time he agreed to serve for the rest of the President's term.[32]

Secretary Hughes Resigns

Secretary Hughes campaigned for the reelection of President Coolidge but he would not permit any officials in the State Department to do so. The results were never in doubt and Calvin Coolidge was reelected by the largest majority that had ever been given to a Republican candidate for the Presidency. Secretary Hughes had notified the President immediately after his reelection that he wished to resign when President Coolidge entered upon his second term, but the secret was kept so closely that when, on January 10, Secretary Hughes's resignation was announced to become effective March 4, 1925, the country was stunned. In his formal letter of resignation to the President, Secretary Hughes declared that after almost twenty years of continuous public service he felt that he must be relieved of official responsibility and be permitted to return to private life. President Coolidge, in his letter of acceptance, expressed his warm commendation for Secretary Hughes's services and his sincere regret at his resignation.[33]

The press was inclined to seek other reasons for Hughes's resignation than his expressed desire to return to private life. It was appreciated that his salary of $12,000 a year as Secretary of State was not sufficient to keep his family and do the necessary entertaining required by his position. It was also known that he could earn ten times as much in private practice with the expenditure of less time and energy than was required by the government. Nevertheless, an ulterior reason was sought. The suggestion that he would be in a better position to run for the Presidency at the end of Coolidge's second term had no basis in fact; that he was unwilling to continue, knowing that his bitter opponent, Senator Borah, would be chairman of the Foreign Relations Committee of the Senate, was wholly contrary to Hughes's character and disposition. If further proof is required, Hugh Wilson, a career foreign-service officer, at that time Chief of the Division of Current Information, went to Mr. Hughes to urge that he remain at the head of the Department. Secretary Hughes explained that, having passed his sixtieth birthday and having given many years to public service, he must go back to private life to make provision for his family.[34]

Both at home and abroad Hughes's resignation was regarded almost as a calamity. With Hughes as Secretary of State it was felt that the United States was safe in any diplomatic encounter where justice was on her side. Otherwise he would dare to oppose even Congress, as was shown by his stand against the crude procedure used to repeal the Gentleman's Agreement with

Japan. Justice Brandeis, speaking somewhat cryptically of Hughes, said: "His is the most enlightened mind of the eighteenth century," but the Washington newspaper man was more forthright who remarked of Hughes's mind that he always had it with him. As an administrator Hughes always took advantage of experience and ability to strengthen his "Department of Peace." He sought to improve the machinery of negotiation at home and abroad, and the Rogers Act owed much to his counsel and his support. He appreciated the need for men of the highest ability to represent the United States abroad. "We need the man," he stated emphatically; "we cannot rely on paper; we cannot rely on direct messages. We need the man in the personal contact with other men transacting the business of their government." [35] His ability to initiate and direct foreign policy was well summarized by J. L. Garvin of the London *Observer*: "Mr. Hughes has steered world policy through the tumult and confusion of the darkest post war years into the New Era, and in that work he has been an honor to his country and an asset to his time."

23

Frank Billings Kellogg

Frank Billings Kellogg—Secretary of State

The country was just as much surprised at the appointment of Ambassador Frank Billings Kellogg as Secretary of State as it was dismayed at the sudden and unexpected resignation of Secretary Hughes. President Coolidge had apparently consulted neither his cabinet members nor leading Republicans with regard to the appointment. Mr. Kellogg acknowledged later that he had received a letter from Secretary Hughes in December, 1924, informing him that President Coolidge wanted him to succeed Mr. Hughes as Secretary of State. After discussing the matter with Mrs. Kellogg, he cabled Secretary Hughes that he would accept. The notification that he had been named officially came to Ambassador Kellogg while he was staying with Ambassador Herrick in Paris on January 13, 1925, the night before the signing of the Dawes Plan agreement.[1] The next day, as Ambassador Kellogg was about to sign, he received a telegram from the Department instructing him not to sign unless a certain reservation were included. He did not think the reservation justified, so he forthwith signed the agreement and instructed Ambassador Herrick to inform the Department that its instructions had come too late.[2] As Secretary of State designate he felt justified in violating instructions which would have delayed and might have nullified the negotiations which he had with such difficulty brought to a successful conclusion.

The press did not regard the appointment with enthusiasm. Mr. Kellogg had been a "trust-busting" lawyer, a senator for one term, during which he was a member of the Foreign Relations Committee, a member of the American delegation to the Fifth Pan American Conference in 1923, and ambassador to the Court of St. James's for a little over two years. He thus had had more diplomatic experience than many of his predecessors, but the consensus of opinion seemed to be that Herbert Hoover would have been a much better choice.

The generally accepted reason for his appointment was that President Coolidge liked him personally and found in him a congenial and cooperative person to work with. He was familiar with the European situation, he was acquainted with the principal European statesmen, and he was immediately available.

Hugh Wilson, Chief of the Division of Current Information when Secretary Kellogg was appointed, found that the Secretary had a very hasty and explosive temper but never bore a grudge nor did he ever fail to back up his subordinates. Whenever the newspapers published something critical of the Department—quite a common occurrence during Kellogg's sojourn—the Secretary would call in all the officials concerned and upbraid them vigorously. Then he would calm down and confer quietly.[3] This was not the kind of temperament likely to produce a successful Secretary of State, and events soon proved that Kellogg's appointment was not a happy one.

Changes in Personnel

It was quickly made evident that President Coolidge intended to play a more important role in the conduct and control of foreign relations than he had when Mr. Hughes was Secretary. The most important position in the Department next to that of Secretary was that of Under Secretary. Inasmuch as the Secretary was regularly a political appointee, the normal procedure was to appoint a career diplomat or an official experienced in international relations as Under Secretary. Although President Coolidge was inexperienced in diplomatic matters and Secretary Kellogg was far from being an expert, Secretary Kellogg suggested that he would like to appoint as Under Secretary of State Dwight Morrow, a banker from the House of Morgan, with no diplomatic background, in the place of Joseph C. Grew, a very able career officer with over twenty years' experience. The two Under Secretaries preceding Grew, William Phillips and Henry P. Fletcher, had been experienced diplomats; their predecessors, Norman H. Davis and Frank L. Polk, although not of the career service, had served in the Department or abroad. Mr. Morrow was a very close friend of President Coolidge's and had helped materially in his election; he was a banker of outstanding reputation and ability; nevertheless, the President wisely suggested that Mr. Grew be retained as Under Secretary.

Secretary Kellogg was able to make one political appointment in the upper echelons of the Department. Assistant Secretary of State MacMurray, an authority on the Far East, was appointed minister to China in April, 1925, upon the resignation of Dr. Jacob Gould Schurman. To fill MacMurray's place, Secretary Kellogg brought in Robert E. Olds, a good friend and former law partner, who had served as European commissioner in charge of American Red Cross operations after the First World War, but who was wholly without experience in the State Department or the Foreign Service.

The other principal changes in the Department which occurred during the first year of Secretary Kellogg's administration were not of the political variety. Green H. Hackworth, who succeeded Charles Cheney Hyde as Solicitor, had served both as Assistant Solicitor and as Acting Solicitor before his promotion. Nelson T. Johnson, a career officer with over twenty years' service in China, was appointed Chief of the Division of Far Eastern Affairs. On January 16, 1926, the Division of Passport Control had its name changed, by a Departmental order, to Passport Division. Its former Chief, George L. Brist, who had risen from the job of laborer and later clerk at $900 a year to become Chief of the Division at $3,300, was replaced by an experienced Foreign Service officer, J. Klahr Huddle, at his regular salary of $6,000. The Passport Division was still the second largest division in the Department—Indexes and Archives was the largest. In addition to sixty clerks, it had three Foreign Service officers besides Chief Huddle. John J. Scanlan was now designated Technical Adviser, and F. Virginia Alexander had been made Assistant Chief.

It was not a new appointment, but the retention by Secretary Kellogg of a negro messenger with fifty-five years of service received the most attention in the press. Edward Augustine Savoy at seventy had served under nineteen secretaries of state, and Secretary Kellogg intervened personally to set aside the rules to permit him to serve two more years. Eddie's proudest experience occurred in connection with the Spanish-American War. Secretary of State Day instructed him to deliver his passports to the Spanish minister and then report to the Department. Since Eddie's father had served as a butler in the Spanish legation, Eddie was well known to the minister. Upon delivering the passports, Eddie expressed his regret at the minister's departure and requested as a memento the minister's autograph on the envelope in which the passports were delivered. The Spanish minister obliged and Eddie returned to the Department. He was summoned into the presence of President McKinley and Secretary Day and asked if he had delivered the passports in person. "Yes, sir," he said; "here is the proof." President McKinley remarked to the Secretary that it was very clever of Eddie to have thought of that.

Inasmuch as the Republicans remained in power, very few changes occurred in the diplomatic service. Myron T. Herrick remained as ambassador to France and Alanson B. Houghton was transferred from Germany to London, and Jacob Gould Schurman from Peking to Berlin. The three important appointments which were purely political were Charles MacVeagh, a New York lawyer, as ambassador to Japan, John B. Stetson, Jr., a hat manufacturer, as minister to Poland, and Ogden H. Hammond, a wealthy New Jersey businessman, as ambassador to Spain.

The Department Under Fire

From the very beginning of the Kellogg incumbency the Department of State came under criticism of liberal and leftist elements of the public. The National Women's Party made an issue of the fact that a newspaper woman, Ruby Black, who was married to Herbert A. Little, was refused a passport in her maiden name. The matter was appealed to the Secretary, who agreed to issue the passport under the name Ruby Black provided the marriage was noted and the husband's signature appended. This compromise satisfied neither the National Women's Party nor Miss Black.

An incident occurred in September, 1925, which aroused the Civil Liberties Union against the Department of State. The Interparliamentary Union was scheduled to meet in Washington and a Communist member of the British House of Commons by the name of Shapurji Saklatvala signified his intention of coming. When the Department learned that a number of British members of Parliament had declared that if S—— came they would stay away, Secretary Kellogg revoked Saklatvala's passport on the ground that a speech which he had made in Parliament indicated that he intended to carry on Communist propaganda while he was in the United States.

Hardly had the agitation over this question died down before a more serious criticism was aroused over the refusal of the Department to admit the Countess Karolyi, wife of the former president of Hungary. The countess had begun a lecture tour in the United States in 1924 and was taken sick before completing it. Her husband, Count Karolyi, had been admitted by Secretary Hughes with the understanding that he should engage in no political discussions while in the United States. He obeyed the order but later made some disparaging remarks regarding the Department after crossing into Canada. In October of 1925 when the countess applied in Paris for a visa to enter the United States for a visit the visa was refused. A New York law firm took up the case and the Department was asked to state the grounds for the refusal. Assistant Secretary Castle, after some little delay, cited the statutes which allegedly covered the case and declared that the action was taken "pursuant to duties imposed and authority conferred by these laws." Inasmuch as both laws were on the statute books when Secretary Hughes had admitted the countess the preceding year, a more specific ruling was requested. Appeals were made to Secretary Kellogg and to President Coolidge, but to no avail. The countess finally brought suit for a writ of mandamus in the Supreme Court of the District of Columbia to compel Secretary Kellogg to revise his ruling and permit her entry to visit friends and complete her lecture tour.[4] When Secretary Kellogg insisted on the ban, an appeal was taken to the Circuit Court. This court also ruled against the countess and the visit was dropped.[5] According to the *New Republic,* Secretary Kellogg inadvertently confessed that the real reason was that the Department was irritated by the remarks of Count Karolyi after his visit.[6] In 1929 Secretary Stimson allowed the Karolyis to enter with no restriction on lectures.

The most extreme case of restrictive action occurred in the case of Madame Alexandra Kollontai, a Russian diplomat who had been appointed as ambassador to Mexico after a very creditable record as minister to Norway. While in Berlin en route to Mexico in the fall of 1926, Madame Kollontai applied for a visa on her passport permitting her to pass through the United States. By order of Secretary Kellogg she was refused on the ground that she was an outstanding member of the Russian Communist party. As one news writer phrased it: "No Bolshevik must touch the sacred soil of America even though bonded for transit." This was too much even for Kellogg's good friend Senator Borah, who protested the action vigorously.

Mexico Insulted

Perhaps the most serious diplomatic mistake made by Secretary Kellogg came in regard to our relations with Mexico. Secretary Hughes had been able to work out certain agreements in 1923 which settled at least temporarily the problem of confiscation of American agricultural lands and the nationalization of subsoil deposits involving American property rights. The Department of State had also signed two satisfactory claims conventions with Mexico. As a result the United States had recognized the government of Mexico, and during the year 1924 the relations between the two countries were quite cordial. Upon taking over the Department, Secretary Kellogg asked Ambassador Sheffield to return to Washington to report on Mexican conditions. After their conference Secretary Kellogg issued what one of his former colleagues described as "an unmannerly and unjustifiable" public statement. Noting that conditions in Mexico were not satisfactory, Kellogg declared that he had seen statements published in the press that another revolutionary movement might be impending. If so, the United States would

use its influence and support in behalf of stability and orderly constitutional procedure, but it should be made clear that this Government will continue to support the Government in Mexico only so long as it protects American lives and American rights and complies with its international engagements and obligations. The Mexican Government is now on trial before the world.[7]

This statement was bitterly resented in Mexico and widely criticized in the United States. President Calles thought it strange that the United States should manifest its interest in the maintenance of order in Mexico by suggesting that revolutionary movements were said to be impending. If the suggestion that Mexico was on trial before the world meant in the guise of a defendant, the imputation was an insult and was rejected absolutely.[8] The *New York World* felt that the Secretary had "confused strength with impoliteness," and the *Macon Telegraph* declared it to be the "worst diplomatic blunder in American history." Certainly it was not in accordance with normal diplomatic procedure for the Secretary of State to broadcast his scarcely veiled threats to the world without sending a preliminary note of protest to the Mexican government responsible. The result was to unite all factions behind Calles and to fan the slumbering fears of Yankee imperialism throughout Latin America.

The situation between the two countries was rendered even more critical at the beginning of 1927 by the introduction of a new factor. The Department of State had received information which seemed to indicate that Mexico was supporting a revolutionary government in Nicaragua hostile to the United States and permitting arms and munitions to be shipped from her ports. Numerous congressional resolutions requested that information concerning the situation in Mexico and Nicaragua be furnished to the House of Representatives, and on January 10, 1927, President Coolidge, in a message to Congress, gave an impartial statement of the facts and the position taken by the administration.[9] Unfortunately, Secretary Kellogg, two days later, gave a statement to the press, following his testimony at an executive session of the Senate Committee on Foreign Relations, which connected Mexico with Moscow in a way which was unwarranted by his evidence. The *New York Times* found the accusations unworthy of the State Department; the *New York World* declared the statement either "utterly irresponsible or deliberately unfriendly;" and the *Baltimore Sun* doubted that "ever before in the history of the nation has the head of the State Department appeared in public in a state of such utterly indecent intellectual exposure." [10]

Learning of Ambassador Sheffield's impending resignation, Secretary Kellogg once more approached President Coolidge on the subject of utilizing Dwight Morrow, and this time the President agreed. Secretary Kellogg sounded out Morrow, who seemed a bit dubious about the President's attitude. Coolidge took occasion to broach the subject a little later while Morrow was visiting him in Washington, and on July 14, 1927, the President wrote Morrow, offering him the post of ambassador to Mexico, but without putting any pressure upon his friend to accept. However, he did indicate that Ambassador Sheffield felt that Mexico offered the greatest possible opportunity for service.[11] Morrow accepted, and by his broadminded, fair, and intelligent procedure in dealing with the Mexican government, he was able to secure an immediate improvement in the relations between the two countries.

The Outlawry of War

Fortunately for Mr. Kellogg's future reputation he seized one diplomatic opportunity, after several hesitant and ineffectual efforts to sidestep the responsibility, and carried it to a notable and successful conclusion. On February 14, 1923, Senator Borah, the militant isolationist, introduced a resolution outlawing war as the means for the settlement of international disputes and making it a crime under the law of nations. The World Court issue broke about ten days later and the Borah resolution went almost unnoticed. Borah again introduced his resolution on December 6, 1926, but again with no apparent results. Professor James T. Shotwell of Columbia University, who was lecturing in Berlin in the spring of 1927, was passing through Paris when he learned that Foreign Minister Briand intended to deliver an address to the American people on April 6, 1927, commemorating the tenth anniversary of the entrance of the United States into the war. Professor Shotwell had an interview with M. Briand and persuaded him to insert in his address a proposal that the two great democracies enter into an engagement mutually outlawing war. Briand willingly agreed and included Professor Shotwell's suggestion. When the message received little attention in the United States, President Nicholas Murray Butler of Columbia University wrote a letter to the *New York Times* on April 25, urging the United States to give consideration to the French proposal. The subject was immediately taken up by individuals and organizations and a widespread discussion followed in the press. Neither the President nor the Secretary of State, however, manifested the slightest interest in the proposal of the French foreign minister.

Two weeks later, while Senator Borah was speaking in Cleveland on American foreign relations, in reply to a question to suggest an alternative to the League of Nations the senator answered that he would take M. Briand's proposal to outlaw war between France and the United States and extend it to all nations.[12] The State Department still evidenced no interest; in fact, on several occasions when interrogated by representatives of the press regarding the Briand proposal, Secretary Kellogg replied that he had been too busy to look into the matter. Meanwhile, in Paris an American lawyer, Salmon O. Levinson, the originator of the phrase "outlawing of war," had been putting pressure upon the Quai d'Orsay to approach the State Department directly with a proposal. M. Briand thereupon requested Ambassador Herrick to find out whether the United States would object to entertaining a proposal for outlawing war between the two nations. The State Department could hardly refuse such a friendly gesture, and so on June 20, 1927, M. Briand, through the American ambassador at Paris, transmitted the draft of a Pact of Perpetual Friendship between France and the United States which provided that the two countries condemned recourse to war and renounced it as an instrument of their national policy toward each other.[13]

The Department of State was still loath to act and over six months elapsed before Secretary Kellogg returned an official reply to the Briand proposal. Secretary Kellogg has explained that his hesitancy was due to a number of reasons. He saw no practical advantage to such a treaty if limited to the United States and France; other nations might object to the United States making such a treaty unless we were ready to make similar treaties with them; the Senate had adjourned and neither the President nor Secretary Kellogg wished to propose such an agreement without having some assurance that the Senate would approve.[14] Finally, inasmuch as the United States was on the point of negotiating a new arbitration treaty with France to replace the existing arrangement, which was about to expire, Secretary Kellogg thought that the new agreement might be utilized to cover the Briand proposal. In fact, in the draft of the arbitration treaty submitted to the Foreign Relations Committee of the Senate, war was condemned. This did not satisfy Senator Borah, who insisted that the United States propose to France that all of the nations be invited to enter into a multilateral pact to outlaw war. The other members of the committee expressed their approval of the position of the chairman. Secretary Kellogg in his memorandum states that this suggestion of a multilateral pact accorded exactly with what he already had in mind, and he forthwith accepted M. Briand's proposal with the proviso that the treaty be concluded by the principal powers and open to all nations of the world.[15]

M. Briand, however, was not pleased with the idea of a multilateral pact and found various reasons for his inability to accept. Secretary Kellogg now showed that once started he was not to be thwarted, and his dogged determination and indefatigable persistence overcame every barrier raised in opposition. In the long continued exchange of notes which followed, Secretary Kellogg would accept no compromise on principle nor any excuse for delay. He took advantage of the rising ground swell of public opinion against war by conducting his negotiations wholly in the open. In fact, public opinion played such an important role that Professor Shotwell, the originator of the idea, while lauding the "courage and idealism" of M. Briand and the "cooperation and persistent diplomacy" of Mr. Kellogg, gives the ultimate credit for the achievement to the people themselves.[16]

The Kellogg-Briand Pact, or the Pact of Paris, as it was officially known, was signed in Paris on August 27, 1928, by the fifteen powers originally invited. Secretary Kellogg made a special trip abroad to sign it in person. To prevent opposition in the Senate, he insisted that the pact be divorced from domestic partisan politics, and as a result the Senate approved its ratification by a vote of eighty-five to one. Secretary Kellogg was justly proud of his achievement and regarded the antiwar pact as his greatest contribution to world peace while Secretary of State. As evidence of the world's appreciation of his labors in behalf of the outlawry of war, Mr. Kellogg was awarded the Nobel Peace Prize for 1929.

Maladministration of the Rogers Act

Before we finish with Secretary Kellogg's administration of the Department of State, it is necessary to consider a much criticized development in the Department as a result of the administration of the Rogers Act of 1924. In accordance with the terms of the Act, President Coolidge, by an executive order dated June 7, 1924, had authorized the appointment of a Foreign Service Personnel Board to examine into the efficiency records of Foreign Service officers and to recommend for promotion on the basis of these records. The Foreign Service Personnel Board consisted of the Under Secretary of State, two Assistant Secretaries of State, and an executive committee composed of three Foreign Service officers of high rank. Unfortunately, in making promotions the diplomatic and consular services were considered separately by the Personnel Board and the diplomatic branch got more than its proportional share. It was also alleged that members of the Foreign Service Personnel Board gave themselves and their friends preference both in promotions and posts. As evidence it was noted that during the spring of 1927 two members of the board, J. Butler Wright and Hugh Wilson, received choice diplomatic appointments to Hungary and Switzerland, and shortly afterward Under Secretary Grew, chairman of the board, was appointed ambassador to Turkey.

The latter accusation had no basis in fact. Secretary Kellogg stated that he was responsible for recommending to the President the names of Mr. Wright and Mr. Grew, and the latter accepted the Turkish post most reluctantly. In the case of Mr. Wilson, although Under Secretary Grew favored his promotion, the original recommendation had come from Hugh Gibson, who had just been promoted from minister to Switzerland to become ambassador to Belgium.

The other complaint was proved to have been justified. Called before the Foreign Affairs Committee of the House, Secretary Kellogg conceded that a disproportionate number of promotions had occurred in the diplomatic branch, and he promised to make an equal number of promotions in the consular branch to equalize the situation. The Senate was not satisfied, and Senator Harrison of Mississippi, on December 17, 1927, introduced a resolution in the Senate requesting an investigation of the administration of the Foreign Service Personnel Board. The investigation showed that of a total of 214 promotions in the Foreign Service during the first two and one-half years of the new legislation, 63 per cent of all diplomatic officers were advanced while only 37 per cent of the consular officers were so favored. The initial injustice in the application of the Act arose from the use of a double list—one diplomatic and one consular—in making promotions, a procedure not contemplated by the Act. Inasmuch as the diplomatic branch exercised the greater influence in the operation of the Rogers Act, the greater benefits had been obtained for that group.[17] The committee made a series of recommendations to remedy these faults, and they were subsequently included in large part in the Moses-Linthicum Act of 1931.

Kellogg Supports the Foreign Service

On the other hand, Secretary Kellogg supported the career service, both in his appointments at home and abroad, throughout his four years in office. Except for his friend Robert E. Olds, who was at first named Assistant Secretary of State and later Under Secretary when Under Secretary Grew was named as ambassador to Turkey, we find no evidence of political appointments to important positions in the Department of State. When Assistant Secretaries of State Leland Harrison and J. Butler Wright were named ministers to Sweden and Hungary respectively in 1927, two officers of long experience replaced them: one, William R. Castle, Jr., from the Department, and the other, Nelson T. Johnson, from the career service. The work of each Assistant Secretary was assigned as far as possible in accordance with his previous experience.

The new Chiefs of the geographical divisions, brought in from the field in 1926 and 1927 to take the places of career officers sent abroad in accordance with the terms of the Rogers Act, were all career officers: John K. Caldwell, Chief of the Division of Far Eastern Affairs; Stokeley W. Morgan, Chief of the Division of Latin American Affairs; J. Theodore Marriner, Chief of the Division of Western European Affairs; G. Howland Shaw, Chief of the Division of Near Eastern Affairs; Arthur Bliss Lane, Chief of the Division of Mexican Affairs; and Robert F. Kelley, Chief of the Division of Eastern European Affairs.

The new Chief of the Passport Division, appointed in 1927, was Parker W. Buhrman, a career Foreign Service officer. When Mr. Buhrman was assigned to Berlin in 1928, Ruth B. Shipley was named Chief of the Passport Division, an appointment based upon merit and experience. Mrs. Shipley had entered the Department in 1914 as a clerk and by 1924 she had become Assistant Chief of the Office of Coordination and Review. As Chief of the Passport Division she was destined to serve for more than twenty years and to make a record outstanding in the annals of the Department.

In the place of Hugh Wilson, Chief of the Division of Current Information, who was named minister to Switzerland, Secretary Kellogg appointed Assistant Chief Michael J. McDermott, whose experience included work with

General Tasker H. Bliss in Paris and Elihu Root at The Hague, in addition to his services in the Department of State. Mr. McDermott remained as Chief of the Division of Current Information until it was abolished in 1944, and then he was made Special Assistant to the Secretary of State for Press Relations, a position which permitted him to serve as personal adviser to the Secretary in all matters pertaining to both press and radio.

A few important changes in the organization of the Department were made during the Kellogg regime. The United States had been exceedingly remiss in providing suitable living quarters for its representatives abroad—in fact, until the Lowden Act of February 17, 1911, American diplomats and consuls, with few exceptions, were expected to find for themselves suitable quarters in which to live and to carry on their duties. The Lowden Act authorized the Secretary of State to acquire in foreign countries sites and buildings for the use of diplomatic and consular establishments but limited the amount to be expended in any one year to $500,000.

At the time that the Lowden Act was passed, the United States possessed only one suitable embassy building, the embassy in Constantinople, which had been authorized in 1906. A fairly satisfactory legation building was owned by the United States in Peking, China, but the legations in Bangkok, Siam, and Tokyo, Japan, were very unsatisfactory. Five consulates were owned by the United States: at Amoy, China; Tangier, Morocco; Tahiti, Society Islands; Seoul, Korea; and Yokohama, Japan, of which only the building in Tahiti was suitable. Progress under the Act of 1911 was so slow that after fourteen years only eight embassy and legation buildings had been acquired, of which one was a gift. On May 7, 1926, the Foreign Service Building Act was passed, which authorized the appropriation of a Foreign Service Building Fund not to exceed $10,000,000 of which only $2,000,000 could be spent in any one year for the acquisition of buildings and property for the use of diplomatic and consular establishments. A Foreign Service Building Commission, which included the Secretaries of State, Treasury, and Commerce, was to direct the program, and a Foreign Service Buildings Office was set up in the Department on June 23, 1926, to supervise its execution. Although the United States today has adequate diplomatic and consular establishments in many parts of the world, the program is still far from completion.

New Agencies Established

Although some agency has existed in the Department of State ever since it was first established to make such translations as might be required, it was not until October 18, 1928, that the Translating Bureau was established. Secretary McLane, in his reorganization of 1833, had set up a Translating and Miscellaneous Bureau, but in the following year Secretary Forsyth joined the duties of Translator with those of Librarian and the two positions remained merged for approximately twenty years. In 1870, when Secretary Hamilton Fish reorganized the Department, Henry Livingston Thomas was appointed Translator and held this position until his death in 1903. Although Mr. Thomas had never been to college, he knew almost all ancient and modern languages and could speak many of them as well as read and write in them. He once wrote a letter in Hebrew which John Hay signed; he was called to testify in court as an expert in modern Greek; and in Latin he could quote poetry with Gildersleeve. It was said that on one occasion he corrected the Spanish of a Latin American envoy. In his report of his work submitted in 1897, Mr. Thomas declared that the major portion of the Translator's work consisted of notes from the various embassies and legations in Washington and that the principal languages were Spanish, French, German, and Italian. Letters received at the Executive Mansion not only used these four languages, however, but also Swedish, Danish, Dutch, Portuguese, Greek, and Hebrew. On one occasion the Translator had to translate enclosures from the American consulate in Cuba covering the entire court proceedings of the trials of two American citizens accused of rebellion. At times telegrams had to be deciphered and translated, although they arrived in such condition as to be almost devoid of meaning.[18] Mr. Thomas was succeeded by Wilfred Stevens, who, it was claimed, had a working knowledge of some thirty languages and who served for about twenty years. John S. Martin, Jr., who succeeded Mr. Stevens, served more than twenty-four years as Translator or Assistant Translator. When the bureau was set up in 1928, Emerson B. Christie, a specialist in Spanish and French, was named Chief. He was given four Assistant Translators and a clerk to perform the duties of his "clearing house for the Tower of Babel."

Diplomatic ceremonial has always been a rather important consideration in foreign offices, but the United States was hesitant to recognize the fact. It was not until 1919 that Charles Lee Cooke was named Ceremonial Officer and given charge of the ceremonial section in the office of the Third Assistant Secretary of State. Protocol service was found to be so useful that by a Departmental order, dated February 11, 1928, Secretary Kellogg established the Division of Protocol. Its duties covered not only arrangements for the agréation and presentation of diplomats and for the ceremonial for White House and State Department functions, but also included preparations for international congresses and conferences. As a result the name was changed in 1929 to Division of International Conferences and Protocol. Career Foreign Service officer James C. Dunn was appointed chief of the new division, and Charles Lee Cooke remained as Ceremonial Officer.

The work in the Department of State pertaining to the preparation for, and the negotiation of, treaties had increased so considerably during Secretary Kellogg's direction of the State Department—some eighty-one treaties were negotiated during the period—that on April 21, 1928, a Departmental order was issued setting up the Treaty Division. Its duties included such procedural functions as were involved in treaty making as well as the supplying of information regarding existing and prospective agreements. In the case of multilateral treaties of a technical nature, a very considerable amount of preliminary research was required before the division could commence the drafting of proposed agreements. Charles M. Barnes, who was named Chief of the Treaty Division, had entered the Department of State in 1912 and in 1920 he had been named Assistant Solicitor.

One important change in personnel occurred in the Department toward the close of Kellogg's incumbency when on June 30, 1928, Under Secretary Robert E. Olds resigned to become associated with the New York law firm of Sullivan and Cromwell. At first it was expected that a career man would be chosen, but President Coolidge, after delaying six weeks, named an eminent international lawyer, J. Reuben Clark, Jr. Mr. Clark had served as Assistant Solicitor and Solicitor in the Department of State for seven years, from 1906 to 1913, and subsequently as counsel on various claims commissions. His background and experience and proven ability made his appointment a highly commendable one.

Secretary Kellogg let it be known shortly after Herbert Hoover was elected President in November, 1928, that he did not expect to serve in the new administration. He was approaching his seventy-third birthday and the strain of Washington life had made itself felt. Secretary Kellogg had not been a great Secretary of State. He was vacillating, hesitant, and at the same time obstinate. He was a hard worker, sincere, and socially minded, but he possessed neither the background, the ability, nor the flexibility to be rated among the outstanding statesmen who have held the office. His greatest success was the Kellogg-Briand Peace Pact but even here he stumbled awkwardly into achievement and fame. He hardly deserved the nickname of "Nervous Nelly" that was applied to him, but he was inclined to overemphasize the dangers of Bolshevism. He showed his political courage in keeping the Pact of Paris out of national politics, even though he knew that his attitude would not help him with President-elect Herbert Hoover. His departure was regarded as a natural routine political adjustment by the press. His kindly disposition and his unflagging devotion to his duties in the Department had gained the appreciation and respect of his subordinates. Although he had not been able to obtain vitally needed appropriations to provide a staff adequate for the work, it was generally conceded that the Department of State had a higher morale and was functioning more efficiently when he left than when he entered.

24

Henry L. Stimson

Henry L. Stimson—Secretary of State

President Herbert Hoover entered the Presidency with a world-wide reputation for administrative efficiency. He had proved it in business, in European relief work, and as Secretary of the Department of Commerce. It was therefore taken for granted that he would choose a cabinet whose members would be men of experience and ability rather than well groomed representatives of the party. The names suggested as Secretary of State were all men possessing either wide diplomatic or equivalent experience. Those most commonly mentioned were Senator William E. Borah, chairman of the Foreign Relations Committee, and career diplomat Henry P. Fletcher, who had accompanied President-elect Hoover as advisor on his good-will trip to Latin America. Senator Edge suggested that Dwight Morrow, who had done so well in Mexico, would be an ideal choice. Ex-Secretaries of State Root and Hughes thought that Henry L. Stimson, currently serving as governor general of the Philippine Islands, would make an excellent Secretary of State.

President Hoover first offered the State Department post to Senator Borah, although he conceded that the Senate would be the loser if he accepted. Borah, without hesitation, refused, partly because of the financial obligations which would be entailed, but also because he felt that he ought not to give up his work in the Senate. He further felt that the two might not agree on foreign policy, which would entail resignation on Borah's part.[1] According to Harold Nicolson, President-elect Hoover, because of the urgent recommendation of President Coolidge, next approached Dwight Morrow, but since Mr. Morrow felt that he should finish his job as ambassador to Mexico,[2] Mr. Hoover did not offer him the Secretaryship of State. The third potential nominee, Colonel Henry L. Stimson, rated high in Hoover's estimation, and the President considered him suitable either as Secretary of State or as Attorney General. Through his law partner George Roberts, Mr. Stimson let it be known that he

292

would accept the Department of State post, but would not be interested in heading the Justice Department. On January 30, 1929, Colonel Stimson was informed that Mr. Hoover would appoint him Secretary of State.[3] Inasmuch as Colonel Stimson could not conveniently take up his new duties immediately after the inauguration, Secretary Kellogg was persuaded to remain until his successor arrived.

Henry L. Stimson entered upon the duties of his office on March 28, 1929. Although born to wealth, Stimson had a passion for public service, and he had already served his government in many capacities. As U.S. attorney for the Southern District, New York, he distinguished himself so that he was chosen as the Republican candidate for governor. His aloofness and aristocratic bearing were too great a handicap in a campaign against Tammany Hall, and he failed of election. President Taft soon afterward took the sting out of this defeat by appointing Stimson Secretary of War. His next call by the government was to serve as the personal representative of President Coolidge to go to Nicaragua, investigate the revolutionary conditions, and, if possible, to suggest a workable solution. His mission achieved such satisfactory results that almost immediately upon his return President Coolidge appointed him governor general of the Philippine Islands. In this position he proved equally successful in conciliating the Filipinos. Colonel Stimson came to his new position as Secretary of State with the advantage of a wide background of national and international administrative and political experience.

Secretary Stimson appreciated the fact that in President Hoover he would have a chief far more interested in, and better acquainted with, foreign affairs than was President Coolidge. No previous President possessed the firsthand information concerning foreign countries which President Hoover had acquired through his work as a mining engineer and later through his humanitarian services in Europe. A good-will tour covering eleven Latin American republics, taken between the time of his election and his inauguration, had given the President-elect an opportunity to feel the pulse of the neighbors to the south. It was only natural, therefore, that the new President should have certain definite ideas with regard to the foreign relations of the United States.

Changes in Personnel

The new administration made few immediate changes in the Department of State personnel. By far the most important was the appointment of Joseph P. Cotton, a well known and highly respected New York lawyer, as Under Secretary of State to replace J. Reuben Clark, Jr., who had resigned on June 19, 1929. Mr. Cotton had served with the United States Food Administration as its European representative and President Hoover had a high regard for his administrative ability, but the appointment was made at the request of Secretary Stimson. Although a corporation lawyer reputed to earn $100,000 a year, Mr. Cotton was an inveterate foe of established precedent and possessed distinctly liberal tendencies. It had been widely rumored that Assistant Secretary Castle would be named Under Secretary upon the resignation of Mr. Clark—in fact, his name, among others, was suggested by President Hoover—but Secretary Stimson wished to reorganize the Department and felt that an outsider like Mr. Cotton would be in a better position to approach the problem impartially. The untimely death of Under Secretary Cotton on March 10, 1931, seemed to make Castle a natural choice, and he was commissioned Under Secretary on April 1, 1931. Mr. Castle had entered the Department in 1919 and had headed the important Division of European Affairs from 1921 to 1927, when he became Assistant Secretary of State. Secretary Stimson concedes that Castle was not his choice, and that afterward he regretted that he had allowed the President to persuade him to make the appointment.[4] The vacancy caused by the elevation of Mr. Castle to the position of Under Secretary was filled on June 10, 1931, by the appointment as Assistant Secretary of State of Harvey H. Bundy, a lawyer skilled in finance but unacquainted with either the State Department or international affairs. Secretary Stimson found that his financial experience was very useful in the complicated problems of defaulted private loans and war debts. The other Assistant Secretaryship[5] was not filled until February 27, 1931, and then it was given to James Grafton Rogers, dean of the law school at the University of Colorado. Although wholly inexperienced in governmental or international matters, Rogers had been a newspaper man, and Secretary Stimson used him as liaison officer with the press. Bertram D. Hulen, who as a correspondent assigned to the Department of State by the Associated Press and later by the New York Times, declared that Rogers explained and clarified policies "with a frankness that has never been exceeded in the Department of State." [6] The appointment of Allen T. Klots as Special Assistant to the Secretary was a personal appointment made by the Secretary, and one that proved eminently satisfactory.

One change was made in the Department's organization for which Secretary Stimson was widely criticized—his decision to eliminate the State Department's code-cracking office, the so-called Black Chamber. This agency of cryptography had been functioning for sixteen years under the direction of Herbert O. Yardley, who originated and perfected its procedure.[7] The reason given was: "Gentlemen do not read each other's mail." [8]

In the policy-formulating geographical divisions all changes of personnel were based upon merit or experience. The Divisions of Far Eastern Affairs, Near Eastern Affairs, and European Affairs were the strongest. Stanley K. Hornbeck, Chief of the Division of Far Eastern Affairs, with firsthand experience in the Far East and Near East and with a keen analytical mind, had three experienced Foreign Service officers as advisers, John K. Caldwell, Ransford S. Miller, and Joseph E. Jacobs. In addition to these he had Maxwell M. Hamilton, a former Foreign Service officer who had served as an interpreter in China, and another retired Foreign Service officer with governmental and business experience in the Far East, Stuart J. Fuller. In the Near Eastern Division the Chief was suave and efficient Wallace S. Murray, a former Foreign Service officer with broad experience in the Near East. His assistants were expert career officers of outstanding ability: Paul H. Alling, Maynard B. Barnes, and Jefferson Patterson. Another adviser was retired Foreign Service officer Clayson W. Aldridge, who had already served for five years in the Near East when he became divisional assistant in the Department. J. Theodore Marriner, Chief of the Division of Western European Affairs, was a brilliant Foreign Service officer with ten years of experience in Europe when he was appointed as head of the Western European Division in 1927. Secretary Stimson had the most complete confidence in Marriner's judgment and advised with him constantly. Marriner had a very capable group of noncareer assistants, such as Prentiss B. Gilbert, John F. Carter, Jr., and Paul Culbertson, as well as the experienced career officers Pierre de L. Boal and John Dewey Hickerson. The Division of Eastern European Affairs, with Robert F. Kelley as Chief, was not as highly rated as the other divisions, partly because its principal function appeared to be to find reasons for not recognizing the Soviets. The Division of Latin American Affairs lost a very able officer when its Chief, Dana G. Munro, was sent as minister to Haiti in 1930. Its new chief, Walter C. Thurston, a career officer, had not achieved the reputation of his predecessor, but since both President Hoover and Secretary Stimson were personally familiar with this area, they were inclined to take the lead in the initiation of Latin American policies. In the same way Ambassador Dwight Morrow and his successor, J. Reuben Clark, Jr., so completely dominated Mexican policy that the Division of Mexican Affairs had little to say regarding the making of policy.

The Office of the Legal Adviser

A logical change in the Department's organization occurred when the Office of the Solicitor was changed in 1931 to the Office of the Legal Adviser. From the very beginning the Department had one clerk assigned to claims, but the first official claims clerk dated from 1848. In 1870 the Examiner of Claims in the State Department was placed under the Department of Justice and received his salary from that agency. The Examiner of Claims was designated Solicitor in 1887 and served as head of the Law Bureau of the State Department. The Solicitor, although acting as the legal adviser of the Department of

State, continued to be paid by the Department of Justice until the Office of Legal Adviser was authorized by the Act of February 23, 1931. Although this office concerned itself with questions of extradition, recognition, boundary disputes, the implications of treaties, and various other legal matters, its most important function had always been the handling of claims. These have varied in amounts from $500 to $13,000,000 and have included claims dating back more than a hundred years.[9] The head of the Office of Legal Adviser was Green H. Hackworth, who had been appointed law clerk in the Department in 1916 and Solicitor in 1925. When designated Legal Adviser, Mr. Hackworth had twenty-one assistants and three clerks. The new arrangement brought him an increase in salary from $8,500 to $9,000, placing him on a financial parity with the Assistant Secretaries of State.

The Historical Adviser

Just before Secretary Stimson entered the Department of State, the Division of Publications was designated as the Office of the Historical Adviser. As formerly, it was responsible for the publication of all official documents issued by the Department, including the selection and editing of those appearing in the *Foreign Relations of the United States*. The Geographer, the library, which now possessed some 175,000 volumes, and all the archives of the Department up to August 14, 1906, were under the jurisdiction of this office. The law section of the office compiled and edited the Statutes at Large and prepared drafts of executive orders and proclamations. A definitive edition of the treaties and other international acts of the United States was being compiled and edited by the Historical Adviser himself. Incredibly enough, no edition of the treaties and agreements to which the United States was a party had ever been published where the original texts and translations had been carefully checked. The proposed collection was to include the original texts of all treaties with the translations and with notes giving the background and history of the treaty with relevant citations of legislative acts and judicial decisions.[10]

The Congress in 1925 and in 1929 had authorized the collection, editing, and publication of the official papers of the Territories, and this was begun in 1931 under the direction of Clarence E. Carter. Dr. Tyler Dennett, a historian of high reputation who had been Chief of the Division of Publications since 1924, was designated Historical Adviser on February 15, 1929. Upon Dr. Dennett's resignation in April, 1931, he was succeeded by Hunter Miller. The latter, who had served as legal adviser to the House mission and later to the American mission to negotiate peace, had been acting as Editor of Treaties since 1929. When in 1933 the Office of Historical Adviser was divided, Mr. Miller became Historical Adviser and the Assistant, Dr. Cyril Wynne, was made Chief of the Division of Research and Publications. The Historical Adviser under this new arrangement was expected to advise with the Secretary of State on historical and constitutional questions as well as in matters of policy relating to current questions before the Department. Hunter Miller soon became so engrossed in the new edition of treaties that he devoted the rest of his life to this task. At the present time some seven volumes of the Miller treaty series have been published.

Diplomatic Appointments

In the appointment of diplomats the Hoover administration was seriously criticized, even though for the first time in history more than four-fifths of the posts abroad were filled by men named from the career service. The harsh criticism in the liberal press resulted from the three appointments to the most sought after posts, London, Paris, and Berlin. It has already been indicated that these posts are almost never given to career diplomats or even to men experienced in international law or diplomacy. They are posts of vital importance, yet all too often appointees must have served the party well, either politically or financially, to gain them. Of the nine ambassadors who preceded Charles Gates Dawes to the Court of St. James's, John Hay was the only one with substantial diplomatic experience. Whitelaw Reid had served previously briefly in Paris, and Alanson B. Houghton had been American ambassador to Berlin for three years, but both were far removed from being career diplomats. Bayard had been Secretary of State before going to London. The others—Choate, Page, Davis, Harvey, Kellogg—were totally devoid of any previous experience even kindred to diplomacy. Nevertheless, Choate and Davis proved to be among America's greatest diplomats and Page and Kellogg were not without honor.

The appointment of Charles G. Dawes to the London post was the least criticized of the three. General Dawes had proved himself a genius in cutting red tape and getting results as Procurement Chief in the First World War. He had made a fine record as the first Director of the Bureau of the Budget. He had even given the Vice Presidency a status never before enjoyed, and his so-called Dawes Plan had been the first sane economic approach to the reparations question. Dawes was picturesque, an expert on international finance, a musician of parts, and he could maintain the American embassy in a way impossible to a representative dependent upon the wholly inadequate salary and representation allowance provided by his government. But Dawes liked to violate conventions and play to the gallery, and the Court of St. James's was not a congenial locale for a boisterous Midwestern Yankee.

The appointment of Senator Walter E. Edge as ambassador to France also provoked somewhat unjustifiable outcries. Edge had been governor of

New Jersey and was serving his second term in the Senate. He was a business-man who had succeeded in the advertising business so well that he had agencies abroad as well as at home, and he was personally familiar with the work of his agency in Paris. It was he who had suggested to Ambassador Herrick the con-struction of a building to house all American governmental activities in Paris, and as a member of the Senate Foreign Relations Committee he had intro-duced a bill authorizing the appointment of a Foreign Service Buildings Com-mission to purchase property abroad to house American governmental agencies.

The appointment of Senator Frederic M. Sackett as ambassador to Ger-many was perhaps more deserving of criticism because of his complete lack of experience in international affairs. But here, too, it could be argued that Mr. Sackett was a very successful businessman who had proved his ability in the public service as Federal Food Administrator for Kentucky and a man who was capable of improving our trade relations with Germany. Furthermore, since Dawes, Edge, and Sackett had all been good friends in the Senate, they would be inclined to cooperate in carrying out their duties abroad.

Increased Salaries and Improved Morale

Both President Hoover and Secretary Stimson were determined to improve the Department of State by an increase in salaries and by the addition of per-sonnel. In his Armistice Day address on November 11, 1929, President Hoover declared: "Our State Department . . . must be strengthened and supported as the great arm of our government, dedicated to the organization of peace." [11] In his first appearance before the House Committee on Appropriations, Secre-tary Stimson told the members that he had personally made a careful investiga-tion of the Department and he found that it "was understaffed and under-manned and to a very large extent underpaid." [12] It should be noted that the salary situation in the Department had been somewhat improved by an amend-ment to the Classification Act of 1923 known as the Welch Act and passed in 1928. Under its provisions the Under Secretary and four Assistant Secretaries were given the highest rating in the so-called Clerical Administrative and Fiscal Service (C A F 15) which amounted to $9,000. In the appropriation bill for 1930 the salary of the Under Secretary was raised to $10,000. The Secretary of State had been receiving $15,000 since 1925, the year when Secretary Kellogg took office. Under the Welch Act classification the Solicitor was raised from $7,000 to $8,500, and the Economic Adviser from $6,000 to $8,000.

Under a new professional and scientific rating the Division Chiefs could receive $8,000, which cut the unfair discrepancies between the salaries of For-eign Service officers assigned to the Department and permanent employees of the Department. Secretary Stimson requested that the Under Secretary be paid

$12,000, the Assistant Secretaries $10,000, and the heads of geographical divisions $8,000 to $9,000. He also requested sufficient funds so that the forty-odd Foreign Service officers who had been brought into the Department because of its lack of personnel could be replaced so that they could man the posts where they were urgently needed.[13] The amount appropriated for the Department of State proper in 1929 was $1,464,465, and in 1930, $1,692,835. Mr. Stimson's estimates for 1931 were $2,368,273 and the amount appropriated was $2,364,273, an almost incredible success for Secretary Stimson in his financial dealings with Congress.

It was the general expectation that Henry L. Stimson, with his background of wealth and his predilection for the War Department and all of its works, would be even less liberal than his predecessor in the administration of the State Department. He soon made it evident that such was not the case. The appointment of Joseph P. Cotton as Under Secretary indicated the Secretary's appreciation of vigorous liberalism. Stimson reversed the Kellogg ruling which barred Count Karolyi, and allowed the Hungarian revolutionary free ingress to the United States. He authorized the granting of a passport to the militant pacifist Dorothy Detzer in spite of her refusal to bear arms in support of the United States. Although not sympathetic to the Soviets' theories and practices, he was calm and rational about it. He instituted an innovation at his beautiful Woodley estate when, instead of inviting the wives of the Assistant Secretaries to pour tea in accordance with established custom, he asked certain efficient feminine officials in the Department, notably Ruth B. Shipley and Margaret M. Hanna, to do him the honor.

In his inaugural address on March 4, 1929, President Hoover had expressed his high regard for the Pact of Paris, and shortly after his inauguration, at a special ceremony in the White House, the President proclaimed the Pact to be in effect. But President Hoover saw the need for more and better instrumentalities for the peaceful settlement of disputes, and both he and Secretary Stimson favored the adhesion of the United States to the Permanent Court of International Justice as one "peculiarly identified with American ideals." At the close of the Coolidge administration Elihu Root, at President Hoover's request, had gone abroad and had worked out an acceptable agreement with the signatory powers to take care of the Senate reservation regarding the court's procedure in rendering advisory opinions. Hoover was dubious about senatorial approval, but since Stimson was insistent the President submitted the protocols to the Senate on December 10, 1930, with a strong message urging acceptance. The Senate, however, was still obdurate and favorable action was not taken. Nevertheless, despite its failure to join the World Court, the United States in the four years of the Hoover-Stimson regime entered into twenty-five new treaties of arbitration and seventeen new treaties of conciliation.[14]

The London Naval Conference

As a further effort to establish a peaceful world, the Hoover administration favored greater limitation of armament. In his Memorial Day address of May 30, 1929, President Hoover suggested that such action might be made possible by utilizing a rational yardstick with which to make reasonable comparisons of naval units.[15] Almost simultaneously, Secretary Stimson outlined and discussed with the President and Ambassador Dawes the latter's address containing specific proposals which he would present in his forthcoming speech before the Society of Pilgrims in London. To obtain the most exact possible phraseology, President Hoover and Secretary Stimson, with the aid of Ambassador Dawes and Theodore Marriner, Chief of the Division of Western European Affairs, finally worked out a formula which they felt might establish approximate parity even though the fleets differed in characteristics.[16]

In carrying on the negotiations with Ramsay MacDonald through Ambassador Dawes, Secretary Stimson was in constant conference with the President. It was finally decided to invite the British prime minister to come to Washington where President Hoover and Premier MacDonald might work out a formula in spite of the relentless opposition of the naval authorities on both sides. While Secretary Stimson and Under Secretary Cotton struggled with the admirals in Washington, President Hoover and Ramsay MacDonald reached a satisfactory agreement on policy at the President's summer camp on the Rapidan in Virginia. Taking as a basic assumption that war between the two countries was definitely banished, the problem was largely one of technical adjustments.

At times the President and Secretary Stimson became somewhat incensed at the efforts of the naval board to juggle figures in applying the Hoover "yardstick." On one occasion the President, by figuring out the formulas himself, found the naval board almost 100 per cent wrong. When Secretary Stimson requested an explanation, the naval board excused their figures by intimating that the "yardstick" was only a camouflage and that it was their duty to protect their country's interest. Secretary Stimson replied coldly, "Gentlemen, the United States in its international negotiations is not in the habit of camouflaging." [17] President Hoover and the State Department were also handicapped by vicious propaganda against limitation of armament put out by the Navy League and by a paid propagandist, William B. Shearer. President Hoover skilfully met the attack by utilizing a lawsuit, brought by Mr. Shearer against certain shipbuilding corporations to collect for past services, to bring into the open the sinister influences which were opposing the government's policies.[18]

An agreement was finally reached to hold the conference for further limitation of naval armament in London in January, 1930. Secretary Stimson headed the American delegation and Ambassadors Charles G. Dawes, Hugh Gibson, and Dwight Morrow were assigned to assist him. Determined to be prepared for any question that might arise, Secretary Stimson turned over the Department to Under Secretary Cotton and spent most of the month preceding the conference at Woodley, concentrating on the agenda.

That the London Naval Conference failed to achieve what was originally hoped was not the fault of President Hoover, Secretary Stimson, or the American delegation. The French representatives refused to compromise or to cooperate unless guaranteed security could be obtained. Only a consultative pact including the United States and which would cover the Mediterranean and the Atlantic with guarantees similar to the Four Power Pact in the Pacific would satisfy them. Personally, both the President and the Secretary of State might have been willing to accept such a consultative pact as a basis of agreement, but they knew very well that the Senate would not.

It must be conceded that neither the State Department contingent nor the career Foreign Service played the leading roles at the London Conference. Perhaps the three most successful negotiators on the American delegation were Ambassador to Mexico Dwight Morrow—"the little man with the untidy hair" —the dynamic but crafty parliamentarian, David A. Reed, and the experienced specialist in international conferences, Hugh Gibson. Practically all of the political advisers were career officers from either the Department or the field. J. Theodore Marriner, Chief of the Division of Western European Affairs, came from the Department; Minister Hugh Wilson came from Geneva, Ray Atherton was counselor of the American embassy at London, and Norman Armour held the corresponding position in Paris. The secretary to the delegation was F. Lammot Belin, first secretary at the London embassy, and the press officer was Michael J. McDermott, Chief of the Division of Current Information in the Department.[19] Secretary Stimson, although he had rented a large estate with a golf course at Stanmore, spent most of his time at the Ritz Hotel with the American delegation, and no delegate, with the exception of Dwight Morrow, put in longer hours or worked more strenuously. In his address of April 13, 1930, in London, summarizing the results of the conference, Secretary Stimson expressed his appreciation of the work of the American delegation, the assistance of the naval officers, and the advice of "the loyal and capable staff of the Department of State and the American Embassy in London."

The London Conference had resulted in a substantial saving in appropriations for naval armament but had not considered limitation of armament on land. President Hoover, appreciating both the human and economic wastage of war preparations, felt that the World Disarmament Conference, which was scheduled to occur in Geneva in 1932 under the auspices of the League of Nations, should be supported by the United States. So that the United States might be adequately informed of the European political situation, Secretary Stimson made a preliminary trip to Europe in the summer of 1931, visiting Rome, Paris, Berlin, and London. Although he felt that the conference would have a greater chance of success if certain political problems of the European states could be settled first, Stimson agreed with the President that the United States should participate and do its best to ensure success. The American delegation, headed by Hugh Gibson, quickly realized that the world was not ready to disarm. When the conference seemed impotent to reach any satisfactory agreement, Secretary Stimson, although weak from illness, went over personally to stimulate action. Again France refused to commit herself without adequate guarantees of security. Secretary Stimson returned home empty-handed.

As a last resort President Hoover decided to make a personal appeal, and he accompanied it by an original, sane, concrete proposal which would cut the bill for armaments materially and strengthen the position of peace-loving states. Writing it out in longhand without consulting the experts, President Hoover prepared a memorandum proposing the abolition of weapons largely offensive, such as tanks, bombing planes, and mobile guns, and the reduction of armament on land, sea, and air by one-fourth to one-third. It was a simple and feasible suggestion and appealed to many of the delegations. But the French were against it, the British were cold, and the Japanese uninterested. Only the technical advisers overwhelmingly supported the Hoover proposal.[20]

Relations with Latin America

The Latin American policy of the Hoover administration was the result of the closest sort of collaboration between the President and the Secretary of State. During his good-will tour of Latin America before his inauguration, President Hoover, through his good offices, had been able to bring about a settlement of the long-standing Tacna-Arica dispute.[21] It was while he was on this journey that Mr. Hoover repeatedly used the term "good neighbor," which was publicized so extensively by President Roosevelt.

With regard to intervention, that bête noire of Latin American relations, in his address to the Gridiron Club on April 13, 1929, the President declared "that it never has been and ought not to be the policy of the United States to intervene by force to secure or maintain contracts between our citizens and foreign states and their citizens." [22]

To prove that its nonintervention policy was genuine, Secretary Stimson felt that the United States must withdraw its marines from the Caribbean. As a safeguard against the raids of General Sandino, the Secretary of State, on April 17, 1931, informed Americans that the United States could no longer protect them in the interior of Nicaragua and urged them either to leave the country or withdraw to the towns on the coast.[23] Shortly after this the United States began to withdraw its marines from Nicaragua and by January, 1933, not a single marine was left in the country.

One much publicized incident in Secretary Stimson's relations with Latin America must be noted in passing. When Dr. Getulio Vargas seized the government of Brazil by a *coup d'état*, the State Department, at the urgent solicitation of the Brazilian ambassador, placed an embargo upon shipments of arms to the Federal government. Within a few days the revolutionists were victorious, assumed the government, and were forthwith recognized by the United States. The United States was bound by a treaty with Brazil to prohibit the shipment of arms to the rebels, so that the Department was justified in its position, but its failure to explain its sudden shift of policy was much criticized in the press.[24] It was alleged that Assistant Secretary White, in charge of Latin American affairs, had completely overlooked the treaty in seeking for an excuse for the embargo. Secretary Stimson later pointed out that even without the treaty the United States was justified, both by a joint resolution of the Congress in 1922 and by the fact that the revolutionists had not yet been recognized as belligerents either by the Brazilian government or the United States.[25]

Relations with the Far East

By far the most important problems of foreign policy which faced the Department of State while Mr. Stimson was Secretary arose in the Far East. Shortly after signing the Kellogg-Briand Pact, Russia broke off diplomatic relations with China and mobilized her armed forces on the Manchurian frontier. Since the United States had sponsored the Pact of Paris, Secretary Stimson felt that this government was morally bound to remind both China and Russia of their obligations and to enlist the aid of the other signatory powers in an effort to prevent war.[26] When direct negotiations failed and Russia attacked and defeated the Chinese defenders in Manchuria, Secretary Stimson sent a more forceful reminder to the two powers. Unfortunately, this second appeal reached Russia after peace negotiations had begun and the Soviet Foreign Commissar took occasion to administer a harsh rebuke to the United States for its unjustifiable interference, particularly since it had steadily refused to enter into official relations with the Soviet government.[27]

A much more serious situation occurred in the fall of 1931, when the Japanese suddenly invaded Manchuria and occupied vast areas of Chinese territory. Again the Department of State intervened and reminded the Japanese government of its obligations under the Pact of Paris. Realizing the importance of popular support in his valiant effort to sustain the commitments of the

Kellogg-Briand Pact, Secretary Stimson not only held his regular press conferences in the Department, but supplemented them with invitations to the senior Washington journalists to meet with him from time to time at his home in Woodley. Secretary Stimson also gave full credit to the advice and assistance which he obtained from the officials both in the Department and abroad. In the first place both President Hoover and Secretary Stimson had lived in the Far East and had personally known conditions there. In the Department, Under Secretary Castle had been ambassador to Japan, and Dr. Stanley K. Hornbeck, Chief of the Division of Far Eastern Affairs, "combined long personal experience in the Far East with careful and accurate study of Oriental problems and history." [28]

When the Secretary of State was convinced that there was no further possibility of solving the Manchurian problem by discussion and conciliation, he decided to try to find "some way of formally expressing the moral disapproval of the world against the breach of peace in Manchuria, and if possible to put behind that expression a sanction." [29] It was at this point that the President and the Secretary of State differed on procedure. According to Secretary of the Interior Ray Lyman Wilbur, the State Department and some members of the cabinet felt that only by vigorous efforts and united action on the part of the nations involved could the Japanese be restrained. On the other hand President Hoover opposed sanctions either by economic means or by force and insisted upon a "policy of non-recognition of whatever territorial conquests the Japanese might make." The President presented his thesis "so vigorously and efficiently that it soon dominated over all other ideas." [30]

Secretary Stimson prepared a note which President Hoover approved, stating categorically that the United States would neither admit the legality of nor recognize any treaty or agreement which impaired the treaty rights of the United States, including the territorial integrity of China and the open-door policy; nor would it recognize any situation brought about by means contrary to the obligations of the Pact of Paris.[31] The United States had reason to expect both Great Britain and France to support her stand, but neither was willing to associate itself with the American *démarche*, and so the United States acted wholly on her own responsibility.

Japan, encouraged by this diplomatic rebuff to the Department of State, now proceeded to attack Shanghai, an international city where British and French interests were superior to those of the United States. When President Hoover and Secretary Stimson decided to send warships to protect American citizens and their property, the British were now willing to cooperate. Some of the member states of the League of Nations favored the imposition of economic sanctions against Japan and the State Department was willing to consider the idea of participation. But again President Hoover stood strongly against the idea on the ground that it would merely spread the war and might involve the United States.[32]

The Hoover-Stimson Doctrine

As it became clearer that Japan was determined to encompass the dismemberment of China, Secretary Stimson, with the approval of the President, decided to invoke the Nine Power Treaty of Washington, which specifically provided that the signatory powers respect the sovereignty, independence, and territorial integrity of China. At the same time President Hoover suggested that a notice of nonrecognition, such as was contained in the note of January 7, "be brought forward as an appropriate determination to be announced by the signatories of that treaty." [33] Secretary Stimson thereupon sought a joint *démarche* along these lines with the British, but again Sir John Simon retreated behind the bulwark of the League of Nations and its more deliberate procedure. Forced again to go it alone, and spurred on by the Japanese recognition of the spuriously sovereign state of Manchukuo, Secretary Stimson had a brilliant inspiration. He would make a public statement of the views of the United States in a letter to Senator Borah, chairman of the Foreign Relations Committee of the Senate.

Utilizing as background, memoranda prepared by Dr. Stanley K. Hornbeck, Chief of the Division of Far Eastern Affairs, Secretary Stimson, aided by Assistant Secretary James G. Rogers and Special Assistant Allen T. Klots, prepared a letter which outlined the proposed policy of the United States and the basis upon which it rested. He pointed out that the United States was following closely the path trod previously by John Hay and Charles Evans Hughes. The principles of this policy were the territorial integrity of China and the maintenance of the open door, both of which had been accepted by Japan in the Nine Power Treaty. The United States still stood upon these principles and had formally notified Japan and China "that it would not recognize any situation, treaty or agreement entered into by those governments in violation of the covenants of their treaties." Secretary Stimson then suggested that if the other governments of the world would take the same stand, a caveat would be placed upon aggressive action which would bar the legality of titles or rights sought to be obtained in violation of treaties.[34]

This proposal, subsequently known as the Hoover-Stimson Doctrine, was, according to its author, intended as a message of encouragement to China, an explanation of policy to the American people, a suggestion of action to the League of Nations, and, perhaps most important of all, a reminder to Japan that its violation of treaties would release other powers from treaty obligations which Japan might wish maintained. To stimulate action by the League Assembly which British indecision was delaying, Secretary Stimson instructed our representative in Shanghai, who had been cooperating actively with the British, to withdraw from all conferences until further notice. He then notified the British foreign minister, who was in Geneva, that our action in Shanghai depended upon British action in Geneva. Sir John Simon could hedge no longer, and a resolution of nonrecognition of any situation brought about by means contrary to the League Covenant or the Pact of Paris was introduced by the British and passed unanimously.[35] President Hoover and Secretary Stimson had at last brought the United States and the League of Nations into full agreement in the imposition of a sanction against aggression whereby the public opinion of the world could be quickly and effectively marshaled.

Reparations and Debts

The Department of State played a constant and important role in the Far Eastern crisis, but on the question of reparations and Allied debts the President took the initiative and the responsibility. It was the Hoover moratorium, the Hoover-Laval conversations; and it was the President who authorized Secretary Stimson to prepare the calling of an international monetary and economic conference. When the November elections of 1932 made Franklin D. Roosevelt the next incumbent of the White House, President Hoover made every effort to work out a joint policy whereby the questions of debts and the questions to be discussed at the forthcoming World Economic Conference might be joined. Both he and Secretary Stimson had several conferences with the President-elect, but the latter preferred to let matters drift until the new administration could take over.

Departmental Changes

A few changes in organization and personnel not yet noted occurred in the State Department during the Stimson regime. The Division of International Conferences and Protocol was divided on September 11, 1931, and career officer James C. Dunn was appointed Chief of the Division of International Conferences and career officer Warren D. Robbins was named head of the Division of Protocol. Charles Lee Cooke remained as Ceremonial Officer. On January 1, 1931, the Bureau of Indexes and Archives was given a new name, the Division of Communications and Records—indicating that it was a living organism rather than a mortuary of obsolete documentary materials. This division, the largest in the Department, with over 150 employees, was the vital link between the Foreign Service and the Department. It handled as many as a million pieces of mail and fifty thousand telegrams in a single year. David

A. Salmon, who entered the Department in 1906, remained Chief of the Division.

Chief Clerk E. J. Ayers died on April 30, 1931, after seven years' service in this office. The position was filled temporarily by Harry A. McBride and then by Percy F. Allen until January 1, 1932, when a career officer, Clinton E. MacEachran, was appointed Chief Clerk and Administrative Assistant. The Economic Adviser's Office, which since Arthur N. Young's resignation in 1929 had been under the direction of Frederick Livesey as Acting Economic Adviser, was given to Dr. Herbert Feis.

The most important change in our representation abroad came early in 1932, when Secretary of the Treasury Andrew W. Mellon succeeded Ambassador Charles G. Dawes at the Court of St. James's. President Hoover desired Mr. Dawes to serve as President of the Reconstruction Finance Corporation, for which he was peculiarly well equipped by background and experience. It was problematical whether Secretary Mellon would be willing to accept a diplomatic post. He had served successfully during three administrations in a position which appealed particularly to him. However, Mellon was not in sympathy with Hoover's policies of cushioning the depression, and the London post offered the opportunity for a graceful retirement.[36]

Secretary Stimson had been able to obtain for the Department of State substantial increases in personnel and salaries during the fiscal years 1931 and 1932 for essential duties. There had been a steady increase in the work and practically no increase in personnel since 1919. For example, whereas the correspondence between 1924 and 1927 increased 25 per cent, the increase in appropriations for current expenses of the Department amounted to 3 per cent. As Assistant Secretary Carr pointed out: "An average increase of approximately $5,000 annually in an appropriation amounting to $1,340,000 had been added during the preceding seven years for the general work of the Department." [37] Congress, at the urgent request of the Secretary, increased the appropriations for the Department proper by $657,438 in 1931 and by an additional $137,845 for 1932. The increases allowed the Foreign Service for the same two years were $1,948,989.11 and $679,028.66.[38] The total appropriation for the Department of State proper for 1931 was $2,364,273, and for 1932, $2,502,118. The business depression brought about an Economy Act on the part of the Congress which not only cut salaries and allowances but reduced personnel. Thus the total appropriations for the Department for 1933 were cut to $2,265,540 and the estimates for 1934 dropped to $2,083,012.[39] Nevertheless, Assistant Secretary Carr, speaking on November 23, 1932, was able to declare: "Our organization now, we think, at least is the best we have ever had; I mean as to business organization and as to quality of personnel." [40]

In evaluating the services of Colonel Henry L. Stimson as Secretary of

State, great credit must be given for the improvement of the morale of the Department as a result of his success in obtaining increased appropriations. Many delayed promotions were granted and the strain of overwork was lessened. He chose able assistants and delegated responsibility. He was liberal toward questions of protocol and procedure. He made a valiant effort to support the League of Nations both on the limitation of armament and in maintenance of peace. He fought the aggression of Japan with every peaceful procedure available and helped the President devise new ones. Although the final results were unquestionably not commensurate with the efforts put forth, the failure to achieve lay in causes beyond the power of the American government. It is doubtful whether any statesman could have built better with the materials which were available than did Secretary of State Henry L. Stimson.

CORDELL HULL

25

Cordell Hull

Cordell Hull—Secretary of State

The administration of Franklin D. Roosevelt, which began officially on March 4, 1933, had already been functioning in the field of foreign relations for several months. As a result of President Hoover's request for a joint policy on foreign debts, President-elect Roosevelt utilized his so-called "brain trust," particularly Professor Raymond Moley of Columbia University, to assist him in stalling until after the inauguration.[1] In fact, it was in late November, 1932, that Roosevelt offered Moley the position of Assistant Secretary of State.[2] Nevertheless, the President-elect quickly indicated that he intended to make his own decisions on foreign policy, in spite of all opinion to the contrary. Without consulting his brain trust and, in fact, directly in opposition to its collective opinion, Roosevelt approved the Hoover-Stimson Doctrine in the Far East. When Moley and Tugwell protested his action as a tragic mistake, the President-elect called their attention to the fact that since his ancestors used to trade with China he had always had the deepest sympathy for the Chinese. "How could you expect me not to go along with Stimson on Japan?"

Franklin D. Roosevelt neither sought nor took advice on his cabinet appointments. He talked from time to time about a suitable appointee to head the State Department and gave some attention to a half dozen names: Newton D. Baker, Robert W. Bingham, Cordell Hull, Key Pittman, Joe Robinson, and Owen D. Young. The only two names given serious consideration, however, were those of Hull and Young, and the latter would not have been popular with the left-wing Democrats because of his affiliation with big business. Senator Cordell Hull was popular with the Southern Democrats and with the more conservative Northern elements in the party.

Moley, a New Dealer, was appalled at the thought of trying to serve as Assistant Secretary of State and as close confidential adviser to the President on economic affairs under a Secretary of State such as Cordell Hull. The latter's predilection for tariff reduction was notorious and Moley had no illusions as to Hull's certain resentment at a subordinate who would be closer to the President than the Secretary himself. Moley pointed out the difficulty and asked that he be relieved of the proposed position in the State Department. Roosevelt, however, insisted that Hull knew all about Moley's status, and to reassure him he dictated a statement of his duties. They were to include "the handling of the foreign debts, the world economic conference, supervision of the economic adviser's office and such additional duties as the President may direct in the general field of foreign and domestic government." [3]

Senator Cordell Hull had no intimation that he would be asked to serve as Secretary of State. In fact, when he was offered the position personally by the President-elect in January, 1933, Senator Hull asked for time to think the matter over. He declares in his *Memoirs* that he told Roosevelt frankly that the post of Secretary of State had not been any part of his personal planning for the future.[4] Most of his political friends advised him against taking the position, but after careful consideration he decided to accept. He had long since felt that the world's sad economic plight was primarily caused by restrictive trade barriers and thought that he might, as Secretary of State, be able to lead the way toward better international economic relations. He accepted on February 17, 1933, with the understanding that his duties as Secretary meant more than merely carrying on correspondence with foreign governments. It would mean the formulation of policy with the aid of the State Department's experts and the recommending of such policy to the President for his approval or disapproval. President Roosevelt expressed his acceptance of this interpretation. At the same time it was understood that Raymond Moley was to be named Assistant Secretary of State so that he might continue to serve as the President's political and economic adviser.[5]

The background of Cordell Hull hardly prepared him for his new position. Born in a small town in Tennessee, he had studied law and practiced briefly while serving in the state legislature. He volunteered during the Spanish-American War, and after service in Cuba and Trinidad as captain, he returned to civil life and a circuit judgeship in Tennessee. He entered Congress in 1907 and except for two terms, served steadily from 1907 to 1931. He was elected senator in 1930 and had still three years to serve when he was named Secretary of State. In the House he had fathered the Federal income-tax system and had been a consistent and ardent opponent of the high protective tariff. He fought the Smoot-Hawley Tariff bill and felt that its passage had much to do with the world-wide depression which followed. In spite of his predilection for domestic affairs, Hull was not wholly unversed in foreign policy. He had always been a close observer of international affairs, he had supported Wilson in his fight for the League of Nations, he had visited some nine countries in Europe in 1925, and had made a number of speeches on foreign policy.

Roosevelt and Hull Make Appointments

When he entered upon his new duties, Cordell Hull had the great advantage of being well acquainted with Washington and on friendly terms with its outstanding leaders. Norman H. Davis, a friend and fellow Democratic Tennessean, had been representing the United States in the disarmament conference sponsored by the League of Nations, and Hull persuaded the President to allow him to continue under the new administration as ambassador-at-large in charge of the American delegation at Geneva. Hull was well acquainted with Secretary of State Stimson, British Ambassador Sir Ronald Lindsay, and French Ambassador Paul Claudel. In the ten days before taking office, the new Secretary of State consulted all of them. The able and experienced, though intermittent envoy extraordinary William C. Bullitt, a close friend of the President's, lived in the same hotel as Hull and became a friend and adviser.

The Department of State at this time was functioning under the Economy Act of June 30, 1932, made necessary by the depression. It was not possible to carry on the work and make a substantial cut in the personnel, and so the procedure followed was to give the staff the regular twenty-four working days but vacations without pay, which meant the saving of one month's salary to the government. In the field, however, during the fiscal year 1932-1933, 171 clerks in the Foreign Service were dropped without being replaced, which made a saving of about $180,000.[6] The total number of employees in the Department at this time was 804 and the salary roll was $1,867,100. No new bureau or agency had been established since 1930 except the Division of Protocol, which had become a separate agency instead of being joined with international conferences.

As was expected, the new Democratic regime changed a considerable number of the top positions in the Department, particularly those appointed upon a political basis. For example, Under Secretary William R. Castle, Jr., was a very close friend of President Hoover's, and Assistant Secretaries Rogers and Bundy were appointees wholly political in character. Their resignations were promptly accepted. Nevertheless, Secretary Hull was strongly opposed to bringing domestic politics into international affairs. He stated his position clearly as regards changing personnel.

I carefully investigated the character and fitness of officers of the Department, especially those in key positions. Although I weeded out an official here and there who for one cause or another was not equipped to perform the most efficient service, I retained the seasoned, experienced persons in key positions.[7]

Inasmuch as Secretary Hull was not prepared, either temperamentally or financially, to carry the burden of entertaining extensively, a new Under Secretary who could relieve him in this respect was necessary. A career man for this vital post was advisable, and at the recommendation of Louis Howe President Roosevelt appointed William Phillips. Phillips had been in the diplomatic service for some twenty years, had served in the Department of State as Assistant Secretary on several occasions, and had proved himself an able Under Secretary under Secretary Hughes from 1922 to 1924. The position of Under Secretary had been created to maintain continuity in foreign policy in spite of changes in the political character of the administration. Phillips's appointment assured this desirable aim. Assistant Secretary Carr, who had just celebrated his fortieth year of service in the Department, was retained as Assistant Secretary in charge of administration in accordance with the wishes of both the President and the Secretary of State. Francis White, a career officer who had served as Assistant Secretary of State in charge of Latin American affairs since 1927, was named minister to Czechoslovakia on July 3, 1933. Meanwhile, Sumner Welles, another able career officer with much experience in the Latin American field, had been appointed on April 6, 1933, as Assistant Secretary of State in his place. When the Cuban situation under President Machado became very serious, President Roosevelt requested Assistant Secretary Welles to go as his ambassador to see whether he could tender his good offices in what had become an intolerable political situation.[8] Jefferson Caffery, another top-rank career officer, who had recently served as minister in Guatemala and ambassador to Colombia, was named as Assistant Secretary to serve until Welles's return.

One of the new Assistant Secretaries of State, Harry F. Payer, proved to be a most unfortunate appointment. The position had first been offered to Breckinridge Long, who had held the position for three years under Secretary Lansing, but Long, having served previously on terms of equality with William Phillips, was unwilling now to serve under him. There was need of one Assistant Secretary trained to handle legal matters; and Assistant Secretary Moley, while directing the Cleveland Foundation in its studies of crime and law enforcement, had made the acquaintance of Payer, who was serving as the chairman of judicial reform of the Cleveland Bar Association. At Moley's suggestion Mr. Payer was offered the position, which he was only too delighted to accept. Payer had, it soon appeared, a completely false idea of the social requirements for an Assistant Secretary of State. His extreme sartorial elegance, his super-de-luxe automobile, and his overeager desire to shine in diplomatic society did not fit well with the New Deal appeal to the masses. In less than six months he resigned.

Even before this time Raymond Moley had found his position of Assistant Secretary under Cordell Hull more difficult than he had anticipated, and when

President Roosevelt let them both down at the London Economic Conference, he decided to resign as quickly as he gracefully could. The opportunity was afforded when the President requested him to make a survey for the Department of Justice with regard to more adequate legislation against kidnaping. This was in Professor Moley's specialized field of criminal law administration. He accepted and resigned on September 7, 1933, exactly six months after he had, with misgivings, accepted the office of Assistant Secretary of State.

In Moley's place Secretary Hull appointed a close friend and old crony, Robert Walton Moore, to aid in legal matters. Moore had served as counsel for various railway and steamship companies and had been elected as a congressman for Virginia from 1919 to 1931. The only criticism raised against Moore was his age—he was seventy-four years old at the time of his appointment. The other vacancy, which occurred when Payer resigned, was filled by Francis B. Sayre, onetime professor at Harvard Law School and Woodrow Wilson's son-in-law. Sayre had acted as legal adviser to the king of Siam and was an authority in the widely separate fields of international administration and criminal law.

In December of 1930 a new position, entitled Special Assistant to the Secretary of State, had been created. The salary was $8,000 a year, the same as that received by the Assistant Secretaries of State. Assistant Secretary Moley had been impressed with the broad background and recent European contacts of William C. Bullitt, who lived, as did Hull and Moley, at the Carlton Hotel. Moley also felt that Bullitt deserved some recompense for the harsh treatment he had received from the Wilson administration for telling the truth as he saw it in regard to Bolshevik Russia. Moley would have liked to see Bullitt an Assistant Secretary of State, but Under Secretary Phillips opposed that, so it was finally agreed to make him Special Assistant to the Secretary. Secretary Hull was agreeable and the President was finally prevailed upon to make the appointment.[9] Bullitt later became one of the President's closest advisers and unquestionably had much to do with the recognition by the United States of the Soviet government of Russia.

Secretary Hull was determined to retain in office in the Department all the experienced officials of merit, so that very few changes in personnel were made in the heads of divisions. Green Hackworth remained Legal Adviser and Herbert Feis, Economic Adviser. Stanley K. Hornbeck continued to direct the Division of Far Eastern Affairs and Wallace Murray remained at the head of the Division of Near Eastern Affairs. Career officers Edwin C. Wilson, Jay Pierrepont Moffat, and Herschel V. Johnson were retained as Chiefs of the Divisions of Latin American Affairs, Western European Affairs, and Mexican Affairs. Robert F. Kelley, a former Foreign Service officer who as Chief of the Division of Eastern European Affairs for seven years had been furnishing arguments against the recognition of the USSR, now was continued in office with instructions to show good reasons why the Soviet government should be recognized. Clinton MacEachran, a Foreign Service officer, remained as Chief Clerk and Administrative Assistant; Michael J. McDermott in charge of press relations; and Hunter Miller as Historical Adviser. The two outstanding feminine Chiefs of Division, Ruth B. Shipley at the head of Passports and Margaret M. Hanna in charge of Coordination and Review, were retained.

Cordell Hull in his *Memoirs* has painted a graphic picture of the Department's organization and procedure in the early days of his incumbency. He usually reached his office about nine o'clock in the morning. Immediately his secretary, able and experienced career officer Harry McBride,[10] brought in the important communications from ambassadors, ministers, and consuls abroad which analyzed conditions in the areas in which they were stationed. After going over these, the Secretary received a confidential report of the Departmental activities of the preceding day with suitable suggestions. As far as possible Secretary Hull made decisions on the problems presented without further consideration and issued the necessary instructions for their execution. The most important might require consultation with the policy-making officials of the Department and final consideration by the President himself. Secretary Hull did not limit his conferences to the top-level officials. He called in every person in the Department conversant with the subject and requested his opinion upon the problem. Secretary Hull believed that it was not possible to consult too many qualified persons and he followed this policy consistently.

An ordinary list of the day's engagements would include ambassadors, ministers, cabinet members, senators, representatives, Departmental officials, and Foreign Service officers returned from abroad. But the regular engagements were constantly being changed by emergency questions which required a complete rearrangement of the time schedule. On Monday mornings at eleven o'clock a meeting of all the principal policy officers was held in the Secretary's office to summarize existing conditions and to plan ahead for desirable action. These officers included the Under Secretary, the Assistant Secretaries, the Legal Adviser, the Economic Adviser, and the political advisers or heads of geographical divisions for all parts of the world. Secretary Hull inaugurated the system of daily press conferences, and no matter how busy he was he always insisted upon having a certain time to receive representatives of the press and radio. The burden of work was so heavy that Secretary Hull regularly took papers and documents home to study them at night, and his Sunday mornings were often spent at the office, either alone or discussing important questions with the key officials of the Department.

In his relations with the diplomatic corps Secretary Hull believed in a policy of complete frankness. Shortly after he took office as Secretary of State, he received the entire diplomatic corps of some seventy members individually and assured each one that he intended to deal with him openly and tell him the exact truth. The Secretary insisted that his subordinates follow the same policy. In order to have more time to see the foreign representatives personally, Secretary Hull, from the very beginning, refused almost all luncheon and dinner engagements. He frankly explained his reasons for this policy and the diplomatic corps accepted it as a reasonable procedure.

Diplomatic Appointments

In the appointment of American ambassadors and ministers President Roosevelt took the major responsibility, but Secretary Hull urged the President to make at least 50 per cent of the appointments from career men in the Foreign Service. The top diplomatic post, the ambassadorship to Great Britain, was given to Robert W. Bingham, the publisher of the Louisville *Courier-Journal* and a substantial contributor to the Democratic campaign fund. Bingham was much admired by Colonel House and his name had been mentioned for the position of Secretary of State. Both Secretary Hull and Secretary of Commerce Daniel C. Roper recommended Bingham for the London post. Although inexperienced in diplomacy, Mr. Bingham had studied in Germany and had traveled often and extensively in Europe. He had many friends in Great Britain and had spent many summers in the British Isles.

Another heavy contributor to the Roosevelt campaign chest, Jesse Straus, president of the R. H. Macy store in New York, was named ambassador to France. Straus had been led to believe that he would be named Secretary of Commerce, but when McAdoo insisted that Roper be given a cabinet position, Straus was offered the Paris post.[11] This post requires a very considerable personal outlay to maintain the position of ambassador adequately, and according to Mr. Straus he called a family conference and requested their views as to whether they were willing that he spend a part of what they might ultimately receive in maintaining the prestige of the United States in France. The family approved his acceptance.

An appointment which caused considerable comment was the choice of Josephus Daniels as ambassador to Mexico. Daniels had been Secretary of the Navy under Woodrow Wilson, and the Assistant Secretary of the Navy was Franklin D. Roosevelt. The President wished to honor his former chief and Daniels was informed that an ambassadorship might be offered. Forgetting completely, as did the President, that the shelling of Vera Cruz had been ordered by himself as Secretary of the Navy, Daniels informed Secretary of Commerce Roper that if an ambassadorship was to be offered he would prefer to go to Mexico. The appointment was made, and in spite of protests by the American colony and the Mexican Communists, the *agrément* was speedily granted. The Mexican government had not forgotten Vera Cruz, but it also remembered who was Assistant Secretary of the Navy at the time of the incident.[12]

One of the most difficult posts to fill at this time was the Berlin embassy. The rise of Adolf Hitler and the Nazi government took away the glamor of the post for the wealthy campaign-contributor type. Furthermore, the situation required an able official who would protect American interests and report the political developments of the Nazi regime intelligently and objectively. The position was first offered to former presidential candidate James M. Cox, but he declined. Other names were mentioned—Dave Hennen Morris, who was later appointed as ambassador to Belgium, and Robert P. Skinner, an able and experienced career officer who was named ambassador to Turkey. Finally, on June 13, 1933, President Roosevelt, upon the advice of Secretary of Commerce Daniel C. Roper, named Professor William E. Dodd of the University of Chicago. Dr. Dodd had studied in Germany and held a doctor's degree from the University of Leipzig. He was an outstanding historian and had just been elected president of the American Historical Association. With Dodd as ambassador and the outstandingly able George S. Messersmith as consul general in Berlin, the Department of State was kept accurately and completely informed of the sinister development of the Nazi threat to world peace.

A number of career diplomats were retained in their posts, notably Joseph C. Grew in Japan, Nelson T. Johnson in China, Fred M. Dearing in Peru, and Hugh Wilson in Switzerland—the last a Republican. Hugh S. Gibson, another Republican and career diplomat of long experience, who had made a signal success as ambassador to Belgium, was not expected to be retained because of his close friendship with President Hoover. Secretary Hull, however, was able to retain his services by sending him as ambassador to Brazil. Alexander W. Weddell, a former career officer, was named to Argentina to replace Robert Woods Bliss, who retired after thirty years of diplomatic service abroad. Out of fifteen ambassadorships filled, five were career officers; out of thirty-four legations, sixteen were filled from the Foreign Service.

It was not possible, nor did dispenser of patronage Postmaster General Farley think it desirable, to overlook the supporters of the party in choice diplomatic appointments. Claude G. Bowers had written and spoken very effectively for the Democratic party, and he wanted a quiet diplomatic post to continue his literary activities. When Farley, Moley, and President Roosevelt all looked favorably upon Bowers's request to be made ambassador to Spain, his appointment was assured. Less satisfactory political appointments were George H. Earle, III, to Austria, and Henry H. Sevier to Chile. Mayor Jim Curley of Boston wanted to go to Rome as ambassador, but Under Secretary of State Phillips was so strongly opposed that President Roosevelt decided to name the experienced Breckinridge Long, who had been offered and refused the position of Assistant Secretary of State.[13] William C. Bullitt finally achieved his ambition to go as ambassador to Moscow, but he quickly found that his ardent aid in obtaining recognition of the Soviet government went wholly unappreciated by the rulers in the Kremlin. President Roosevelt broke a precedent by naming a woman, Ruth Bryan Owen, as minister to Denmark. Since 1924 women had been eligible to enter the Foreign Service, but outside of one notable exception, Frances Willis, no woman had made a real success in the career service. It was rumored that Mrs. Owen had been chosen to be Assistant Secretary of State, but that Secretary Hull did not listen kindly to the suggestion.

In addition to the regular diplomatic corps, President Roosevelt from time to time utilized special agents who were sent as his personal representatives, usually on *ad hoc* missions. Harry Hopkins often served in this capacity, and numerous others, such as Patrick J. Hurley, William J. Donovan, Henry Wallace, Myron C. Taylor, and W. Averell Harriman. Neither the Department of State nor the heads of missions abroad approved of this practice, but they were in no position to object. Secretary Hull felt that the sending of these special envoys "tended in many instances to create havoc with our ambassadors or ministers in the capitals they visited, even though the envoys themselves had no such intention." [14]

Changes in Organization

Owing to the need to utilize more fully the services of Dr. Hunter Miller, the Historical Adviser on matters of policy relating to current questions before the Department, a new division was established by a Departmental order dated November 1, 1933, named Division of Research and Publication. Its functions included preparation of the *Foreign Relations of the United States* series; supervision of the Department's library; supervision of the work of the Editor of the *Territorial Papers of the United States*; editing and compiling the Session Laws, Statutes at Large, Executive Orders and Proclamations; and the preparation and distribution of Departmental publications. Dr. Cyril Wynne, a former Foreign Service officer and onetime Assistant Solicitor in the Department, was named as Chief of the new division. Dr. E. Wilder Spaulding was appointed Assistant Chief. Dr. Hunter Miller continued to edit the great treaty collection of the United States, which bears his name, in addition to his advisory duties.

The Trade Agreement Program

Secretary of State Hull had long been an active crusader for the reduction of tariff barriers between nations, and almost immediately after taking office the Department of State drafted a bill for submission to the Congress which would authorize the President to negotiate reciprocal trade agreements on a most-favored-nation-clause basis. The President directed that an Executive Committee on Commercial Policy be formed, with representatives from The Departments of Treasury, Commerce, and Agriculture and other interested agencies, and with the State Department's representative serving as chairman. Under Secretary Phillips served as temporary chairman until Assistant Secretary of State Sayre became the permanent chairman. This committee was won over to Hull's point of view and drafted a trade-agreements bill which fully supported Secretary Hull's stand. The bill was approved on June 12, 1934. To carry out its provisions, a Departmental order, dated May 27, 1935, established a Division of Trade Agreements in the Department of State and Secretary Hull placed the new division under the direction of Dr. Henry F. Grady. The appointment was an excellent one inasmuch as the new Chief was not only a strong advocate of lower tariffs, but his experience included work as trade commissioner and commercial attaché abroad, and in the Bureau of Foreign and Domestic Commerce at home.

The new division was given three Assistant Chiefs, twelve officers, and fifteen clerks to do the work of coordinating the efforts of the various governmental agencies concerned with carrying out the trade-agreements program. Within a year it had expanded to twenty-four officers, including the Chief and his Assistants and twenty-nine clerks. On August 1, 1936, Harry C. Hawkins, the Assistant Chief, was promoted to head of the division, and Secretary Hull later declared that Hawkins was a "tower of strength" to the Department throughout the development of the trade-agreements program.

The personnel of the Department of State did a magnificent job in explaining the program to the American people. Secretary Hull, Under Secretary Phillips, Assistant Secretary Sayre, Assistant Secretary Welles, Dr. Grady, Alvin H. Hansen, Green Hackworth, Wallace McClure, Henry L. Deimel, and Lynn R. Edminster gave addresses covering every phase of the program, and the publicity this obtained did much to secure congressional approval when the program came up for renewal. The success of the reciprocal trade agreements-program was a great personal victory for Secretary Hull over the resolute opposition of isolationists, protectionists, and New Dealers, and in spite of the wavering support of an opportunist President.

New Machinery and Procedure

Another new agency established in the Department in the fall of 1935 also resulted from an Act of Congress. As a means of keeping the United

States out of foreign wars, a joint resolution of Congress, approved August 31, 1935, prohibited the export of munitions and implements of war to belligerent countries,[15] and provided for the registration and licensing of persons engaged in the manufacture, export, or import of implements of war. A National Munitions Control Board, consisting of the Secretary of State as chairman and the Secretaries of Treasury, War, Navy, and Commerce Departments as members, was to direct the execution of the resolution. To administer this directive, Secretary Hull, by a Departmental order dated September 19, 1935, established the Office of Arms and Munitions Control in the Department of State whose duty it was to register all manufacturers, exporters, and importers of implements of war, and to issue licenses for exportation and importation of arms and implements of war under such regulations as might be promulgated by the Secretary of State. The Chief of the new agency was Joseph C. Green, an officer in the Division of Western European Affairs in the Department of State.

The last agency in the Department of State to be established during the first administration of President Roosevelt was the Office of Philippine Affairs, which was set up to carry out the provisions of the Philippine Independence Act of March 24, 1934, in so far as they related to the Department of State. The Chief of the Office was Joseph E. Jacobs, a Foreign Service officer of more than twenty years' experience in the Far East.

A few changes occurred in the geographical divisions as a result of the requirement that career Foreign Service officers could not remain in the Department for more than four years continuously: James C. Dunn relieved Jay Pierrepont Moffat as Chief of the Division of Western European Affairs, Edward L. Reed was transferred from the field in place of Herschel V. Johnson as Chief of the Division of Mexican Affairs, and Laurence Duggan, a non-career appointee, became Chief of the Division of Latin American Affairs in place of career officer Edwin C. Wilson. Duggan's appointment was a well merited but exceptionally speedy promotion for the Department of State. Entering the Department as a Divisional Assistant on November 1, 1930, at a salary of $3,200, in less than five years he had been made Chief of Division at $8,000—a record for rapid advancement in the State Department up to this time. Two other changes which occurred during this period should be noted. Foreign Service officer John Farr Simmons was brought in from the field and became Chief of the Visa Division, relieving Foreign Service officer A. Dana Hodgdon, who was assigned as consul at Moscow, and Foreign Service officer Richard Southgate was advanced from Assistant Chief to Chief of the Division of Protocol and Conferences when its former Chief James C. Dunn was appointed Special Assistant to the Secretary of State.

The President and Foreign Policy

In his inaugural address of March 4, 1933, President Roosevelt gave no evidence of his keen interest in foreign affairs. In this speech of over eighteen hundred words only fifty-four related to foreign policy—the sentence in which he dedicated this nation to the policy of the good neighbor.[16] President Roosevelt was so beset by domestic problems during his first term that he left Mr. Hull in almost full charge of foreign affairs. The Secretary of State kept the President completely informed on all major developments, but the President expected Secretary Hull to furnish the initiative in policy and action.[17] In fact, throughout his tenure in the State Department Secretary Hull found that in the majority of cases he had to make his own decisions. The President only made one visit to the Department of State, and that was after hours to look over offices to be used by some of his "anonymous assistants."

The question of disarmament was one of the first confronting the new administration. The two American delegates, Norman Davis and Hugh Gibson, felt that unless the United States should make some positive declaration the conference was headed for failure. Both the President and the Secretary of State favored action to support the policy of arms limitation, and the President decided to send an appeal direct to the heads of all the states, urging support of both the disarmament conference and the coming economic conference. The State Department cooperated both in the preparation and dispatch of this appeal. On May 22, Secretary Hull cabled Ambassador Norman Davis the authorization to supplement the President's appeal by a statement that the United States was prepared to consult with other nations in the event of a threat to peace, and to refrain from any action tending to defeat collective action against a state which should violate its international obligation. To carry out this pledge an effort was made, as had been made previously in the Hoover administration, to obtain legislation giving the President the right to embargo shipments of arms to any aggressor state. Secretary Hull appealed personally to the leaders of the House Committee on Foreign Affairs and of the Senate Committee on Foreign Relations. The House passed the resolution in the form desired by the State Department, but the Senate changed it to a blanket embargo on arms to all belligerents. Since such a procedure nullified all the value of an embargo against the aggressor state, the Department ceased to be interested in its passage.

Secretary Hull was more successful in obtaining the approval by the Senate of the Convention for the Supervision of the International Trade in Arms and Ammunition and in Implements of War which had been signed by the United States in 1925. Unfortunately the Senate had added a reservation, suggested by the Persian minister and introduced by Senator King of Utah without consulting the State Department, conceding any rights of sovereignty which Persia might have in the Persian Gulf. The State Department could not accept this reservation, and Secretary Hull informed the Persian minister that his action in by-passing the State Department was inexcusable. The Convention was finally approved without the King reservation, but the long delay was fatal to obtaining the requisite number of ratifications.[18] In spite of its failure to obtain international cooperation, the Department of State was able to exert considerable pressure to prevent the export of arms from the United States to Germany by a public statement declaring that this government would view such exportation with grave disapproval.

The Department of State was considerably handicapped in one phase of the trade in arms by the Nye Commission of the Senate, which was investigating the munitions industry. In its efforts to obtain headline publicity the committee did not hesitate to publish confidential documents which had been furnished by the Department of State with the definite understanding that they were to remain confidential. Secretary Hull informed Senator Nye on various occasions that the publication of communications from other governments without their permission violated international comity, but the committee paid little attention. As a result the Department was bombarded with protests from the representatives of foreign governments. Secretary Hull appealed to the President with little result, and finally decided that the Department would cooperate henceforth with the committee only upon the assurance of mutuality.[19]

The London Economic Conference

The second and third problems mentioned by President Roosevelt as vital to recovery were the reduction of trade barriers and the stabilization of currency. It was hoped that the forthcoming World Economic and Financial Conference to be held in London in the summer of 1933, under the sponsorship of the League of Nations, would take effective action in both of these fields. It was evident that the President intended to keep close control of the American delegation and that he did not expect much in the way of results. In fact, about ten days before the delegation sailed, a radio address made by Assistant Secretary of State Moley without the permission of, or consultation with, Secretary Hull, questioned the possibility of reducing tariff barriers and seemed to discount the beneficial results of the conference.[20]

The delegation, chosen by the President without consulting with Secretary Hull, who was its chairman ex-officio, was a heterogeneous group including Key Pittman, chairman of the Senate Foreign Relations Committee, who favored high tariffs, and Representative Samuel D. McReynolds, chairman of the Foreign Affairs Committee of the House, a low-tariff advocate. Its vice chairman was former Democratic Governor of Ohio James M. Cox, an internationalist; and a fourth member was Republican Senator James Couzens, an isolationist. William Bullitt, Special Assistant to the Secretary of State, was the chief executive officer, and Herbert Feis, Economic Adviser of the State Department, was the chief technical adviser. Most of the other experts, such as the financial adviser James P. Warburg and the technical advisers Charles W. Taussig and Rexford G. Tugwell, were picked from the group of New Dealers who were confidential advisers to the President. Since Secretary Hull had not chosen the delegates, he could neither instruct them nor prevent them from making individual statements to the press.

The conference proved to be a complete fiasco and was perhaps the most serious setback encountered by Secretary Hull during his twelve years as Secretary of State. The blame for its failure rested to a very considerable extent upon the vacillating and inept policies of the President of the United States. Hardly had Secretary Hull sailed before President Roosevelt reneged on his implied promise to support the State Department bill authorizing the negotiation of reciprocal trade agreements permitting substantial tariff reductions, such agreements not to require senatorial approval. Such a refusal took away one of the most important possibilities entertained by Secretary Hull to start the world back to mutually advantageous trade relations. The next gaff was the sending of Assistant Secretary of State Moley as liaison officer, but with all the appearance of being the personal and confidential representative of the President. Moley was received with the greatest enthusiasm by the foreign officials and popularly vested with an authority and position which he himself neither claimed nor sought. It was an embarrassing situation for the Secretary of State, but he accepted it and made the most of it. However, by the time that Assistant Secretary Moley had worked out what he regarded as a completely innocuous stabilization agreement, President Roosevelt had conferred with other advisers at home, and in what was known as a "bombshell message" he repudiated the recommendations of his "liaison officer." Only the most arduous diplomatic endeavors of the American Embassy and a moving plea on the part of Secretary Hull prevented the conference from adjourning immediately after passing a resolution placing the full responsibility for the failure of the conference at the door of the United States. Assistant Secretary Moley returned to the United States soon afterward and resigned from the Department.[21]

An unfortunate aftermath of hard feelings resulted when excerpts from a critical confidential report upon the American delegation, made by Assistant Secretary Moley to the President, were shown to the members of the delegation. President Roosevelt attempted to placate the justifiable resentment of Secretary Hull by declaring: "Secretary Hull with magnificent force prevented the Conference from final adjournment and made it possible . . . for a renewal of its discussions in the broad field of international relationships." [22] Even the press for once did not place the blame for a diplomatic failure upon either the Secretary or the Department of State.

The Montevideo Conference

After the failure of both the Disarmament Conference at Geneva and the Economic Conference in London, it appeared as though the forthcoming International Conference of American States, which was to convene in Montevideo in December, 1933, would have little chance to succeed. Secretary Hull was far from being optimistic, but he felt that the conference should be held and that he should head the American delegation. He was determined, however, to have something to say regarding the personnel of the delegation. President Roosevelt agreed to let him choose both the delegates and the experts, and except for Dr. Sophonisba P. Breckinridge, who was appointed at the request of Mrs. Roosevelt, all the delegates and experts were authorities in the Latin American field. The official delegation consisted of Secretary of State Cordell Hull, former Under Secretary of State J. Reuben Clark, Jr., who had also served as ambassador to Mexico; J. Butler Wright, a career diplomat and at the time minister to Uruguay, and Spruille Braden, a businessman with wide experience in Latin America. Secretary Hull could be assured that this delegation would function cooperatively as a team and that he could count upon their wholehearted support at all times.

Secretary Hull and the Department of State fared much better in Montevideo than they had in London at the Economic Conference. In the first place President Roosevelt and Secretary Hull held identical views in favoring a Good Neighbor Policy. As is often the case, it was the Department of State which prepared the President's Pan American Day speech of April 12, 1933, wherein he redefined his Good Neighbor Policy as possessing the essential qualities of a true Pan Americanism, and defined the Monroe Doctrine as a "Pan American doctrine of continental defense." [23] Secretary Hull had helped draft the plank in the Democratic platform of 1932 advocating "no interference in the internal affairs of other nations." In the second place Secretary Hull had been able to get the President's support of a resolution looking toward lower tariffs, and the abolition of trade restrictions. And, finally, Secretary Hull was eager to give as well as take, and was in a position to prove it. Instead of waiting for the formal calls required by protocol, he went informally to make the first calls upon the heads of every Latin American delegation. He accepted the Argentine Antiwar Pact. He invited the Argentine delegate, Carlos Saavedra Lamos, to make the speech urging acceptance of the various unsigned treaties in the maintenance of peace, including her own. As proof of its serious purpose, Secretary Hull pledged the promise of the United States against intervention during the Roosevelt administration. By submerging himself and the American delegation in order to obtain wholehearted cooperative action for the welfare of all, instead of personal prestige and praise, Secretary Hull made the Good Neighbor Policy a vital force for better understanding in the Americas.

The Good Neighbor Policy in Action

Throughout the administration of the State Department by Secretary Hull, every effort was made to implement the Good Neighbor Policy. In doing so, Secretary Hull not only had the constant and effective assistance of Assistant Secretary Sumner Welles, but also of an outstanding group of experts in the Division of Latin American Affairs, including its Chief Edwin C. Wilson, the Assistant Chief Joseph F. McGurk, and Willard L. Beaulac, all career Foreign Service officers, and a number of officers not in the Foreign Service, such as Laurence Duggan, Warren Kelchner, and William R. Manning.

When the Department of State suggested that it might be advantageous to call an extraordinary Inter-American Conference devoted entirely to the maintenance of peace in the Western Hemisphere, President Roosevelt quickly fell in with the idea. To give the proposal additional prominence, he decided to violate protocol and write directly to the presidents of the neighboring republics instead of going through the Department of State. He also decided to attend the opening of the conference in person and deliver the speech of welcome. To get Argentine cooperation it was suggested that the conference be held in Buenos Aires. The agenda as prepared by the Department of State emphasized particularly the need of consultation in case of the threat of war.

Secretary Hull again served as chairman of the American delegation, and Assistant Secretary Welles and Ambassador to Argentina Weddell were the ranking delegates. Other members of the Department on the delegation were Mr. Southgate, Chief of the Division of Protocol and Conferences, who acted as secretary general; Mr. Reed, Chief of the Division of Mexican Affairs, who was assistant to the chairman; the special adviser R. Henry Norweb, United States minister to Bolivia, and Dr. Feis, economic adviser; the technical advisers Messrs. Baker, Carr, Kelchner, and Stinebower and Marjorie Whiteman. However, in spite of President Roosevelt's request for cooperation for peace in the opening address and Secretary Hull's efforts to obtain a consultative pact with machinery to make it effective, the Argentinians were adamantly opposed. The Department of State was disappointed but not discouraged.

The Recognition of Russia

The problem of recognizing the Union of the Socialist Soviet Republics had faced every President and Secretary of State from the time of its establishment in 1917, and it faced President Roosevelt and Secretary Hull. The Secretary of State favored it both because of the uncertain world situation and because he wanted the two great nations to be on friendly terms. Nevertheless, since it was known that Russia was eager for recognition, Secretary Hull felt that certain conditions ought to be met first—particularly as regards payment of debts, noninterference in domestic matters, and religious freedom—before discussing the question of recognition. President Roosevelt agreed with the principles but not with the procedure. He preferred to consider the two questions at the same time. Also, the President decided to deal with President Kalinin directly rather than through the channels of the Department of State; he therefore sent a personal letter to the Soviet president, offering to receive a representative from Russia to discuss all outstanding questions.[24] President Kalinin agreed and forthwith dispatched Maxim Litvinov.

The Division of Eastern European Affairs, headed by Robert F. Kelley, was assigned the task of drafting a treaty. Kelley and his assistants, who were for the most part experienced Foreign Service officers personally familiar with the Russian psychology, examined some twenty-six treaties which Soviet Russia had signed with other governments and prepared the draft, using the identical phraseology found in sentences which fitted the case. It was a clever procedure, because when Litvinov later protested that Russia could not agree to certain provisions, he was informed that his government had already done so, and the case was cited. Under Secretary of State Phillips and Special Assistant Bullitt worked with President Roosevelt and Secretary Hull before Litvinov's arrival; and when Secretary Hull left for Montevideo, Assistant Secretary Walton Moore was charged with preparing the final draft. Before the Secretary left, he and President Roosevelt agreed that if negotiations succeeded, William Bullitt would be named as the first ambassador from the United States to Soviet Russia. The exchange of notes and recognition took place, but the results were unsatisfactory. The Soviet government's interpretation of the debt payment differed from the Department of State's, and it made no effort to prevent the propaganda of the Third International in the United States. The sole advantage of recognition was to strengthen the Far Eastern position of the United States as regards Japan, and that only temporarily.

The Department Feels the Depression

Both the Department of State and the Foreign Service of the United States were seriously handicapped during the first Roosevelt administration by the financial depression. The work of the Department both at home and abroad constantly increased, nevertheless the cuts in appropriations necessitated a diminished personnel. The total budget for the Department of State for the years 1931 and 1932 was approximately $18,000,000, while for 1933 it was about $13,500,000, and for 1936 about $16,000,000. It was not until 1937 that the amount appropriated topped the 1931-1932 levels.[25] The situation as to the personnel of the Department of State in Washington was not nearly as serious as the conditions of the personnel abroad.

The result of the Roosevelt administration going off the gold standard and its revaluation of the dollar had a dire effect upon the American Foreign Service. It meant a reduction in salaries of over 50 per cent, inasmuch as in addition to the depreciation of the value of the dollar there was the 15 per cent cut in all governmental salaries and a reduction of 65 per cent in rental allowances. Assistant Secretary Carr, in a hearing before the Committee on Foreign Affairs of the House, declared that "the distress in the Foreign Service today is greater than at any time within the memory of those of us in the Department of State." He then proceeded to illustrate with the specific examples of one ambassador having a mental breakdown as a result of worry, of a minister who had to remove his children from school and defer payments on his life-insurance policy, of a consul general who had to sell his automobile and send his wife and baby to the United States, one case of insanity, and at least one case of suicide.[26]

As a result of the strenuous efforts of Secretary Hull and Assistant Secretary Carr and the friendly publicity of the press, the Congress restored post allowances and allowed a substantial increase in rent allowances. The exchange bill of March 26, 1934, took care of the losses due to devaluation and exchange conditions incurred by Foreign Service officers abroad. President Roosevelt subsequently refused to believe that the cost of living in Venezuela as claimed by Foreign Service officers was over 100 per cent higher than in Washington, D. C. and asked Harry Hopkins to find out without letting the State Department know. A report proved that the State Department's figures were correct.[27]

The Congress also restored 5 per cent of the salary cut on February 1, 1934, and another 5 per cent on July 1 of the same year. The State Department appropriation bill for 1936 permitted the restoration of the final 5 per cent cut. On September 16, 1935, Secretary Hull announced that the first promotions of Foreign Service officers in the upper grades would be effective on October

1, 1935, and that the first new appointments since March 28, 1932, to the number of forty-three, would be made on the following day.[28]

According to a study made of the Department's organization and work by the Division of Research and Publications, the total number of employees in the Department in Washington as of January 1, 1936, was 753, and the number of divisions, offices, and bureaus was 33. As of the same date there were 3,662 employees abroad in 57 diplomatic missions and 288 consular offices.[29]

26

Secretary Hull Carries On

Personnel and Organization Changes

The reelection of Franklin D. Roosevelt in November, 1936, brought few changes in the personnel of the Department of State. Secretary of State Cordell Hull had done an outstanding job, and no suggestion of a change was made even in the press. The principal problem facing the Secretary in regard to personnel was to fill the position of Under Secretary of State. Ambassador Breckinridge Long had asked to be relieved of his post at Rome and Under Secretary of State William Phillips had been sent as his successor. A long delay arose in filling the post of Under Secretary due to the rivalry between Assistant Secretaries Welles and Moore to obtain the appointment. Secretary Hull preferred his old friend, R. Walton Moore, who had served as Secretary of State while Hull attended the conference at Buenos Aires. However, he hesitated to make a recommendation since he felt that President Roosevelt preferred Welles. After a delay of over six months, the problem was settled by the reestablishment of the position of Counselor, to which Moore was appointed, and Welles was made Under Secretary. The two positions were equal in rank and salary— $10,000 a year—except that in the absence of the Secretary, the Under Secretary became Acting Secretary of State. The Congress was not adverse to the change inasmuch as the Department had agreed not to fill the post of Assistant Secretary which had been vacated by Judge Moore.

Two new Assistant Secretaries were needed, one to fill the position held formerly by Assistant Secretary Welles, and the second to fill that of Assistant Secretary Carr. The latter, after forty-five years of service in the Department under seventeen different Secretaries of State, had been named minister to Czechoslovakia so that he might have for a brief period, at least, the experience of serving at the transmitting end of the line. It was hardly expected that a little more than a year after his arrival Czechoslovakia would be "sold down the river" and that his mission would end with the downfall of the state to which

328

he was accredited. To take his place, Secretary Hull appointed career officer George S. Messersmith, who had recently done an excellent job of protecting Americans as consul general in Berlin and as minister in Vienna. Mr. Messersmith was fully conversant with the European situation, and his reports had accurately foretold the progress of Hitler's aggression. In making the appointment Secretary Hull declared: "I consider him as the most capable person in the Service who is available for such an assignment." [1] The other Assistant Secretary named was Hugh R. Wilson, a Foreign Service officer who at the time was the United States minister to Switzerland. Wilson had been in the diplomatic service for some twenty-five years. It was understood that his duties would be for the most part in the field of policy making, whereas Messersmith would be concerned with the administration of the Department.

In his conference with the press on May 21, 1937, Secretary Hull declared that for some two years he and his colleagues had been contemplating certain readjustments and changes looking toward greater efficiency, both in the Foreign Service and in the Department. Steps had already been taken to weed out some forty to fifty Foreign Service officers who were not up to the desired standard. It was now proposed to send certain members of the State Department out into the field to get a refresher course in the work of a diplomat and consul abroad. It was also proposed to amalgamate certain agencies and to coordinate the work of others.[2] On the same day a Departmental order was issued consolidating the Division of Latin American Affairs and the Division of Mexican Affairs into a single agency to be designated Division of the American Republics. Laurence Duggan was named Chief of the new division, and the three Assistant Chiefs were Willard L. Beaulac, Donald R. Heath, and Richard C. Tanis. The first two were experienced Foreign Service officers, and the latter had been in the Department for twenty-seven years, during most of which he had served as Assistant Chief of the Division of Mexican Affairs.

In similar fashion, on June 15, Departmental orders were issued which combined the Western European Division, the Eastern European Division, and the Near Eastern Division into two divisions to be designated as the Division of European Affairs and the Division of Near Eastern Affairs. The first of these was increased materially in size, from twelve officers and seven clerks to eighteen officers and thirteen clerks. James C. Dunn was made Chief and he was assigned four Assistant Chiefs: John Hickerson, Paul T. Culbertson, Harold H. Tittmann, Jr., and Orsen N. Nielsen. The first two had been Assistant Chiefs of the Division of Western European Affairs, and the last two were career Foreign Service officers. The Division of Near Eastern Affairs remained almost unchanged with Wallace Murray as Chief, and Paul H. Alling and Maynard B. Barnes as Assistant Chiefs. It might be noted in passing that a woman, Amy C. Holland, had risen from clerk to divisional assistant in this division, the only woman who had as yet broken into the ranks of the policy-making officers in the Department.

A new agency, called the Office of Fiscal and Budget Affairs, was created by a Departmental order on July 6, 1937, to be responsible for all budgetary matters of the Department. Its Chief would be expected to help prepare the Department's budget and then justify it in the hearings before Congress. Charles B. Hosmer was appointed Chief of the office, and Ella A. Logsdon, Assistant Chief. The office was to function directly under the Assistant Secretary of State in charge of administration.

Perhaps the greatest innovation of the reorganization of 1937 was the attempt to give more opportunity to the ranking officials to consider long-term policies, instead of being forced to devote all of their time and energies to immediate problems of policy and administration. The reestablishment of the position of Counselor was a step in this direction by relieving the Secretary of certain difficult technical legal questions. Another move was to establish a group of advisers whose functions would be essentially analytical and advisory in the formulation of policy. The first of these advisers was set up by a Departmental order on June 17, 1937, under the designation of Adviser on International Economic Affairs, and Dr. Herbert Feis, formerly Chief of the Office of Economic Affairs, was appointed. Subsequently, similar advisers on political affairs were appointed on a regional basis, James C. Dunn, who had been Chief of the Division of European Affairs, and Stanley K. Hornbeck, formerly Chief of the Division of Far Eastern Affairs. Two more Advisers of Political Relations were subsequently appointed, Laurence Duggan, Chief of the Division of American Republics, on October 24, 1940, and Wallace Murray on March 13, 1942. The results were not as satisfactory as had been hoped, because it was difficult for these advisers—all of whom had been Chiefs of political divisions—to surrender entirely their former administrative tasks. As a consequence they found themselves carrying on a considerable amount of their former work on a slightly higher level.

The other changes made in the reorganization of 1937 were for the most part routine changes of personnel. An exception should be made, perhaps, in regard to the Division of Protocol and Conferences, which was again divided into its component parts on July 29, 1937, as a result of the increased work in both fields. The history of this agency seems to be one of marriage and divorce. The Division of Protocol, set up in 1928, became the Division of International Conferences and Protocol in 1929. It was split into two divisions in 1931, and the two were joined together again in 1933. By the latest order the Division of International Conferences was made responsible for matters pertaining to international civil aviation in addition to its duties in regard to international conferences. Richard Southgate, a former Foreign Service officer and former Chief of the Division of Protocol and Conferences, was named head of the new division. The new Division of Protocol had charge of all matters pertaining to ceremonial, and George T. Summerlin, a career officer serving currently as minister to Panama, was named Chief.

Several of the old civil-service employees in the Department, who had served for many years in their positions, were made Foreign Service officers and sent to the field. Robert F. Kelley, who before becoming Chief of the Division of Eastern European Affairs in 1928 had been in and out of the Foreign Service, was again sent to the field as first secretary in Istanbul. Herbert C. Hengstler, Chief of the Division of Foreign Service Administration, who had entered the Department as a clerk in 1898, was given the status of Foreign Service officer of Class 1 and sent as consul general to Toronto. Career officer Nathaniel P. Davis was given Hengstler's position in the Department. Margaret M. Hanna, who had served in the Department three years longer than Mr. Hengstler and had been Chief of the Office of Coordination and Review for thirteen years, was made Foreign Service officer of Class 5 and assigned to Geneva. Just before her departure Miss Hanna, in collaboration with Alice M. Ball, had completed the preparation of the Department of State Correspondence Manual, an invaluable guide to the officers of the Department in the drafting of correspondence. Blanche Rule Halla, who had been in the Department some twenty years and Assistant Chief of the office since 1928, was promoted to be Chief.

Other routine changes in the Department during 1937 occurred in the Division of Foreign Service Personnel, where Foreign Service Officer G. Howland Shaw replaced Chief Thomas M. Wilson, who by law was required to return to the field. Clinton E. MacEachran, who had been acting as Chief Clerk and Administrative Assistant since 1933, was assigned to Halifax as consul general, and a lawyer from the United States and Mexican Claims Commission, Edward Yardley, took the post in the Department. The Director of the Foreign Service Officers' Training School, Lowell C. Pinkerton was sent abroad, and J. Klahr Huddle returned from Warsaw to take his place. One notable change occurred when William McNeir, Chief of the Bureau of Accounts, retired on April 30, 1937, after more than fifty-five years in the service. He had been Chief of the Rolls and Library and Chief Clerk before taking over the Bureau of Accounts. Secretary Hull wrote him a cordial letter of appreciation, and his colleagues presented him with a silver punch bowl and silver cup in honor of his long and excellent service. In all of these changes experience and merit were regularly the basis of appointment, and the purposes of the Rogers Act of 1924 and the Moses-Linthicum Act of 1931, to exchange officers between the Department and the field, were most faithfully observed in practice.

Changes in Diplomatic Personnel

Very few changes in the diplomatic representation abroad came as a result of the Roosevelt reelection. A few important changes had occurred earlier. When Jesse Isidor Straus resigned as ambassador to France because of health, William Bullitt was transferred from Moscow to Paris, and Joseph E. Davies was appointed ambassador to Russia; also, when Breckinridge Long resigned as ambassador to Italy, William Phillips was named to succeed him. Perhaps the most noteworthy political appointment was that of Florence Jaffray Harriman, vice chairman of the Democratic National Committee, as minister to Norway. She succeeded Anthony Joseph Drexel Biddle, Jr., another political appointee, who had been made ambassador to Poland. Most of the changes made were within the career service, and President Roosevelt, wherever it was possible, promoted outstanding Foreign Service officers to the highest posts in the diplomatic service.

In the period from 1938 until the outbreak of the war in Europe in September, 1939, there were a number of changes of a routine nature which should be noted in the personnel of our diplomatic service. The most important occurred when Ambassador Bingham asked to be relieved of his post at London because of serious illness which brought about his death a week after his resignation. President Roosevelt immediately named Joseph P. Kennedy, chairman of the Maritime Commission, a wealthy but very democratic individual, to this important post; on the same day, January 17, 1938, Assistant Secretary of State Hugh R. Wilson was named ambassador to Germany to fill the post vacated by William E. Dodd. Career officer Norman Armour, who was serving as minister to Canada, was appointed ambassador to Chile. Two appointments outside of the career service occurred when Joseph Davies was transferred from Moscow to Brussels, and when Spruille Braden, a mining engineer with many years' experience in South America, was named ambassador to Colombia. Braden had served with noteworthy success as the chairman of the American delegation at the Chaco Peace Conference in Buenos Aires from 1935 to 1938. The President's brain truster Adolf Berle, Jr., was appointed Assistant Secretary of State to fill the position vacated by Hugh Wilson. The post at Moscow, which had remained vacant since Ambassador Davies had been transferred to Brussels, was finally filled in May, 1939, when Laurence Steinhardt, ambassador to Peru, was transferred to Russia.

The Messersmith Reorganization

No Assistant Secretary of State had ever possessed a broader background of service in the field than George E. Messersmith, and as budget and fiscal officer of the Department, as well as chief administration officer, he was equipped to work out plans for the reorganization of the Department so that it might more effectively try to solve the increasingly numerous and complex problems of world politics.

One of the most important innovations was the establishment of the Division of Cultural Relations in the Department of State by a Departmental order dated July 28, 1938. Until this time the United States had neither cultural nor press attachés in its embassies and legations abroad, nor any agency in the Department of State to stimulate intellectual cooperation between the United States and its sister states. The defined function of this agency was to cultivate closer cultural relations by the exchange of professors, teachers, and students, by the dissemination abroad of representative intellectual and cultural work of the United States, and to cooperate in the fields of music, art, literature, and other intellectual and cultural attainments.

Although the emphasis at first was to be placed upon improving the cultural relations of the United States with its Latin American neighbors, the program was expected ultimately to embrace the entire world. The man chosen to head the new organization was Professor Ben M. Cherrington, chairman of the Department of International Relations at the University of Denver. Dr. Cherrington had traveled widely in Europe and had been a representative of the Institute of International Education at the World Peace Congress in Brussels in 1936. The appointment came to Dr. Cherrington wholly unsolicited. The new division was expected to work closely with the various foundations and as far as possible to stimulate and coordinate their activities.

The other entirely new division created in 1938 to meet a pressing need was the Division of International Communications. This was established on August 19, 1938. The vast improvement in the fields of aviation and telecommunication had raised many problems of an international character, but hitherto these had been handled by experts in the various agencies of the government. The new division was to centralize and coordinate the handling of these activities by placing the various experts in the fields of aviation, shipping, and telecommunications into one division comprising three sections. Thomas Burke, a division Chief in the Department of Commerce with wide foreign experience, was made Chief of the new division.

A slight reorganization was brought about in 1938 in regard to work being done by Hunter Miller, the editor of the definitive collection of treaties and other international acts of the United States. He had just completed the fifth volume of his monumental work, bringing the series up to 1852. Since his work had become primarily limited to the editing and compiling of these instruments, he was given the official title of Editor of Treaties in an office of that name. The other duties of the now defunct Office of the Historical Adviser were transferred to the Division of Research and Publication, including the Office of the Geographer. Carlton Savage, formerly Assistant Historical Adviser, was designated Assistant to the Counselor of State. The archives and documents of the former office, under the direction of able archivist Natalia Summers, were at first put under the custody of the Chief Clerk and then transferred, with Mrs. Summers still in charge, to the National Archives Building.[3] On January 15, 1944, the Office of the Editor of Treaties was abolished and its functions and responsibilities transferred to the Division of Research and Publication.[4]

The State Department and Neutrality Legislation

It will be remembered that beginning in 1933 the Congress, disturbed by the threatening situation in Europe, by the Italian invasion of Ethiopia, and by the Japanese aggression in Manchuria, had passed a series of Acts to keep the United States out of war. The Acts went by the name of neutrality legislation, although in reality they were far more stringent than required by the generally accepted principles of international law. The State Department was opposed to such legislation, since by placing an embargo on the sale of arms it seriously limited the influence of the United States in world affairs. In the spring of 1939 the Department of State felt so strongly that the embargo on arms to belligerents was aiding the aggressive policies of Germany and Japan that Secretary Hull made urgent personal pleas to both Senator Pittman, chairman of the Senate Committee on Foreign Relations, and to Representative Bloom, chairman of the House Committee on Foreign Affairs, to introduce and support legislation repealing the embargo provisions of the neutrality legislation as a deterrent to the dictators' threats to go to war to achieve their ends. The President supported the State Department in its efforts, but the Congress refused to see the danger. Senator Borah went so far as to disparage the State Department sources of information and asserted that reports which had reached him privately made him confident that a European war was not imminent.[5]

The one feature of the neutrality acts strongly favored by the Department was the machinery created to control the traffic in arms and ammunition. The work of the Office of Arms and Ammunition Control was increased to such an extent by the revolution in Spain and by the so-called "cash and carry" provisions of the law of 1937 that it was found necessary to expand the office. By a Departmental order dated November 22, 1938, the office was designated Division of Controls, and its personnel was increased from five officers and six clerks to nine officers and ten clerks. The division could now help initiate policy as well as supervise and administer the contracts established to prevent the involvement of the United States in war through the international traffic in arms. Joseph C. Green remained Chief, and Charles W. Yost, Assistant Chief.

In a statement issued by the Secretary of State on May 15, 1936, he declared that 131 persons and companies engaged in the manufacture, export, or import of arms had registered with the Secretary of State. On July 1, 1938, the Department of State addressed to all manufacturers and exporters of aircraft a circular stating that the Department would with great regret issue any licenses authorizing the exportation of aircraft or aerial bombs to countries where armed forces were making use of airplanes for attack upon civilian population. Secretary Hull reported as of January 12, 1939, that all but one American aircraft company had observed this moral embargo.[6] By December, 1940, 422 persons and companies had registered according to the provisions of the law, and the value of arms, ammunition, and implements of war authorized during the year 1940 amounted to almost $875,000,000. In the five years of control operations Great Britain had received arms and equipment valued at over $700,000,000 and France, amounts valued at over $100,000,000. The total value of arms and equipment of war exported was valued at over $1,000,000,000.[7]

One incident which occurred in regard to the control of exports illustrates the friction between Federal agencies and the tendency to blame the Department of State for an incident for which it was not responsible. The National Munitions Control Board, of which Secretary Hull was chairman, had granted an allotment of helium gas to Germany for dirigibles, and the license had been issued. Secretary of Interior Ickes, who had already approved the transaction, now refused to supply the helium. Secretary Hull felt that to castigate Hitler for tearing up treaties and then to violate a written contract with him was not the way to carry on foreign relations satisfactorily. Although President Roosevelt supported the stand of the State Department in principle, he permitted Secretary Ickes to refund the German payments and cancel the contract.[8]

Perhaps the most important reorganization effected under the administrative direction of Assistant Secretary Messersmith was one which related more to the Foreign Service than to the Department of State. The Reorganization Act of 1939 gave the President wide powers of combining agencies, and on May 9, 1939, he transferred the activities and personnel of the foreign service of the Department of Commerce and the Department of Agriculture to the State Department, consolidating them with the Foreign Service of the United States.[9] Mr. Messersmith had advocated this consolidation for many years as an important means of unifying effort and reducing to a minimum the duplication of services abroad.

An important change in the Department's personnel occurred when President Roosevelt, on July 26, 1939, nominated Assistant Secretary of State Francis B. Sayre as high commissioner to the Philippine Islands. Assistant Secretary

Sayre had been concerned primarily with economic and financial matters and with the development of the trade-agreements program. The choice of Dr. Henry F. Grady as his successor betokened a continuation of the same policies by a man peculiarly well equipped, both theoretically and practically, to ensure their widest application. Dr. Grady had served for two years as Chief of the Division of Trade Agreements and was vice chairman of the Tariff Commission at the time of his appointment.

The Department lost an able official in September, 1939, with the death of Dr. Cyril E. Wynne, Chief of the Division of Research and Publications. Few officers had a wider experience in the field of foreign relations. He had served with the army overseas and had been on detail with the American commission to negotiate peace in Paris in 1919. He was a Foreign Service officer for three years, then was made Assistant Solicitor in the Department, later Acting Historical Adviser, and in 1933 Chief of the Division of Research and Publications. His successor was Dr. E. Wilder Spaulding, who had been Dr. Wynne's assistant since the establishment of the division.

27

The Department Prepares for War

Efforts to Prevent War

During the second administration of Franklin D. Roosevelt the United States was constantly being drawn more closely into the vortex of European power politics, and the Department of State was being faced with ever more serious problems of policy. When Czechoslovakia was threatened by Hitler's program of expansion, the President was urged by Ambassador Bullitt and Under Secretary Welles to make a personal appeal to the heads of the European states most deeply concerned. Secretary Hull was not too sympathetic to the suggestion since he was not convinced that any good would come of such action. However, when the President decided to make the appeal, the Department of State, through Under Secretary Welles and Assistant Secretary Berle, aided the President in preparing the text. The President sent his appeal of September 26, 1938, directly to Chancellor Hitler and President Beneš, whereas the message to the British and French premiers went through Departmental channels. Chancellor Hitler's long reply blaming the situation upon Czech persecution of Sudeten Germans seemed to require a special answer, and the President, with the aid of Under Secretary Welles, drafted another message urging Hitler to continue negotiations. Secretary Hull's prescience was correct. Hitler had no intention of changing his plans. The State Department had spent many hours of concentrated effort on these messages of the President, and Secretary Hull paid particular tribute to the efforts of Under Secretary Welles, Assistant Secretaries Messersmith and Berle, to the European experts Dunn and Moffat, and to Press Officer McDermott. Nor did he overlook the underpaid, overworked personnel of the Code Room.[1]

The President made one more effort to prevent the war which threatened Europe by personal appeals to both Hitler and Mussolini. Hitler had taken over Austria and Czechoslovakia, and Mussolini, after annexing Ethiopia, now moved into Albania. Again Secretary Hull was dubious as to results, but Ambassador Bullitt in Paris had urged the President to make a final effort, and such a plea would at least make the position of the aggressor states plain before the bar of world opinion. In this instance President Roosevelt followed State Department usage to the extent that since Mussolini was not the legal head of the Italian state, the plea to him was signed by Secretary Hull. Since Hitler now was the titular head of the German state, the message to him was signed by President Roosevelt. The two dictators did not reply directly, but contented themselves by making addresses rejecting disdainfully the President's offer.

Relations with Latin America and Japan

During this period the Department of State could not limit its active interest to Europe. Latin America and the Far East engaged its attention almost equally with Europe. The eighth Inter-American Conference met in Lima, Peru, in December, 1938, and it was necessary for the State Department to work on the agenda and then to send a substantial number of State Department officials to aid the American delegation. Secretary Hull again headed the delegation from the United States, and Assistant Secretary of State Berle, Ambassador to Peru Steinhardt, Minister to the Dominican Republic Norweb, and Legal Adviser Hackworth were members of the official American delegation of twelve. Economic Adviser Feis, Chief of the Division of American Republics Duggan, Chief of the Division of Cultural Relations Cherrington, and Foreign Service Officer Nyhus acted as advisers to the American delegation. Dr. Warren Kelchner was secretary general, and Michael J. McDermott was press officer. The remarkable American-Peruvian or Peruvian-American, Dr. Albert A. Giesecke, who served as a cultural attaché at the Lima embassy many years before such a position was authorized, was the encyclopedia of local information for the delegation.

Argentina was again in opposition, and it was only after Secretary Hull, contrary to all diplomatic practice, appealed directly to President Ortiz over the head of the Argentine delegation that Argentina began to cooperate. The result was the vitally important Declaration of Lima, which not only promised to defend continental solidarity against foreign intervention, but provided the machinery to make it effective.

The relations of the United States with Japan, which Secretary Hull aptly characterized as a chain whose links were "incident, protest, investigation, regret, promises," and then the same over again, were deteriorating rapidly. In her undeclared war against China, Japan had utterly disregarded the principles of international law. Although Japan had given assurance to the United States after the sinking of the *Panay*, that American rights would be respected, the Department of State, throughout the year 1938, sent note after note to Tokyo protesting violations. When Japan not only continued to violate the Nine Power Treaty but began to expand southward, closer to American interests, the United States decided to act.

Senator Vandenberg had already introduced a resolution requesting the President to give Japan the six months' notice of the government's intention to denounce our commercial treaty with Japan. President Roosevelt and Secretary Hull decided such a procedure was too slow, and on July 26, 1939, without any preliminary notice, the Secretary of State wrote a polite communication to the Japanese ambassador, giving notice of our desire to terminate the Treaty of Commerce and Navigation between the United States and Japan signed February 21, 1911.

One other rather unique procedure was used by the State Department to bring home to Japan the increasingly hostile attitude of the American people toward Japan's flagrant violation of American rights in the Far East. Ambassador Grew had been back in the United States during the summer of 1939, and he suggested to the Department that upon his return to Tokyo he utilize the opportunity afforded by an address which he proposed to give before the America Japan Society to let the Japanese people know exactly how the American people felt regarding Japan's policy of ruthless conquest. Both the President and the Department of State approved the idea. An original draft was prepared by the Division of Far Eastern Affairs and amplified and revised by Ambassador Grew, but owing to changed conditions and the possibility of improved relations, Ambassador Grew, with the Department's approval, toned down the original draft very drastically. Nevertheless, the address, "straight from the horse's mouth," pictured very frankly American resentment against Japan's aggressive and imperialistic policies. The repercussions indicated that the Japanese people had not appreciated the American point of view, and for a period of time, at least, it strengthened the position of the liberal elements in Japan.[2]

The Department Faces War

In August of 1939, in spite of Washington's heat, the Department of State worked strenuously to keep abreast of the world's critical situation. For several years the personnel of the Department had worked overtime with no additional compensation, but with the increasing tension in Europe and the Far East the number of hours put in by the employees beyond the regular hours for which compensation was rendered almost doubled. In the month of August, 1938, the number of overtime hours worked in the Department amounted to 17,644, whereas in 1939 it amounted to 21,840 hours. In September the comparison was much more striking: in 1938 it amounted to 11,151, but in 1939, when war broke, it reached 21,282 hours.[3] These figures did not include the relatively higher number of overtime hours put in by the ranking officials. A night watch in the Secretary's office was established consisting of two Foreign Service officers, William D. Moreland, Jr., and Aaron S. Brown, and an officer of the Department, Henry Allen. They were given wide discretionary authority and were authorized to take appropriate action on all matters which came to their attention.

The Department was apprised by its representatives in the various capitals of Europe that Hitler was determined upon war and would probably attack Poland the last week in August. The news of the German attack was telephoned by Ambassador Bullitt in Paris directly to President Roosevelt instead of to his Chief, Secretary of State Hull, and the President forthwith telephoned the news to Secretary Hull. The Secretary of State went immediately to his office at three-thirty in the morning and called in his principal assistants: Under Secretary Welles, Assistant Secretaries Berle and Messersmith, Legal Adviser Hackworth, Ambassador to Germany Hugh Wilson—called back for consultation—the political advisers Dunn and Hornbeck, Economic Adviser Feis, Chief of the European Division Moffat, Assistant to the Counselor Savage, and Assistant Chief of the Far Eastern Division Ballantine. Upon telephoning to Ambassador Kennedy in London, it was learned that the British had not yet been informed of the invasion.[4]

The Department of State Aids Americans

In 1914, at the outbreak of the First World War, a Welfare and Whereabouts Section had been established in the Consular Bureau of the Department of State to assist Americans stranded in the war areas.[5] At its peak the section employed ninety persons working on day and night shifts, and a period report by Nathaniel P. Davis, head of the section, indicated that 64 per cent of the work of the section was devoted to welfare and whereabouts inquiries and transmission of funds; the other 36 per cent of the section's time was devoted to reports from consuls on inquiries and payments, certification of documents, prisoners of war, whereabouts of persons in the United States, and travel conditions. After the war the section became a mere skeleton organization, and in 1924 it was made a part of the Division of Foreign Service Administration. The advent of the Nazi regime in Germany, the revolution in Spain, and the undeclared war in the Far East increased the amount of protection, welfare, and whereabouts work. In the division files there were some 12,000 cards on cases in Spain for the revolutionary period, and about double that number for the long period of undeclared warfare in the Far East. On September 13, 1938, Mr. Davis, Chief of the Division of Foreign Service Administration, wrote a memorandum pointing out the necessity for an expanded organization to handle whereabouts and relief cases and similar cases in the event of a major war. Assistant Secretary of State Messersmith was sympathetic to the idea, and the two officials worked out a tentative program. A confidential instruction was sent to certain diplomatic officers indicating the intention of setting up a division in the Department to handle special problems arising from the war, such as welfare, relief, and repatriation of Americans, and suggesting that similar sections be established in our missions abroad. A central card index giving relevant data pertaining to citizens sought or assisted was a basic requirement of the program.

Immediately upon the outbreak of World War II the Special Division was set up by a Departmental order dated September 1, 1939. Former Ambassador to Italy Breckinridge Long, Special Assistant to the Secretary, was put in charge of the new division. He was assisted by former Ambassador to Germany Hugh R. Wilson. Foreign Service Officer George L. Brandt was made Administrative Officer. The division began operations with twelve Foreign Service officers home on temporary duty in the Department and nineteen clerks and stenographers. The head of the clerical staff was Madge M. Blessing, who had been handling welfare and whereabouts work for over twenty years. The large card index of cases was transferred and became the basis of operations of the new agency.

The first problem was the repatriation of American citizens from the war zones. More than 100,000 Americans were in Europe at the outbreak of hostilities, and foreign shipping was largely withdrawn from service. The Special Division arranged for the dispatch of a half dozen additional ships, for an increased passenger-carrying capacity on the regular transatlantic steamers, and for their quicker turnaround. By the spring of 1940 more than 80,000 Americans were safely returned to the United States. By an instruction dated March 21, 1939, Foreign Service officers had been authorized, in case of need, to assist Americans to get in touch with relatives or friends in the United States to obtain funds for their passage back. Such telegrams could be sent to the Department at government expense. In cases where no funds were available, the Department of State made allotments of public funds to its officers abroad and authorized them to advance funds for relief and evacuation of American citizens. Such loans were to be covered by promissory notes signed by the beneficiaries. During the twelve-month period from September 1, 1939, to August 31, 1940, the Special Division transmitted approximately $550,000 from Americans in the United States. In the same period the Special Division arranged for the granting of over $240,000 in loans against promissory notes to bona fide

American citizens in the war areas needing funds for transportation expenses to the United States.

Inquiries by Americans in the United States concerning their relatives and friends abroad flooded the Department of State upon the outbreak of the war. For a time the Special Division dispatched as many as three hundred telegrams daily, and in its first year the division handled approximately 26,000 inquiries from Americans in the United States desiring information regarding the welfare and whereabouts of relatives and friends in the war-stricken areas of Europe. With the aid of the Foreign Service officers abroad, the division was successful in obtaining the desired information in about 95 per cent of these inquiries.

Another important function added to the new division was the representation of the interests of various belligerent governments that requested this service of the United States. This meant taking charge of the represented government's diplomatic and consular property and archives, the handling of whereabouts and welfare inquiries in respect to its citizens, the receipt and payment of funds to them, and the providing for their repatriation when possible. According to the Geneva Prisoners of War Convention of 1929, the protecting government was required to inspect prisoners-of-war camps, and to report the condition of the camps and inmates to the proper officials of the represented government. Almost immediately after the outbreak of war the United States took over the interests of France, Great Britain, Canada, Australia, and New Zealand in Germany, and indicated its willingness to assume representation of the interests of certain other governments in Europe in the event the war should spread. A closely related function of the new division was the maintenance of liaison with the Red Cross and other American organizations that conducted war-relief operations and received and furnished information for humanitarian purposes.

Diplomatic Problems of the War

The outbreak of war necessitated a proclamation of neutrality on the part of the United States. The existing legislation regarding the shipment of arms required that the Department of State prepare two proclamations: the first, a general one covering the activities of the United States as a neutral under the rules of international law; the second, to carry out the provisions of the Neutrality Act of 1937 forbidding the export of arms and implements of war to belligerents. Both were issued under the President's name. It was now regarded as essential to repeal the arms-embargo provisions. President Roosevelt called a special session of the Congress, and Senator Pittman prepared and introduced a bill to this effect but with needlessly harsh restrictions on American shipping. The Department of State, after mature consideration, prepared a revised draft, but Pittman refused to compromise. Secretary Hull appealed to key members in both Houses and obtained a few minor improvements. The bill passed and became law on November 4, 1939, and the State Department forthwith issued the proclamations and regulations to make our neutrality effective.

Even before the outbreak of the war the President and the Department of State had been considering the renewal of diplomatic relations with the Vatican, which had been severed after the Pope had lost his temporal powers. Under Secretary Welles wrote personally to American Ambassador to Italy Phillips, asking his opinion. Phillips favored the idea but suggested that a Protestant be chosen. Secretary Hull thought that the envoy must be a personal representative from the President to the Pope. After the usual diplomatic preliminaries, the President announced that Myron C. Taylor had been appointed as his personal representative to the Vatican so that close cooperation might be possible in working toward world peace and the alleviation of human suffering.

The Welles Mission to Europe

Early in 1940 President Roosevelt decided to send Under Secretary of State Sumner Welles to the principal belligerent countries to see whether there was still any possibility of obtaining a peaceful settlement before the war should spread further and make peace still more difficult to achieve. Apparently Roosevelt and Welles had discussed the matter before Secretary Hull was informed of it. Under Secretary Welles declared that early in January the President proposed the possibility of such a mission, whereas Secretary Hull did not learn about the suggested trip until early in February.[6] Secretary Hull was confident from Roosevelt's statements that Welles had suggested the mission and had persuaded the President to let him make it. The Secretary of State not only resented keenly the fact that the trip had been arranged behind his back, but felt that no good results would be achieved. In fact, by seeming to offer false hopes for peace the mission might be extremely harmful in its results. Secretary Hull made it very clear that he did not favor the mission; and he insisted that no peace feelers be proposed, but that the mission be confined solely to a first-hand study of the situation in each country in order that the United States might be the better prepared to formulate its own policy. President Roosevelt agreed to this conception of the mission's purpose.

Accompanied by the Chief of the Division of European Affairs Jay Pierrepont Moffat and Foreign Service Officer Lucius Hartwell Johnson,[7] Mr. Welles visited Rome, Berlin, Paris, and London. He talked with Mussolini and Ciano, with Hitler and von Ribbentrop, with Daladier and Herriot, with Chamberlain and Lord Halifax, and with numerous others. Under Secretary Welles kept religiously within the sphere of his instructions and limited himself as far as possible to the role of listener and observer. However, to put an end to rumors, Secretary Hull cabled Mr. Welles on March 18 that the press had been informed that his mission was purely one of fact finding and that he was not acting in a capacity to receive or convey any proposals for peace.[8] Under Secretary Welles made a comprehensive report of his findings to the President upon his return, but they were all pessimistic. Perhaps the most unfortunate aspect of the mission was that it brought the latent antagonism between Secretary Hull and Under Secretary Welles into such an active state that they could no longer work together satisfactorily in the Department.

This situation was partly due to the tendency of President Roosevelt to disregard regular channels of procedure whenever he felt so disposed. Inasmuch as he liked Welles personally—they had both gone to Groton and Harvard—and had full confidence in his ability, the President quite often wrote Welles notes or chits directly and discussed matters of foreign policy with him personally without bothering to mention it to Secretary Hull. Similarly the Under Secretary would send to the President information which might particularly interest him, or even seek his opinion on important questions. Inasmuch as Secretary Hull was away from time to time, and in such cases Under Secretary Welles acted as Secretary of State, it was a natural tendency to deal directly with the President even when the Secretary was on duty. Paradoxically enough, Welles did not find it inappropriate to protest a directive proposed by Secretary of Treasury Morgenthau regarding export licenses for arms on the ground that the State Department had already assumed jurisdiction and was handling the matter satisfactorily.

State Department Difficulties

Appreciating the fact that the war would have consequences of a lasting nature on the future foreign relations of the United States, and that when it ended problems of readjustment to peacetime production would be presented, Secretary Hull appointed a committee in the Department to gather data on and study both the immediate and long-range results of overseas war measures and the manner in which the problems arising from them might best be handled.[9] Under Secretary Welles was made chairman, Hugh Wilson, vice chairman; Counselor R. Walton Moore, chairman of the Subcommittee on Disarmament, and Special Assistant to the Secretary Leo Pasvolsky, chairman of the Subcommittee on Economic Problems. The importance of this committee may be the better appreciated when it is realized that the whole postwar program for Dumbarton Oaks and the Charter for the United Nations had their beginnings in this organization.

The year 1940 was a very difficult one for the Department of State. In attempting to prevent the war from spreading, particularly the effort to keep Italy neutral, the President took control. At the urgent solicitation of the Pope, of Ambassador Phillips in Rome, and Ambassador Bullitt in Paris, President Roosevelt sent a series of appeals to Mussolini. He also acted as an intermediary for Prime Ministers Churchill and Reynaud in their offer to consider sympathetically Italy's territorial claims and also to permit Italy to have an equal place at the peace conference. Each reply from Mussolini was more hostile than the preceding. Finally, Secretary Hull opposed vehemently any further appeals "to a bandit who was determined on war to satisfy his own vanity and wish for glory," and the last appeal suggested by the President and Under Secretary Welles was not sent.[10] The much quoted sentence of President Roosevelt's speech at Charlottesville, Virginia, on June 10, 1940, "the hand that held the dagger has struck it in the back of its neighbor," [11] was in the State Department draft, but eliminated by the President at Under Secretary Welles's suggestion, and reinserted by the President just before he delivered the address.

When the defeat of France was no longer in doubt, President Roosevelt and the Department of State recognized that purely from the selfish viewpoint of security of the United States that every effort must be made to keep the French fleet out of the hands of the Germans. The day after the French requested an armistice Secretary Hull sent one of the strongest instructions of his career when he declared that if the French surrendered their fleet to Germany the French government would permanently lose the friendship and good will of the United States.[12] Similar appeals were made to the British. As an earnest of American support, neutrality regulations were amended to permit American pilots to deliver planes to Canada for export to Britain. The Department's Chief of the Division of Controls, Joseph C. Green, discovered that a statute of 1917 permitted the return of army and navy aircraft to the manufacturers, who could then resell to the Allies.

When the German armies were about to invest Paris, the French government went first to Tours and then to Bordeaux. Ambassador Bullitt, just as his predecessor, Ambassador Herrick, in World War I, decided to remain in Paris. Secretary Hull felt that Bullitt would be much more useful to the United States if he kept his contacts with the French government, but Bullitt, knowing the Department's attitude, dealt directly with President Roosevelt. Even after Secretary Hull stated the Department's position and the reasons for it, President Roosevelt, although recommending that Bullitt go with the French government, permitted the ambassador to use his discretion. Bullitt stayed in Paris and during this crucial period sent his cables in private code to the President, leaving the Department uninformed as to his actions.[13] Secretary Hull thereupon authorized Ambassador Biddle, accredited to Poland, to represent the United States with the French government.

As a means of greater protection for the Western Hemisphere, Secretary Hull declared that Greenland was definitely under the purview of the Monroe Doctrine. To be certain that the United States would be kept in close contact with the situation in Greenland, career officer James K. Penfield was dispatched with authority to cooperate with the Greenland officials in planning the defense of the island. In similar fashion the State Department opened up a consulate in Reykjavik, Iceland. On April 9, 1941, an executive agreement signed by Secretary Hull and by the Danish minister in Washington, without the permission of the Nazi-controlled Danish government, gave the United States the right to protect Greenland and to prevent her territory from serving as a base of attack against the Western Hemisphere.[14] As was expected, the agreement was protested by the Danish government and the minister recalled. Nevertheless, the Danish minister remained in Washington, and Secretary Hull declared that the United States would continue to regard him as the minister of Denmark. In spite of German pressure and letters from King Christian of Denmark insisting upon Minister de Kauffmann's recall, the State Department maintained its position.[15]

Security and Neutrality

Perhaps the most important transaction in 1940 for the mutual advantage of the United States and their allies was the exchange of fifty over-age destroyers on the part of the United States for eight naval and air bases on the part of the British. The original proposal of France and Great Britain was to purchase a number of the older type of destroyers. The President was not sympathetic to the suggestion at first, but when the British offered to make available naval and air-base facilities in the Caribbean and near Newfoundland, the idea of a trade seemed more feasible. Under Secretary Welles began the negotiations in the absence of Secretary Hull, and the latter took charge toward the end of August. Although there was a serious problem involved with regard to the maintenance of American neutrality, the vital question facing the President was how would the people react. The difficult problem for the Department was to reconcile the British desire for the transaction to take the form of reciprocal gifts, with that of the United States to make it on a *quid pro quo* basis. William Allen White and his Committee to Defend America by Aiding the Allies proved to the President's satisfaction that an Executive agreement for an exchange along the lines proposed would be very popular in the country. Legal Adviser Green H. Hackworth solved the Department's problem by suggesting that the British lease some of the bases as a gift and the others in return for the destroyers. Since self-preservation is the primary law of a state and the deal was clearly advantageous for national security, the quibbling as to whether the transaction violated international and constitutional law was purely academic. To make the arrangement fit in with the Good Neighbor Policy, Secretary Hull declared that the bases would be made available to all the American republics in the common defense of the Hemisphere.

The major problem of the Department from the time of the passage of the Neutrality Act, signed November 4, 1939, until the United States entered the war was the enforcement of neutrality. When war broke, the President had created an Interdepartmental Neutrality Committee upon which the Department of State was represented, and on November 22, 1939, a Departmental order established a committee consisting of Counselor Moore, Assistant Secretary Berle, Legal Adviser Hackworth, and Chief of the Division of Controls Green to act as its secretariat. The Department was flooded with inquiries by firms and citizens as to how the restrictions worked. One section of the law required an examination of contributions for relief in belligerent countries by the State Department. The fact that by February, 1940, some 241 organizations were registered for collection of funds and supplies for belligerent countries, and that they had collected over $1,750,000 in the first four months of the war indicates the burden imposed upon the Department.[16] Even American diplomats were not always neutral in their statements, and the speeches of Minister to Canada Cromwell in Toronto on March 19, 1940, and Ambassador to Belgium Cudahy in London on August 6, 1940, were so unneutral that both were immediately recalled for consultation. The Department, however, might well have been accused of inconsistency, inasmuch as on August 18, 1940, in Philadelphia, the President's close friend, Ambassador to France Bullitt, in a powerful plea for the United States to prepare for war, went so far as to ask his listeners whether they wanted "to see Hitler in Independence Hall making fun of the Liberty Bell." *The State Department Bulletin* gave this address first place in its issue of August 24, 1940.

Personnel and Organization Changes

The Trade Agreements Act came up for renewal by the Congress in 1940, and the Department made every effort to publicize the advantages which had already accrued to the country. Agreements had been signed with twenty-one countries and American exports had increased by almost $1,000,000,000. It seemed advisable to establish a permanent agency in the Department to take charge of the negotiation and administration of all commercial treaties and agreements. Assistant Secretary of State Messersmith, in appearing before the

House Committee on Appropriations, pointed out that the proposed Division of Commercial Treaties and Agreements was not only vitally essential, but that it was merely a permanent substitute for the temporary existing Trade Agreements Division. He also assured the committee that no additional expense would be entailed since the same eighty-four employees would be retained.[17]

The plea was successful and a Departmental order, dated July 1, 1940, established the Division of Commercial Treaties and Agreements. Harry C. Hawkins was retained as Chief of the new division. An additional function was assigned to this division on April 16, 1941, when a Departmental order made it responsible for coordinating the activities of the Department in assisting foreign governments to purchase and export articles under the provisions of the Lend-Lease Act of March 11, 1941. Lynn R. Edminster, Special Assistant to the Secretary, was also given certain duties in conducting the Department's activities under Lend-Lease.[18] On October 7, 1941, the division changed its name to Division of Commercial Policy and Agreements, and its responsibilities included correspondence and contacts with American export-import interests and making arrangements with the foreign representatives negotiating for supplies.

The Consular Commercial Office, charged with the protection and promotion of American commercial and agricultural interests abroad, was also raised in status, and by a Departmental order dated February 26, 1940, became the Division of Commercial Affairs. James J. Murphy, Jr., its first Chief, was succeeded almost immediately by another Foreign Service officer, Raymond H. Geist. An agency very secretive as to its functions was created on November 22, 1940, under the somewhat ambiguous title of Division of Foreign Activity Correlation. A Departmental order of October 31, 1941, was somewhat more specific as to its functions. The division was directed to interview all foreign political leaders promoting movements in the interests of their peoples and committees of foreign-born groups visiting the Department, and to give information on their activities and obtain all possible relevant information regarding their purpose, organization, and membership.[19]

The most important change in Departmental personnel which occurred in 1940 was the appointment of Assistant Secretary Messersmith as ambassador to Cuba and his replacement by Breckinridge Long as Assistant Secretary of State for Administration. Mr. Long had served as Third Assistant Secretary of State during the First World War and later as ambassador to Italy from 1933 to 1936. Just prior to his nomination as Assistant Secretary, Mr. Long had been serving as Special Assistant in charge of the Special Division. Owing to his keen interest in its work of repatriation of Americans and the protection of prisoners of war, Assistant Secretary Long retained the Special Division under his organization. When on March 4, 1941, a reorganization of the work of the Assistant Secretaries took place, Assistant Secretary Long largely relinquished his work in administration and assumed the supervision of liaison activities with the Senate and House of Representatives and the general representation of the Department of State at hearings before congressional committees.

Other changes in 1940 which should be noted were the promotion of Warren Kelchner from Acting chief to Chief of the Division of International Conferences, and the promotion of Assistant Chief Charles A. Thomson to Chief of the Division of Cultural Relations. A particularly meritorious promotion came to Ella A. Logsdon, who after twenty years of outstanding service was appointed Chief of the Office of Fiscal and Budget Affairs.

The year 1940 was election year, but the Department, except for two addresses on foreign policy by Secretary Hull, kept strictly out of the campaign. It had been President Roosevelt's original idea that Secretary Hull succeed him in the Presidency, but the victories of Hitler and Hull's disinclination to run, joined with the constant clamor of the New Dealers that their leader must not let them down, persuaded the President to violate the third-term tradition. The Department helped prepare a foreign-policy plank for the Democratic platform, but in spite of Secretary Hull's strong support it was not accepted. President Roosevelt won the election and henceforth gave almost his entire attention to the conduct of foreign affairs. The keynote of his future policy was sounded in his world-wide radio fireside chat of December 29, 1940: "We must be the great arsenal of democracy. . . . There will be no bottlenecks in our determination to aid Great Britain." The Department of State prepared the material, but the White House wrote the speech.

28

The Department Goes to War

The Department on the Eve of War

The development of the Department of State up to the year 1941 was one of gradual increase in numbers and functions in accordance with the requirements of the situation. No over-all reorganization had occurred since World War I, but as shown in the annual hearings before the appropriations committee of the Congress, a constant effort was made to curtail expenses and maintain the Department with the minimum staff commensurate with a fair degree of efficiency. Perhaps the chief criticism that could be leveled at the Department was that it had never sought adequate funds to carry on its activities without imposing an undue strain upon its personnel. The fact that the officials in the Department put in 156,000 hours of unpaid overtime in the year 1940 would seem to bear out this criticism. A critical survey of the organization at the close of the year 1940 would show no Departmental agency that did not perform an essential function and, generally speaking, perform that function well. Although salaries were low, they were not out of line with other governmental positions nor with the cost of living. Morale was high, on the whole, because tenure was certain and practically all positions were based upon civil-service regulations. Promotion, although very slow at times, was based upon merit, and if deserved could generally be counted upon.

The Secretary of State now received a salary of $15,000 a year, and the Under Secretary and the Counselor each $10,000. The Assistant Secretaries and Legal Adviser received $9,000 a year. The political advisers, the Economic Adviser, and the Special Assistants to the Secretary ranged in salary from $8,500 to $9,000. The heads of divisions, except in the case of Foreign Service officers, who had their own scale of salaries, were generally paid $8,000 a year. The principal discrepancy here seemed to favor those who came under the professional and scientific classification as compared with those who were classed as clerical, administrative, and fiscal, although at times the work could hardly

350

be differentiated. For example, it would be hard to justify a salary of only $6,500 for the services of the head of the large, important, and highly technical Passport Division when the Chiefs of the Divisions of International Conferences, of Cultural Relations, of International Communications, and of the Foreign Service Buildings Office were paid $8,000. The salaries of thirty-odd Grade 1 clerks and stenographers, who under clerical classification received only $1,260 a year, also left something to be desired.

The total personnel of the Department of State in 1940 was 971 employees, and the sum appropriated for the State Department proper, not counting the Foreign Service or international obligations, was slightly under $3,000,-000. The appropriations requested for 1941, in spite of the serious international situation, were very little larger. Inasmuch as it was difficult to foresee just what emergency needs might arise, it was thought preferable to ask the Congress for supplemental appropriations when necessary.

Expansion of Economic Work

By far the most notable development in the Department brought about by the war was the increase in agencies of an economic character. At the end of 1940 only three agencies—the Adviser on Economic Affairs, the Division of Commercial Affairs, and the Division of Commercial Treaties and Agreements—with less than one hundred personnel,[1] were concerned with international economic affairs; whereas when the war ended, some twenty economic units, with a personnel of about five hundred, were functioning in this field. Their activities were largely of a wartime character and were concerned primarily with coordinating the international policies of the much larger independent agencies, such as the Board of Economic Warfare, the War Production Board, and the Office of Lend-Lease Administration. The growth of the Department in this direction was abnormal, but the situation at the time seemed to warrant the expansion.

Even in 1940 the Adviser on International Economic Affairs and his assistants were engaged in stock-piling strategic materials and instituting measures of economic warfare as well as advising on international economic policy.[2] The first of the economic agencies of a strictly wartime character was the Division of World Trade Intelligence, which was brought over from the Office of the Coordinator of Inter-American Affairs and set up in the Department of State on July 21, 1941. A so-called Proclaimed List of Certain Blocked Nationals had been issued by the United States to prevent any trading with the United States on the part of firms in any way affiliated with the Axis powers. The Department of State was made responsible for its enforcement. The first duty was to analyze and evaluate the information required to decide what persons and firms should be placed upon the Proclaimed List. The division also helped to prepare for the Board of Economic Warfare a List of Unsatisfactory Consignees, also known as the Confidential List. The Division of World Trade Intelligence had a substantial nucleus of officers and clerks when it was transferred to the Department of State, and by the end of 1941 it had approximately twenty officers and forty clerks. In 1944 and 1945 it reached a maximum of about twenty-five officers and fifty clerks.

The Chief of the Division was John S. Dickey, its Assistant Chief Francis H. Russell, and Philip W. Thayer was the Acting Assistant Chief. The division was divided into five sections of which the Western Hemisphere Section was the most important since most of the Proclaimed List firms were in Latin America. The Newspaper, Radio, and Motion Picture Section had to determine what information agencies putting out propaganda against the United States were being subsidized by the Axis, and such were placed upon the Proclaimed List. The World Trade Intelligence Division prepared and kept up to date a remarkable index file containing information on over 300,000 persons and firms in Latin America and 100,000 persons and firms in Europe. When the Board of Economic Operations was established in the Department of State on October 7, 1941, the Division of World Trade Intelligence became one of its component parts.

According to Departmental Order 973, which set up the Board of Economic Operations, its duty was to carry out the Department's functions in connection with the economic defense of the United States. However, to understand what the Department's functions were it must be remembered that President Roosevelt had already expanded existing agencies and established numerous outside emergency agencies to carry on the program of economic warfare and economic defense of the United States. For example, the Treasury Department controlled foreign funds, the Maritime Commission, shipping, the Economic Defense Board, exports, and the Board of Economic Warfare, the procurement of strategic materials. But since the Department of State assisted the President in over-all foreign policy and the Foreign Service furnished the principal contacts abroad, the Department had to advise and guide these operating agencies so that their work would be properly coordinated. The members of the board were Assistant Secretaries Acheson and Berle, Economic Adviser Feis, Special Assistant Pasvolsky, and the Chiefs of divisions primarily concerned.

A reorganization of the Department's economic activities was announced simultaneously with the setting up of the Board of Economic Operations on October 7, 1941. The Division of Commercial Treaties and Agreements now became the Division of Commercial Policy and Agreements. It retained all of its previous duties, and it was in addition called upon to serve as contact agency for American representatives abroad and foreign representatives in the United States to work out arrangements for the many and complex wartime agreements in which time was of the essence. At the same time a new agency called the Division of Exports and Defense Aids was set up and made responsible for the policy involved in the government's exports and requirements work, including export control, lend-lease, and priorities and allocations for exports. This division was placed under the direction of Charles Bunn, a law professor from the University of Wisconsin, who had been in the Department about a month. However, it had as Assistant Chiefs Charles W. Yost and Granville O. Woodward, both of whom had been Foreign Service officers and also had considerable experience in the foreign economic work of the Department of State.

Another much smaller agency, called Division of Defense Materials, was established and made responsible for the foreign policy aspects of the government's procurement program, which included the preclusive buying of strategic materials, a function previously carried out by the Economic Adviser's Office. Thomas K. Finletter, a well known New York lawyer, who had been acting as Special Assistant to the Secretary of State, was placed in charge of this agency. Similarly, a Foreign Funds and Financial Division under Frederick Livesey was created and made responsible for policy matters involving foreign funds control. Finally, a Division of Studies and Statistics was created to do all research work required by the Board of Economic Operations. Lynn R. Edminster, a top economic analyst of the Department of State, headed this division which only lasted until June 18, 1942, when its functions were transferred to the Division of Commercial Policy and Agreements. It had already become apparent that each division preferred to do its own research.

Inasmuch as all of these agencies were a part of the Board of Economic Operations, and all reported either to Assistant Secretary Acheson or to Assistant Secretary Berle or to both, the Department of State exercised a certain amount of coordination in the wartime economic policies. A simpler procedure would have been to have made all of these divisions sections of the Division of Commercial Policy and Agreements. However, the Department was bound by civil-service requirements in recruiting, and the factors of salary and prestige had to be taken into consideration.

In the period from October, 1941, to June, 1943, during which the Board of Economic Operations was functioning, several changes in the organization occurred which should be noted. Within six weeks of its establishment the Foreign Funds and Financial Division was split into two parts. Mr. Livesey remained head of the Financial Division, and Donald Hiss, an assistant in the Legal Adviser's Office, was made head of the Foreign Funds Control Division. A sort of anomalous growth in the Board of Economic Operations was the American Hemisphere Exports Office, an agency created originally to see to it that Latin American countries were supplied with essential commodities on a parity with civilians in the United States. It gradually took over various responsibilities involving Latin America from the functional divisions, as, for example, shipping priorities and Lend-Lease to Latin America. Although it only operated for approximately a year, its growth was phenomenal and in the fall of 1942, under its Chief, Foreign Service Officer Christian M. Ravndal, there were five Assistant Chiefs, thirty-eight officers, and forty clerks.

Space precludes more than a mere mention of the activities of these wartime economic agencies nor is opportunity afforded to discuss the continuous conflicts in jurisdiction between the Board of Economic Warfare and the Department of State. Assistant Secretary of State Dean Acheson, who served as chairman of the Board of Economic Operations, soon became as unpopular with the personnel of the Board of Economic Warfare as their Milo Perkins was with the economic agencies of the Department of State.

During the year 1941 there were a number of important changes in the Department's top personnel. The Counselor of the Department, R. Walton Moore, died at the age of eighty-two. He had served four years as Assistant Secretary and four years as Counselor, and his death was a serious loss to his close friend Secretary Hull. No one was named to succeed him. Assistant Secretary Henry F. Grady resigned at the end of December, 1940, and on February 1, 1941, Dean G. Acheson was appointed in his place. On March 4, 1941, G. Howland Shaw, a Foreign Service officer with almost twenty-five years' experience in the Department and abroad, was appointed Assistant Secretary of State in charge of the administration and budget matters of the Department. Mr. Shaw had been serving in the Department for the past four years as Chief of the Division of Foreign Service Personnel. Foreign Service Officer John G. Erhardt succeeded to Mr. Shaw's previous position.

New Visa Control Procedure

The war in Europe and the threat to the security of the United States through the efforts of certain foreign governments to introduce agents into the United States in the guise of immigrants, visitors, or seamen required that a greater degree of care be exercised in granting admission to foreigners. The Department felt that the best method of control would be to centralize all visa control in the Department.

A Departmental order, dated June 20, 1941, established the new procedure whereby aliens seeking permanent residence, temporary entry, or transit to a foreign destination were required to submit to the Visa Division of the Department of State a biographical statement and two affidavits of sponsorship. An interdepartmental advisory committee representing State, Justice, the Federal

Bureau of Investigation, and the intelligence services of the army and navy thereupon considered the applicants' cases from the standpoint of national security. The Visa Division then referred the cases back to the permit-issuing authority, usually an American consul, with appropriate recommendations. A formal review procedure was established with a final appeal to an appeal board for cases refused by the interdepartmental committee.

In the first seven months of its work, that is, from July 1, 1941, until January 31, 1942, the committee considered 22,100 cases, of which 14,100 were approved, 5,200 disapproved, and 2,800 deferred. The new procedure entailed a large expansion of the Visa Division's staff. In October, 1940, its personnel numbered 47, and by June 30, 1942, the number had reached 278.[3] Owing to the pressures constantly exerted upon the Chief of the Visa Division by members of Congress and others to admit particular aliens, the Department regularly named a Foreign Service officer of high classification to this post, thereby rotating the position. Avra M. Warren, who was appointed Chief on January 21, 1941, was a Class 1 officer with previous experience in the office. The Assistant Chief Eliot B. Coulter, a former Foreign Service officer, has held his position since 1930 and has become the recognized authority on all questions of the highly complicated and technical visa procedure.

New Passport Regulations

The various neutrality acts and the imminence of war also had a profound effect upon the Passport Division. The passport is an ideal device for the control of the movements of American citizens, therefore it was logical that this division be made responsible for the enforcement of the regulations forbidding American citizens to travel on the ships of belligerent states. The division was also concerned with getting army and navy personnel, merchant seamen, intelligence officers, and defense experts to various areas of the world. The law of June 21, 1941, authorized the President to impose rules and regulations governing the entry into, and the departure from, the United States of all aliens and citizens. This included seamen who had never before been required to carry passports. This one requirement necessitated the issuance of over 300,000 seamen passports during the war period.

To increase the security of the United States, all the old red passports were replaced by a new-style green document more difficult to forge. At the same time, by this means the division was able to remove from circulation all fraudulent or altered passports and to remove passports from the hands of undesirables. As an additional safeguard, passports of American citizens returning to the United States were taken up, forwarded to the State Department, and carefully examined for alteration or violation of the Neutrality Act.

Such passports were retained in the Department until further facilities were granted to the bearers. The change in the emphasis of the division's work from protection of the individual to the security of the state necessitated a considerable increase in personnel. At the outbreak of the war in 1939 there were 76 officers and clerks in the Passport Division. When the United States entered the war in 1941, it had increased to 121 in Washington and 19 in the passport agencies in Boston, Chicago, New York, and San Francisco. In January, 1945, there were 239 officers and clerks and 44 more positions authorized. Ruth B. Shipley, who at the time of writing (September, 1948), still heads the division, was appointed Chief on June 1, 1928, after having already served fourteen years in the Department. No Division in the Department has been administered with greater courage and efficiency than the Passport Division.[4]

The Caribbean Office of the Department of State and the Anglo-American Caribbean Commission

With the coming of the Second World War, the protection of the Caribbean area was essential to the security of the Western Hemisphere. The exchange of fifty destroyers for the right to construct a number of naval and air bases on British islands of the Caribbean increased considerably the responsibilities of the United States in this area. The genesis of the Caribbean Office, set up in the State Department in 1941, and the Anglo-American Caribbean Commission came from a suggestion made by Charles W. Taussig to President Franklin D. Roosevelt. Being very familiar with the area, Mr. Taussig felt that the United States must face the serious economic and social problems which existed in the islands where it was proposed to construct these fortified bases. In a meeting in Under Secretary Welles's office, held on October 30, 1940, Mr. Taussig presented his views and was named as the head of a commission of three to visit the British West Indies, study the situation, and report back.

In his report Mr. Taussig recommended the creation of a joint advisory committee with the British to consider the various problems raised by the proposed developments. This later became the Anglo-American Caribbean Commission. A memorandum prepared under Mr. Welles's signature proposed the establishment in the Department of State of an Office of Caribbean Affairs to handle questions recommended by the commission, but not to conflict with the Division of American Republics. A Departmental order, dated October 9, 1941, established this office with Foreign Service Officer Coert du Bois in charge, and on October 30 the President announced the appointment of

Charles W. Taussig, Rexford G. Tugwell, and Coert du Bois as American members of the joint commission.

The new agencies held a series of conferences, and the results were invaluable to the war effort. Emergency food caches were stored at strategic places in the islands and stockpiles built up. Local food production was stimulated and fishing facilities augmented and improved. As a result the threat of famine conditions due to the submarine menace was overcome. An emergency land-water highway to avoid submarine attack utilized trucks, railways, barges, and schooners. A million and a half tons of Cuban sugar came to the United States by such means. Mr. du Bois established a West Indies Schooner Pool which proved to be of the greatest service and at the same time showed handsome profits. Arrangements were made for labor requirements, and public health and disease control were improved. The Caribbean Office, having fulfilled its functions, was abolished by the Departmental order of January 15, 1944, but the Anglo-American Commission, now known as the Caribbean Commission, is still functioning as a successful international agency for regional cooperation.

Changes in Diplomatic Personnel and Activities

Although few changes occurred in the diplomatic service of the United States in 1941, the war conditions made a number of necessary adjustments in the representation of the United States in European countries. For example, Ambassador Anthony J. Biddle, Jr., acted as ambassador to the governments of Belgium, Poland, Norway, the Netherlands, Czechoslovakia, Yugoslavia, and Greece, all established in England. No ambassador was sent to Germany after the return of Ambassador Hugh R. Wilson in 1939, but Alexander Kirk and subsequently Leland B. Morris, the counselors of the embassy, acted as chargés d'affaires ad interim. Admiral William D. Leahy [5] was appointed ambassador to the Vichy government in France in November, 1940, after Bullitt's resignation, and Robert D. Murphy acted as counselor. In the place of Ambassador Joseph P. Kennedy, who had resigned from his post in London, President Roosevelt, on February 11, 1941, appointed former governor of New Hampshire John G. Winant. Ambassador Winant had been serving as Director of the International Labor Office at Geneva for several years and consequently was fully conversant with European political and economic conditions. Career officer Frederick A. Sterling retired as minister to Sweden in 1941 after twenty-seven years in the Foreign Service, and was replaced by Foreign Service Officer Herschel V. Johnson. Nelson T. Johnson, ambassador to China, who had entered as student interpreter in China in 1907, accepted a reduction in rank and salary to go as minister to Australia in February, 1941.

In addition to the regular corps of diplomatic representatives, President

Roosevelt constantly utilized the services of special agents to perform particular missions. His close friend and adviser, Harry Hopkins, was constantly called upon to undertake special missions as the personal representative of the President. Secretary Hull, although not sympathetic to this proclivity of the President, concedes that in the case of Harry Hopkins there was never any attempt to interfere with the Department's policies.

The work of the American embassies and legations abroad and the State Department at home was augmented materially from the outbreak of the war by assuming a very considerable representation of foreign interests until the United States became a belligerent. For example, before December 8, 1941, the United States served as the protecting power at Berlin for Great Britain and the members of the British Commonwealth of Nations, as well as for France, Belgium, Luxembourg, Egypt, Panama, Haiti, and Costa Rica.

The Special Division in the State Department was made responsible for the various problems of representation, and a Representation Section in this division was established in May, 1940. The protecting power was expected to take custodial charge of the represented government's official property, protect its nationals, and be responsible for the receipt and payment of funds provided by the represented government to its nationals for their subsistence, and for their repatriation when possible. Protection of prisoners of war and civilian internees was another very important duty included in representation. Over $2,000,000 yearly was advanced by the represented governments to be used for financial assistance to protected nationals, for the upkeep of buildings used as embassies, legations, and consular offices, and for the packing, storage, and shipping of the effects of the official staffs of the represented governments.

Presidential Diplomacy

It was in 1941 that President Roosevelt began more and more to conduct the foreign affairs of the country personally. In a world-wide broadcast sent by short wave on March 15, 1941, in every European language, the President promised ever increasing aid to the embattled democracies until total victory had been won. Early in August, 1941, the President informed Under Secretary Sumner Welles that, considering the world situation, he felt that a public declaration of the principles of human and moral decency and the need for states to fashion their conduct according to the principles of international law was in order. About a week later the President informed Mr. Welles that he had arranged to meet with Mr. Churchill, and that inasmuch as Mr. Churchill was being accompanied by the British Undersecretary of State for Foreign Affairs, he would like Under Secretary Welles to accompany him.[6]

In order to keep the meeting absolutely secret, the President left ostensibly for a fishing trip, and Welles flew in a navy plane to join him. The meeting took place in the harbor of one of the recently acquired naval bases in Newfoundland, and the Atlantic Charter was the result of the conference. No other members of the State Department were present. Secretary Hull had been apprised of a possible conference of this sort at the end of May, but he was recuperating at White Sulphur Springs when the meeting took place. The idea of a joint declaration regarding the basic principles of the postwar world seems to have been broached first by the British prime minister. The President asked Welles to prepare a draft with the British undersecretary. The final draft was considered word for word by Roosevelt, Churchill, Welles, Hopkins, and Cadogan. An unsigned joint communiqué was thereupon issued, now known as the Atlantic Charter, which served as the fundamental basis of American foreign policy in the years immediately following.

Not only did President Roosevelt deal directly with Churchill. He sent personal communications to Marshal Pétain and General Weygand on numerous occasions, urging that France retain her fleet and defend her colonies overseas. Upon at least two occasions he appealed directly to the French people. He helped prepare the instructions to Ambassador Leahy and from time to time he wrote to him directly. He conferred in person with the Vichy French Ambassador Henry-Haye. He wrote directly to Joseph Stalin, offering supplies up to the value of $1,000,000,000 under the Lend-Lease Act, without any payment of interest. On July 24, 1941, the President had a long talk with Ambassador Nomura in which he protested vigorously against the Japanese move into Indo-China, and two days later he issued an Executive order freezing Japanese assets in the United States. When in September the Japanese government proposed that President Roosevelt and Premier Konoye meet to work out an agreement, the President would only accept providing his preliminary demands regarding Japanese action should be met. Finally, President Roosevelt on December 6, 1941, sent a long message to the emperor of Japan, making a last appeal for a peaceful solution of the crisis which had been reached in the Far East.[7]

The Break with Japan

On the whole, however, in the relations with Japan preceding the attack on Pearl Harbor, the Department of State was given the responsibility for both the formulation and execution of American policy. Secretary Hull took charge personally of all dealings with the Japanese ambassador. Not only did he see Nomura in the State Department, either alone or with President Roosevelt on certain occasions, but he discussed the situation with him in some forty to fifty meetings in the Secretary's apartment, first at the Carlton Hotel and later at the Wardman Park Hotel.[8]

Secretary Hull notes that in formulating the Department's Far Eastern policy he depended upon his "three ranking Far Eastern experts—Stanley K. Hornbeck, Maxwell M. Hamilton, and Joseph W. Ballantine." All three had had firsthand experience in the Far East and had been following developments in that area for the past decade, either in the Department or in the field.

At this time the Division of Far Eastern Affairs had on assignment to the Department four Foreign Service officers in addition to Ballantine, all specialists in the Far East, and several others who had been formerly Foreign Service officers in this area. With these trained experts in the Department of State and with the long experienced and capable career officer Joseph C. Grew as ambassador in Tokyo, the failure of diplomacy in dealing with Japan was not due to lack of expert negotiation.

Both Secretary Hull and the Department of State have been accused of forcing the Japanese into war by the so-called "ultimatum" of November 26. Such an accusation overlooks three important facts. The first is the *modus vivendi* which Secretary Hull wished to accompany the ten-point peace proposal. This offer compromised to such an extent that China objected to it violently, and the British were rather cold to its provisions. Under the circumstances the Department decided to withdraw it. In the second place the proposal submitted to the Japanese was a mere restatement of the long held American position, and it did not close the door to further discussion. Finally, the Japanese had already chosen the date for breaking off negotiations, and their plan of attack had been completed and orders to carry it out given.

The Department was still less at fault for the catastrophe at Pearl Harbor. Secretary Hull had repeatedly declared that diplomacy had failed and that the responsibility belonged henceforth to the army and navy. He warned that a surprise attack might be expected momentarily. On December 5 he instructed the representatives of the United States in the Far East to be ready to destroy their codes and secret archives. The State Department had done all in its power to prevent the break, and when failure was evident in this direction, to delay war as long as possible. There is not the slightest justification in this case for blaming either the Department of State or the American embassy in Tokyo.

When the Japanese ambassadors on December 7 came to the Department to declare that the United States offer was unsatisfactory, Secretary Hull already knew their instructions and he had just received our own report that Pearl Harbor had been attacked. The Secretary received the two Japanese representatives coldly and did not invite them to sit down. After glancing through the document with whose contents he was already familiar, he delivered one of the most caustic utterances in American diplomatic annals:

In all my fifty years of public service I have never seen a document that was more crowded with infamous falsehoods and distortions—infamous falsehoods and distortions on a scale so huge that I never imagined until today that any Government on this planet was capable of uttering them.

He then waved them out. Secretary Hull that same afternoon called a conference of his principal advisers and prepared a statement for the press. They also discussed the draft of the message which the President would deliver to the Congress the next day. The Department of State went on a war footing but unfortunately was not invited to participate in the war councils. The President as Commander in Chief regarded all questions pertaining to the conduct of war as military rather than diplomatic and not only did not consult his Secretary of State, but at times left him in ignorance. The ill effects of this procedure have been almost universally recognized.

The Department's War Problems

One of the first tasks of the Department after the outbreak of war was to prepare a statement of principles to which the democratic states at war with the Axis might subscribe and which would bind them to unified action until victory was achieved. The procedures of World War I were examined, and the declarations of cooperation made at the Pan American conferences and the various declarations of the President regarding unity were considered. Secretary Hull directed Maxwell M. Hamilton, Chief of the Division of Far Eastern Affairs, to prepare the original draft of such a declaration and another setting up a Supreme War Council. The two drafts were worked over at great length by the Department, with Under Secretary Welles, Assistant Secretary Berle, Economic Adviser Feis, Legal Adviser Hackworth, and Special Assistant Carlton Savage aiding materially in the many revisions. The two drafts were considered at a cabinet meeting with the President presiding. Prime Minister Churchill and Ambassador Halifax were consulted and made certain suggestions which were incorporated. The Russian Ambassador Litvinov made a few changes, and as finally agreed upon, a single joint declaration was issued under the title suggested by President Roosevelt: "Declaration by the United Nations." The work was completed so that on January 1, 1942, President Roosevelt, Prime Minister Churchill, Ambassador Litvinov, and Minister T. V. Soong affixed their signatures to it. Within twenty-four hours the document had been signed by the representatives of twenty-six nations.[9]

Immediately upon receiving news of the attack on Pearl Harbor, the republics of Latin America proved that their promised cooperation could be counted upon. On December 9, 1941, in accordance with the procedure agreed upon at Havana in 1940, the minister of foreign affairs of Chile requested the chairman of the governing board of the Pan American Union, in view of the aggression by a non-American power against the United States, to consult with the American governments as to the advisability of convoking a third meeting of the ministers of foreign affairs to consider the situation.[10] Owing to the many serious problems facing the United States, it was decided by the President that the Secretary of State should remain in Washington and that Under Secretary Sumner Welles should head the American delegation. A large delegation accompanied Mr. Welles—twenty-seven including the clerical staff. Of the twenty officers, thirteen were from the Department of State in addition to the Under Secretary. They included Dr. Kelchner, Chief of the Division of International Conferences, Dr. Collado, Special Assistant to the Under Secretary, Mr. Daniels, Assistant Chief of the Division of American Republics, and Dr. Marjorie Whiteman, Assistant to the Legal Adviser.

In his address at the opening session of the Rio Conference, Under Secretary of State Welles made it clear that the only sure way to stamp out the Axis methods of poisoning inter-American intercourse was by breaking off diplomatic relations. This policy had been agreed upon in the State Department before the delegation sailed. A cable sent by Assistant Secretary Berle to Mr. Welles at the request of Secretary Hull supported this position even at the expense of unanimity. All of the American republics supported a resolution to break relations except Argentina and Chile, but they insisted upon a formula recommending rupture as each country should determine. Rather than insist to the extent of not obtaining unanimous support, Mr. Welles accepted the compromise. He did this without consulting Secretary Hull, who, when he learned of it, sharply reprimanded Welles for his change of position. Secretary Hull felt that the American front had been weakened more by giving way to Argentina than by letting her go her own way. President Roosevelt stepped in as arbiter and accepted the Welles agreement.[11]

Secretary Hull's bitter disappointment at the failure of the Rio Conference and the heavy work entailed by the outbreak of the war affected his health, and he was compelled to leave the Department for several months to recuperate. Under Secretary Welles forthwith became Acting Secretary of State, but it was evident that it would be even more difficult in the future for Mr. Hull and Mr. Welles to work satisfactorily in the same Department.

The Department of State, December, 1941

The Department of State at the time of the outbreak of the war had increased very materially in size compared with January, 1941. As 1941 ended, the Department had approximately 1,000 permanent employees and over 600 on a temporary status. The appropriations for the fiscal year ending June 30, 1942, for the Department of State proper amounted to $3,318,440, of which $2,724,440 was allocated to salaries. The Department as organized at the end of 1941 consisted of the Secretary, the Under Secretary, and four Assistant Secretaries as the chief directing officers of policy and administration. The Secretary had an assistant and four Special Assistants, the first to assist him in the office routine and the other four to advise on matters assigned to them from time to time. To carry out defense arrangements, three Special Assistants to the Under Secretary were appointed during 1941: Charles P. Curtis, Jr., to assist in the coordination of international political and economic policies of the United States; Max Thornburg, an oil company official as consultant on petroleum matters; and Emilio G. Collado, an economist, to assist in matters of export control. Five advisers, one legal, one economic, and three political, were concerned with matters of immediate and long-range policy in the fields indicated by their titles.

The Division of Communications and Records was now by far the largest agency in the Department: its telegraph section had a chief, an assistant chief, two supervisors, and 107 clerks; its telephone section, a chief operator, assistant chief operator, and thirteen operators; the records section, divided into seven sections—general, immigration, passport, personnel, political, mail, and war-trade board—numbered, together with its supervisor, assistants, chiefs, assistant chiefs, clerks, and messengers, 269, making a total personnel of 393. The cost of the telegraph messages alone amounted annually to almost $500,000. In the fiscal year 1940-1941, about 1,125,000 pieces of correspondence passed through the division, and in 1941-1942 this was almost doubled. This division, which worked twenty-four hours a day and 365 days a year, put in annually over 21,000 hours of unpaid overtime.[12]

The increase in the size of the Department required more space than was available in the vast structure on Pennsylvania Avenue. Although the space formerly assigned to the army and navy had been vacated, new agencies, such as the Executive Offices of the President, the Administrative Assistants to the President, the Bureau of the Budget, and the National Resources Planning Board, had moved into the Department of State Building. By the fall of 1941 seven additional buildings were required to house the activities of the Department of State: the Winder Building across from Old State on 17th Street; an apartment building at 515 22nd Street, N.W.; the annex to the American Institute of Architects Building at 1735 New York Avenue; the Metropolitan Club Annex at 1712 H Street; the Hill Building at 17th and Eye streets; a building at 1126 21st Street, N.W., and a part of the Commerce Building.

One result of the critical international situation was the institution, beginning August 14, 1941, of an identification pass system to regulate the admission of employees and visitors to the Department of State Buildings. Three types of employees' passes were issued. The most important officials had what was called the gold pass, which admitted the holder into any Department building at any time and also permitted its holder to carry official papers into, or out of, any Department building. The second admitted the holder into all Department buildings at regular hours or into the building in which the holder worked at any time; the third was valid for admission to any Department building at regular hours. Visitors were directed to an information desk where upon identification and statement of reason for the visit the information was recorded and a visitor's pass issued. If any question arose, the officer to be seen would be called on the telephone and queried as to the action desired. All visitors' passes had to be surrendered upon departure. Special permission had to be given for all property taken from the buildings by visitors or employees.[13]

29

The Role of the Department of State in the North African Invasion

The Division of Near Eastern Affairs

At this point it seems desirable to discuss a much criticized policy of the State Department in relation to the conduct of the war. Inasmuch as this policy was for the most part initiated and carried out under the direction of the Division of Near Eastern Affairs, the opportunity is afforded to examine the methods employed by a geographical division whose primary function is the formulation and development of policy.

At the outbreak of World War II in 1939, the Division of Near Eastern Affairs consisted of a Chief, an Assistant Chief, seven desk officers, and four clerks. Wallace Murray, Chief of the Division, was a former Foreign Service officer who had been made Chief in 1929. His work, like that of other Chiefs of policy divisions, included advising with the Secretary of State and other government officials in the formulation of policy in relation to the countries of his area, interviewing foreign diplomatic officers, American businessmen, and missionaries regarding problems affecting American interests arising in the area, and supervising the work of the division. His Assistant Chief, Paul H. Alling, also a former Foreign Service officer, carried on similar duties as designated by the Chief. The desk officers or divisional assistants read all the incoming dispatches and telegrams regarding the territories under their jurisdiction and familiarized themselves in every way possible with the countries concerned. Four of the divisional assistants or desk officers were Foreign Service officers detailed to the Department: Gordon P. Merriam, a Near Eastern specialist who had served in seven different diplomatic or consular posts in the Near East, had charge of our relations with India, Burma, Iran, and Afghanistan; Henry S. Villard was concerned with Saudi Arabia, Iraq, and most of Africa; J. Rives Childs, was responsible for Egypt, the Anglo-Egyptian Sudan, Sudan, Palestine, Morocco, and Tangier; and George V. Allen was charged with affairs in Greece, Turkey, the Lebanon, and Syria. Desk officer Morrison P. Giffen handled Ethiopia, Liberia, and the European colonies and mandates; James J. Durhan, an economist, specialized in the raw-material problems in African territories and served as the division's representative in trade-agreements negotiations; Amy Holland kept the archives of the division and did special research.

Inasmuch as Greece, North Africa, and Egypt, three primary theaters of the war, were under the division's jurisdiction, it was faced with such problems as the protection of American interests in the region, the acquisition of stocks of strategic materials, the maintenance of Turkish neutrality as a bulwark against German aggression in the Near East, and giving aid to the French in North Africa to prevent or at least delay as long as possible German occupation of that territory. It was this last problem that became a major policy of the Department of State, and one so effectively carried out that it was one of the principal factors in the success of the invasion of North Africa by American troops.

Economic Aid to Morocco

On September 9, 1940, General Weygand had been appointed as delegate general of the Vichy government to organize the French African colonies for defense and to coordinate their administration. Although General Weygand was too devoted to Marshal Pétain to violate his instructions from Vichy, he had shown a tendency to oppose the Laval policy of close cooperation with Germany, particularly in the colonial domains. When the ranking officers of the Division of Near Eastern Affairs first learned of Weygand's appointment, they agreed that France might try to guard this region against German occupation. A report from A. G. Reed, general manager of the Socony-Vacuum Oil Company in Morocco, indicated that the French protectorate authorities were willing to exchange certain stocks of minerals, such as manganese and cobalt, for small quantities of petroleum products. This interested the State Department because of certain manifest strategic advantages. It was felt that Morocco might be less likely to succumb to the Axis if the economic situation were improved, and at the same time such an arrangement would not only preserve the organization of the Socony-Vacuum Oil Company, with its five hundred employees in Morocco, but also furnish the United States with strategic and other materials. The Division of Near Eastern Affairs thereupon prepared a memorandum entitled the *Political Implications of American Moroccan Trade*, strongly urging that every effort should be made to support the economic situation in North Africa. Unfortunately the Adviser on Economic Affairs, Mr. Feis, opposed the project vehemently until he was finally overruled by Assistant Secretary Berle. As a result, the memorandum and instructions to American

Consul General Cole in Algeria and Diplomatic Agent White in Tangier to confer with the French authorities along these lines were delayed almost a month.[1]

As a preliminary to any exchange of commodities with North Africa, it was first necessary to make an arrangement with the British to relax their blockade. When the State Department emphasized the advantages of such a trade policy and pointed out that failure to arrange for it might lead to disintegration of the internal political situation, the British reluctantly agreed. They did not have much faith in Weygand's resistance and made as a condition that no re-export should be permitted. To enforce this requirement they suggested that observers be sent to control the distribution.

Meanwhile, it was necessary to get firsthand information as to the attitude of the French leaders in North Africa. Robert D. Murphy, formerly consul general in Paris and subsequently counselor of embassy in Paris and Vichy, was chosen to visit North Africa and report back to the Department. He left Vichy on December 18, 1940, and traveled through Algeria, Tunis, Morocco, and Dakar, visiting the governors general of each area, as well as Delegate General Weygand and High Commissioner Boisson. All were opposed to Axis domination of North Africa and favored American economic aid, but all were loyal to Pétain and Vichy. A draft memorandum for economic assistance was prepared by Murphy which included the control of shipments by American officials and was initialed by Weygand. The State Department approved it, and Admiral Darlan put his signature to the arrangement on March 10, 1941.

Inasmuch as the Foreign Service did not have available the necessary personnel to control the shipments, the War and Navy departments agreed to assign carefully selected officers to this task. They were to be known as Foreign Service Technical Advisers and were commissioned as noncareer vice consuls by the Department of State. Mr. Murphy was to direct the control organization, and although ostensibly he was still counselor of the embassy at Vichy, in reality he was high commissioner for North Africa.

Jurisdictional Difficulties

In spite of the manifest importance of the program in the over-all foreign policy of the United States, the Department of State failed to receive the proper cooperation of other Federal agencies. The Office of Production Management, by refusing to grant the necessary priorities, threatened the success of the plan. As a result of decisions made by the Office of Price Administration and the Board of Economic Warfare, numerous difficulties arose which, although partly due to overlapping jurisdictions, were often caused by an inexcusable lack of desire for cooperation. The Board of Economic Warfare officials were particularly obstructionist. They attempted to have the Treasury Department refuse permits for North African purchases without written authority of the board; appointments with the French representative requested by the Near Eastern Division were delayed, and a two-day delay in the sailing of the accord vessels was caused by the order of a board official. Other difficulties arose with the Treasury Department which controlled the unblocking of funds for the purchase of the goods involved.

Even in the State Department itself there were influences tending to thwart the program, particularly on the part of the Adviser on International Economic Affairs, by investigations and restrictions which seemed to discount the careful supervision exercised in the North African posts by the control officers. Both Secretary Hull and Under Secretary Welles had protested vigorously to President Roosevelt at the Executive Order of April 13, 1942, which permitted the Board of Economic Warfare to send their own representatives abroad to carry on negotiations with foreign governments on economic matters. The Department of State was well equipped through its Foreign Service and through its contacts with the foreign representatives in Washington to perform this function, and the new arrangement was bound to produce a duplication of effort and conflict of jurisdictions. The Presidential order had been obtained by Vice President Wallace because the President had been led to believe that the State Department had agreed to it. The President on this matter was finally induced to issue a Clarification and Interpretation of the April 13 Order which categorically stated:

In the making of decisions the Board and its officers will continue to recognize the primary responsibility and position under the President of the Secretary of State in the formulation and conduct of our foreign policy and our relations with foreign nations . . . that it is the function of the Department of State to conduct or authorize the conduct of all negotiations with foreign governments in Washington and abroad.[2]

The idea of extending *military* aid to the French in North Africa was suggested by several of the French advisers of Weygand, and Counselor Murphy raised the question in letters to the State Department during the summer of 1941. In a letter to Under Secretary Welles, he pointed out that assurances of support from the United States could strengthen immeasurably General Weygand's determination to resist. The State Department discussed the matter but Murphy was not authorized to give any assurance of military support. When on November 18, 1941, General Weygand was recalled and Admiral Darlan, the collaborationist, assumed full control, the United States suspended its program of economic assistance to French North Africa. However, it was quickly recognized that without continuing economic aid the United States would have no excuse for maintaining the control officers in North Africa. These men had made such excellent contacts and such complete reports regarding conditions that after careful consideration the Department decided that the advantages of retaining the dozen control officers and the strengthening of French resistance warranted a renewal of the program. The fact that up to January 1, 1942, six small freighters and three tankers, all of French nationality, had brought all the cargo received made the price of the economic-assistance policy a very cheap one.

On the other hand the policy of dealing with Vichy aroused violent criticism of the State Department in the United States. Popular opinion tended to support De Gaulle and the Free French movement, and the Department was in no position to explain the great advantages accruing from having control officers in North Africa. Still less was it possible to let it be known that President Roosevelt and Prime Minister Churchill, during the latter's visit to Washington in December, 1941, had decided that an Anglo-American expeditionary force should be sent to North Africa and that General Weygand was to be asked to return secretly to North Africa and cooperate with the allies.

The policy of the Department was even more bitterly assailed when it took a stand against the seizure of the two islands Saint-Pierre and Miquelon by Admiral Muselier of the Free French. Inasmuch as the Department had just made an agreement with Admiral Robert, the principal Vichy representative in the Western Hemisphere, guaranteeing the status quo of the French possessions, the Department was compelled to protest vigorously. However, in the public statement issued on December 25, 1941, by the Department, the phraseology condemning the seizure was unfortunate in that it declared that "the action taken by the three so-called Free French ships at St. Pierre-Miquelon was an arbitrary action." [3]

Secretary Hull made every possible effort to secure the support of President Roosevelt and Prime Minister Churchill to compel the Free French forces to withdraw from the islands. But expediency on the part of the British prevailed, and the President refused to make an issue of it. Secretary Hull, whose health was being jeopardized by overwork, was so exasperated at the unwillingness of the President to take a stand in his support that early in January, 1942, he contemplated sending in his resignation. Only the critical situation in Europe and the Far East held him to his task.[4]

Invasion of North Africa

When Weygand made it clear that he was not interested in supporting a North African revolt, the matter was dropped temporarily. However, when Churchill refused to consider a cross-Channel invasion in 1942 and President

Roosevelt insisted that some operation should take place, the two leaders again turned to North Africa. Meanwhile, the meager shipments resulting from the economic agreement had discouraged the French and had produced a feeling of resentful disillusionment. Admiral Leahy, Counselor Murphy, and the Division of Near Eastern Affairs urged strongly that the program of sending supplies be stepped up, but the Board of Economic Warfare continued to follow its obstructionist policy. Mr. Murphy was placed in charge of the diplomatic front, and he immediately proceeded to get in touch with the various French officials heading the interventionist groups. He was able to make the necessary contacts and devise plans for the invasion. He arranged for the secret meeting of General Mark Clark and the French officials on the North African coast about seventy-five miles west of Algiers.

General Clark, who was in command of the American forces, soon found that French officers in North Africa refused to accept the leadership of General Giraud.[5] Admiral Darlan was the only officer whom both the army and navy would obey. Under these circumstances an agreement with Darlan was vital, and after considerable pressure it was obtained. Admiral Darlan gave the order to cease firing and he agreed to a joint command with General Giraud. Again a storm of criticism was raised against the State Department and Counselor Murphy for dealing with Darlan and Vichy. Yet Darlan was the only Frenchman who had control over the army and navy, and his order to cease fire unquestionably saved the lives of thousands of American soldiers. General Eisenhower summarized the situation succinctly: "I played ball with Darlan because it would take me ten divisions to hold my lines of communications open if I didn't; and I couldn't get ten divisions here in a year while I'm fighting this war." [6]

It should be noted here that the arrangement between General Clark and Admiral Darlan was essentially a military arrangement made without either the knowledge or consent of the Department of State. In fact, when the Department wished to send instructions to its representative, Robert Murphy, that only such Vichy officials against whom no well founded objection could be raised should be retained in office, General Marshall refused to clear the instructions on the ground that they seemed to include Admiral Darlan. Although Secretary Hull, when informed of the agreement by President Roosevelt, declared it to be an unfortunate step diplomatically, he conceded that from the military standpoint it had every justification.[7] In order that the situation might be made clear to the public, Secretary Hull persuaded the President to issue a statement pointing out that the arrangement was "only a temporary expedient justified solely by the stress of battle," and at the same time explaining the military advantage of the arrangement.[8]

The results proved the wisdom of the North African policy and the methods used to put it into operation. The State Department's role and the part played by its representatives abroad were essential to its success. Secretary Hull, Under Secretary Welles, Adviser Wallace Murray, Assistant Chief Henry S. Villard, and Foreign Service Officer Thomas C. Wasson directed the policy in the Department. In the field, Ambassador Leahy in Vichy labored strenuously to strengthen Pétain and support Weygand; in North Africa Counselor Murphy carried the burden of the whole program with the assistance of Colonel William A. Eddy, naval attaché at Cairo, whose assignment was to coordinate military and naval intelligence and keep constantly in touch with Murphy. The Foreign Service officers Childs in Tangier, Doolittle and Springs in Tunis, and Cole and Taft in Algiers, were of the greatest value. But of equal value were the dozen control officers whose reports and contacts paved the way for the military effort. The French possessions in North Africa were kept intact and served as the spearhead for the successful invasion of Europe. Credit is the more deserved considering the constant and inexcusable difficulties encountered as a result of conflicting jurisdictions and jealous interference of competing government agencies.

Departmental Adjustments to Meet War Problems

During 1942, the first year in which the United States participated in the war, the Department of State made a number of changes to meet the war requirements. The number of personnel increased materially: by the end of the year more than 2,500 persons were employed by the Department outside of the Foreign Service.[9] However, to carry the extra burdens it was also necessary to increase the hours of work. Beginning on February 2, 1942, the hours of work for all employees of the Department were from 9:00 A.M. to 5:30 P.M. from Monday through Friday, and from 9:00 A.M. to 1:00 P.M. on Saturdays. Various economies of time and materials were instituted. Much of the memoranda and correspondence was henceforth to be single-spaced. Stenographers were instructed to make corrections to avoid rewriting, extra flimsies were restricted, greater care was requested with regard to the use of white and kraft envelopes.[10] To relieve the excessive burden of code work, a departmental order directed that airgrams, a suggestion of Foreign Service Officer George J. Haering's, be used instead of telegrams. The messages were to be marked nonconfidential, confidential, or strictly confidential, and to be handled like telegrams. Their dispatch by air pouch, air courier, or regular air mail was authorized. Arrangements were made for daily dispatching of air pouches. The service began in the Western Hemisphere, where many posts could be reached within twenty-four hours, and was subsequently extended to the entire world.[11]

One of the big problems of the Department was to correlate the war activities of other departments and agencies in the foreign relations field. To establish an orderly procedure and to prevent duplication of effort and to centralize control the Department of State set up a committee of three consisting of Under Secretary Welles, and Assistant Secretaries Shaw and Acheson. This committee was to consider, with the interested government agencies, all plans and proposals which required the dispatch of personnel on official business outside of the United States. At the same time the instructions made it clear that all official representatives of the United States were at all times responsible to the chief of mission in the country in which they were operating. Army and navy personnel were excepted from this prescribed procedure.[12]

Assistant Secretary Shaw's office was the center of the control system, and his assistant, William E. De Courcy, directed the work. The interested divisions were consulted, and no passport was issued until clearance was obtained. Once cleared, the Division of Foreign Service Administration notified the appropriate field officers about the project. The control system worked quite successfully, and in approximately 95 per cent of the cases clearance was obtained within four days, and often within forty-eight hours or less. Between March, 1942, and March, 1944, over three thousand cases of personnel assignments abroad were dealt with. The principal difficulties were with the Foreign Economic Administration, the Office of War Information, and the Office of the Coordinator of Inter-American Affairs. All of these agencies sent a very considerable number of persons abroad.

A Liaison Office in the Office of the Under Secretary gave consideration to questions which were both military and political in character, and saw to it that information of this sort was transmitted to the War and Navy Departments and to the Inter-American Defense Board. Upon request the Liaison Office arranged for the transmission through State Department channels of urgent messages emanating from War and Navy Departments to officers abroad who were without facilities for confidential communication. Special agreements with other American republics for assignment of military, naval, and air missions were drafted by the Liaison Office. In 1943 over four hundred documents passed through the Liaison Office daily. The Advisers on Political Relations collaborated with the Joint Chiefs of Staff, with the Lend-Lease Administration, with the President's Administrative Assistant, with the Board of Economic Warfare, and with other agencies of the war effort. The geographical divisions and the Divisions of Cultural Relations and Current Information aided in the program of psychological warfare by collaborating with the Office of War Information, the Office of Censorship, and the Office of the Coordinator of Inter-American Affairs. The Department appointed a representative, Carl B. Spaeth, to serve on the Emergency Advisory Committee for Political Defense, set up in Montevideo by the Rio Convention of 1942, to combat acts of aggression, including sabotage, espionage, and subversive propaganda by the Axis powers against the nations of the Western Hemisphere. Finally, on November 2, 1942, a Committee on Political Planning was established to develop and lay before the Secretary and Under Secretary plans in the field of the Department's political activity. The four political advisers, the Economic Adviser, ranking members of Foreign Activity Correlation, Current Information, and World Trade Intelligence, and, upon occasion, representatives from other agencies were to constitute the committee. Political Adviser James C. Dunn served as chairman.

Personnel and Organizational Changes

During 1942 very few important changes took place in the Department, either in personnel or in structural organization. Wallace Murray, Chief of the Division of Near Eastern Affairs, was appointed Adviser of Political Relations on March 13, 1942, and his assistant, former Foreign Service Officer Paul Alling, became Chief. Philip W. Bonsal, who had entered the Foreign Service in 1938, was made Chief of the Division of American Republics in 1942—a phenomenal rise in rank and responsibility in a Department where rapid promotion had always been the exception.[13] It should be noted, however, that Mr. Bonsal had had considerable experience in Latin America before entering the government service. Joseph C. Grew, former ambassador to Japan, was assigned to the Department and made a Special Assistant to the Secretary of State. Foreign Service Officer Avra M. Warren, Chief of the Visa Division, was sent out to the field as minister to the Dominican Republic, and Foreign Service Officer Howard K. Travers was brought back from Budapest to act as Chief of the Visa Division.

The Chief Clerk's Office, which had existed from 1789 until 1939, was reestablished on August 6, 1942, under the title of Chief Clerk and Administrative Assistant. Millard L. Kenestrick, who had served in the Department for twelve years, was appointed to the position. However, the salary was now fixed at $3,800, whereas Chief Clerk Edward Yardley in 1937 received $4,600, and as Chief of the Division of Personnel Supervision and Management—the glorified title for Chief Clerk established in 1939—he received $5,600. However, no money was being saved, because due to the crying need for additional personnel, the new Division of Departmental Personnel was created and its Chief given the additional title of Executive Officer of the Department. The duties assigned to the head of this new division were so extensive and varied that more than five hundred words were required to enumerate them.[14] No one human being could possibly perform the manifold functions required—it is doubtful whether two people could. However, the elaborate recital satisfied the Civil Service Commission that the new position could be classified as Grade 8 of the

Professional and Scientific Service, which provided a salary of $8,000. John C. Ross, Assistant Chief of the Division of Commercial Policy and Agreements, a very able officer, was given this hydra-headed job. Mr. Ross made a valiant effort to carry out the assigned functions, but Mr. Ross was not Superman.

In November of 1942 the Office of Foreign Territories was established to deal with problems of a nonmilitary character resulting from the military occupation of foreign territories by American forces. Paul Appleby of the Department of Agriculture was loaned temporarily to the Department of State to inaugurate the new agency. The proposal for the new agency, which came from the Combined Chiefs of Staff, was originally made to Milo Perkins, Director of the Board of Economic Warfare, but at the request of the President it was redrafted and directed to the Secretary of State. The immediate problem was North Africa, and simultaneously with the establishment of the Office of Foreign Territories the Department also organized an interdepartmental Economic Mission to North Africa. The two State Department representatives on the Economic Mission were Paul T. Culbertson, Assistant Chief of the European Division, and Donald Hiss, Chief of the Division of Foreign Funds Control.

In the Department proper the Office of Foreign Territories labored under jurisdictional difficulties. The office was located in the Division of European Affairs, and that agency felt that the office should be restricted to economic problems only and that the division would take care of political matters. This attitude pleased neither the Office nor the Near Eastern Division, which had done all the spadework for the North African occupation. Mr. Appleby, who had been Under Secretary of the Department of Agriculture, was given the title of Special Assistant to the Secretary of State. As Special Assistant, he thought that he should report directly to the Secretary, whereas the administration of his office made him subject to the Chief of the Division of European Affairs. Not being able to get a ruling on the jurisdiction of his office, and not being willing to be held responsible for matters which he could not control, Mr. Appleby resigned at the end of six weeks. Six months later the office was abolished and its functions redistributed. It deserves credit for two achievements—the organizing of the interdepartmental Economic Mission to North Africa, and for setting up the procedure for the shipments of nonmilitary supplies to North Africa and sending the first shipment. Its ultimate failure was the fault of the President's tendency to set up new agencies without any consideration given to the jurisdictions of those already functioning.

It is pleasant to relate that upon at least a few occasions the State Department officials were able to disregard jurisdictional limitations and, either by a broad interpretation of the law or by a considerable extension of administrative authority, achieve the results which common sense demanded. An illustration of this occurred in connection with an agreement between the United States and Canada to protect the Aleutian Islands and Alaska. According to the arrangement, in case of an invasion by the Japanese the American air forces in Alaska would advance into the Aleutians and be replaced by Canadian air forces which would thereupon enter Alaska. However, when the action occurred, the American customs officer insisted that some of the Canadian equipment was dutiable. This was a ridiculous contretemps; nevertheless, since it was the law the Treasury officials felt that they must uphold him. Fortunately, John D. Hickerson, Assistant Chief of the European Division, remembered that the Secretary of State could permit distinguished visitors to enter the United States without being subject to customs procedure. Secretary Hull thereupon wrote the Treasury that since these airmen were the first foreigners since Lafayette to join with the forces of the United States to protect the nation they were distinguished visitors and could enter without examination.[15] In similar fashion Foreign Service Officer Coert du Bois made an unauthorized agreement with the British to permit commercial fishing off the Bahamas to meet the threatened famine in that area, an agreement which, if they had known about it, would have given the officers of the Treaty Division some very unhappy moments.

30

Postwar Planning

Office of Foreign Relief and Rehabilitation Operations

On November 21, 1942, President Roosevelt announced from the White House that Governor Lehman of New York was resigning in order to serve as Director of a new agency in the Department of State which would be designated as the Office of Foreign Relief and Rehabilitation Operations. On December 3, 1942, the President, under his authority over emergency funds, issued a letter of allocation declaring that a sum of $500,000 was being set aside for the use of the Department of State for the reconstruction and rehabilitation of territories occupied by the armed forces of the United Nations. The next day a very brief Departmental order stated that Governor Herbert H. Lehman would direct the Office of Foreign Relief and Rehabilitation Operations thereby established in the Department of State. This unique procedure of setting up a new agency in the State Department indicated that the Department was probably not consulted and would have little to say in the direction of the new agency, OFRRO, as it was immediately designated.

Although the President, in his letter of November 18, 1942, had declared that the Secretary of State would take the lead in dealing with "economic, political, and fiscal questions which were developing in the wake of the advancing American armies," in a letter dated March 19, 1943, to Governor Lehman,[1] the President authorized him "to plan, coordinate, and arrange for the administration of this Government's activities for the relief of victims of war in areas liberated from Axis control through the provision of food, fuel, clothing, and other basic necessities." [2] However, in the very next paragraph the Director was informed that in any specific area abroad his operations were subject to the approval of the United States military commander during the occupation period, and that in matters of general foreign policy he would be guided by the directives of the Secretary of State.[3]

This extensive but indefinite grant of power was certain to provide bitter jurisdictional disputes with numerous other governmental agencies interested in the foreign field. For example, the Office of Lend-Lease Administration, which was to furnish the money, wanted to share in preparing the estimates for the liberated areas. The Board of Economic Warfare insisted that it participate in the formulation of policies governing distribution of the supplies. The Treasury Department felt that it must be consulted in financial matters covering the fixing of exchange rates and the expenditure of funds. Finally, in the State Department itself the recently established Office of Foreign Territories seemed to have jurisdiction over approximately the same field.

Early in April of 1943 Thomas K. Finletter, Special Assistant to the Secretary of State, suggested that the desired cooperation might be obtained by vesting supervisory authority in a Director appointed by and responsible to the Department of State. Governor Lehman strongly objected to such a solution. When the Bureau of the Budget officials also failed to work out an acceptable compromise, President Roosevelt again issued a directive, dated June 3, 1943, outlining the relief and rehabilitation responsibilities of the individual agencies and giving a plan for the coordination of the economic operations of the United States civilian agencies in areas liberated from enemy control.[4] To coordinate these activities, the State Department was directed to reexamine its internal organization and procedure in order that it might assume the position of leadership required.

As a result of this directive there was established in the Department of State, by a Departmental order dated June 24, 1943, an Office of Foreign Economic Coordination (OFEC). The Defense Materials, Exports and Requirements, Foreign Funds Control, and World Trade Intelligence divisions were to be considered as component parts of OFEC. The Office of Foreign Territories and the Board of Economic Operations were thereby abolished.

The President's plan, as prepared by the Bureau of the Budget, required two interdepartmental committees representing War, Navy, Treasury, BEW, Lend Lease, and OFRRO, one a Policy Committee and the other a Coordinating Committee. Both of these were organized under the chairmanship of Assistant Secretary of State Acheson. Area committees for various European regions were established with a chairman and secretariat for each provided by the Department of State. Serious friction immediately developed in the Coordinating Committee when Mr. Acheson proposed a more integrated organization abroad. Director Lehman opposed the proposal on the ground that if adopted it would transfer responsibility for field operations from OFRRO to OFEC.

The State Department officials also differed with those of OFRRO as regards the jurisdictional limits of the Area Directors. Finally, a basic conflict developed with respect to the organization of the representatives of the civilian agencies in the field. OFEC wanted all personnel integrated into a single organization with appropriate functional divisions, whereas OFRRO insisted that each agency be allowed to send separate missions to the field which would report to the parent agency in Washington rather than to the Area Directors. The dispute finally culminated in a direct appeal to the President by the Director of OFRRO on August 30, 1943, to make the relief and rehabilitation of all liberated areas a "single unitary job." The President requested that Secretary Hull reply to Governor Lehman's strictures. On September 4 the Secretary sent the President a memorandum pointing out that relief was only a small part of our foreign policy and that responsibility for total coordination had been, in his opinion, properly placed in the Department of State by the Presidential action of June 3. Each communication was quite critical of the other's position, and on September 6 the Secretary and Director met to discuss the jurisdictional problem, but it soon became clear that no compromise was possible.

Foreign Economic Administration

The President finally cut the Gordian knot by his famous Executive Order No. 9380 of September 25, 1943, which set up a new agency, Foreign Economic Administration (FEA). The various organizations for foreign operations, such as the Office of Lend-Lease Administration, the Office of Foreign Relief and Rehabilitation Operations, the Office of Economic Warfare, and the Office of Foreign Economic Coordination, were all merged into the new agency. Mr. Lehman was appointed Special Assistant to the President and made responsible for representing the United States in the creation of the United Nations Relief and Rehabilitation Administration.[5] The only three economic divisions now surviving in the Department of State were the Division of Commercial Policy and Agreements, with its continuing responsibility for the trade-agreements program, the Financial Division, and the Division of World Trade Intelligence, with its special Proclaimed List functions.

Planning for Peace

The shadows of war grew steadily darker in the fall of 1939, and it was just as the storm broke that President Roosevelt, in an address given on September 3, 1939, declared: "It seems to me clear even at the outbreak of this great war that the influence of America should be consistent in seeking for humanity a final peace which will eliminate, as far as it is possible to do so, the continued use of force between nations." [6] The State Department assisted in the preparation of this address and began immediately to implement it. On September 16, 1939, Secretary Hull appointed Leo Pasvolsky, an economist who had previously served as Assistant to the Secretary of State, as Special Assistant to begin to work on the problem of postwar organization for peace. Several preliminary studies along this line were worked out by Dr. Harley Notter in the Office of Under Secretary Welles as a basis of discussion.

The work in the beginning was largely exploratory, but in addition to papers and discussions, conversations were held with forty-seven governments of neutral states regarding the establishment of a sound international economic system, and the limitation of armament. One result of these preliminary efforts was the appreciation of the need for basic organized research in the Department of State in the field of postwar problems. On November 22, 1940, Mr. Pasvolsky had proposed that a Division of Special Research be set up to analyze and appraise developments arising from the disturbed international conditions, and on February 3, 1941, the Division of Special Research was established with Leo Pasvolsky as Chief, Harley A. Notter, Assistant Chief charged with political security, territorial, and armament matters; Henry J. Wadleigh, economic affairs, and Charles W. Yost, administration. The departmental order establishing the division was kept confidential in accord with the prevailing policy concerning war and postwar problems.

The division undertook, among other tasks, to compile and analyze the official views and policies of allied and neutral governments regarding postwar planning. The Division of Special Research was handicapped both by insufficient personnel and by the lack of defined lines of function in postwar matters within the Department. A few new officers were gradually added during the summer and fall of 1941: Dr. C. Easton Rothwell and Virginia Hartley to the political section, and John V. Evans and Margaret H. Potter to the economic staff. Considering the type of problems to be studied, the research staff not only needed to carry on advanced research, but needed to think in terms of policy. Consequently, the necessity for specialists and experts meant tapping the reservoirs of the great universities and research foundations. A large increase occurred in June and July, 1942, and a second in September and October, 1942. Among the consultants brought in at this time were experts known both at home and abroad, such as Clarence Berdahl, George H. Blakeslee, Clark M. Eichelberger, Halford L. Hoskins, Grayson L. Kirk, William P. Maddox, and Norman J. Padelford. On January 1, 1943, when the Division of Special Research was reorganized (infra p. 380), its personnel numbered sixty-nine—a staff of historians, political scientists, and international lawyers well equipped by training and experience to meet the many and complex problems of postwar planning.

It was the opinion of Mr. Pasvolsky that the former Advisory Committee on Problems of Foreign Relations should be renewed to consider the organization of peace.[7] The entrance of the United States into the war gave the needed impetus, and on December 22, 1941, Secretary Hull wrote the President, enclosing for his approval the names of the members of the proposed Advisory Committee on Postwar Foreign Policy whose duty would be to translate into a program of specific policies the principles enunciated in the Atlantic Charter, and other pronouncements on postwar policy. The tentative list included Secretary Hull, Under Secretary Welles, Assistant Secretaries Acheson and Berle, Economic Adviser Feis, Legal Adviser Hackworth, Chief of the Division of Commercial Policy Hawkins, and Chief of the Special Research Division Pasvolsky, as well as a half dozen eminent outsiders: Norman H. Davis, Myron C. Taylor, Hamilton Fish Armstrong, Benjamin Cohen, and Anne O'Hare McCormick. The President approved both the proposal and the list of suggested members.

Shortly after the committee started work, its membership was materially increased by enlisting specially qualified persons from the Congress, from the State, War, Navy, and other departments and agencies of the government, as well as representatives from the public. The membership, which was strictly nonpartisan, finally reached forty-eight persons, of whom eleven came from the Department of State. In addition to the members mentioned above, Assistant Secretary Breckinridge Long, Special Assistant to the Secretary of State John Van A. MacMurray, and Chief of the European Division Ray Atherton were asked to serve. Dividing into subcommittees, the Advisory Committee studied and prepared preliminary proposals on every kind of postwar problem which seemed likely to require determination of American policy. Territorial adjustments, regionalism, dependent areas, economic and social problems, security, and the bases and procedures of an international organization for the maintenance of peace were among the problems considered.

The work in the Department of State in research and the formulation of potential policies became so heavy that on January 1, 1943, the Division of Special Research was separated into a Division of Political Studies and a Division of Economic Studies.[8] Both were placed under the general supervision of Leo Pasvolsky, with Harley A. Notter, Chief of the first, and Leroy D. Stinebower, Chief of the second. The scope of the research in the Division of Political Studies is shown by the fact that five Assistant Chiefs were named to cover the ramifications of the postwar political problems: Philip E. Mosley in charge of territorial problems; Durward V. Sandifer, international organization and security; David Harris, Central Europe; S. Shepard Jones, administration, and C. Easton Rothwell, central services. By the end of 1943 almost one hundred specialists were preparing special studies and advising on political problems which seemed likely to need consideration for the establishment of a just and permanent peace. The Division of Economic Studies, although less elaborate in organization and jurisdiction, utilized four Assistant Chiefs, H.

Julian Wadleigh, Bernard F. Haley, Melvin M. Knight, and Paul T. Ellsworth, with some thirty odd specially qualified experts.

The following illustration indicates one type of problem and the procedure followed in meeting it. On May 18 Dr. Isaiah Bowman was asked by President Roosevelt to prepare a memorandum on Libya which he might use in preparation for a conference with Prime Minister Churchill which was scheduled for May 23. On the afternoon of the same day the assignment was given to a group of qualified experts on the research staff of the Department with instructions to prepare a main text with facts and an analysis of them, a summary not to exceed two pages, and a set of interpretative maps. Conferences of specialists were held daily, relevant materials were obtained from the Department of State, the Library of Congress, and the American Geographical Society of New York. By the late afternoon of May 22 the material as requested was delivered to the White House usher, who forwarded it by two secret-service men to the President, who had gone to the country.

By the end of 1943 the various committees and subcommittees working with the State Department's corps of research workers had explored and prepared tentative drafts on every phase of international relations. The question of international organization was given particular attention, and a special subcommittee on this subject, with Under Secretary Welles as chairman, after a vast amount of research and analysis finally worked out a proposed charter. Here again the Secretary and Under Secretary clashed, because Mr. Welles leaned toward a regional approach somewhat similar to the one functioning in the Western Hemisphere, whereas Mr. Hull favored an organization of universal character. The composite draft as finally issued with seven analyses became the basis of discussion for the proposals at Dumbarton Oaks.

Resignation of Under Secretary Welles

The outstanding change in personnel occurring toward the end of the year 1943 was the resignation of Sumner Welles as Under Secretary of State. Secretary Hull and Under Secretary Welles had never been compatible, and the gulf which separated them widened steadily. Secretary Hull resented the tendency of the President to discuss many matters directly with the Under Secretary and to encourage Mr. Welles to follow the same procedure. Under Secretary Welles's visit to Europe in 1940, concerning which Secretary Hull had not been consulted until the decision had been made, rankled deeply. On various occasions when Secretary Hull was ill he felt that Mr. Welles as Acting Secretary of State did not keep him adequately informed as to important developments, nor was he consulted upon occasions when the situation seemed to him to warrant it. The specific disregard of his instructions at the Rio Conference, although the Under Secretary was able to justify it plausibly, was a flagrant violation of accepted Departmental procedure. Matters had almost reached a head in the late spring of 1942 when Secretary Hull accused Mr. Welles of formulating and announcing new lines of foreign policy in public addresses which had not been shown to the Secretary.

In the summer of 1943, when the friction had become so acute that even President Roosevelt appreciated the fact that one or the other must go, the President found himself on the horns of a serious dilemma. The President liked the Welles approach to a diplomatic problem, with its cold objective analysis resulting in a clear-cut, prompt decision. The Hull method of weighing every possibility, of discussing the question with all available specialists, and even then being a bit hesitant over making an absolute decision was less in keeping with the Roosevelt manner.

Other factors, however, had to be taken into consideration. Since the President had broken the two-term tradition, it was conceivable that he might want to seek even a fourth term. He could not afford to weaken his chances by antagonizing one of the most outstanding and representative Democrats in the party, and perhaps the most popular member of the administration. Under Secretary Welles, in spite of his great ability, had no political influence whatsoever. Even if the President should nominate Mr. Welles for the position of Secretary of State, it was extremely doubtful that the Senate would confirm the nomination. The President wisely decided that it would be the part of political judgment to accept the resignation of Mr. Welles. Both the President and Secretary Hull favored appointing Mr. Welles as a roving ambassador to Latin America, or to sending him on a special mission to Russia. Welles, however, refused to accept the arrangement, and on September 25, 1943, the President announced his resignation. Unquestionably the country lost one of its ablest and most experienced experts in foreign affairs, but Secretary Hull, who had suffered long and not too patiently the constant irritation which Welles caused him, felt relieved of the most serious handicap in his conduct of the Department. The veteran Washington correspondent Arthur Krock thus summarized the situation, "The State Department will function smoothly and effectively when the President permits the Secretary to be the real undisputed head of a loyal staff." [9]

Under Secretary Stettinius

The appointment of Edward R. Stettinius as Under Secretary of State was at complete variance with the conception of the office of Under Secretary. Inasmuch as the Secretary of State is necessarily a political appointment, and since the foreign affairs of a country are supposedly nonpartisan and at the same time exceedingly complicated, the need of a certain degree of continuity and experience is essential, and the Under Secretary's position was established to provide these two requirements. The majority of the appointments to the position of Under Secretary had been either career Foreign Service officers of top rank, or men who had already served in the Department on a high level. Under Secretaries Frank Lyon Polk, Joseph C. Grew, William R. Castle, Jr., William Phillips, and Sumner Welles all fulfilled the traditional requirements. It was, therefore, not surprising that when it was rumored in the press that Under Secretary Welles was about to retire, the men who were immediately discussed as an appropriate successor to Welles were of this type: Norman Armour, Breckinridge Long, and George Messersmith. Mr. Stettinius possessed neither the background nor experience warranting his appointment as Under Secretary of State.

As a businessman he seemed destined to carry on the excellent traditions established by his father, who had been a partner with J. P. Morgan. Edward R. Stettinius, Jr., had arrived at the commanding position of chairman of the board of the United States Steel Corporation before he had reached his thirty-eighth birthday. His phenomenal rise in business seemed to warrant his appointment as chairman of the War Resources Board and in 1941 as Administrator of Lend-Lease. Two possible reasons might be advanced for the appointment of Mr. Stettinius as Under Secretary of State at this time. The Department of State was given large responsibilities in the carrying out of the Lend-Lease program, and Mr. Stettinius as its administrator was quite familiar with its work and procedure. In the second place the Department had been expanding so rapidly and in so many directions simultaneously that it was expected that Mr. Stettinius would coordinate similar activities and perhaps effect a thorough reorganization of the Department. As a matter of fact Mr. Stettinius brought about two reorganizations which were so drastic that the morale of the Department has not yet completely recovered from these operations.

Changes in Personnel

Very few other important changes of personnel occurred during 1943.[10] One other notable resignation was that of Herbert Feis, who had served as Economic Adviser in the Department since 1931. As the importance of the economic aspect of world affairs increased, the work of the Adviser on International Economic Affairs became steadily more complex and difficult. Since almost every political problem in any part of the world seemed to have an economic aspect, the Economic Adviser's Office became a bottleneck which slowed up operations. We have already noted the obstruction in the economic program for North Africa. Some idea of the ramifications of the problems facing the Economic Adviser have been given recently by Mr. Feis.[11] When he resigned in October, 1943, the wartime requirements had already increased the economic aspects of the Department's work to such an extent that Assistant Secretary Acheson and six divisions were functioning in this field. Assistant Secretary of State Acheson was chairman of the Executive Committee on Commercial Policy; chairman of the Board of Economic Operations; member of the Frozen Funds Committee; member of the Requirements Committee of the War Production Board; Director of the Office of Foreign Economic Coordination; chairman of the Policy Committee and Coordinating Committee of the Committee for Economic Policy in the Liberated Areas. He was at the same time responsible for the Divisions of Reports and Requirements, World Trade Intelligence, War Commodities, Blockade and Supply, and the agencies pertaining to Liberated Areas Matters and Economic Warfare Matters—all in the Department of State. When the reorganization of January 15, 1944, was put into effect, the Assistant Secretary of State for Economic Affairs was made responsible for eleven divisions concerned with some phase of economic matters, and the Office of the Adviser on International Economic Affairs was abolished.

A few routine changes occurred also in the Department's personnel. Maxwell M. Hamilton, Chief of the Division of Far Eastern Affairs, was appointed Foreign Service officer of Class 1 and sent to Moscow as counselor of embassy. He was replaced by Joseph W. Ballantine, also a Class 1 Foreign Service officer with over thirty years' experience in the Far East. In similar fashion Foreign Service Officer Harrison Freeman Matthews, who was counselor of embassy with the honorary rank of minister in London, was brought back to act as Chief of the Division of European Affairs in place of Ray Atherton, who was slated to go as minister to Canada.

Carlton Savage, who had been serving as assistant to the Assistant Secretary of State, was named General Consultant. Mr. Savage had just supervised the editing of a volume which speedily became one of the largest best sellers that had ever come out of the Department. The book was entitled *Peace and War*, and it was a survey of the foreign policy of the United States during the years 1931-1941. The original printing was 2,500 copies, but in less than a month 47,000 copies were sold. The printings for the United States finally reached 135,000 copies, and the British government published an edition which reached 30,000 copies. Translations were made in Portuguese, Spanish, and French. Although very well received, the volume had a number of very serious flaws due doubtlessly to the haste in compilation, and the failure to consult the experts in the Division of Research and Publications who regularly withdraw from the files the documents to be published in the *Foreign Relations* volumes. For example, there was practically nothing on the civil war in Spain, very little on the United States' relations with China, and no dispatches at all from Ambassador Dodd in Germany. This last omission was the more glaring since Ambassador Dodd's diary had already been published, showing that he had an unusually clear grasp of the Nazi situation and had so indicated in many dispatches to the Department which were well worthy of quotation. As often happens, the Division of Research and Publications received all the criticism for the gaps, although they were not consulted in the preparation of the volume nor were they responsible for its publication.

The Division of Communications and Records

The huge Division of Communications and Records, on August 7, 1943, swallowed up the Division of Commercial Affairs, which had already been divested of several of its functions. However, the Chief of the Division of Commercial Affairs, Foreign Service Officer Raymond H. Geist, became Chief of the enlarged Division of Communications and Records. David Salmon, who had been in the State Department for thirty-seven years and Chief of the Division of Communications and Records since 1931, was made Assistant Security Officer for the Department.

The war had almost demoralized the work of this division. Owing to the low salaries paid to its personnel and the pressure of work which constantly necessitated overtime, the Division of Communications and Records had long been very unpopular with its employees. A survey of salaries indicated that from 1936 to 1940 the Department of State personnel had received an average salary increase of 5.91 per cent, while the increase in the Division of Communications and Records was only 0.51 per cent; in other words, the Department's average increase was eleven times greater than that of the Division of Communications and Records. As a result of the low morale, the work of the division was unsatisfactory and under constant criticism. Incoming communications were delayed in distribution, papers were misplaced or lost, and inadequate records made it difficult to locate them. Serious errors were made in the code room. Backlogs existed in every section. It was customary to have approximately 15,000 documents in the records branch which were neither indexed nor listed on the purport sheets. The vitally important telegraph section was on several occasions as much as two days behind in the coding and decoding of messages. The first requirement insisted upon by Mr. Geist was a complete reclassification of positions so that salaries commensurate with the work might be available. This was begun immediately and resulted in a considerable improvement in speed and accuracy. The other requirement was an improvement of the procedure within the division.

The huge backlog in the telegraph section required emergency action. The War Department was asked to help out, and twenty enlisted men trained in cryptography were loaned temporarily, and within forty-eight hours the backlog of 200,000 words, or groups of words, was completely eliminated. Thereafter, from six to eight code clerks from the War Department remained to keep the work current. As soon as possible, high-speed equipment was added to eliminate the slow, cumbersome manual labor of decoding. For example, a machine will decode about 20 words, or word groups, per minute as against 2.7 to 3 words manually, and the results are more accurate. Working conditions were improved. Air conditioning made it possible to endure the heat generated by the mechanical cipher devices. Fluorescent lights reduced the percentage of error. The average time required for a message in the code room was reduced from forty-eight to six hours. The introduction of airgrams also helped materially in reducing the strain in the code room.

The records branch was completely reorganized between August, 1943, and June, 1945, but the changes were gradual, thus permitting the adjustments to be made without slowing up the work of the division. A functional organization was adopted so that material coming into the records branch would move from section to section as each performed the assigned function. A records-retirement program was introduced, and a new tally system kept the division informed at all times of the location of papers.

The distribution and liaison section carried on the work formerly performed by the Division of Commercial Affairs, transmitting information to, and maintaining liaison with, some fifty governmental agencies. The work included the processing and distribution of dispatches and reports from the Foreign Service and the processing and distribution of telegrams and airgrams. The effect of the war on the work of this section is shown by these figures: the number of incoming airgrams and telegrams received and acted upon per month by the distribution and liaison section increased from 246 in January, 1942, to 4,397 in January, 1944. The number of dispatches and reports received for action and distribution in the same period increased from 2,740 to 6,433.

Diplomatic Appointments and Diplomacy

On the whole, President Roosevelt had made a good record for his administration in making diplomatic appointments, but on one occasion he made a selection, which produced such a storm of protest that he was finally compelled to withdraw the nomination. On January 8, 1943, the President wrote as follows to Edward J. Flynn, chairman of the Democratic National Committee:

DEAR EDDIE:

I am sending your nomination to the Senate on Monday as Minister to Australia. In addition, I am appointing you my personal representative with the rank of Ambassador. I do so because in the very large area of the South West Pacific I want to feel free to avail myself of your services on various other forms of activity over and above your duty as Minister.

When Mr. Flynn informed the press of his nomination before the official announcement came from the White House, the newspapers throughout the country attacked the appointment. Not only was Mr. Flynn wholly inexperienced in the diplomatic field, but he had received considerable unfavorable publicity through the alleged use of city-owned paving blocks upon his country estate. Senator Bridges made a series of accusations against Flynn in the Senate, and the Senate Foreign Relations Committee held public hearings. However, although the committee approved the nomination 13 to 10, it seemed probable that the Senate would not accept its committee's findings. Flynn ended the controversy by requesting the President to withdraw his name.

The only other diplomatic change of importance which occurred in 1943 was the resignation of Admiral Standley as ambassador to Russia. The President thereupon named a well known businessman, William Averell Harriman, to the post. Relations with Russia had become so important during the year that Secretary Hull, in spite of the state of his health, attended the Moscow Conference of Foreign Ministers in October, 1943. It was largely due to Secretary Hull's initiative that the four powers, the United States of America, the United Kingdom, the Soviet Union, and China, agreed to cooperate both in the prosecution of the war and in the establishment of an organization to maintain international peace and security. Upon his return, Secretary Hull made a report of his mission before a joint session of the Congress, the first time in history that such an honor was accorded to a Secretary of State.

An interesting example of what might be called house-top diplomacy occurred in the relations between the United States and Argentina in August of 1943. The United States had become weary of waiting for the Argentine break with the Axis powers, and Ambassador Armour decided to return to Washington for consultation. Before leaving, Mr. Armour suggested that Foreign Minister Storni give him a definite statement as to Argentina's position and intentions, preferably in writing. Storni accepted Ambassador Armour's suggestion and gave him a letter to deliver to Secretary Hull. The purport of this missive was to the effect that the United States had misunderstood Argentina's policy of benevolent neutrality. He suggested that if, as a gesture of friendship, the United States would send airplanes and armaments to Argentina, thus returning her to her former military and naval status in South America, the evolu-

THE DEPARTMENT OF STATE

tion of public opinion against the Axis would be more rapid. Secretary Hull wrote a caustic letter in reply and gave the correspondence to the press. He pointed out Argentina's failure to carry out the commitments of the Rio Conference and made it clear that since the United States was guided by considerations of hemispheric security in sending arms to Latin America, and since Argentina refused to aid in the support of this security, no arms or equipment would be forthcoming. Storni was criticized in Argentina so severely for his diplomatic *faux pas* that he was forced to resign from the cabinet.[12]

31

Reorganizing the Department of State

The Stettinius Reorganization Begins

It was to be expected that Under Secretary Stettinius would make some radical changes in the Department's organization and procedure. As a businessman he was inclined to regard the somewhat cumbersome methods which had developed over the years in the Department of State as ineffective and unsatisfactory. Unquestionably, a reorganization was badly needed; but in an agency like the State Department, where international law, protocol, and diplomatic *savoir-faire* enter into the procedure, such a reorganization must be made slowly and by experts fully conversant with the intangibles in the conduct of foreign policy. Under Secretary Stettinius did not adopt this system. In the first place he brought in three Special Assistants to advise him who were as completely inexperienced as himself in the conduct of international affairs. Robert J. Lynch, who was made responsible for appraising recommendations and proposals requiring the attention of the Under Secretary, had been with Mr. Stettinius for ten years as assistant, and he continued in the same capacity. G. Hayden Raynor, who was charged with drafting of policy determinations and regulations for the Under Secretary and for representing the Under Secretary in various staff meetings of the Department, had joined Mr. Stettinius in 1939 on the staff of the War Resources Board. This was his first experience in the field of diplomacy. The third Special Assistant, John E. Orchard, who was to serve as adviser on questions of high policy and postwar international economic relations, was an economist who had joined Mr. Stettinius's staff in 1941 as an economic adviser in the Office of Production Management.

The situation facing the new Under Secretary was the more difficult in that hardly was he confirmed before Secretary Hull left Washington for a week's rest prior to attending the Moscow Conference of Foreign Ministers. This meant that Mr. Stettinius became Acting Secretary of State and had to assume responsibility for important decisions on policy, for conferring with important foreign officials, for liaison with the White House, for attending cabinet meetings, for holding press conferences, and for carrying on the numerous other duties which fall to the Secretary of State.

Nevertheless, the plan for the reorganization of the Department had a high priority, and on November 29, 1943, Under Secretary Stettinius presided over the first session of the staff group on the Reorganization Plan. A memorandum dated November 10 emphasized the necessity of the reorganization by showing the overload carried by high policy officers in the Department. Assistant Secretary Acheson, who was responsible for economic matters, had not only seven divisions dealing with economic affairs, but also two pertaining to treaties. Assistant Secretary Berle, to whom were assigned the wholly disconnected fields of finance, aviation, Canada, and Greenland, was also responsible for the Passport Division, the Division of International Conferences, and the Translating Bureau. Assistant Secretary Long had the most logical assignment—legislative and special war problems, in both of which he had had considerable experience. But he also shared international communications with Assistant Secretary Berle and directed fisheries and the Office of Philippine Affairs. Assistant Secretary of State Shaw, the fiscal and budget officer, was also responsible for the administration of the Department and the Foreign Service, which meant ten divisions, and in addition he supervised the Division of Research and Publications, the Office of the Geographer, and shared international communications with Mr. Berle. But the Under Secretary had the largest assignment of all. Under his jurisdiction were the four political advisers, the four geographical divisions, the Caribbean Office, the Division of Cultural Relations, the Division of Current Information, the Division of Protocol, the Visa Division, the Office of Coordination and Review, and the Central Translating Office.

The first and simplest part of the reorganization was to attempt a regrouping of cognate matters partly on a functional basis. For example, financial and economic matters were joined so that with the abolition of the Office of the Adviser on International Economic Affairs all matters of international economics and finance came under the jurisdiction of Assistant Secretary Acheson. In similar fashion all of the principal administrative functions and those pertaining to public information were placed under Assistant Secretary Shaw. Assistant Secretary Berle was made responsible for the Offices of Controls and Transportation and Communications. Controls covered Passport, Visa, Special War Problems, and Foreign Activities Correlation. The fields of transportation and communications, including aviation, shipping, and telecommunications, were combined under Assistant Secretary Berle. Assistant Secretary Long, whose principal function was liaison with the Congress, was relieved of all administrative responsibility.

As a means of delegating responsibilities in order to relieve the Assistant

Secretaries and the Under Secretary of many of their administrative functions, twelve offices were created, each headed by a Director and a Deputy Director, and the divisions placed under their immediate direction. No office was responsible for more than six, or less than two divisions. Under this setup the Under Secretary had the four Directors of geographical offices and the Office of Special Political Affairs directly responsible to him. In this way the Under Secretary could keep in close touch with the top policy questions in all parts of the world through the Directors of the Offices of American Republic Affairs, European Affairs, Far Eastern Affairs, Near Eastern and African Affairs, and Special Political Affairs. The huge field of administration and public information, supervised by Assistant Secretary Shaw, was divided into the three Offices of Public Information, Departmental Administration, and Foreign Service Administration. Assistant Secretary Acheson's field of economic affairs was divided into the two Offices of Economic Affairs and Wartime Economic Affairs.

An important feature of this establishment of offices in control of certain geographical areas and the elimination of the political advisers was its tendency to centralize policy making closer to the country desks where the expert might be expected to have a greater influence. At the same time the geographical divisions were increased in number so that where formerly there were only four such divisions, the four offices which took their place were divided into nineteen divisions, which made much greater specialization possible. For example, Political Adviser Duggan, who was now Director of the Office of American Republic Affairs, was in direct relations with the Under Secretary above, and with the Chiefs of the Divisions of Mexican Affairs, Caribbean and Central American Affairs, Brazilian Affairs, Bolivian Affairs, River Plate Affairs, and West Coast Affairs. This change, coupled with the wording of the Departmental order of January 15, 1944,[1] which placed the responsibility for "the coordination of policy and action in regard to *all aspects of relations* with the . . . countries," seemed to indicate an intention to combine economic and political aspects. In other words, "So far as they apply to particular countries, the policies or actions of all other offices are to be coordinated by the *area* offices." [2]

Informational and Social Activities

Perhaps the greatest innovation established by the order of January 15 was the recognition of the importance of public relations and the need to keep both the people and their representatives informed regarding foreign policy. It created an Office of Public Information which not only contained the long established divisions of Current Information and Research and Publication, but also a Motion Picture and Radio Division, and a Division of Science, Education, and Art. The United States had never thought it necessary to appoint either press or cultural relations attachés, but the remarkable success of Nazi propaganda in Latin America had made it clear that we could not continue to remain so handicapped in the future. Another innovation was the creation of a Division of Labor Relations. The international aspects of labor could no longer be overlooked, but this division was also concerned with making international agreements in the fields of health, economic and social welfare.[3] In fact a departmental order, dated November 10, 1944, changed the name to Division of International Labor, Social and Health Affairs.

Policy Planning and Administration

The reorganization also attempted to take care of a long recognized need in the Department that had never been adequately met. Long-range planning was a vital requirement for any successful foreign policy, but the top officials were always so immersed in current problems and administrative requirements that no time or opportunity was afforded to give consideration to over-all future contingencies. The reorganization of January 15, 1944, provided for the creation of two top-level committees—a Policy Committee and a Committee on Postwar Programs. The Secretary of State was to serve as chairman of both of these committees and the Under Secretary as vice chairman. The four Assistant Secretaries, the Legal Adviser, the Secretary's Special Assistant Mr. Pasvolsky, and the twelve Directors of offices were members ex officio of both committees. The Policy Committee supplanted the former lower-level Committee on Political Planning: it was to meet regularly three times a week and "assist the Secretary in the consideration of major questions of foreign policy." It is not quite clear why it was necessary to create an almost identical committee to consider postwar planning, which was certainly a "major question of foreign policy." If, as has been alleged, the objective was to harmonize "postwar planning with top policy,"[4] one committee would have been better than two. On the other hand, the establishment of the Office of Special Political Affairs, with its Division of International Security and Organization and Division of Territorial Studies, was an excellent move since it centralized and correlated the whole program looking toward international organization for peace.

In the administration of the Department a decided improvement in organization was accomplished. Under the new Office of Departmental Administration were created the Division of Budget and Finance, the Division of Administrative Management, and the Division of Departmental Personnel— a seemingly logical arrangement both in theory and practice. The Office of Fiscal and Budgetary Affairs and the Division of Accounts were abolished and their functions transferred to the Division of Budget and Finance. Similarly, the Office of Chief Clerk and Administrative Assistant was abolished and its responsibilities transferred to the Division of Administrative Management. It was hoped that this latter division would serve as a sort of governor of the complicated mechanism of administration.

Weaknesses of the Organization of January 15, 1944

Unquestionably a reorganization was needed, and the organization as created by Order 1218 of January 15 remedied certain outstanding defects. The glaring defects in the plan resulted partly from the hasty way in which the vast reorganization was planned, partly from the secrecy with which it was prepared, and particularly from the failure to consult experienced officials either in working out the plan of organization or permitting them to criticize it before it was put into effect. The result was disastrous to the morale of the Department. Numerous signing officers suddenly found themselves without authority to sign contracts, to requisition funds from disbursing officers of the Treasury, or to approve or certify vouchers. An order dated January 24, 1945 was put through to redelegate such authority. Certain heads of divisions, who had done their work effectively for long periods of time, read in the morning paper that overnight they had been reduced to Acting Chiefs. Assistant Secretary Berle refused to appoint directors for the Office of Controls and the Office of Transportation and Communication. He liked the existing arrangement and preferred to have the division Chiefs report directly to him. Mr. McDermott resented the transfer of the Division of Current Information to the Office of Public Information and persuaded the Secretary of State to appoint him Special Assistant to the Secretary of State in charge of press relations.[5] Similarly, George T. Summerlin objected to being made subordinate to an office Director, with the result that Secretary Hull detached the Division of Protocol from the Office of Departmental Administration and attached it to the Chief of Protocol, Special Assistant to the Secretary.

One of the greatest gaffs was the elimination of the Office of Coordination and Review, the agency best equipped to discover and remedy the mistakes which were bound to be made as a result of the drastic reorganization. The Chief of this office, Mrs. Blanche Halla, was designated as an Executive Assistant to the Secretary of State, and the Assistant Chiefs, Miss Sarah Moore and Miss Helen Daniel, were assigned to the Division of Communications and Records. Although the order provided that the review of outgoing correspondence and the other work performed by the office be transferred to the Division of Communications and Records, the remaining personnel of the office were not mentioned nor was any arrangement made with the Division of Communications and Records to take charge of the work. To prevent utter confusion, the office continued to function extralegally. Meanwhile, the various divisions and officers, who depended so completely upon the office for accuracy and suitability of their communications in both form and content, had registered such vigorous objections that less than a month later a new Departmental order established a Division of Coordination and Review in the Office of Departmental Administration and with the identical personnel of the former office.

In setting up the Telecommunications Division, radio, telegraph, and cable communications were covered, but telephone and mail were omitted. A new Departmental order was required to meet this deficiency. A stupid blunder changed the name of the Division of Near Eastern Affairs to the Office of Eastern and African Affairs. A new Departmental order was required to give it the name intended—Office of Near Eastern and African Affairs. Mr. Rayner, adviser on petroleum policy in the Office of Economic Affairs, wanted a petroleum division: one was created for him and he became its Acting Chief, as well as retaining his position as adviser. The jurisdiction of the Aviation Division was so vague and limited in scope that a new order was issued enumerating eleven specific functions and responsibilities in place of the four originally required. Space prevents even listing the constant stream of amendments and changes which were found necessary to fill gaps, remedy faults, or to improve procedure in the jerry-built Order No. 1218. However, one other illustration deserves mention. In setting up the Office of American Republic Affairs, no mention whatsoever was made of the very important Analysis and Materials Unit, which had been functioning most effectively under various names for several years in the Division of American Republics. Various work sheets were utilized to retain the personnel and carry on the activities until a Departmental order, dated May 3, 1944, established a Division of American Republics Analysis and Liaison in the Office of American Republic Affairs. In all, some thirty-three Departmental orders were issued which specifically amended Order No. 1218 between January 15, 1944, and December 20, 1944, when Order No. 1301 once more completely reorganized the Department.

In regard to the Foreign Service, Order 1218 wisely left the reorganization largely in the hands of experienced Foreign Service officers. An Office of Foreign Service Administration was created with Foreign Service Officer John G. Erhardt as Director; and the Division of Foreign Service Personnel and the Division of Foreign Service Administration were made responsible for functions in these fields. Foreign Service Officer Nathaniel P. Davis was Chief of the first, and Foreign Service Officer Monnett B. Davis, Chief of the second. The Foreign Service Buildings Office and the Office of Foreign Service Furnishings were abolished and their functions vested in the Administration Division. Director Erhardt promptly formed a planning staff to study and anticipate the needs of the Foreign Service and to prepare an integrated program of reforms. One of its first projects was the organization of the Joint Survey Group of seventy-one members and associates who were directed to study and recommend measures to bring the reporting of the Foreign Service to a maximum efficiency.[6]

As regards personnel, the reorganization of January 15, 1944, for the most part utilized the officers who were already in charge of the same or similar functions. In the top echelons of Assistant Secretaries and above no changes were made. With reference to the four Special Assistants to the Secretary currently serving—Messrs. Finletter, Green, MacMurray, and Grew—three were retained and three new ones were named: Messrs. Pasvolsky, Summerlin, and McDermott. Foreign Service Officer MacMurray retired. Robert Woods Bliss was added as Consultant, and Carlton Savage remained as General Consultant. Professor Arthur W. Macmahon, who had helped draft the new organization plan, was retained as Consultant on Administration. Three new advisers were named, but from the Department staff: Frederick Livesey and Leroy D. Stinebower as Advisers to the Office of Economic Affairs, and Charles A. Thomson as Adviser to the Office of Public Information. All of the new Directors of offices were drawn from the Department. The four advisers on political relations, Duggan, Dunn, Hornbeck, and Murray, became Directors of the geographical offices of the regions in which they were specialists—Latin America, Europe, the Far East, and the Near East respectively. Harry Hawkins, Chief of the Division of Commercial Policy and Agreements, became Director of the Office of Economic Affairs. Charles P. Taft, Special Adviser on Supply and Resources, was made Director of Wartime Economic Affairs.

For some unexplained reason Mr. Pasvolsky was not made Director of the Office of Special Political Affairs, which directed postwar planning, his particular field. Instead, Director Dunn of European Affairs became Acting Director of this office. John Dickey, formerly Special Consultant, became Director of the Office of Public Information, and John C. Ross, formerly Executive Officer and Chief of the Division of Personnel, was made Director of Departmental Administration. We have already noted that Foreign Service Officer Erhardt became Director of Foreign Service Administration and that no directors were appointed in the Offices of Controls and Transportation and Communication. Of the fifty-one divisions set up under the line offices, forty-nine were given Chiefs who were experienced Departmental officials, and in two—the Divisions of Supply and Resources and the Division of Science, Education, and Art—Chiefs were not immediately appointed. It was very fortunate for the Department that the personnel knew its lines, regardless of cues, or the results of the reorganization might have been even more harmful. The Department in its press announcement wisely left a loophole for retreat: "The Department does not believe that this new organization chart and the Departmental Order are the final answer to all the Department's administrative problems."

Throughout 1944 plans were being formulated for a further over-all re-organization which could remedy the weaknesses of Order 1218. In a memorandum dated January 29, 1944, Professor Arthur W. Macmahon, Consultant to the Department, proposed a central secretariat for the Policy Committee and the Committee on Postwar Programs. The idea was developed further by Charles W. Yost and Charles Easton Rothwell, the executive secretaries of the two top committees, into plans later carried out for the establishment of a strong single secretariat. To carry out the reorganization effectively, it was felt that the Department needed at least two more Assistant Secretaries of State, and in a report dated February 21, 1944, Acting Secretary of State Stettinius recommended the addition of two additional Secretaries who should serve without numerical designation of rank.[7] The President submitted the draft bill with a message recommending its passage, and on December 8, 1944, Congress authorized the appointment of two more Assistant Secretaries of State.

Before taking up the reorganization plan put into effect on December 20, 1944, it is desirable to note some of the changes in the Department's personnel which occurred during 1944. A praiseworthy tendency to appoint outstanding men of experience in foreign affairs as advisers or Special Assistants to the Secretary of State brought into the Department men like Robert Woods Bliss, Henry P. Fletcher, and Isaiah Bowman. Career men were utilized both to head important agencies or to serve as advisers, as, for example, when long experienced Foreign Service Officers Stanley K. Hornbeck and George A. Gordon were made Special Assistants to the Secretary; Joseph C. Grew was made Director of the Office of Far Eastern Affairs, Edwin C. Wilson, Director of the Office of Special Political Affairs, and Norman Armour was placed at the head of the Office of American Republic Affairs. The latter appointment was particularly important because in the resignation of Laurence Duggan in July, 1944, the Department lost an official who had been of the greatest assistance in building up more cordial relations with Latin America. The appointment of Professor Bernard Haley as Director of the Office of Economic Affairs recognized both his services as Chief of the Commodities Division and his outstanding ability as an economist and as an administrator.

Cordell Hull Resigns

The change in the Departmental personnel which dwarfed all others in importance came late in November, 1944, when after almost twelve years of service, the longest term of office ever held by an American Secretary of State, Cordell Hull resigned because of ill health. In accepting his resignation most

inridge Long and Adolf Berle could probably have been prevailed upon to remain.[9] Dean Acheson, formerly in charge of economic affairs, was retained to take over the relations with Congress formerly carried on by Mr. Long, and in addition he was to be responsible for the Department's participation in international conferences. President Roosevelt nominated Joseph C. Grew for the position of Under Secretary of State, William L. Clayton to be Assistant Secretary in charge of foreign economic affairs, Nelson A. Rockefeller to be Assistant Secretary in charge of relations with the Latin American republics, and Archibald MacLeish to be Assistant Secretary of State in charge of public and cultural relations. Four days later, on December 8, 1944, the same day that the bill creating two new Assistant Secretaries of State was approved, the President sent to the Senate two other nominations for Assistant Secretaries of State, James C. Dunn and Julius C. Holmes.

It is doubtful whether a better selection for Under Secretary of State could have been made than in the appointment of Joseph C. Grew. A career Foreign Service officer since 1904, Mr. Grew was personally familiar with conditions in Europe and the Far East. He had headed the Division of European Affairs in the Department, and had served as Under Secretary of State from 1924 to 1927. After his service as ambassador to Japan, Mr. Grew had been made Special Assistant to Secretary Hull and subsequently Director of the Office of Far Eastern Affairs. When he appeared before the Senate Committee on Foreign Relations, Mr. Grew confessed that only the serious emergency persuaded him to accept the onerous position of Under Secretary of State at this time.

The nomination of William L. Clayton as Assistant Secretary of State in charge of foreign economic affairs was also an excellent one. Mr. Clayton had been in the cotton business on an international scale for over twenty-five years, and he had held numerous important positions in the government, such as Deputy Federal Loan Administrator, Assistant Secretary of Commerce, and Surplus War Property Administrator. He had been uniformly successful as an administrator, and he was an ardent and consistent supporter of Secretary Hull's trade-agreements policy.

Nelson A. Rockefeller, who had been Coordinator of Inter-American Affairs for a period of four and a half years, seemed to be a reasonable choice for the position of Assistant Secretary of State in charge of Latin American affairs. He was an ardent supporter of the Good Neighbor Policy and had contributed effectively to the strengthening of inter-American relationships. He had shown both vision and business ability as president of Rockefeller Center in New York. His interest in government was philanthropic rather than materialistic, and although not as experienced in Latin American diplomacy and politics as a Welles or a Duggan, the appointment could be defended. Foreign Service Officer James C. Dunn, who was to be in charge of the other geographical offices as Assistant Secretary of State, had had twenty-four years of service in either the Foreign Service or the Department. As former Adviser on Political Affairs and as Director of the Office of European Affairs, Mr. Dunn was a logical choice. Some criticism was leveled at his conservative leanings, particularly regarding his partiality toward the Franco regime in Spain, but there were two sides to the story of our relations with Spain.[10]

The position of Assistant Secretary of State in charge of administration has recently become one of the most important and difficult positions in the Department. A most excellent choice was made in picking Brigadier General Julius C. Holmes for this post. He was well equipped by experience and training to assume this position in a very critical period. Mr. Holmes had served as a career officer in the Foreign Service for twelve years and was Assistant Chief of the Division of International Conferences when he resigned from the Department. Subsequently, as Vice President of the New York World's Fair, he was responsible for relations with the Federal government and foreign governments. Shortly after the entrance of the United States into the war, Mr. Holmes, who was then president of General Mills of Brazil, volunteered and was made brigadier general in 1943. The army was loath to release General Holmes, but agreed to do so as a means of bringing about a closer rapprochement between the Departments of State and War. Since General Holmes could not leave his position as Deputy Chief of Staff for Civil Affairs in Paris immediately, John G. Erhardt, Director of the Office of Foreign Service Administration, served as Acting Assistant Secretary of State until General Holmes took the oath of office on January 29, 1945.

The principal opposition to the new appointments was centered upon Archibald MacLeish, the New Assistant Secretary of State in charge of public and cultural relations. It was alleged that as head of the defunct Office of Facts and Figures Mr. MacLeish told what he thought the people ought to know instead of what had happened. Since some senators wished to question Mr. Clayton, and others Mr. Dunn, the Senate followed the unusual procedure of sending the names back to the Committee on Foreign Relations in order that open hearings might be held. Apparently the New Dealers felt that Wall Street was too well represented, while the conservatives didn't like the MacLeish brand of poetry or his ideas on Communism. All were finally confirmed, both in the committee on December 14 and in the Senate on December 19. Grew obtained the highest ratio of support, 66 to 7, and MacLeish the lowest, 43 to 25.[11]

32

The Department of State Reorganizes Again

Reorganization of December 20, 1944

The announcement of another over-all reorganization of the Department of State was made on December 20, 1944, simultaneously with the confirmation of the names of the new Under Secretary and the five new Assistant Secretaries. The day after his nomination had been approved by the Senate as Secretary of State, Mr. Stettinius discussed with John Ross, the Director of the Office of Departmental Administration, four alternative charts which had been prepared for the reorganization of the Department. He chose one between the two extremes of a mild or a sweeping reorganization.

The new organization as prescribed by Departmental Order 1301 revised and extended the organization of January 15, 1944. The first notable change was the substitution of a Staff Committee for the old Policy Committee, and a Coordinating Committee in place of the Committee on Postwar Programs. The new Staff Committee in reality combined both jurisdictions of the two old committees and became the top-level policy committee of the Department. It consisted of the Secretary, the Under Secretary, the six Assistant Secretaries, the Legal Adviser, and the Special Assistant for International Organization. It would meet on call and advise and assist the Secretary in determining current and long-range foreign policy. The Coordinating Committee was a lower-level committee, consisting of the Under Secretary, the twelve office Directors, and the Special Assistant for Press Relations, which would give prior consideration to questions of policy and could also discuss questions of interoffice relations. This new dual-committee organization lent itself to more thorough consideration of problems of policy and more prompt action on the upper level.

A new agency, designated as the Joint Secretariat, was a vital cog in the machinery of operations. Its function was both to collect and to coordinate subject matter for important decisions of policy and procedure and to see to it that such action as was authorized was carried out promptly by the operating agencies. With the development of interdepartmental committees the Joint Secretariat was also expected to keep the Department's representatives informed as to the Department's position in regard to major questions of foreign policy. The Joint Secretariat was also required to keep the official records of the committees and to prepare periodic reports on action taken. Two experienced State Department officials were made executive secretaries of the Joint Secretariat, Charles W. Yost and C. Easton Rothwell.

The new plan improved considerably the coordination of economic matters in the Department by placing all of them under Assistant Secretary Clayton. It had quickly become evident after the January 15 reorganization that a serious problem arises when functional and jurisdictional units exist side by side. Only two weeks after the Eastern Hemisphere Division had been set up in the Office of Wartime Economic Affairs, its Chief, Mr. Labouisse, wrote a memorandum asserting that the economic aspects of our foreign policy had become so merged with the political that except in a limited number of special situations it was impractical and unwise to continue an administrative separation within the Department. He suggested that the political divisions be given primary responsibility for all matters affecting their special areas, economic as well as political, and that the economic units be built along purely functional and commodity lines.

Inasmuch as Assistant Secretary Clayton wished more time to consider the reorganization plan, no change was made in the economic offices on December 20. However, an even greater reorganization was made a month later, on January 26, 1945.[1] The Offices of Economic Affairs and Wartime Economic Affairs were abolished, and in their places the Office of Commercial Policy (soon afterward renamed the Office of International Trade Policy), and the Office of Financial and Development Policy were established. It seemed advisable to give less attention to problems of the war and more to the postwar economic problems which were already beginning to engage the Department. Another step looking toward postwar preparations occurred in the International Trade Policy Office on April 25, 1945, when the War Supply and Resources Division was merged with the Commodities Division. As of May 1, 1945, the other divisions of the Office of International Trade Policy were War Areas Economic Division, Petroleum Division, Commercial Policy Division, and Division of International Labor, Social, and Health Affairs. It might be noted that four of these divisions were functional, and that only one of the so-called "area" divisions remained.

On March 1, 1945, the Office of Financial and Development Policy was given jurisdiction over four divisions: Financial Affairs, Foreign Economic Development, Lend-Lease and Surplus War Property Affairs, and Economic Security Controls.[2] The last division took over the staff of the World Trade

Intelligence Division and continued to enforce the Proclaimed List, the Safehaven program, controls over funds and property, and the collection and evaluation of biographic data. When established in March, 1945, this division had over one hundred persons on its staff. It seemed that the new organization, with its logical administrative allocation of functions and its emphasis upon postwar problems, was equipped to deal with the many and complex tasks facing it.

The importance of the geographic desks in the new reorganization was emphasized by allocating two Assistant Secretaries to direct their activities, James C. Dunn in charge of European, Far Eastern, Near Eastern, and African Affairs, and Nelson Rockefeller in charge of American Republics Affairs. A slight increase in the number of divisions permitted more intensive consideration of certain areas and research pertaining to them.

One of the new divisions was a very successful experiment. It was called the Division of American Republics Analysis and Liaison, and although formally established on May 3, 1944, it had already been functioning most effectively before that time. Its analysis of data and its preparation of special reports proved to be most useful, not only to the Department of State, but to many other outside governmental agencies. The requests for information averaged about one hundred per month, of which over one-fourth were answered on an immediate basis from information available in the files; about one-half required more extensive research, while one-sixth required the preparation of special memoranda. The following illustrate the type of queries: a desk officer wanted information regarding the number, the ownership, and size of the railways of Colombia; the Navy wanted information regarding a deceased South American statesman before christening a boat in his honor; various agencies desired to know the status of our trade agreements with the other American republics; a high governmental official wished to obtain the reaction of the other American republics to Mrs. Roosevelt's visits.

Informational Activities of the Department

By assigning an Assistant Secretary of State to devote his entire attention to the field of public and cultural relations, the new attitude of the Department toward informational activities was emphasized. Before Pearl Harbor the information activities of the Department of State were for the most part confined to press and publication activities supplemented by speeches made by officials of the Department. Neither the motion picture nor radio were utilized to any extent. As a result of the need for close censorship of information during the war, the principal immediate developments were the publication of documentary materials, such as the volume *Peace and War*, and the two-volume publication *Foreign Relations of the United States: Japan 1931-1941*. Whereas in 1941 some 700 press releases were issued, in 1942 they dropped to about 600, and in 1943 to less than 550. On the other hand the Division of Current Information increased materially the information facilities to the officers of the Department and in the field. The *Radio Bulletin,* a compilation of current news sent to the officers abroad, which was first issued on March 30, 1935, was enlarged and editorial comment from representative newspapers was added. The *Information Series,* a confidential survey of world affairs, was expanded, and after January 1, 1944, it was issued weekly instead of monthly. Beginning on October 25, 1943, a concise summary of news relating to the interests of the State Department was prepared each morning and was distributed to the President, the Secretary of State, and to about two hundred officials of the Department. In its new publication the *Bulletin of the Department of State,* published by the Division of Research and Publications, the Department gave a considerable amount of current information which was of great value to the public. By means of carefully prepared signed articles by experts in the Department, many controversial problems were analyzed and clarified. Outstanding addresses of officials of the Department, texts of primary documents, and significant international agreements enhanced the value of the *Bulletin* to scholars.

On June 29, 1943, Secretary Hull appointed John S. Dickey as Special Consultant to formulate a program of closer relationship between the Department of State and private organizations. This was regularized by a Departmental order of September 1, 1943. In a memorandum which Mr. Dickey wrote to Assistant Secretary Shaw, he made a statement which, unfortunately, is probably even closer to the truth today than when he made it. "The point has been reached," he wrote, "where there can be no question concerning the widespread dissatisfaction and doubt which exists in all circles regarding the State Department as an institution." [3] As a first step toward orienting the public on the work of the Department, a series of four radio broadcasts entitled "The State Department Speaks" were given in January, 1944. High departmental officials, including Secretary Hull, Under Secretary Stettinius, and Assistant Secretaries Acheson, Berle, Long, and Shaw, participated. The current reorganization of the Department was explained and assurance was given that the State Department welcomed public interest in its activities.

In the reorganization of January 15, 1944, as we have seen, an Office of Public Information was established, and Mr. Dickey was made Director. One immediate innovation was the establishment of a visitor's reception room in the State Department Building, where the public might receive more considerate treatment than it had in the past. In the reorganization of December 20, 1944, Archibald MacLeish, at that time Librarian of Congress, was made Assistant Secretary of State in charge of Public and Cultural Relations. The name of Mr. Dickey's office was changed to Office of Public Affairs so that the two-way relationship between the Department and the public might be emphasized. The instrumentality used to acquaint the public with Departmental policy was the Division of Public Liaison, which had been established on February 22, 1944. The functions of this division included the Department's relations with private groups interested in the formulation of foreign policy, the collection and analysis of materials relating to public attitudes on foreign policy questions, and the handling of correspondence expressing public views on foreign policy.

To prove the Department's intention to explain its policies to the public, Assistant Secretary MacLeish arranged a series of seven broadcasts covering the following subjects: "America's Foreign Policy," "Main Street and Dumbarton Oaks," "The World Trade and World Peace," "What About the Liberated Areas?" "What About the Enemy Countries?" "America's Good Neighbors," and "It's Your State Department." Of the 2,900 letters received by the Department during these broadcasts, all but fifteen were commendatory.

The reorganization of December 20, 1944, also paid attention to the dissemination of information abroad. This work was originally performed by the Department when the Division of Cultural Relations was established in 1938. The reorganization of January 15, 1944, separated the cultural work of the Department from the informational by dividing up the work of the Division of Cultural Relations into two parts, one which related to the exchange of professors and students and all matters pertaining to international cooperation in the fields of science, education, and art, and the other to the dissemination of information abroad largely by the radio and the motion picture. The Division of Science, Education, and Art, whose name was changed on July 7, 1944, to the Division of Cultural Cooperation, took care of the activities of the first category. The agency responsible for the second was called the Motion-Picture and Radio Division.

The war had brought home the need for effective propaganda abroad, and various agencies, particularly the Office of War Information, the Coordinator of Inter-American Affairs, and the War Department, had engaged in these activities. The Motion-Picture and Radio Division was directed to effect a liaison with these agencies. However, the new agency was also made responsible for the development and execution of cultural programs through these media, thus emphasizing this aspect as well as that of press relations. This meant more jurisdictional difficulties, and due to the persistence of John Begg, Chief of the Division, a new Departmental order, dated August 31, 1944, changed the name to International Information Division and specifically limited its jurisdiction to overseas information activities. As evidence of its work, in January, 1945, the officers of the International Information Division working with the Office of War Information cleared 626 glossy prints, 299 plastic plates, reviewed 40 editions of the OWI news letters, checked 142 feature articles, and examined 47 articles for inclusion in OWI publications. In one instance a pamphlet describing each of the United Nations was reviewed by seventeen divisions of the State Department; so many errors were found that OWI killed the copy. In the fiscal year 1944 the division dispatched for use abroad a total of 2,200 reels of motion pictures to twenty-four posts in twenty different countries.

The Department of State became interested in radio first as a mechanism, and believed that control over broadcasting should be based upon government allocation of frequencies or by licensing control of facilities. The Telecommunications Division was responsible for this aspect. During the war the emphasis of control shifted to the content, and the radio section of the International Information Division was made responsible for liaison between the Department and governmental broadcasting agencies and for planning for broadcasting in the postwar era. One radio project, prepared jointly by the International Information Division and Office of Inter-American Affairs and entitled "Music in American Life," utilized fifty-two programs of a half hour each and received enthusiastic praise in the Latin American republics. A Special Committee on Communications, with Assistant Secretary of State Clayton as chairman, recommended in February, 1945, that direct short-wave broadcasts originating in the United States should be continued after the war on a daily basis.

International Organization and Security

Considerable progress had been made since the organization of January 15, 1944 had established the Office of Special Political Affairs with two divisions, International Organization and Security, and Territorial Studies. It will be remembered that at the Moscow Conference held in October, 1943, the four great powers had agreed to establish an international security organization and that exchanges of views should take place as soon as practicable in Washington. On February 17, 1944, the State Department sent to the British and Russian embassies a list of topics upon which studies were being prepared in regard to international organization. The British had already submitted a list, and the Russians agreed to use the American and British lists as a basis for discussion.

The State Department specialists submitted a series of recommendations on April 12, suggesting that the four nations take immediate steps to reach a consensus of opinion regarding the fundamental features of an international organization plan. They could then convene a general conference to work out an agreement embodying the charter of the organization. The preliminary draft prepared by the American experts was ready on April 24, and Secretary

Hull thereupon submitted it in confidence to Charles Evans Hughes, John W. Davis, and Nathan L. Miller. All three made suggestions and approved the draft. Secretary Hull also gave copies of the draft in confidence to a small select bipartisan committee of the Senate to discuss the principles and procedures of the proposed plan. The senatorial group agreed that the draft should be submitted to the other three powers but were unable to agree upon a public statement. Early in June Secretary Hull followed the same procedure with a bipartisan group of representatives. At the same time Assistant Secretary of State Long was attempting to persuade the Democratic and Republican national conventions to adopt planks favoring an international organization.

On July 17 the State Department announced publicly that conversations regarding an international security organization would take place in Washington in August. On July 18 the United States presented tentative draft proposals for an international organization to both the British and Russian chargés d'affaires and to the Chinese ambassador. The Soviets now requested an extension of time to study the proposals, and the date of the conference was moved back to August 21. The place chosen for the conference was Dumbarton Oaks, the beautiful Georgetown estate which formerly belonged to Robert Woods Bliss, who had donated it to Harvard University.

Secretary Hull from the beginning was determined to keep the question of postwar international organization out of domestic politics. A statement by Governor Dewey of New York, on August 16, that the Dumbarton Oaks Conference, according to reports, intended to place the world under great-power domination disturbed Mr. Hull to such an extent that he immediately called his advisers into conference. It was decided that a statement be issued denying the allegation and explaining the intentions of the four governments. Secretary Hull also agreed to meet Governor Dewey and discuss the matter with him. Governor Dewey accepted the offer and sent the able internationalist John Foster Dulles to represent him. Secretary Hull gave Mr. Dulles a copy of the United States proposals and discussed them at length with him in several long conferences. The two men finally came to an agreement on most of the controversial issues and issued a public announcement to that effect on August 25. This was followed by an exchange of letters between Secretary Hull and Governor Dewey, emphasizing the nonpartisan character of the discussions.

The Conference at Dumbarton Oaks

The American delegation to the Dumbarton Oaks Conference, headed by Under Secretary Stettinius, included the following representatives of the State Department: Dr. Isaiah Bowman and Henry P. Fletcher, Special Assistants to the Secretary of State; Assistant Secretary of State Breckinridge Long; Joseph

C. Grew, Director of the Office of Far Eastern Affairs; James C. Dunn, Director of the Office of European Affairs; Edwin C. Wilson, Director of the Office of Special Political Affairs; Leo Pasvolsky, Executive Director of the Committee on Postwar Programs; Dr. Stanley K. Hornbeck, Special Assistant to the Secretary of State; and Legal Adviser Green H. Hackworth. Michael McDermott acted as Press Officer, and Dr. Harley Notter as General Adviser, Alger Hiss served as Executive Secretary, Easton Rothwell as Assistant Executive Secretary, and James Frederick Green as Documents Officer. A considerable number of the State Department experts who had been working on the various proposals, such as Benjamin Gerig, Durward Sandifer, Charles W. Yost, Esther Brunauer, Clyde Eagleton, Grayson L. Kirk, Laurence Preuss, and Norman Padelford, were also included to serve as the international secretariat. A half dozen military representatives from the top ranks of the army and navy completed the delegation. Secretary Morgenthau asked that a Treasury observer be invited, but his request was refused. After his opening address, Secretary Hull did not participate actively in the conference, but both he and President Roosevelt followed its deliberations carefully.

When the conference had finished its deliberations, the four participating governments issued a statement which included the text of The Proposals for the Establishment of a General International Organization.[4] The State Department immediately began a campaign to publicize the draft Charter so that as much popular comment as possible might be provoked. Teams of speakers from the State Department arranged to discuss the project in off-the-record hearings before picked audiences all over the United States.[5] At a conference on peace organization held in the Department of State under the auspices of Americans United for World Organization and the Commission to Study the Organization of Peace, representatives of ninety-six organizations heard an off-the-record discussion by Under Secretary Stettinius, Dr. Pasvolsky, and Judge Hackworth. Numerous radio broadcasts were made, millions of copies of the text of the Proposals were distributed, and the State Department prepared four Foreign Affairs Outlines on Building the Peace.

The second general reorganization of the Department, on December 20, 1944, retained the Office of Special Political Affairs, but its divisions were changed to meet the new requirements. The Division of International Security and Organization was replaced by the Divisions of International Security, International Organization Affairs, and Dependent Areas. The Division of Territorial Studies was temporarily continued but was abolished as of March 1, 1945, and its personnel transferred largely to the geographic divisions. The Divisions of International Organization Affairs and International Security Affairs were made responsible for the formulation of policy regarding the establishment of the proposed United Nations Organization, and the Division of Dependent

Areas was concerned with the delicate but vitally important problem of trustee-ships. The whole international organization was placed under the jurisdiction of Special Assistant Leo Pasvolsky, with Edwin C. Wilson, a long-experienced career diplomat, as Director of the Office of Special Political Affairs, and Alger Hiss as Deputy Director. Harley Notter, formerly Chief of the Division of International Security and Organization, was made adviser to the office.

Early in 1945 Foreign Service Officer Wilson was transferred as ambassador to Turkey and Deputy Director Alger Hiss, who was subsequently to be placed on trial for his loyalty, was made Director. He was succeeded on March 5, 1947, by Colonel Dean Rusk who after overseas service in the army had entered the State Department as Assistant Chief of the Division of International Security Affairs. Director Rusk was still in charge when the Office of Special Political Affairs in January, 1948, was more appropriately designated Office of United Nations Affairs, and he remained Director till he was named Assistant Secretary of State, January 31, 1949.

Assistant Secretary of State for Administration

One of the most difficult problems of a large fluctuating organization is to obtain a satisfactory efficient administrative organization. The reorganization of December 20, 1944, by divorcing all matters of policy from the administrative agency and by obtaining an exceedingly able administrative officer, General Julius C. Holmes, who had had experience both in the Department of State and in the Foreign Service, made an excellent start. Three offices were established: Departmental Administration, Foreign Service, and Controls. The first of these, under the direction of John C. Ross, was the largest and most unwieldy. Eight divisions were placed under this office, but four of them were comparatively small, highly specialized, and needed practically no supervision. These were the Divisions of Coordination and Review, International Conferences, Protocol, and Cryptography. The other four were large and vitally important to the effective functioning of the entire Department of State; these were the Divisions of Budget and Finance, Management Planning, Departmental Personnel, and Central Services.

The Division of Budget and Finance, as its name indicates, was made responsible for the budgetary, fiscal, and accounting functions of the Department of State. With the increased responsibilities contemplated for the reorganized Department, it devolved upon the Division of Budget and Finance to prepare carefully documented estimates for the expansion of activities and to defend them before the Congress. The appropriations which the Department receives depend to a considerable extent upon the care which is taken in preparing and presenting the budget estimates. One of the important duties of a fiscal nature is the responsibility for handling the Department's emergency fund, which is not subject to review by the General Accounting Office. The fund is strictly for emergency use, and has provided for the repatriation of Foreign Service personnel and their families, for loans to American citizens abroad engulfed by the sudden outbreak of war, for the exchanging of prisoners of war and civilian internees, and for the protection of American interests in enemy and enemy-occupied territory. A part of the Department's official entertaining in Washington, including the expenditures of the Blair and the Blair-Lee houses, is paid from the Emergency Fund. Harry M. Kurth, Chief of the Division, was also Deputy Director of the Office of Departmental Administration.

The Division of Management Planning had as its responsibility the perfection of procedures and organizational structure so that the Department might assume the expanded functions and duties imposed by changes brought about by the war and postwar conditions. The Division of Departmental Personnel was responsible for providing an adequate and efficient personnel, which meant giving attention to such factors as the proper classification of positions, the methods of recruitment and placement of employees, the proper utilization of personnel, an adequate scale of promotion and suitable training, and health and recreation programs.

The Division of Central Services, the largest division in the Department, took over the Division of Administrative Services and the Division of Communications and Records. This division was responsible for all the communications services of the Department, for the maintenance of records and files, and for the procurement and supply activities of the Department. This included the procurement and allocation of space. Inasmuch as the Department was already scattered among some twenty-four buildings and steadily expanding, the problem of space was a very serious one. Foreign Service Officer Raymond Geist, Chief of the Division of Communications and Records, was made Chief of the new Division of Central Services.

The Office of Controls was charged with four divisions, one of which, the Passport Division, was run so efficiently by its Chief, Ruth Shipley, that any attempted outside reorganization or supervision would have been a serious mistake. The Visa Division, which controlled immigration, was always under fire because of its fearless efforts to enforce the laws which the Congress had passed. As a consequence, its Chief was regularly a Foreign Service officer who after about three years of service in this division would be ready to return to the field. Its Chief, Howard K. Travers, appointed in 1942, would soon be transferred abroad. Since Assistant Chief Eliot Coulter was a permanent official and had been in the division almost twenty years, the rotation of Chiefs was less of a handicap. The Special War Problems Division was finishing up its program, and the Division of Foreign Activity Correlation was so secretive as to its activities that even the Secretary of State was not informed of some of its work. The specialists in reorganization wisely made few suggestions for changes in these smoothly functioning divisions under the Office of Controls.

Foreign Service Administration

Although this volume is primarily interested in the State Department in Washington rather than in its representatives abroad, the latter cannot be entirely overlooked. The new duties and activities of the Department required a much more diversified service abroad, and the second reorganization plan was expected to meet the new situation. However, inasmuch as many of the autonomous agencies abroad were not yet ready to disband, the principal changes in Foreign Service administration came in 1945.

Assistant Secretary Holmes, who had been a Foreign Service officer, felt that a first requirement was to make arrangements for improving and expanding the system of consultation with returning Foreign Service officers, both within the Department and with other interested agencies. A Departmental order, dated February 8, 1945, required the returning officer to report at his earliest convenience to the Office of the Foreign Service, whose responsibility it was to see that he should have the opportunity to confer with the appropriate individuals, both in the Department and outside. He was authorized to do trade-conference work with the regional offices of the Bureau of Foreign and Domestic Commerce and to be made available for speaking engagements before representative groups and associations in various parts of the country.

On April 7, 1945, a Departmental order provided for the expansion and complete reorganization of the Office of the Foreign Service to meet the government's need for vigorous and effective representation abroad during the transition from war to peace and in the postwar period. A Division of Foreign Service Planning was created to define and analyze the functions and activities to be carried on by the Foreign Service, to initiate new projects and surveys, and to make any recommendations which would enable the Foreign Service to keep pace with its expanding and increasingly diversified responsibilities. A Division of Training Services was set up to provide basic orientation for junior officers and to offer advanced courses for Foreign Service officers in preparation for high administrative and fiscal duties. Specialized training at selected colleges, universities, and technical schools was an essential part of the program. A Division of Foreign Reporting Services was established to make certain that all governmental agencies, which might utilize it, might be supplied with full and timely information necessary to the discharge of their responsibilities. The Division of Foreign Service Personnel was retained and no radical changes were made in the duties of the three existing bodies concerned with the recruiting, training, and promotion of personnel.

Conclusions Regarding the December 20, 1944, Reorganization

The second reorganization of 1944 was in reality a continuation of the reorganization of January 15, 1944. It was made more slowly, more carefully, and it profited by the previous mistakes. The reorganization of January 15 attempted to combine like functions under a single office; the second went further and grouped the related offices under a single Assistant Secretary. The fact that there were six instead of four Assistant Secretaries, and two other officials—the Legal Adviser and the Special Assistant in charge of International Organization and Security—of approximately the same rank made this allocation possible. An improvement was evident in the grouping of similar functions within offices and divisions. The greatest improvement lay in the channeling of reporting, which reduced very considerably the flow of policy problems to the top-level officers, thus giving more time for consideration of the most vital questions and over-all policy. The two top policy committees, with the coordinating Joint Secretariat, were built upon sounder bases of policy making than their immediate predecessors. There still remained the very serious problem of bringing the various agencies operating autonomously overseas on a wartime basis under the control of the State Department either by a merging operation or by the abolition of their personnel and activities.

33

Secretary Stettinius and Acting Secretary Grew

The Department Organization Under Stettinius

President Franklin D. Roosevelt nominated Edward R. Stettinius, Jr., as Secretary of State on November 27, 1944, and on June 27, 1945, the day after the conference on the United Nations at San Francisco ended, President Harry Truman accepted Mr. Stettinius's resignation. During this seven-month period Secretary Stettinius spent more than half of his time attending international conferences abroad. This meant that Under Secretary Joseph C. Grew, during the absences of Secretary Stettinius, served as Acting Secretary of State. Whereas Secretary Hull had a total staff of about seventy, including all employees, Secretary Stettinius increased the staff of the Secretary's office to a total of 130.

In the Secretary of State's immediate office there were as assistants a number of experienced officers, such as Charles E. Bohlen, a Foreign Service officer responsible for White House liaison both for the Department and for the Foreign Service; Morris N. Hughes, a Foreign Service officer appointed to draft and execute special assignments; and Foreign Service Officer R. Borden Reams, assigned as Information Officer. Blanche Halla, Chief of the Division of Coordination and Review, was made responsible for the review and coordination of all correspondence drafted for the signature of the Secretary, a very wise precaution.

A number of outsiders with no diplomatic or State Department experience were brought in at salaries of $8,000 or more to draft or execute special assignments. Louis Kepler Hyde, Jr., who had served for one year in the Office of Lend-Lease Administration and one year as Deputy Trade Relations Adviser in the Foreign Economic Administration, was appointed at a salary of $8,250 "for compilation, review, and analysis of major policies and actions." There were also a considerable number of Special Assistants, such as Robert J. Lynch, who was in charge of administrative matters and the Secretary's staff; G. Hayden Raynor, who was concerned with policy matters and International Security Organization matters; Leo Pasvolsky, who had jurisdiction over the Office of Special Political Affairs; Michael J. McDermott, in charge of press relations, and George T. Summerlin, Chief of Protocol. Robert Woods Bliss served as Consultant to the Secretary, Hamilton Fish Armstrong, Isaiah Bowman, and Henry P. Fletcher as Special Advisers to the Secretary; Joseph C. Green was Adviser on Arms and Munitions Control, Charles B. Rayner, Adviser on Petroleum Policy, and Charles W. Taussig, Adviser on Caribbean Affairs.

As Under Secretary of State, Mr. Stettinius had a total staff of twenty-one, including clerks, messenger, and chauffeur. When Mr. Grew assumed charge, his total staff, including the messenger, numbered eight. In spite of this limited personnel, Mr. Grew's closely knit, efficient staff not only did the Under Secretary's work, but, as we have indicated, more than half of the time it had to take over the work of the Secretary. Under Secretary Grew's first assistant was career Foreign Service Officer Frances E. Willis. Although Miss Willis had never before served with Mr. Grew, she had had over seventeen years' experience abroad and in the Department and was the highest ranking feminine career officer in the Foreign Service. It was the duty of Miss Willis to read everything, except press material, which came to the office, and to see to it that all important matters were brought to the attention of the Under Secretary, together with any background material required. Miss Willis also received some of the visitors and did some of the special drafting. Nelson Newton, who had served with Mr. Grew in Tokyo, shared some of Miss Willis's work, and was responsible for keeping Mr. Grew posted in regard to pertinent items in the press. Mrs. Marion A. Johnston was Under Secretary Grew's office director. Having worked with him for over twenty years in the Department and outside, she ran the office smoothly and efficiently and made all Mr. Grew's appointments. All three secretaries and the file clerk were old hands in the Department, so that there was no lost motion. By working long hours at top speed, with no friction or duplication of effort, this small corps performed an unbelievable number of tasks promptly and efficiently.

A glance at the personnel required by each Assistant Secretary of State in 1945 gives an indication of the remarkable growth of the Department. Assistant Secretary Dean Acheson, who was primarily responsible for maintaining liaison with the Congress and the Bureau of the Budget, had four Special Assistants, two regular assistants, a Personal Assistant, an Administrative Assistant, and eight clerks. Assistant Secretary William L. Clayton, who was in charge of economic affairs, had not only a deputy and various assistants and Special Assistants, but an Adviser on Refugees and Displaced Persons, an Adviser on German Economic Affairs, and an Acting Economic Information Officer. His total staff numbered forty-seven. Assistant Secretary MacLeish, in charge of public information and cultural relations, had a total staff of nine. Assistant Secretary Rockefeller, in charge of Latin American Affairs, had two Special Assistants and his total staff numbered sixteen. Assistant Secretary Dunn, in charge of all the geographical offices except Latin America, was of the old school, and his total staff, including his two Special Assistants, numbered only eight. Assistant Secretary Julius C. Holmes, who was also trained in the former State Department economy methods, with the largest number of offices and divisions in the Department under his jurisdiction—three offices and eighteen divisions—had only two Executive Assistants and a total of seven, including clerks and messenger.

The Legal Adviser's Office, headed by Green H. Hackworth, now had eleven assistants, four clerks, and a messenger. This office had perhaps greater stability in personnel than any other office in the Department. Of the eleven assistants, Richard Flournoy, the greatest authority in the United States on nationality laws, had been associated with the Department of State for more than forty years. Anna O'Neill had served for thirty years, and Mr. Hackworth had been Legal Adviser for twenty-nine years. Considering State Department's conservatism, it is interesting to note that of ten Legal Assistants, three were women—Anna O'Neill, Marjorie M. Whiteman, and Katherine B. Fite. A comparison of the salaries paid to these able and experienced officers with those given to younger and wholly inexperienced officers in some of the newly established divisions would partly explain the drop in morale in the Department so evident in recent years.

The Department proper, which in 1939 had only 974 employees, in the spring of 1945, had 3,767, an increase of about 400 per cent. The Foreign Service, which numbered 3,730 persons, had now increased to about 7,000. The total cost of the Department of State, including the Foreign Service, just topped $50,000,000.

Secretary Stettinius was socially minded and a master of public relations. In order to become better acquainted and to obtain closer cooperation between the Department of State and other governmental agencies, Secretary Stettinius invited his fellow cabinet members and other government executives to meet with him, with Under Secretary Grew, and with the Assistant Secretaries in a series of luncheons. Instead of following precedent and receiving each of the foreign diplomats stationed in Washington separately, Secretary Stettinius invited them collectively to a reception at Blair House. He made a real effort to get better acquainted with the principal officers of the Department by giving a series of social functions at the Shoreham Hotel. He made a valiant attempt to renovate the State Department building by the use of light-green paint, new plumbing, and modernistic furniture.

On the whole, Secretary Stettinius got on very well with the members of the Congress. While head of the Lend-Lease Administration he frequently appeared before congressional committees, and his pleasing personality and sincere desire to play the game fairly made an excellent impression. Unquestionably, his own appearance before the Senate Foreign Relations Committee helped materially in obtaining approval of his new Assistant Secretaries of State.

The State Department Attends Conferences

Probably during no period in the nation's history has the United States participated in more important conferences than in the first half of 1945. The Crimean Conference at Yalta early in February committed the United States to settlements which may cause the United States trouble for years to come; the United Nations Conference on International Organization held in San Francisco from April 25 to June 26, 1945, brought the United States into a new world organization under the Charter of the United Nations.

The State Department, it must be conceded, did not play a very important role in the Yalta Conference. James F. Byrnes, then Director of the Office of War Mobilization and Conversion, found it a cause for regret that the President and his advisers utterly ignored the complete file of studies and recommendations which had been prepared by the State Department and placed on board the cruiser U.S.S. *Quincy* for their consideration.[1] Secretary Stettinius attended the conference, as did the American ambassador W. Averell Harriman, H. Freeman Matthews, Director of the Office of European Affairs; Alger Hiss, Deputy Director of the Office of Special Political Affairs; and Charles E. Bohlen, Assistant to the Secretary of State. The Department of State had prepared policy statements upon all possible subjects which it was thought might arise at the conference. Ten leading points to be discussed at the conference were given special documentation, with a brief memorandum covering each point. However, the Big Three—Roosevelt, Churchill, and Stalin —were laws unto themselves and made their own decisions upon their own responsibilities.

In addition to the daily meetings by the heads of governments and the foreign secretaries, separate meetings of the three foreign secretaries and their advisers were held daily. These proved so valuable that the conference agreed that permanent machinery should be set up for regular consultation between the three foreign secretaries as often as might be necessary, probably about every three or four months. The President seemed appreciative of the assistance and briefing which he received from the State Department representatives—in fact, he felt that their support strengthened him to such an extent that he said that he would never go to another conference without them.

It is impossible as yet to determine the exact role played by advisers such as Harry Hopkins and Jimmy Byrnes, Admiral William D. Leahy and Ernest J. King, and General George C. Marshall in the Crimean Conference, but unquestionably some of the secret commitments made to Russia, such as the return of the Kurile Islands and southern Sakhalin to the Soviets in return for Soviet participation in the war against Japan, were as much military as diplomatic.

The Inter-American Conference on the Problems of War and Peace convened in Mexico City exactly ten days after the adjournment of the Crimean Conference. This conference did not interest the President to the same extent as the conferences immediately concerned with the war effort and the terms of the peace, consequently the Department of State played a much more important part. Argentina had originally proposed a foreign ministers' conference to consider her relations with the American republics, but the State Department cleverly avoided this by a conference of the American states cooperating in the war effort to consider war and postwar problems. In this way Argentina, which had been sabotaging the war effort of the United States, was left out.

The agenda was considered by the Secretary's Staff Committee, but Secretary Stettinius was almost wholly unfamiliar with Latin America, and Assistant Secretary Rockefeller's interest had been largely cultural. The Office of American Republic Affairs had lost its outstanding experts Laurence Duggan and Philip Bonsal, and Sumner Welles was no longer *persona grata* to the Department. The new Director of the Office of American Republic Affairs, Avra M. Warren, a very able Foreign Service officer, although he had served in a number of Latin American posts, could hardly be called a Latin American specialist. He had been made Director of the Office in December, 1944, after brief sojourns in the Dominican Republic and Panama as American ambassador. His Deputy Director, John E. Lockwood, was wholly inexperienced in diplomacy and in Departmental matters. His sole connection with Latin America was four years' experience as Counselor to the Coordinator's Office.

President Roosevelt appointed Secretary Stettinius as the official delegate of the United States to the conference, and Assistant Secretary Rockefeller as alternate. Secretary Stettinius believed in doing things in the grand manner. Whereas the total Chilean delegation was twenty-one, the Brazilian twenty-five, and even the host country Mexico had but forty-one, the United States sent a delegation of seventy-nine. Of these, thirty-five were from the Department of State or from the American Foreign Service, but of these thirty-five only a dozen might be classified even in the broadest sense as being familiar with Latin American affairs.[2] On the other hand, in the fields of general foreign policy, international economic problems, and the very vital question of international organization, the American delegation was very strong. With

Senators Connally and Austin, Congressmen Bloom and Johnson, and Congresswoman Rogers to take care of political questions, and Acting Secretary of Commerce Taylor, Assistant Secretary of State Clayton, President of the Export-Import Bank Pierson, businessmen Paul G. Hoffman and Eric A. Johnston in charge of economic matters, and Messrs. Pasvolsky, Alger Hiss, and Harley Notter, the State Department specialists in problems of international organization, the interests of the United States were well protected.

Secretary Stettinius arrived at the airport in Mexico City direct from Yalta and Moscow. He immediately read a short prepared statement that will probably remain a classic in diplomatic *faux pas*. Whether through carelessness or by deliberate intent, the underpaid clerk who prepared the statement had him say: "The United States looks upon Mexico as a good neighbor, a strong upholder of democratic traditions in this hemisphere, and *a country we are proud to call our own*." The word "friend" was hastily substituted for "own," but it was a most embarrassing moment for all concerned. The incident showed up the ineptitude of the procedure whereby a public officer in high position is not considered to be competent to prepare and deliver a very simple and forthright word of greeting which expresses his own sentiments. Instead he delivers a hackneyed statement of whose content he is ignorant. The Gettysburg Address was not produced in that way.

The shadow of the forthcoming San Francisco Conference lay over Mexico City, and the Latin American states were not satisfied with the Dumbarton Oaks formula. They wanted a strong regional agreement against the aggressor. The United States feared lest regional agreements might interfere with the new world organization that was to be established. By astute drafting on the part of specialists Pasvolsky and Notter, and clever diplomacy on the part of Secretary Stettinius and Senator Warren Austin, and appreciative understanding of the Latin American point of view on the part of Assistant Secretary Rockefeller and Ambassadors Messersmith and Berle, a satisfactory compromise was worked out. The resulting Act of Chapultepec, while stating that regional action is permissible to maintain peace in the Americas, provides also that any action so taken "shall be consistent with the purposes and principles of the general International Organization."

United Nations Conference at San Francisco

The Department of State had been preparing for a conference such as met in San Francisco to write a charter for the United Nations for a number of years. Following the Dumbarton Oaks Conference, some 1,900,000 copies of the Proposals were distributed by the Department of State, and 260 speeches were made by officials of the Department to explain and publicize these proposals. Motion-picture films and a radio series were utilized, and as a result letters to the Department concerning the Proposals reached a weekly peak of about 20,000 by the month of April, 1945.[3] The time and place of the conference and the names of the official delegation of the United States were announced by President Roosevelt at Yalta on February 13, 1945. Secretary of State Stettinius was named chairman of the United States delegation, Cordell Hull was senior adviser, and the other members were Senators Tom Connally and Arthur H. Vandenberg, Congressmen Sol Bloom and Charles A. Eaton, Commander Harold E. Stassen, and Dean Virginia C. Gildersleeve. Former Secretary Hull was too ill to attend the conference, but he was kept informed concerning important developments, and his advice was sought from time to time.

The date of the conference had been set for April 25, and immediately upon Secretary Stettinius's return from Mexico City on March 13, 1945, the American delegation met from time to time in the Secretary's office. Approximately a dozen meetings were held during which State Department members and committees, which had worked upon the problems of international organization and security, reported upon the work already done. On April 3 the advisers to the American delegation were named. Every Executive Department was invited to send one or more advisers, except the Post Office Department. The State Department named eleven advisers to the American delegation: Messrs. Dunn, Hackworth, Pasvolsky, Bowman, Armstrong, Taussig, Warren, Hickerson, Notter, Stinebower, and the eminent Republican expert on foreign affairs John Foster Dulles; three Assistant Secretaries, Holmes, MacLeish, and Rockefeller, were assigned to the conference; the chairman had seven Special Assistants and seven assistants from the Department; eighteen political and liaison officers represented the geographical divisions of the Department, and twenty-eight experts were drawn from other agencies of the Department.

The preliminary meetings of the United States delegation had been going on for a month when President Roosevelt died suddenly on April 12, 1945, of a cerebral hemorrhage. As soon as President Truman was inaugurated, Secretary Stettinius submitted his resignation, but the new President requested that he continue in office and carry on as chairman of the United States delegation to the conference. On April 13 Secretary Stettinius announced that the President had authorized him to say that there would be no break of continuity in the foreign policy of the United States and that the conference at San Francisco would begin on April 25 as planned.

Inasmuch as the United States was the host nation, in addition to the United States delegation, which numbered, including all the aides and assistants, 175 persons, the personnel of the secretariat must be provided by the United States. This requirement plus the need to make the physical arrangements taxed the facilities of the State Department to the limit. Here again the personnel necessarily included a considerable number of officials from the Department of State. Alger Hiss was named Secretary General, John C. Ross, Deputy Secretary General, and Professor Bernadotte E. Schmitt was appointed as Special Adviser to write up the history of the conference. C. Easton Rothwell was Deputy Executive Secretary and William D. Wright was the Administrative Secretary. So many top-rank State Department officials had gone to the coast that during the two months of the conference the question was raised as to whether the foreign affairs of the country were now being conducted from the Fairmount Hotel in San Francisco. The Washington correspondents who attended the press conferences of Acting Secretary Grew in Washington would not have raised the question.

For some inexplicable reason the management of the San Francisco Conference was not placed under the direction of the Division of International Conferences. Nevertheless, the duties of this division, according to official Publication 2359, issued by the Department simultaneously with the naming of the delegates, were as follows: "Responsibility for the coordination of all administrative aspects of the preparation and conduct of international conferences." Chief Warren Kelchner of this division had been organizing and directing numerous international conferences for the Department of State so that they functioned smoothly and efficiently, yet in this conference, the most elaborate, and perhaps the most important in which the United States had ever participated, the expert services of Dr. Kelchner and his staff were not adequately utilized. The very unsatisfactory distribution of tickets and the bitter complaints regarding housing might have been avoided if Dr. Kelchner and his experts had been given the primary responsibility which their experience and position in the Department warranted.

The American delegation held some sixty-five meetings during the conference to decide upon policy for specific issues. Once agreement was reached, Secretary Stettinius would invite the heads of the British, Soviet, and Chinese delegations—the French were included later—to his penthouse on the top of the Fairmount Hotel. The delegation of the United States, as host to the conference, expected to have Secretary Stettinius chosen as the presiding officer. However, Russia objected and the United States accepted the Russian proposal of four rotating chairmen.

On one occasion Secretary Stettinius had to telephone President Truman in Washington and then to Ambassador Harriman and Presidential Representative Hopkins in Moscow to appeal to Stalin to obtain Molotov's reluctant consent to permit the consideration of a dispute by the Council as a procedural matter.[4] On another occasion Secretary Stettinius had to fly to Washington to report to the President and receive instructions on final policy.

President Truman flew to San Francisco to address the final plenary session, held on June 26, 1945, when the fifty nations represented at the conference signed the United Nations Charter. On the following day President Truman accepted the resignation of Edward R. Stettinius, Jr., as Secretary of State and named him representative of the United States to the United Nations.

The resignation of Mr. Stettinius as Secretary of State was not unexpected. He was manifestly not equipped to carry on the complex duties of such an office in a period of great national crisis. So long as President Roosevelt was alive and the real director of American foreign policy, Secretary Stettinius was an acceptable lieutenant. But President Truman was, on the whole, unfamiliar with foreign affairs, and he needed a Secretary of State who had a broader national and international experience, and one who could both initiate and direct on his own responsibility. In his brief period of office the greatest mistake of Mr. Stettinius was his hasty and radical reorganization of the Department without adequate understanding of the problems involved. His greatest service was to demand and get larger appropriations for the State Department as a vitally essential agency whose functions should be adequately taken care of by the people's representatives. Secretary Stettinius got along well with the President, with his fellow cabinet members, and with the Congress, but in 1945 the United States needed more than a good public-relations man as head of the State Department.

Under Secretary Grew as Acting Secretary of State

Under Secretary Joseph C. Grew was confirmed as Under Secretary of State on December 19, 1944, and he served as Acting Secretary of State for five and one-half months while Secretary Stettinius was attending the conferences at Yalta, Mexico City, and San Francisco. Since Mr. Grew was an exceedingly able as well as long-experienced official both in the Department and in the Foreign Service abroad, he was able to perform all the routine tasks of his position as well as meet, with a minimum of time and effort, the extraordinary problems which arose constantly in contemporary foreign policy. A typical day's work will indicate the duties which are routine with the office. As a signing officer he regularly signed letters to other cabinet officers, as, for example, a letter to the Secretary of Navy explaining the Department's position regarding broadcasting to Japan the story of a Japanese submarine attack upon a United States merchant vessel and the treatment accorded the survivors; a letter to the Director of the Foreign Economic Administration regarding the application to Spain of FEA's policy regarding neutrals; a letter to the Director of War Information informing him that information activities in France were under the jurisdiction of his office rather than under the Department of State; letters to senators and congressmen commenting upon bills; instructions to American representatives in various posts, and notes to foreign representatives in Washington. He must answer phone calls from the President's office and from other Department officials; he must attend staff meetings, receive foreign diplomats, meet the press, converse with government officials and private citizens. He had a vast amount of paper work, which included the reading and answering of dispatches and telegrams from abroad and the review of Departmental memoranda. He had to preside over the Secretary's Staff Committee, which met daily and which considered recommendations made by the Coordinating Committee and prepared policy decisions for the President. One of his most arduous duties was to make at least two major addresses a month on various aspects of American foreign policy, particularly with reference to Japan.

Acting Secretary Grew saw President Truman much oftener than he had President Roosevelt, and during May, 1945, the two officials discussed problems of foreign policy on at least twenty-four different occasions. On the very difficult question of the Yugoslav demand to control Trieste, not only did the President and Secretary confer, but joint conferences included General Marshall, Admiral Leahy, and William Phillips. The latter, former Under Secretary of State, had been persuaded to return temporarily to the Department as Special Assistant to the Secretary of State while so many top officials of the Department were in San Francisco. The problem was also discussed at the weekly meetings of the Secretaries of State, War, and Navy at the Pentagon Building. Acting Secretary Grew was an old friend of Secretary of War Stimson's—Mr. Stimson was Secretary of State when Mr. Grew was appointed ambassador to Japan—and these two officials kept in touch with each other almost daily on the question of Trieste. The relations of the State Department with Secretary of the Treasury Morgenthau as regards our policy in occupied Germany were not nearly so satisfactory.

Organization and Personnel Changes

We have already discussed the changes made in the offices concerned with economic matters. Another substantial reorganization occurred in the Office of the Foreign Service by a Departmental order issued on April 7, 1945. The principal changes consisted of adding three new divisions, one called the Division of Foreign Service Planning, a second, the Division of Training Services, and the third, the Division of Foreign Reporting Services. The first of these divisions was authorized to initiate recommendations for desirable changes through legislation to meet the changing needs of the Foreign Service. The Joint Survey Group was to continue its work assisted by the Foreign Service Planning Division. Closely allied with this idea was the establishment of a Division of

Training Services to work out new training and specialized training programs to equip present and new personnel to carry on the new responsibilities of the war and postwar periods. These programs looked toward administrative and clerical training and specialized training, as well as basic orientation. Inasmuch as reporting is the basic function of Foreign Service officers, any improvement here would be of fundamental value. The third new division was established to improve reporting techniques, to obtain wider circulation for the reports, and give the officers in the field more information regarding the policies and procedures of the Department in Washington. The reorganization of the Foreign Service Office at this time helped to bring about the vastly improved Foreign Service Act of 1946, which will be discussed later. Foreign Service Officer Monnett B. Davis remained director of the Office of the Foreign Service until June, 1945, when he was named minister to Denmark. The Deputy Director, Selden Chapin, another Foreign Service officer of Class 1 rank, became Director.

Very few important changes in personnel were made while Mr. Stettinius was Secretary of State. Alger Hiss, who had been in the Department in various positions since 1935, was advanced from his position as Deputy Director of the Office of Special Political Affairs to Director and given charge of the San Francisco Conference arrangements. Charles P. Taft, son of ex-President Taft, former Director of the Office of Wartime Economic Affairs, was made Director of the Office of Transportation and Communications. Foreign Service Officer Loy W. Henderson, who had been minister to Iraq, was brought back and made Director of the Office of Near Eastern and African Affairs. No post in the Department was more difficult to fill at this time, due to the critical situation which had arisen in Palestine. A man of superb ability and unblemished integrity, Mr. Henderson remained in this office for more than three years, striving constantly to protect American interests under a storm of vituperation and abuse from unscrupulously selfish individuals and groups who put their individual and class interests above the interests of the United States. Almost simultaneously, with the resignation of Secretary Stettinius, Clair Wilcox, an experienced economist and a consultant in the Department of State, was appointed Director of the Office of International Trade Policy.

A few important changes occurred in the diplomatic service during this period. The top-flight career officer Norman Armour, who had been serving as Director of the Office of American Republic Affairs in the Department, was appointed on December 15, 1944, as ambassador to Spain. The constant criticism of the Department's relations with General Franco required the ablest diplomat available for this difficult post. Having supported the admission of Argentina into the United Nations, it was incumbent upon the United States to name an ambassador to Buenos Aires. The vivid and outspoken Spruille

Braden was chosen for this delicate mission. Mr. Braden had been an engineer in South America, had done an excellent job in Buenos Aires as chairman of the American delegation in settling the Chaco dispute, and had subsequently served as ambassador to Colombia. He had been ambassador to Cuba for about four years at the time of his appointment to Argentina. Former Assistant Secretary Adolf Berle was appointed on January 18, 1945, as ambassador to Brazil.

An incident occurred while Under Secretary Grew was Acting Secretary of State which received a considerable amount of unfavorable publicity in the press. For the first time in history an American Foreign Service officer was arrested for an alleged violation of the Federal espionage statute. On June 6, 1945, by a Departmental order, provision was made for a Security Officer to be appointed in the Office of Controls. On the same date Acting Secretary Grew issued a statement to the press that State Department officials had learned that secret information was reaching unauthorized persons. An investigation by the Federal Bureau of Investigation resulted in the arrest of six persons of whom one was Foreign Service Officer John S. Service and the other an employee of the State Department, Emmanuel S. Larsen. The basis of the charges was an article in *Amerasia* containing the verbatim text of parts of a secret report of the Office of Strategic Services. A grand-jury hearing completely vindicated Mr. Service. The sole basis of the charges as far as he was concerned was that having recently returned from China he had talked to several magazine writers at a dinner party, giving them background information. The press alleged that political considerations were involved, since Mr. Service did not get along well with Ambassador Patrick J. Hurley and had been ordered back to Washington. The day after the grand-jury vindication, Mr. Service was reassigned to the Department in the Division of Chinese Affairs and three weeks later sent to Tokyo on the staff of George Atcheson, Jr., political adviser to General Marshall. Emmanuel Larsen, a minor official in the Department, was fined after pleading *nolo contendere*. Mr. Service had the satisfaction of receiving letters from both Secretary of State Byrnes and Under Secretary Grew expressing their pleasure at his vindication and the happy termination of the ordeal.[5]

34

James F. Byrnes

Secretary Byrnes Assumes Control

There were many reasons why President Truman should choose James Francis Byrnes, the eminent South Carolinian, as his Secretary of State. In the first place no Democrat in public life had made a more remarkable record as a government servant. He had served as a member of the lower house of Congress for seven consecutive terms and as a senator for two. During his second term he was a member of the Foreign Relations Committee of the Senate. He had been a Justice of the Supreme Court and had resigned, at President Roosevelt's request, to become Director of Economic Stabilization. Later, as Director of War Mobilization, he had been President Roosevelt's chief executive assistant—he was often called "Assistant President"—with the task of putting the country upon an all-out war basis. While in Congress he had supported Woodrow Wilson on the League of Nations issue and Cordell Hull on his reciprocal trade-agreements program. He was for Lend-Lease and against the keep-out-of-war-at-any-price type of neutrality legislation. He had accompanied President Roosevelt to Yalta and as a result of his early experience as a court reporter he had kept a very complete account of the proceedings there. In the second place President Truman could not forget the fact that President Roosevelt had chosen Byrnes for his running mate in the recent election and that only the serious objections of the CIO had made possible the choice of Truman for that post. Finally, President Truman needed a strong cabinet to support him in his very difficult position, and the appointment of Justice Byrnes would contribute materially to the prestige of the administration.

The day after the death of President Roosevelt, President Truman asked Mr. Byrnes to represent him at the San Francisco Conference. Mr. Byrnes urged the President to keep the existing delegation, which had already been named. The next day President Truman asked Justice Byrnes to serve as his Secretary of State. Mr. Byrnes accepted, but with the understanding that no announcement of the appointment should be made until after the San Francisco Conference had ended. The public nomination of Byrnes as Secretary of State was made by President Truman on Saturday, June 30, 1945, and on the following Monday the appointment was confirmed by the Senate. Although Secretary Byrnes was not an authority on foreign policy, the press was unanimous in its praise of his appointment. As a master legislative strategist, a shrewd negotiator, he would be able to hold his own with the horse-trading diplomats. The late Senator McNary of Oregon was credited with saying: "When I see Jimmy Byrnes coming, I put one hand on my watch, the other on my wallet, and wish to goodness I knew how to protect my conscience." In Congress, Byrnes was recognized as having a remarkable talent for compromise—in fact, he had said, "Where there's politics there's got to be compromise." Unfortunately, as he was to discover later, in dealing with the Russians their idea of give-and-take was United States give and Russia take.

In taking the oath of office, Secretary Byrnes promised that there would be no change in the basic principles of American foreign policy which had been charted by President Roosevelt and reaffirmed by President Truman. He declared that he was asking all of those in the Department, at home or abroad, to remain at their posts and carry on as usual. He confessed that he had asked the Director of the Budget to make an investigation of the structure of the Department, but that no change in personnel would be made until he should receive the report and have time to study it.[1] Inasmuch as he was to leave almost immediately with President Truman to confer with Prime Minister Churchill and Premier Stalin in Berlin, the Departmental personnel was reassured. However, when the Secretary found it necessary to fly to London to attend the meeting of foreign ministers less than a month after he had returned from Berlin, one of the State Department officials, expressing the sentiment of the personnel regarding their uncertainty of status, quipped, "The State Department fiddles while Byrnes roams." [2]

On June 5, 1945, Secretary Byrnes announced that Benjamin Cohen, Donald S. Russell, and Walter Brown had joined his staff as Special Assistants to the Secretary of State. Mr. Cohen had been an assistant to the Director of Economic Stabilization and general counsel to the Office of War Mobilization, and Secretary Byrnes thought very highly of him. He obtained his appointment in time to accompany the President and Secretary of State to Berlin, and in September, 1945, he was appointed Counselor of the State Department. Donald S. Russell, Secretary Byrnes's senior law partner, had also assisted the Secretary in his war work, and he also was invited to make the trip to Berlin. Walter Brown, who had served with Mr. Byrnes on the War Mobilization staff, had been a former Washington correspondent whom the Secretary liked to consult with on political matters, and he too was invited to join the President's group to the Berlin meeting.[3]

No other changes of importance in the Department's personnel occurred until the middle of August, when Under Secretary Grew and Assistant Secretaries Holmes and MacLeish resigned. Mr. Grew had already served the government for forty-one years and was past the age of retirement from the Foreign Service. He had taken the onerous position of Under Secretary to do his part in the war effort, and now that the war was over he wished to return to private life. The State Department was very fortunate in obtaining the services of Dean G. Acheson to replace him. An excellent lawyer, Mr. Acheson gave up his practice to become Under Secretary of the Treasury in 1933. In 1941 he was appointed Assistant Secretary of State and served in that capacity until his resignation on August 13, 1945. A few days later he was asked to return at a higher level, and he was sworn in as Under Secretary of State on August 27, 1945. With Secretary Byrnes necessarily absent from the country so much of the time, an experienced official to serve as Acting Secretary was vitally important. Inasmuch as the Senate was not in session, Mr. Acheson's appointment was not confirmed until September 24, 1945. Before confirmation, however, a lengthy debate took place in the Senate due to an allegation by Senator Wherry of Nebraska that Mr. Acheson had insulted General MacArthur. The "insult" was a statement by Under Secretary Acheson in a press conference that the United States Government, and not the occupation authorities, would determine the policy of the United States toward Japan. Senator Wherry was unable to secure any support for his criticism, and his was the only vote against confirmation.[4]

In the resignation of Assistant Secretary Julius C. Holmes, the Department lost an experienced and able administrator. He had made a number of needed changes in Departmental organization, but in such a way as to strengthen the Department and improve morale. His resignation, after serving only a little over a year and a half, was most regrettable. The choice of his successor was even more so. Colonel Frank McCarthy had made a brilliant record in the army, rising from lieutenant to colonel in five years' time. Colonel McCarthy, however, was wholly without diplomatic experience and completely unfamiliar with the State Department and its work. To give him the very difficult post of Assistant Secretary for Administration at a time when the Department was still in the throes of being overhauled and expanded was questionable judgment. President Truman announced his appointment on August 21, 1945, and his resignation on September 11. The reason given was illness, but the cumulative frustration of attempting to administer the Department of State without any background of experience must have been an important contributing factor.

Colonel McCarthy's successor, Donald S. Russell, was equally inexperienced, but he had one extremely valuable asset—he was Secretary Byrnes's law partner and as such would always have easy access to the Secretary. Mr. Russell was confirmed as Assistant Secretary of State for Administration on September 14, 1945, and assumed his duties on September 24. Mr. Russell, who had accompanied President Truman and Secretary Byrnes to the Berlin Conference as Special Assistant to the Secretary, had had some administrative experience as Deputy Director of the Office of War Mobilization and Reconversion. Nevertheless, Assistant Secretary Russell appreciated fully his lack of preparation for the position and he made every effort to consult and advise with the officials of the Department in all technical Departmental questions.

In the place of Assistant Secretary Archibald MacLeish as Assistant Secretary in Charge of Public and Cultural Relations, the President named William Benton, onetime president of a well known advertising agency and vice president of the University of Chicago. At the University of Chicago Mr. Benton was particularly interested in the development of adult education by utilization of the radio and motion pictures. During the war he had served in various advising capacities for the government, principally in the Latin American field, and seemed ideally equipped for the position he was named to fill.

The Department's New Informational Activities

The President, by an Executive order dated August 31, 1945, had abolished the Office of War Information. Inasmuch as it was felt that some of the foreign-information operations must be continued temporarily, an Interim International Information Service was established in the Department of State to carry on these activities until December 31, 1945. On September 14 Ferdinand Kuhn, Jr., a veteran newspaper writer who had headed the *New York Times* bureau in London for twelve years and for the past two and a half years had served as Deputy Director of the Office of War Information, was named Director of the new agency. The Executive order also transferred to the Department of State the foreign-information functions of the Office of Inter-American Affairs. Testifying before the House of Representatives Appropriations Committee on October 4, 1945, Assistant Secretary Benton indicated the tentative lines of the Department's policy in the field of overseas information. First noting the urgent requests from the heads of American missions abroad that the information services in their areas be continued, Mr. Benton declared that in his opinion the soundest procedure was for the State Department to determine American needs in the various fields of overseas information—news, motion pictures, publications, and the rest—and then to support and help private industry to do everything it could to meet those needs. The State Department should do the rest.

Speaking more specifically before the House Foreign Affairs Committee on October 16, Assistant Secretary Benton declared that the reduction of our radio output from forty to eighteen languages had been ordered, and the publication of certain wartime magazines, such as *Victory*, *USA*, and *En Guardia*, had been discontinued. However, in the case of short-wave radio, twenty-three of the thirty-six stations now in use were built by or for the government after Pearl Harbor, and to stop programming them at once would not seem intelligent from the standpoint of future national interest. He also urged an increase in the exchange of students and the promotion abroad of American books, authors, and libraries.[5]

Assistant Secretary Benton might have also noted that in the year July 1, 1944, to June 30, 1945, some 164 persons from the United States and 89 from South and Central America were awarded grants for professional visits to other American republics or the United States.[6] During the years 1944 and 1945 "Basic Libraries" of some 250 volumes, including works on American history, political science, philosophy, education, agriculture, literature, art, and music, were sent to 28 universities and colleges in 12 countries of the East, Middle East, and Africa. Another avenue of particular value was the cultural centers, of which there were 27 independent and 20 branch centers in the other American republics. The State Department paid the salaries of 20 directors and 27 American teachers and about 20 per cent of the local operating expenses. The main activity of these centers was the teaching of English, and the total number of students enrolled to study English had reached 20,000 by July, 1945.[7]

As a means of publicizing the international information policy of the United States in a new series of broadcasts instituted over the NBC network on "Our Foreign Policy" and beginning on December 15, 1945, Assistant Secretary Benton, Director Stone of the Office of International Information and Cultural Affairs, and Director Henderson of the Office of Near Eastern and African Affairs attempted to explain to the world the attitude and position of the United States so as to counteract the widespread false impression that the United States is either an Uncle Santa Claus or an Uncle Shylock.[8]

On December 31, 1945, a very thorough reorganization of the Office of International Information and Cultural Affairs was announced. Its two former divisions of Cultural Cooperation and International Information were abolished, and the Central Translating Division was transferred to the Office of Departmental Administration. Ten new divisions were established as follows: Divisions of International Press and Publications, International Broadcasting, International Motion Pictures, International Exchange of Persons, Libraries, and Institutes, and five area divisions—Europe, Near East and Africa, Far East, American Republics, and Occupied Areas. The fundamental responsibility of the office was to promote a better understanding of the aims, policies, and institutions of the United States among foreign peoples "to eliminate the areas of mass ignorance and ill-will." [9] The new organization was based to a considerable extent upon a study by Professor Arthur W. Macmahon of Columbia University and entitled *Memorandum on the Postwar International Information Program of the United States.*[10] The Director of the new office was William T. Stone, a journalist, who had served as Director of the Economic Warfare Division of the American embassy in London.

The Department of State's New Intelligence Program

Another addition to the operational activities of the State Department as a result of the liquidation of war agencies was the assumption of the functions of the Office of Strategic Services. By an Executive order of September 20, 1945, President Truman terminated the Office of Strategic Services and transferred its research and analysis branch and presentation branch to an Interim Research and Intelligence Service in the Department of State. At the same time there was established the position of Special Assistant to the Secretary of State in charge of Research and Intelligence. Acting Secretary Acheson announced on September 27 the appointment of Colonel Alfred McCormack, Director of Military Intelligence in the War Department, as Special Assistant to set up the new agency.

Colonel McCormack explained the work of the Department's agency as mainly a research program. "The intelligence needed by the State Department" he declared, "is primarily information on the political and economic factors operating in other countries of the world, and on the potential effect of those factors in relations with this Government." He estimated that approximately 1,600 OSS personnel were transferred to State, a number soon reduced by about 50 per cent. Two offices were created, an Office of Research and Intelligence under Dr. Sherman Kent, with five geographical intelligence divisions corresponding roughly to the Department's geographic organization, and the Office of Intelligence Collection and Dissemination under Colonel George R. Fearing, who had served with distinction as an intelligence officer with the army. Colonel McCormack indicated that most of the work would be done in Washington, but that from fifty to seventy-five representatives with special training would be attached to embassies overseas to do particular types of work. As examples of the work done, Colonel McCormack cited the report made on the transportation system of North Africa, which was invaluable to the American forces of invasion, and a study of the industrial organization and capacity of Germany.

Once created, the intelligence program underwent a series of revisions and modifications. For example, established as a self-sufficient intelligence unit on a geographic basis, the service was changed in April, 1946, in accordance with the so-called Russell Plan, so that the geographic intelligence functions were transferred to the political offices, thereby limiting the functions of the Office of Intelligence and Research to matters which cut across geographic lines.[11] At the same time an Office of Intelligence Coordination and Liaison was established to formulate, in consultation with the geographic and economic offices, a Departmental program for basic research. The day after the Departmental regulations making this radical change were issued, Colonel Mc-Cormack resigned on the ground that he regarded the new organization as unworkable and unsound and felt that it would make impossible the establishment of a real intelligence unit within the Department. On February 6, 1947, the original type of organization was reinstituted when the Office of Intelligence and Liaison was changed to the Office of Intelligence Research and the geographical divisions were restored to its jurisdiction.[12]

It must be confessed that the new intelligence agency did its best to baffle any attempt to follow up its organizational nomenclature and administration. For example, on January 1, 1946, the Division of Geography and Cartography was abolished, its functions transferred to the Office of Research and Intelligence, and its name changed to the Division of Map Intelligence and Cartography. On May 1, 1946, the Division of Map Intelligence and Cartography became the Division of Map Intelligence, and on August 20 it once more became the Division of Map Intelligence and Cartography. On February 4, 1947, it again changed its name to simply Map Division, and two days later it was transferred to the Office of Information Collection and Dissemination. Here it remained until December 29, 1947, when it was transferred to Central Intelligence Agency, where it may be today—Central Intelligence does not say.

Although the rest of the intelligence service did not change as much as the division cited above, it was by no means a stabilized organization. Both in name and personnel there seemed to be a state of flux. On April 29, 1946, Professor William L. Langer of Harvard, who had headed the Division of Research and Analysis in the Office of Strategic Services, was made Special Assistant in charge of Research and Intelligence in the State Department. On July 1, 1946, a Departmental regulation raised this position to rank with the Assistant Secretaries of State. A few weeks later Professor Langer resigned, and Colonel William A. Eddy, American minister to Saudi Arabia, was appointed. He remained till the end of September, 1947, when he resigned and was succeeded by Deputy Director William Park Armstrong, Jr. At the present time the Office of Intelligence Research, under the direction of Allan Evans, has four geographical divisions plus the Division of International and Functional Intelligence. The Office of Intelligence Collection and Dissemination, George R. Fearing, Jr., Director, has three Divisions: Acquisition and Distribution, Reference, and Biographic Information. The total agency at present has approximately 550 persons on its staff.

There is no question but that a complete and accurate knowledge of all pertinent facts is essential to the formulation of successful policy. The establishment of a large, trained staff of research workers available to all policy divisions would seem to be an essential requirement. As to whether it is better to have the centralization of all intelligence personnel in one office or to assign intelligence research activities to the operational geographic offices is a much debated question. Both systems have been employed, but the weight of informed opinion seems to favor the centralized system, which is now in operation.

Department of State Takes Over War Agencies

By an Executive order dated September 27, 1945, President Truman terminated the Foreign Economic Administration and its agencies and transferred to the Department of State its functions pertaining to the United Nations Relief and Rehabilitation Administration, to the procurement of supplies in liberated areas, to the planning of measures for the control of occupied areas, and for the gathering and reporting of economic and commercial information.[13] To carry out these provisions, there were organized in the Department of State an Interim Foreign Economic and Liquidation Service, an Office of Foreign Liquidation, and a Foreign Liquidation Commission.[14] Most of the personnel engaged in this work were transferred temporarily to the Department but kept out of the "main stream" of its economic organization. Economic problems which arose in connection with the occupation of ex-enemy states necessitated the creation at the same time (October 19, 1945) of the Office of Economic Security Policy with three divisions. The divisions of Japanese and Korean Economic Affairs and German and Austrian Economic Affairs were concerned with formulating economic policy toward the occupied nations of Asia and Europe. The Division of Economic Security Policy was responsible for the winding up of the economic warfare programs, such as the Safehaven program, which was aimed at preventing the Axis powers from salvaging any economic assets from the war.[15] Thomas B. McCabe was appointed Foreign Liquidation Commissioner, and John K. Galbraith was made Director of the Office of Eco-

reluctantly, President Roosevelt paid his first assistant a charming tribute when for sentimental reasons he requested that the acceptance be dated so that Secretary Hull might fill out the third term together with the President.[8] Messages of sincere regret at this resignation and wishes of a speedy recovery came over the cables from almost every democratic country in the world. Even the Peoples Commissar for Foreign Affairs of the Soviet Union, V. M. Molotov, hoped that Mr. Hull's knowledge and experience would "continue to serve the cause of collaboration between the United States and the Soviet Union," and Joseph V. Stalin's regards and wishes of good health were included. Secretary Hull's sincerity, his courage, his high purpose in championing the cause of justice, his unflagging support of the ideal of decent human conduct made him endeared to the many and respected by all. His valiant and successful struggle to establish in concrete form the basic principle of international economic cooperation and to make it effective in his reciprocal trade-agreements program will always remain a monument to his name. Secretary Hull was a great Secretary of State, a great statesman, but, above all, a great man. Working with a President like Franklin D. Roosevelt in wartime, when the President felt that the emergency required that he rule the United States temporarily as an absolute dictator, Secretary Hull's achievement was all the more noteworthy.

Stettinius Becomes Secretary of State

President Roosevelt moved quickly in picking a successor to Secretary Hull. Hardly had the press begun to discuss the possibility of Norman Armour, James F. Byrnes, Sumner Welles, or Henry Wallace when on November 30, 1944, the White House announced the appointment of Edward R. Stettinius, Jr., as Secretary of State. It was everywhere realized that the President intended to be his own Secretary of State, and under these circumstances Under Secretary Stettinius seemed a suitable choice. Through his experience as Acting Secretary of State while Secretary Hull was ill, he had already become somewhat familiar with the position and he could always be depended upon to carry out instructions loyally and with a minimum of friction. The Senate confirmed his appointment with but a single senator in opposition.

Inasmuch as the third term of President Roosevelt was coming to an end, the top political appointees of the government, including the Assistant Secretaries of State, sent in their resignations in *pro forma* fashion, as is customary.

It was the cause for considerable surprise when all but one of the four Assistant Secretaries of State had their resignations accepted. Career Foreign Service officer G. Howland Shaw, with twenty-seven years of service in the government behind him, was eager to return to private life, but both Breck-

nomic Security Policy. He was succeeded in November, 1946, by Hamilton Robinson.

A report on the disposition of foreign surplus property abroad made a fine tribute to the excellent work of Foreign Liquidation Commissioner Thomas B. McCabe and his corps of assistants. By the end of June, 1946, surplus property, which cost the United States originally about $3,500,000,000 had been sold for slightly over $1,000,000,000. The amount disposed of was three-fifths of the amount of salable surplus declared currently available and about one-half of the total amount of salable overseas surplus expected to be available. The sales were not merely commercial transactions, but in the words of Acting Secretary of State Acheson, they furnished "a substantial contribution to the rehabilitation of a war-torn world." For example, two million cases of emergency army rations which were retailed at cost to hungry Filipinos aided materially in preventing a threatened famine in the Philippine Islands. The sales of commodities to UNRRA in China included medical supplies, ten army hospitals, food, blankets, tractors, trucks, and jeeps. The items sold varied from airplanes and vessels to tobacco and rock candy. The largest deal was the sale to the French government of $1,400,000,000 surplus located in France for $300,-000,000. This agency was aptly termed "one of the blood banks for a bleeding world." [16] Perhaps one of the most important results of this vast financial transaction will be the exchange of thousands of students and professors made possible by earmarking some $30,000,000 for cultural exchanges under the provisions of the Fulbright Act.

The vast increase in foreign economic responsibilities imposed too great a burden upon the Assistant Secretary of State for Economic Affairs. The new international agencies, such as the Economic and Social Council of the United Nations, the United Nations Food and Agricultural Organization, the International Monetary Fund, and the International Bank for Reconstruction and Development would increase the scope of these responsibilities. To meet the situation, it was recommended that a new position be established for a two-year period in the Department of State to be called the Under Secretary of State for Economic Affairs. By continuing the office of the Assistant Secretary for Economic Affairs, with Willard L. Thorp in charge, the vast number of economic duties could be shared. Congress was favorable to the idea, and on August 17, 1946, Assistant Secretary William L. Clayton took the oath of office as Under Secretary of State for Economic Affairs.

Rockefeller Out, Braden In

A very important change in the Department's personnel occurred early in Secretary Byrnes's term when Nelson A. Rockefeller resigned as Assistant Secretary of State in charge of Latin American affairs. Mr. Rockefeller had long been interested in strengthening the bonds between the United States and Latin America, and both as Coordinator of the Office of Inter-American affairs and as Assistant Secretary of State he had been engaged in a labor of love. Unfortunately, some of his agents in Latin America had been unwilling to ask the advice of the experienced American consular officers and as a result expended sums in ways that were scarcely beneficial to the stimulation of more friendly relations. To advertise in Nazi-controlled newspapers or to urge travel when no facilities were available were mistakes which could easily have been avoided. However, compared with the general over-all achievements of the program, the few errors were not of great importance. Nevertheless, Mr. Rockefeller was attacked vigorously in the Senate by Senator Hugh Butler of Nebraska on November 26, 1943, for his allegedly wasteful expenditures for propaganda. Mr. Rockefeller was able to prove that of over $79,000,000 available, approximately only $29,000,000 had been used, and of that over one-third had been spent on programs of food, health, sanitation, and emergency rehabilitation.[17] Nevertheless, there was a certain feeling that the United States had been exploited and that Mr. Rockefeller was too idealistic.

Considering the tense relations with Argentina, it seemed advisable to secure the services of someone particularly conversant with political problems in Latin America and, if possible, familiar with the situation in Argentina. Spruille Braden, who had spent many years in Latin America as an engineer, businessman, and diplomat, seemingly filled these qualifications. The only fact militating against the appointment was President Perón's bitter hostility to Braden resulting from Braden's action while ambassador to Argentina in vigorously opposing Perón's election. Such an appointment would seem to indicate that the United States had no intention of seeking a working arrangement with the Perón administration. In fact, Secretary Byrnes, in his statement on the appointment, declared that "as Assistant Secretary, in charge of Latin American affairs, it will be his duty to see that the policies, which he had so courageously sponsored in the Argentine, are continued with unremitting vigor." [18] Nevertheless, the same administration which appointed Braden and commended his policies sent Ambassador George Messersmith to Buenos Aires about six months later with instructions to reach a friendly agreement with the same Perón government.

Office of Transport and Communications

A few other changes in important personnel occurred in the fall of 1945 and spring of 1946. Charles P. Taft resigned as Director of the Office of Transport and Communications and was succeeded on September 14, 1945, by Colonel George P. Baker. Colonel Baker had been Professor of Transportation at Harvard and was assigned during the war to the War Department General Staff. Although Colonel Baker only served until June of 1946, when he resigned to accept the James J. Hill Professorship of Transportation at Harvard, during his nine-month period in the Department he received high commendation for giving life to the interdepartmental committees so that there could be participation in, and understanding of, a uniform governmental policy through all agencies concerned. He was succeeded by Deputy Director Garrison Norton.

A thorough reorganization of the office had been worked out and became effective on June 1, 1946. Although the office still consisted of three divisions, Aviation, Shipping, and Telecommunications, the units in these divisions were arranged so as to carry out more effectively policies concerned with international transport and communications.[19] The office played a leading role in the development of world air transport of passengers and freight. It supported the so-called "five freedoms of the air;" it worked toward the acceptance of multilateral agreements; and when success in this direction was not immediately realizable, the less satisfactory bilateral agreement was substituted. By the summer of 1948 some forty of these had been negotiated by the United States. The office consistently emphasized the principle that the stimulation of international air travel is a means of promoting friendly understanding and good will among peoples.[20]

Changes in Personnel

Dr. Ralph J. Bunche, Acting Chief of the Division of Dependent Area Affairs and formerly head of the Political Science Department at Howard University, was named by President Truman on September 1, 1945, as United States Commissioner of the Anglo-American Caribbean Commission, a token of well merited recognition of his outstanding ability. On September 20 John Carter Vincent, a career diplomat, was made Director of the Office of Far Eastern Affairs, replacing Foreign Service Officer Joseph W. Ballantine. Mr. Vincent had had over twenty years' experience in the Foreign Service, mostly in the Far East. Foreign Service Officer Ellis O. Briggs was named Director of the Office of American Republic Affairs on October 22, 1945, succeeding Foreign Service Officer Avra M. Warren, who had been commissioned ambassador to Nicaragua. On November 21, 1945, the Division of Budget and Finance was raised to office status, and its Chief, Harry M. Kurth, became the Director of the new agency.

Early in February, 1946, it was announced that Green H. Hackworth, Legal Adviser of the Department of State, had been elected judge of the new International Court of Justice.[21] No person in the history of the State Department had been the head of the Legal Department as long as Mr. Hackworth. He entered the Department's Legal Office in 1916 and became its head in 1925. For the next twenty-one years he served in this capacity. Just before his election the government had published his *Digest of International Law* in eight volumes, which supplemented the previous *Digest* by John Bassett Moore. Judge Hackworth was chairman of the Committee of Jurists which had prepared, prior to the San Francisco Conference, the preliminary draft of a Statute for the International Court, and at San Francisco he was adviser on both the text of the Charter and the Statute. In Judge Hackworth's place Secretary Byrnes chose former Solicitor General of the United States Charles Fahy. Since he was currently in Berlin helping prepare the cases of the war criminals, General Clay requested that Mr. Fahy not assume his duties as Legal Adviser until May 15, 1946.

A word must be said at this point about an agency which was not a part of the State Department but in which the Department played an important role, the State-War-Navy Coordinating Committee—SWNCC, as it is usually written. This agency was established in December, 1944, to improve existing methods of obtaining for the State Department advice on politico-military matters and of coordinating the views of the three Departments in the field of foreign policy. Assistant Secretary Dunn was chairman of the committee, and in his absence H. Freeman Matthews, Director of the Office of European Affairs, took his place. The committee helped prepare policy directives for the control of postwar Japan, Germany, and Austria. Working in close liaison with the Joint Chiefs of Staff, they prepared SWNCC papers in the form used by the Joint Chiefs of Staff. In the war period and in the troubled postwar situation it was hoped that the coordination afforded by this agency would be of great value in joining the policy makers of the State Department more closely and satisfactorily with the officers of the armed services whose duty it was to implement and carry out the policies in the field.[22]

Inasmuch as United States policy as regards occupied areas would be a most important phase of American foreign policy in the postwar period, on February 27, 1946, the White House announced the appointment of Major General John H. Hilldring as Assistant Secretary of State for Occupied Areas. General Hilldring had been a member of the United States delegation to the Berlin Conference in 1945 and chairman of the meeting on bizonal arrangements for Germany in Washington in 1946. A directive issued by Secretary of State Byrnes as of April 8, 1946, made General Hilldring the State Department member of SWNCC on all matters of occupation policy, and it was his duty to take the initiative in submitting to SWNCC such policy matters as might require study, consideration, or action. As interpreted by Assistant Secretary Hilldring, it was not the function of his office to make policy but rather to coordinate and expedite all Departmental policy for occupied enemy territories:

The need for such a point of contact from which the armed services might get policy decisions and get them on time has existed for the past three years. . . . The best testimony of the success of our program is found in the fact that we have accomplished more in two months than had been planned for four months.[23]

State Department Under Attack

It has already been noted that Secretary Byrnes left for the Potsdam Conference on July 6, 1945, three days after he had been sworn in as Secretary of State. In the next eighteen months he spent more time in Berlin, London, Moscow, and Paris than he did in Washington.[24] Although the State Department was in the able and experienced hands of Acting Secretary Dean Acheson, the task of carrying on simultaneously the two responsibilities of Secretary and Under Secretary in the unwieldy and ever expanding Department was more than one human being could hope to perform with complete success. The problem was made the more difficult by two unfortunate procedures: presidential appointments both in the Department and abroad of men wholly untrained and unsuited for the practice of diplomacy and presidential interference in the conduct of foreign policy based upon domestic political expediency rather than upon the broad international interests of the United States.

On November 30, 1945, newspapers in New York and Oklahoma simultaneously laid down a barrage of criticism of the way in which American foreign policy was formulated and executed. The *New York Herald Tribune* pontificated:

There is a tangled legacy from all sorts of conflicting policies and personalities being administered by an equal tangle of conflicting agencies and authorities. . . . The United States cannot indefinitely leave its foreign policy to the accidental interplay of the brilliant amateur, the opinionated, eccentric, and the bureaucratic intriguer.

The *Tulsa Tribune* was more laconic: "Our fellow townsman Patrick J. Hurley has given the State Department a sock in the jaw it needs." The basis for these two outbursts was the sudden resignation of Mr. Hurley as the President's representative to China. Coincident with his resignation he had blasted both the Foreign Service and the State Department, claiming that the chief opposition to his mission came from the career diplomats in the embassy in Chungking and from the officials of the Far Eastern Division of the State Department. More specifically, he declared that the Roosevelt-Hull-Truman-Byrnes policy in the Far East was being sabotaged by the State Department and Foreign Service officers, and the result was to encourage Chinese Communistic imperialism.[25]

In rebuttal Secretary Byrnes was able to prove to the Foreign Relations Committee of the Senate that Counselor Atcheson, the principal target of Ambassador Hurley's attack, in his report as chargé d'affaires at Chungking of the current situation in China, was making an honest effort to assist the Department in the formulation of its future policy in China. Furthermore, since Mr. Atcheson had suggested that the Department seek the views of Ambassador Hurley, then in Washington, it could hardly be said that the chargé d'affaires was trying to circumvent his superior officer. The other Foreign Service officer criticized, John S. Service, was attached to the staff of General Stilwell as a political observer in Yenan when he wrote the memorandum criticized by Ambassador Hurley. The memorandum was addressed to General Stilwell, and its conclusions were not endorsed by the embassy. When it was circulated later in the Department, the Division of Chinese Affairs attached a covering memorandum stating that while its contents were informative, many of its conclusions were regarded as incorrect.[26] Ambassador Hurley clearly failed to make a case, and his resignation as ambassador was accepted by the President.

The most serious setback which Secretary Byrnes and the Department received came at the hands of Secretary of Commerce Henry Wallace. In an address made at a political rally in New York on September 12, 1946, while Secretary Byrnes was in Paris working upon the treaties to end the war, Secretary Wallace attacked the foreign policy of the United States as being too friendly toward Britain and too critical of Russia.[27] Secretary Byrnes, completely fed up with the Soviet's stubborn refusal to cooperate with the democratic powers, had made a brilliant exposition of American foreign policy at Stuttgart on September 6, criticizing Russia for failure to carry out the Potsdam agreements and declaring categorically that the United States intended to support them to the end.[28] Wallace objected strongly to this stand which he characterized as "get-tough-with-Russia policy." The effect of this speech in Paris was almost disastrous to the American delegation, particularly as the press reports quoted President Truman as having approved the address prior to its delivery. Anne O'Hare McCormick, writing from Paris, declared that the speech "has weakened United States bargaining power, needled the British, increased the assurance of the Russians, and confused everybody." The immediate reaction to the Wallace address in the United States was so critical, except in the case of the Communists and left-wing liberals, that President Truman modified Voltaire's famous aphorism by declaring that he meant to indicate his approval of the right of the Secretary of Commerce to deliver the speech, but that he did not mean to approve the speech as constituting a statement of American foreign policy.[29] Secretary Byrnes telegraphed the President asking the President to accept his resignation immediately unless he could keep Mr. Wallace from speaking on foreign affairs.[30] Meanwhile, Secretary Wallace made public a letter to the President dated July 23 even more critical of American policy than his address.[31]

Senator Vandenberg's statement that he wanted to cooperate with the administration but that he could only cooperate with one Secretary of State at a time pointed the way to the President's action. On September 20 the President asked for and obtained the resignation of Secretary of Commerce Wallace. In the statement from the White House the President declared:

The Government of the United States must stand as a unit in its relations with the rest of the world. . . . No change in our foreign policy is contemplated. No member of the executive branch of the government will make any public statement as to foreign policy which is in conflict with our established foreign policy. Any public statement on foreign policy shall be cleared with the Department of State.[32]

The New York Times did not mince words in its editorial in the issue of September 23, 1946.

Mr. Truman has dropped Mr. Wallace as the best available means, first of indicating his complete support of Mr. Byrnes, next of putting an end of speculation about possible changes in our foreign policy, and finally of repairing damage caused in large part by his own earlier ineptitude, hesitation, and equivocation.

Secretary Byrnes Resigns

We have already noted the important role played by Secretary Byrnes in international political conferences during his administration of the Department of State. In all of these conferences he was ably assisted by a large corps of State Department advisers. At Potsdam, where both President Truman and

Secretary Byrnes participated, we find Ambassadors Robert D. Murphy and W. Averell Harriman, Assistant Secretaries of State Clayton and Dunn, and nine other officials from the Department of State. At the various sessions of the Council of Foreign Ministers, the Secretary always had a corps of from ten to twenty-five experts from the Foreign Service or the Department of State. At the Peace Conference at Paris, which continued from July 27, 1946, until October 17, 1946, a large number of advisers and experts from the State Department participated. The American delegation, headed by Secretary of State James F. Byrnes, consisted of Under Secretary William L. Clayton, Assistant Secretary Willard L. Thorp, Counselor Benjamin V. Cohen, and Ambassadors Jefferson Caffery, James C. Dunn, W. Averell Harriman, and W. Bedell Smith, and Special Representative of the President Edwin W. Pauley. Ten political experts from the Department of State were, with one exception, Foreign Service officers of the upper ranks. Michael McDermott served as press attaché, and William W. Bishop, Jr., as the legal expert. Four of the economic experts were drawn from the Department, and various assistants, secretaries, and stenographers brought the total number of the American delegation to over seventy-five persons.

The documents setting forth the deliberations and recommendations of the Paris Conference have been compiled and edited in a most satisfactory manner by Velma H. Cassidy of the Division of Historical Policy Research of the Department of State.[33] Inasmuch as the United States was host at the New York meeting of the Council of Foreign Ministers, the State Department was responsible for preparing the final texts of the treaties and the accompanying maps. Since each treaty appeared in English, French, and Russian, as well as in the language of the state concerned, the five treaties required twenty versions, which in all resulted in 44,000 volumes and 143,000 maps. Dr. Warren Kelchner and his staff worked for over two months on this task after the council had adjourned. The task was a Herculean one, and the cost of the printing and binding of these documents amounted to many tens of thousands of dollars.

Although Secretary Byrnes had little opportunity to take part in domestic politics, on one occasion he was able to perform a minor miracle in behalf of the Foreign Service. The Foreign Service Act of 1946, which was the result of over two years' study by the Department of State to strengthen and improve the overseas agency for the conduct of American foreign relations, was in a legislative jam in the closing days of a long congressional session. Returning to Washington in July, 1946, Secretary Byrnes was apprised of the situation. Within a few days he had talked to the right congressmen and senators, answered objections, explained provisions, emphasized advantages. The legislation, which increased salaries and allowances, created a better promotion system, provided for additional training, and in every way raised the standard of the Foreign Service, passed both houses with speed and overwhelming support. It was signed by the President on August 13, 1946, and became law the following November.

The long grueling struggles in the meetings of the Foreign Ministers' Council and the Peace Conference at Paris had laid a heavy toll upon the Secretary of State. Mr. Byrnes had been ordered by his physician to slow down long before he went to the Paris Peace Conference, and on April 16, 1946, he had written President Truman, asking to be relieved, but since he felt that he should attend the forthcoming meeting of the Council of Foreign Ministers and the Peace Conference in Paris, he fixed the date ahead to July 1. When the Paris Conference dragged on throughout summer and fall, Secretary Byrnes continued on to complete the work. But once the treaties with the five satellite states were completed and the date of signature fixed, Secretary Byrnes again submitted his resignation to become effective on January 10, 1947, or as soon thereafter as his successor should be appointed.

The unexpected resignation started rumors of a split with the President, but in his letter of December 19, 1946, Secretary Byrnes reiterated his former statement of having always received the full support of the President. It was, however, well known that Secretary Byrnes had been largely autonomous in the conduct of foreign policy. At times he consulted neither President nor advisers. One well known newspaper correspondent declared that Secretary Byrnes had possessed "greater authority over the conduct of United States foreign policy than any other person in modern times."

Secretary Byrnes's greatest weakness at first was his willingness to compromise, but once he learned that the Russians interpreted compromise as weakness he took a position and maintained it resolutely. He outgeneraled Molotov in the final stand in the satellite-state treaties, and it was Molotov who finally made the concessions. Few Secretaries of State in history faced as many and as thorny diplomatic situations as had Mr. Byrnes. Far East, Near East, Latin America, and Europe all furnished difficult and dangerous problems, with the Soviets always playing the role of the old man of the sea. Once cognizant of Russian tactics, Secretary Byrnes, although patient and friendly, became adamant in standing by his avowed principles. At Stuttgart he laid down the policy of the United States toward Germany which has been followed consistently ever since: "As a great power . . . we have a responsibility, veto or no veto, to see that other states do not use force except in defense of law. We must discharge that responsibility." Such a statement, made by a man who had patiently tried every possible means to reconcile conflicting opinions, meant that appeasement was ended. History may decide that Secretary of State James F.

Byrnes was overly patient, but it cannot find that he was weak. But whatever the final judgment, one cannot overlook the contemporary attitude; and *Time* magazine, just a few days before the resignation was announced, picked James F. Byrnes as "Man of the Year" for 1946, representing "the firm and patient voice of the United States in the Councils of the World."

35

Secretary of State George C. Marshall

The Appointment of General Marshall

The announcement of the nomination of General George C. Marshall as successor to Secretary Byrnes was made on January 7, 1947, simultaneously with the news of Mr. Byrnes's resignation. Senator Vandenberg, chairman of the Senate Foreign Relations Committee, reported his committee's approval and urged speedy action by the Senate "to notify the world that unity still prevails" in United States foreign policy. The Senate confirmed the nomination unanimously and immediately—waiving its rules for at least a day's layover. At the time of the appointment General Marshall was returning from China where he had been serving as the President's personal representative. He did not reach Washington until January 21, 1947, and was sworn in as Secretary of State on that date. General Marshall's mission to offer his assistance to reconcile the conflict between the Chinese government and the Communist factions had failed, but seemingly it had in no way diminished his prestige. In fact, his very frank statement on the situation in China to the press upon his return presaged a greater degree of open diplomacy, with corresponding popular understanding and support of the country's foreign policy.

Although the mission to China was General Marshall's most important diplomatic assignment before becoming Secretary of State, he was an old hand in the field of world politics. His first commission as second lieutenant in 1902 took him to the recently acquired Philippines. He returned in 1913, and it was upon this occasion that, suddenly appointed chief of staff for the defending forces in the maneuvers, he dictated a battle order which is still regarded as a classic. During the First World War, Marshall served with the First Division on various fronts. He drafted the plans for the Saint-Mihiel offensive, and later acted as chief of operations in the Meuse-Argonne battle. For six months he was chief of staff for the Eighth Army Corps; he was then made aide-de-camp

GEORGE CATLETT MARSHALL

to General Pershing and remained with him in this capacity until 1924. At this time he was assigned again to the Far East, in Tientsin, China.

General Marshall's diplomatic experience began in 1939 when as deputy chief of staff he headed the American military mission to Brazil. Upon his return he was appointed chief of staff. It was in this capacity that General Marshall participated in meetings of international military groups and allied heads of governments where both wartime strategy and peace problems were considered. In 1942 General Marshall and the late Harry Hopkins went to London to discuss the ways and means of the projected North African invasion with the British imperial general staff. He accompanied President Roosevelt to the conference when the Atlantic Charter was formulated. He attended the great-powers conferences at Casablanca, Quebec, Cairo, Teheran, and the fateful conference at Yalta whose results were to plague him as soon as he became Secretary of State. Following the death of President Roosevelt, General Marshall went with President Truman to the Potsdam Conference.

Few Secretaries of State have been as conversant with the contemporary world political scene as was General Marshall at the time of his appointment. Considering the world situation and the bellicose attitude of Russia, Secretary Marshall's military background was an additional asset. The Soviet government would respect the new Secretary of State even if it would not like him. The consensus of opinion throughout the nation was expressed by the *Chicago Daily News*: "One great American succeeds another as Secretary of State." [1]

Changes in Organization and Personnel

It was not anticipated that any immediate or considerable change in personnel would follow Secretary Byrnes's resignation. In a press conference on February 7, 1947, the new Secretary of State declared that the only change of any importance contemplated was the amalgamation of the various coordinating and administrative bodies into a single Secretariat. This agency was named the Executive Secretariat and it embraced a number of existing agencies, such as the Division of Protocol and the Division of Coordination and Review as well as certain servicing units, such as the policy registry branch and the committee secretariat branch. The Director of the new agency was Carlisle H. Humelsine, formerly Director of the Office of Departmental Administration, who had organized the Executive Secretariat in the Pentagon Building for General Marshall during the war.

In spite of this promised stability, the top officials, as is customary, offered their resignations to the new Secretary of State, and in the case of several the action was more than a mere formality. For example, Assistant Secretary of State for Administration, Donald S. Russell, law partner of Secretary Byrnes, had entered the Department as a personal favor to Mr. Byrnes and was only too willing to be relieved of the arduous and complex duties of his office. On January 23, 1947, Secretary Marshall announced the appointment of John E. Peurifoy as Deputy Assistant Secretary, and two months later Mr. Peurifoy was made Assistant Secretary of State for Administration. Mr. Peurifoy had entered the Department of State in 1938 as an economic analyst. By 1945 he had risen to the position of Deputy Director of the Office of Information and Cultural Affairs and held at the same time the position of Deputy Director of Public Affairs. In March, 1946, he became Special Assistant to Under Secretary of State Dean Acheson, and it was from this position that he was promoted. Shortly after Mr. Peurifoy's appointment, the Department announced that the Deputy Assistant Secretary would be Charles M. Hulten, who would thus transfer from the field of public affairs, where he had been Deputy to Assistant Secretary Benton, to the field of administration.

Owing to the vast increase in problems concerning aviation, shipping, and telecommunications,[2] it was decided to establish the position of Assistant Secretary for Transportation and Communications. Garrison Norton, Director of the Office of Transport and Communications, was given this position and Walter A. Radius, Deputy Director, was made Director of the office. In the fall of 1948 it was felt advisable to reorganize this agency in such a way as to transfer to the appropriate geographic offices of the Department responsibility for all day-to-day transportation and communication matters concerning a single geographic area and to retain all policy making in the field of aviation, inland transportation, shipping, and telecommunications in the hands of the Assistant Secretary and his staff.

The most important immediate change in organization and procedure inaugurated by Secretary Marshall was the creation of a Policy Planning Staff modeled somewhat upon a section of the general staff of the army. The fact that Secretary Marshall was informed of the British withdrawal from Greece just as he was ready to leave for Moscow at the end of February, 1947, and had to interrupt his preparations to meet the new situation unquestionably impressed him with the need for long-range planning. The United States could no longer afford to improvise in its foreign relations or to "make policy on the cables."

The Secretary's Staff Committee, established in 1945 to carry on long-range policy planning, had not been successful, and the Policy Planning Staff was set up in its place. Established in the Office of the Under Secretary of State, its purpose was to diagnose trends and to aid in the development of long-range policy which might serve as a framework for program planning and a guide for current policy decisions. To ensure its freedom from administrative duties, the staff was specifically enjoined from issuing directives or instructions either to the operational organizations of the Department or to missions in the field. As Director of the Policy Planning Staff George F. Kennan was chosen, a Foreign Service officer of career-minister rank who had had over twenty years' experience in European posts. With a naturally philosophical trend of mind and an intimate familiarity with Russia and her military masters, Kennan proved to be an excellent choice. The staff as originally created was a small but representative group. It consisted of several Foreign Service officers, such as John P. Davies, just back from an assignment in the Far East; Ware Adams, a specialist on Germany and Austria; several members of the State Department staff, such as Jacques J. Reinstein, an expert in economic and financial matters; Joseph E. Johnson, an authority on the United Nations; and Henry S. Villard, a specialist on the Near East. Carlton Savage, who had served in the Department in various capacities for some twenty years, was named Secretary. The staff was to be assisted by panels of special advisers from the operating branches of the Department of State as well as from other departments and agencies, and by experts outside of the government.

The most serious loss to the Department of State was the resignation of Under Secretary of State Dean Acheson shortly after General Marshall's appointment. Mr. Acheson, finding it impossible to maintain his financial position satisfactorily upon his $12,000 salary, had attempted to resign upon several previous occasions and had only consented to remain upon the urgent solicitation of President Truman. His experience as Assistant Secretary, as Under Secretary, and as Acting Secretary of State during Secretary Byrnes's many sojourns abroad, his success in his relations on the Hill, and his extraordinary ability in presiding over all sorts of diplomatic conferences had given Mr. Acheson an enviable and deserved reputation.

Secretary Marshall chose Robert A. Lovett, former Assistant Secretary of War for Air, to fill the vacancy. Mr. Lovett, a banker by profession, had proved himself to be an able administrator and was responsible for the success of the War Department's heavy-bomber program. Although without diplomatic experience, he was thoroughly informed as regards European economic and financial matters. With his pleasantly sardonic sense of humor, his acumen, his astonishing memory and immense capacity for work Lovett was very highly regarded by his associates. He insisted upon serving as assistant to Under Secretary Acheson for a month before taking over the responsibilities of the office. He had so well mastered the problems facing the Department that when he went before the Congress to explain the European Recovery Program, the rabidly economy-minded Congressman Taber conceded that Lovett "does his homework and knows his stuff."

There had been considerable criticism both in the Senate and in business circles of Assistant Secretary Spruille Braden's harsh policy toward the Perón government in Argentina. The ace career diplomat George Messersmith had been brought back from Mexico and instructed to continue the effort to get rid of Nazi influence in Argentina, but without antagonizing Perón. Messersmith achieved considerable success but only by reversing the role played formerly by Ambassador Braden. To retain Braden as Assistant Secretary in charge of Latin American affairs in the Department when his policies were being reversed in the field was neither feasible nor desirable. Braden's resignation was accepted and it was decided to put a single Assistant Secretary in charge of all the geographical offices. To fill this extremely difficult assignment required a diplomat of exceptional ability and one familiar with both European and Latin American problems. Former Ambassador to Argentina Norman Armour, who before retiring had had over thirty years' experience in the Foreign Service at various posts in Europe, the Far East, and Latin America, was persuaded to reenter the government service and become Assistant Secretary of State for Political Affairs.

The last important changes in the Department's upper echelons occurred in the positions of Under Secretary for Economic Affairs and Counselor. The position of Under Secretary for Economic Affairs had been created by the Congress on August 6, 1946, as an emergency position which was to last but two years. Assistant Secretary for Economic Affairs William L. Clayton had been appointed to this position and had filled it brilliantly. However, the strain had been very great, and after making an exhaustive report upon the need for American assistance to prevent an economic debacle in Europe, Under Secretary Clayton asked to be permitted to return to private life. His resignation was accepted with the promise that he would remain on call in case of a special need for his services.

The resignation of Benjamin V. Cohen as Counselor of the Department was not unexpected. Mr. Cohen had been one of the original Roosevelt brain trusters and had been a close friend and confidant of Secretary Byrnes's. Since the Department was lacking in ranking officials with diplomatic experience, Secretary Marshall wisely chose in his place a career Foreign Service officer, an expert on Russian affairs who had been present at the Moscow, Teheran, and Crimean conferences and who had also served as adviser at the conferences of Foreign Ministers in Berlin, London, Moscow, and Paris. Charles E. Bohlen, although only forty-three years of age at the time of his appointment, had been in the Foreign Service nineteen years and had risen to the top by reason of an excellent record. The Counselor's duties as now defined were concerned primarily with liaison duties with the Congress; and an expert in this field, Florence K. Kirlin, was made Staff Assistant. The appointments of General Charles E. Saltzman as Assistant Secretary of State for Occupied Areas in place of General John H. Hilldring, and Colonel Ernest A.

New State Building 1948–
Twenty-first Street and Virginia Avenue

Gross [3] as Legal Adviser in place of Charles Fahy were regarded as personal choices of General Marshall. Both had served in the army during the war and were highly regarded by the chief of staff. The criticism of these appointments on the ground that too much brass was going into the Department of State was unjustified, because most of the appointees were "war-inducted officers." [4]

The Department of State Moves to Foggy Bottom

The huge many-pillared granite building on Pennsylvania Avenue which had housed the Department for over half a century had become too small for the increased personnel even after the War and Navy Departments moved out. Unfortunately, instead of utilizing all of the space for the State Department, President Franklin D. Roosevelt moved his ever expanding Bureau of the Budget into the rooms vacated by the military departments. Instead of building a large annex across Pennsylvania Avenue on the tract of land utilized by the Court of Claims, as had been contemplated, office buildings and apartment buildings were rented in various parts of the city to take care of the overflow. Some were well suited and convenient of access, such as the Winder Building on F Street, directly across from the side of the State Department Building. The Passport Division took over this building and had it renovated and remodeled. Today this is an attractive and adequate edifice well located and satisfactory both to the officials of the Division and to the public. The Walker-Johnson Building on New York Avenue was also a reasonably satisfactory building for the Division of Personnel. But to place the Visa Division in the distant Standard Oil Building on Constitution Avenue and to scatter other agencies from the Washington Loan and Trust Building on Ninth Street to Du Pont Circle was a most unsatisfactory arrangement.

Various arguments supported retaining the old State Department Building as the permanent home of the Department. It was close to the White House, thereby facilitating a closer relationship between the President and the Secretary of State. If the whole building were given over to the State Department and its interior remodeled to eliminate waste space, and if the annex were constructed as originally planned, and the Winder Building retained, the entire Department, reorganized upon a peacetime basis, could have been housed in this most desirable location. The purchase of the Blair House and the Blair-Lee House, directly across Pennsylvania Avenue, to house the nation's guests was an additional inducement to keep the State Department in this location.

With the appointment of General Marshall as Secretary of State, all plans to retain the old State Department Building were discarded. The new modernistic War Department Building on Virginia Avenue in "Foggy Bottom" was available, since the vast Pentagon Building could take care of the needs of the

War Department. The suggestion of such a move had been made early in 1946 and a plan developed by the Public Buildings Administration and White House aides. It was opposed by many in the Department, and Secretary Byrnes did not favor it. Secretary Marshall, however, favored the move, and on January 22, 1947, the first unit of the Department moved into the new State Department building. On April 19 the Secretary and his principal assistants and all of the offices and divisions in the old building except the economic and financial agencies moved to the new quarters. This was the seventeenth time the Department had moved since its original location at No. 13 South 6th Street, Philadelphia.[5] The very excellent library of the Department remained temporarily in the old building, a rather serious handicap for those officials whose work included research of any sort. However, the removal permitted the elimination of a considerable number of temporary quarters and a concentration in buildings surrounding the new State Department building. Whereas in the latter part of 1945 the Department's personnel was scattered through forty-seven different buildings, by August of 1947 the number had been reduced to twenty-five, and by May, 1948, to seventeen, of which none were more than a mile distant from the New State Building. According to plans already prepared, it is hoped ultimately to house the entire Department under one roof.[6]

The Informational Program of the Department of State

On September 2, 1947, Assistant Secretary of State for Public Affairs William B. Benton sent in his resignation to take effect at the end of the month. His information program, particularly the Voice of America, had been the target of congressional attacks ever since it had been instituted. Both President Truman and Secretary Marshall had supported the program, and the Congress had finally been won over reluctantly, but its sanction was not obtained until after the Benton resignation.

The radio could cross state boundaries, it was not subject to censorship, and it was an ideal instrumentality to furnish foreign peoples with a fair and adequate picture of the United States. The United States Government had utilized the radio in its Voice of America program during the war, tripling the number of transmitters, establishing relay points overseas, and broadcasting in thirty-four languages over eleven hundred program hours weekly.

When the State Department took charge, it continued the Voice of America broadcasts but on a considerably reduced scale. During 1946 the International Broadcasting Division of the Department broadcast approximately 390 hours per week in twenty-five languages to foreign countries. The short-wave broadcasts went directly or were relayed to all the principal countries in

Latin America, Europe, and the Far East. Beginning February 17, 1947, programs were broadcast to the Soviet Union through the Munich transmitter. It was estimated by Kenneth Fry, Chief of the International Broadcasting Division of the Department of State, that as of the spring of 1947 short-wave radio sets outside of the United States numbered about 30,000,000 and the potential audiences numbered over 150,000,000.[7] The importance of these broadcasts was shown by the fact that when the Polish government suppressed Secretary Byrnes's famous speech at Stuttgart of September 5, 1946, the Voice of America broadcast of the address went through on three successive days. As a result the censors finally released the speech to the newspapers.

Secretary Byrnes felt—and Secretary Marshall and Assistant Secretary Benton agreed—that the Department of State possessed neither the facilities nor the funds adequate to present a "full and fair picture" of the acts and purposes of the United States. Consequently, on March 24, 1947, the State Department asked the Congress to create a public corporation, to be known as the "International Broadcasting Foundation of the United States," to take charge of the nation's international short-wave broadcasting. It would be administered by a board of trustees of fourteen outstanding private citizens, with the Secretary of State the fifteenth member. The foundation would assume full responsibility for all voice international broadcasting of the United States with the purpose of disseminating information "pertaining to American life, policy, industry, techniques, culture and customs."

The State Department's program was not acceptable to the Congress, and in its place Representative Mundt introduced a bill, known as the United States Information and Cultural Exchange Act, which placed the responsibility for the entire information and cultural program in the Department of State, with advisory commissions to formulate and recommend programs. The bill passed the House on June 24, 1947, by a large majority, but it was delayed in the Senate and did not become law until January 27, 1948.[8] The Act specifically provided that the Secretary should use to the maximum extent practicable the services and facilities of private agencies.

Meanwhile, the Congress had cut the budget of the Office of International Information and Cultural Affairs from a current expenditure of $20,000,000 to $12,400,000 in spite of Secretary Marshall's personal plea in its behalf. This necessitated a reduction of the Voice of America programs by 40 per cent. At the same time the name of the operational agency in the State Department was changed to the Office of Information and Educational Exchange to conform with the language of the Mundt bill. Large cuts in personnel followed, and as rapidly as possible all programs except those going to Central and Eastern Europe and the Far East were turned over to private companies. On October 1, 1947, the Department announced that effective immediately the National

Broadcasting Company and the Columbia Broadcasting System would take over all English and foreign-language programs to France, Italy, Germany, Spain, Latin America, Indo-China, Siam, and Indonesia. This comprised about 75 per cent of the total broadcast.

Assistant Secretary of State Benton's resignation became effective on October 1, 1947, but the year ended with no one appointed to fill his position. It was not until January 8, 1948, that George V. Allen, a Foreign Service officer currently serving as ambassador to Iran, was named Assistant Secretary for Public Affairs. The State Department's budget came before the appropriations committees of Congress early in February, 1948, before Assistant Secretary Allen had returned from Iran and been confirmed. However, following a survey made by a joint committee, headed by Congressman Mundt and Senator Smith, in twenty-two countries of Europe and the Near East of the results of the Voice of America program, the Congress had passed the Smith-Mundt Act and was more favorably disposed to the whole information program. An unfortunate contretemps occurred, however, when Senator Capehart of Indiana took the floor in the Senate on May 26, 1948, and read selected sentences from an earlier series of programs broadcast in Spanish to Latin America for the Department by the National Broadcasting Company. Entitled "Know North America," the information broadcast disclosed that: Wyoming was the most primitive of states, Texas was founded by sin and New England by hypocrisy, in Las Vegas, Nevada, people got married, and in Reno they got divorced, while in Utah men had as many wives as they could support.

An investigation showed that the Congress had cut appropriations to such an extent that the State Department did not have the personnel to supervise programs which had been farmed out to private broadcasting companies. It also showed that the broadcasting companies objected to State Department supervision and that the Senate Committee on Appropriations held similar views. Inasmuch as it was the Congress that had insisted upon giving private companies the responsibility for broadcasting the majority of the Voice of America programs on the ground that private companies could do the job "more effectively and efficiently" than the State Department, the Congress could hardly escape a certain amount of responsibility. Assistant Secretary Allen, who had taken charge after these programs had been discontinued, frankly stated the State Department's position: "It is my best judgment that the programs have been left fully in the hands of private companies because the Department of State felt that was the intent of Congress." [9] As a result of the hearings all existing contracts with private companies were permitted to expire, and the new contracts provided for supervision by the Department of State of all programs, with sufficient funds appropriated so that the job could be done adequately.

Public Affairs Reorganization

Assistant Secretary of State Allen was sworn in on March 31; and about three weeks later, on April 22, 1948, the Department announced a complete reorganization of the Public Affairs Area except for the UNESCO Relations Staff. This agency, with Charles A. Thomson as Director, remained responsible for UNESCO matters in the State Department and served as the Secretariat of the United States National Commission for UNESCO. The Office of Information and Educational Exchange was abolished and in its place the Office of International Information (OII), the Office of Educational Exchange (OEX), and an Executive Staff were established. William T. Stone, formerly Director of OIE became Director of OII, but on June 21, 1948, he was superseded by Lloyd A. Lehrbas, a newspaperman with wide Associated Press experience, both in Washington and abroad. Mr. Stone was appointed Special Assistant to Assistant Secretary Allen. Kenneth Holland, Assistant Director for Cultural Affairs of OIE, was made Director of the new OEX, and when he returned to Paris as United States Adviser on UNESCO affairs, Dr. William C. Johnstone, Jr., dean of the School of Government at George Washington University but currently acting as public-affairs officer at New Delhi, India, was appointed Director. Leland Barrows, formerly Deputy Director of OIE, was named Director of the new Executive Staff. The new OII was specifically made responsible for the development, coordination, and execution of the United States information policies in the field of international relations. With over $7,000,000 as compared with $6,000,000 of the previous year provided for international broadcasting, the Voice of America might be expected to present a "full and fair picture" of the United States which would satisfy both the Department of State and the Congress.

The other principal agency, the OEX, had already become a very important factor in promoting the foreign relations of the United States in the field of educational, scientific, and cultural affairs, and would become more so as soon as the Fulbright program got thoroughly under way. By the end of 1947 the sale of United States surplus property overseas had made about $140,000,000 available to twenty-two countries for the educational exchanges provided by the Fulbright Act;[10] the Board of Foreign Scholarships to make awards had been organized, and the State Department was prepared to carry out the program.

Shortly after taking over the position of Assistant Secretary for Public Affairs, Mr. Allen declared that "the Department of State has a responsibility not only to keep the public informed on foreign affairs, but to seek public support and assistance in the formulation of foreign policy." [11] Increased efforts were made to carry out this policy. The *Department of State Bulletin* continued to carry current articles on policy and events, and in April, 1948, a new publication called *Documents and State Papers* was issued by the Division of Publications of the Office of Public Affairs to complement the *Bulletin*. It included specially prepared policy reports, basic background studies, and selected official documents. A new four-sheet publication entitled *Foreign Affairs Highlights* was first issued on August 1, 1948, by the Public Liaison Division of the Department for free distribution. This gave a brief summary of the principal subjects with which the Department was concerned for the preceding month. The Division of Publications also continued to publish a large number of pamphlet series covering every phase of foreign policy. For example, from October 1, 1927, to January 1, 1948, the *Commercial Policy Series* carried 109 issues, the *Conference Series*, 105; the *European Series*, 31, and the *Inter-American Series*, 37. The nonserial publication list included such titles as *International Control of Atomic Energy, American Policy in Occupied Areas, Aspects of Current American Foreign Policy*, and *The United States and the United Nations*. The Government of the United States was finally prepared to furnish both an overseas and a domestic-information program under the jurisdiction of the Department of State, utilizing radio, motion pictures, institutes, libraries, publications of various kinds, and the exchange of persons, which would present a true and adequate picture of the United States as it really is.

The Foreign Service Institute [12]

The Department of State had for many years, particularly after the passage of the Rogers Act of 1924, carried on a program of limited training for Foreign Service officers who had just been inducted into the service. The Foreign Service Act of 1946 authorized a much more comprehensive training program, and in accordance with its provisions the Department, on March 13, 1947, established the Foreign Service Institute. The Institute provided, in addition to the traditional basic training for the newly selected officers, more advanced and specialized training for the experienced officers both in the Department and in the Foreign Service.

The Institute's School of Basic Officer Training offered a nine to twelve weeks' orientation course to acquaint the young officer with the requirements and functions of the Foreign Service. Lectures, conferences, and practice work were utilized, covering all phases of Foreign Service operations. Advanced-officer training was of various types. Refresher courses might be taken by the officers who had been abroad for many years, in order to familiarize themselves with recent developments in the United States in the fields of history, economics, and political science. Some officers with particular interests were given comprehensive training assignments in a functional specialization in the Institute; others were detailed to other departments of the government for training, or they might be assigned to university graduate schools which afforded specialized programs. A few of the officers of Classes 2 and 3 might be sent to the National War College for a ten months' course in the study of international problems facing the United States. The Language Training School's instruction was based upon the conception that language required at the same time a knowledge of the culture and institutions of the people who use it. Full-time intensive instruction was offered in eleven foreign languages, including Arabic, Russian, and Chinese, and part-time semi-intensive instruction, in thirty-one, including Bengali and Icelandic.

At present the Foreign Service Institute is housed in an eight-story former apartment house quite close to the new State Department building. Dr. William P. Maddox, a professor of political science who was chosen to head the institute, served during the war as Chief of the intelligence branch in the European and Mediterranean theaters with the Office of Strategic Services. Some idea of the utilization of the Institute may be gained from the report of a typical month, July, 1947, when over 500 personnel received part or full-time training either provided or arranged by the Institute. This number included 64 new Foreign Service officers in basic training, 36 staff officers taking full or part-time training for periods of two to six weeks, 102 Foreign Service clerks attending classes for a month, 130 Department supervisors taking brief training conferences, and 50 members of the Special Mission to Greece being given intensive indoctrination. About 220 were studying languages at the Institute and others at various universities in the United States and under the auspices of the Institute abroad. Ultimately it was planned that the Institute would offer a program for senior officers in policy planning and diplomatic procedures comparable to the staff colleges of the armed services.

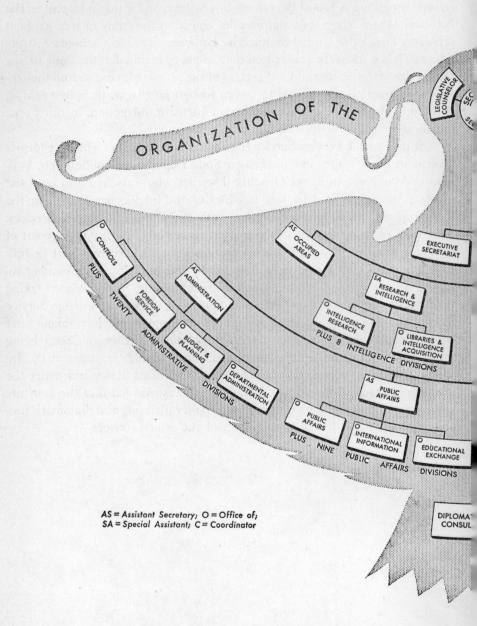

ORGANIZATION OF THE

LEGISLATIVE COUNSELOR

SEC

EXECUTIVE SECRETARIAT

O CONTROLS

AS OCCUPIED AREAS

SA RESEARCH & INTELLIGENCE

PLUS TWENTY ADMINISTRATIVE DIVISIONS

AS ADMINISTRATION

O FOREIGN SERVICE

O BUDGET & PLANNING

O DEPARTMENTAL ADMINISTRATION

O INTELLIGENCE RESEARCH

O LIBRARIES & INTELLIGENCE ACQUISITION

PLUS 8 INTELLIGENCE DIVISIONS

AS PUBLIC AFFAIRS

O PUBLIC AFFAIRS

O INTERNATIONAL INFORMATION

O EDUCATIONAL EXCHANGE

PLUS NINE PUBLIC AFFAIRS DIVISIONS

AS = Assistant Secretary; O = Office of;
SA = Special Assistant; C = Coordinator

DIPLOMAT
CONSUL

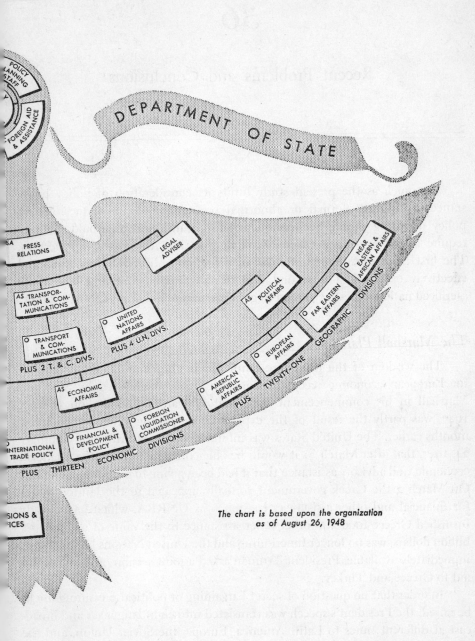

DEPARTMENT OF STATE

POLICY PLANNING STAFF

FOREIGN AID & ASSISTANCE

SA PRESS RELATIONS

LEGAL ADVISER

AS TRANSPORTATION & COMMUNICATIONS

O TRANSPORT & COMMUNICATIONS

PLUS 2 T. & C. DIVS.

UNITED NATIONS AFFAIRS

PLUS 4 U.N. DIVS.

AS POLITICAL AFFAIRS

O NEAR EASTERN & AFRICAN AFFAIRS

O FAR EASTERN AFFAIRS

O EUROPEAN AFFAIRS

GEOGRAPHIC DIVISIONS

AS ECONOMIC AFFAIRS

O AMERICAN REPUBLIC AFFAIRS

PLUS TWENTY-ONE

INTERNATIONAL TRADE POLICY

O FINANCIAL & DEVELOPMENT POLICY

FOREIGN LIQUIDATION COMMISSIONER

ECONOMIC DIVISIONS

PLUS THIRTEEN

SIONS & ICES

The chart is based upon the organization
as of August 26, 1948

36

Recent Problems and Conclusions

Inasmuch as the present study limits its consideration of policy to instances illustrating normal or abnormal procedure only, two questions of policy occurring during Secretary Marshall's administration would seem to require attention—the so-called Marshall Plan and the Palestine question. The first is an excellent illustration of a foreign policy well conceived and effectively executed. The second is a flagrant example of a policy which sacrificed national prestige abroad to gain partisan political advantage at home.

The Marshall Plan

The wisdom of the procedure employed in the carefully prepared plan for European economic reconstruction so casually introduced by Secretary Marshall in his commencement speech at Harvard University on June 6, 1947, was partly the result of the experience in dealing with Greece a few months earlier. The United States was informed by Great Britain on February 24, 1947, that after March 31 it would be obliged to discontinue the financial, economic, and advisory assistance that it had been giving to Greece and Turkey. On March 3 the Greek government formally appealed to the United States for financial and other assistance. Inasmuch as UNRRA, which had already furnished Greece food and other relief assistance to the value of a third of a billion dollars, was no longer functioning and the United Nations had no funds immediately available, President Truman asked a joint session of Congress for aid to Greece and Turkey.

In order that no question of secret bargaining or political pressuring might be raised, the President's speech was translated into eight languages and broadcast at different times to Latin America, Europe, the Soviet Union, and the Far East. Summaries of the address were also broadcast several times in the twenty-five languages of the Voice of America program. On March 28 Warren

R. Austin, United States Representative to the United Nations, explained the proposed action of the United States to the Security Council and stated that any agreements entered into would be registered with the United Nations for publication by the Secretary General. Nevertheless, the United States was severely criticized, both at home and abroad, for having allegedly by-passed the United Nations. Inasmuch as the United Nations was notified before the Congress authorized any financial assistance to Greece and since the urgent need could be met neither by the United Nations nor any other nation than the United States, the State Department's explanation that the United States was implementing by the use of its own resources its responsibilities and commitments under the Charter seemed plausible and reasonable.

There was also some question as to whether the program of aid to Greece and Turkey was a White House policy hastily arranged without the assistance and support of the Department of State. To allay such doubts, Secretary Marshall telegraphed from Moscow that he had participated in the formulation of the Greek-Turkish aid program, that he regarded it as very urgent, and that he supported the position taken by Acting Secretary of State Acheson, who had explained it and urged its passage before the Foreign Relations Committee of the Senate.

The Congress approved a $400,000,000 aid program to Greece and Turkey, but this met only the most urgent danger. The Department of State had now been compelled by unimpeachable and overwhelming evidence to face the fact that all Europe was in dire need of aid and that delay might mean disaster. The United States had already contributed almost $3,000,000,000 for foreign relief; it had subscribed almost $6,000,000,000 to the International Bank for Reconstruction and Development and the International Monetary Fund; it had increased the facilities of the Export-Import Bank to lend abroad, and it had made a direct loan to Great Britain of $3,750,000,000. On February 21, 1947, President Truman had recommended another appropriation of $350,000,000 for relief to the people of the liberated areas, this to be essentially restricted to the basic necessities of life, such as food and medical supplies, and to be administered exclusively by the United States. Congress accepted the recommendation and authorized the expenditure by a law which the President signed on May 31, 1947. The terrible destruction of the war, however, had been coupled with severe droughts, winter storms, and floods, and a blizzard which swept over all northern Europe. A still greater effort and on a broader basis was necessary. Under Secretaries Acheson and Clayton discussed the emergency with President Truman, and on May 8, 1947, Under Secretary Acheson, as a trial balloon, painted a clear picture of the situation in a speech at Cleveland, Mississippi. The Department, meanwhile, had consulted Senator Vandenberg, who counseled that a carefully prepared long-range program be worked out and submitted to the Congress. The Policy Planning Staff believed that the European nations should take the initiative and work out a plan to which the United States could lend its support. Secretary Marshall approved but insisted that all Europe, including Russia and its satellite states, be included in the program.

Taking advantage of the opportunity afforded by speaking at the Harvard commencement exercises, Secretary Marshall made his epoch-making proposal. After describing the serious situation in Europe and the responsibility of the United States to help in meeting it, Secretary Marshall declared:

It would be neither fitting nor efficacious for the Government to undertake to draw up unilaterally a program designed to place Europe on its feet economically. . . . The initiative, I think, must come from Europe. The role of this country should consist of friendly aid in the drafting of a European program and of later support of such a program so far as it may be practical for us to do so. The program should be a joint one, agreed to by a number, if not all, European nations.[1]

The European nations, in the words of Foreign Minister Bevin of Great Britain, "seized the proposal with both hands." Only the USSR and her satellite countries refused. Sixteen European nations met in Paris and formed a Committee of European Economic Cooperation. Meanwhile, several groups of specialists in the United States had investigated the problem and made reports to the President. The State Department studied all the reports, and Secretary Marshall made a statement before a joint session of the Senate Foreign Relations Committee and the House Committee on Foreign Affairs on November 10, 1947, urging support of the European Recovery Program as finally formulated. He recommended an appropriation of approximately $6,375,000,000 for the first fifteen months of the program. President Truman called a special session of the Congress to convene on November 17, 1947, to consider the crisis in Western Europe and made a strong plea in behalf of the proposal for European recovery submitted by the State Department. Secretary Marshall appeared before Senate and House committees and made numerous addresses to the public. Other members of the Department and various agencies of the government which had assisted in preparing the original plan and in making special studies for the congressional hearings explained and defended it. Three committees in the Department directed the ERP planning: the Interdepartmental Steering Committee, the Interdepartmental Correlation Committee, and the Departmental Committee for European Recovery. During peak stages as many as 350 departmental employees worked from half to full time on the ERP program,

The Congress had to be convinced that the expenditure of such a vast sum abroad was vital to the interests of the United States, and it was in no hurry to pass the bill as drawn by the administration. Two factors outside of the Department's efforts aided in its passage. The Politburo had engaged in a vigorous campaign throughout Europe to sabotage the program, and a Communist coup in Czechoslovakia was an added inducement. The unexpected inclusion by the House of Franco's Spain in the program, contrary to both presidential and Departmental policy, delayed passage slightly, but this provision went out in conference. The Foreign Assistance Act of 1948 was passed on April 3 and it included an additional $275,000,000 for military aid to Greece and Turkey. One final barrier remained—the necessary appropriations had to be passed by the Congress. The House of Representatives, in spite of its previous approval, cut approximately $1,000,000,000 from the sum which had been agreed upon as the minimum amount to carry out the program. Senator Vandenberg vigorously attacked the House "meat-axe technique" and the Senate committee restored most of the amount in question. The Foreign Aid Appropriation Act of 1948, which provided funds for the first year of the ERP and for aid to Greece, Turkey, and China, was signed by the President on June 28, 1948. The total appropriation was $6,030,710,228, of which $4,000,000,000 was for economic cooperation with Europe. Since this could be used in one year instead of fifteen months, the original requirements of the program were substantially met. Although the President and the State Department spearheaded the initiative, the other agencies of the government and the bipartisan, statesmanlike attitude of the Congress were equally important in securing its acceptance.

The Question of Palestine[2]

The Palestine question has long been a factor in domestic party politics in the United States, but only since 1944 has it been a disturbing influence in the conduct of our foreign relations. A large number of American Jews seemed to favor the Zionist movement, and as a well organized minority it could exert strong pressure upon members of Congress. Resolutions were introduced by Senators Taft of Ohio and Wagner of New York and by Representatives Compton of Connecticut and Wright of Pennsylvania—the first in the Senate requesting that the United States use its good offices to persuade Great Britain to abrogate the British White Paper on Palestine which limited immigration and would prohibit it entirely on March 31, 1944, and the second in the House favoring the establishment of a Jewish commonwealth in Palestine and its endorsement by the United States.

The occasion seemed most inopportune for such action, both to the War

Department and to the State Department, and General Marshall, then chief of staff, informed the Senate Foreign Relations Committee that he would not be responsible for its military effects on the Moslem world if the resolution passed. Secretary of War Stimson wrote to the committee that the resolution's passage would be prejudicial to the successful conclusion of the war. Secretary of State Hull also favored the postponement of the resolution. When at the close of the year the resolution in an amended form passed the House, and the Senate Committee on Foreign Relations inquired as to the attitude of the Department of State, the answer given was that while the Department had the utmost sympathy for the persecuted European Jewish people, it considered that "the passage of the resolution at the present time would be unwise from the standpoint of the general international situation." [3]

Hardly had President Truman assumed the duties of President before he, too, was subjected to pressure regarding Palestine. A joint letter from Senator Brewster of Maine and Representative Celler of New York urged that he "insist" that Prime Minister Winston Churchill open Palestine to Jewish immigration. The President acceded to the extent of calling for the free settlement of Palestine by the Jews to a point consistent with civil peace.

Earl G. Harrison, the United States representative on the Intergovernmental Committee on Refugees who had been sent by the President on a mission to inquire into the condition of displaced persons in Germany, particularly Jews, reported that he was led to believe that most of the Jews wished to go to Palestine and recommended that 100,000 immigration certificates be made immediately available.[4] President Truman, following this suggestion, wrote to British Prime Minister Attlee, enclosing a copy of the report and supporting the proposal that 100,000 Jews be permitted to enter Palestine.

This interference in the conduct of British foreign policy did not please the British and it enraged the Arabs. A communication from King Ibn-Saud of Arabia bitterly protested the violation on the part of the United States of the promise made by President Roosevelt, both verbally and in writing, that the United States would take no decision with respect to the basic situation in Palestine without full consultation with both Arabs and Jews. President Truman at first was not cognizant that any such commitment had been made, but when Ibn-Saud proposed to publish the correspondence, the State Department released the two letters.[5]

Great Britain subsequently suggested a joint Anglo-American Committee of Inquiry to examine the whole question. This was set up, and President Truman, by an Executive order, authorized all agencies of government in the United States to furnish upon request of the American chairman of the committee any of their relevant records or documents unless such disclosure would be prejudicial to the interests of the United States.

The report and recommendations of the Anglo-American Committee satisfied neither the Jews nor the Arabs, the British government was reserved, and the United States was not entirely pleased with the findings.[6] President Truman was happy that his request for the admission of 100,000 Jews into Palestine, as rapidly as conditions would permit, had been unanimously endorsed and that the abrogation of the land and immigration provisions of the British White Paper of 1939 had been recommended. Prime Minister Attlee particularly wished to know to what extent the United States would share the military and financial responsibilities before accepting the proposals.

In a formal note to the Arab governments, Acting Secretary of State Dean Acheson promised to make no definite decisions regarding Palestine before consulting both Arabs and Jews, and on May 21, 1946, the Department of State announced that the United States and Great Britain had initiated consultations with Jewish and Arab leaders. The Department also addressed letters to those organizations in the United States interested in the problem to submit their views. The United States at the same time dispatched technical experts to London to work on the details of moving 100,000 Jews into Palestine, and on July 2, 1946, President Truman, in a conference with representatives of the Jewish Agency for Palestine, stated that the Government of the United States was prepared to assume technical and financial responsibility for the transportation of the 100,000 Jewish immigrants from Europe to Palestine. A week later the President announced the establishment of a Cabinet Committee on Palestine, composed of the Secretaries of State, War, and Treasury, to assist in considering the recommendations of the Anglo-American Committee. The alternates of this committee, headed by Ambassador Henry F. Grady, had left the preceding day for London to discuss the implementation of the report.

The report of the alternates, generally known as the Morrison-Grady Plan, was submitted on July 24, 1946, but although published in Great Britain, it has never been released officially in the United States.[7] The plan advocated a system of provincial autonomy leading ultimately to a binational state or, alternatively, to partition. The Zionists opposed it vigorously, and although Secretary of State Byrnes approved it, the President did not support it but continued to urge immediate immigration. When, in a letter dated October 15, 1946, King Abdul-Aziz of Saudi Arabia expressed his incredulity at the contradictions in the President's promises, President Truman attempted to prove that his support of immigration of Jews into Palestine was not inconsistent with his promises to the Arabs.

The Department of State was not only by-passed during much of the policy making, but some of its most experienced and able officials were harshly criticized for having the courage to support objectively the interests of the United States. One of the members of the Anglo-American Committee of Inquiry, whose knowledge of the Near East stemmed from his few months' experience on the commission, obtained a few moments of notoriety by declaring that the middle level of State Department officials had frustrated American policy toward Palestine, and he demanded the resignation of Loy W. Henderson, Director of the Office of Near Eastern and African Affairs, a career diplomat of outstanding ability who had spent many years in Russia and the Near and Middle East in the service of his country. Actually, the President had taken over American foreign policy regarding Palestine, and the Department of State could only attempt to keep the policy coherent.

When after prolonged efforts to find an area of agreement no compromise between Arabs and Jews seemed possible, the British government decided early in February, 1947, to refer the Palestine problem, without any recommendations, to the United Nations General Assembly, which was to meet in September. The United States was not averse to a settlement by the United Nations, and in a speech before the opening session of the General Assembly on September 17, 1947, Secretary of State Marshall promised that the United States would do all in its power to assist in finding a solution. Herschel V. Johnson, United States Deputy Representative to the General Assembly, in a statement made at the meeting of its *ad hoc* Committee on Palestine of the General Assembly, declared that "the United States Delegation supports the basic principles of the unanimous recommendations and the majority plan which provides for partition and immigration."

This statement of the American attitude favoring partition unquestionably influenced some of the smaller states, and the position of the United States just before the vote was taken had become so pronounced that the Arabs and some British correspondents alleged that coercion was being used. Major General John H. Hilldring, former Assistant Secretary of State and a member of the United States delegation, conceded afterward that "we tried as best we could to persuade other countries of the logic and justice of our position," but he insisted that no intimidation or pressure was used. It was noted, however, that Haiti, the Philippines, and Liberia all shifted their stand to favoring partition at the last moment; and it was common knowledge that thousands of telegrams from private sources in the United States were received by Assembly representatives, some threatening the withholding of credits unless partition was supported.[8]

The representatives of the Arab states refused to accept the decision, claiming that it had been obtained by pressure exerted by some of the great powers. When it was evident that the Arab states were preparing to resist by force, a new problem faced the United Nations. The emergency was underscored by the fact that the United Kingdom had served notice that it would terminate its Palestine Mandate on May 15, 1948; while the General Assembly's Palestine

Commission officially reported to the Security Council on Feb. 16, 1948 that partition could only be carried out by force.

Hostilities quickly broke out in Palestine, and the State Department, in accordance with the laws previously enacted, placed an embargo on arms to all Arab countries, including Palestine. Numerous congressmen now demanded that the embargo be lifted as regards the Jews in Palestine. A group of thirty congressmen sent a letter of inquiry to Secretary Marshall regarding shipments of arms by the British to the Arab states and the future policy of the United States regarding Palestine. Secretary Marshall answered the questions frankly and fully.[9] He was all too well aware of the steadily increasing menace of the Soviet Union and the necessity of not permitting the Palestine problem to bring about a split between the two great English-speaking democracies who were the sole dependable bulwark against the Communist menace. The State Department had reluctantly agreed to support partition but the safety of the United States had now become the issue. President Truman was so advised by those responsible for the maintenance of that security.

The first indication of a reversal in policy was shown by the address of Ambassador Warren R. Austin, the United States Representative on the Security Council, on February 24, 1948. The substance of his statement was that the Security Council did not have the power to enforce a political settlement pursuant to a recommendation of the General Assembly.[10] In a statement made on March 19, 1948, Mr. Austin, conceding that partition could not be effected peaceably, as indicated by the report of the Palestine Commission, recommended that the commission should suspend its efforts to implement the proposed partition plan and that instead the Security Council should recommend a temporary trusteeship for Palestine to be established under the Trusteeship Council of the United Nations without prejudice to the eventual political settlement.[11] This policy was a recognition of the realities of the situation, that a mistake had been made, and that the security of the United States took precedence over all other interests. The next day, speaking in Los Angeles, Secretary of State Marshall declared:

The course of action with respect to the Palestine question which was proposed on March 19 by Ambassador Austin appeared to me to be the wisest course to follow. I recommended it to the President and he approved my recommendation. . . . The interest of the United States in a peaceful settlement in Palestine arises not only out of deep humanitarian considerations but also out of vital elements of our national security.[12]

The opinion of the former chief of staff and current Secretary of State meant nothing to the more fanatical Zionists. Representative Emanuel Celler of New York introduced a resolution in the House of Representatives calling for an investigation of the State Department couched in language almost vituperative. A few sentences will illustrate the tone of the resolution:

Whereas the activities of the Near Eastern Division have brought the State Department into disrepute; and whereas the activities of that Division indicate bad faith, ineptitude, indecision and obscure motives . . . and whereas the said Division has deliberately contravened established policy by untoward instructions to our consular and diplomatic agents in the Middle East . . .[13]

One further act in the diplomatic tragedy of errors remained. A special session of the Assembly was called to consider the United States' trusteeship proposal. While the Assembly was still debating the question, and without the American delegation receiving the slightest intimation, the news was brought that President Truman had again reversed himself and had recognized the provisional government of the new state of Israel exactly ten minutes after it had been self-proclaimed. It was later learned that the President was so eager to be the first to accord recognition that he granted it even before the request for recognition had reached him. Since the State Department did not learn of the President's decision until the very day that the State of Israel proclaimed its independence neither the American representatives at Lake Success nor the American ambassador in London were given any previous notice of the President's intention.

The entire behind-the-scenes story has not been told, but dependable sources have indicated that certain Democratic leaders in Washington and New York and certain White House advisers, rather than the Department of State, influenced the final decision. A successful American foreign policy can hardly be expected when the President accepts the questionable advice of self-seeking politicians instead of the objective counsel of experienced and disinterested experts of the Department of State.

Secretary Marshall's resignation was announced on January 7, 1949. He had been forced to undergo a serious operation and his health could not support further the overwork, strain, and frustration of the top cabinet position. He had consistently followed a bipartisan foreign policy and his resignation was sincerely regretted by leaders of both parties. His fair and convincing presentation of the justice of American policy toward the Soviet Union had brought an overwhelming majority of the members of the United Nations to give their support to the United States. Secretary Marshall's outstanding services had unquestionably assured him a position among America's great Secretaries of State.[14]

Suggestions and Conclusions

As the problems of foreign policy have become more complicated, the need for adequate machinery to handle them becomes more necessary. Much of the criticism of the State Department in the formulation of policy is unjustified because, as has been shown, the President in this field is in control and must assume the responsibility. But in the execution of foreign policy the Department is in charge, and if it fails here, criticism is justified. It must be conceded that at the present time the Departmental machinery is somewhat antiquated and cumbersome and there is too much of it. The Department is still suffering from the forced expansion after the Second World War, when it was compelled to absorb the thousands of employees of war agencies which were being disbanded. Neither has it recovered from the series of drastic reorganizations hastily conceived and carried out by persons not sufficiently familiar with the development of the Department.

In a recent investigation of the Department's organization, one of the principal criticisms was that it failed to effect the close relationship necessary between political, economic, cultural, and intelligence matters. The result was that more conferences were held than was necessary, thereby consuming a needlessly large amount of time. The report laid down as an essential requirement that "the men interested in all of the phases of activity in a particular country should be grouped together organizationally and if possible physically." Another charge made was that the Department had "an overabundance of units, sections, branches, divisions and offices," and it was alleged that this detailed organization was established to increase the personnel that could be given a title.[15]

Both of these complaints were justified and the Department is aware of it. In a recent memorandum prepared for Secretary Marshall by Assistant Secretary Peurifoy, it was noted as a preliminary that the present organization

disperses responsibility and authority in the Department, precludes expeditious action when several interests may be involved; requires excessive committee work and coordinating staff to produce action; and dilutes control of United States Foreign relations by engaging the Department in work not essential to its major role.

It was further pointed out that overseparation existed between the Departmental and the Foreign Services and between the functional and regional staffs.

A careful plan of reorganization has been prepared by the experienced officials of the Department working with the Hoover Commission, which will reduce organizational units, eliminate certain operational functions, simplify the assignment of work, speed up action, and fix responsibility. Recognizing that an "appalling burden has fallen on the Secretary and Under Secretary of State," a basic change will be an integrated and responsible administration of economic, informational, and political affairs in four geographic-area offices, each headed by an Assistant Secretary of State. A Deputy Under Secretary for Administration will coordinate the Departmental and Foreign Service agencies, and a Second Deputy Under Secretary will oversee high-level policy matters. An Assistant Secretary will be responsible for congressional affairs, another for public affairs, a seventh for interdepartmental coordination, and an eighth for international organization affairs. Ultimate amalgamation of the Foreign Service and State Department personnel is approved.

In a world of ruthless power politics it is vital that the Department of State be made an efficient and responsible agency capable of formulating and carrying out a foreign policy which will maintain, strengthen, and improve the status of the United States in world affairs. Such a reorganization, put into effect gradually, with a minimum of friction, would add materially to the stature of the Department of State as the most important Department in the government. However, this is not enough. It is also necessary to make it possible and desirable to attract and keep in the Department of State the ablest minds in the country. To achieve this end either top-level salaries must be substantially increased or adequate allowances must be provided, so that able officials can afford to serve. It is also necessary that greater stability and responsibility be effected. The President should not only choose the best available advisers, but he should be guided by their counsel. Domestic party politics should stop at the frontiers.

Finally, public opinion must be informed and its support obtained. A democracy can achieve success in no other way. Never before in history have the problems of foreign policies been more difficult and acute than today, and never before has it been so essential that they be solved by peaceful means. Inasmuch as the primary causes of war are conflicts in foreign policy, our first line of defense is adequate machinery for the conduct of foreign relations. We need the best army, navy, and air force to support our foreign policy, but this policy must merit defense. It must be a policy so wisely formulated that its execution will appeal to the citizens as both reasonable and necessary. A well organized, effective Department of State capable of advising the administration intelligently can and must perform this fundamental function.

NOTES

CHAPTER 1

1. *Secret Journals of Congress* (Boston, 1820), II, 36.
2. George C. Wood, *Congressional Control of Foreign Relations During the American Revolution* (New York University thesis, 1919), p. 35.
3. *Revolutionary Diplomatic Correspondence of the United States*, ed. Francis Wharton (6 vols., Washington, 1889), III, 288.
4. *Correspondence and Public Papers of John Jay*, ed. H. P. Johnston (4 vols., New York, 1890-1893), I, 440. Hereafter cited as *Jay Papers*.
5. Wood, *op. cit.*, pp. 53-55.
6. *Journals of Congress*, XVI, 428; XVII, 1156; XIX, 42.
7. *Secret Journals of Congress* (4 vols., Boston, 1821), II, 580.
8. *Journals of the Continental Congress* (Library of Congress ed.), XIX, 43.
9. *Revolutionary Diplomatic Correspondence*, V, 199-202.
10. Gaillard Hunt, *The Department of State of the United States* (Yale University Press, 1914), p. 31.
11. Thomas A. Bailey, *A Diplomatic History of the American People* (New York, 1940), p. 11.
12. *Revolutionary Diplomatic Correspondence*, I, 597.
13. *Ibid.*, p. 292.
14. The peace treaty was signed before Jefferson was able to embark.
15. William Jay, *The Life of John Jay* (New York, 1833), I, 188-189.
16. Gaillard Hunt, *op. cit.*, p. 45.
17. *Jay Papers*, III, 251.
18. Hunt, *op. cit.*, pp. 50-51.
19. George Bancroft, *History of the Formation of the Constitution of the United States* (New York, 1882), I, 479-480.
20. *Jay Papers*, I, 395.
21. *Secret Journals of Congress*, IV, 452.
22. *Ibid.*, pp. 185-257.
23. William Jay, *op. cit.*, II, 179.
24. *Ibid.*, p. 191.
25. Samuel Flagg Bemis, *Jay's Treaty, A Study in Commerce and Diplomacy* (New York, 1923), p. 207.
26. S. F. Bemis, "John Jay," in *American Secretaries of State and Their Diplomacy* (New York, 1927), I, 252-259.
27. William Jay, *op. cit.*, I, 200-201.
28. Paul L. Ford, *Pamphlets on the Constitution of the United States* (Brooklyn, 1888), p. 72.
29. *Secret Journals of Congress*, IV, 454.
30. Francis Wharton, *Digest of International Law*, 2nd ed., III, 919.

CHAPTER 2

1. *U.S. Statutes at Large*, V, 25-29.
2. *Ibid.*, I, 65.
3. Quoted by James Schouler, *History of the United States of America*, rev. ed. (New York, 1894), I, 120.
4. *The Writings of George Washington*, ed. John C. Fitzpatrick (Washington, D. C., 1939), XXX, 509-511.
5. *The Writings of Thomas Jefferson*, ed. Paul L. Ford (New York, 1895), V, 223.

6. *Ibid.*, p. 231.

7. *The Writings of James Madison*, Cong. ed. (New York, 1900-1910), I, 369; *Writings of Jefferson*, Ford ed., V, 336.

8. *Writings of Jefferson*, Ford ed., VI, 199.

9. *Ibid.*, p. 259.

10. *Ibid.*, p. 451.

11. *American State Papers: Foreign Relations* (Washington, 1833), I, 300-304.

12. *Writings of Washington*, Fitzpatrick ed., XXXIII, 231.

13. See below, pp. 25-26.

14. Department of State MSS.: *Washington Papers*, Record Book, Vol. 20, quoted by Hunt, *The Department of State of the United States*, p. 110.

15. *Writings of Jefferson*, Ford ed., II, 468.

16. Hunt, *op. cit.*, p. 96.

17. Hunt, *op. cit.*, p. 110.

18. *Writings of Jefferson*, Ford ed., VI, 74-77.

19. *The Writings of Thomas Jefferson*, ed. Andrew A. Lipscomb (Washington, 1904), VIII, 71-94.

20. *Ibid.*, XIII, xxxv.

21. Moncure D. Conway, *Omitted Chapters of History Disclosed in the Life and Papers of Edmund Randolph* (New York, 1889), p. 213.

22. Dice R. Anderson, "Edmund Randolph," in *American Secretaries of State and Their Diplomacy*, ed. S. F. Bemis (New York, 1927), II, 104.

23. John Bassett Moore, *Digest of International Law* (Washington, 1906), IV, 465-466.

24. Jared Sparks, *Life of Gouverneur Morris* (Boston, 1832), II, 449.

25. *American State Papers: Foreign Relations*, I, 689.

26. Anderson, *op. cit.*, p. 113.

27. See S. F. Bemis, *Jay's Treaty, A Study in Commerce and Diplomacy* (New York, 1923).

28. John B. Moore, *History and Digest of International Arbitrations* (Washington, 1895), I, 310.

29. The text in French may be found in M. D. Conway, *op. cit.*, pp. 272-281; a translation is given in *A Vindication of Mr. Randolph's Resignation* (Philadelphia, 1795), pp. 41-48, and a detailed explanation by Randolph in the same, pp. 61-96.

30. Randolph, *op. cit.*, pp. 9-17.

31. Octavius Pickering and C. W. Upham, *Life of Timothy Pickering* (Boston, 1873), III, 226.

32. For sympathetic accounts see Anderson, *op. cit.*, pp. 152-156, and Conway, *op. cit.*, pp. 262-289; for a very critical account see Schouler, *op. cit.*, I, 313-316.

33. Moore, *Digest of International Law*, IV, 693.

CHAPTER 3

1. Pickering and Upham, *Life of Timothy Pickering*, III, 229.

2. Henry Jones Ford, "Timothy Pickering," in *American Secretaries of State* (New York, 1927), II, 186.

3. *American State Papers: Foreign Relations*, I, 645.

4. Pickering and Upham, *op. cit.*, III, 233-237.

5. H. J. Ford, *op. cit.*, II, 206.

6. *American State Papers: Foreign Relations*, I, 746.

7. H. J. Ford, *op. cit.*, II, 217.

8. Schouler, *History of the United States of America*, I, 426-427.

9. H. J. Ford, *op. cit.*, II, 225.

10. Pickering and Upham, *op. cit.*, III, 488.

11. Hunt, *The Department of State of the United States*, p. 142.

12. *Ibid.*, pp. 351-352.

13. Albert J. Beveridge, *Life of John Marshall* (New York, 1916), II, 492.

14. *American State Papers: Foreign Relations*, II, 486-490.

15. Quoted by Beveridge, *op. cit.*, II, 525.

16. *The Life and Works of John Adams* (Boston, 1854), IX, 85.

CHAPTER 4

1. *The Writings of James Madison*, ed. Gaillard Hunt (New York, 1900), I, 141.

2. William C. Rives, *History of the Life and Times of James Madison* (Boston, 1860-1868), III, 382, note.

3. *The Writings of Thomas Jefferson*, ed. Andrew A. Lipscomb (Washington, 1904), X, 313.

4. *Ibid.*, p. 317.

5. James D. Richardson, *Messages and Papers of the Presidents* (New York, 1911), I, 339.

6. Livingston was somewhat disgruntled at this apparently unfair discrimination and sent a gentle protest to Madison. He was assured that no distinction in grade was meant and that the two ranks were regarded as on a parity. *American State Papers: Foreign Relations*, II, 554, 566.

7. *American State Papers, op. cit.*, p. 567.

8. *Writings of Jefferson*, ed. P. L. Ford, VIII, 246.

9. Charles E. Hill, "James Madison," in *American Secretaries of State and Their Diplomacy*, ed. S. F. Bemis (New York, 1927), III, 104.

10. See particularly the letter to Monroe dated Jan. 5, 1804. *American State Papers: Foreign Relations*, II, 730-732.

11. *Ibid.*, III, 183.

12. Henry Adams gives an excellent picture of the results of Jefferson's "Canons of Etiquette," *History of the United States* (New York, 1898), II, 365.

13. Francis Wharton, A *Digest of the International Law of the United States* (Washington, 1887), I, 733.

14. For a sympathetic treatment see Charles C. Tansill, "Robert Smith," in *American Secretaries of State and Their Diplomacy*, ed. S. F. Bemis (New York, 1927), III, 151-197. Henry Adams in his *History* is much more critical.

15. During the period between March 3, 1809, the date of Madison's retirement, and March 6, 1809, when Smith entered upon his duties there was no Secretary of State nor Acting Secretary of State.

16. *American State Papers: Foreign Relations*, III, 295-296.

17. *Ibid.*, pp. 300-319.

18. *The Writings of James Madison* (Philadelphia, 1865), II, 499.

19. Henry Adams, *History*, V, 163.

20. The entire episode is described in detail by Madison in a lengthy memorandum; see *Writings of Madison*, Hunt ed. (New York, 1910), VIII, 137-149.

21. *American State Papers: Foreign Relations*, III, 439.

22. *American Historical Review*, XIII, 303-310 (Jan., 1908).

23. *Annals of Congress*, April 1, 1812, p. 1593.

24. *The Writings of James Monroe*, ed. Stanislaus M. Hamilton (New York, 1901), V, 205-212.

25. Julius W. Pratt, "James Monroe," in *American Secretaries of State*, ed. S. F. Bemis, III, 252.

26. See Monroe's strong protest to the British government, *American State Papers: Foreign Relations*, III, 693.

27. E. D. Ingraham, *Sketch of the Events Which Preceded the Capture of Washington* (Philadelphia, 1849).

28. *American State Papers: Documents Legislative and Executive*, II, 252.

29. Monroe retired from the Secretaryship of State on Sept. 30, 1814, but was again commissioned on Feb. 28, 1815.

30. Wharton, *Digest of International Law*, I, 635.

31. *Ibid.*, II, 2.

32. *Annals of Congress*, 14th Congress, 1st session, p. 1735.

33. Wharton, *op. cit.*, III, 565-566.

CHAPTER 5

1. In letters written before his inauguration to both Thomas Jefferson and to Andrew Jackson, Monroe emphasized the necessity of picking the Secretary of State from the East. Adams's outstanding qualifications for the position were given second place. See *The Writings of John Quincy Adams*, ed. W. C. Ford (New York, 1916), VI, 166, note 1.

2. *Memoirs of John Quincy Adams*, ed. Charles F. Adams (Philadelphia, 1875), IV, 388.

3. *Writings of J. Q. Adams*, VI, 132-133, note 1.

4. *Ibid.*, p. 179.

5. Graham became a commissioner to South America and later, in 1819, minister to Portugal.

6. *Memoirs of J. Q. Adams*, IV, 27.

7. *Ibid.*, p. 307.

8. *Ibid.*, p. 193.

9. *Writings of J. Q. Adams*, VI, 228.

10. *Ibid.*, p. 354.

11. *Memoirs of J. Q. Adams*, IV, 98.

12. *Ibid.*, p. 100.

13. *Ibid.*, p. 340.

14. House Document No. 194, 15th Congress, 1st session, VII, Serial 11.

15. *Memoirs of J. Q. Adams*, IV, 224.

16. Adams often opposed appointments suggested by the President, but regularly made out the commissions after the President had made a decision.

17. *Memoirs of J. Q. Adams*, IV, 366.

18. *Ibid.*, p. 435.

19. *Ibid.*, p. 37.

20. *Ibid.*, p. 411.

21. *Ibid.*, V, 125, 130, 134, 135, 147, 148.

22. *Ibid.*, pp. 166-167.

23. *Ibid.*, pp. 239-240.

24. *Ibid.*, pp. 288-289.

25. Stanley Lane-Poole, *The Life of the Right Honorable Stratford Canning* (London and New York, 1888), I, 309.

26. *Writings of J. Q. Adams*, VII, 171.

27. *Memoirs of J. Q. Adams*, V, 289.

28. Francis Wharton, *A Digest of the International Law of the United States* (Washington, 1887), I, 522.

29. *Memoirs of J. Q. Adams*, IV, 205.

30. *Ibid.*, IV, 92.

31. *Writings of J. Q. Adams*, VI, 318.

32. *Memoirs of J. Q. Adams*, VI, 152.

33. *The Writings of James Monroe*, ed. S. M. Hamilton (New York, 1898), VI, 325.

34. *Writings of Thomas Jefferson*, ed. P. L. Ford, X, 277-278.

35. *Writings of James Madison*, ed. S. M. Hamilton, IX, 161-162.

36. *Memoirs of J. Q. Adams*, VI, 177-179.

37. *Ibid.*, p. 163.

38. "Genesis of the Monroe Doctrine," *Proceedings of the Massachusetts Historical Society*, ed. W. C. Ford (1901, 1902), Second Series, XV, 412.

39. *Memoirs of J. Q. Adams*, V, 47.

40. *Ibid*, pp. 400-401.

41. Wharton, *op. cit.*, III, 259-261.

42. *Memoirs of J. Q. Adams*, VI, 166.

43. *Writings of Albert Gallatin*, ed. Henry Adams (Philadelphia, 1879), II, 242.

CHAPTER 6

1. Carl Schurz, *Life of Henry Clay* (New York, 1899), I, 310.

2. Senate Document No. 109, 21st Congress, 1st session.

3. Schurz, *op. cit.*, I, 299.

4. *The Private Correspondence of Henry Clay*, ed. Calvin Colton (Cincinnati, 1856), p. 194.

5. John C. Fitzpatrick, "The Autobiography of Martin Van Buren," *Annual Report of the American Historical Association*, 1918, II, 224.

6. *Correspondence of Andrew Jackson*, ed. John Spencer Bassett (Washington, 1929), IV, 4.

7. See Denis Tilden Lynch, *An Epoch and a Man* (New York, 1929), p. 326.

8. *Ibid.*, p. 328.

9. Fitzpatrick, *op. cit.*, p. 232.

10. *Ibid.*, p. 421.

11. See Peter Force, *National Calendar*, 1829, 1830, 1831.

12. Fitzpatrick, *op. cit.*, p. 262.

13. *Ibid.*, p. 270.

14. J. B. Moore, *Digest of International Law*, IV, 786-787; see also *Memoirs of John Quincy Adams*, VIII, 264.

15. Charles Havens Hunt, *Life of Edward Livingston* (New York, 1864), pp. 356-357.

16. *Ibid.*, p. 361.

17. *Ibid.*, pp. 368-369.

18. Graham H. Stuart, *American Diplomatic and Consular Practice* (New York, 1936), pp. 169-171; see also House Document No. 94, 22nd Congress, 2nd session (Feb. 7, 1833), and Senate Document No. 83, 22nd Congress, 2nd session.

19. *The Correspondence of Andrew Jackson*, ed. John Spencer Bassett (Washington, 1931), V, 102.

CHAPTER 7

1. John C. Fitzpatrick, "The Autobiography of Martin Van Buren," *Annual Report of the American Historical Association*, 1918, II, 593.

2. James D. Richardson, *Messages and Papers of the Presidents* (Washington, 1899), II, 461-462.

3. House Document No. 177, 27th Congress, 2nd session (April 8, 1842), pp. 14-15.

4. Fitzpatrick, *op. cit.*, II, 611.

5. House Document No. 247, 24th Congress, 1st session (April, 1836).

6. *Ibid.*, Sec. B.

7. Richardson, *op. cit.*, III, 100-106.

8. Senate Document No. 63, 24th Congress, 1st session, No. 50.

9. John S. Bassett, *Correspondence of Andrew Jackson* (Washington, 1926, 1935), V, 363.

10. Richardson, *op. cit.*, III, 158-160. This entire episode is fully treated in J. S. Bassett, *The Life of Andrew Jackson* (New York, 1911), 663-667, and in Marquis James, *Andrew Jackson: Portrait of a President* (Indianapolis, 1937), Chap. XXXVIII.

11. House Report No. 931, 25th Congress, 2nd session.

12. House Executive Document No. 73, 25th Congress, 2nd session, 7, 8.

13. Senate Document No. 50, 25th Congress, 3rd session (Jan. 5, 1838).

14. Senate Document No. 13, 26th Congress, 1st session (Dec. 27, 1839).

15. See Lewis H. Campbell, *Patent System of the United States* (Washington, 1891).

CHAPTER 8

1. *The Private Correspondence of Daniel Webster*, ed. Fletcher Webster (Boston, 1857), II, 87.

2. Claude Moore Fuess, *Daniel Webster* (Boston, 1930), II, 94.

3. For Webster's letter to the House of Representatives and the Report on the Commercial Regulations of Foreign Nations, see House Document No. 29, State Department, 27th Congress, 3rd session (Dec. 27, 1842).

4. House Document No. 177, 27th Congress, 2nd session (April 8, 1842).

5. House Document No. 39, 27th Congress, 3rd session (Jan. 4, 1842).

6. House Document No. 84, State Department, 27th Congress, 3rd session (Jan. 25, 1843).

7. George T. Curtis, *Life of Daniel Webster* (New York, 1870), II, 68.

8. Ashburton's wife was the eldest daughter of Senator Bingham of Pennsylvania, an heiress in her own right.

9. *Niles' National Register*, LXIII, 37.

10. See *Treaties and Other International Acts of the United States of America*, ed. Hunter Miller (Washington, 1933), III, 328-351, and H. B. Adams, *Life and Writings of Jared Sparks* (Boston, 1893), II, 393-398.

11. J. B. Moore, *Digest of International Law*, I, 476.

12. *Ibid.*, IV, 15.

13. Curtis, *op. cit.*, II, 212.

14. John W. Foster, *A Century of American Diplomacy* (New York, 1900), p. 283.

15. Henry Cabot Lodge, *Daniel Webster* (Boston, 1883), p. 261.

16. As a matter of fact, it might be claimed that while Derrick served as Secretary of State ad interim, the position of Chief Clerk was in reality vacant.

17. Document No. 341, *Proceedings of the Senate*, 28th Congress, 1st session (May 16, 1844), p. 26.

18. Executive Document No. 2, 28th Congress, 1st session (Dec. 5, 1843), p. 42.

19. Senate Document No. 240, 28th Congress, 1st session, communicated March 8, 1844.

CHAPTER 9

1. According to John Tyler, Jr., President Tyler never forgave Wise for his action. See Olive Perry Chitwood, *John Tyler* (New York, 1939), p. 287.

2. Chitwood, *op. cit.*, pp. 286-287; also St. George L. Sioussat, "John Caldwell Calhoun," in *American Secretaries of State and Their Diplomacy*, ed. S. F. Bemis (New York, 1928), V, 128-129.

3. *Correspondence of John C. Calhoun*, ed. J. Franklin Jameson (Washington, 1900), p. 577.

4. *Ibid.*, p. 586.

5. House Document No. 59, 28th Congress, 2nd session, II, 1.

6. *Correspondence of Calhoun*, ed. Jameson, p. 648.

7. George Ticknor Curtis, *The Life of James Buchanan* (New York, 1883), I, 547-548.

8. *Ibid.*, pp. 548-549.

9. House Report No. 552, 29th Congress, 1st session (April 6, 1846). For the clerical personnel of the Department of State for the year 1848, see Executive Document No. 30, 30th Congress, 2nd session (Jan. 16, 1849), p. 2.

10. *The Works of James Buchanan*, ed. John Bassett Moore (Philadelphia, 1909), VI, 194-204.

11. *Ibid.*, Instructions, Buchanan to Slidell, Nov. 10, 1845, pp. 304-305.

12. House Executive Document, No. 12, 29th Congress, 2nd session (Dec. 12, 1846).

13. *The Diary of James K. Polk During His Presidency*, ed. M. M. Quaife (Chicago, 1910), I, 201.

14. J. B. Moore, *Digest of International Law*, III, 566.

CHAPTER 10

1. Mary W. Williams, "John Middleton Clayton," in *American Secretaries of State and Their Diplomacy*, ed. S. F. Bemis (New York, 1928), VI, 13.

2. House Executive Document No. 43, 31st Congress, 1st session (Feb. 21, 1850).

3. "Clayton Papers," VII, Despatches to France, XXXI-XXXII, cited by Williams, *op. cit.*

4. Quoted by Mary W. Williams, *op. cit.*, VI, 71-72.

5. *Writings and Speeches of Daniel Webster*, National ed. (Boston, 1903), XII, 181-186.

6. *Ibid.*, XVI, 586.

7. Senate Executive Document No. 9, 31st Congress, 2nd session (Dec. 30, 1850), pp. 4-13.

8. Senate Executive Document No. 46, 32nd Congress, 1st session (March 8, 1852).

9. House Report No. 298, 34th Congress, 1st session (Aug. 2, 1856).

10. J. B. Moore, *Digest of International Law*, IV, 760.

11. Senate Document No. 13, 32nd Congress, 2nd session (Jan. 5, 1853), pp. 15-23.

12. James Ford Rhodes, *History of the United States from the Compromise of 1850* (New York, 1893), I, 294.

13. Paul Revere Frothingham, *Edward Everett* (New York, 1925), p. 339.

14. Foster Stearns, "Edward Everett," in *American Secretaries of State and Their Diplomacy*, ed. S. F. Bemis (New York, 1928), VI, 138.

CHAPTER 11

1. *Works of James Buchanan*, ed. J. B. Moore, VII, 508.

2. Henry Barrett Learned, "William Learned Marcy," in *American Secretaries of State and Their Diplomacy*, ed. S. F. Bemis (New York, 1928), VI, 168.

3. The subject is discussed in detail by John W. Foster, *The Practice of Diplomacy* (New York, 1906), VII; see also Senate Executive Document No. 31, 36th Congress, 1st session (April 2, 1860).

4. Graham H. Stuart, *American Diplomatic and Consular Practice* (New York, 1936), p. 277.

5. *Congressional Globe*, March 2, 1855, XXIV, 1106, 33rd Congress, 2nd session.

6. 7 *Opinions of the Attorney General*, pp. 186-229.

7. House Executive Document No. 30, 34th Congress, 3rd session (Jan. 5, 1857).

8. House Executive Document No. 93, 33rd Congress, 2nd session, pp. 128-132.

9. *Memoirs of John Quincy Adams*, XI, 338.

10. *Register of the Officers and Agents in the Service of the United States on September 30, 1857* (Washington, 1857), pp. 1-2.

11. *Works of James Buchanan*, X, 103.

12. Mr. Cass to Lord Napier, April 10, 1858, Senate Executive Document No. 49, 35th Congress, 1st session, pp. 42-48.

13. J. B. Moore, *Digest*, II, 943; see excellent summary of the entire question in *Ibid.*, pp. 914-951.

14. James D. Richardson, *Messages and Papers of the Presidents*, V, 507.

15. Mr. Cass to Mr. Mason, minister to France, June 27, 1859, MS. Instruction to France No. 190, XV, 455.

16. House Executive Document No. 67, 35th Congress, 2nd session (Jan. 25, 1858).

17. Trescot, an author of several important books on diplomacy, had also served as Secretary of Legation in London. He became Assistant Secretary of State on June 11, 1860, immediately after the resignation of John Appleton.

18. *Works of James Buchanan*, XI, 59.

19. J. B. Moore, *Digest*, III, 573-579.

CHAPTER 12

1. F. W. Seward, *Seward at Washington* (New York, 1891), II, 481.

2. *The Complete Works of Abraham Lincoln*, ed. J. G. Nicolay and John Hay (New York, 1890), I, 659.

3. F. W. Seward, *op. cit.*, II, 487.

4. *Ibid.*, p. 497.

5. *Ibid.*, p. 519.

6. F. W. Seward, *Reminiscences of a War-Time Statesman and Diplomat* (New York, 1916), pp. 142-143.

7. F. W. Seward, *Seward at Washington*, II, 633-634.
8. *Ibid.*, p. 519.
9. F. W. Seward, *Reminiscences*, pp. 147, 148.
10. F. W. Seward, *Seward at Washington*, II, 535.
11. *Ibid.*, p. 541.
12. The text of the original instructions and the changes made by Lincoln are shown in J. G. Nicolay and John Hay, *Abraham Lincoln* (New York, 1890), IV, 270-275. In final form it is found in *Diplomatic Correspondence—1861*, Nos. 10, 71.
13. F. W. Seward, *Seward at Washington*, II, 581.
14. *Ibid.*, III, 21.
15. Senate Executive Document No. 8, 37th Congress, 2nd session, Vol. 4.
16. C. F. Adams, *Charles Francis Adams* (New York, 1900), p. 338.
17. *Ibid.*, p. 342.
18. F. W. Seward, *Seward at Washington*, III, 17-20.
19. C. F. Adams, *op. cit.*, p. 356.
20. *Ibid.*, p. 354.
21. F. W. Seward, *Seward at Washington*, III, 343.

CHAPTER 13

1. Grant was impressed by wealth, never having acquired any himself, and having dined at the Fish's, he was taken with the urbanity and charm of his host.
2. *Register of the Department of State for the Year* 1869-70 (Washington, 1870).
3. See *List of Officers of the Department of State on September* 30, 1859; also *List of Officers of the Department of State Corrected to January* 1, 1862 (Washington, 1862).
4. *Register of the Department of State—*1869-70 (Washington, 1869), p. 7.
5. House Executive Document No. 19, 41st Congress, 2nd session (Dec. 6, 1869), p. 2.
6. House Miscellaneous Document No. 31, 41st Congress, 2nd session (Jan. 17, 1870).
7. Allan Nevins, *Hamilton Fish* (New York, 1936), p. 863.
8. See *Register of the Department of State*, Oct. 1, 1870 (Washington, 1870).
9. *Revised Statutes of the United States* (1878), p. 1093.
10. 17 U. S. *Statutes at Large*, p. 509.
11. Nevins, *op. cit.*, p. 140.
12. Cf. *Nation*, XV, 342 (Nov. 28, 1872).
13. The whole affair is treated exhaustively in Nevins's *Hamilton Fish*, pp. 201-212.
14. Senate Executive Document No. 11, 41st Congress, 3rd session (Jan. 9, 1871). See particularly Instruction No. 15, Secretary Ford to Chargé d'Affaires Moran, pp. 27-37.
15. See Nevins, *op. cit.*, p. 379.
16. See the monograph by Charles C. Tansill, *The United States and Santo Domingo, 1798-1873* (Baltimore, 1938).
17. House Report 579, 44th Congress, 1st session.
18. Fish to Grant, July 13, 1874, quoted by Nevins, *op. cit.*, p. 727.
19. Nevins, *op. cit.*, pp. 730-739.
20. John Russell Young, *Around the World with General Grant* (New York, 1879), II, 273-275.
21. *Diary and Letters of Rutherford B. Hayes*, ed. C. R. Williams (Ohio State Historical Society 1922-26), III, 402; also C. R. Williams, *Life of Rutherford Birchard Hayes* (New York, 1914), II, 17.
22. William Maxwell Evarts, *Arguments and Speeches*, ed. Sherman Evarts (New York, 1919), I, 667.
23. Brainerd Dyer, *The Public Career of William M. Evarts* (Berkeley, California, 1933), p. 188.
24. Chester L. Barrows, *William M. Evarts* (Chapel Hill, North Carolina, 1941), p. 344.
25. Andrew D. White, *The Autobiography of Andrew Dickson White* (New York, 1905), I, 528.
26. Senate Executive Document No. 53, 46th Congress, 3rd session, p. 2.

CHAPTER 14

1. According to records available it was not until July 1, 1874, that any women were appointed to clerical positions in the Department.

2. *Regulations of the Department of State to December, 1880* (Washington, 1880).

3. The salary was now $4,500, but the income meant little to Hay, who had married the daughter of the Cleveland millionaire, Amasa Stone.

4. *Letters of Mrs. James G. Blaine* (New York, 1908), I, 203.

5. Gail Hamilton, *Biography of James G. Blaine* (Norwich, Conn., 1895), pp. 494-495.

6. *Letters of Mrs. James G. Blaine* (New York, 1908), I, 191.

7. Perry Belmont, *An American Democrat* (Columbia University, 1941), p. 219.

8. James G. Blaine, *Political Discussions—Legislative, Diplomatic, Popular* (Norwich, Conn., 1887), p. 411.

9. *Letters of Mrs. James G. Blaine*, I, 313.

10. Mrs. James G. Blaine once wrote that his last name should have been Aider.

11. *Register of the Department of State* (Washington, 1882), pp. 5-11.

12. Thomas Hunt, *The Life of William H. Hunt* (privately printed, Brattleboro, Vermont, 1922), pp. 253-256.

13. Samuel Flagg Bemis, *A Diplomatic History of the United States* (New York, 1942), p. 576.

14. Thomas A. Bailey, *A Diplomatic History of the American People* (New York, 1942), p. 436.

15. Philip Marshall Brown, "Frederick T. Frelinghuysen," in *American Secretaries of State and Their Diplomacy*, ed. S. F. Bemis (New York, 1928), VIII, 43.

CHAPTER 15

1. See Charles C. Tansill, *The Foreign Policy of Thomas F. Bayard, 1885-1897* (New York, 1940), pp. xvii-xx.

2. Senate Report No. 507, Part 3, 50th Congress, 1st session.

3. Gaillard Hunt, *The Department of State of the United States*, p. 190.

4. Allan Nevins, *Grover Cleveland* (New York, 1933), p. 207.

5. J. B. Moore, *Digest of International Law*, IV, 480-484.

6. A star in brown gold and green enamel with 130 diamond brilliants.

7. Upon his return, Cox recounted his experience in a book entitled *Diversions of a Diplomat in Turkey* (New York, 1887).

8. Lester B. Shippee, "Thomas Francis Bayard," in *American Secretaries of State*, ed. S. F. Bemis, VIII, 50-51.

9. The whole affair is objectively and exhaustively treated in the scholarly work, *The Foreign Policy of Thomas F. Bayard*, by Charles C. Tansill (New York, 1940), Chaps. 6-11; see also J. B. Moore, *Digest*, V, 216-218.

10. Quoted in Tansill, *op. cit.*, pp. 104-105.

11. *Ibid.*, p. 111.

12. The "Murchison" correspondence may be found in *Foreign Relations* (1888), II, 1667-1718; see also Moore, *Digest*, IV, 536-548.

13. Quoted by Thomas A. Bailey, *A Diplomatic History of the American People*, p. 441.

14. Gail Hamilton, *Biography of James G. Blaine* (Norwich, Conn., 1895), p. 618.

15. *Ibid.*, pp. 651-652.

16. *Ibid.*, p. 653.

17. *Letters of Mrs. James G. Blaine*, II, 244.

18. *Official Register of the United States, July 1, 1889* (Washington, 1889), I, 22-23.

19. Royal Cortissoz, *Life of Whitelaw Reid* (New York, 1921), II, 124-125.

20. See Nevins, *op. cit.*, pp. 437-451, for detailed discussion of this issue.

21. John W. Foster, *Diplomatic Memoirs* (Boston, 1909), II, 25.

22. See Bailey, *op. cit.*, p. 448, note 15.

23. The correspondence is found in *Relations with Chile*, House Executive Document No. 91, 52nd Congress, 1st session; see also Alice Felt Tyler, *The Foreign Policy of James G. Blaine* (University of Minnesota Press, 1927), pp. 135-164.

President	*Secretary of State*
	John Quincy Adams, of Massachusetts. Commissioned March 5, 1817; entered upon duties September 22, 1817; retired March 3, 1825.
John Quincy Adams, of Massachusetts March 4, 1825-March 4, 1829	Daniel Brent, of Virginia (Chief Clerk). *Ad interim* March 4-7, 1825. Henry Clay, of Kentucky. Commissioned and entered upon duties March 7, 1825; retired March 3, 1829.
Andrew Jackson, of Tennessee March 4, 1829-March 4, 1837	James A. Hamilton, of New York. *Ad interim* March 4-27, 1829. Martin Van Buren, of New York. Commissioned March 6, 1829; entered upon duties March 28, 1829; retired May 23, 1831. Edward Livingston, of Louisiana. Commissioned (recess of the Senate) and entered upon duties May 24, 1831; recommissioned January 12, 1832; retired May 29, 1833. Louis McLane, of Delaware. Commissioned (recess of the Senate) and entered upon duties May 29, 1833; retired June 30, 1834. John Forsyth, of Georgia. Commissioned June 27, 1834; entered upon duties July 1, 1834.
Martin Van Buren, of New York March 4, 1837-March 4, 1841	John Forsyth continued from preceding administration; retired March 3, 1841.
William Henry Harrison, of Ohio March 4-April 4, 1841	Jacob L. Martin, of North Carolina (Chief Clerk). *Ad interim* March 4-5, 1841. Daniel Webster, of Massachusetts. Commissioned March 5, 1841; entered upon duties March 6, 1841.
John Tyler, of Virginia April 6, 1841-March 4, 1845	Daniel Webster continued from preceding administration; retired May 8, 1843. Hugh S. Legaré, of South Carolina (Attorney General). *Ad interim* May 9-June 20, 1843 (died). William S. Derrick, of Pennsylvania (Chief Clerk). *Ad interim* June 21-23, 1843. Abel P. Upshur, of Virginia (Secretary of the Navy). *Ad interim* June 24-July 23, 1843; commissioned (recess of the Senate) and entered upon duties July 24, 1843; recommissioned January 2, 1844; died February 28, 1844. John Nelson, of Maryland (Attorney General). *Ad interim* February 29-March 31, 1844. John C. Calhoun, of South Carolina. Commissioned March 6, 1844; entered upon duties April 1, 1844.
James K. Polk, of Tennessee March 4, 1845-March 4, 1849	John C. Calhoun continued from preceding administration; retired March 10, 1845. James Buchanan, of Pennsylvania. Commissioned March 6, 1845; entered upon duties March 10, 1845.
Zachary Taylor, of Louisiana March 5, 1849-July 9, 1850	James Buchanan continued from preceding administration; retired March 7, 1849. John M. Clayton, of Delaware. Commissioned March 7, 1849; entered upon duties March 8, 1849.
Millard Fillmore, of New York July 10, 1850-March 4, 1853	John M. Clayton continued from preceding administration; retired July 22, 1850. Daniel Webster, of Massachusetts. Commissioned July 22, 1850; entered upon duties July 23, 1850; died October 24, 1852.

President	Secretary of State

| President | Secretary of State |

President — *Secretary of State*

Charles M. Conrad, of Louisiana (Secretary of War). *Ad interim* October 25-November 5, 1852.

Edward Everett, of Massachusetts. Commissioned (recess of the Senate) and entered upon duties November 6, 1852; recommissioned December 9, 1852; retired March 3, 1853.

Franklin Pierce, of New Hampshire
March 4, 1853-March 4, 1857

William Hunter, Jr., of Rhode Island (Chief Clerk). *Ad interim* March 4-7, 1853.

William L. Marcy, of New York. Commissioned March 7, 1853; entered upon duties March 8, 1853.

James Buchanan, of Pennsylvania
March 4, 1857-March 4, 1861

William L. Marcy continued from preceding administration; retired March 6, 1857.

Lewis Cass, of Michigan. Commissioned and entered upon duties March 6, 1857; retired December 14, 1860.

William Hunter, Jr., of Rhode Island (Chief Clerk). *Ad interim* December 15-16, 1860.

Jeremiah S. Black, of Pennsylvania. Commissioned and entered upon duties December 17, 1860.

Abraham Lincoln, of Illinois
March 4, 1861-April 15, 1865

Jeremiah S. Black continued from preceding administration; retired March 5, 1861.

William H. Seward, of New York. Commissioned March 5, 1861; entered upon duties March 6, 1861.

Andrew Johnson, of Tennessee
April 15, 1865-March 4, 1869

William H. Seward continued from preceding administration; retired March 4, 1869.

Ulysses S. Grant, of Illinois
March 4, 1869-March 4, 1877

Elihu B. Washburne, of Illinois. Commissioned and entered upon duties March 5, 1869; retired March 16, 1869.

Hamilton Fish, of New York. Commissioned March 11, 1869; entered upon duties March 17, 1869; recommissioned March 17, 1873.

Rutherford B. Hayes, of Ohio
March 5, 1877-March 4, 1881

Hamilton Fish continued from preceding administration; retired March 12, 1877.

William M. Evarts, of New York. Commissioned and entered upon duties March 12, 1877.

James A. Garfield, of Ohio
March 4-September 19, 1881

William M. Evarts continued from preceding administration; retired March 7, 1881.

James G. Blaine, of Maine. Commissioned March 5, 1881; entered upon duties March 7, 1881.

Chester A. Arthur, of New York
September 20, 1881-March 4, 1885

James G. Blaine continued from preceding administration; retired December 19, 1881.

Frederick T. Frelinghuysen, of New Jersey. Commissioned December 12, 1881; entered upon duties December 19, 1881.

Grover Cleveland, of New York
March 4, 1885-March 4, 1889

Frederick T. Frelinghuysen continued from preceding administration; retired March 6, 1885.

Thomas F. Bayard, of Delaware. Commissioned March 6, 1885; entered upon duties March 7, 1885.

Benjamin Harrison, of Indiana
March 4, 1889-March 4, 1893

Thomas F. Bayard continued from preceding administration; retired March 6, 1889.

James G. Blaine, of Maine. Commissioned March 5, 1889; entered upon duties March 7, 1889; retired June 4, 1892.

| *President* | *Secretary of State* |

William F. Wharton, of Massachusetts (Assistant Secretary). *Ad interim* June 4-29, 1892.

John W. Foster, of Indiana. Commissioned and entered upon duties June 29, 1892; retired February 23, 1893.

William F. Wharton, of Massachusetts (Assistant Secretary). *Ad interim* February 24, 1893, to close of administration.

Grover Cleveland, of New York
March 4, 1893-March 4, 1897

William F. Wharton continued, *ad interim*, from preceding administration to March 6, 1893.

Walter Q. Gresham, of Illinois. Commissioned March 6, 1893; entered upon duties March 7, 1893; died May 28, 1895.

Edwin F. Uhl, of Michigan (Assistant Secretary). *Ad interim* May 28-June 9, 1895.

Richard Olney, of Massachusetts. Commissioned (recess of the Senate) June 8, 1895; entered upon duties June 10, 1895; recommissioned December 3, 1895.

William McKinley, of Ohio
March 4, 1897-September 14, 1901

Richard Olney continued from preceding administration; retired March 5, 1897.

John Sherman, of Ohio. Commissioned March 5, 1897; entered upon duties March 6, 1897; retired April 27, 1898.

William R. Day, of Ohio. Commissioned April 26, 1898; entered upon duties April 28, 1898; retired September 16, 1898.

Alvey A. Adee, of the District of Columbia (Second Assistant Secretary). *Ad interim* September 17-29, 1898.

John Hay, of the District of Columbia. Commissioned (recess of the Senate) September 20, 1898; entered upon duties September 30, 1898; recommissioned December 7, 1898, and March 5, 1901.

Theodore Roosevelt, of New York
September 14, 1901-March 4, 1909

John Hay continued from preceding administration; recommissioned March 6, 1905; died July 1, 1905.

Francis B. Loomis, of Ohio (Assistant Secretary). *Ad interim* July 1-18, 1905.

Elihu Root, of New York. Commissioned (recess of the Senate) July 7, 1905; entered upon duties July 19, 1905; recommissioned December 6, 1905; retired January 27, 1909.

Robert Bacon, of New York. Commissioned and entered upon duties January 27, 1909.

William Howard Taft, of Ohio
March 4, 1909-March 4, 1913

Robert Bacon continued from preceding administration; retired March 5, 1909.

Philander C. Knox, of Pennsylvania. Commissioned March 5, 1909; entered upon duties March 6, 1909.

Woodrow Wilson, of New Jersey
March 4, 1913-March 4, 1921

Philander C. Knox continued from preceding administration; retired March 5, 1913.

William Jennings Bryan, of Nebraska. Commissioned and entered upon duties March 5, 1913; retired June 9, 1915.

Robert Lansing, of New York (Counselor). *Ad interim* June 9-23, 1915; commissioned (recess of the Senate) June 23, 1915; entered upon duties June 24, 1915; recommissioned December 13, 1915; retired February 13, 1920.

Frank Lyon Polk, of New York (Under Secretary). *Ad interim* February 14-March 14, 1920.

[No Secretary of State or Acting Secretary of State, March 15-21, 1920.]

Bainbridge Colby, of New York. Commissioned March 22, 1920; entered upon duties March 23, 1920; retired March 4, 1921.

President	*Secretary of State*
Warren Gamaliel Harding, of Ohio March 4, 1921-August 2, 1923	Charles Evans Hughes, of New York. Commissioned March 4, 1921; entered upon duties March 5, 1921.
Calvin Coolidge, of Massachusetts August 3, 1923-March 4, 1929	Charles Evans Hughes continued from preceding administration; retired March 4, 1925. Frank Billings Kellogg, of Minnesota. Commissioned February 16, 1925; entered upon duties March 5, 1925.
Herbert Clark Hoover, of California March 4, 1929-March 4, 1933	Frank Billings Kellogg continued from preceding administration; retired March 28, 1929. Henry Lewis Stimson, of New York. Commissioned March 5, 1929; entered upon duties March 28, 1929; retired March 4, 1933.
Franklin Delano Roosevelt, of New York March 4, 1933-April 12, 1945	Cordell Hull, of Tennessee. Commissioned and entered upon duties March 4, 1933; retired November 27, 1944. Edward R. Stettinius, Jr., of Illinois. Commissioned and entered upon duties December 1, 1944.
Harry S. Truman, of Missouri April 12, 1945-	Edward R. Stettinius, Jr., continued from preceding administration; retired June 27, 1945. James Francis Byrnes, of South Carolina. Commissioned and entered upon duties July 3, 1945; retired January 7, 1947. Dean G. Acheson, of Connecticut (Under Secretary). *Ad interim* January 7-January 21, 1947. George Catlett Marshall, of Pennsylvania. Commissioned and entered upon duties January 21, 1947; retired January 7, 1949. Robert A. Lovett, of Texas (Under Secretary). *Ad interim* January 7-January 21, 1949. Dean G. Acheson, of Connecticut. Commissioned and entered upon duties January 21, 1949.

Index

495